Liz,
Hope your
birding goes
well this
summer!
Mary

The Birdwatcher's Handbook

The Birdwatcher's Handbook

A Guide to the Natural History of the Birds of Britain and Europe

Including 516 species that regularly breed in Europe and adjacent parts of the Middle East and North Africa

Paul R. Ehrlich, David S. Dobkin, and Darryl Wheye, with species treatments by Stuart L. Pimm

Illustrated by Shahid Naeem

Oxford   New York   Tokyo
OXFORD UNIVERSITY PRESS
1994

Oxford University Press, Walton Street, Oxford OX2 6DP

Oxford   New York   Toronto
Delhi   Bombay   Calcutta   Madras   Karachi
Kuala Lumpur   Singapore   Hong Kong   Tokyo
Nairobi   Dar es Salaam   Cape Town
Melbourne   Auckland   Madrid
and associated companies in
Berlin   Ibadan

Oxford is a trade mark of Oxford University Press

A catalogue record for this book is available from the British Library

Library of Congress Cataloging in Publication Data
Ehrlich, Paul R.
   The birdwatcher's handbook: a guide to the natural history of the birds of
Britain and Europe: including 516 species that regularly breed in Europe
and adjacent parts of the Middle East and North Africa / Paul R. Ehrlich,
David S. Dobkin, and Darryl Wheye, with species treatments by
Stuart L. Pimm; illustrated by Shahid Naeem.
   Includes bibliographical references (p. 531) and indexes.
   1. Birds–Europe–Handbooks, manuals, etc.   2. Birds–British Isles–
Handbooks, manuals, etc.   3. Bird watching–Europe–Handbooks, manuals, etc.
4. Bird watching–British Isles–Handbooks, manuals, etc.   I. Dobkin,
David S.   II. Wheye, Darryl.
III. Title.
QL690.A1E38   1994   598.294–dc20   93–41606
ISBN 0–19–858407–5

Typeset by Footnote Graphics, Warminster, Wilts and Focal Image Ltd, London
Printed in Great Britain on acid-free paper by the Bath Press

Acknowledgements

We thank Jared Diamond, Pete Myers, and David Wilcove for contributions so crucial to our earlier book on North American birds, *The birder's handbook*, that they appear throughout this book too.

In checking essays, the material for treatments, and the endpapers we thank: Arturo Ariño, Tony Cain, John Harte, Rob Hengeveld, R. Jordano, Josef Kren, John Lawton, Esa Ranta, Dafila Scott, Uriel Safriel, and Staffan Ulfstrand. Michael Brooke of the University of Cambridge was kind enough to read all the essays critically and to provide excellent suggestions and additions. Christopher Perrins was especially helpful, and graciously consulted with us on a variety of issues.

Shahid Naeem took time from his other duties at the University of Michigan to adapt illustrations and some of the icons from *The birder's handbook* for use here.

At Stanford University, P.R.E. and D.W. thank Zoe Chandik, Joan Dietrich, Jill Otto, and Joe Wible of the Falconer Biology Library for their persistence in tracking down obscure source material. We also thank Steve Masley and Pat Browne for invariably efficient handling of the extensive photocopying which accompanies a project of this size. Once again, Peggy Vas Dias of the Biology Department provided a vital link among widely dispersed authors and their overseas publisher.

At Rutgers University, D.S.D. extends his gratitude to Libby Hart and her staff at the Camden Library for cheerfully filling the requests for research materials needed through interlibrary loans. D.S.D. is grateful to the High Desert Museum of Bend, Oregon, and its staff for providing a supportive and stimulating environment during completion of his work on this book. He thanks Robbie Cortez for his help with the final assembly of the bibliography.

At the University of Tennessee, S.L.P. thanks Sean Kinane, Andrew Redfearn, and Gregory Witteman for assistance, and Fred and Raisa Killeffer for much hospitality. His wife Julia provided extensive help and enthusiastic support. The Alexander Library of the Edward Grey Institute, Birds of the Western Palearctic Ltd., and the British Trust for Ornithology provided access to essential sources of literature. John Lawton at the Centre for Population Biology, Imperial College, hosted S.L.P.'s stay in England. S.L.P. also thanks the many individuals who took and accompanied him bird watching, from his teens in the Derbyshire Ornithological Society, to later years across the Palearctic from the Russian Arctic to the Spanish Coto Doñana, from the west coast of Ireland to Afghanistan. A special debt is owed to the late Olli Järvinen for his efforts on behalf of this book.

We are all especially grateful to the staff at Oxford University Press, who not only caught many errors and infelicities, but tailored and assembled the 516 treatments and 170 essays into a comprehensive package.

Finally, we are indebted to the generations of ornithologists, birdwatchers, and conservationists whose efforts to understand and protect the birds of Britain, Europe, and adjacent areas made this book possible.

The book was sponsored in part by the Center for Conservation Biology of Stanford University. The Center, established in 1984, carries out biological and policy research and education activities associated with preserving biological diversity.

Stanford	P.R.E.
Bend	D.S.D.
Palo Alto	D.W.
Knoxville	S.L.P.

To the memory of Olli Järvinen

PRE *To Jared Diamond, for rekindling my interest in birds*
DSD *To Donna, Gabe, Adria, and Elliot Dobkin, with special thanks to Gertie*
DW   *To my father, the late Owen Wheye*
SLP *To Julia*

Contents

Essays

Introduction

How often have you come across a bird on a spring morning and stood motionless in an effort to determine what it was doing; to see whether it was near its nest, and if so, what kind of nest it built, or to see why it was holding its tail in an unusual position? Have you wondered what it ate, how many mates it had, how many eggs would occupy its nest, how long it would take them to hatch, or how helpless its hatchlings would be? While there are excellent field guides to help identify that bird, none provide comprehensive information on what it is doing and why. This field guide takes up where the others leave off — that is, once you have identified the bird. First, you can refer to an up-to-date condensed description of the biology of the species you have in view, and then you can read brief essays which expand on that information and fit your bird into 'the big picture' of avian ecology, behaviour, and evolution. As you become familiar with this book's format, you will find that it also serves as a guide to what is *not* known about the biology of the birds of Britain, Europe, and adjacent areas. We have indicated where, by making careful observations, you can contribute to the science of ornithology (see Observing and Recording Bird Biology, p. xxxiii).

The birdwatcher's handbook includes accounts of the 516 bird species known to nest regularly in Europe, North Africa, and the Middle East, north of 30°N and west of 40°E. This area includes Iceland, but not islands off the west coast

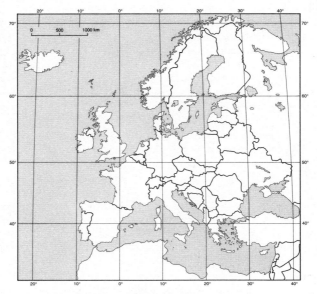

The area covered by this guide

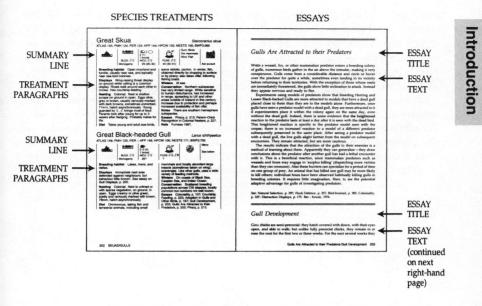

SUMMARY LINE — TREATMENT PARAGRAPHS — SUMMARY LINE — TREATMENT PARAGRAPHS — ESSAY TITLE — ESSAY TEXT — ESSAY TITLE — ESSAY TEXT (continued on next right-hand page)

of Africa; it includes the Nile delta of Egypt, but not the Red Sea Coast; and it includes all but the far eastern part of Turkey. We have excluded some exotic species that have escaped from captivity and have only very local distributions. We have also excluded birds whose ranges have retreated beyond the limit of this area.

Just as some identification guides present text on left-hand pages and illustrations on right-hand pages, this guide puts facing pages to different uses. Short synopses, called 'species treatments', describing the biology of individual species are on left-hand pages of the main section of the book. The species are arranged in the same order as in *The birds of the Western Palearctic*, the nine-volume work edited by Cramp and colleagues. Other field guides follow this order more or less closely. (We have not followed the new sequence derived from studies of bird DNA by Sibley and Monroe (1990) in their *Distribution and taxonomy of birds of the world*, because this radical change would confuse those who know the old sequence. However, we do refer to this important new work in a number of places.) At the end of each species treatment you will find a list of essays (and the page number on which each starts) giving especially pertinent background material, followed by several references cited in the Bibliography (p. 531) which provide entry to the detailed literature on the species.

The essays are presented on the right-hand pages facing the species treatments. They vary in length and cover important and interesting biological topics — how flamingos feed, how different species of tits and warblers divide hunting areas in trees, how raptors can be conserved, why shorebirds sometimes stand on one foot, why some birds rub themselves with ants, how migrating birds find their way, why the Great Auk became extinct, and what information duck displays convey, just to name a few of the many topics addressed. As far as possible, these essays are placed opposite species to which they are most relevant. (Further essays not included here because of space limitations can be found in the version of this book that deals with North American birds, *The birder's handbook* by Paul R. Ehrlich, David S. Dobkin, and Darryl Wheye (Simon and Schuster, 1988).)

We have attempted in this single volume to compress the information that otherwise can be found only in a library of ornithological books and journals. To achieve compactness we have had to use a highly condensed format for the presentation of data on the species treated. It therefore is important to read the next section, How to Use This Book, so that the information will be readily accessible to you when birdwatching.

How to Use This Book

Read this section and the treatments of some familiar birds before you use the book in earnest. Because the information in the treatments is concentrated, it will take a little practice before you gain access to details rapidly.

Right-hand pages — Essays

Whenever possible, essays are placed close to species to which they relate. If you are searching for information on a particular topic, refer to the subject index (p. 613) or to the list of essays on p. xi which will help you delve more systematically into the topics covered in the *Handbook*. At the end of each essay we have cross-referenced other essays.

For instance, the essay 'Parasitized Ducks' deals with ducks laying eggs in the nests of other ducks — an example of 'brood parasitism'. The first essay referenced at the end of 'Parasitized Ducks' is 'Brood Parasitism', which gives a more general discussion of the phenomenon. Lists of references at the ends of the essays direct you to further readings on the same general topic.

Left-hand pages — Species treatments

Treatments of the 516 species that regularly breed in the area covered are given on the left-hand pages in the main section of the book. Decisions on which species to exclude were sometimes 'judgement calls'. Sometimes the decision will surprise you: the familiar wader, the Knot, does not breed in the area of this guide and is not included, but the Sanderling is, on the basis of a very small breeding population in the area we cover. We have separated Rock and Water Pipits but excluded the Semi-collared Flycatcher because its distinctness was recognized too late for inclusion in this edition. We excluded the Green Warbler because its occurrence in the area covered by this book is a recent discovery.

Each treatment is divided into three parts: the heading, the summary line, and the text.

Treatment heading

The first line of the heading consists of the common name of the species, followed by its scientific name. The latter is given in two parts, a generic name (always capitalized) and a specific name (never capitalized). The generic name identifies the immediate group to which the bird belongs, and the specific name denotes the exact member of the genus. The scientific name of the Blackbird is *Turdus merula*. *Turdus* is a genus of large thrushes; other members of that genus include *T. torquatus*, the Ring Ouzel; *T. pilaris*, the Fieldfare; *T. philomelos*, the Song Thrush; *T. iliacus*, the Redwing; and *T. viscivorus*, the Mistle Thrush.

Finally, so that you can quickly find a picture of the bird being described, the second line of the heading lists the pages where the species is discussed in recent editions of the standard field identification guides and some other important reference books. The following abbreviations are used.

ATLAS   *An atlas of the birds of the Western Palearctic*, by C. Harrison (1982). (This is not a field guide, but a small book replete with information about the ranges and habitats of the birds in the area.)

PMH   *Birds of Britain and Europe* (**5th edn**), by R. Peterson, G. Mountford, and P. A. D. Hollom (1993).

PER   *New generation guide to birds of Britain and Europe*, by C. Perrins (1987).

HFP   *The birds of Britain and Europe with North Africa and the Middle East*, by H. Heinzel, R. S. R. Fitter, and J. Parslow (1979).

HPCW   *Birds of the Middle East and North Africa*, by P. A. D. Hollom, R. F. Porter, S. Christensen, and I. Willis (1988).

NESTS   *A field guide to the nests, eggs, nestlings of British and European birds*, by C. Harrison (1985).

BWP   *The birds of the Western Palearctic*. The nine-volume series (see Cramp in the Bibliography) that covers all the species in this book. BWP2:113 means, for example, volume two of the series, page 113.

Note that in some cases birds' names have changed since the above books were published and will not match those found in this guide. We follow the nomenclature of *The birds of the Western Palearctic*. Names commonly used by other guides are indicated in the **Notes** line of the species treatment.

Summary line

Immediately beneath the heading is an abbreviated, partly pictorial 'summary line' presenting a combination of symbols, words, abbreviations, and numbers, that supplies the following basic information at a glance.

Column 1: Typical nest location and height; alternative nest locations.

Column 2: Type of nest; how sexes divide the task of nest building; predominant type of breeding system (whether the species is monogamous, a co-operative breeder, etc.).

Column 3: Whether eggs are marked or unmarked; usual number of eggs in a clutch, the range of numbers of eggs laid, and the number of broods per year; how sexes divide the task of incubation; usual number of days from start of incubation to hatching (often given as a range).

Column 4: Stage of development at hatching (precocial/altricial); how the sexes divide the task of caring for the young; usual number of days between hatching and fledging (often given as a range).

Column 5: Major and secondary types of food eaten during the year.

Column 6: Basic methods of obtaining food (foraging).

The summary line for an imaginary bird is shown below. The full list of symbols is given in the front endpaper and fully explained on pp. xxi–xxix.

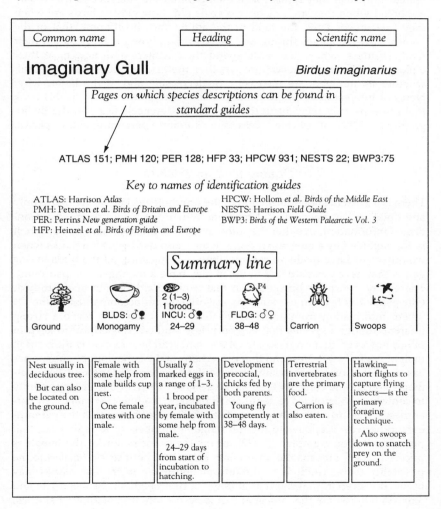

Common name · Heading · Scientific name

Imaginary Gull
Birdus imaginarius

Pages on which species descriptions can be found in standard guides

ATLAS 151; PMH 120; PER 128; HFP 33; HPCW 931; NESTS 22; BWP3:75

Key to names of identification guides

ATLAS: Harrison *Atlas*
PMH: Peterson *et al. Birds of Britain and Europe*
PER: Perrins *New generation guide*
HFP: Heinzel *et al. Birds of Britain and Europe*

HPCW: Hollom *et al. Birds of the Middle East*
NESTS: Harrison *Field Guide*
BWP3: *Birds of the Western Palearctic Vol. 3*

Summary line

Ground	BLDS: ♂♀ Monogamy	2 (1–3) 1 brood INCU: ♂♀ 24–29	P4 FLDG: ♂♀ 38–48	Carrion	Swoops
Nest usually in deciduous tree. But can also be located on the ground.	Female with some help from male builds cup nest. One female mates with one male.	Usually 2 marked eggs in a range of 1–3. 1 brood per year, incubated by female with some help from male. 24–29 days from start of incubation to hatching.	Development precocial, chicks fed by both parents. Young fly competently at 38–48 days.	Terrestrial invertebrates are the primary food. Carrion is also eaten.	Hawking— short flights to capture flying insects—is the primary foraging technique. Also swoops down to snatch prey on the ground.

Text

The largest part of the treatment, several short sections giving expanded information on the biology of the species, follows the summary line. The sequence of topics is: **Breeding habitat**: the habitats in which the birds nest; **Displays**: the common displays that might be observed; **Nesting**: whether the bird is territorial or colonial, the kind of nest, the colour and size of the eggs, whether the eggs hatch on the same day or not, details of how the young are reared, how long they remain with their parents and, for species which may not breed when they are one or two years old, how old the birds are when they first breed; **Diet**: the food of the adults and, if different, that of the young, how it changes throughout the year, and how the birds obtain their food; **Winters**: where the birds spend their winters and aspects of their biology in winter; **Conservation**: whether the bird is widespread or local, whether its numbers are increasing or decreasing and, if the latter, why; **Notes** of interest in addition to the previous categories; **Essays** in this book that are especially relevant to the species; **Ref[erence]s** listed in the Bibliography (p. 531) that provide access to the literature pertaining to the species.

Dealing with uncertainty

There is a great deal of information in the ornithological literature that is only anecdotal and in need of confirmation. Where we have presented unconfirmed information, in either the summary line or the treatment paragraph, it is accompanied by a question mark. We have also used question marks when we ourselves have made an extrapolation. For instance, all the birds in one genus that have been studied in detail may have a monogamous pair bond. There may, however, be species in that genus that have not been studied. Our policy has been to use such guesswork (always accompanied by the '?') where information from a closely related species can help make a strong inference about a species that has been less studied. It is critical to keep in mind, however, that even closely related birds can be remarkably different in their biological attributes, and that projections of the behaviour of one species based on that of a close relative can be dead wrong. Throughout the treatments you should consider the '?' to be a signal to alert you to an opportunity to contribute to knowledge about avian biology. If a question mark is in parentheses, the uncertainty applies only to the information within the parentheses; otherwise it applies to the full range of numbers or to both sexes that preceded it. For example, ♂ (♀?) means the participation of the female is uncertain; ♂ ♀? means the uncertainty extends to both sexes. Be alert to the possibility that exceptions to the information given in the summaries may occur. If we report that the typical range of nest heights is between 1 m and 3 m, do not assume that a nest at 5 m is necessarily that of another species; recorded ranges are seldom all-inclusive. Finding something that differs markedly from the information given is a sign that caution and careful observation are called for. If you just saw a Long-tailed Tit lay an egg in an open cup nest, double check the identity of the bird; it would be an unusual event indeed, but not impossible.

What follows is a key to the treatment summary line and then a detailed description of the text.

Key to the summary lines

Column 1

Nest location

Since many species are quite flexible about where they place their nest, the symbol often represents only the most likely location. The symbol for the primary site is given at the top of the summary line. Secondary locations are indicated by words or abbreviations shown below that symbol. For a very few unusual sites the location is given by a word only (no symbol). In the summary line, the numbers just under the location information indicate the range of heights (in metres) at which nests of the species have been found. A species whose nests are found in trees as high as 10 metres, in shrubs, and on the ground will be shown as 0–10 m.

Locations defined by topographic features

 Bank Includes river banks, areas of soft soil on steep island slopes, etc., where nest burrows are excavated.

 Ground Includes nests placed among the roots, or in niches among the roots of fallen trees, on bare rock, or simply scraped in the dirt or sand.

 Cliff Includes nests situated in natural crevices or on ledges of cliffs typically offering a commanding view of a defensible position, and sometimes chosen when no suitable trees are available. *We also use 'cliff' for many species that originally used cliffs but now utilize structures such as buildings and bridges.*

Locations defined by supporting plant structures

 Shrub Includes nests placed within any multi-stemmed woody plant (i.e. one that does not have a distinct single trunk extending several metres between the ground and the lowest branching point).

 Deciduous tree Includes nests placed in any broad-leafed tree, whether it sheds all of its leaves in the autumn ('deciduous') or not ('live'): oaks, maples, poplars, beeches, etc. Also used for species that use a mixture of deciduous and coniferous trees.

Coniferous tree Includes nests placed in any tree that bears cones: pines, spruces, junipers, firs, etc. *We also use 'Coniferous tree' for species that nest in deciduous trees (like birches) which are interspersed through extensive northern coniferous forests.*

Vine tangle Includes nests in vines, brambles, brush piles, etc.

Floating on water Almost always anchored to live emergent or submerged vegetation.

Reed-beds Includes nests supported by reeds and other aquatic vegetation.

Column 2

Nest type

The symbol shows the type of nest most frequently used by that species. Birds of the same species tend to construct similar nests, but the materials available often differ from area to area. (See essays: Nest Evolution, p. 345; Nest Sites and Materials, p. 443; Nest Lining, p. 439.) Secondary nest types are listed beneath the symbol and usually discussed in the treatment paragraph.

Scrape A simple depression usually with a rim sufficient to prevent eggs from rolling away. Those of many duck species are almost bowl-shaped. Occasionally lining is added.

Cup Typical of songbirds, this is the archetypal 'bird nest'. Hemispherical inside with a rim height several times the diameter of the eggs. In some cases bulky, but always with a deep depression.

Saucer A shallow cup with the height of the rim not more than twice the diameter of the eggs. Also a flattened nest of pliable vegetation as in some wetland birds.

Platform A structure usually big enough for the bird to land on, in a tree, on a cliff, *or providing a dry place in marshy ground or above water*, with or without a distinct depression to hold the eggs. Typical of many raptors and birds of wetlands.

Cavity Either excavated, as is typical of woodpeckers, or in a dead or dying limb or tree. Sometimes a cup or other structure is built within.

Crevice Eggs placed in a crack in the face of a cliff, between boulders, in a human-made structure, etc.

Burrow Eggs placed in chamber at the end of a tunnel. Tunnels either excavated by the birds (most kingfishers, puffins, storm-petrels), or usurped from small mammals, especially those in desert and grassland habitats.

 Pendant An elongate sac-like nest suspended from a branch.

 Spherical Globe-shaped or ball-shaped. A roughly round structure, fully enclosed except for a small opening on the side or on the top or bottom.

Who builds the nest

The male ♂ and/or female ♀ symbol(s) after 'BLDS' below the nest symbol indicate which sex participates in nest-building. If both sexes participate, but one does much more than the other, the symbol for the sex doing more work is filled in (♀ or ♂). A dash indicates that no nest building is involved.

Breeding system

The following terms, found at the bottom of Column 2, indicate which breeding system is typical for the species.

Monogamy One female mates with one male (see essay: Monogamy, p. 335).

Polygyny One male mates with two or more females (see essay: Polygyny, p. 265).

Polyandry One female mates with two or more males (see essay: Polyandry, p. 195)

Cooperative breeder Two females rear broods in the same nest simultaneously and/or non-breeding birds serve as helpers at the nest of one or more breeding pairs (see essay: Cooperative Breeding, p. 275).

Some species, such as the Dunnock, have very complicated mating systems. For these species there is no simple description and we refer you to the text below the summary line for details.

Monogamy is by far the most commonly recorded mating system in birds. Note that very often a small percentage of birds in a population deviate from the mating system of the majority. It is not, for example, unusual in an otherwise monogamous population to find 5 per cent of the males polygynous. *For all categories except 'monogamy', the use of the category means that the particular system is common in the species, but not necessarily the predominant system.* For instance, in many of the species we have described as polygynous, the majority of the males may have only one mate, and some (particularly young males) may have none. *We have used the non-monogamous categories to indicate mating systems that are reasonably common in the species,* common enough for a careful observer to notice them. Careful observations are needed to see if non-monogamous systems, especially polygyny, are more widespread than currently thought. As information accumulates, fewer and fewer species are found to have the strictly monogamous mating system they were once thought to have.

Column 3

Eggs, clutch size, and broods

At the top of the third column, the symbol 🥚 is used if the egg has markings, ⬭ if it is unmarked. The number(s) just below the symbol indicate the most common clutch size, or the range (there is often individual and/or geographic variation in clutch size). The number(s) in parentheses to the right on the same line indicate the more extreme values recorded in the literature. In many species data on clutch size are limited. Furthermore, it is often difficult to determine when clutch sizes at the higher end of the range indicate the production of two or more females laying in the same nest and when clutch sizes at the lower end of the range indicate incomplete production (we have tried to exclude such values here). Clutch size can also be affected by a female's age, by whether the clutch is produced early or late in the season, by whether it is the female's first clutch or a replacement clutch, as well as by other factors (see essays: Average Clutch Size, p. 31; Variation in Clutch Sizes, p. 55; Brood Parasitism, p. 249; and Cooperative Breeding, p. 275).

The number of broods per year is printed below the information on clutch size.

Incubating sex

The male ♂ and/or female ♀ symbols after 'INCU' indicate whether both parents, or only one parent incubates. As in nest construction, if both sexes participate, but one does much more than the other, one symbol is filled in to indicate which sex does more work. Sometimes only the female incubates, but the male may still contribute by defending the territory, guarding the nest, or feeding the female.

Length of incubation

The number(s) below the line detailing who incubates is the usual number of days (or recorded range of days) from the start of incubation to hatching. Note that hatching of a clutch is often synchronized by delaying the start of incubation until the last egg is laid. In species where the eggs do not hatch synchronously, the incubation time for each egg may be more or less fixed, and the time for the entire clutch dependent on how many eggs are laid. Where we know the time for each egg we have indicated this; unless otherwise indicated, the time is for the entire clutch in a nest with a typical number of eggs.

Incubation time is somewhat geographically variable within species, and your accurate observations could add to knowledge of that variation. Numbers appearing in parentheses represent recorded extreme values.

Column 4

Stage of development at hatching

Bird species show great variation in their degree of development at hatching, and we show the maturity of hatchlings at the top of the fourth column. In Britain and Europe there are no fully developed ('Precocial 1') young at hatching. The most fully developed young at hatching, such as ducklings and wader chicks, are classified 'Precocial 2'. They are downy, open-eyed, mobile at birth, and find their own food while following their parent(s). At the opposite extreme, songbirds are 'Altricial' — born naked, immobile, and wholly unable to feed themselves.

Developmental patterns are explained fully in the essay Precocial and Altricial Young (p. 401). In Britain and Europe seven categories of young at hatching are found.

 P2 **Precocial 2** Mobile, downy, eyes open, follow parents, find own food.

 P3 **Precocial 3** Mobile, downy, eyes open, follow parents, are shown food.

 P4 **Precocial 4** Mobile, downy, eyes open, follow parents, fed.

 SP **Semiprecocial** Mobile, downy, eyes open, remain at nest, fed.

 SA1 **Semialtricial 1** Immobile, downy, eyes open, fed.

 SA2 **Semialtricial 2** Immobile, downy, eyes closed, fed.

 A **Altricial** Immobile, downless, eyes closed, fed.

Other than in the summary line, the word 'precocial' used alone in this guide refers collectively to the first four categories; similarly, the word 'altricial' refers collectively to the last three categories.

Who tends the young

How the parents share the feeding of the young is shown below the development symbol, following 'FLDG'. For precocial species whose young are not fed by the parents, we indicate who tends the young while they feed. The symbols of the sex of the tending parent(s) are the same as those used in Columns 2 and 3.

Time from hatching to fledging

The number(s) printed under who looks after the young are the usual number of days (or range of days) until precocial young are able to fly competently and the time required before altricial young leave the nest (altricial species may not be able to fly competently when they depart from the nest). Numbers in parentheses represent recorded extreme values. Again, fledging times are variable and your accurate observations may be useful. Note that fledging rarely means the end of parental care. Precocial young of some species, such as geese, stay with and are helped by the parents long after they can fly, and indeed often stay with their parents on their first migration. Altricial young may be fed more than twice as long as fledglings as when they were nestlings.

Deciding how long it takes to reach flying competence is very difficult in some species. Some altricial birds leave the nest when they can almost fly and are not easy to observe once they have left. Other species, especially partridges and pheasants, have young that can fly, after a fashion, long before they are fully grown.

Column 5

Diet

At the top of the fifth column, the symbol shows the primary type of food eaten during the year. Secondary types of food commonly taken may be shown by words or abbreviations below the symbol. Additional specific food items taken less frequently are listed in the treatment paragraph and details of primary food types are often given there (since the symbols cover broad categories). Remember, many species change their diets during the year and have different diets in different parts of their range. In some species, the adults (and often the young) feed on insects in the summer but switch to seeds and other plant materials in the winter. We have a special symbol for this. In other species, there are major seasonal shifts in diet for which we cannot provide a simple symbol.

Animal foods

 Small mammals Anything from shrews to squirrels and rabbits, but most often small rodents.

Birds May include their eggs, in which case this will be mentioned in the treatment paragraph.

 Small terrestrial vertebrates other than mammals and birds, including reptiles (lizards, snakes) and amphibians (frogs, toads). *Sometimes used to mean a wide range of small vertebrates, including mammals and birds, in which case this will be mentioned in the treatment paragraph.*

 Fishes Sometimes includes fry and eggs.

 Terrestrial invertebrates Includes insects, *but also a wide range of other invertebrates such as spiders, mites, snails, slugs, earthworms, millipedes.* Usually a predominance of insects.

 Aquatic invertebrates May include aquatic insects, shrimp and other crustaceans, snails, bivalves, etc.

 Carrion Prey found dead, either on land or on water (such as the waste from fishing boats).

Plant foods

 Nectar The sugary solution found in many flowers.

 Fruits Includes berries which are simple fleshy fruits.

 Greens May include leafy parts of both aquatic and terrestrial plants. May also be used for birds which take a wide range of plant parts (seeds, leaves, buds, fruit, etc.), in which case this will be noted in the treatment paragraph.

 Seeds Includes grains, sunflower seeds, conifer seeds, etc.

Omnivore A variety of plants and animals too diverse to specify here; neither plant nor animal food usually comprises less than one-third of the diet.

Insects in the summer, seeds in the winter Many species of birds, especially songbirds, switch from insects in the summer to seeds in the winter.

Although seed-feeding birds frequently consume gravel to aid in grinding seeds, we have not included gravel in our description of diets.

Column 6

Foraging techniques

The primary method each species uses to obtain food during its breeding season is at the top of the far right-hand column of the summary line. The symbol is often supplemented by a code word or abbreviation below that indicates less frequently used foraging techniques. Note both primary and secondary techniques may be used to obtain primary food items.

Techniques for picking food from ground surface or plants while walking or clinging

 Ground gleaning Picks up items from the surface of soil, turf, sand, etc. Includes scavenging aquatic organisms from shorelines.

 Gleaning from foliage and occasionally from branches. Takes invertebrates and/or fruit from vegetation, not from the surface of the ground.

 Gleaning from tree trunks and branches Includes excavating and drilling into bark.

Hovering techniques

 Gleaning while hovering Takes insects or berries from plants above the ground, while hovering.

 Hovering and pouncing Hovers before swooping or dropping down on prey.

Other flying techniques

 Hawking Sallies from perch on short flights to capture flying insects.

 Aerial foraging While in prolonged continuous flight, captures flying insects.

 Aerial pursuit Chases and catches birds in mid-air, stoops (drops on flying birds from above, killing them in mid-air with a blow from the talons), or snatches them from their perches.

Swoops Snatches up prey from ground in talons after descent from perch.

 High patrol Soars at high altitude in search of carrion or prey.

 Low patrol Seeks prey in low searching flight.

Aquatic techniques

 High dives Drops from height into water, usually to catch fish.

 Skims Flies low over water and snatches up fishes or aquatic invertebrates.

 Surface dives Floats and then dives; swims under water using feet and/or wings.

 Surface dips Takes food from the water's surface or from just below while floating or swimming on the surface.

 Dabbling Floats on surface in shallow water, pivots head-first downwards while raising hindquarters above water to reach submerged plants or animals on or near substrate (mud, sand).

Stalks and strikes Hunts by standing on bank or in water and spearing fishes, frogs, etc.

 Probes below surface Forages for food beneath surface of substrate (mud, sand) either in or near shallow water. Also often includes taking food from within the water column.

Interpreting the treatment paragraphs

As in the summary line, the information in the treatment paragraph is also necessarily condensed, so you should be aware of the following assumptions. First, birds are complex, adaptable animals, and although certain aspects of the behaviour of some species are relatively stereotyped, many vary with local environmental conditions. Thus a species that normally lines its nest with fine grasses may substitute a bit of fleece snagged on a barbed-wire fence surrounding a sheep pen, or shredded plastic, if either is conveniently near the nest site. In addition to behaviour, the physiological, reproductive, and other biological characteristics of most widespread birds vary geographically. For instance, a species may raise only one brood per season in the northern part of its range, but rear two or even three farther south. Within a species, clutch and egg sizes may differ between birds nesting in desert regions and those in well-watered localities. Western coastal populations may have access to insects during the rather mild winters, while eastern representatives may be restricted mostly to berries after the first hard frost.

Thus, because space limitations in the book prevent detailing these patterns of variation, we present the most common biological features and behaviours, and try to indicate the range of variation. But not every individual bird will fall within a given range.

The statements in the paragraph are telegraphic and most of the material is self-explanatory, but keep the following in mind.

Breeding habitat. Only the breeding habitat — where nesting occurs — is given. Birds may very often be found in quite different kinds of environments during foraging, after breeding, on migration, or in the winter.

Displays. Territorial and courtship displays have not been described systematically in many birds, particularly those active at night. If described in the literature, we attempt here to give at least some major features of these displays. In addition, as you will see in various essays, displays used in courtship and in aggression are frequently similar. Because of space constraints, in many cases you will have to infer the form of the display from its name (e.g. 'head pumping' meaning moving the head up and down). Careful observations of display behaviour and the contexts in which it occurs are badly needed for many species.

Nesting. Positions of nests (e.g. relative to the trunk for cup nests in trees) are often listed, as are alternative sites, but materials used tend to be so extremely variable (see essays, Nest Sites and Materials, p. 443; Nest Lining, p. 439) that information has usually been condensed to a minimum. Eggs vary in colour and pattern, even within clutches. Colours may change as incubation advances, and eggs often become stained in the nest, particularly if it is situated on the ground. Egg identification thus is often very difficult even when a photograph is available. It is, however, usually easy to exclude many possibilities on the basis of our brief description of colour, markings, and average size. Average egg size (length) is given in millimetres (mm). Remember that one inch is 25.4 mm. Note that egg size is also variable: if one species is listed as having an average length of 19 mm and another of 18 mm, it is quite likely that some eggs of the first species will be smaller than some of the second species, and vice versa. If, on the other hand, one species is listed as 15 mm and the other 25 mm, egg size will provide a pretty good clue to which species' nest you are observing. Also bear in mind that eggs may vary in size with the order in which they are produced and that eggs from early clutches often tend to be larger than later ones. *Above all, remember it is illegal to disturb the eggs and young of most species.*

Diet. This usually expands on information on diet presented in the summary line, may list food eaten during the non-breeding season if different, and adds brief comments on foraging methods.

Winters. This section describes where the birds winter, the habitat they choose, their migration or movements, if any, and miscellaneous details about the birds' winter ecology. Information about the wintering range provides important clues about the future conservation status of migrants travelling to Africa, where accelerating deforestation and desertification are having major impacts on many migratory species. Therefore we describe here the wintering range in some detail if significant numbers of individuals spend the non-breeding season outside of Britain and Europe.

Conservation. Critical as wintering grounds can be to the survival of a species, remember that many threats to the persistence of the avifauna involve human activities. Significant documented interference by humans (hunting, habitat destruction associated with civilization and concomitant land, water, and food contamination, competition from introduced species) is listed here. The species range, whether extensive or local, is also discussed. Inclusion in the European Community Birds Directive (p. 528) is noted here as well. Standard enemies are not discussed here. Given the chance, predators such as domestic cats or raptors will snatch up any small birds; and foxes, jays, ravens, and many others will rob any nest. Such predators may become more important where large blocks of forests have been fragmented into many smaller woodlands, for these predators are often common along forest edges.

Notes. In this section we include interesting additional information that does not conveniently fit elsewhere. Some of the most important unusual aspects of the biology of the species will be described here.

Essays. Near the end of the treatment paragraphs we list a few of the essays that seem especially pertinent to the species, and give the page numbers on which those essays begin. For instance, after watching one of the several species that have leks, you may wonder what all these bizarre displays involve. We deal with some of your questions in an essay on leks. Naturally, we cannot list every pertinent essay in every species treatment, so each essay itself is cross-referenced to other essays on related topics. By referring to cross-linked essays we hope that it is possible gradually (and relatively painlessly) to acquire an overview of bird biology. We hope that each time you see an especially interesting bird in the field, you will try to read some of the associated essays, and that they will enhance your appreciation of the species you have under observation. For an overview of the topics covered in the essays, see the List of Essays, p. xi.

References. Citations in this section direct you to sources listed in the Bibliography (p. 531) that can give you further information on a species. By far the most important reference is the monumental *Birds of the Western Palearctic* — a nine-volume work edited by Cramp and others. Seven volumes have been published as we go to press. We have included the volume and page number for the description of each species at the head of each species treatment (see section on Treatment headings, p. xvii). There are a number of other important references which are less encyclopaedic and deal with either birds of a particular region (such as Paz (1987) *The birds of Israel*), particular topics (such as Marchant *et al.* (1990) *Population trends in British breeding birds*), or particular species (such as Lack (1956) *Swifts in a tower*).

We have included only a few references to technical literature in the species treatments. Many more of these references are cited in *Birds of the Western Palearctic*, but, of course, the first volume of that work is more than fifteen years old and there have been important advances since then. One example is the remarkable range expansion of the Barnacle Goose — it now nests in Sweden. We must emphasize that the present handbook is a guide and not a reference book for professional ornithologists, and consequently a comprehensive list of technical references gleaned from a wide range of national and international journals cannot be included with each species' treatment. (For example, we do not refer to K. Larsson *et al.*'s work on the Barnacle Goose.) We hope colleagues will not feel slighted when they recognize their work, yet do not find it cited directly. Space constraints are less severe with the essays and so they are followed by an extensive list of technical references.

Observing and Recording Bird Biology

We wrote this field guide largely to provide birdwatchers with a portable, easily accessed source of information on the birds of the region. Throughout the book, we specify, by the use of a question mark, areas where knowledge of the avifauna is incomplete or unconfirmed, or where information is entirely lacking. For many species, even common ones, the literature provides only anecdotal reports on, for example, the length of incubation and fledging periods. Similarly, for many widespread species, data on breeding biology are often based on a limited number of studies from only a restricted portion of the species' range. Because many features (such as clutch size, prey items fed to young, incubation and fledging periods, and even the preferred nest site) can vary geographically, the understanding of even comparatively abundant species may be incomplete. Thus one use of this book is as a guide to the kinds of observations needed to advance knowledge of British and European birds. Active birdwatchers are constantly refining their ability to watch, interpret, and record various aspects of bird behaviour and ecology. The most important habit is that of carrying a small field notebook and writing down observations in the field while the details are still fresh in the mind.

How to record

There are several ways to organize a notebook; the two most popular are by species and by date. Other possibilities include organizing by habitat, by geographic region, etc. Most people find that in a notebook organized by species, it is most convenient to include observations for only one species per page, although entries for more than one date (in chronological order) can go on the same page. Organization by date is usually more convenient for entering data, but often is not so convenient when the time comes to look up what you recorded. In either case, each day's entry should start with the date, the geographic location, any pertinent information concerning the habitat, a brief description of weather conditions, and the time of your observations. Time is most conveniently noted with a 24-hour clock, so that 6 a.m. is 0600 and 6 p.m. is 1800. If you prefer not to do this, be sure to include a.m. and p.m. in order to avoid confusion. Scientists ordinarily keep a second copy of their notes for safety's sake. If observations are worth making, they are worth preserving; be sure to store your duplicate notes in a different building from the originals. If you have a computer, you may wish to enter your notes each day into a database and to keep a back-up disc in another building for safety.

What to record

Many useful data can be obtained simply by recording counts: how many eggs in a clutch, how many fledglings being fed, how many birds in a wader flock, how many standing on one leg, and so on. Similarly, behaviours can be easily quantified. For example, one can note the number of feeding trips made to the nest by parent birds per 10 minutes of watching the nest, or the duration of dives made by a duck. It is very important, and far more useful for making comparisons, to quantify your observations wherever possible rather than simply describing a situation in general terms. For example, say that you are watching the foraging behaviour of a Willow Warbler on a sunny day. Rather than simply recording: 'Willow Warbler foraging for insects in a tree, 1300–1320', you could quantify your observations by recording.

'Willow Warbler foraging for insects in variety of deciduous trees (list species of trees if known), 1300–1320: *hawking* — 3 times, *foliage gleaning* — 6 times, *hovering and gleaning* — 13 times.'

You now have a 20-minute sample of foraging behaviour for one individual at one point in the breeding cycle, at a given time of day, in a given type of habitat under certain weather conditions. Additional information that might be recorded includes height for each foraging attempt, diameter of the branch on which each attempt occurred, surface of the leaf (top or bottom) gleaned for each instance of foliage gleaning, and other birds foraging in the vicinity. You might wish to sample for shorter periods of time — say 10 minutes of continuous observation of one bird — and then move on to locate a different individual and similarly observe and record its foraging behaviour. Repeating this procedure over a number of days and at different times of day would soon give you a pretty good picture of the relative use of different foraging techniques by Willow Warblers under different circumstances.

Another observational strategy involves locating one or more active nests and following the families throughout the breeding cycle. Again, it is important to quantify your observations and record clutch size, which bird incubates, the duration of the incubation period, which bird feeds the nestlings, the duration of nestling period, etc. Here too, more detailed aspects of behaviour can be quantified, such as the duration of incubation by one bird before it leaves to forage or is relieved by the other parent, or the proportion of time spent singing by the territorial male during the course of the breeding cycle. The latter will tell you whether singing decreases or increases at different points in the cycle.

In all of your birdwatching it is extremely important to remember that you are an observer, not a participant. In other words, you want to be as unobtrusive to the bird as possible. Do not interfere with nests, and always remain at sufficient distance from the birds you are watching to avoid modifying the very behaviours that you are seeking to observe. Remember that capture or marking of virtually all species of wild birds and even possession of dead ones, except by individuals possessing valid permits or authorization from the appropriate government agencies, are prohibited by law in most countries. Remember also that what a bird does and why it does it are two different things. You can readily devise ways of quantifying and recording the behaviour of a bird, but you should resist the temptation of attributing motivations to that behaviour — e.g. 'the male sang an average of 9 songs during each 3-minute period, trying to attract a mate'. In fact, the male may have been already mated and was singing quite aggressively towards the male on an adjacent territory. What you do know unambiguously, however, is that he sang an average of 9 songs every 3 minutes.

What to do with your data

A fine way to make your observations widely available to the birding community, and thus add to the growing body of information on British and European birds, is to contribute them to the literature on birds or to join one of many cooperative programmes organized by different ornithological groups.

First, here is a list of organizations in Britain and Ireland.

British Ornithologists' Union
Zoological Museum
Tring
Hertfordshire
HP23 6AP
Tel. 0442 890080

(publishes the journal *Ibis*)

British Trust for Ornithology
National Centre for Ornithology
The Nunnery
Thetford
Norfolk
IP24 2PU
Tel. 0842 750050

(publishes the journal *Bird Study* and organizes many internationally important efforts requiring your help)

International Council for Bird Preservation
 (now known as BirdLife International)
Wellbrook Court
Girton Road
Cambridge
CB3 0NA
Tel. 0223 277318

(has sections for Britain and most European countries)

Royal Society for the Protection of Birds (RSPB)
The Lodge
Sandy
Bedfordshire
SG19 2DL
Tel. 0767 680551

(The RSPB is Britain's foremost bird conservation organization. They publish *Birds*. They have local offices in Edinburgh, Munlocky (Ross and Cromarty), Glasgow, Newtown (Powys), Newcastle upon Tyne, Brighouse (West Yorks), Droitwich, Norwich, Lincoln, West Shoreham, and Exeter.)

World Pheasant Association
PO Box 5
Lower Basildon, near Reading, Berkshire RG8 9PF

Hawk and Owl Trust
The National Centre for Owl Conservation
Wolterton Park
Erpingham
Norwich
NR11 7LY

The Game Conservancy
Fordingbridge
Hampshire
SP6 1EF
Tel: 0425 652381

Wildfowl and Wetlands Trust
Slimbridge
Gloucester
GL2 7BT
Tel. 0453 890333

(publishes the Journal *Wildfowl*)

Scottish Ornithologists' Club
21 Regent Terrace
Edinburgh
EH7 5BT
Scotland
Tel. 031 556 6042

Irish Wildbird Conservancy
Ruttledge House
8 Longford Place
Monkstown
Co. Dublin, Ireland
Tel. 2804322

There are many comparable organizations throughout Europe and adjacent areas.

There are also many journals about birds. The editors are often ornithologists at institutes or universities. Because these journals change editors from time to time, it is not always easy to provide up-to-date addresses for them. Here we list a selection of countries and their journals. Some journals — like *British Birds* — you are likely to find in even a small local library. Others, you may find only in university libraries with special collections — such as the Alexander Library, in the Edward Grey Institute, Department of Zoology, Oxford University (tel. 0865 271275). Many journals are published by societies, in which case we have indicated which society in parentheses.

Austria
   Egretta (Österreichische Gesellschaft für Vogelkunde)

Belgium
   Gerfaut (Institut Royal des Sciences Naturelles de Belgique)
   Aves (Société d'Etudes Ornithologiques)
   L'Homme et l'Oiseau (Comité de Coordination pour la Protection des Oiseaux)

Croatia
   Larus (Institute of Ornithology, University of Zagreb)

Denmark
   Fuglevaern
   Tidsskrift
   Feltornithologen (Dansk Ornithologisk Forening)

Egypt
   Courser (Ornithological Society of Egypt)

Finland
   Ornis Fennica (Finnish Ornithological Society)
   Lintumies (Lintutieteellisten Yhdistysten Liittoo)

France
   L'Oiseau (Ligue Française pour la Protection des Oiseaux)
   Alauda (Société d'Etudes Ornithologiques)
   La Revue Française d'Ornithologie (Société Ornithologique de France)

Germany
 Die Vogelwarte (Bird Stations on Heligoland and at Radolfzell)
 Die Vogelwelt (Dachverband Deutscher Avifaunisten)
 Der Falke
 Journal für Ornithologie (Deutsche Ornithologen-Gesellschaft)
 Wir und die Vogel (Deutsche Bund für Vogelschutz)

Gibraltar
 Alectoris (Gibraltar Ornithological Society)

Great Britain and Ireland
 British Birds
 Ibis (British Ornithologists' Union)
 Bird Study (British Trust for Ornithology)
 Irish Bird Report (Irish Ornithologists' Club)
 Annual Report (The Wildfowl Trust)
 Birds (The Royal Society for the Protection of Birds)
 Seabird (Seabird group)
 Scottish Birds (Scottish Ornithologists' Club)
 Zoological Record: Aves (Zoological Society of London)

Hungary
 Aquila (Institutus Ornithologicus Hungaricus)

Iceland
 Bliki (Islands Naturhistoriska Museum and Islands Fågelskyddsförening)

Israel
 Tzufit (Sunbird) (Israel Ornithological Society)

Italy
 Rivista Italiana di Ornitologia (Societa Italiana di Scienze Naturali)
 Avocetta (Centro Italiano Studi Ornitologici)

Netherlands
 Ardea (Nederlandse Ornithologische Unie)
 Limosa (Nederlandse Ornithologische Unie)
 Vogels (Nederlandse Vereniging tot Bescherming van Vogels)

Norway
 Cinclus (Norsk Ornitologisk Förening)
 Vår Fuglefauna (Norsk Ornitologisk Förening)
 Sterna (Stavanger Museum)

Poland
 Acta Ornithologica (Musei Zoologici Polonici)
 The Ring (Polish Zoological Society)

Portugal
  Cyanopica (Sociedade Portuguesa de Ornitologia)

Scandinavia
  Ornis Scandinavica (Skandinavisk Ornitologisk Union)

Spain
  Ardeola (Sociedad Española de Ornitología)
  Acta Vertebrata (Estación Biologica de Doñana)

Sweden
  Vår Fågelvärld (Sveriges Ornitologiska Förening)
  Fauna och Flora (Naturhistoriska Riksmuseet)
  Anser (Skanes Ornitologiska Förening)
  Calidris (Olands Ornitologiska Förening)

Switzerland
  Nos Oiseaux (Société Romande pour l'Etude et la Protection des Oiseaux)
  Der Ornitologische Beobachter (Schweizerische Gesellschaft für Vogelkunde und Vogelschutz)
  Ornis (Schweizer Vogelschutz)

Species Treatments
and
Essays

Red-throated Diver
Gavia stellata

ATLAS 45; PMH 30; PER 62; HFP 20; HPCW 13; NESTS 47; BWP1:43

		2 (1–3) 1 brood			
	BLDS: ♂♀ Monogamy	INCU: ♂♀ 24–29	FLDG: ♂♀ 38–48	Aq inverts	

Breeding habitat Deep freshwater lakes to shallow pools or marine inlets. Nests on small pools, so adults must fly to lakes or sea to feed.

Displays Flies over territory, calling. Courtship includes bill-dipping and splash-diving; fast underwater rushing. Pairs duet.

Nesting Nest is saucer or scrape of vegetation on muddy ground within 0.5m of water; occasionally platform of mud and vegetation. Lined with vegetation and few feathers. Eggs greenish- or brownish-olive, spotted blackish, 75mm, hatch asynchronously. Young ride on backs of adults. Adults use distraction display to lure predators from nest.

Diet Mostly fish, captured by seizing (not spearing), but also includes frogs, aquatic invertebrates, and insects. Young fed invertebrates and then small fish.

Winters At sea, along inshore waters, S to Mediterranean.

Conservation Widely distributed across N Europe, Asia, N America; perhaps increasing in UK, though has declined in Scandinavia, Finland due to human disturbance. See p. 528.

Notes Eyes adapted for both aerial and underwater vision. Can take off more easily from water than other divers, and can land on and take off from land.

Essays Adaptations for Flight, p. 511; Birds and Oil, p. 225; Colour of Eggs, p. 161; Distraction Displays, p. 175.

Refs Marchant et al. 1990.

Black-throated Diver
Gavia arctica

ATLAS 45; PMH 30; PER 62; HFP 20; HPCW 13; NESTS 46; BWP1:50

		2 (1–3) 1 brood			
	BLDS: ♂♀ Monogamy	INCU: ♂♀ 28–30	FLDG: ♂♀ 60–65	Aq inverts	

Breeding habitat Large freshwater lakes to small pools in boreal to arctic waters. Avoids lakes where water level fluctuates.

Displays Very vocal on territory. Courtship includes bill-dipping and splash-diving in pairs, followed by underwater rushing.

Nesting Nest is wet mass of vegetation and mud lined with vegetation, built mainly by the ♂ at edge of shallow water. Completed after 1st egg laid. Up to 3 false nests built by ♂. Eggs greenish-to-olive-brown, spotted blackish, 85mm, hatch asynchronously.

Diet Mostly fish, with a few insects, crustaceans, and sometimes much aquatic vegetation. Often flies to salt water to feed. In winter takes almost entirely fish.

Winters At sea, inshore waters, S to Mediterranean.

Conservation Widely distributed across northern latitudes. While susceptible to human disturbance from boats, there is evidence of range increase. See p. 528.

Essays Adaptations for Flight, p. 511; Birds and Oil, p. 225; Colour of Eggs, p. 161.

Classifying Birds

TAXONOMY (sometimes called 'systematics') is the science of classifying organisms. The Linnaean system of classification was developed more than two centuries ago by the great Swedish botanist Carolus Linnaeus (born Karl von Linné). It is a hierarchical system — that is, each organism belongs to a series of ranked taxonomic categories, such as subspecies, species, genus, family, class, etc. At any rank (level) in the hierarchy any organism can belong to only one taxon, or taxonomic group. For instance, the Red-throated Diver can be a member of only one genus and one class. Each taxon is given a formal, unique, latinized name that is recognized by scientists around the world. Nomenclature is a formal system of names used to label taxonomic groups.

Birds are the class Aves, which is in the phylum Chordata (which also includes mammals, reptiles, amphibians, fishes, and tunicates) — everything with an internal skeletal rod called a 'notochord', which in vertebrates is enclosed in cartilage or within a backbone. The living (non-fossil) members of the class Aves are placed into more than two dozen orders, such as the Passeriformes (perching birds) and Piciformes (woodpeckers, etc.). The orders are divided into about 160 families, an average of 6–7 families per order. Family names can be recognized because they all end in 'idae'. For example, in the order Passeriformes are such families as the Prunellidae (accentors), the Laniidae (shrikes), the Sylviidae (Old World warblers), and the Emberizidae, a large family that includes, among others, the buntings and New World sparrows.

The next commonly used category is the genus: the Red-throated Diver is in the genus *Gavia*, along with other similar species. Its latinized specific name is *Gavia stellata*, made up of the name of the genus combined with a 'trivial name' to distinguish it from congeners (other members of the same genus).

SEE: Species and Speciation, p. 325; 'Passerines' and 'Songbirds', p. 351. REF.: Mayr, 1969.

Brood Patches

ONCE a bird's egg is laid, it must be heated if it is to develop. With rare exceptions, birds use their body (metabolic) heat to incubate their eggs. This presents them with a problem, however. Since birds are 'warm-blooded',

Great Northern Diver

Gavia immer

ATLAS 44; PMH 31; PER 62; HFP 20; HPCW 13; NESTS 45; BWP1:56

  2 (1–3) 1 brood INCU: ♂♀ 24–25 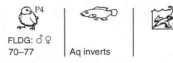 FLDG: ♂♀ 70–77 Aq inverts

BLDS: ♂♀
Monogamy

Breeding habitat   Close to deep, large freshwater lakes.

Displays   Yodel call signals territorial ownership. Courtship includes bill-dipping, splash-diving, and 'penguin dancing' with birds in vertical position and wings outstretched.

Nesting   At edge of shallow water. Nest lined with vegetation, perennial, continues to be built during incubation. Occasionally a simple scrape is used. Eggs greenish- or olive-brown, spotted brown, 90mm, hatch asynchronously; adults perform distraction display when threatened by predators. Chicks ride on adults' backs.

Diet   Fish, pursued and swallowed underwater, some aquatic invertebrates, especially crustaceans. Young fed small fish, aquatic invertebrates.

Winters   At sea in coastal waters, S to Spain. Birds use individual feeding territories during day, but gather into rafts at night.

Conservation   Iceland population is small, but is at edge of species range; no obvious change in numbers. Widely distributed across northern N America, where locally threatened by acid rain.

Notes   Eyes adapted for both aerial and underwater vision.

Essays   Adaptations for Flight, p. 511; Birds and Oil, p. 225; Colour of Eggs, p. 161; Swimming and Underwater Flight, p. 61.

White-billed Diver

Gavia adamsii

ATLAS 45; PMH 32; PER 62; HFP 20; HPCW -; NESTS 45; BWP1:62

 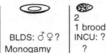 2 1 brood INCU: ? FLDG: ?? ? Aq inverts

BLDS: ♂♀?
Monogamy

Breeding habitat   In low-rimmed, sometimes shallow coastal lakes beyond the tree-line.

Displays   Courtship of bill-dipping and splash-diving, followed by search-swimming and inviting. Territorial behaviour including calls, alert posture, circle dance, bill dipping, and silent splash diving. Also rushing, jumping, and fencing-posturing in which the bird rises nearly straight up, treads water with bill held to breast, and wings folded or extended.

Nesting   Nest sometimes lined with vegetation. ♂ selects site. Eggs buffish- or greenish-brown, spotted with black, 90mm, hatch asynchronously. Young brooded in nest or elsewhere on shore for first few days. Chicks ride on back of swimming adults.

Diet   Mostly fish, a few aquatic invertebrates.

Winters   At sea at high latitudes.

Conservation   Low numbers and restricted habitats may mean that this species will be threatened by the increasing exploitation of the high Arctic, but is widely distributed around Arctic Ocean.

Notes   Eyes adapted for both aerial and underwater vision.

Essays   Adaptations for Flight, p. 511; Birds and Oil, p. 225; Colour of Eggs, p. 161.

they must be very careful about losing heat to the environment, yet be able to transfer heat to their eggs.

Heat is lost from a bird's surface, and the more surface it has relative to its volume, the more readily the heat will be lost. The smaller of two objects with the same shape will always have the greater surface/volume ratio. For example, a 1-centimetre cube has a surface area of 6 square centimetres, and a volume of 1 cubic centimetre. It has a surface/volume ratio of 6/1. A 2-centimetre cube has a surface area of 24 square centimetres (6 sides, each with 4 square centimetres) and a volume of 8 cubic centimetres. Its ratio then is 3/1 — only half the surface/volume ratio of the smaller cube. Most birds are relatively small, and thus have a large surface-to-volume ratio.

One of the main functions of the feathers is to insulate the bird — to prevent its body heat from being dissipated through the body surface. Most birds have 'solved' the dilemma posed by the need to both transfer and preserve heat by evolving 'brood patches'. These are areas of skin on the belly that lose their feathers toward the end of the egg-laying period. In the majority of birds the feathers are shed automatically, but geese and ducks pluck their brood patch and use the plucked feathers to make an insulating lining for their nests (hence 'eider down'). The brood patch also develops a supplemental set of vessels that bring hot blood close to the surface of the skin. In at least some birds, the female is able to regulate heat transfer to the eggs by adjusting her metabolic heat production and the flow of blood to the brood patch.

When birds return to the nest to resume incubating, they go through characteristic settling movements in order to bring the brood patch into contact with the eggs. In precocial birds, after the chicks have hatched, the insulating feathers grow back. In passerines, and presumably other altricial birds, the re-growth of the feathers is delayed, and the patches remain functional through early brooding. Then they gradually disappear, restoring the adult's thermoregulatory integrity about the time the young are fledged.

The placement of brood patches differs among groups of birds. There may be a single brood patch in the middle of the belly, as in hawks, pigeons, and most songbirds. Waders, auks, and skuas have one on each side, and gulls and game birds combine these two patterns by having three brood patches. Pelicans, boobies, and gannets have none at all. Instead they normally incubate by placing their webbed feet on the eggs. However, tropical boobies sometimes need to prevent the eggs overheating, in which case the eggs are rested on top of the webs. Emperor Penguins (*Aptenudytes forsteri*), which nest on Antarctic ice, cradle their single egg on their feet and cover it with a warming fold of abdominal skin.

When just one parent incubates, it alone develops a brood patch. If both parents incubate, both may produce brood patches, or one may cover the eggs without a patch, warming it less efficiently but at least retarding heat and water loss from the egg.

SEE: Incubation: Controlling Egg Temperatures, p. 273; Temperature Regulation and Behaviour, p. 163; Feathers, p. 363. REFS: Bailey, 1952; Haftorn and Reinertsen, 1982.

Little Grebe

Tachybaptus ruficollis

ATLAS 48; PMH 33; PER 62; HFP 22; HPCW 14; NESTS 50; BWP1:69

BLDS: ♂♀
Monogamy

4–6 (–10)
2 (3?) broods
INCU: ♂♀
20–21

FLDG: ♂♀
44–48

Aq inverts

Breeding habitat Wide range of aquatic habitats, but generally shallow, small lakes, exceptionally up to 1500m above sea level.

Displays Water courtship occurs all year, with hunched display and vocal trilling. Small groups may wing-wave in upright position and then patter along water. Advertising (by either sex) with long series of calls with neck erect. Birds may face each other, in hunched display, with duetting trills. There is a head-skating display, and a 'penguin dance' with birds erect in the water.

Nesting Nest is floating platform of weeds anchored to submerged vegetation. Eggs white or cream becoming stained, 38mm, hatch asynchronously.

Diet Mainly insects, some molluscs, crustaceans. Young fed mainly insects and some plants.

Winters Resident, or E populations move S; on more open waters than in summer; sometimes in loose flocks. Pairs may hold territories in winter.

Conservation Widely distributed across Europe, Africa, Asia. Declines in areas where there has been extensive drainage. In N, vulnerable to cold winters.

Essays Wetland Conservation, p. 145.

Refs Marchant et al. 1990.

Great Crested Grebe

Podiceps cristatus

ATLAS 46; PMH 33; PER 64; HFP 22; HPCW 14; NESTS 48; BWP1:78

BLDS: ♂♀
Monogamy

4 (1–6)
1–2 broods
INCU: ♂♀
27–29

FLDG: ♂♀
71–79

Aq inverts

Breeding habitat Well-vegetated fresh water, including man-made lakes, shallow sheltered bays on large lakes.

Displays ♂s (usually) defend territory with head and neck lowered over water. Courtship displays are subject of a classical study in behaviour and are complex. They involve head-shaking, and a weed dance where birds carry weeds to each other and rise quickly into vertical position, paddling rapidly and turning heads.

Nesting Nest is floating heap of vegetation anchored to other plants; well concealed. Eggs white becoming stained, 54mm, hatch asynchronously. Young carried on adults' backs. Adults split up brood and each looks after one group, favouring it over the other. Adults aggressively defend eggs and young and warn the young to dive by splash-diving.

Diet Fish, some aquatic invertebrates. Young fed small fish, insects.

Winters Resident; E populations move S. Also on more open water, estuaries, and inshore on sea.

Conservation Widely distributed across Europe, Asia. Declined to <50 pairs in England in 1860 and similarly threatened elsewhere by plumage trade. Has now recovered to over 6000 pairs in Britain, in part because of protection and ability to exploit such man-made habitats as gravel pits. Expanding N into Scandinavia.

Essays Visual Displays, p. 33; Nest Lining, p. 439; Transporting Young, p. 9.

Refs Marchant et al. 1990.

Black and White Plumage

ALL else being equal, black or dark-coloured objects more readily absorb heat than do white or light-coloured objects. Therefore, compared to birds with white plumage, birds with black plumage should be better able to absorb radiant solar energy and use it to warm themselves at low temperatures. For the same reason, dark-coloured birds should have a problem with overheating in hot environments. In nature, however, 'all else' is rarely equal, and this simple dichotomy of black plumage as a good absorber of radiant energy and white plumage as a good reflector seldom holds true. If it did, birds with black or dark plumage would not occur in arid regions or other habitats with abundant sunshine and little shade, and birds with white or very light plumage would not be found in very cold environments. In fact, black or dark-coloured birds such as Bald Ibis, vultures, several hawks, eagles, and herons, as well as Black Lark, several wheatears, Tristram's Grackle, and ravens all inhabit deserts and arid grasslands or savannas that have high daytime temperatures and abundant sunlight. Likewise, Ptarmigan, Willow Grouse, light-coloured gulls and egrets are found at higher altitudes and latitudes with cooler temperatures.

This apparent paradox can be resolved by considering other avenues of heat exchange between a bird and its environment. Heat will be gained from or lost to the environment depending on whether a bird is hotter or cooler than its surroundings. If body temperature is lower than the air temperature, then heat will tend to flow from the external environment to the bird, which will warm up and possibly face a problem of overheating. The reverse is true when the bird's temperature exceeds the environmental temperature — it may become chilled. The bird's structural adaptations and behaviour mediate heat gain and loss by means of conduction (by placing some portion of the body in contact with a surface of different temperature), convection (by exposing the body surface to the wind), radiation (by either emission or absorption of radiant energy, a passive result of the bird/environment temperature difference), and evaporation (by losing body heat via wetting of the plumage or skin, or through water vapour in exhaled breath).

The relationship between plumage colour and radiative heat gain and loss is therefore not straightforward. The simple rule of black/absorbing and white/reflecting is modified by whether feathers are sleeked or erected, by wind speed, and by how deeply the absorbed radiation actually penetrates through the plumage. At low wind speeds and with feathers sleeked, black plumages acquire higher heat loads than do white plumages, but the heat is absorbed mostly near the outer surface. As wind speed increases, the relative heat gains by white and black plumages converge; the portion of radiation that is not reflected by white plumage penetrates deeper than in black plumage and convection is thus less effective at removing heat from white than

Red-necked Grebe
Podiceps grisegena

ATLAS 46; PMH 33; PER 64; HFP 22; HPCW 14; NESTS 49; BWP1:89

		4–5 (2–6) 1 (2) broods	P4		
BLDS: ♂♀ Monogamy	INCU: ♂♀ 20–23	FLDG: ♂♀ 75?	Fish	Surface dips

Breeding habitat Small lowland waters rich in vegetation; sometimes rivers. Associates with gull colonies.

Displays On water ♂ and ♀ call together; call ends like horse whinny. ♂ and ♀ approach, head and bill at 45°, birds nearly facing until close, then swim in parallel while calling.

Nesting Nest is anchored mass of floating vegetation; several platforms built before actual nest. Eggs white becoming stained, 51mm, hatch asynchronously. Young carried by one parent may be fed by the other. Young early in the season are sometimes brooded on nest. Parents aggressively defend young.

Diet Aquatic invertebrates, especially insects, taken by diving or picked off surface; some fish.

Winters Mainly on estuaries and coastal habitats in western Europe.

Conservation Has been lost from many areas following habitat drainage. Occurs from E Europe, across Asia and N America.

Essays The Avian Sense of Smell, p. 13; Birds and Oil, p. 225; Empty Shells, p. 199; Moulting, p. 373; Swimming and Underwater Flight, p. 61; Temperature Regulation and Behaviour, p. 163; Nest Lining, p. 439; Swallowing Stones, p. 135; Transporting Young, p. 9.

Slavonian Grebe
Podiceps auritus

ATLAS 47; PMH 34; PER 64; HFP 22; HPCW 14; NESTS 49; BWP1:97

		4–5 (1–7) 1 (2) broods	P4		
BLDS: ♂♀ Monogamy	INCU: ♂♀ 22–25	FLDG: ♂♀ 55–60	Fish	

Breeding habitat Shallow, well-vegetated ponds and lakes; compared to Black-necked Grebe, lakes have less dense vegetation on margins.

Displays Elaborate courtship of varied postures including rushing (both birds rise out of water while side by side), weed ceremony, and much head shaking.

Nesting Nest is anchored pile of floating vegetation, usually in cover; started by ♂. Eggs chalky white becoming stained, 46mm, hatch asynchronously. Parents defend young aggressively with splash-diving distraction display.

Diet Mostly insects and fish, obtained by diving; fish in winter. Young fed insects in some areas, small fish in others. Dives are often long and birds travel far underwater.

Winters Across Europe on open reservoirs, estuaries, shallow coastal waters; sometimes in large groups.

Conservation Occurs across N central Europe, Asia, and N America; increasing in N and W. Vulnerable to human disturbance. See p. 528.

Essays Birds and Oil, p. 225; Empty Shells, p. 199; Moulting, p. 373; Precocial and Altricial Young, p. 401; Swimming and Underwater Flight, p. 61; Temperature Regulation and Behaviour, p. 163; Nest Lining, p. 439; Distraction Displays, p. 175; Transporting Young, p. 9.

Refs Sharrock 1976; Marchant et al. 1990.

from black plumages. With erect feathers, black plumage actually gains less heat than white plumage when wind speeds are moderate or high. Thus, under conditions routinely encountered in arid habitats, birds with dark-coloured plumage stay cooler than birds with light-coloured plumage! Conversely, at low ambient temperatures and higher wind speeds, erect white plumage gains heat better and is more resistant to heat loss because of better penetration by solar radiation and better resistance to convective heat loss.

This is not to say that thermoregulatory considerations have been the only, or even the most important, selective forces in the evolution of white and black plumages. Surely white plumage in some high latitude birds has been of overriding importance as camouflage. Similarly, black plumage is very conspicuous in open or light-coloured surroundings that are typical of deserts, grasslands, and marshes. Hence, its value as a long-distance visual signal must also be considered when viewing the evolution of dark plumages in birds of arid or other open habitats. And finally, some plumages, such as the wingtips of many gulls and terns, apparently are black because the dark pigment, melanin, increases the durability of the feathers.

SEE: Metabolism, p. 281; Temperature Regulation and Behaviour, p. 163; Feathers, p. 363; Colour of Birds, p. 137; Spread-wing Postures, p. 17. REFS: Ellis, 1980; Walsberg, 1982; Walsberg *et al.*, 1978; Wunder, 1979.

Transporting Young

MUCH like the lore of babies being delivered by a stork, the accounts of fledglings being carried from elevated tree nests by a parent appear to be fairy tales — or, at best, descriptions of very atypical behaviour. Reports of chicks leaping to the ground are far more common.

Aerial carrying has been reported in 16 species of seven waterfowl groups as well as in coots, moorhens, woodcocks, and a cuckoo. Nevertheless, the behaviour is not well documented and ornithologists remain uncertain of the conditions leading to it or of how it is accomplished. Making observations is difficult, given that aerial transport occurs either discreetly under the cover of dim light or in panic situations when a parent is confronted by a predator. Thus, most information remains anecdotal. It is not clear, for example, whether a parent holds its chick in its bill, carries it on its back, or clutches it between its legs.

Much more is known about birds that carry their young while swimming. Worldwide, three species of swans, at least seven species of ducks, grebes and various other wetland birds commonly chauffeur their young. In all cases, the young initiate the ride and are readily able to hang on by clamping their bills over the feathers of the adult should it decide to dive. It is thought

Black-necked Grebe

Podiceps nigricollis

ATLAS 47; PMH 34; PER 64; HFP 22; HPCW 14; NESTS 50; BWP1:105

		3–4 (1–6) 1 (2) broods			
	BLDS: ♂♀ Monogamy	INCU: ♂♀ 20–22	FLDG: ♂♀ 21?	Fish	Surface dips

Breeding habitat Well-vegetated shallow ponds and lakes; often in association with colonies of gulls and terns.

Displays Courtship and pair-bond maintenance; penguin dance with partners facing; stereotyped preening; one bird, submerged, approaches the other, which raises its crest and its folded wings.

Nesting Nest is mass of floating vegetation anchored to other vegetation in cover of reeds or sedges. Several nests may be built before final one, and sometimes eggs laid in each one. Eggs chalky white becoming stained, 44mm, hatch asynchronously. Young sometimes cared for in crèche; ride on parents' backs when small. Sometimes parents split brood and each looks after one group.

Diet Mainly aquatic insects, some molluscs, amphibians, and small fish. Collected from shallow water or surface. Young fed mostly insects.

Winters Across S and C Europe in a variety of habitats: open reservoirs, estuaries, shallow coasts; in large concentrations in N America.

Conservation Sporadic breeder in the western part of Europe, occurs across Asia and N America.

Essays The Avian Sense of Smell, p. 13; Birds and Oil, p. 225; Empty Shells, p. 199; Moulting, p. 373; Precocial and Altricial Young, p. 401; Swimming and Underwater Flight, p. 61; Temperature Regulation and Behaviour, p. 163; Nest Lining, p. 439; Swallowing Stones, p. 135; Transporting Young, p. 9.

Fulmar

Fulmarus glacialis

ATLAS 48; PMH 35; PER 64; HFP 24; HPCW 15; NESTS 52; BWP1:121

		1 (2) 1 brood			
Bank	BLDS: – Monogamy	INCU: ♂♀ 52–53	FLDG: ♂♀ 41–57	Carrion	Surface dives

Breeding habitat On cliffs near sea, but also on inland cliffs up to 1000m above sea level.

Displays ♀ resting on ledge, ♂ alights, bill open, head back, waving head side to side and up-down with loud cackling calls. Also displays on water near colonies.

Nesting Colonial. Nest site has no material and is on bare rock or small depression on ground. Eggs white, 74mm, clutches of 2 probably produced by 2 ♀s. First incubation is by ♀ for about 1 day, then ♂ has 7-day spell, then sexes alternate with spells 3–4 days each. Adults defend young by spitting oil. 6–12 years old when first breed.

Present at colonies most of year.

Diet Mainly crustaceans, squid, fish, and fish offal from boats. Seized from surface, though sometimes by diving. Young fed by regurgitation.

Winters At sea in N Atlantic; nomadic, but sometimes large feeding flocks.

Conservation Has increased greatly over last 200 yr, spreading from Iceland to Britain, France, and Germany and is now widespread in N Atlantic.

Essays The Avian Sense of Smell, p. 13; Disease and Parasitism, p. 315; Drinking, p. 313; Feeding Young Petrels, p. 11; Seabird Nesting Sites, p. 233; Sleeping Sentries and Mate-guarding, p. 73; Commensal Feeding, p. 27.

that ferrying by adults over water is most advantageous in species that fly infrequently, that have large bodies and small broods, and whose young grow slowly.

In addition to aerial and aquatic carrying there are also a few reports of birds using their wings to clap chicks to their sides and proceeding on foot. But there is one note of caution in documenting how frequently and under what circumstances parent birds carry their young: some species such as the Woodcock feign carrying their young, and such distraction displays may as effectively fool birdwatchers as predators.

SEE: Parental Care, p. 171; Carrying Eggs, p. 99; Distraction Displays, p. 175; Precocial and Altricial Young, p. 401. REFS: Johnsgard and Kear, 1968; Lowe, 1972.

Feeding Young Petrels

PETRELS, albatrosses, shearwaters, and fulmars are commonly known as 'tubenoses'. All are marine birds with extremely large nostrils (thus the name) and a well-developed olfactory centre in the brain. Experiments have shown that smell is important and perhaps crucial in finding food. More contentiously smell may also aid petrels to find their nest sites.

Tubenoses often feed very far from land, converting the oil-rich prey in their stomachs into a store of oil and partially digested flesh. The birds regurgitate the mix for their young when they return to their nests, often after an absence of days or weeks.

Tubenoses always produce a clutch of one, and the single chick matures very slowly. At one extreme, the larger albatrosses may take almost a year to fledge, while small storm-petrels are flight-ready in about two months. Tubenose young store large deposits of fat that may function to tide them over the long intervals between feedings. But the young of species such as Manx Shearwaters, that are fed frequently (only about 5 per cent of feeding intervals extend beyond three days) also have abundant fat deposits. These stores may allow for earlier fledging or may safeguard against uncertainties in hunting success after fledging.

Field studies have been conducted to examine whether foraging rates of the adults are determined by unpredictable food supplies or instead are dictated by the needs of the chicks. In one such study, a detailed analysis of feeding rates (frequency of feeding and meal size) was undertaken for Leach's Storm Petrels on an island in the Bay of Fundy, New Brunswick, Canada. The results showed that time between consecutive feedings was only rarely as long as the period that the chicks could survive on their fat stores. Indeed the rate at which the Storm Petrel chicks were fed seemed

Cory's Shearwater

Calonectris diomedea

ATLAS 49; PMH 36; PER 66; HFP 26; HPCW 17; NESTS 53; BWP1:136

	BLDS: ♂♀ Monogamy	1 1 brood INCU: ♂♀ 52–55

SA1		
FLDG: ♂♀ 85–95?	Aq inverts	Surface dips

Breeding habitat   Offshore islands.

Displays   Very noisy at breeding colonies. In courtship, birds face each other, then preen each other. During copulation, call loudly, and then ♀ nibbles ♂'s tail.

Nesting   Colonial. Nest has little or no material in burrow in soil; sometimes excavated by both sexes; visits nest only at night. Eggs white, 69mm. Assembles off shore near colonies before sunset, before moving to nests. ♂ incubates first, then ♀, with shifts lasting about 6 days.

Diet   Mainly fish, squid, and zooplankton, but will scavenge offal. Feeds nocturnally, skimming surface and surface feeding, occasionally shallow diving.

Winters   At sea from UK southwards.

Conservation   Abundant nester on islands in Atlantic and Mediterranean. At some colonies, large numbers of young were taken for food, down, and oil. Now protected: see p. 529.

Notes   Sometimes forms dense rafts on ocean.

Essays   The Avian Sense of Smell, p. 13; Feeding Young Petrels, p. 11; Skimming: Why Birds Fly Low over Water, p. 67; Swimming and Underwater Flight, p. 61; Soaring, p. 79; Commensal Feeding, p. 27.

Manx Shearwater

Puffinus puffinus

ATLAS 49; PMH 37; PER 66; HFP 26; HPCW 19; NESTS 53; BWP1:145

	Crevice BLDS: ♂♀ Monogamy	1 1 brood INCU: ♂♀ 47–55

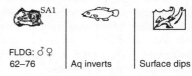

SA1		
FLDG: ♂♀ 62–76	Aq inverts	Surface dips

Breeding habitat   Offshore islands.

Displays   Calls near burrows, often duetting, except on moonlit nights; breeding displays little known.

Nesting   Colonial. Nest has no material or small amount of vegetation in excavated burrows or crevices. Visits only at night. Eggs white, 61mm. Birds establish long-term bonds and tend to reuse same burrow. ♂ incubates first, then sexes alternate with spells lasting about 6 days. Young deserted by parents before fledging. Young adults visit colony as early as second year, coming earlier each year as they get older; start to breed at 5 or 6 years.

Diet   Mostly small fish, some cephalopods, zooplankton. Feeds during day, pursuing prey after dives or seizing prey on surface; sometimes in small flocks. Young fed pre-digested fish.

Winters   At sea; to the coast of S America.

Conservation   In Britain, some colonies became extinct following introductions of rats; major decreases in France. Widespread and abundant in N Atlantic and Mediterranean. See p. 529.

Essays   Feeding Young Petrels, p. 11;The Avian Sense of Smell, p. 13; Skimming: Why Birds Fly Low over Water, p. 67; Swimming and Underwater Flight, p. 61; Soaring, p. 79; Commensal Feeding, p. 27; Orientation and Navigation, p. 503; Parent–Chick Recognition in Colonial Nesters, p. 227.

Refs   Brooke 1990 is a book about this species.

determined by their needs rather than by the ability of the adults to find food. More research will be required to determine whether this is true for all tubenoses and, if so, to examine further the true function of fat storage in the chicks of these birds.

SEE: Coloniality, p. 107; Average Clutch Size, p. 31; Seabird Nesting Sites, p. 233; The Avian Sense of Smell, p. 13. REF.: Ricklefs *et al.*, 1985.

The Avian Sense of Smell

MOST birds are primarily 'sight animals' as their superb eyes, colourful plumage, and non-acoustic signals attest. But their sense of hearing is obviously also very acute — as in the case of night-hunting owls, which use sound to locate their prey. Most birds seemingly would have little use for smell; in the airy treetops odours disperse quickly and would be of minimal help in locating obstacles, prey, enemies, or mates. Yet the apparatus for detecting odours is present in the nasal passages of all birds. Based on the relative size of the brain centre used to process information on odours, physiologists expect the sense of smell to be well developed in rails, cranes, grebes, and nightjars and less developed in passerines, woodpeckers, pelicans, and parrots. By recording the electrical impulses transmitted through the bird's olfactory nerves, physiologists have documented some of the substances that birds as diverse as albatrosses, shearwaters, ducks, vultures, chickens, pigeons, and sparrows are able to smell.

The sense of smell seems better developed in some avian groups than others. Kiwis, flightless birds that are the national symbol of New Zealand, appear to sniff out their earthworm prey at night. Sooty Shearwaters and Fulmars are attracted from downwind to the smell of fish oils, squid, and krill, and when tested, investigate the area around a wick releasing such odorants. Other tubenoses are also attracted to the same stimuli.

When they return at night from foraging in eastern Canada's Bay of Fundy, Leach's Storm Petrels appear to use odour to locate their burrows on forested Kent Island, New Brunswick. They hover above the thick spruce-fir canopy before plummeting to the forest floor in the vicinity of their burrows. Then they walk upwind to their burrow, often colliding with obstacles on the way. In one experiment the petrels moved toward a stream of air passing over materials from their own burrow, rather than one passing over similar materials from the forest floor. However the crucial test, to determine whether the birds could distinguish the smell of their own burrow from the smell of other individuals' burrows, was not undertaken. The matter is not conclusively resolved. Perhaps smell is more important for petrel burrow location in heavy forest cover, less so on unforested Pacific islands. Similarly, Manx Shearwaters do not appear to use smell to find their burrows in an

Storm Petrel

Hydrobates pelagicus

ATLAS 51; PMH 39; PER 66; HFP 28; HPCW 21; NESTS 54; BWP1:163

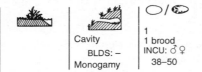 

	Cavity	1 brood			
	BLDS: –	INCU: ♂♀	FLDG: ♂♀		
	Monogamy	38–50	56–73	Fish	

Breeding habitat Offshore islands.

Displays Include nocturnal display flights circling over burrow. Birds (both sexes?) have purring call in burrow and preen each other; otherwise behaviour in burrow little known.

Nesting Colonial. Nest has no or little material in excavated burrow in soft soil or in rock crevices. Eggs white, 28mm. Pair bond for life, perhaps because both birds return to same nest hole. Incubation alternately by both sexes with about 3 days per spell. Young fed almost until fledging. Young adults return to colony at 2 years and start to breed at 4 or 5 years.

Diet Surface zooplankton, small fish.

Feeds during day from surface without landing, alone or in small groups. Young fed regurgitated, mashed food.

Winters At sea, sometimes inshore. S to coast of South Africa.

Conservation Marked decreases on some islands, but an abundant nester from Iceland to Mediterranean. See p. 529.

Essays Geometry of the Selfish Colony, p. 15; Feeding Young Petrels, p. 11; Monogamy, p. 335; Swimming and Underwater Flight, p. 61; Commensal Feeding, p. 27; Feeding Birds, p. 357; Birds and Oil, p. 225; Feeding Young Petrels, p. 11; Parental Care, p. 171; Salt Glands, p. 237.

Leach's Storm-Petrel

Oceanodroma leucorhoa

ATLAS 51; PMH 39; PER 66; HFP 28; HPCW 21; NESTS 54; BWP1:168

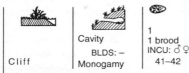 

	Cavity	1 brood			
	BLDS: –	INCU: ♂♀	FLDG: ♂♀		
Cliff	Monogamy	41–42	63–70	Fish	

Breeding habitat Offshore islands.

Displays Nocturnal display flight including communal displays and sexual chases. A rapid, erratic flight often centred above burrow. Also a slower flight, vibrating wings and hovering with legs trailing. Birds may stand with raised wings. Calls start after dark, peaking near midnight; also calls in burrow when both birds present. Frequent, long duets.

Nesting Colonial; in burrows in soft soil or in rock crevices, walls. Nest has no material. Eggs white, 33mm. Nocturnal. Pair for life, choosing the same site each year. First breeding at 5 years, though young adults return to colony earlier.

Diet Plankton and small fish. Feeds in daytime from surface while flitting above it and rarely settles. Follows feeding whales and seals for leftovers.

Winters At sea as far S as South Africa.

Conservation Europe is on edge of species range; the major colonies are in N America. No noticeable declines, and small colonies may be overlooked. See p. 529.

Notes In a homing experiment, birds released in England returned to Canada 4800km away within 14 days.

Essays The Avian Sense of Smell, p. 13; Feeding Young Petrels, p. 11; Geometry of the Selfish Colony, p. 15; Seabird Nesting Sites, p. 233; Monogamy, p. 335; Swimming and Underwater Flight, p. 61; Commensal Feeding, p. 27; Feeding Birds, p. 357; Birds and Oil, p. 225; Feeding Young Petrels, p. 11; Parental Care, p. 171; Salt Glands, p. 237; Orientation and Navigation, p. 503.

unforested colony. Interestingly, there is also some evidence that the smells in air currents near their lofts help pigeons navigate in some parts of the world.

There has been a long controversy over the degree to which New World vultures use odour to help them find food. Mostly the argument has been over whether sight or smell is more important, but it has also been suggested, by those with a flair for the absurd, that vultures listen for the noise of the chewing of carrion-feeding rodents or insects or even use an as yet undiscovered sense. Nonetheless, the sight–smell argument remains unsettled. While North American Turkey Vultures (*Cathartes aura*), for example, seem to have a good sense of smell, quite likely it is not good enough to detect the stench of decomposing food from their foraging altitudes. Experiments have shown that their threshold for detecting the odours of at least three different products of decay is too high to permit sniff location from high altitude. Whether or not the birds are more sensitive to the smells of other components of decomposition remains to be determined. More work will be required to determine whether New World vultures use sight or smell or both to locate the dead animals they feed on. Old World vultures probably rely solely on sight.

SEE: Eyes like a Hawk, p. 89; What Do Birds Hear?, p. 255; How Owls Hunt in the Dark, p. 251. REFS: Bang and Wenzel, 1985; Grubb, 1974; James, 1986; Smith and Paselk, 1986; Wenzel, 1973.

Geometry of the Selfish Colony

IN a classic article entitled 'The geometry of the selfish herd', the behavioural ecologist W. D. Hamilton presented a model to explain why animals often are found in aggregations — flocks, herds, schools, etc. The basic assumption of the model was rather simple: animals do not crowd together to benefit the group, but for purely 'selfish' reasons.

Hamilton's scheme assumed that a predator would always attack the nearest prey. In that circumstance, it would always be to the advantage of potential victims to approach each other. Side by side, two of them would each have only half the 'domain of danger' that one alone would have, since each would be closer to a predator approaching from only half the possible directions. If four crowd together, each is exposed to predation from only one quarter of the possible directions (that is, the domain of danger is halved again). And so it goes — the larger the herd or colony, the less the exposure of a given individual. Those able to reach the centre of the crowd would be safest of all.

Some evidence of this can be seen in observations of fishes attempting to

Gannet

Sula bassana

ATLAS 56; PMH 40; PER 68; HFP 30; HPCW 23; NESTS 56; BWP1:191

 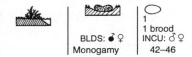

	BLDS: ♂♀ Monogamy	1 1 brood INCU: ♂♀ 42–46	FLDG: ♂♀ 84–97	Surface dives

Breeding habitat Offshore islands or cliffs.

Displays Nest sites are in limited supply and are defended by both sexes, but particularly ♂ with gripping, pushing, and loud calling. Nest exchange sequence: pair faces, wings slightly raised, tails spread, bow, sky-point, and repeatedly dip bill to breast of mate, then preen.

Nesting Colonial. Nest is of seaweed and other flotsam. Eggs bluish-white, becoming stained, 79mm. Young brooded continuously for first 14 days on top of parent's feet. Adults pair for life; birds come to colony in 4–5 year to pair, typically nest the following year.

Diet Fish taken by spectacular plunge dives from heights of up to 40m. Also feeds from surface.

Winters At sea S to West Africa.

Conservation Has increased throughout region, following earlier persecution, and is common and widespread in N Atlantic. Major colonies are in Britain.

Notes Has special reinforced skull to cushion impact of dives.

Essays Bills, p. 391; Disease and Parasitism, p. 315; Incubation: Controlling Egg Temperatures, p. 273.

Refs Nelson 1978 is a book about this species.

Cormorant

Phalacrocorax carbo

ATLAS 53; PMH 40; PER 68; HFP 32; HPCW 23; NESTS 58; BWP1:200

		3–4 (3–6) 1 brood		
Decid tree	BLDS: ♂♀ Monogamy	INCU: ♂♀ 28–31	FLDG: ♂♀ 50?	

Breeding habitat Mostly in sheltered coastal waters in W, fresh water on continent.

Displays Limited nest sites are defended by ♂ by pecking, lunging head forward with loud calls. ♂ advertises for ♀, with 'wing-waving': uttering no call but raising wing tips upwards and outwards, revealing white rump patches. After eggs are laid, birds greet each other with gaping display, ♂ points closed bill, head, and neck up, swinging head and neck slowly backwards and opening bill with loud call, touching base of tail. ♀'s greeting is similar.

Nesting Colonial. Nest is of seaweed and twigs; on broad cliff ledges, in trees, or flat ground on islands. Eggs pale blue, overlaid chalky white, 66mm; incubated by both sexes changing over twice a day; hatch asynchronously. Sometimes

young fed in crèche by parents from whom they beg food. Begin to nest at 4–5 years.

Diet Entirely fish, mainly flatfish and other bottom feeders obtained during day by diving from the surface and pursuing prey underwater. Feeds in shallow waters.

Winters In breeding habitats, but also disperses inland.

Conservation Common and widespread across Europe, Asia, and into N America, N Africa. Efforts have led to increases in the UK, but species is vulnerable to disturbance and to deliberate nest destruction elsewhere. See p. 528.

Notes Used by fishermen in SE Asia to capture fish.

Essays Spread-wing Postures, p. 17.

Refs Sharrock 1976.

move into the middle of a school when a predator approaches, sheep trying to butt their way into the centre of a flock when harried by sheep dogs, and Mexican Gray-breasted Martins (*Progne chalybea*) trying to remain near the centre of nocturnal roosting aggregations on power lines. Could Hamilton's model fit other aggregations of birds? Research by Susan E. Quinlan, of the Alaska Department of Fish and Game, who studied predation by river otters on storm-petrel colonies at Fish Island in the Gulf of Alaska, indicates that it could. Quinlan suggested that river otters prey heavily on seabirds only under such special circumstances as a decline in the availability of an important aquatic food. She found that in 1976 and 1977 the otters were the primary cause of mortality among breeding Fork-tailed Storm Petrels on Fish Island, killing about a quarter of those breeding in burrows on the soil-covered plateau in the island's centre. (The petrels breeding in the other habitat, rocky slopes dropping to the shoreline, suffered little predation, but exact data could not be obtained because of the difficulty of locating the nests.)

The density of Fork-tailed Storm Petrel nests varied over the plateau, and depredations by the otters were greatest where the density was lowest. Birds in denser parts of the colony were safer, even though there is no mobbing reaction to intruders to explain the greater security of 'inside' birds. Quinlan suggested that although the probability of detection for a group of nests increased as they crowded close together, above a certain density this disadvantage was overcome by the reduction in the chance of being eaten. This could be due to the selfish herd effect; in high-density areas the domains of danger of each nest would be very small. She predicted that large colonies in general will suffer less than small ones from irregular otter predation. Similarly, in a Guillemot colony in Wales, scattered nests suffered higher predation rates than those in dense groups.

More research needs to be done to test whether these birds really do constitute a 'selfish colony', but Quinlan's results show that here, as elsewhere, ecological theory can suggest reasons for observed bird behaviour — in this case why some Fork-tailed Storm Petrel nest burrows have as many as five other burrows within a radius of two metres. A good model may eventually prove to be incorrect or inapplicable in a given case, but models provide a framework for designing field research.

SEE: Mobbing, p. 261; Sleeping Sentries and Mate-guarding, p. 73. REFS: Birkhead, 1977; Hamilton, 1971; Kharitonov and Siegel-Causey, 1988; Quinlan, 1983; Watt and Mock, 1987.

Spread-wing Postures

SOME birds adopt characteristic poses in which they extend and often slightly droop their wings. This behaviour is commonly described as 'sun-bathing' or

Shag

Phalacrocorax aristotelis

ATLAS 54; PMH 41; PER 68; HFP 32; HPCW 24; NESTS 58; BWP1:207

 Ground | Cavity BLDS: ♂♀ Monogamy | 3 (1–6) 1 brood INCU: ♂♀ 30–31 | FLDG: ♂♀ 48–58 | | High dives

Breeding habitat   Coastal, especially on rocky coasts and islands. Unlike Cormorant avoids very shallow water.
Displays   ♂s (sometimes ♀s) bill-point with head shaking to defend nest site. ♂s advertise to ♀s by drawing head back over body, rapid darting upwards and forwards showing gape. Mates often preen each other.
Nesting   In loose colonies, sometimes dense colonies. Nest on narrow cliff ledge or in boulders is of seaweed, twigs; better nests have higher success, as young fall out of poorly built ones. ♂s sometimes bigamous where nest sites scarce. Eggs pale blue, overlaid with chalky white, 63mm, hatch asynchronously. Young beg for food, holding head up and waving it side to side while calling, will preen each other and adults. Breeds for first time at 2 (♂s) or 3 (♀s) years.

Diet   Fish caught under water, following dive from surface, but sometimes from air. Takes free-swimming fish, especially sand eels, in deep water (compare with Cormorant). Young fed regurgitated fish.
Winters   Along coasts.
Conservation   Common along coasts from Iceland, W Europe, and around Mediterranean; has increased when freed from human persecution. See p. 529.
Essays   Disease and Parasitism, p. 315; Natural Selection, p. 297; Visual Displays, p. 33; Colour of Eggs, p. 161; *Hesperornis* and Other Missing Links, p. 129; Who Incubates?, p. 285; Swimming and Underwater Flight, p. 61; Spread-wing Postures, p. 17; Temperature Regulation and Behaviour, p. 163; Bird Droppings, p. 485.
Refs   Sharrock 1976.

Pygmy Cormorant

Phalacrocorax pygmeus

ATLAS 55; PMH 41; PER 68; HFP 32; HPCW 24; NESTS 59; BWP1:216

 | BLDS: ♂♀ Monogamy | 4–6 (3–7) 1 brood INCU: ♂♀ 27–30 |  FLDG: ♂♀ 70?

Breeding habitat   Usually densely vegetated, standing or slowly flowing fresh waters; often with herons.
Displays   Poorly known.
Nesting   Colonial. Nest is of twigs and reeds in trees or reedbeds. Eggs pale blue, overlaid with chalky white, 47mm, hatch asynchronously. At few weeks old, leave nest and move around colony.
Diet   Fish. Often dives after watching for prey from a perch near surface.
Winters   Disperses away from breeding areas, in flocks or small family parties.

Conservation   Has restricted and fragmented range in SE Europe and SW Asia and has declined because of habitat drainage. See p. 528.
Essays   Wetland Conservation, p. 145; Visual Displays, p. 33; Colour of Eggs, p. 161; *Hesperornis* and Other Missing Links, p. 129; Who Incubates?, p. 285; Swimming and Underwater Flight, p. 61; Spread-wing Postures, p. 17; Temperature Regulation and Behaviour, p. 163; Bird Droppings, p. 485.

'wing-drying'. Cormorants and darters frequently assume these postures, which are also seen in some pelicans, storks, herons, vultures, and hawks.

The structure of cormorant and darter feathers decreases buoyancy and thus facilitates underwater pursuit of fishes. Hence their plumage is not water-repellent, but 'wettable'. It has been suggested that the function of spread-wing postures in these birds is to dry the wings after wetting. Biologists once thought that deficient production of oils from the preen gland necessitated wing-drying behaviour. We now know, however, that the degree of feather waterproofing is primarily due to their microscopic structure, not to their being oiled. In addition to helping wing feathers to dry, other suggested functions for these postures include regulating body temperature ('thermoregulation'), realigning feathers, forcing parasites into motion to ease their removal, and helping the perched bird to balance.

Spread-wing postures may serve different purposes in different species. Darters, for example, have unusually low metabolic rates and unusually high rates of heat loss from their bodies. Whether wet or dry, they exhibit spread-wing postures mostly under conditions of bright sunlight and cool ambient temperatures, and characteristically orient themselves with their backs to the sun. Thus, it appears that darters adopt a spread-wing posture primarily for thermoregulation. They absorb solar energy to supplement their low metabolic heat production and to partly offset their inordinately high rate of heat loss due to convection and (when wet) evaporation from their plumage.

Cormorants, in contrast, apparently use spread-wing postures for drying their wings, not for thermoregulation. Although cormorant plumage also retains water, only the outer portion of the feathers is wettable, so cormorants maintain an insulating layer of air next to the skin when swimming underwater. This difference in feather structure may explain why cormorants can spend more time foraging in the water and inhabit cooler climes than darters, which are restricted to shorter foraging bouts and are limited to tropical and subtropical waters.

An alternative explanation comes from the observation that African Reed Cormorants were more likely to spread after catching fish, and less likely after failure. The occurrence of the posture was not dependent on the length of time spent in the water. Could the birds have been signalling their success to other cormorants?

Spread-wing postures appear to serve for both thermoregulation and drying in many vultures, such as Lappet-faced and Griffon, but the most detailed studies are of American Turkey Vultures (*Cathartes aura*). Field observations of wing spreading in vultures indicate that the incidence of this behaviour is related to the intensity of sunlight and also occurs more frequently when the birds are wet.

SEE: Metabolism, p. 281; Temperature Regulation and Behaviour, p. 163; Black and White Plumage, p. 7. REFS: Clark, 1969; Clark and Ohmart, 1985; Elowson, 1984; Hennemann, 1982, 1983, 1985; Jones, 1978; Mahoney, 1984; Simmons, 1986.

White Pelican
Pelecanus onocrotalus

ATLAS 56; PMH 41; PER 68; HFP 30; HPCW 25; NESTS 56; BWP1:227

BLDS: ?	2 (3–5?) 1 brood		
Monogamy	INCU: ♂♀ 29–36	FLDG: ♂♀ 65–70	

Breeding habitat Large freshwater marshes and shallow coastal waters.
Displays At nest, birds defend by a display involving stretching bill upwards towards rival. Sexes develop coloured patch of bare skin on forehead in breeding season. ♀s with coloured patches attract ♂s who compete, and groups of ♂s with coloured patches may have a group display. In pairing, ♂ uses strutting walk with head and neck extended, follows ♀.
Nesting Colonial. Nest is large pile of vegetation sometimes lined with feathers. Eggs chalky white, 94mm, hatch asynchronously. At 20–30 days young leave nest and form crèche. Birds breed at 3–4 years.
Diet Fish, caught in bill with gular sac held open to form a scoop. Often feeds cooperatively with birds in a semi-circle moving forward. Young chicks given liquid pre-digested food.
Winters Migrates southwards, sometimes in spectacular concentrations; wintering range of European birds not well known, but includes Egypt.
Conservation Has very restricted, fragmented distribution in Europe, S and C Asia, and Africa. Is vulnerable to habitat drainage and direct persecution. See p. 529.
Essays Drinking, p. 313; Wetland Conservation, p. 145; Spread-wing Postures, p. 17; The Avian Sense of Smell, p. 13; Moulting, p. 373; Communal Roosting, p. 81; Crèches, p. 45.

Dalmatian Pelican
Pelecanus crispus

ATLAS 57; PMH 42; PER 68; HFP 30; HPCW 26; NESTS 57; BWP1:233

Floating	BLDS: ♂♀ Monogamy	2–4 (5–6) 1 brood INCU: ♂♀ 30–32	FLDG: ♂♀ 85?	

Breeding habitat Large freshwater marshes and shallow coastal waters, often shared with White Pelican.
Displays Display to rivals is waving of wide open bill. In pair formation, ♂ turns to ♀ and does bowing display, drooping joints of closed wing and spreading tail widely, then bowing.
Nesting Colonial. Nest is heap of reeds, sticks, etc. built by ♀ from material brought by ♂. Eggs chalky white, 95mm, hatch asynchronously. First breed at 3 years.
Diet Fish, caught in gular scoop used as a sack. Like White Pelican, birds may fish in groups.
Winters Disperses from breeding areas, some migrating through Turkey into Egypt.
Conservation Fragmented and local distribution, from SE Europe to C Asia, reduced by marsh drainage and disturbance. Said to number in the millions in Romania in the 1800s, but now in the thousands. See p. 529.
Essays Wetland Conservation, p. 145; Spread-wing Postures, p. 17; The Avian Sense of Smell, p. 13; Moulting, p. 373; Communal Roosting, p. 81; Colour of Eggs, p. 161; Skimming: Why Birds Fly Low over Water, p. 67; Bird Droppings, p. 485; Birds on Borders, p. 95.

Marine birds show a wide variety of foraging strategies. From left to right above the waterline: a gull picks up floating offal; a tern and a Gannet plunge after fishes near the surface; a storm-petrel 'walks on water'; and a pelican floats as it forages on the surface. Below the waterline: a Shag uses its legs to propel it after a fish; a shearwater (above the Shag) and a Razorbill use their wings to 'fly' in pursuit of prey; and a Scaup 'flies' down to forage for crabs on the bottom.

Bittern

Botaurus stellaris

ATLAS 63; PMH 42; PER 70; HFP 38; HPCW 28; NESTS 67; BWP1:247

Floating	BLDS: ♀ Monogamy Polygyny	⬭/🥚 3–6 (7) 1 brood INCU: ♀ 25–26	SA1 FLDG: ♀(♂?) 50–55	Sm verts

Breeding habitat   Large dense reed beds.

Displays   Distinctive booming call of the ♂ in breeding season carries great distances. Pair displays poorly known because of dense habitat.

Nesting   Nest is mound of reeds, near or over water. May be close to other nests when up to 5 ♀s share one ♂. Eggs olive-brown, sometimes lightly speckled with dark spots, 53mm, hatch asynchronously. Young may leave nest at 2 weeks old and ♀ may build a second nest for them.

Diet   Fish, amphibians, insects, and a variety of other animal prey. Takes prey while slowly wading or waiting near cover, in day or evening.

Winters   In nesting areas, if these do not freeze over, or moves S.

Conservation   Many breeding areas abandoned due to drainage and persecution, but some recovery, as in the UK following the establishment of reserves. Fragmented distribution across Europe and Asia. See p. 528.

Notes   Well-known camouflage stance involves neck and body fully stretched upward, remaining still or swaying with the reeds for hours.

Essays   Feathers, p. 363; Incubation: Controlling Egg Temperatures, p. 273; Polygyny, p. 265.

Refs   Sharrock 1976.

Little Bittern

Ixobrychus minutus

ATLAS 63; PMH 43; PER 70; HFP 38; HPCW 28; NESTS 67; BWP1:255

Decid tree	BLDS: ? Monogamy	⬭ 5–6 (4–9) 1 (2) broods INCU: ♂ ♀ 17–19	SA1 FLDG: ♂ ♀ 25–30	Sm verts

Breeding habitat   Dense marsh vegetation.

Displays   ♂ chases off rival ♂s with flight attack. Advertising call of ♂ given in day and at night; attracts ♀ to nest he has built. Change-over on nest preceded by exchange in which birds appear to threaten each other with opening and closing of bill, ruffling feathers on back, and raising and lowering crown.

Nesting   Nest is pile of reeds or twigs. ♂ may build several if he fails to attract a ♀ to one. Mating is on nest. Eggs white, 36mm, hatch asynchronously. First breeds at 1 year.

Diet   Fish, amphibians, and insects, taken while waiting in cover or at edge of water; at dawn and dusk.

Winters   E Africa.

Conservation   Widespread across Europe, Asia, Africa, Australia, but has fragmented range within S and W Europe. Vulnerable to marsh drainage. See p. 528.

Notes   Has bittern-like stance: see above.

Essays   Feathers, p. 363; Incubation: Controlling Egg Temperatures, p. 273; Polygyny, p. 265.

Plume Trade

DURING two walks along the streets of New York in 1886, the American Museum of Natural History's ornithologist, Frank Chapman, spotted 40 native species of birds including sparrows, warblers, and woodpeckers. But the birds were not flitting through the trees. They had been killed, and for the most part, plucked, disassembled, or stuffed, and painstakingly positioned on three-quarters of the 700 women's hats Chapman saw. The North American feather trade was in its prime; across the Atlantic, it was enjoying a resurgence.

Fashions using plumes of the Ostrich (*Struthio camelus*) go back at least to the early Greeks and Romans and can be traced through the Middle Ages to the present. Three thousand years ago peacock plumes were traded, although the birds were rare until the time of Alexander the Great. By the days of Cicero, guests at court were using Peacock tail feathers as fly swatters. In Europe, the plume trade seems to have peaked by the time of the French Revolution. Hair fashion for ladies of the Court, it is said, had become so embellished with ornamental plumes and *objets d'art* that when riding in closed carriages these women found it necessary to kneel or hold their heads outside windows. Conditions, of course, changed, and feathered apparel, having lost its allure, did not truly revive until the last half of the nineteenth century. By then, plumes from birds of paradise and herons entered Europe with surprising regularity. An estimated 80 000 birds of paradise were killed yearly for their feathers from the turn of the century until World War I.

The Great White Egret and the more delicately plumed Little Egret evolved extravagant breeding plumage as sexual advertisements to attract their mates. The feathers, apparently, had such a similar effect on nineteenth-century men, particularly in France, that sources of supply began to disappear. So extensive was the slaughter in North America, that egrets were adopted as the symbol of the bird preservation movement. Writers such as Herbert Job began to focus protests on the robbing of heron and egret rookeries:

Here are some official figures of the trade from one source alone, of auctions at the London Commercial Sales Rooms during 1902. There were sold 1,605 packages of . . . herons' plumes. A package is said to average in weight 30 ounces. This makes a total of 45,240 ounces. As it requires about four birds to make an ounce of plumes, these sales meant 192,960 herons killed at their nests, and from two to three times that number of young or eggs destroyed. Is it, then, any wonder that these species are on the verge of extinction?

The plume trade, however, had become too lucrative to control easily. 'In 1903', Job continued, 'the price for plumes offered to hunters was . . . about twice their weight in gold.' Nonetheless, the heron slaughter would prove to

Night Heron

Nycticorax nycticorax

ATLAS 62; PMH 43; PER 70; HFP 38; HPCW 28; NESTS 63; BWP1:262

Shrub	BLDS: ♂♀ Monogamy	3–5 (1–8) 1 (2) broods INCU: ♂♀	SA1 FLDG: ♂♀	Sm verts
		21–22	40–45	

Breeding habitat In trees and bushes near fresh water in wide range of habitats up to 2000m above sea level.

Displays Threat displays of both sexes include upright posture. ♂s give advertising displays to attract ♀s; includes bowing. After pairing ♂ may bring twigs and ceremoniously present them to ♀. Followed by mutual preening or bill fencing.

Nesting Colonial. Nest of twigs, reeds, etc. built by ♀ from material gathered by ♂. Eggs pale greenish-blue, 50mm, hatch asynchronously. Young leave nest and perch on branches at 20–25 days, but are fed in nest.

Diet Mainly fish, amphibians, insects, taken by stalking in shallow water or after waiting. Largely nocturnal. Young fed partly regurgitated fish etc.

Winters In Africa.

Conservation Distributed worldwide and uses a wide variety of habitats, so is less vulnerable than other herons to habitat losses. See p. 528.

Essays Colour of Eggs, p. 161; Feathers, p. 363; Monogamy, p. 335; Pellets, p. 257; Precocial and Altricial Young, p. 401; Spread-wing Postures, p. 17; Communal Roosting, p. 81; Declines in Forest Birds: Europe and America, p. 339; Visual Displays, p. 33; Commensal Feeding, p. 27; Birds on Borders, p. 95; Plume Trade, p. 23; Swallowing Stones, p. 135.

Squacco Heron

Ardeola ralloides

ATLAS 61; PMH 44; PER 70; HFP 36; HPCW 29; NESTS 63; BWP1:273

Shrub	BLDS: ♀ Monogamy	4–6 (7) 1 brood INCU: ♀	SA1 FLDG: ♂♀	Sm verts
		22–24	45?	

Breeding habitat Freshwater marshes and lakes, with dense vegetation.

Displays Nest defended against intruder by body pushed forward, low, and bill pointed at rival. Pair displays include holding each other's bill, mutual preening, and passing sticks from one to the other.

Nesting Colonial. Nest is platform of reeds or twigs, built by ♀ from material supplied by ♂. Eggs pale greenish-blue, 39mm, hatch synchronously. Young leave nest at 30–35 days and scramble about colony.

Diet Amphibians, fish, and insects; at dawn and dusk; from cover, but sometimes in the open.

Winters In tropical Africa.

Conservation Vulnerable to habitat destruction and, in the past, to the plumage trade. Has fragmented distribution in Europe, though is more widespread in Africa. See p. 528.

Essays Colour of Eggs, p. 161; Feathers, p. 363; Monogamy, p. 335; Pellets, p. 257; Precocial and Altricial Young, p. 401; Spread-wing Postures, p. 17; Communal Roosting, p. 81; Declines in Forest Birds: Europe and America, p. 339; Visual Displays, p. 33; Commensal Feeding, p. 27; Birds on Borders, p. 95; Plume Trade, p. 23; Swallowing Stones, p. 135.

be of central importance in bringing the problem of over-exploitation to the attention of the public.

The plume trade heyday, which lasted to the 1920s, is thought to have been prompted by general prosperity that encouraged the purchase of fashionably elaborate non-essentials. Emulating the genteel elite, men selected fedoras with feather trim and women adorned their hair, hats, and dresses with 'aigrettes' (sprays of breeding plumage). Women's hats became larger, hat ornamentation (reminiscent of that found on dress military headgear) became more lavish, and, accordingly, the feather trade expanded. North American activist William T. Hornaday recorded 61 avian families and species viewed as threatened by the London and continental feather market.

In their attempts to defend the industry, the millinery establishment stood fast against claims of cruelty and exploitation, contending that the bulk of feather collection was limited to shed plumes — those found scattered on the ground within rookeries. In truth, those 'dead plumes' brought only one-fifth the price of the live, unblemished, and little-worn sprays. To counteract the charges of cruelty, assertions were circulated that most feather trim was either artificial or produced on foreign farms that exported moulted feathers. Between 1880 and 1920 the debate raged. Anti-plumage groups were formed to counter industry claims that feather farming and dead plumes were all that was at issue. In England in 1885, Rev. Francis O. Morris, Lady Mount-Temple, and others founded the Plumage League. That was followed by formation of the Selbourne League (later called the Selbourne Society) which was broadly devoted to protecting nature. Three years later, in 1889, the Society for the Protection of Birds (SPB) was established. SPB membership was nearly entirely female and absolutely unanimous in its outrage over Britain's enormous importation of feathers. Within a year the SPB received support in print from sixty parish magazines, local newspapers, ladies' magazines and *The Times*. Three years later it had 9000 members.

SPB members were discouraged from wearing all but ostrich feathers, and by 1899 Queen Victoria issued an order for the British Army to replace its ceremonial egret aigrettes with ostrich plumes. In 1904, Edward VII granted the Society permission to use the prefix 'Royal' in its title and within two years the Queen lent her name in support of bird protection. Through a series of leaflets published by the RSPB and with the support of other wildlife organizations, as well as ornithological activists and nature writers, the public came to understand the complexities of the issues.

The RSPB and its affiliates in Ireland, India, Australia, and Western Europe campaigned to bring more information on endangerment, cruelty, and ecological damage to public attention. They assembled information on plumes taken from a variety of bird groups including sunbirds, vultures, storks, hawks, eagles, and owls that were shipped from British, Dutch, French, and German colonies to London, New York, and Parisian fashion houses. Members of the Linnaean and Zoological Societies, along with members of local natural history and humane organizations, also worked to refute industry accusations of public over-reaction to the yearly killing of many millions of birds by plume hunters.

Cattle Egret

Bubulcus ibis

ATLAS 60; PMH 44; PER 70; HFP 36; HPCW 30; NESTS 62; BWP1:279

 Shrub BLDS: ♂♀ Monogamy | 4–5 (3–9) 1 (2) broods INCU: ♂♀ 22–26 | SA1 FLDG: ♂♀ 30 | |

Breeding habitat Wetlands, but often away from water in fields; avoids coastal marshes.

Displays At nest, threat display with body forwards and crest erect, lunging at rivals. During advertisement ♂ is very aggressive in use of forward display and is vocal. Pair displays include mutual preening and back biting, and a greeting display with fully raised scapular plumes.

Nesting Colonial. Nest is pile of twigs, reeds, etc. in trees and bushes. Eggs pale greenish-blue, 45mm, hatch asynchronously. Young leave nest for nearby branches at 20 days. First breeds at 2 years.

Diet Mainly terrestrial insects, often those disturbed by cattle and horses; walks steadily or sometimes runs, jabbing downwards. Also feeds in shallow water. Often in flocks. Diurnal.

Winters Disperses from colonies.

Conservation Abundant and widespread; a marked range increase with the colonization of S and then N America, Australia, and New Zealand. Benefits from human activities.

Essays Commensal Feeding, p. 27; Mixed-species Flocking, p. 429; Colour of Eggs, p. 161; Monogamy, p. 335; Pellets, p. 257; Precocial and Altricial Young, p. 401; Spread-wing Postures, p. 17; Communal Roosting, p. 81; Visual Displays, p. 33; Commensal Feeding, p. 27; Birds on Borders, p. 95; Plume Trade, p. 23; Swallowing Stones, p. 135.

Little Egret

Egretta garzetta

ATLAS 60; PMH 44; PER 70; HFP 36; HPCW 30; NESTS 62; BWP1:290

 Shrub BLDS: ♂♀ Monogamy | 3–5 (6–7) 1 (2?) broods INCU: ♂♀ 21–22 | SA1 FLDG: ♂♀ 40–45 | Sm verts |

Breeding habitat Shallow marshes; open ditches, including estuaries and freshwater.

Displays At nest, has forward pointing display to rivals – like other herons. ♂ advertises with short flap wing displays, attracting both other ♂s and ♀s. Pairs have both flap-flight and bill-rattling, over mate's back. Greeting ceremony at nest exchange involves birds with all plumes erect.

Nesting Colonial. Nest platform in tree is of twigs, brought by ♂, built by ♀ and sometimes ♂. Eggs pale greenish-blue, 46mm, hatch asynchronously. Young leave nest at 30 days and perch nearby.

Diet Small fish, amphibians, insects, and a variety of animal prey, taken as bird wades, sometimes up to belly, as it stalks prey. Diurnal.

Winters Spain, Africa.

Conservation Widespread across S Europe, S Asia to Australia, and Africa; declines and extinctions in the 1800s due to plumage trade. Some recovery in this century; is relatively tolerant of human activity. See p. 528.

Essays Plume Trade, p. 23; Colour of Eggs, p. 161; Feathers, p. 363; Monogamy, p. 335; Spread-wing Postures, p. 17; Communal Roosting, p. 81; Visual Displays, p. 33; Commensal Feeding, p. 27; Birds on Borders, p. 95; Plume Trade, p. 23; Swallowing Stones, p. 135.

Preservationists struggled to enact laws to prevent the killing, possession, sale, and importation of plume birds and ornamental feathers. In 1900 a RSPB branch was established in India and within two years export of all wild bird skins and feathers from British India was forbidden. Nonetheless, between 1900 and 1910 Britain imported £20 million in feathers — some 6000 tonnes. Although the first plumage bill in the House of Lords, introduced by Lord Avebury in 1908, died in the Commons, two years later Inter-Departmental Government Committees were established to discuss the questions surrounding the plumage market. In 1917 the Board of Trade passed an importation of plumage regulation and, finally, in 1921 the Importation of Plumage (Prohibition) Bill was passed. Thus ended the 'Age of Extermination' and the embellishment of attire with breeding plumes. How much this change was due to the effects of hunting and trade regulations and how much was the result of rising prices for dwindling supplies is still not clear. Nor is it evident whether changes in the everyday lives of women simply eliminated opportunities to wear oversized, constraining hats and accessories, or whether a growing inclination toward promoting humanitarian ideals reduced the allure of feathered garb. Regardless of the predominant reason, displaying breeding plumage in Britain and on the Continent became, once again, primarily an avian trait.

Today, the RSPB has over three-quarters of a million members (including its junior branch) and a substantial endowment. It has evolved from a tiny society whose aim was to prevent cruelty to fledglings in rookeries into the most important conservation organization in Britain. While it continues to police illegal egg collectors, falconers, traders, and gamekeepers, it is also involved in purchasing reserves, providing information on birds to foresters, farmers, hydro-developers, and landowners, manoeuvring to get its questions asked in the political arena, and it is on the forefront of correlating the changes in land use with fluctuations in avian populations.

SEE: Birds and the Law, p. 521; Ducking the Bird Laws, p. 523; Feathers, p. 363.
REFS: Bent, 1926; Brooke, 1989; Buchheister and Graham, 1973; Doughty, 1975.

Commensal Feeding

SOME birds eat alone. For those that do not, the choice of partners can be surprising. Why should a phalarope associate with an Avocet, or a coot with a swan? Such dining partners tend to benefit from company; their foraging success and/or protection from predators may be enhanced. In North America, for example, by simply standing close to a foraging White Ibis (*Eudocimus albus*) a Great White Egret (*Egretta alba*) can snatch prey scared to the surface beyond the ibis's reach. In return, the egret warns the shorter, less wary ibis of predators. But not all foraging associations are mutually beneficial.

In commensal associations, members of one species increase the foraging

Great White Egret

Egretta alba

ATLAS 59; PMH 45; PER 72; HFP 36; HPCW 31; NESTS 61; BWP1:297

 Decid tree | BLDS: ♂♀ Monogamy | ⬭ 3–5 (2–6) 1 brood INCU: ♂♀ 25–26 |  FLDG: ♂♀ 42? | Sm verts |

Breeding habitat Large dense reedbeds, lakes, and rivers, sometimes to high elevations.

Displays Has forward display (like other egrets) at nest, also upright display of erect bird. ♂s gather some nest material as a display area. Pairing involves mutual preening and stick passing. Greeting ceremony involves raising scapular plumes.

Nesting Colonial. Nest in bushes or trees is large pile of thin twigs or reeds. Eggs pale blue, 61mm, hatch asynchronously. Young wander from nest at about 20 days, stay with parents until migration.

Diet Fish, aquatic insects; either stalks prey or waits with neck extended. Wades in shallow water or waits on edge of deep water. Chicks fed insects.

Winters Moves S and towards coast of Mediterranean.

Conservation Declines in the 1800s due to plumage trade. Threatened by habitat destruction, especially in the west of range, but very widely distributed throughout the world. See p. 528.

Essays Commensal Feeding, p. 27; Birds on Borders, p. 95; Plume Trade, p. 23; Wetland Conservation, p. 145; Colour of Eggs, p. 161; Feathers, p. 363; Precocial and Altricial Young, p. 401; Spread-wing Postures, p. 17; Communal Roosting, p. 81; Declines in Forest Birds: Europe and America, p. 339; Visual Displays, p. 33; Birds on Borders, p. 95; Swallowing Stones, p. 135.

Grey Heron

Ardea cinerea

ATLAS 58; PMH 45; PER 72; HFP 34; HPCW 32; NESTS 60; BWP1:302

 Reeds | BLDS: ♂♀ Monogamy | ⬭ 4–5 (1–10) 1 (2) broods INCU: ? 25–28 |  FLDG: ♂♀ 42–45 | Sm verts |

Breeding habitat Wide range of water margins, including parks in cities.

Displays ♂ defends nest site against rivals with an arched neck, upright display. Advertises, calling loudly, with neck stretched up and bill pointed skyward. Pairs mutually bill and preen. Greeting ceremony with raised crest and neck feathers.

Nesting Colonial. Nest is pile of twigs in tall trees, but sometimes in reedbeds; often reused. ♂ brings material, ♀ builds. Eggs light blue, 61mm, hatch asynchronously. Young clamber about nearby at 20–30 days. First breeds at 2 years.

Diet Fish, amphibians, insects, and a variety of animal prey.

Winters In wide range of habitats, including estuaries, moves S and W to avoid frozen lakes.

Conservation Widely distributed across Europe, Asia, and Africa, with expansion in N, perhaps declines in S.

Notes Unusually well-studied populations (from 1928 in UK) show the importance of infrequent severe winters in determining densities.

Essays Pesticides and Birds, p. 115; Feathers, p. 363; Monogamy, p. 335; Pellets, p. 257; Precocial and Altricial Young, p. 401; Spread-wing Postures, p. 17; Communal Roosting, p. 81; Commensal Feeding, p. 27; Birds on Borders, p. 95; Plume Trade, p. 23.

Refs Marchant et al. 1990.

success of members of another species, but incur no significant costs and receive no benefits. One of the more common commensal associations involves 'beaters', which stir up prey, and 'attendants', which simply follow in their wake taking whatever comes their way. Robins, for example, use animals as diverse as moles, wild boars, and human beings as beaters. Other beater-follower associations on land include cattle-attending Cattle Egrets, Black-headed Gulls that follow ploughing tractors, and Buzzards that follow combine-harvesters. In snow-covered areas Ptarmigan 'follow' the diggings of caribou and hare. In tropical regions African drongos (jay-sized insectivores) follow many species of mammals and birds. Interestingly, an African drongo can sustain itself by following a single elephant, but when following small antelopes, it requires a small herd. In the New World tropics, some antbirds are 'professional ant followers' obtaining virtually all their food by eating fugitives from army ant swarms.

Some wetland birds attend particular beater species or groups of similar species. Great Egrets, for example, attend North American species of mergansers. Others, such as American Coots (*Fulica americana*, an accidental in Europe), attend a variety of beaters including Bewick's Swans, Mallards, and Pintails. Among seabirds, Gannets are known to associate with a fair number of beaters, including 10 of the 13 cetaceans commonly observed in the North Atlantic. Gulls, Fulmars, auks, shearwaters, and phalaropes may make use of the prey-rich mud plumes brought to the surface by bottom-foraging gray whales. These whales strain sediment through their baleen, discharging whole and damaged invertebrates. Many seabirds, in fact, follow seals, porpoises, and whales, fishing vessels, ocean liners and other non-fishing vessels that provide galley scraps. Shearwaters, albatrosses, petrels, and, especially, Fulmars that once followed whaling vessels now follow the fishing fleet.

The distance separating avian attendants from their avian beaters is not uniform. It depends on the habitat, the type of prey and ease of its capture, and the speed of the feeders. Consequently, it may be difficult to determine whether two birds seen near each other are feeding commensally. In his North American study of White Ibises and Little Blue Herons (*E. caerulea*), ornithologist James Kushlan compared the foraging success of the attendant herons venturing to within one metre of the ibis and non-attendants (those staying farther away). Kushlan found that attending herons caught twice as many prey as those feeding alone and that the increase reflected more frequent feeding attempts (presumably because the beater stirred up more prey), rather than more successful strikes.

Commensal feeding arrangements can also involve recycling. House Sparrows sometimes eat the legs removed from large beetles by feeding thrushes, and Chaffinches have been recorded eating seeds from crab-apples opened by Fieldfares. In New Guinea, the diet of Shining Starlings (*Aplonis metallica*) includes fruits with large, hard pits. The starlings digest the fleshy coating and regurgitate the pit. Opportunistic Emerald Doves (*Chalcophaps indica*), whose digestive tracks can grind tough materials, consume the stripped pits. Sparrows and finches feed on seeds in horse manure. Seabirds

Purple Heron

Ardea purpurea

ATLAS 58; PMH 46; PER 72; HFP 34; HPCW 32; NESTS 61; BWP1:312

Decid tree

BLDS: ♂♀
Monogamy

4–5 (2–8)
1 brood
INCU: ♂♀
24–28

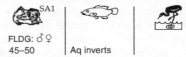

FLDG: ♂♀
45–50

Aq inverts

Breeding habitat   Wetlands with reed beds or thick cover.

Displays   ♂ defends nest with upright (bittern-like) stance and forward displays, like other herons; also include puffed out chin feathers. In greeting ceremony, birds face away from each other. Birds also preen each other.

Nesting   Colonial. Nest is of dead reeds, near water level, though sometimes in trees; built by both birds. Eggs pale blue, 57mm, hatch asynchronously. Young leave nest for nearby at 8–10 days. First breeds at 1 year.

Diet   Fish and insects, but a variety of animal prey.

Winters   Africa.

Conservation   Widely distributed across S Europe, C and S Asia, and S Africa; local increases, but special nesting habitat means vulnerable to wetland drainage. See p. 528.

Essays   Birds on Borders, p. 95; Colour of Eggs, p. 161; Feathers, p. 363; Monogamy, p. 335; Pellets, p. 257; Precocial and Altricial Young, p. 401; Spread-wing Postures, p. 17; Communal Roosting, p. 81; Declines in Forest Birds: Europe and America, p. 339; Visual Displays, p. 33; Commensal Feeding, p. 27; Plume Trade, p. 23; Swallowing Stones, p. 135.

Black Stork

Ciconia nigra

ATLAS 66; PMH 46; PER 72; HFP 42; HPCW3 4; NESTS 71; BWP1:323

Cliff

BLDS: ♂♀
Monogamy

3–5 (2–6)
1 brood
INCU: ♂♀
35–36

FLDG: ♂♀
65–71

Insects

Breeding habitat   Forests with areas of wet meadows, marshes, sometimes lakes.

Displays   ♂ gives head shaking crouching display when mate approaches. At nest exchange mutual up-down display: stand horizontally, with wing tips raised, each extends neck with head tossing, bobbing up and down with weak whistles. Mutual preening common. ♂ clatters bill after mating.

Nesting   Not colonial. Nest is large mass of twigs in tall trees, but also cliffs. Eggs white, 65mm, hatch asynchronously. Age of first breeding 3

years.

Diet   Fish, but also other small vertebrates and insects, taken while walking or standing in shallow waters.

Winters   Spanish population resident, others migrate to Africa, India.

Conservation   Has retreated from much of its range in western Europe; the population in Spain is very isolated from the rest of the species' range, from E Europe across Asia. See p. 529.

Essays   Birds on Borders, p. 95; Spread-wing Postures, p. 17; Plume Trade, p. 23; Transporting Young, p. 9; Nonvocal Sounds, p. 263.

feed on the stomach contents of sperm whales that are vomited during chases by whalers or feast on the whales' periodic regurgitations of indigestible cephalopod beaks. Small petrels feed on the faeces of pilot whales.

The line between commensalism and competition, however, may be difficult to draw. In 1772, Gilbert White noted that

... If we do not much wonder to see a flock of rooks usually attended by a train of daws, yet it is strange that the former should so frequently have a flight of starlings for their satellites. Is it because rooks have a more discerning scent than their attendants ... Perhaps then their associates attend them on the motive of interest, as greyhounds wait on the motions of their finders; and as lions are said to do on the yelpings of jackalls. Lapwings and starlings sometimes associate.

There may be no outright exceptions to the ecological slogan, 'There is no free lunch', but some species definitely gain from the actions of others with whom they forage while not obviously damaging their benefactors.

SEE: Mixed-species Flocking, p. 429; Coevolution, p. 239; Interspecific Territoriality, p. 421. REFS: Burton, 1985; Diamond, 1981; Diamond et al., 1977; Evans, 1982; Goodwin, 1978; Kilham, 1980; King, 1988; Kushlan, 1978; Obst and Hunt, 1990; Palfery, 1989; Smith, 1989; Warren, 1989; Williams, 1953; Willis and Oniki, 1978.

Average Clutch Size

CLUTCH size is the number of eggs laid in a single nesting. When clutch sizes within populations are censused and the number of young successfully reared is later determined, it often turns out that the average clutch size is slightly below that which produces the greatest number of successfully reared young. One would expect evolution to establish clutch sizes that maximize reproduction. Why, then, would females lay 'too few' eggs in a clutch? One explanation of this has been that evolution should, if possible, maximize reproduction *over the lifetime of a female*, not reproduction *per brood*. By being slightly conservative in the size of the clutches they produce, females might reduce the stresses of brood rearing and increase their chances of living through the following winter and producing more clutches.

Careful studies of reproduction by Great Tits and Collared Flycatchers, however, did not support this notion of higher survivorship of reproductively conservative females. Rather, tit pairs varied in their ability as parents and proved best able to raise the number of young produced by the clutches they laid. Each pair maximized its reproduction. In the flycatchers, experimentally enlarging clutches resulted in lower survival of juveniles, and the future reproduction of both the experimental adults and the offspring from the experimentally-enlarged broods was reduced. But adult survival was not.

White Stork

Ciconia ciconia

ATLAS 66; PMH 46; PER 72; HFP 42; HPCW 36; NESTS 70; BWP1:328

BLDS: ♂♀
Monogamy

4 (1–7)
1 brood
INCU: ♂♀
29–30

SA1
FLDG: ♂♀
58–64

Insects

Breeding habitat Marshes and wet open ground, often near people using buildings in towns.

Displays Nest defended actively against other birds. Much bill clattering, and up-down display throwing head upward and backward; up-down display used in pair's mutual greeting.

Nesting Colonial or solitary. Nest is large mass of twigs on trees, cliffs, or buildings. Eggs white 73mm, hatch asynchronously. Birds breed first at 4 years. Pairs often only for the one season, ♂ accepting first ♀ to arrive.

Diet Variety of small vertebrates and large insects, taken while walking with bill pointed downward. May concentrate on mice or grasshoppers, etc., if these are in unusual numbers. May feed together in large flocks.

Winters Africa and India; not in family groups.

Conservation Occurs across Europe into N Africa, and isolated populations in Asia. Decreases in north and west; no longer breeding in Belgium, Switzerland, Sweden, but does associate with humans. Rapid increase in Estonia. See p. 529.

Notes On migration soars in thermals, so concentrating across Straits of Gibraltar and the Bosporus.

Essays Raptors at Sea Crossings, p. 93; Nest Lining, p. 439; Nest Sites and Materials, p. 443; Birds on Borders, p. 95; Spread-wing Postures, p. 17; Plume Trade, p. 23; Transporting Young, p. 9; Migration, p. 377; Nonvocal Sounds, p. 263.

Glossy Ibis

Plegadis falcinellus

ATLAS 64; PMH 47; PER 72; HFP 40; HPCW 36; NESTS 68; BWP1:338

Shrub

BLDS: ♂♀
Monogamy

3–4 (5–6)
1 brood
INCU: ♂♀
21

SA1
FLDG: ♂♀
28?

Breeding habitat Shallow marshes, wet meadows, particularly reed beds.

Displays At nest pairs have mutual bowing, billing, and preening.

Nesting Colonial. Nest is pile of twigs or reeds, in trees or bushes in water; built by ♀ from material brought by ♂. Eggs blue, 52mm, hatch synchronously. Young leave for feeding grounds with parents.

Diet Insects, possibly small vertebrates; feeds by probing ground, mud, or shallow water with bill. Often feeds in flocks.

Winters Africa, India, small numbers around Mediterranean; in a wider variety of wetland habitats than for nesting.

Conservation In Europe has fragmented distribution and there has been a contraction of range because of drainage. Sensitive to human disturbance. Distributed almost worldwide. See p. 528.

Essays Wetland Conservation, p. 145.

Some birds, rather than laying fewer eggs than they can successfully rear, almost always lay more. Lesser Spotted Eagles and most cranes, including the endangered North American Whooping Cranes, lay clutches of two eggs but almost always rear only one young. Only a fifth to a third of Eurasian Crane nests fledge both young from a pair of eggs. Presumably, it takes relatively little energy to lay the second egg, even though usually only one chick can be reared. The second egg is 'insurance' against loss of the other egg to accident or predation. Conservationists sometimes take advantage of an insurance egg by removing it from the nest to hatch the chick for captive or foster breeding programmes. For example 'spare' Whooping Crane eggs have been hatched under the more abundant Sandhill Cranes.

SEE: Variation in Clutch Sizes, p. 55; Indeterminate Egg Layers, p. 437; Natural Selection, p. 297; Hatching Asynchrony and Brood Reduction, p. 507. REFS: Gustafsson and Sutherland, 1988; Koenig, 1984; Lack, 1947, 1968; Pettifor et al., 1988; Saether, 1990; Winkler and Walters, 1983.

Visual Displays

WHEN a bird moves or holds itself in a way that signals information to another bird of the same or different species, it is said to be performing a 'display'. Thus a pigeon leaping into flight at the sight of a hawk, only coincidentally alerting other members of its flock in the process, is moving but not displaying. In contrast, a male Black Grouse strutting on a lek (a traditional courting ground) is displaying — passing information about its desirability as a mate to females of its own species. Displays may include vocalizations, as they do in the case of the grouse, and displays by females may be elicited by specific vocalizations by males. Indeed, in the broad sense, vocalizations alone are displays. But because ornithologists often consider vocalizations separately, for our discussion we will define as displays only ritualized movements or postures.

Displays are usually classified according to their apparent function: courtship, aggression, begging, greeting, and so on. The strutting male grouse is performing one of the many kinds of courtship displays seen in birds. Often courtship displays accent a striking feature of the bird's plumage. Thus the male Black Grouse raises his tail while displaying, thereby emphasizing the unusual shape and the contrasting white undertail coverts. Many birds of open areas such as Tree Pipits and Skylarks have 'song flights' that involve singing during stereotyped flights over their territories.

On the other hand, some male birds do not advertise with physical attributes; they demonstrate skills. Male terns court females by displaying a fresh-caught fish. Courting male Grey Herons perform ritualized hunting move-

Bald Ibis
Geronticus eremita

ATLAS 65; PMH 242; PER - ; HFP 40; HPCW 37; NESTS 69; BWP1:343

| | BLDS: ♂♀ Monogamy | 2–4 (1–7) 1 brood INCU: ♂♀ 24–28 | SA1 FLDG: ♂♀ 40–45 | Sm verts | |

Breeding habitat Rocky cliffs; in arid regions, but usually near rivers.

Displays At nest, rivals peck each other with open bills, or give threat display with erect back feathers, head pulled in, and bill lifted then lowered. ♂ advertises with bill pointing and calls. Pairs have mutual billing, preening, and neck entwining.

Nesting Colonial. Nest is made of small branches, lined with softer materials, on cliff ledges. Eggs pale whitish-blue with small spots and blotches of reddish-brown, 63mm, hatch asynchronously. Does not breed every year, depending on rainfall, and fledging success is low in dry years. First breed when 6 years old.

Diet A variety of large invertebrates and small vertebrates, taken by probing, under stones, into cracks and vegetation. Feeds in dry, open areas, pastures, and tilled fields; sometimes in groups.

Winters Disperses away from colony, into small feeding flocks.

Conservation Critically endangered with less than 300 birds in the wild. The population in Turkey declined from 23 pairs in 1973, to 13 in 1977, to extinction in 1989. The surviving population in Morocco had 250 pairs in 1975 and was down to 119 pairs in 1977. Once found in central Europe and throughout N Africa. Pesticides may be responsible for decline.

Essays Birds and the Law, p. 521; Black and White Plumage, p. 7.

Spoonbill
Platalea leucorodia

ATLAS 65; PMH 47; PER 74; HFP 40; HPCW 37; NESTS 68; BWP1:352

| Decid tree 0–5m | BLDS: ♂♀ Monogamy | 3–4 (–7) 1 brood INCU: ♂♀ 24–25 | SA1 FLDG: ♂♀ 45–50 | Fish | See below |

Breeding habitat Dense reed-beds in shallow wetlands,.

Displays Rivals peck and snap bills at each other. Pairs mutually preen. At nest exchange, bird on nest spreads head feathers and calls.

Nesting Colonial. Nest is of reeds and twigs, generally near ground, but sometimes in trees. Eggs white, sometimes with darker blotches, 67mm, hatch asynchronously.

Diet Insects, some small fish, tadpoles.

Feeds in small flocks wading, with slightly open bill swept from side to side.

Winters On estuaries; some in Europe but most S to Africa.

Conservation Fragmented, scattered range, reduced in W Europe through drainage (and direct destruction). The colonies in Spain and Holland are isolated from range from SE Europe across Asia. See p. 529.

Essays Birds on Borders, p. 95; Wetland Conservation, p. 145.

ments, erecting head feathers, pointing their bills downward and clashing their mandibles together. Many male passerines, when courting, also lower their bills as if pecking at something below them. Perhaps, next to singing, the most common component of courtship displays in male songbirds is vibration of the wings; other components include fluffing of the body feathers, bill-raising, thrusting the head forward, and running using short steps.

Birds also use a great diversity of agonistic displays (those used in threats and actual combat). Stock Doves may bow repeatedly when defending their nest sites. Geese often pump their heads up and down just before attacking. Aggressive geese may rear up and spread their wings when on land; aggressive divers rear up in the water. In aggressive displays between rival male Robins, the orange breast is normally pointed toward the enemy before an attack. Male Great Tits will threaten rivals with a head-down wings-spread display, or by a 'head-up' display of its black breast-stripe. In established dominance hierarchies, dominant birds often use threat displays against subordinates. Subordinates signal their submission with other displays — in passerines often by crouching with feathers fluffed and head withdrawn.

Quite different from these sexual and agonistic displays are begging displays, which are employed both by chicks to solicit parental feeding and by some females to solicit courtship feeding. Greeting displays are used by many species when one parent relieves the other at the nest, and may serve to prevent aggressive interactions. Pairs of adult Adelie Penguins perform bowing displays and exchange vocal greetings at 'changings of the guard', thus making large colonies extremely noisy. And, finally, there are social displays that apparently help to keep flocks unified. Displays are, in fact, a major part of the 'glue' that binds avian groups.

How this glue evolved remains a matter of conjecture and dispute. It was the courtship display of the Great Crested Grebe that led the pioneering British behaviourist and evolutionist Julian Huxley to develop the concept of 'ritualization' — the gradual evolutionary transformation of an everyday movement into an increasingly effective signal. For instance, pre-flight movements — crouching, slight spreading of the wings, and raising of the tail — have been modified in many birds into signals. When wooing a female, the male Cormorant begins an exaggerated take-off leap, but does not leave the ground.

One of the most interesting ideas on the origins of display behaviour was developed in the middle of this century by the celebrated ethologist (student of behaviour) Niko Tinbergen and his colleagues. Tinbergen suggested that internal conflicts between different behavioural 'systems' or tendencies — such as the desire to threaten and the urge to court — are responsible for the generation of displays.

For example, after vigorously defending its territory, a male bird may approach a female with ambivalence over whether to attack or woo her. As a result, he may do neither, but instead channel his energies into behaviour that is irrelevant to either aggression or mating — say pulling at a tuft of grass or preening. Such 'displacement activities' can then become incorporated into courtship displays and 'emancipated' from their previous functions. Thus

Greater Flamingo

Phoenicopterus ruber

ATLAS 67; PMH 47; PER 74; HFP 42; HPCW 38; NESTS 72; BWP1:359

| BLDS: ♂♀ | 1 (2) 1 brood | SP | Filters |
| Monogamy | INCU: ♂♀ 28–31 | FLDG: ♂♀ 70–75 | |

Breeding habitat Shallow salt lagoons in very restricted locations.

Displays Communal displays may serve to bring all the colony into breeding condition, start 8–10 weeks before breeding. Up to 40 birds of both sexes in a group, with necks stretched upwards move heads side to side giving short calls. Then, simultaneously spread wings, stretch neck upwards or forwards in a bow. In courtship during feeding, birds walk side by side repeating soft calls.

Nesting Highly gregarious in location, very erratic in timing. Nest is cone-shaped dome of mud. Eggs white becoming stained, 90mm. Young leave nest at day 10 and move into crèche of young of similar age, fed by parents; stay in crèche until day 100. First breeding at 2–3 years. Pair bond for life.

Diet Zooplankton: see essay, p. 37.

Winters Resident, but there is movement between breeding sites, with many ringed Camargue birds being recovered in Spain.

Conservation Breeding is irregular even at the highly restricted and isolated sites across S Europe, C Asia, C America, and C and S Africa. Very susceptible to disturbance, by tourists for example. See p. 528.

Essays Flamingo Feeding, p. 37; Bird Milk, p. 243; Swallowing Stones, p. 135; Crèches, p. 45.

Mute Swan

Cygnus olor

ATLAS 68; PMH 49; PER 74; HFP 44; HPCW 39; NESTS 73; BWP1:372

| BLDS: ♂♀ | 5–8 (1–11) 1 brood | P2 | | |
| Monogamy | INCU: ♂♀ 36 (35–41) | FLDG: ♂♀ 120–150 | | Ground glean |

Breeding habitat Mostly freshwater lakes and rivers, some on brackish or salt water, readily uses artificial habitats.

Displays Breeding territory vigorously defended, by both sexes, with feathers raised above back, neck ruffled, and head and neck arched. Courtship consists of mutual head turning. Triumph ceremony when pair has seen off rival, similar to threat, but by both birds accompanied by chin lifting. Lacks loud calls of other swans, but hisses when threatened.

Nesting Nest is a mound of reeds and other vegetation near water. Eggs pale greenish-white, 113mm, hatching synchronously; cygnets carried on back of ♀. Young remain with parents until plumage is mostly white, then driven off. First breeds at 3–4 years.

Diet Aquatic vegetation obtained by completely up-ending or by immersing head and neck. Also grazes on vegetation near water's edge or in pastures.

Winters Resident, except where lakes freeze over, when moves SW.

Conservation Generally tolerant of human activities; vulnerable to picking up lead shot (mistaken for small stones) and locally many birds die from lead poisoning. Widely introduced, and now occurs across Europe, C Asia, N America, S Africa, Australia, New Zealand.

Essays Swallowing Stones, p. 135; Moulting, p. 373; Monogamy, p. 335; Piracy, p. 213.

Refs Johnsgard 1965; Marchant et al. 1990. Birkhead and Perrins 1986 is a book about this species.

when displacement preening becomes part of courtship, it also becomes more conspicuous and stereotyped than normal preening, and becomes useful as a signal rather than an aid in maintaining the bird's feathers. Similarly, males of many species have incorporated components of courtship fighting (battles between rivals during the courtship season) into their courtship displays; among passerines, bill-raising is used widely, in fighting by some species, in courtship by others, and in both contexts by a few species. In many finches the preliminary male courtship display is a modified head-forward threat posture.

Although some ethologists think that virtually all displays arise from conflicts between internal tendencies, experiments have so far failed to confirm this. As a result, scientists are now turning away from Tinbergen's approach, and looking at the possible evolution of displays without reference to conflicting 'underlying tendencies' in the nervous system. Evolution has modified an enormous variety of activities into displays, from courtship feeding (originating as food exchange between parent and chick), to stylized fishing movements (used in heron courtship). We expect the perspectives of those researchers investigating the overt behaviour of the animal and those studying the functioning of its nervous system gradually to converge. That convergence, we hope, will supply a deeper understanding of displays and other behavioural phenomena.

SEE: Leks, p. 123; Territoriality, p. 397; Distraction Displays, p. 175; Dominance Hierarchies, p. 131; Wader Displays, p. 181; Duck Displays, p. 47; Bird Badges, p. 433; Vocal Development, p. 479. REFS: Andrew, 1961; Baerends, 1975; Hinde, 1955; Tinbergen, 1953; West and King, 1988; Wilson, 1975.

Flamingo Feeding

FLAMINGOS are filter feeders, and in that respect resemble whales and oysters more than they do most birds. Many complex rows of horny plates line their beaks, plates that, like those of baleen whales, are used to strain food items

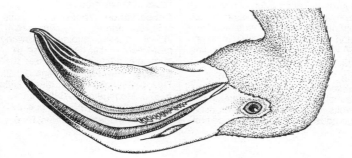

Bewick's Swan
Cygnus columbianus

ATLAS 68; PMH 49; PER 74; HFP 44; HPCW 39; NESTS 74; BWP1:379

	BLDS: ♂♀ Monogamy	3–5 (2–6) 1 brood INCU: ? 29–30

FLDG: ♂♀ 40–45		Ground glean

Breeding habitat Marshy tundra.

Displays Threat displays even on wintering grounds, but not between members of families. Birds call frequently. Courtship has head turning with neck feathers erect as ♂ and ♀ face each other. After mating, birds spread wings and call.

Nesting Solitary. Nest is mound of vegetation on bank, ♂ passes material to ♀ who builds. Eggs off-white, 103mm, hatch synchronously. Monogamous, long-lasting pairing. Birds start to breed at 5 or 6 years, pairing a year or two earlier. Young adults may rejoin parents on wintering grounds, but not on nesting areas.

Diet Vegetation, obtained by up-ending in shallow water; grazes on roots in flooded pastures. Mainly in day, also early night.

Winters In W Europe in freshwater marshes, open fields; in flocks.

Conservation Large increases in winter range in UK (and on migration in Finland) following active conservation efforts. Changes in numbers breeding in Russian Arctic are unknown. Also found in N America, where called the Tundra Swan. See p. 529.

Notes The wintering flock at Slimbridge, UK, has the bill markings of each bird recorded, giving a unique opportunity to follow the behaviour and family history of each individual.

Essays The Bewick's of Slimbridge, p. 39; Commensal Feeding, p. 27; Moulting, p. 373; Monogamy, p. 335.

Refs Johnsgard 1965.

Whooper Swan
Cygnus cygnus

ATLAS 68; PMH 49; PER 74; HFP 44; HPCW 39; NESTS 74; BWP1:385

	BLDS: ♂♀ Monogamy	3–5 (4–7) 1 brood INCU: ♀ 35 (31–42)

FLDG: ♂♀ 87 (78–96)		Ground glean

Breeding habitat Northern wetlands usually south of tundra.

Displays Threat displays in winter flocks involve neck extended down at angle, calling, and body shaking. Also there is triumph ceremony between paired birds following eviction of rival birds from lakes; wings half open in lifted position, neck bobbed as birds face each other and call loudly. Courtship (also can occur in winter flocks) has head bobbing greeting, with head turning.

Nesting Solitary. Nest is mound of vegetation. Eggs off-white,113mm, hatch synchronously. Young remain with adults into winter. Long-term monogamous pairings. Birds breed first at 4 years, pairing at 2 years.

Diet Aquatic vegetation obtained by up-ending, but also grazes in fields.

Winters Across Europe on lakes, marshes, sheltered marine inlets, and grassy fields south of breeding areas; in flocks of family groups.

Conservation Widespread across N Europe and Asia. Recent spread in Finland and Scandinavia following protection; earlier declines due to hunting and egg collection. See p. 529.

Essays How Fast and High Do Birds Fly?, p. 63; Feathers, p. 363; Moulting, p. 373; Monogamy, p. 335; Piracy, p. 213; Commensal Feeding, p. 27.

Refs Johnsgard 1965.

from the water. The filter of the Greater Flamingo traps crustaceans, molluscs, and insects an inch or so long. The Lesser Flamingo (*Phoenicopterus minor*) has such a dense filter that it can sift out single-celled plants less than half a millimetre in diameter.

Flamingos feed with their heads down, and their bills are adapted accordingly. In most birds a smaller lower mandible works against a larger upper one. In flamingos this is reversed; the lower bill is much larger and stronger. To complete the jaw reversal, the upper mandible is not rigidly fixed to the skull. Consequently, with the bird's head upside down during feeding the upper bill moves up and down, permitting the flamingo's jaws to work 'normally'.

Part of the flamingo's filter feeding is accomplished simply by swinging the head back and forth and letting the water flow through the bill. The fat tongue, lying within the bill's deep central groove, can be used as a pump to pass water through the bill's strainer more efficiently. It moves quickly fore and aft in its groove, sucking water in through the filter as it pulls backward, and expelling it from the beak as it pushes forward. The tongue may repeat its cycle up to four times a second.

Flamingos are not the only avian filter feeders, however. Some penguins and auks have simple structures to help them strain small organisms from the water, and one Southern Hemisphere genus of petrels (*Pachyptila*, prions or whalebirds) and some ducks have filtering devices. With its long, broad bill the Shoveler is the most highly developed filter feeder among waterfowl. It has specialized plates lining the sides of both upper and lower mandibles. The Mallard also has a broad bill, horny plates, and an enlarged tongue. But the pumping action of these ducks is different from that of flamingos, and their tongues are housed in the upper mandible, rather than in the lower.

The flamingo's marvellously adapted tongue almost became its downfall. Roman emperors considered it a delicacy and were served flamingo tongues in a dish that also included pheasant brains, parrotfish livers, and lamprey guts. Roman poets decried the slaughter of the magnificent birds for their tongues (much as early American conservationists lamented the slaughter of bison for theirs). One poet, Martial, wrote (as Stephen Jay Gould recently translated):

> *My red tongue gives me my name, but epicures regard my tongue as tasty.*
> *But what if my tongue could sing?*

SEE: Wader Feeding, p. 187; Bills, p. 391; Swallowing Stones, p. 135. REFS: Gould, 1985; Jenkin, 1957; Olson and Feduccia, 1980.

The Bewick's of Slimbridge

SIR Peter Scott founded the Wildfowl Trust in 1946 and established its headquarters at Slimbridge, Gloucestershire, England. Slimbridge quickly became a centre for the study of wetland species.

Bean Goose
Anser fabalis

ATLAS 70; PMH 50; PER 76; HFP 46; HPCW 39; NESTS 76; BWP1:391

BLDS: ♀ Monogamy	4–6 (3–8) 1 brood INCU: ♀ 27–29	FLDG: ♂♀ 40?	Seeds

Breeding habitat Arctic rivers and lakes, in forested and tundra areas.

Displays Threat postures include forward display, with low bow and stretched neck. Displays poorly known, but include triumph ceremony after rivals chased off.

Nesting Solitary. Nest is lined with moss etc. and down from ♀. In banks or at base of tree; often near water, but sometimes far from it. Eggs creamy, 84mm, hatch synchronously. Young are defended by both parents. Breeds first at 3 years.

Diet Grasses, grains, berries; grazes in arable land in winter.

Winters In flocks in grassy fields in western Europe in family parties. Roosts communally.

Conservation Decline in western part of range and in the numbers wintering in the UK. Has extensive range from Scandinavia throughout arctic Russia.

Essays Copulation, p. 87; Flying in V-Formation, p. 43; Habitat Selection, p. 423; Monogamy, p. 335; Diet And Nutrition, p. 493; How Fast and High Do Birds Fly?, p. 63; Birds on Borders, p. 95.

Refs Johnsgard 1965.

Pink-footed Goose
Anser brachyrhynchus

ATLAS 70; PMH 50; PER 76; HFP 46; HPCW - ; NESTS 76; BWP1:397

BLDS: ♀ Monogamy	3–5 (1–9) 1 brood INCU: ♀ 26–27(25–28)	FLDG: ♂♀ 56?	Seeds

Breeding habitat Open arctic tundra but river gorges in Iceland.

Displays Very little known, probably similar to Bean Goose.

Nesting Solitary or in loose colonies. Nest is low mound of vegetation lined with moss and down from ♀. Eggs cream, 78mm, hatching synchronously. First year young winter with parents. Pairs for life, probably in third year.

Diet Vegetation, grasses, grains, and roots, including potatoes; in natural areas and in farm lands.

Winters Farm land and less often saltmarsh in large flocks around North Sea.

Conservation Has increased considerably, perhaps due to better protection on wintering grounds in UK, Holland, Denmark, but has very limited breeding range from Greenland, Iceland to Spitzbergen.

Essays Birds and Agriculture, p. 365; Copulation, p. 87; Flying in V-Formation, p. 43; Habitat Selection, p. 423; Monogamy, p. 335; Diet And Nutrition, p. 493; How Fast and High Do Birds Fly?, p. 63; Birds on Borders, p. 95.

Refs Johnsgard 1965.

Bewick's Swans under study at Slimbridge are identified by differences in the coloration of their bills. (Drawing by Darryl Wheye.)

Bewick's Swans, long-distance Arctic migrants, were once rare Slimbridge visitors. Most travelled between the Siberian breeding grounds and the Netherlands, with smaller numbers going to Germany, Denmark, England, and Ireland. A few regularly visited Wales, Scotland, and France, or appeared as vagrants near the Mediterranean. By the 1930s, however, those birds en route to Ireland had begun to fly over England (rather than crossing Scotland), and a series of hard winters helped to build up a tradition of wintering in England. In 1948, a wild male Bewick's was caught at Slimbridge and within two years was bred with a wild-caught adult female obtained from Holland. By 1964, with help of decoys and wheat left out as feed, Bewick's began landing on the pond in view of Scott's Slimbridge studio window. And 24 individuals remained until March.

Scott and his associates quickly realized that the patterns of yellow and black coloration of individual Bewick's bills were as unique as fingerprints and identifiable at a distance. They began recording the variation and maintaining long-term histories of families and individuals. Interference with the birds was minimized and within eight years of moving to the pond, the Slimbridge population expanded to 626 birds. Population growth made it possible to collect valuable data on social structures, aggressive behaviour, dominance hierarchies, aspects of flight and the effects of weather on the swans' behaviour. Research also expanded beyond the confines of Slimbridge. Recoveries of ringed individuals were recorded in the Soviet Union, Germany, Denmark, Northern Ireland, among other areas, and researchers travelled to various staging areas along migration routes to collect data on individuals that they identified by bill pattern.

Interestingly, somewhat similar populations of two other swans (Whooper and eastern Bewick's) began to expand under the care of a farmer and his son at Suibara, near Niigata, Japan. There, with the help of winter feeding and protection, the swan population grew from 15 birds in 1955 to over 1000 within 15 years. That 'swan lake', some 400 metres in diameter, became a National Monument attracting at times some 10 000 people.

Wetland refuges such as Slimbridge have become an invaluable resource for birds and researchers alike. Until recently, no behavioural study had been made of Bewick's Swans breeding in the wild, making the data Scott and his colleagues collected from wintering birds as well as from individuals in Slimbridge's captive breeding programme of particular importance. In 1991 scientists at Slimbridge began a collaborative programme of research with Russian biologists, and a study of breeding Bewick's Swans began at the

White-fronted Goose
Anser albifrons

ATLAS 71; PMH 51; PER 76 HFP 46; HPCW 39; NESTS 77; BWP1:403

BLDS: ♂♀
Monogamy

5–6 (3–7)
1 brood
INCU: ♀
27–28

FLDG: ♂♀
40–43

Breeding habitat   Arctic tundra; close to rivers and lakes.

Displays   Forward posture threat display like other geese. Pair displays probably similar to Greylag Goose.

Nesting   Solitary. Nest is of vegetation, lined with vegetation and down from ♀; on mound of bank with view of surrounding area. Eggs cream, 79mm, hatch synchronously. First year birds stay with parents. Pairs for life. Probably starts to breed in third year.

Diet   Vegetation, including tubers, berries, and seeds, obtained by grazing.

Winters   Wet grassy fields and estuaries from UK across Europe to Iraq; in flocks.

Conservation   No obvious changes, occurs across arctic from CIS to Greenland. See p. 528.

Essays   Copulation, p. 87; Flying in V-Formation, p. 43; Habitat Selection, p. 423; Monogamy, p. 335; Diet And Nutrition, p. 493; How Fast and High Do Birds Fly?, p. 63; Birds on Borders, p. 95.

Refs   Johnsgard 1965.

Lesser White-fronted Goose
Anser erythropus

ATLAS 70; PMH 51; PER 76; HFP 46; HPCW 40; NESTS 76; BWP1:409

BLDS: ♀
Monogamy

4–6 (2–8)
1 brood
INCU: ♀
25–28

FLDG: ♂♀
35–40

Breeding habitat   Bushy, arctic and alpine tundra (south to 65°N); generally further south than White-fronted Goose.

Displays   Poorly studied; probably similar to other grey geese.

Nesting   Solitary. Nest is flattened pile of grasses lined with down from ♀; usually close to water. Eggs cream, 76mm, hatch synchronously. Young remain with adults until one year old. Breeds first at 3 years. Pairs for life.

Diet   Grazes vegetation.

Winters   In flocks in grasslands from SE Europe eastwards.

Conservation   Very little data, perhaps slight decrease in west of range, in some areas marked decline, but difficult to census. Occurs from Scandinavia across Russian arctic. See p. 528.

Essays   Copulation, p. 87; Flying in V-Formation, p. 43; Habitat Selection, p. 423; Monogamy, p. 335; Diet And Nutrition, p. 493; How Fast and High Do Birds Fly?, p. 63; Birds on Borders, p. 95.

Refs   Johnsgard 1965.

mouth of the Pechora River in Arctic Russia. For the first time a known individual was re-sighted in Russia at its nest on the tundra, and then subsequently re-sighted at its traditional wintering site, the Wildfowl and Wetlands Trust reserve at Martin Mere in Lancashire. Sadly, however, he had failed to raise young successfully.

Unlike migratory ducks, Bewick's families remain together, with parents helping young cygnets, until it becomes necessary for them to return to Arctic Russia. Observations of naturally 'marked' individual Bewick's at Slimbridge helped to identify aspects of group behaviour and parental care. Basic research is clearly essential for effective wildlife management, but perhaps of more urgent importance, refuges such as Slimbridge have become critical centres for helping to maintain wetland ecosystems and, ultimately, the ecosystem services they provide to civilization. Information on the Wildfowl and Wetlands Trust (as the Wildfowl Trust was renamed in 1989) and the International Waterfowl and Wetlands Research Bureau (also headquartered at Slimbridge) is available from Wildfowl and Wetlands Trust, Slimbridge, Gloucestershire GL2 7BT, England.

SEE: Orientation and Navigation, p. 503; Wetland Conservation, p. 145. Migration, p. 377. REFS: Berman, 1978; Evans, 1975; Scott, 1988; Scott and the Wildfowl Trust, 1972.

Flying in V-Formation

WE commonly see ducks and geese flying in a regular V-shaped formation, but why they do so remains something of a mystery. One theory has been that all but the lead bird are able to gain lift from the wing-tip vortices produced by the bird in front of them. Those vortices are formed by air rushing up over the tip from the high-pressure area under the wing into the low-pressure area above the wing. The following bird, if it is in just the right position, will remain within the upward flow of the vortices. Calculations indicate that such an advantage could represent a 15 per cent saving in power and so greatly boost the range of a flock of birds over that of a bird flying alone.

Theoretically, to be most efficient, the wing-tip of a following bird should remain within about one-fourth of a wingspan from that of a bird in front of it. Motion pictures of flying flocks of Canada Geese reveal, however, that in practice they do not travel in formations that allow flight efficiency to be much increased by this mechanism. Instead, flying in V-formation may be a way of maintaining visual contact and avoiding collisions, or of teaching young birds migration routes. Further study is clearly required before the advantages of flying in V-shapes will be understood.

SEE: How Do Birds Fly?, p. 217; Skimming: Why Birds Fly Low over Water, p. 67. REFS: Gould and Heppner, 1974; Lissaman and Schollenberger, 1970; May, 1979.

Greylag Goose

Anser anser

ATLAS 69; PMH 51; PER 76; HFP 46; HPCW 40; NESTS 75; BWP1:413

 Reeds | BLDS: ♀ Monogamy |  4–6 (3–12) 1 brood INCU: ♀ 27–28 | P2 FLDG: ♂♀ 50–60 | Seeds | Dabbles

Breeding habitat A wide variety of marshes and lakes from the tundra south to the Mediterranean; typically in lakes with rich vegetation.

Displays Aggressive displays include forward display with neck stretched forward horizontally or diagonally 45° upwards at rival. Triumph ceremony between pairs common all year. ♂ leaves ♀ and attacks real or imaginary rival. ♂ returns to ♀ calling, with neck in diagonal position, then both birds give cackling calls. Pairs greet each other following separation.

Nesting Nest on ground, often in reed-beds, and generally close to water, is pile of vegetation lined with grass and some down. Eggs cream, 85mm, hatch synchronously. Sometimes large numbers of eggs in nest indicate egg dumping by other ♀s. Young stay with parents for first winter. Monogamous; pairing first at 3 or 4 years.

Diet Leaves, roots, grains, and fruits, taken from ground or by up-ending on water.

Winters Resident, in flocks comprised of family parties, also moves to milder areas, including estuaries, and uses farmlands for feeding.

Conservation Has been successfully reintroduced or has recolonized areas from which it was once lost due to persecution. Is still vulnerable to habitat drainage in some parts of its range across N Europe, SE Europe, and Asia.

Essays Birds and Agriculture, p. 365; Copulation, p. 87; Flying in V-Formation, p. 43; How Fast and High Do Birds Fly?, p. 63.

Refs Johnsgard 1965; Marchant et al. 1990.

Canada Goose

Branta canadensis

ATLAS 73; PMH 53; PER 78; HFP 48; HPCW - ; NESTS 78; BWP1:424

 | BLDS: ♀ Monogamy |  5–6 (3–11) 1 brood INCU: ♀ 28–30 | P2 FLDG: ♂♀ 40–48 | | Dabbles

Breeding habitat Wide range of freshwater lakes, rivers, also in parks in or near cities.

Displays Threat display includes head-pumping (moving head up and down from straight to curved neck), head-tossing (waving head from side to side), and a forward posture that often precedes physical attack. Hisses. Pairs have triumph ceremony similar to other geese.

Nesting Often colonially. Nest is pile of vegetation lined with quantities of down from ♀, often on island, but nearly always near water, near base of tree or bush. Eggs cream, 86mm, hatch synchronously. Young stay with parents through first winter. First breeds at 3–4 years.

Diet Plant material including roots, leaves, etc. obtained mostly by grazing on land, also up-ends in the water.

Winters Resident (although highly migratory in its native range), in flocks.

Conservation Introduced into UK and Scandinavia from N America and increasing, in part because of continued introductions.

Essays Visual Displays, p. 33; Flying in V-Formation, p. 43; Crèches, p. 45; Copulation, p. 87; Birds on Borders, p. 95.

Refs Johnsgard 1965; Marchant et al. 1990.

Crèches

THE fledglings of some British and European bird species such as the Greater Flamingo, Canada Goose, Common Shelduck, King and Common Eiders, Long-tailed Duck, Velvet Scoter, Red-breasted Merganser, Goosander, and Sandwich Tern, sometimes separate from their parents and form groups called 'crèches'. Supervision of the crèche is usually assumed by a small number of guardians who, of course, are related to only a portion (often a small one) of the young in the group. It is curious that the altruistic guarding of unrelated young, presumably a dangerous, tiring responsibility, has evolved, but upon closer scrutiny the behaviour may be less altruistic than it appears.

Chick crèching generally occurs among birds that breed in large, loose colonies and whose broods hatch at about the same time. Whether or not the young remain dependent on their parents for food, crèching is a form of care which frees the adults to spend more time foraging. Crèching tends to be more prevalent if adults must travel to remote areas to forage and if their diet differs from that of their young. Thus among ducks, crèching is more common among those that dive, such as eiders, than among dabbling species. Crèche formation comes about in a number of ways including chance encounters among broods, as a response to the appearance of a predator, or from mutual attraction among fledglings, all of which depend somewhat on the openness of the habitat. Forming groups may make it easier to detect predators or permit a fledgling to lose itself in the crowd and reduce its risk of predation (dilution principle) as in eiders, penguins, and pelicans. Crèche size varies widely, with groups of up to 100 found in Shelducks. In one study in Scotland, more Shelduck ducklings reared in crèches died than did those reared in family groups, but crèche survivors grew faster and were more likely to live through the post-fledging period than were family-reared young.

Although crèching potentially emancipates adult birds, there may be circumstances which necessitate that the ratio of adults to chicks does not fall too greatly. Thus adult penguins may be needed to shield chicks from cold. Alternatively adult pelicans may shelter chicks from excessive heat.

Although larger crèches tend to be attacked more commonly than smaller ones, individuals in large crèches have a higher chance of survival in the face of lone attackers. When, however, a crèche attracts a group of predators crèching may prove disastrous. Evolutionary theory suggests that crèching is likely to develop when the young reared in a group have a higher chance of surviving than those reared alone, so that those birds practising crèche formation contribute more of their genes to the next generation than those that do not. Since the mixing of broods within a crèche may make it impossible for the females to keep track of their own young, selection for generalized defence of crèches may have evolved, leading guardians to defend unrelated individuals or even members of a different species. The evolution of crèching,

Barnacle Goose

Branta leucopsis

ATLAS 72; PMH 53; PER 78; HFP 48; HPCW 40; NESTS 78; BWP1:430

  4–5 (2–9)
1 brood
BLDS: ♀ INCU: ♀
Monogamy 24–25 (28)

 FLDG: ♂♀
40–45

Breeding habitat Arctic tundra, particularly cliffs overlooking sea or on small islands (but see recent colonization of Sweden, below).

Displays Threat postures and pair's triumph ceremony like Canada Goose, also includes a wing-flicking. In pre-mating display ♂ has exaggerated lifting of wings.

Nesting Colonial. Nest shallow pile of vegetation lined with down from ♀. Eggs cream, 77mm, hatch synchronously. Young follow parents to wintering grounds and first breed at 3 years.

Diet Vegetation, grazes mainly on grasses and sedges.

Winters In flocks in grasslands close to sea; salt-marshes around North Sea.

Conservation Once restricted in range from Greenland to Russia; colonized Gotland in Sweden (once a stopover on migration) as a breeding site in 1971 (one pair). Increased to 450 pairs by 1985, and there are sporadic records in Estonia and Finland. This is one of the most remarkable range increases in birds: Gotland is about 2000km from previous breeding areas. Has benefited from the protection of wintering sites. See p. 528.

Essays Breeding Season, p. 293; Copulation, p. 87; Flying in V-Formation, p. 43; Habitat Selection, p. 423; Monogamy, p. 335; Diet And Nutrition, p. 493; How Fast and High Do Birds Fly?, p. 63; Birds on Borders, p. 95.

Refs Johnsgard 1965.

Brent Goose

Branta bernicla

ATLAS 72; PMH 53; PER 78; HFP 48; HPCW 40; NESTS 78; BWP1:436

  3–5 (1–8)
1 brood
BLDS: ♀ INCU: ♀
Monogamy 24–26(21–28)

 FLDG: ♂♀
40?

  Ground glean

Breeding habitat Arctic tundra with pools, close to sea.

Displays Not well known. Has head tossing like Canada Goose, and pre-mating displays include head dipping.

Nesting Colonial. Begins before snow melts. Nest is lined with vegetation and down from ♀; on small hummocks, often on islands. Eggs cream, 71mm, hatch synchronously. Young stay with parents through first winter, breed first at 2–3 years.

Diet Grazes on land and in shallow water, submerging head or up-ending and pulling up underwater plants.

Winters In flocks, in shallow estuaries and salt marshes, grassy fields, near sea in western Europe.

Conservation There was a perhaps 75 per cent decline in the numbers of one subspecies in the 1930s following the loss of the main food plant eel grass, *Zostera*. Numbers have increased since then. Widely distributed above 75°N.

Essays Breeding Season, p. 293; Copulation, p. 87; Flying in V-Formation, p. 43; Habitat Selection, p. 423; Monogamy, p. 335; Diet And Nutrition, p. 493; How Fast and High Do Birds Fly?, p. 63; Birds on Borders, p. 95.

Refs Johnsgard 1965.

in this respect, may be similar to that of mobbing.

It is difficult to predict which adults will adopt guarding behaviour. The role of leading and defending the crèche may be taken by breeding females or by non-breeding but 'broody' females (those that are hormonally-charged to brood, but are broodless or have lost their broods). In some birds, such as shelducks, breeding or broody females apparently attract more fledglings. Guardianship, however, may also be taken by females who exhibit no broodiness (beyond the tendency to lunge at predators during an attack), as well as by neutral females who may be attracted to the crèche.

In Common Eiders, guardians loosely cooperate among themselves rather than compete to retain exclusive responsibility for crèche defence. Cooperation tends to occur when there is considerable turnover among guardians; 'recent mothers' appear, while guardians who have completed their stint and whose hormone-driven broodiness is abating, leave the crèche, often departing for foraging grounds. Crèche guardianship in some species, however, contrasts sharply with the pattern seen in eiders. In the African Ostrich, for example, dominant pairs compete for the opportunity to gather the young of others into their group. Such herding of young is reminiscent of an African catfish that gathers the offspring of cichlid fishes into a school of its own young. Within schools, the little cichlids are kept to the outside, where they (rather than the young of the catfish) are the first to be taken by predators. Data are needed for crèching birds in Britain and on the Continent to identify the relative positions and mortality rates of chicks most closely related to crèche guardians. Until then, we can only speculate on whether supervision is altruistic or not.

SEE: Geometry of the Selfish Colony, p. 15; Parental Care, p. 171; Parent–Chick Recognition in Colonial Nesters, p. 227; Altruism, p. 245. REFS: Gorman and Milne, 1972; Hurxthal, 1986; Munroe and Bédard, 1977a, 1977b; Schmutz et al., 1982; Weatherhead, 1979b; Williams, 1974.

Duck Displays

MOST ducks confine their displays to the water (or land) surface, since their heavy weight relative to their wing area ('high wing loading') dictates continuous flapping and makes complex manoeuvres, such as hovering and soaring, difficult or impossible. Aerial communication is thus largely restricted to short, ritualized flights (ordinarily close to the water surface) and vocalizations, including contact calls that help maintain flock coherence in these rapid flyers.

Most first observations of duck behaviour probably are of Mallard courtship. Mallards perform in the autumn and winter as well as the spring, so there is plenty of opportunity to watch their displays. They are also often rather tame, and perform in the open — this is a good thing since, while

Egyptian Goose

Alopochen aegyptiacus

ATLAS 73; PMH 54; PER 78; HFP 50; HPCW 60; NESTS 79; BWP1:447

		◯ 8–9 (6–12) 1 brood INCU: ♂♀ 28–30	FLDG: ♂♀ 70–75	
Decid tree	Cavity BLDS: ♀ Monogamy			

Breeding habitat In UK mostly on well-vegetated lakes in Norfolk, but also on rivers.

Displays Threat posture has wings lifted slightly away from body to show white wing-coverts. There is a bent-neck display with head lowered against breast and bill pointed downwards. Also a forward display (like other geese) with head and neck stretched forward. ♂s advertise by strutting, and pairs have a triumph ceremony (also like other geese).

Nesting On ground in vegetation or even in trees. Nest is a pile of vegetation lined with down. Eggs cream, 69mm, hatch synchronously. Young stay with parents for several weeks. Probably first breeds at 1 year.

Diet Grazes on grasses and crops.

Winters Resident in flocks.

Conservation Introduced into UK, where increasing; apparently declining in Egypt, but widely distributed in Africa.

Essays Duck Displays, p. 47; Monogamy, p. 335.

Refs Johnsgard 1965; Marchant et al. 1990.

Ruddy Shelduck

Tadorna ferruginea

ATLAS 74; PMH 55; PER 78; HFP 50; HPCW 41; NESTS 79; BWP1:451

		◯ 8–9 (6–12) 1 brood INCU: ♀ 28–29(27–30)	FLDG: ♂♀ 55?	Dabbles
Decid tree	Cavity BLDS: ♀ Monogamy			

Breeding habitat Fresh water from coasts to very high elevations (in Asia). Sometimes far from water.

Displays See essay on Duck Displays, p. 47. Poorly known, but in threat displays wings partly spread to show white markings, and tail fanned. Pair formation started by ♀ who joins ♂ and invites with outstretched neck and calls. Pre-mating display includes mutual head-dipping on water.

Nesting Often in holes in banks, but also other cavities. Nest is shallow depression lined with down. Eggs cream, 68mm, hatch synchronously.

Diet A variety of plant foods on land and in water; also crustaceans and molluscs; largely nocturnal.

Winters Often on or near breeding areas, Asian populations migrate S.

Conservation Has local and fragmented range in Europe, N Africa, though has more extensive range in Asia. Vulnerable to habitat loss. See p. 529.

Essays Duck Displays, p. 47; Wetland Conservation, p. 145; Crèches, p. 45.

Refs Johnsgard 1965.

frequent, their displays are subtle and brief. Males swimming in the presence of females may be seen shaking their heads (head-shake display) and tails (tail-shake), often doing the former with their breasts held clear of the water and their necks outstretched. They also raise their wingtips, heads, and tails briefly and then swim with their necks outstretched and held close to the water (head-up-tail-up). Groups of four to five males may swim around females, arching their necks, whistling, then lowering their bills below the water surface and jerking their bills up to their breasts while spurting water toward the preferred female (water-flick or grunt-whistle). The water-flick may take only a fraction of a second to complete. The drakes in male groups give short, nasal 'raeb-raeb' (two-syllable) calls, and short high-pitched whistles.

Female Mallards and other female ducks often demonstrate (inciting displays) and call to provoke males to attack other males or females. In some circumstances these displays may allow the female to observe the performance of males and to evaluate them as potential mates. To elicit displays from a group of males, a female Mallard may swim with her neck outstretched and her head just above the water (nod-swimming). When a strange male approaches she often will do an inciting display, swimming after her preferred mate while emitting a rapid staccato series of quacks and flicking her bill back and downward to the side. As pairs are formed, both sexes may be observed lifting a wing, spreading the feathers to expose the speculum (the patch of bright colour at the trailing edge of the wing), and placing the bill behind the raised wing as if preening. Then just before copulation, the male and female typically float face-to-face and pump their heads up and down.

Similar courtship can be seen in other dabbling, 'puddle', or 'river' ducks, the tribe Anatini (in Europe members of the genus *Anas* and the Marbled Teal, all of which are able to spring into the air without running across the water surface). Significant differences in patterns of communication exist among members of the genus *Anas*, differences that have evolved in response to varying ecological situations. Shovelers, for example, are specialized for the time-consuming process of sieving plankton from the waters of small, permanent ponds. A male defends a small, discrete territory around his mate, with whom he has a strong relationship; consequently he rarely spends time in 'extramarital' pursuits.

Shovelers, Garganey, and their close relatives in North America (Blue-winged Teal, *A. discors*, and Cinnamon Teal, *A. cyanoptera*) are known collectively as the 'blue-winged ducks' because of their powder-blue or greyish upper-wing coverts. Blue-winged ducks have evolved a conspicuous 'hostile pumping' display. The head, with crown feathers depressed and bill slightly elevated, is repeatedly raised high while giving 'took' calls out of phase with the pumping. This sequence is used both as a short-distance territorial display ('stay away from my mate/nest') and long-distance territorial threat display ('stay out of my feeding territory').

Unlike relatively sedentary Shovelers, Pintails (again, a member of the genus *Anas*) range far and wide to forage in temporary bodies of water, and tend to nest in sparse cover at a great distance from water. In addition, male

Common Shelduck

Tadorna tadorna

ATLAS 74; PMH 55; PER 78; HFP 50; HPCW 41; NESTS 79; BWP1:455

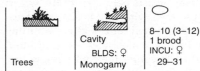 Trees	Cavity BLDS: ♀ Monogamy	8–10 (3–12) 1 brood INCU: ♀ 29–31	P2 FLDG: ♂♀ 45–50		Dabbles

Breeding habitat Shallow coasts and estuaries in western Europe, inland saline lakes across Asia.

Displays See essay on Duck Displays, p. 47. ♂s display with rotating pumping movements of head. Courtship flights involve several ♂s following single ♀s in wide circles. ♀ incites ♂s with displays, and mating is preceded by head-dipping on water.

Nesting In holes, on ground but also in trees, nest is depression lined with down from ♀. Eggs cream, 66mm, hatch synchronously. ♂ guards nests. Young remain in brood for 15–20 days until adults leave for moult, then young form into crèches of up to 100 birds. First breeds at 2–4 years.

Diet Invertebrates, mainly molluscs, and crustaceans, obtained by digging into surface or mud, or dabbling in water.

Winters In NW, breeders and immatures leave nesting grounds (and ducklings in crèches in the care of a small number of adults) for an annual moult in the German Waddenzee area. When moult is complete, some birds remain, others migrate, yet others return to breeding grounds, generally in flocks.

Conservation Increasing in the NW Europe; isolated populations from SE Europe across C Asia; SW Europe and N Africa populations small and decreasing from disturbance.

Essays Duck Displays, p. 47; Crèches, p. 45.

Refs Johnsgard 1965; Marchant et al. 1990.

Mandarin Duck

Aix galericulata

ATLAS 74; PMH 55; PER 80; HFP 50; HPCW 42; NESTS 82; BWP1:465

Ground 0–15m	Scrape BLDS: ♀ Monogamy	9–12 (14) 1 (2?) broods INCU: ♀ 28–30	P2 FLDG: ♀ 40–45	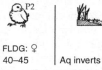 Aq inverts	Surface dips

Breeding habitat Wooded lakes and rivers.

Displays See essay on Duck Displays, p. 47. Has communal courtship with group of ♂s and one or more ♀s. Consists of chases and threats between ♂s and displays on water, involving bill being flicked upwards. ♂s erect crest and their wing 'sails'.

Nesting In hole, lined with down from ♀, some nests on ground. Eggs cream, 51mm, hatch synchronously. ♂s may mate with other ♀s when first mate is incubating.

Diet Mainly vegetation, but some insects and molluscs; feeds in both daytime and night-time, from surface or up-ending. Young feed mainly on insects.

Winters Resident, though migratory in its native range.

Conservation Introduced in UK, where increasing rapidly, and possibly into other areas on continent, where status is not clear. A native of CIS, Japan, and China.

Essays Duck Displays, p. 47.

Refs Johnsgard 1965; Marchant et al. 1990.

Pintails spend only part of their time with their mates, devoting some of it to attempts at copulating with other females; as a result female Pintails tend to be frequently harassed. It seems likely that close defence of a territory is profitable for the male Shoveler because concentrated food resources allow him to provide an area where his mate can obtain sufficient food free from harassment. No such strategy is feasible for the male Pintail because of the dispersed nature of that species' food resources. Therefore Pintails and most of their relatives (e.g. teal) have not evolved a conspicuous long-range territorial threat display; they need only guard nests and mates, not feeding territories.

This description of some dabbler displays only scratches the surface of the complexity and variety of duck displays. Among other species, there is the 'saluting' of the Red-breasted Merganser, the 'pouting' of the Smew, the 'burping' of the Mandarin, the 'vertical calling' of the Shelduck, the 'bubbling' of the Ruddy Duck, and on and on. Each of these is just one of the numerous displays performed by the species. Consider, for example, the results of Robert Alison's studies of the displays of the Long-tailed Duck, whose 'ahr-ahr-ahroulit' vocalizations are familiar background music to those who have spent time in the northern tundra. He distinguished a dozen distinct displays performed by courting males alone: the lateral head-shaking, bill-tossing, rear end, porpoising, wing-flapping, body-shaking, parachute, breast, turning-the-back-of-the-head, bill-dipping, steaming, and neck-stretching displays. Some of these are accompanied by unique vocalizations. Females, in turn, perform chin-lifting, soliciting, and hunch displays. Although the precise functions of the various Long-tail displays are still unclear, they occur with different frequencies in different situations: male–male encounters; male–female encounters; pre- and post-copulation; etc.

The problem of thoroughly analysing such displays is not trivial. The American behaviourist Benjamin Dane and his colleagues studied 6700 metres of film of displaying Common Goldeneyes. They used a stop-action projector to view each frame individually, counting frames (the film was exposed at a constant 24 frames per second) to determine the duration of a given display. It was thus possible to time each action accurately and to determine the probability of one display following another at each stage of the courtship. The projector was also used to analyse display-response interactions between individuals. One of the most interesting findings was the rather uniform timing of some of the displays — the 'head-throw' took an average of 1.29 seconds to perform, and some 95 per cent of head-throws were timed at between 1.13 and 1.44 seconds.

The great complexity of duck courtship displays probably has evolved because ducks tend to concentrate in small areas to breed, and closely related species often give their displays in plain view of each other (and of human observers, which makes them a joy to study). This has created considerable evolutionary pressure for each species to develop distinctive displays, so that hybridization among different species displaying together will be minimized. Thus, for example, the displays of Barrow's Goldeneyes are very different from those of Common Goldeneyes until the pre-copulatory stage is reached. In spite

Wigeon

Anas penelope

ATLAS 76; PMH 56; PER 80; HFP 52; HPCW 42; NESTS 83; BWP1:473

BLDS: ♀	8–9 (6–15)
Monogamy	1 brood INCU: ♀ 24–25

FLDG: ♀ 40–45	Surface dips

Breeding habitat North-temperate to low arctic lakes and marshes.

Displays See essay on Duck Displays, p. 47. Both sexes have threat displays with head forward, open bill, and chin-lifting. ♂s have wing-up display with wing tips crossed and wings raised above back, showing white wing patches. Has communal courtship with several ♂s displaying to one ♀ on water, or chasing her in flight.

Nesting On ground, in cover, usually near water. Nest is a shallow depression lined with down from ♀ and some vegetation. Eggs cream, 55mm, hatch synchronously.

Diet Mostly plants, obtained by grazing on land, from surface of water or under water by ducking head.

Winters Migrates south and west to winter in flocks on estuaries and inland marshes, and nearby grassy fields.

Conservation No declines except in Iceland; has increased its range in UK; widely distributed across N Europe, N Asia.

Essays Brood Parasitism, p. 249; Eclipse Plumage, p. 53; Wetland Conservation, p. 145.

Refs Johnsgard 1965; Marchant et al. 1990.

Gadwall

Anas strepera

ATLAS 75; PMH 57; PER 80; HFP 52; HPCW 42; NESTS 83; BWP1:485

BLDS: ♀	8–12 (6–15)
Monogamy	1 brood INCU: ♀ 24–26

FLDG: ♀ 45–50	Dabbles

Breeding habitat Wide range of freshwater habitats, but usually shallow waters with good cover.

Displays See essay on Duck Displays, p. 47. Threat displays include head and neck forward and bill open. Has communal courtship, with a head-up, tail-up display, with several ♂s and one ♀, and courtship flights of ♀ chased by many ♂s. During pair formation has mock preening display.

Nesting On ground close to water, in cover, nest is lined with leaves and down from ♀. Eggs cream, 55mm, hatch synchronously. ♂s may attempt to mate

with other ♀s while their mates are incubating.

Diet Plants obtained by dipping head under water or sometimes up-ending.

Winters Migrates south and westwards to winter in flocks on lakes and estuaries.

Conservation Apparently increasing and perhaps is being deliberately introduced; widely distributed across Europe, NC Asia, N America. UK population is largely feral.

Essays Eclipse Plumage, p. 53; Piracy, p. 213.

Refs Johnsgard 1965; Marchant et al. 1990.

of this, some hybrids between Barrow's and Common Goldeneyes occur, but with nowhere near the frequency of hybrids in North America between Mallards and Black Ducks (*Anas rubripes*), which have very similar displays.

A major problem that needs more investigation is exactly how context affects communication. Does a certain display given by a mated male convey different information from the same display given by a courting male? Does the distance between signaller and receiver influence meaning? How about orientation (face-to-face, side-to-side, etc.)? When and why does consistent alternation of two displays occur?

Recent advances (and price reductions) in portable video cassette recorder systems may open wide the door to advanced analysis of duck behaviour. With the participation of increasing numbers of birdwatchers and ornithologists, the meaning of many of the complex (and often rapidly performed) displays may be clarified, and thus increase our understanding of why these displays have evolved.

SEE: Visual Displays, p. 33; Wader Displays, p. 181; Sexual Selection, p. 149. REFS: Alison, 1975; Cramp and Simmons, 1977; Dane and Van der Kloot, 1964; Johnsgard, 1965; McKinney, 1975; Rohwer and Anderson, 1988.

Eclipse Plumage

WHEN their breeding efforts are complete, the males of most duck species in the Northern Hemisphere moult from their brightly coloured nuptial plumage to a dull, cryptic plumage. Their brilliance is dimmed — they go into 'eclipse'. The transformation usually occurs rapidly in the depths of marshes where flocks of males retreat for a flightless period. The eclipse plumage is generally retained for a brief time — in many species for as little as one to three months (which is what differentiates it from the non-breeding plumage of most birds), but some species (e.g. Garganey) remain at least partly in eclipse plumage until the following spring. With the next moult, the male returns to his fancy breeding garb. In those species that lose their eclipse plumage early, the rapid loss of their camouflage pattern is apparently more than compensated for by the advantage of impressing females in advance of the impending breeding season.

SEE: Moulting, p. 373; The Colour of Birds, p. 137; Feathers, p. 363.

Teal
Anas crecca

ATLAS 76; PMH 58; PER 80; HFP 54; HPCW 42; NESTS 84; BWP1:494

		$\bigcirc$ 8–11 (7–15) 1 brood	P2	Summer: Aq inverts Winter: seeds	
	BLDS: ♀ Monogamy	INCU: ♀ 21–23	FLDG: ♀ 25–30		Surface dips

Breeding habitat Wide range of streams and marshes; mainly moorland ponds in UK.

Displays See essay on Duck Displays, p. 47. ♂s threaten with chin-up display and much chasing and fighting. Has communal courtship like other *Anas* ducks, including a head- and tail-up posture, and pursuit flights.

Nesting On ground in thick vegetation, close to water. Nest lined with vegetation and down from ♀. Eggs cream, 45mm, hatch synchronously. ♂ deserts ♀ as soon as she starts incubation.

Diet Vegetation, particularly seeds in winter, but aquatic invertebrates important in summer. Walks and slowly filters mud in beak, or swims with head dipped under water. Feeds more at night than in day.

Winters Migrates to shallow fresh waters and estuaries mainly south and west of breeding areas; in flocks. On continent large moult migrations in autumn.

Conservation Has declined in some areas following wetland drainage. Widely distributed, in Europe, Asia, and N America.

Essays Mixed-species Flocking, p. 429.

Refs Johnsgard 1965.

Mallard
Anas platyrhynchos

ATLAS 75; PMH 58; PER 80; HFP 52; HPCW 43; NESTS 82; BWP1:505

		$\bigcirc$ 9–13 (4–18) 1 (2?) broods	P2		
Decid tree	Cavity BLDS: ♀ Monogamy	INCU: ♀ 27–28	FLDG: ♀ 50–60	Aq inverts	Surface dips

Breeding habitat Almost all waters, but mainly fresh, with good cover. Readily exploits man-made lakes.

Displays See essay on Duck Displays, p. 47. Threat involves chases with neck extended and lowered (see other ducks and geese). There is communal courtship as with other ducks, and pursuit flights. In the water-flick display, ♂ dips bill, rises in water, and flicks spray of water droplets sideways with bill in the direction of ♀. ♀s incite ♂s to mate as in other ducks.

Nesting Often on ground, but also in holes in trees, usually close to water, but up to 2km away. Nest is depression of grass and leaves, lined with down from ♀. Eggs creamy to greenish, 57mm, hatch synchronously; large numbers of eggs may indicate presence of 2 ♀s in nest. ♂s attempt to mate with many ♀s during communal displays, and may desert ♀ when her incubation starts and pair with another ♀.

Diet A wide variety of plant and animal foods, obtained by dabbling, dipping head under water, grazing, and diving. Feeds during day and night.

Winters Some resident, but others move from areas where lakes will freeze; some on sea; usually in flocks.

Conservation Adapts to wide variety of habitats and is widely distributed across Europe, Asia, and N America. Some local declines may be due to intensive hunting.

Essays Indeterminate Egg Layers, p. 437; Parasitized Ducks, p. 67; Sleeping Sentries and Mate-guarding, p. 73; Commensal Feeding, p. 27.

Refs Johnsgard 1965; Marchant et al. 1990.

Variation in Clutch Sizes

THE number of eggs in a set laid by a female bird is a recognizable feature of taxonomic groups. Usually petrels, albatrosses, and shearwaters lay 1 egg, auks and vultures lay 1 or 2, terns and gulls 2–3, waders and cormorants 3–4, hawks 2–5, grouse 5–12, ducks 7–12, and pheasants and partridges 8–18. Clutch sizes differ not only among major taxonomic groups and among species, but also among populations and individuals of the same species (as is apparent from the ranges of clutch sizes given for many species in this guide). For instance, both the Robin and the Snow Bunting lay larger clutches in the northern than in the southern parts of their ranges. In addition, older females of some species lay more eggs than do younger females.

Few topics have fascinated students of birds more than the causes of such variations in clutch size. Why do birds near the equator lay fewer eggs than do related birds near the poles? Why do seabirds that forage close to shore lay more eggs than those that forage far from shore? Why do tropical rain-forest birds generally have smaller clutches than those that dwell on tropical savannas? Why do birds that are colonial or nest at relatively high densities often lay fewer eggs than do solitary relatives? Why, in multiple-brooded birds, does clutch size often decline as the breeding season progresses? Why do small species tend to have larger clutches than do large species?

The English ornithologist David Lack was the first to realize that all these breeding patterns were the product of the same thing — natural selection. Each bird species lays the number of eggs that allows individual birds to raise the maximum number of young that will survive to become breeders themselves. A female laying too many eggs may lose them all as a result of being unable to incubate them properly, may attract nest robbers, may be too weakened by the reproductive effort to survive the winter, or (most likely) may be unable effectively to care for the young. On the other hand, by laying too few eggs, a bird will fledge fewer young than it is capable of rearing.

Consider some more detailed explanations of trends in clutch size. Ornithologist N. P. Ashmole has offered an explanation of one of these trends, the increase in the number of eggs per clutch from equator to pole. Such 'latitudinal variation' in clutch size is related to seasonal variation in the amount of food produced per unit area of habitat. More specifically, clutch size is positively related to resource abundance during the breeding season relative to the density of bird populations (abundance per unit area) at that time. If, when the birds are not breeding, their population sizes are limited by food shortages, then population density would be low at egg-laying time. And if resources increase only slightly during the breeding season, then natural selection would not favour large clutches, since food for the hatchlings would be limited. But if the increase in food were large during the breeding season, then, everything else being equal, raising a large brood

Pintail

Anas acuta

ATLAS 77; PMH 59; PER 27; HFP 56; HPCW 43; NESTS 84; BWP1:521

 | | ○ 7–9 (6–12) / 1 brood / BLDS: ♀ INCU: ♀ / Monogamy 22–24 | P2 / FLDG: ♀ 40–45 | Aq inverts | Ground glean

Breeding habitat Lakes and marshes, often shallow and open.

Displays See essay on Duck Displays, p. 47. Similar to other ducks; threat display includes bill being raised and lowered with neck stretched up. Communal courtship, water-flicks, head-up, tail-up display, pursuit flights, ♀ incitement of ♂ to mate, like other *Anas* ducks.

Nesting On ground, usually near water. Nest is of vegetation and down from ♀. Eggs creamy to greenish, 55mm, hatch synchronously. ♂s desert ♀s, often when eggs laid, and certainly by the time they hatch.

Diet Wide variety of plant and animal foods, mainly from mud at bottom by up-ending, but also grazes on land; feeds both in day and at night.

Winters Migrates south and west to winter in flocks, mainly in coastal waters. Widespread inland in small numbers.

Conservation Sporadic breeding in west Europe, but very widely distributed across Europe, Asia, and N America.

Essays Commensal Feeding, p. 27; Eclipse Plumage, p. 53.

Refs Johnsgard 1965.

Garganey

Anas querquedula

ATLAS 76; PMH 59; PER 82; HFP 54; HPCW 43; NESTS 84; BWP1:529

 | | ○ 8–9 (6–14) / 1 brood / BLDS: ♀ INCU: ♀ / Monogamy 21–23 | P2 / FLDG: ♀ 35–40 | Seeds | Dabbles

Breeding habitat Shallow freshwater marshes, and sheltered lakes.

Displays See essay on Duck Displays, p. 47. Communal courtship, water-flicks, head-up, tail-up display, chase flights, ♀ incitement of ♂ to mate, like other *Anas* ducks. Has laying head-back display, when head is flung right back so that the crown touches the lower back, with bill pointing upwards.

Nesting On ground in thick vegetation, close to water. Nest is of plant material and down from ♀. Eggs creamy, 46mm, hatch synchronously.

Diet Insects, molluscs, crustaceans, seeds, and other plant parts; taken while swimming with head dipped under water; less often up-ends. Feeds in the daytime.

Winters Unlike other *Anas* ducks is totally migratory with birds wintering south of Sahara and India; in flocks.

Conservation Nests sporadically in W Europe, which is edge of its range, so numbers fluctuate considerably. Widespread across E Europe and N Asia, probably declining as habitats are lost.

Essays Eclipse Plumage, p. 53.

Refs Johnsgard 1965; Marchant et al. 1990.

should be possible. Thus the largest clutches should be found in high latitudes, where there is an enormous increase in productivity in the spring and summer (as anyone who has braved northern mosquitoes knows only too well), and the smallest clutch sizes might be expected in non-seasonal tropical rain forests, where productivity is rather uniform throughout the year.

According to Ashmole's hypothesis, there should be considerable uniformity of clutch size within a locality, since the seasonality of production should affect all the local birds. Such uniformity is precisely what has been found in tests conducted by avian ecologist Robert Ricklefs. In both the Western and Eastern Hemispheres, for instance, the most common number of eggs in the wet tropics is 2 or 3, but in temperate and arctic regions it is 4 to 6. For one series of 13 localities spread from Borneo to Alaska, 48–88 per cent of the passerine species in each locality had average clutch sizes that fell within a one-egg range. For example, in an equatorial rain forest in Borneo, 86 per cent of the species laid an average of 2–3 eggs, and in another rain forest in west Java 75 per cent were in that range. In a thorn forest in Oaxaca, Mexico, about one half of the bird species laid an average of 3–4 eggs, and on an Alaskan tundra all of the species averaged between 4.5 and 5.5.

Most important, average clutch size under Ashmole's hypothesis is predicted to be closely and inversely related to resource productivity during the *non-breeding* season; the lower the off-season productivity, the larger should be the clutch. In order to test the hypothesis, Walter Koenig of the University of California tabulated the sizes of 411 complete clutches of Northern Flickers (a North American woodpecker, *Colaptes auratus*) from a wide range of localities. He found that, as predicted, clutch size declined significantly as one moved from localities where resources are scarce in the winter to ones where they are abundant. Koenig found that, as predicted by Ashmole's hypothesis, flicker clutch size is not related to resource productivity during the breeding season; he found no correlation between the two.

On the other hand, average clutch size should be positively related to breeding season resource productivity *per breeding pair* of birds. Such a relationship was found in a series of localities spread from Costa Rica to Alaska. Thus it isn't the breeding season productivity *per se* that counts, but that productivity in relationship to the bird density at that season. When there are few winter survivors, breeding density is low. In this situation nesting birds will not seriously compete for breeding season resources, and so will have a chance to raise large broods.

Seasonal differences in food resources seem to explain latitudinal (and, similarly, other geographic and habitat) trends in clutch size. Food is also obviously the key to the difference between onshore and offshore feeding seabirds. The former can rear more chicks because they can visit the nest with food more often. Competition for food also probably explains why clutch sizes are smaller in dense rather than sparse populations. Declining food resources may also explain why late breeders lay smaller clutches.

Although the broad evolutionary influences on clutch size seem reasonably well understood, a great deal remains to be done before the full array of factors determining the number of eggs per clutch is worked out in detail.

Shoveler

Anas clypeata

ATLAS 77; PMH 60; PER 82; HFP 56; HPCW 44; NESTS 85; BWP1:539

BLDS: ♀	○ 9–12 (6–14) 1 brood
Monogamy	INCU: ♀ 26

FLDG: ♀ 40–45	Seeds	Dabbles

Breeding habitat In small productive shallow lakes, marshy meadows.

Displays See essay on Duck Displays, p. 47. Distinctive threat display with head raised and bill pointed slightly upwards.

Nesting On ground, close to water. Nest is of shallow vegetation and down from ♀. Eggs buffish-white to greenish, 52mm, hatch synchronously. ♂s may remain with ♀ in early stages of incubation and promiscuous behaviour of ♂s less pronounced than in other *Anas* species.

Diet A variety of planktonic crustaceans, insects, molluscs, and plants, obtained by feeding on the surface, swimming with head and neck submerged, or up-ending. When surface-feeding sweeps bill from side to side.

Winters Moves S and W into more open marshes, mostly on fresh water in flocks.

Conservation Fluctuates and breeds sporadically in western part of range but is widely distributed in N Europe, N Asia, and N America. Major increases over last century in W.

Essays Flamingo Feeding, p. 37; Wetland Conservation, p. 145.

Refs Johnsgard 1965; Marchant et al. 1990.

Marbled Teal

Marmaronetta angustirostris

ATLAS 77; PMH 61; PER 82; HFP 56; HPCW 45; NESTS 85; BWP1:548

BLDS: ♀	○ 7–14 (5–18) 1 brood
Monogamy	INCU: ♀ 25–27

FLDG: ♀ ?	Greens	Dabbles

Breeding habitat Fresh water to saline, shallow lakes, often close to cover.

Displays See essay on Duck Displays, p. 47.

Nesting On ground in thick vegetation close to water. Nest is of plant material and down from ♀. Eggs cream to buff, 46mm; hatch synchronously; unusually large clutches are probably nests of two ♀s.

Diet Poorly known; probably aquatic insects and plants taken near surface; up-ends, sometimes dives, and will also probe along muddy shores.

Winters Moves away from lakes that dry up. Movements not well understood.

Conservation Is vulnerable to habitat destruction. A marked decline in Spain. Highly fragmented and restricted range, Spain, N Africa, SW Asia. See p. 529.

Refs Johnsgard 1965.

Some biologists feel, for example, that clutch size in passerines will be negatively related to the chance that the nest will be robbed — vulnerable populations should produce smaller clutches. The reasons that have been given include: smaller nests should be more difficult for predators to find, the adults will have more energy to invest in a second brood if the first clutch is lost, and (since less time is invested in the first nest) re-nesting can begin earlier while spring conditions still prevail. Recent research indicates that, at least in the European avifauna, species in which adult survival rates are low have larger clutch sizes (and begin reproduction earlier in life).

It has not yet been possible fully to sort out the determinants of clutch size, and it seems likely that they will remain the subject of ornithological research for some time to come.

SEE: Average Clutch Size, p. 31; Indeterminate Egg Layers, p. 437; Brood Patches, p. 3; Natural Selection, p. 297. REFS: Ashmole, 1963; Koenig, 1984; Lack, 1947, 1968; Murphy and Haukioja, 1986; Nur, 1987; Ricklefs, 1980; Saether, 1988, 1990; Slagsvold, 1982a; Winkler and Walters 1983.

Botulism

ANNUALLY, millions of waterfowl around the world die because of a toxin produced by a bacterium, *Clostridium botulinum*. The bacterium is 'anaerobic' — it is poisoned by oxygen. It thus multiplies in the oxygen-poor environments created by decaying plant and animal matter. The toxin can be acquired by birds feeding on rotting plants or flesh. It affects the birds' nervous systems, causing as the most obvious symptom a paralysis that prevents flight. The neck may be held to the side ('limberneck'), and walking may be difficult or impossible. Birds die from drowning or respiratory failure.

Botulism most commonly attacks aquatic birds. Indeed, it is sometimes called 'duck sickness'. An estimated quarter of a million ducks succumbed on North America's Great Salt Lake in 1932. It has also, however, been identified in over 20 avian families, including waders and gulls. Epidemics usually occur in the summer when high temperatures, low water levels, low oxygen levels, and high alkalinity in lakes and marshes create ideal conditions for the multiplication of *Clostridium* and, therefore, production of the toxin.

Some nine-tenths of waterfowl could probably be cured of botulism if they received antitoxin injections, fresh water, and shade to rest in. Such measures are usually impractical, however. Instead wildlife managers must monitor habitats and discourage birds from foraging in waterways where conditions favour the multiplication of *Clostridium*.

SEE: Disease and Parasitism, p. 315.

Red-crested Pochard

Netta rufina

ATLAS 78; PMH 82; PER 61; HFP 56; HPCW 45; NESTS 85; BWP1:553

	BLDS: ♀ Monogamy	8–10 (6–14) 1 brood INCU: ♀ 26–28	FLDG: ♀ 45–50	Aq inverts	Dabbles

Breeding habitat Large, usually moderately deep freshwater lakes, with reed-beds; also saline ponds.

Displays See essay on Duck Displays, p. 47. Has communal courtship, pursuit flights; also courts at dusk and on moonlit nights. Has courtship feeding, with ♂ bringing food or twigs to ♀ after dive.

Nesting On ground in thick vegetation, near water. Nest is of vegetation lined with down. Eggs creamy to pale, 58mm, sometimes laid parasitically in nest of other ducks; hatch synchronously. Large numbers of eggs are probably dumps

by other ♀s (see essay on Parasitized Ducks, p. 67).

Diet Mainly vegetation, but some insects obtained by diving or up-ending, during daytime.

Winters In flocks in similar habitats to summer, but also coastal wetlands; northern populations move southwards.

Conservation Very fragmented distribution in Europe but more widespread in C Asia; some recent increases in range.

Essays Eclipse Plumage, p. 53.

Refs Johnsgard 1965.

Pochard

Aythya ferina

ATLAS 79; PMH 61; PER 82; HFP 58; HPCW 47; NESTS 86; BWP1:561

	BLDS: ♀ Monogamy	8–10 (4–22) 1 brood INCU: ♀ 25 (24–28)	FLDG: ♀ 50–55	Aq inverts

Breeding habitat Open freshwater lakes, with densely vegetated fringes and small islands for nests.

Displays See essay on Duck Displays, p. 47. Has communal courtship and pursuit flights. ♂ has head-throw display, quickly bringing head back so that crown touches back and bill points upwards, then head comes forward again.

Nesting On ground, close to water, in dense cover. Nest mat of vegetation and down from ♀. Eggs are pale greenish, 62mm; more than 15 eggs probably due to 2 ♀s (see essay on Parasitized Ducks, p. 67). Eggs hatch synchronously.

Diet Dives for underwater plants, aquatic invertebrates, tadpoles, and small fish. Sometimes stirs up bottom sediments by paddling with feet.

Winters S and W of breeding areas on more open waters including reservoirs; in flocks.

Conservation Widespread across N Europe, N Asia, local further S. Considerable increases in range in N and W.

Essays Nest Sites and Materials, p. 443.

Refs Johnsgard 1965; Marchant et al. 1990.

Swimming and Underwater Flight

ONE of the most graceful sights in the animal world is a penguin swimming underwater. With seemingly no effort, it rockets around using its wings to 'fly' through the ocean. A swimming penguin changes the angle of the leading edge of its wings, lowering them on the downstroke and raising them on the upstroke, so that both strokes propel the bird forward, resulting in smooth progression through the water. The penguin's body feathers are short, and thus trap little air, and penguin bones are quite solid for birds. Both features reduce buoyancy, thereby helping penguins to remain submerged.

Underwater 'flyers' are mostly short-winged seabirds, such as auks, and diving petrels. To work well in water, wings must be both short and stiff. Long, slender wings are fine for soaring, but are poor instruments for flying in a medium as dense as water — they cannot be moved rapidly against the resistance. But with their stubby wings, underwater flyers tend to make poor aviators, and some, such as penguins, have given up flying altogether. Diving petrels, however, fly reasonably well with rapid wing beats, and upon plunging into water simply continue to fly through it.

Most birds that swim in fresh water propel themselves with their feet, as do underwater flyers when they are on the surface. The most advanced foot-paddlers are the divers. Veritable submarines, divers are long, slender, and streamlined, with two powerful flattened legs attached to the rear of their body and tipped with webbed feet. Like penguins (and other diving birds such as auks, grebes, and cormorants) they have relatively solid bones and

Diving ducks. On the left, a Common Scoter keeps its wings partially extended to help in propulsion and manoeuvring; on the right, a Pochard propels itself with legs alone.

Ferruginous Duck

Aythya nyroca

ATLAS 79; PMH 62; PER 82; HFP 58; HPCW 45; NESTS 87; BWP1:571

 | BLDS: ♀ Monogamy | ⬭ 8–10 (6–14) 1 brood INCU: ♀ 25–27 | P2 FLDG: ♀ 55–60 | Aq inverts | Dabbles

Floating

Breeding habitat Shallow, well-vegetated fresh water lakes and marshes, often with much floating vegetation.

Displays See essay on Duck Displays, p. 47.

Nesting On ground, close to water, or in reed-beds. Nest is pile of vegetation with down from ♀. Eggs pale buff, 53mm, hatch synchronously.

Diet Mainly plants, some aquatic insects, taken from surface, up-ending, or diving.

Winters Moves S; more open and coastal waters, less often in flocks than other ducks.

Conservation Species has very fragmented distribution in W, with erratic fluctuations in numbers. More widespread from E Europe into C Asia. See p. 528.

Refs Johnsgard 1965.

Tufted Duck

Aythya fuligula

ATLAS 78; PMH 62; PER 84; HFP 58; HPCW 46; NESTS 86 ; BWP1:577

 | BLDS: ♀ Monogamy | ⬭ 8–11 (3–22) 1 brood INCU: ♀ 25 (23–28) | P2 FLDG: ♀ 40–45 | Aq inverts | Dabbles

Breeding habitat Relatively deep, open freshwater lakes and ponds, free of floating vegetation, including reservoirs and gravelpits.

Displays See essay on Duck Displays, p. 47.

Nesting Often on small islands, on ground near water or in water, sometimes in an open site among nesting gulls. Nest is of vegetation and down from ♀. Eggs pale grey with green tinge, 59mm. Nests with >14 eggs are those of 2 ♀s (see essay on Parasitized Ducks, p. 67); eggs hatch synchronously.

Diet Plants, molluscs, crustaceans, and insects, often taken from the bottom after dives, but sometimes feeds by up-ending in shallow water. Young take mostly aquatic insects.

Winters Resident or moves south and west to larger open waters including reservoirs, estuaries; in flocks.

Conservation Marked increase in W, in part because species can use man-made lakes. Occurs widely across N Europe, N Asia.

Essays Feeding Birds, p. 357.

Refs Johnsgard 1965.

float low in the water. And, like submarines, they can dive deep; Great Northern Divers have been recorded at incredible depths of over 180 metres in the North American Great Lakes.

Other birds that dive but are also accomplished flyers, such as terns, gannets, and pelicans, are quite buoyant because of their hollow bones, numerous air sacs, and the air that remains trapped in their feathers. They submerge much as buoyant human beings often do — by diving from a considerable height and allowing their momentum to help carry them well below the surface. Kingfishers seem to use a similar technique, but more often take their prey very close to the surface. In contrast, grebes can squeeze much of the air out of their feathers and partially deflate their air sacs, 'trimming' themselves to float at any level or to submerge. Cormorants and darters have wettable feathers that help them sink but which also apparently commit them to long sessions of sun-drying with spread wings.

Birds that are foot-propelled in water generally fold their wings tightly while diving and swimming, so as to streamline the body. Eiders and scoters, however, keep their wings partially open and use them for both paddling and steering. Oddly, dippers often just walk along the bottom. When suspended in mid-water, however, these passerines use their wings to swim.

SEE: How Do Birds Fly?, p. 217; Soaring, p. 79; Feet, p. 289; Dipping, p. 333. Spread-wing Postures, p. 17.

How Fast and High Do Birds Fly?

GENERALLY birds follow the facetious advice often given to pilots — 'fly low and slow'. Most cruise speeds are in the 30-to-50-kph range, with a Common Eider having the fastest accurately clocked cruise speed of about 75 kph. During a chase, however, speeds increase; ducks, for example, can fly 100 kph or even faster, and it has been reported that a Peregrine can stoop at speeds of 320 kph (160 kph may be nearer the norm). Interestingly, there is only a weak relationship between the size of a bird and how fast it flies. Both hummingbirds and geese can reach roughly the same maximum speeds.

There is, of course, a considerable difference between the speed at which a bird *can* fly and the speed at which it normally *does* fly. When the bird is 'around home' one might expect it to do one of two things; minimize its energy use per unit time (that is, minimize its metabolic rate), or maximize the distance it travels per unit of energy expended. A vulture loitering in the sky in search of prey might, like the pilot of an observation aircraft, maximize endurance; a seabird travelling to distant foraging grounds might, like a Concorde encountering headwinds on a transoceanic flight, maximize range. Staying up longest does not necessarily mean going farthest. A bird might be able to stay aloft 6 hours at 25 kph (maximum endurance, covering 150 km) or

Scaup

Aythya marila

ATLAS 78; PMH 63; PER 84; HFP 58; HPCW 46; NESTS 86; BWP1:586

Floating	BLDS: ♀ Monogamy	8–11 (6–15) 1 brood INCU: ♀ 26–28

FLDG: ♂♀ 40–45	Seeds	Surface dips

Breeding habitat Freshwater lakes, northern lakes, also on Baltic Sea.

Displays See essay on Duck Displays, p. 47.

Nesting Often with gulls and terns, on ground or floating in shallow water. Nest is of grass with down from ♀. Eggs greenish, pale, 62mm; >15 eggs in a nest probably indicates egg dumping - that is, use of nest by more than 2 ♀s (see essay on Parasitized Ducks, p. 67); hatch synchronously. ♂ may stay with ♀ at nest longer than in other ducks.

Diet A variety of plant and animal foods, but often molluscs, taken during dives. In Scotland, will take waste grain spilled by whisky distilleries.

Winters In large flocks often in marine habitats, S to Mediterranean.

Conservation Decline in N; is widely distributed in N Europe, N Asia, N America.

Essays Eye Colour and Development, p. 85.

Refs Johnsgard 1965.

Common Eider

Somateria mollissima

ATLAS 80; PMH 63; PER 84; HFP 60; HPCW - ; NESTS 87; BWP1:595

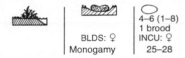 

	BLDS: ♀ Monogamy	4–6 (1–8) 1 brood INCU: ♀ 25–28

FLDG: ♀ 65–75		Dabbles

Breeding habitat Northern coasts, into estuaries in some places.

Displays See essay on Duck Displays, p. 47; has communal displays, with ♂s giving dove-like cooing calls frequently.

Nesting Colonially, on ground, sometimes sheltered by rocks, but often in the open, and often in tern colonies, near shore. Nest slight hollow lined with thick layer of down from ♀, provides special insulation in this largely arctic species. Eggs pale greenish-grey, 77mm, hatch synchronously. ♀ leaves eggs relatively infrequently. Young form crèches on sea, with attendant adult ♀s, while parents leave to feed. First breeds at three years, and ♂s show immature plumages until then.

Diet Mainly benthic molluscs, but also crustaceans and sea-urchins, taken from dives, or by up-ending in shallow water.

Winters On coasts, on or near breeding areas; in flocks. There is a large moult migration of ♂s assembling in large flocks off SW Jutland.

Conservation Declined in the 19th century because of human exploitation, but has largely recovered. Dutch population declined in the 1960s due to pollution of the Rhine; has now recovered. Dramatic increase in the Baltic in recent decades. Occurs widely across N Europe, N Asia, N America.

Essays The Colour of Birds, p. 137; Crèches, p. 45; Skimming: Why Birds Fly Low over Water, p. 67.

Refs Johnsgard 1965; Marchant et al. 1990.

5 hours at 32 kph (maximum range, covering 160 km). Birds can also choose to maximize speed, as when chased by a predator or racing to defend a territory. Or they can choose some compromise between speed and range. In order to determine what birds normally do, Gary Schnell and Jenna Hellack of the University of Oklahoma used Doppler radar, a device similar to that used by police to catch speeders, to measure the ground speeds of a dozen species of seabirds (gulls and terns) near their colonies. They also measured wind speeds with an anemometer, and used those measurements to estimate the airspeeds of the birds. (The wind speeds were generally measured closer to the ground than the birds flew, which led to some errors of estimation since friction with the surface slows air movement near the ground.)

Airspeeds were found to be mostly in the 15-to-65-kph range. The power requirements of each bird at each speed could be calculated, and that information was used to establish that the birds were generally compromising between maximizing their range and minimizing their metabolic rates — with more emphasis on the former. Airspeeds varied a great deal, but near the minimum metabolic rate rather large changes in airspeed did not require dramatic increases in energy consumption. For example, a gull whose maximum endurance airspeed was 35 kph could fly at any speed between 25 and 40 kph without increasing its metabolic rate more than 15 per cent.

Most birds fly below 150 metres except during migration. There is no reason to expend the energy to go higher — and there may be dangers, such as exposure to higher winds or to the sharp vision of hawks. When migrating, however, birds often do climb to relatively great heights, possibly to avoid dehydration in the warmer air near the ground. Migrating birds in the Caribbean are mostly observed around 3000 m, although some are found half and some twice that high. Generally long-distance migrants seem to start out at about 1500 m and then progressively climb to around 6000 m. Just like jet aircraft, the optimum cruise altitude of migrants increases as their 'fuel' is used up and their weight declines. Vultures sometimes rise over 3000 m in order to scan larger areas for food (and to watch the behaviour of distant vultures for clues to the location of a feast). Perhaps the most impressive altitude record is that of a flock of Whooper Swans which was seen on radar arriving over Northern Ireland on migration and was visually identified by an airline pilot at 8850 m. Birds can fly at altitudes that would be impossible for bats, since bird lungs can extract a larger fraction of oxygen from the air than can mammal lungs.

SEE: Wing Shapes and Flight, p. 269; Soaring, p. 79; Flying in V-Formation, p. 43; Adaptations for Flight, p. 511; Migration, p. 377. REFS: Murphy, 1986; Schnell and Hellack, 1978, 1979.

King Eider

Somateria spectabilis

ATLAS 80; PMH 63; PER 84; HFP 60; HPCW - NESTS 88; BWP1:605

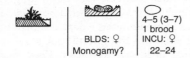

	4–5 (3–7) 1 brood	P2		
BLDS: ♀ Monogamy?	INCU: ♀ 22–24	FLDG: ♀ ?		Surface dips

Breeding habitat Freshwater tundra pools.

Displays Not well known, but see essay on Duck Displays, p. 47; has cooing calls like Common Eider in communal displays.

Nesting Usually not colonial, near water often on small islands. Nest is slight hollow, lined with down from ♀. Eggs light olive, 67mm, hatch synchronously. ♂ may help guard nest for the first few days of incubation, then leaves. ♀ leads young to ocean shortly before they can fly. Sometimes form crèches, like Common Eider.

Diet Benthic invertebrates; mainly molluscs, but also crustaceans and echinoderms. Also takes food while swimming on surface. Young, on freshwater lakes, take mainly insects.

Winters In flocks on coastal seas, to edge of ice, further from shore than Common Eider. Has spectacular moult migration with vast flocks assembling in some areas.

Conservation Hunted, but little known about numbers as it nests in remote areas around Arctic Ocean in Russia, to N America.

Essays The Colour of Birds, p. 137; Crèches, p. 45; Eclipse Plumage, p. 53.

Refs Johnsgard 1965.

Harlequin Duck

Histrionicus histrionicus

ATLAS 82; PMH 64; PER 84; HFP 62; HPCW - ; NESTS 88; BWP1:620

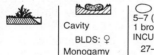

	5–7 (3–10) 1 brood	P2		
Cavity BLDS: ♀ Monogamy	INCU: ♀ 27–29	FLDG: ♀ 60–70?		Surface dips

Breeding habitat Fast-flowing arctic streams and rivers.

Displays See essay on Duck Displays, p. 47; visual displays not as obvious as other sea-going ducks. Has communal courtship and pursuit flights.

Nesting On ground, in cover, sometimes in rock cavity. Nest is depression mainly lined with down from ♀. Eggs cream to pale buff, 58mm, hatch synchronously. ♀ may lead young down rivers to sea. First breeds at 2 years.

Diet Molluscs, crustaceans, taken from dives or while swimming on surface; young take mainly insects.

Winters In rocky coastal waters, near shore; in flocks.

Conservation Within Europe, only occurs in Iceland (where it is protected). Is widely distributed in N America, NE Asia.

Essays The Colour of Birds, p. 137; Eclipse Plumage, p. 53.

Refs Johnsgard 1965.

Skimming: Why Birds Fly Low over Water

A flock of seaducks or Oystercatchers skimming low over the water is a common seashore sight. Further offshore shearwaters often closely follow the contours of the waves, and gaggles of Little Auks fly rapidly just above the water. Such low-level skimming permits the birds to take advantage of an aerodynamic phenomenon known as 'ground effect', and save up to 20 per cent of the mechanical power required for flight by doing so. Skimmers are, appropriately, masters of the tactic.

Energy is saved because the patterns of air-flow around a wing operating close to a smooth surface are modified in a way that reduces drag (the resistance of the air to the progress of the wing). Heavily-laden planes that can maintain flight close to the ground are sometimes incapable of climbing above the ground effect zone. Similarly, large waterbirds like swans and pelicans benefit particularly from ground effect during take-off.

Although it is more energetically efficient to fly close to a surface, the effect only operates when the flying object is within one wingspan of the surface. To maintain this proximity is generally too hazardous for landbirds and so the habit is largely restricted to waterbirds.

SEE: How Fast and High Do Birds Fly?, p. 63; How Do Birds Fly?, p. 217; Soaring, p. 79. REF.: Pennycuick, 1975, 1989.

Parasitized Ducks

A Cuckoo laying its egg in the nest of a small warbler is pretty obvious to us, so such *inter*specific brood parasitism has received a great deal of attention from ornithologists. On the other hand *intra*specific brood parasitism, an individual laying eggs in the nest of another of the same species, is not nearly as easily detected by birds or people. Parasitic eggs and young are essentially identical to those of the host. If both the host and parasite female are un-ringed, even an observed incident of one female laying in another's nest may go unrecognized as such.

Intraspecific parasitism is common among Ostriches and their relatives, gallinaceous birds, a few passerines (such as North American Cliff Swallows, *Hirundo pyrrhonota*), and many ducks. A female duck that is parasitized by

Long-tailed Duck

Clangula hyemalis

ATLAS 81; PMH 65; PER 84; HFP 64 HPCW 46; NESTS 90; BWP1:626

○
6–9 (5–11)
1 brood

BLDS: ♀
Monogamy

INCU: ♀
24–29

FLDG: ♀
35–40

Breeding habitat Arctic tundra pools, upland lakes, coastal islands.
Displays See essay on Duck Displays, p. 47. ♂ has head-back display with head touching back and bill upwards, and also unique rear-end display, with ♂ raising head, then throwing it forward, as tail goes up vertically and feet kicked backwards, raising rear out of water. Has loud, far-reaching courtship calls. and continuous noisy behaviour.
Nesting On ground, in cover, near water. Nest is a depression lined with some vegetation and down from ♀. Eggs creamy yellow, 54mm, large numbers may be eggs of two ♀s (see essay on

Parasitized Ducks, p. 67). Eggs hatch synchronously; two broods may join together. ♂s may stay halfway through incubation. First breeds at 2 years.
Diet Crustaceans and molluscs, insects in freshwater habitats, taken during dives.
Winters Mainly at sea, in flocks.
Conservation Decreases in Iceland, and species is very vulnerable to oil spills, perhaps because it mistakes the slicks for smooth, quiet water. Widespread around Arctic Ocean.
Essays Crèches, p. 45.
Refs Johnsgard 1965.

Common Scoter

Melanitta nigra

ATLAS 82; PMH 65; PER 86; HFP 62; HPCW 46; NESTS 88; BWP1:634

○
6–8 (5–11)
1 brood

BLDS: ♀
Monogamy

INCU: ♀
30–31

FLDG: ♀
45–50

Breeding habitat Freshwater lakes on tundra and even moorland away from water.
Displays See essay on Duck Displays, p. 47.
Nesting On ground, in cover, near water. Nest is hollow lined with grass and down from ♀. Eggs creamy to buff, 66mm, large numbers of eggs probably involve 2 ♀s, hatch synchronously. Two broods may join together. First breeds at 2–3 years.
Diet Mainly molluscs, taken by diving; insects in freshwater habitats.

Winters Almost exclusively in shallow coastal waters, in flocks; may concentrate in large numbers during moult migrations.
Conservation Inshore feeding habits make it sensitive to oil spills. Marked decline in Finland may be due to illegal hunting. Occurs widely across N Europe, N Asia, more locally in N America.
Essays Skimming: Why Birds Fly Low over Water, p. 67.
Refs Johnsgard 1965; Marchant et al. 1990.

another of the same species may have her own reproductive output reduced in several ways. Both hatching success of her own eggs and survival of her hatchlings may be reduced, and the larger brood may attract more predators. The female may face the numerous risks and stresses of reproduction for relatively little benefit, if a substantial portion of the clutch is not her own.

What can the host female do in the face of parasitic attack? She can desert the clutch and start again, thus not spending her efforts on a mix of her own and 'adopted' offspring, but then she wastes the resources tied up in her own eggs. She can identify the parasitic eggs and discard them. Or if she senses from the presence of more eggs in the nest than she laid that she has been parasitized, but cannot discriminate the other female's eggs, she can adjust the number of eggs she lays subsequently so as to maximize survival of her own offspring.

Female Goldeneyes are apparently incapable of recognizing foreign eggs, perhaps because Goldeneyes nest in deep, dark cavities. A test was carried out in a Swedish population of Goldeneyes in which there was evidence of a regular decline in fledging success with increased clutch size. Experimenters simulated parasitism by adding one, four, or seven eggs to clutches of Goldeneye females in nest boxes. The Goldeneyes' reactions were recorded: did they continue to lay, start to incubate, or desert the nest? When one or four eggs were added to the females' clutches, the rate of nest desertion was no higher than it was in 'control' nests, which had no added eggs. If seven eggs were added, however, the female never incubated.

When females were 'parasitized' with only one additional egg, they laid significantly more eggs than if four 'parasitic' eggs were added to their clutches. In addition, if four eggs were added before a female had laid five eggs of her own, she adjusted her final output downward, whereas if the four interloper eggs were added to the nest after the female had laid five to eight eggs of her own, she did not reduce her output (natural clutch sizes are mostly in the range of eight to twelve).

These experiments clearly showed that Goldeneye females can adjust their egg-laying to compensate for parasitic eggs added to their clutches. This is not surprising, since Goldeneyes are indeterminate layers — they do not always lay exactly the same number of eggs in each clutch.

Why should intraspecific brood parasitism have evolved so commonly in ducks? One suggestion is that many ducks, especially cavity nesters, suffer from a shortage of suitable nest sites. This could drive several females to lay in the same nest, but in the Goldeneye population under study, less than a third of the nest boxes were used, so this is certainly not a universal reason. In addition, ducks seem better able than smaller birds to find the nests of others of their own species. Also ducklings are precocial, which can lessen the host's burden when caring for the young of parasites. Altricial birds, in contrast, should be under heavy selection to avoid being parasitized by their own kind. Loss of young to starvation is commonly observed in altricial birds, indicating that a high price would be paid for attempting to rear an 'adopted' offspring.

Another factor may be that a female duck often returns to nest near the place of her birth. Thus sisters or mothers and daughters would tend to nest

Velvet Scoter

Melanitta fusca

ATLAS 83; PMH 66; PER 86; HFP 62; HPCW 46; NESTS 89; BWP1:644

 | 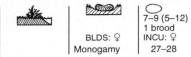 | P2 | |

BLDS: ♀
Monogamy

7–9 (5–12)
1 brood
INCU: ♀
27–28

FLDG: ♀
50–55?

Surface dips

Breeding habitat Freshwater or brackish lakes or offshore islets.

Displays See essay on Duck Displays, p. 47.

Nesting On ground, in cover, near water, but up to 3km away from it. Nest is shallow cup lined with vegetation and down from ♀. Eggs cream to buff, 72mm, hatch synchronously; large clutches are eggs of two ♀s. First breeds at 2 years.

Diet Mainly molluscs, some crustaceans, taken by diving or while swimming on surface; ducklings take insects from surface.

Winters Along exposed coasts, but sometimes inshore in estuaries; in flocks.

Conservation Decreases in many areas, but widely distributed in N Europe, N Asia, N America.

Essays Crèches, p. 45; Eye Colour and Development, p. 85.

Refs Johnsgard 1965.

Barrow's Goldeneye

Bucephala islandica

ATLAS 83; PMH 66; PER 86; HFP 64; HPCW - ; NESTS 89; BWP1:652

 | | P2 | |

BLDS: ♀
Monogamy

8–11 (6–14)
1 brood
INCU: ♀
28–30

FLDG: ♀
?

Breeding habitat Clear, arctic and alpine lakes and rivers.

Displays See essay on Duck Displays, p. 47; very aggressive towards rivals.

Nesting In hole or crevice among rocks (in tree holes in N America), near water. Nest has little or no material, lined with down from ♀. Eggs bluish-green, 62mm, hatch synchronously. Large numbers of eggs due to two ♀s. First year ♀s spend much of first year looking for nest sites.

First breeds in second year.

Diet Insects, molluscs, and crustaceans, from diving, and (rarely) by up-ending.

Winters Resident, but avoids frozen waters, and may move to marine bays, sometimes in small flocks.

Conservation In Iceland, population is apparently stable; species is widely distributed in NW America.

Refs Johnsgard 1965.

in the same general vicinity, and therefore in many cases would parasitize each other. This would reduce somewhat the evolutionary costs of being parasitized, since the host often would be rearing young carrying copies of the same genes. That, in turn, would reduce selection pressures on the hosts to evolve defences against being parasitized.

Finally, ducks, unlike many passerines, do not defend the immediate vicinity of their nests during the laying period, easing the access of parasitic females to the nest. This exposes ducks to interspecific parasitization as well, generally by other ducks. The Redhead (*Aythya americana*), a close relative of the Pochard, appears to be the most persistent parasitic duck. In one Canadian study on artificial islands in reservoirs in Alberta, Redheads parasitized 19 per cent of 685 duck nests, laying an average of 2.7 eggs per parasitized nest. Mallard nests were most frequently parasitized, but the percentage of parasitic eggs per nest was highest when Lesser Scaups (*Aythya affinis*) were the hosts. Red-crested Pochards are known to parasitize Pochards as well as their own species. This perhaps happens most frequently when Red-crested Pochard females have lost clutches and are pressed for time before starting their moult migration (movement to the area where they moult). Laying in the nests of the later-migrating Pochard saves them having to delay departure.

Why don't more passerines exhibit intraspecific parasitism? Have they evolved powerful defences to prevent parasitism by members of their own species? Studies were done in which the eggs of three colonial passerines — Swallows, Pinyon Jays, and Great-tailed Grackles (the latter two, *Gymnorhinus cyanocephalus* and *Quiscalus mexicanus* restricted to the New World) — were exchanged between nests of the same species. The experiments produced no evidence that members of these species can discriminate between their own eggs and foreign eggs. Perhaps the birds have other mechanisms for repelling brood parasites of the same species, such as defence of the nest. Another possibility is that the costs of being a parasite are too high for most birds with altricial young. Nest failures are frequent, and time taken sneaking around trying to parasitize another nest must be subtracted from time that could be used in building nests, laying eggs in the home nest, feeding, and other activities that affect the success of the bird's own nesting attempt. In short, the costs of being a parasite may often outweigh the benefits in altricial birds, which may explain why intraspecific parasitism does not seem to be wide-spread in passerines.

SEE: Brood Parasitism, p. 249; Altruism, p. 245; Precocial and Altricial Young, p. 401; Breeding Site Tenacity, p. 219. REFS: Amat, 1985; Andersson and Eriksson, 1982; Bezzel, 1961; Giroux, 1981; Lanier, 1982; Yom-Tov, 1980.

Goldeneye

Bucephala clangula

ATLAS 83; PMH 67; PER 86; HFP 64; HPCW 46; NESTS 89; BWP1:657

Ground	BLDS: ♀ Monogamy	8–11 (5–13) 1 brood INCU: ♀ 27–32	FLDG: ♀ 57–66		

Breeding habitat Forests near freshwater lakes or rivers.

Displays See essay on Duck Displays, p. 47; communal courtship most intense in late winter, while still on wintering areas, and may be intense with many ♂s and several ♀s. ♂ jerks head back, bill pointed up in display.

Nesting In hollow trees; nest boxes where provided. Site used repeatedly, and often sites are in very limited supply. Nest has little lining except down from ♀. Eggs bluish-green, 59mm, hatch synchronously. ♂ may stay near nest. Large numbers of eggs are from more than one ♀ (see essay on Parasitized Ducks, p. 67). On leaving nest, at 1–2 days, young sometimes may be taken to rearing areas up to 2km away.

Diet Molluscs, crustaceans, and insects, from diving, rarely from dabbling.

Winters In sheltered coastal waters and a variety of freshwater habitats; in flocks.

Conservation Widely distributed in N Europe, N Asia. N America, and no marked changes in numbers, although increases where nest boxes provided (e.g. Scotland), and decreases where forests felled.

Essays Monogamy, p. 335; Eye Colour and Development, p. 85; Breeding Site Tenacity, p. 219.

Refs Johnsgard 1965; Marchant et al. 1990.

Smew

Mergus albellus

ATLAS 84; PMH 67; PER 86; HFP 66; HPCW 46; NESTS 91; BWP1:668

	BLDS: ♀ Monogamy	7–9 (5–11) 1 brood INCU: ♀ 26–28 (30)	FLDG: ♀ ?	Aq inverts	

Breeding habitat Usually northern, wooded freshwater lakes, rivers.

Displays See essay on Duck Displays, p. 47.

Nesting In tree holes, often those made by Black Woodpeckers, but will use nest boxes. Nest is lined with down from ♀. Eggs buffish-cream, 52mm, large numbers are from 2 ♀s (see essay on Parasitized Ducks, p. 67). Probably breeds at 2 years.

Diet Fish and insects, from dives.

Winters Moves S into more open waters including reservoirs, sheltered sea bays, estuaries; in small flocks.

Conservation Little known about numbers; recent increase in Finland. Nests sporadically outside northern Russia.

Essays Bills, p. 391.

Refs Johnsgard 1965.

Sleeping Sentries and Mate-guarding

EVEN when apparently asleep, birds open their eyes and peek around. Peeking is limited to the phase of sleep referred to as dozing or 'quiet sleep'. During the remaining 'active-sleep' portion of their slumber, birds' eyes remain shut.

Animal behaviourist Dennis Lendrem found that among ducks, peeking typically occurs about once every two to six seconds. Which ducks in the flock do the most peeking depends on the size of the flock, a bird's position within it, and the time of year. Members of smaller flocks peek more, as do ducks in less-protected positions. During the breeding season, males peek more than females.

As the number of females in a flock of birds increases, so do mating opportunities for promiscuous males. Among colonial Guillemots, for example, extra-pair copulations (EPCs) occur at a higher rate than that found in birds with dispersed nesting. Most EPCs occur when the male of the pair is either absent, asleep, or otherwise engaged. Among Lendrem's ducks, males kept an eye on each other, lessening the threat of their mates (willingly or unwillingly) copulating with others, which might explain why mated males peek more than bachelors. Males that successfully avoided cuckoldry were at an advantage, especially if they attempted to obtain EPCs themselves.

Promiscuity among generally monogamous species is surprisingly commonplace and has been recorded, for example, in Fulmars, Teals, Mallards, Ptarmigans, Swallows, Sand Martins, Rooks, Starlings, Chaffinches, and House Sparrows. Preventing EPCs through close guarding by male partners prior to and during the laying period has been reported in over 50 species, most of which are passerines. Accordingly, the timing of an EPC is critical to its success, and some of the cues that males use to increase their chances have been isolated. Male Swallows, for example, use the intensity of mate-guarding as a signal, while male Sand Martins cue into the heaviness of female flight which reveals which females are actively egg-laying and fertile.

The potential for sperm competition in birds is high. Unlike most mammals, female birds can store sperm for a prolonged period. The shortest known viability for stored sperm is six days in the Ring Dove (*Streptopelia risoria*), but sperm 'shelf-life' is known only for domesticated birds and is highly variable. In the Zebra Finch (*Poephila guttata*) sperm from the last male to mate has precedence over prior matings, so that a single extra-pair copulation can be disproportionately successful in fertilizing an egg. That some males compete to be the last to mate with a particular female may explain why those at risk of EPCs copulate many more times than is necessary to fertilize their mate's eggs. Fulmars copulate some 30 times before the only egg is laid. Ospreys copulate more than 100 times for each clutch. Rates are

Red-breasted Merganser
Mergus serrator

ATLAS 84; PMH 67; PER 86; HFP 66; HPCW 47; NESTS 90; BWP1:673

BLDS: ♀	◯ 8–10 (6–14) 1 brood INCU: ♀ 31–32(29–35)
Monogamy	

 FLDG: ♀ 60–65

Breeding habitat By lakes and rivers and sheltered marine bays and estuaries.

Displays Even during breeding season, spends night communally, and such gatherings are a focus of social behaviour. See essay on Duck Displays, p. 47.

Nesting On ground, among roots, in hollows, or in thick vegetation. Nest is shallow depression lined with down from ♀. Eggs greenish or buffish, 65mm, hatch synchronously. Large number of eggs in one nest indicate use by more than one ♀. Sometimes different broods join together into crèches, often with only one ♀ in charge. First breeds at 2 years.

Diet Fish. Finds prey by swimming with head under water and then catches them by diving. Sometimes several birds feed cooperatively, with line of birds driving prey into shallower water, where prey are more easily captured.

Winters Moves S, into mostly sheltered marine habitats; in flocks.

Conservation Increasing; in UK, first bred in northern England and Wales in the 1950s. Persecuted on some salmon rivers. Widely distributed in N Europe, N Asia, N America.

Essays Bills, p. 391; *Hesperornis* and Other Missing Links, p. 129; Crèches, p. 45; Commensal Feeding, p. 27; Skimming: Why Birds Fly Low over Water, p. 67.

Refs Johnsgard 1965; Marchant et al. 1990.

Goosander
Mergus merganser

ATLAS 84; PMH 68; PER 86; HFP 66; HPCW 47; NESTS 90; BWP1:680

BLDS: ♀	◯ 8–11 (4–13) 1 brood INCU: ♀ 30–32
Monogamy	

 FLDG: ♀ 60–70

Breeding habitat Large freshwater lakes and rivers, in forested or mountainous areas.

Displays See essay on Duck Displays, p. 47.

Nesting In holes, sometimes those excavated by Black Woodpeckers, only rarely uses nest boxes. Usually close to water, but up to 1km away. Nest is a hollow of material lined with down. Eggs creamy, 68mm, large numbers are eggs of 2 or more ♀s. Young may be led some distance from nest, and different broods may join together into crèhes. Breeds first at two years.

Diet Fish, obtained by diving. Like Red-breasted Merganser, several birds often feed together, apparently cooperatively.

Winters Moves S onto large freshwater lakes, much less often on sea; in flocks.

Conservation Has colonized UK within the last century; widely distributed in N Europe, N Asia, N America.

Essays Diet And Nutrition, p. 493; Crèches, p. 45.

Refs Johnsgard 1965.

also high in polyandrous species (those species where one female mates with more than one male).

While there are certain limitations to using copulation frequency as a simple measure of reproductive success, peeking frequency may also be of limited use as an indicator. Breeding male ducks, for example, out-peek females not only to guard their own reproductive contribution, but also because their bright breeding plumage is presumably quite conspicuous to predators. Breeding males peek much less frequently after they return to eclipse plumage when, all other factors being equal, their peeking rates drop to those of females.

SEE: Communal Roosting, p. 81; Flock Defence, p. 257; Geometry of the Selfish Colony, p. 15; Monogamy, p. 335. REFS: Birkhead, 1987; Goodburn 1984; Lendrem, 1983, Westneat, *et al.*, 1990.

Nest Sanitation

THE very fragility of a nest may be adaptive in forcing many birds to build a new one every year; nests that do not deteriorate over the winter can harbour potentially lethal parasites or pathogens that may withstand the cold and await returning nesters. Indeed, despite their appearance as peaceful retreats, nests are often alive with invertebrates that feed on the birds, on their waste products, or on each other.

Infestations of parasites (fly maggots, fleas, ticks, and mites) or pathogens (bacteria and fungi) are discouraged by various means that include removing the fecal sacs of the young, and adding nest material containing natural chemicals that deter invertebrates. Ectoparasites can also be dodged by laying eggs directly on the substrate (as in nightjars and some seabirds) and by avoiding old nests that have not deteriorated over the winter. When heavy parasite infestations do occur, nestling mortality rises, nests may be deserted, and in extreme cases, entire colony sites are abandoned.

The first gelatinous faecal sacs produced by passerine nestlings are normally eaten by the parents (the inefficiency of chick digestion allows the adults to obtain some nutrition this way); later sacs usually are carried some distance from the nest and dropped. In open nests, young either signal the ejection of a faecal sac or eject it on to the nest rim to be removed by the parent. In some dove species, adult droppings may help to strengthen otherwise flimsy nests, and in some cliff-nesting seabirds, guano accumulation on narrow ledges helps to prevent eggs from accidentally rolling off.

Two thousand years ago Pliny noted that the Swallow brings sprigs of celandine to its nest. Recent work has shown that some birds repeatedly add green leaves or cedar bark with pesticidal properties to their nests. This behaviour has been recorded for numerous birds of prey that re-use old

Ruddy Duck
Oxyura jamaicensis

ATLAS 85; PMH 68; PER 88; HFP 66; HPCW - ; NESTS 92; BWP1:689

 | |

		P2
BLDS: ♀	6–10 1 brood INCU: ♀	FLDG: ♀	Seeds
Monogamy	25–26	50–55	

Breeding habitat Freshwater, especially small lakes.

Displays See essay on Duck Displays, p. 47; ♂ has head-up, tail-cocked posture.

Nesting In thick cover, nest is floating mass of vegetation anchored to reeds etc. with little or no down. Eggs buff-white, 62mm, hatch synchronously. Large numbers of eggs are from more than one ♀ (see notes and essay on Parasitized Ducks, p. 67). ♂s accompany ♀s with nests or young for longer than other ducks. Birds breed in second year.

Diet Insect larvae and aquatic plants, obtained by diving and then straining the benthic mud.

Winters Resident, typically moving onto reservoirs in flocks.

Conservation Introduced to UK from N America in 1960, numbers increased, but now appear stable. Parasitic habits may harm native ducks.

Notes In N America, this species commonly parasitizes the nests of other species of ducks.

Refs Johnsgard 1965; Marchant et al. 1990.

White-headed Duck
Oxyura leucocephala

ATLAS 85; PMH 69; PER 88; HFP 66; HPCW 47; NESTS 91; BWP1:694

 | | |

		P2		
		BLDS: ♀	5–10 1 brood INCU: ♀	FLDG: ♀
Ground	Monogamy	25–26?	?	Aq inverts	Dabbling

Breeding habitat Open, shallow, fresh or brackish lakes, with well-vegetated margins.

Displays Not well known. See essay on Duck Displays, p. 47; ♂ has head-up, tail-cocked posture.

Nesting On lake margins. Nest is floating mat of vegetation anchored to reeds etc. Eggs white, 67mm, probably hatch synchronously; large numbers of eggs are from more than one ♀.

Diet Aquatic vegetation, some insects and other invertebrates, obtained from diving, or less often dabbling.

Winters Resident or locally disperses, sometimes onto larger lakes, in flocks.

Conservation There must be considerable concern about this species. It has a scattered, fragmented distribution from Spain to C Asia. Many populations threatened by habitat destruction. See p. 528.

Essays Feathers, p. 363.

Refs Johnsgard 1965.

nests (some kites, many hawks, and most eagles) and for some passerines (especially secondary cavity nesters). Experiments with Starlings (a secondary cavity nester) show that they can discriminate among leaves and select those with biochemical properties that deter lice and bacteria. Interestingly, rather than adding greens, nuthatches (also secondary cavity nesters) ritually smear pitch and rub insects (both containing chemicals that may discourage parasites) around their nest hole entrance.

SEE: Nest Evolution, p. 345; Nest Sites and Materials, p. 443; Nest Lining, p. 439; Disease and Parasitism, p. 315; Incubation: Controlling Egg Temperatures, p. 273. REFS: Clark and Mason, 1985; Collias and Collias, 1984; Wimberger, 1984.

Bird Guilds

GUILDS are groups of species in a community that exploit the same set of resources in a similar manner, but are not necessarily closely related taxonomically. Birds that hunt for insects on the floor of a deciduous forest constitute a guild; tropical American hummingbirds and butterflies jointly form a guild of daytime nectar feeders; Rock Sparrows, ants, and rodents are members of a seed-eating guild. Members of guilds often differ in their precise food requirements, reducing the potential for competition among them when resources are limited. Thus members of a dabbling duck guild in Finland differ in neck and body length, which permits them to feed at different depths.

In a given locality, the membership of a guild can change through the year as migrants are added or subtracted. For example a guild of foliage-gleaning birds in northern Finland has been analysed using statistical techniques. The guild included the Chaffinch, Brambling, and Willow Warbler as summer visitors. Willow Tits, Crested Tits, Treecreepers, and a portion of the Goldcrest population were resident. The guild members differed most in their foraging habits, especially in the part of the tree where they fed and the species of tree in which they fed. There was even less overlap in foraging behaviour in winter, apparently because food is scarcer then and the potential for competition higher — not because of the departure of the migrants.

SEE: Bills, p. 391; Songbird Foraging, p. 417; Hartley's Titmice and MacArthur's Warblers, p. 425. REFS: Alatalo, 1982; Pöysä, 1983a, 1983b; Root, 1967; Wagner, 1981.

Honey Buzzard

Pernis apivorus

ATLAS 93; PMH 70; PER 92; HFP 76; HPCW 47; NESTS 101; BWP2:13

| 10–20m | BLDS: ♂♀ Monogamy | 2 (1–3) 1 brood INCU: ♂♀ 30–35 | SA1 FLDG: ♂♀ 40–45 | Sm verts | |

Breeding habitat Open woodland, avoids marshes and open agricultural land.

Displays Pair may circle high over nest. Have long complex aerial display, with plunges and swoops. Bird may dive, swoop upwards into stall with wings held high and quivering.

Nesting Territorial. Nest is of twigs in tree, with much fresh, green vegetation. Eggs white or pale buff, heavily marked, 52mm; hatch asynchronously. Initially ♂ brings food to ♀ who feeds young; even after young can feed on own, both parents also provide food and they help young until several weeks after fledging, young often returning to the nest to be fed.

Diet As name suggests, has remarkable habit of feeding on the larvae and adults of social insects, which it finds by watching from a perch or by following flying insects, then excavating nest. Snips off the stingers with beak before eating. Also feeds on a variety of small vertebrates, and ground insects which it pursues on foot.

Winters Migrates to Africa, S of Sahara. Large concentrations of birds, where species tries to avoid water crossings (see essay).

Conservation Widespread across Europe and NC Asia. Changes not well known; local decreases especially where shot. See p. 528.

Notes Has dense, scale-like feathers on face that minimize stings.

Essays Raptors at Sea Crossings, p. 93; Raptor Hunting, p. 113; Piracy, p. 213. Migration, p. 377; Differential Migration, p. 323.

Refs Brown and Amadon 1968.

Black-winged Kite

Elanus caeruleus

ATLAS 88; PMH 70; PER 92; HFP 72; HPCW 37; NESTS 95; BWP2:23

| 3–20m | BLDS: ♂♀ Monogamy | 3–4 (2–6) 1 brood INCU: ♀ 26 (25–28) | SA1 FLDG: ♂♀ 30–35 | Insects | Low patrol |

Breeding habitat Open forest or cultivated land with trees in dry to arid areas.

Displays Not well known. Pairs may circle to great heights, and have slow-flapping, 'butterfly' flight display. When pair perched both may slowly cock tails with wings drooped.

Nesting Territorial. Nest of twigs and grass in tree, built by ♀ with material brought also by ♂. Eggs cream with dark blotches, 39mm, hatch asynchronously. ♀ normally feeds young. Adults may remain together from year to year, even outside breeding season, and accompany young until after fledging.

Diet Small vertebrates and large insects, obtained by first hovering and then dropping onto prey. Also flies low over ground to surprise prey.

Winters Mainly resident, though in Africa disperses to take advantage of locally abundant insects and rodents.

Conservation Scattered and fragmented distribution, but possibly increasing. More widely distributed in Africa, S Asia, Americas. See p. 528.

Notes Also known as Black-shouldered Kite.

Essays Raptor Hunting, p. 113.

Refs Brown and Amadon 1968.

Soaring

SOME land birds, such as vultures, eagles, and buzzards, sustain flight for long periods without flapping their wings. They take advantage of updrafts produced when the wind blows over hills and mountain ridges or make use of rising columns of warm air called 'thermals'. Vultures stay within thermals by flying slowly in tight circles. They have short, broad wings and a low wing loading (ratio of bird weight to wing area) that allows them to remain aloft and to be highly manoeuvrable at slow speeds. They also have a low aspect ratio (ratio of wing length to width), something that is dictated by their take-off requirements. Low-aspect-ratio wings generally produce a lot of drag — that is, resistance from the air through which they are moving. Air from high-pressure areas beneath the wings tends to flow over the wingtips into the low-pressure areas above the wings. That flow produces wingtip turbulence, which disturbs the smooth flow of air and increases drag. The broad tips of low-aspect-ratio wings create a great deal of drag and that is very undesirable in a soaring bird.

A soaring Black Vulture spreads its primary feathers so that each acts as a small, high-aspect-ratio wing. This reduces turbulence at the wingtips and lowers the stall speed, helping the vulture to stay aloft while circling slowly in thermals (columns of rising warm air).

Vultures alleviate this problem slightly by flying with their primary feathers spread, thus creating slots between them. Each primary serves as an individual high-aspect-ratio wing, reducing wingtip turbulence and lowering the stalling speed of the wing so that the bird can remain aloft at a slower speed. This helps vultures to circle in thermals, maintaining thrust by gliding downward, but staying aloft by sinking at a rate slower than the hot air is rising.

It has been possible to measure a vulture's rate of sink by flying sailplanes in close formation with them. North American Turkey Vultures (*Cathartes aura*) have a minimum sink rate of 60 cm per second, while North American Black Vultures (*Coragyps atratus*) have a minimum rate of 80 cm per second.

Black Kite
Milvus migrans

ATLAS 88; PMH 71; PER 94; HFP 72; HPCW 48; NESTS 95; BWP2:27

		2–3 (1–5) 1 brood	SA1
	BLDS: ♂	INCU: ♂♀, ♀	FLDG: ♂♀	
8–15m	Monogamy	26–38?	42?	Carrion

Breeding habitat Wide range of open country and human settlements; often near water.

Displays Has high, circling flight display near nest. Pairs have mock fights, higher bird drops to attack bird below and birds may lock talons, briefly, as the birds tumble over in the air.

Nesting Solitary, but sometimes colonial. Nest is of twigs, often decorated with rubbish and green vegetation, built by ♂, who may give mate choice of more than one site. Eggs dirty white, usually spotted or blotched, 54mm, hatch asynchronously. Food brought by both parents, but ♀ feeds young. Young fed for up to 7 weeks after fledgling. Pairs may remain together for several years.

Diet A wide variety of vertebrates and insects, also steals food from other birds of prey, and frequently scavenges.

Winters Migrates to Africa and India, with concentrations of birds at the Bosporus and Strait of Gibraltar (see essay). Often gregarious.

Conservation Wide distribution in Old World to Australia; often in large numbers in urban areas. See p. 528.

Essays Raptors at Sea Crossings, p. 93; Commensal Feeding, p. 27; Mixed-species Flocking, p. 429; Nest Sanitation, p. 75; Migration, p. 377; Differential Migration, p. 323.

Refs Brown and Amadon 1968.

Red Kite
Milvus milvus

ATLAS 87; PMH 71; PER 94; HFP 72; HPCW 48; NESTS 94; BWP2:36

		1–3 (1–5) 1 brood	SA1
	BLDS: ♂♀	INCU: ♂♀, ♀	FLDG: ♂♀	
12–15m	Monogamy	31–32	48–70	Carrion

Breeding habitat Open country with woods and trees.

Displays Has displays similar to Black Kite.

Nesting Nest is of dead twigs in fork of large tree, often decorated with rubbish (but not greenery). Built by ♀ from material brought by ♂. Eggs white, blotched reddish-brown, 57mm hatch asynchronously. Fledging period depends greatly on amount of available food. Young fed for few weeks after fledging. Pairs probably remain together from year to year.

Diet A wide variety of vertebrates and insects; also scavenges. Hunts by soaring and circling, swooping down on prey.

Winters UK and S Europe populations resident, others move south within Europe; some cross into Africa.

Conservation Considerable decreases in some areas due to human persecution. Once found throughout UK, but now restricted to a relict population in Wales, where increasing slowly, and where attempts are being made to reintroduce the species. Has limited range in S and C Europe. See p. 528.

Essays Raptor Hunting, p. 113; Listing Birds in Danger, p. 526; Commensal Feeding, p. 27; Ducking the Bird Laws, p. 523; Mixed-species Flocking, p. 429; Nest Sanitation, p. 75.

Refs Brown and Amadon 1968.

Black Vultures therefore need stronger thermals than Turkey Vultures, which helps to explain why they are restricted to the southern United States while Turkey Vultures can penetrate the relatively cool climes of southern Canada.

Albatrosses and other seabirds such as shearwaters and petrels also soar. But their techniques are different from those of vultures. Albatrosses have long, slender wings with a high aspect ratio. They have the longest wings of any birds; the wingspan of the Wandering Albatross is in the vicinity of 3 metres. The high-aspect-ratio wings of soaring seabirds minimize drag, since the amount of wingtip is small in comparison with the length of the wing. The wing loading of albatrosses is very high also. Indeed, it is thought that albatrosses are close to the structural limits of wing length and wing loading.

Albatrosses and other soaring seabirds use their high wing loading and high-aspect-ratio wings to take advantage of the slope lift, updrafts created on the windward slopes of waves in the same manner as updrafts are created on mountain ridges. Albatrosses are able to proceed upwind by zigzagging along in the slope lift, and can even soar in windless conditions if there are waves. The waves push air upward as they move, and the albatrosses stay in that rising air. Seabirds can also extract some energy from an altitudinal gradient in the wind. The flow of air over the ocean is slowed close to the water by friction with its surface, and increases in speed with height. Employing that gradient has been called 'dynamic soaring', but recent work by a leading authority on bird flight, Colin Pennycuick, indicates that slope soarers gain relatively little energy in that way. For instance, in typical wind conditions in the South Atlantic, dynamic soaring would permit albatrosses to rise about 3 metres above the surface, but they are regularly observed soaring to near 15 metres.

SEE: How Do Birds Fly?, p. 217; Wing Shapes and Flight, p. 269; How Fast and High Do Birds Fly?, p. 63. REFS: Pennycuick, 1982; Raspet, 1950; Rayner, 1988.

Communal Roosting

WHEN flocks of a million or more Starlings make pests of themselves by spending the night close to human habitation, the phenomenon of communal roosting comes to local attention. These gigantic swarms, however, hardly approach the record for communal roosting birds. The Red-billed Quelea (*Quelea quelea*, a weaver, related to the House Sparrow) is so abundant that it may be considered the avian equivalent of a locust plague when invading African grain fields *en masse*. Quelea roosts may number tens of millions of individuals; poisons, explosives, and even flamethrowers have been used in attempts to control local outbreaks. The record-holding communal rooster, however, was North American; the now-extinct Passenger Pigeon roosted

White-tailed Sea Eagle *Haliaeetus albicilla*

ATLAS 87; PMH 72; PER 90; HFP 70; HPCW 49; NESTS 93; BWP2:48

  | 2 (1–3) 1 brood | SA1 | |

BLDS: ♂♀ Monogamy
INCU: ♂♀, ♀ 38 (34–46)
FLDG: ♂♀ 70–75 | Carrion
3–10m

Breeding habitat Rocky shores or inland waters, from steppes to Arctic.

Displays Includes high circling above nesting area, with upper bird swooping down to lower bird, which rolls out of way, and then drops down to first bird, so that both may roll and spin. Talons may touch briefly. Much calling near nest, mainly by ♂, but sometimes as a duet, involves sky-pointing, with head thrown back.

Nesting Territorial. Nest is huge pile of branches and twigs on cliff ledge or in tree, often added to each year. ♂ brings material to ♀ who builds. Eggs dull white becoming stained, 77mm, hatch asynchronously, and larger chick often intimidates smaller one. Young fed by parents for several weeks after fledging. Probably pairs for life.

Diet Fish, but also birds, mammals, and carrion. Locates prey from perch or when soaring, then drops down in stoop. Snatches fish from surface but also plunges. Sometimes gets fish by wading in shallows, often takes stranded fish.

Winters Resident in many coastal areas, but moves S from northern Russia.

Conservation Considerable declines, with local extinctions, from human persecution, intentional poisoning, and pesticides. Has benefited from aggressive conservation efforts in Scandinavia. Range is fragmented in west, though perhaps more extensive across E Europe and N Asia. See p. 529.

Essays Raptor Hunting, p. 113; Conservation of Raptors, p. 103; Listing Birds in Danger, p. 526; Ducking the Bird Laws, p. 523.

Refs Brown and Amadon 1968.

Lammergeier *Gypaetus barbatus*

ATLAS 98; PMH 72; PER 88; HFP 82; HPCW 50; NESTS 105; BWP2:58

  | 1–2 (3) 1 brood | SA1 | |

BLDS: ♂♀ Monogamy
INCU: ♂♀ 55–60
FLDG: ♂♀ 100–110?

Breeding habitat Mountains, to high elevations if free of snow, lower elevations in Asia.

Displays Has courtship flights involving high circling, and cartwheeling descents, with talons interlocked. Visits several alternative nesting sites.

Nesting Nest in small cave or on sheltered cliff ledges, is massive pile of branches, lined with wool, fur, and other materials. Eggs whitish, blotched, and stained brown and yellow, 84mm, hatch asynchronously, and second nestling (if any) rarely survives. Young remain with adults for several months after fledging. Usually monogamous, life-long pairing, first breeding at five years or more. Some birds are polyandrous. See essay, p. 528

Diet Has spectacular feeding habits. Eats the bones, but also meat, of freshly killed mammals, tortoises, and birds usually after other vultures have finished. Small bones may be swallowed whole, but large bones are dropped from heights, repeatedly, if need be, until they are broken and the marrow is extracted. Will sometimes harass ill or injured animals.

Winters Resident.

Conservation Rare or threatened, and declining in Europe, with local extinctions; more common and widespread in Asia. Isolated European populations total less than 100 pairs. See p. 528.

Refs Brown and Amadon 1968.

(and nested) in gigantic colonies containing billions of individuals and covering several square kilometres.

All birds roost — that is, have a period of inactivity analogous to sleep in human beings. Some birds do it alone; others (including vultures, herons, pelicans, pigeons, and crows) with mobs of compatriots. Some change their roosting habits with the season: female Starlings remain in their nest holes with eggs or young in summer, but crowd together with the males at night during the rest of the year. Birds that roost communally do so in a wide variety of situations. In severe winter cold, small groups of nuthatches, treecreepers and Long-tailed Tits spend the night huddled together for warmth in cavities. Some vultures roost on cliffs, and others on the tops of trees; many seabirds roost on islands, and swallows may roost on telephone lines. Starlings choose an enormous diversity of roost sites — many kinds of woodlands, reeds, and numerous kinds of buildings, to name a few.

The question of why some birds roost communally and others roost solitarily is related to the question of why there are both communal and solitary nesters. One possibility is that older, more experienced birds are better able to find food; hence younger birds roost with them in order to follow their elders to better foraging grounds (the 'information centre hypothesis'). The older birds accept this social parasitism because they tend to be dominant, and are able to appropriate more central and therefore safer positions in the roosting crowd. Older Choughs, Red-winged Blackbirds (*Agelaius phoeniceus*), and Brown-headed Cowbirds (*Molothrus ater*, a North American blackbird with cuckoo-like breeding habits), for example, are concentrated in the centres of their roosts. As long as the costs of increased competition are outweighed by the benefits of increased safety from predators for the older birds, and the benefits of locating rich food supplies for the young outweigh any reduction in night-time safety for them, roosting should be communal.

In a Mexican mixed-species roost of marsh birds, Snowy Egrets (*Egretta thula*) and Great White Egrets (*Egretta alba*) displaced others from the higher (and presumably safer) positions in the trees; other species have been found to get more food if they forage near Snowy Egrets, and other birds tend to be attracted more to dummies of Snowy Egrets placed in foraging sites than to dummies of other species. No studies have yet been done to determine whether the egrets are actually followed to foraging sites from the mixed-species roosts, however. These observations, and those of the blackbirds and cowbirds, are consistent with the notion that older and younger birds (or species with divergent capacities to locate food) get different benefits from joining communal roosts.

Further support for this notion comes from observations of Swallows in Denmark. Older birds were more successful in finding food than younger ones, and also displaced the youngsters from the safest roosting positions. Evidence was also found that the young Swallows were somehow able to evaluate the feeding success of adults and preferentially follow the well-fed ones when they left the roost the next day.

Even in larger roosts in which huddling does not occur, more central

Egyptian Vulture

Neophron percnopterus

ATLAS 98; PMH 72; PER 88; HFP 82; HPCW 50; NESTS 104; BWP2:64

  2 (1–3)
1 brood
INCU: ♂♀
42

BLDS: ♂♀
Monogamy

 SA1
FLDG: ♂♀
70–90

Breeding habitat Wide range of open habitats from mountains to hot lowlands, from remote areas to close to villages.

Displays Not well known. Include high circling and steep dives and climbs. Pairs roll in flight.

Nesting Solitary, nesting area is defended against rivals. Nest pile of branches on sheltered ledge on cliffs, in caves, or, rarely, in trees. Eggs dirty white, mottled, and stained, 66mm, hatch asynchronously. Birds breed first at probably 4–5 years.

Diet Carrion and a wide variety of organic refuse, particularly near human settlements. With its small bill, it feeds mainly on scraps left by other vultures. One of a small, but remarkable group of birds that uses tools. In this case, stones are thrown at or dropped onto eggs of Ostriches to break them.

Winters Migrates to Africa and India, concentrating over the Strait of Gibraltar and the Bosporus.

Conservation Like other vultures, has declined throughout Europe, and has scattered and isolated populations there. More widespread in Africa and Asia. See p. 529.

Notes Has remarkable eyesight, apparently with twice the visual powers of resolution of humans.

Essays Raptors at Sea Crossings, p. 93; Diet And Nutrition, p. 493; Tool-using, p. 459; How Fast and High Do Birds Fly?, p. 63; Spread-wing Postures, p. 17; Coloniality, p. 107; Birds on Borders, p. 95; Plume Trade, p. 23; Migration, p. 377.

Refs Brown and Amadon 1968.

Griffon Vulture

Gyps fulvus

ATLAS 100; PMH 73; PER 88; HFP 84; HPCW 51; NESTS 106; BWP2:73

 ◯/◐
1
1 brood
INCU: ♂♀
48–54

BLDS: ♂♀
Monogamy

 SA1
FLDG: ♂♀
110–115

Breeding habitat Mountainous areas, but comes down to plains especially to feed .

Displays Mainly high circling flights of pairs above colony. One bird (♂?) follows other closely, carrying twig in its bill. Birds are highly aggressive to each other when feeding, spreading wings, ruffling mantle feathers, and pushing other birds away.

Nesting Typically in colonies on cliff ledges, nest is pile of twigs. Egg whitish, sometimes speckled darker, 92mm. Young fed by regurgitation. Monogamous, probably life-long pairing, probably first breeds at 4 or 5 years.

Diet Carrion of mammals, often domestic species such as sheep, cows, horses, and dogs; often assembles in large numbers on carcass, tearing off pieces of flesh. May consume so much that they cannot take off.

Winters Largely resident.

Conservation Declines throughout Europe. Now has fragmented and isolated populations, with more extensive distribution from Turkey through to India. See p. 529.

Essays How Fast and High Do Birds Fly?, p. 63; Spread-wing Postures, p. 17; Coloniality, p. 107; Diet And Nutrition, p. 493; Birds on Borders, p. 95; Plume Trade, p. 23; Eye Colour and Development, p. 85.

Refs Brown and Amadon 1968.

positions may often be thermally advantageous as a result of denser vegetation (relative to the periphery of the roost) and a greater mass of bird bodies per unit area. Both of these factors may act to reduce the loss of heat from individual birds, primarily by reducing the cooling effects of wind. That reduction, however, would rarely be enough to compensate for the energy lost flying the extra distance to the roosting site. In addition, there is some evidence that birds in the lower positions in colonial roosts lose heat because the rain of droppings from higher birds reduces the insulating properties of their plumage. It thus seems unlikely that thermoregulation is a prime reason for communal roosting in most species.

SEE: Coloniality, p. 107; Mixed-species Flocking, p. 429; Temperature Regulation and Behaviour, p. 163; Commensal Feeding, p. 27; Flock Defence, p. 257; Geometry of the Selfish Colony, p. 15. REFS: Gori, 1988; Still *et al.*, 1987; Ward and Zahavi, 1973; Weatherhead, 1985; Yom-Tov, 1979.

Eye Colour and Development

THE colour of a bird's eye (usually the colour of the iris) results both from pigments and from physical phenomena such as the diffraction of light. Avian eye colours range from dark brown and yellow through red, blue, and green to metallic silver and gold. In some species, eye colour differs between the sexes, as in pale grey or white-eyed male and brown-eyed female Velvet Scoters. The nearly identical sexes of the Starling can be differentiated by the presence of a yellow ring along the edge of the iris in females.

In many species, eye colour changes as the bird matures and can serve as a means of determining age. Although the physiology of iris pigmentation is poorly understood, changes in colour with age and with season are likely to be under hormonal control, especially where colours are closely associated with the sexual cycle. Changes of eye colour with age are found in a wide variety of avian families including divers, grebes, ducks, hawks, rails, pheasants, gulls, alcids, woodpeckers, and babblers. Species requiring more than a year to pass from juvenile to adult plumage (such as Bonelli's Eagle and Herring Gull) generally show a concurrent change in eye colour. Specific examples of age-related changes occur in the Gannet in which eye colour turns from dark brown in nestlings to grey blue in juveniles to nearly white in adult birds, in Hen Harriers which transform gradually from brown in young birds to yellow in adults, and in Griffon Vultures whose eyes remain hazel for five years and then gradually become yellow-brown. Eye colour reportedly can be used to distinguish between sub-adults and adults in both Goldeneye and Scaup but further study with known-age birds is needed. In Brown Babblers, both age-related and sex-differentiating changes occur: young birds have dull grey irises that change colour during their first year to pale yellow

Lappet-faced Vulture

Torgos tracheliotus

ATLAS 98; PMH 244; PER -; HFP 82; HPCW 52; NESTS 105; BWP2:83

		1 1 brood	SA1		
	BLDS: ♂♀ Monogamy	INCU: ♀ ?	FLDG: ♂♀ 125?		

Breeding habitat   Desert or savannah regions and up into mountains, usually where there are herds of large mammals.

Displays   High circling above nest. Birds are very aggressive at carcasses, and have threat walk with raised feathers on ruff and mantle, with head low, with slow walk, and exaggerated side to side pivoting.

Nesting   Territorial. Nest is of sticks, cup lined with fur, dung, and grass; in trees. Eggs dull white, spotted and blotched with brown. Monogamous pair-bond maintained at least throughout year; adults will accompany young for several months after fledging.

Diet   Carrion; is often first species at carcass, tears off strips of meat and hide. Will steal from other vulture species.

Winters   Resident.

Conservation   Extensive range in Africa, S of Sahara, but has decreased on edge of its range in North Africa. Israel population, of about 30 pairs in the 1940s, declined to zero in 1990, due to decline in nomadic Bedouin herds. A reintroduction effort is planned.

Essays   How Fast and High Do Birds Fly?, p. 63; Spread-wing Postures, p. 17; Coloniality, p. 107; Diet And Nutrition, p. 493; Birds on Borders, p. 95; Plume Trade, p. 23.

Refs   Brown and Amadon 1968; Paz 1987.

Black Vulture

Aegypius monachus

ATLAS 99; PMH 73; PER 88; HFP 84; HPCW 52; NESTS 105; BWP2:89

Cliff 10–20m	BLDS: ♂♀ Monogamy	1 1 brood INCU: ♂♀ 50–55	SA1 FLDG: ♂♀ ?		

Breeding habitat   Open areas but usually near forested hills with herds of large mammals.

Displays   High circling of pair above nest, with mutual cartwheeling displays and flight rolls. Aggressive at carcasses, raises neck ruffles, may dance from one foot to the other with wings half open.

Nesting   Generally solitary. Nest is large mass of twigs and branches in a tree or cliff ledge. Eggs whitish, variably blotched with browns, 90mm. Monogamous, probably life-long pairing, first breeds at 5–6 years.

Diet   Carrion, often of domesticated animals. Tears off flesh and hide with large bill. Often only one individual at carcasses with other vulture species.

Winters   Largely resident.

Conservation   Marked decline, species no longer breeds in many former nesting areas in SE Europe. Populations in Spain and on island of Mallorca are isolated from rest of range in Greece, Turkey, and east through Asia. See p. 529.

Essays   How Fast and High Do Birds Fly?, p. 63; Spread-wing Postures, p. 17; Coloniality, p. 107; Diet And Nutrition, p. 493; Birds on Borders, p. 95; Plume Trade, p. 23.

Refs   Brown and Amadon 1968.

in most males and dark brown in females. The evolutionary significance of all these changes is not clear, but in some birds they may serve to help signal the maturity of potential mates.

SEE: The Colour of Birds, p. 137; How Long Can Birds Live?, p. 497; Bird Badges, p. 433. REF.: Trauger, 1974.

Copulation

UNLIKE the testes of mammals, those of birds vary greatly in size with the seasons. During the breeding season they may be several hundred times larger than they are during the rest of the year and can account for as much as a tenth of the male's body weight. Their massive enlargement is triggered in temperate-zone birds by day length (curiously enough not timed by the amount of light received by the eyes, but by light passing through the skull and stimulating photoreceptors on the brain). As the days lengthen in the spring, increases in hormones produced by the brain initiate the enlargement of the testes. This stimulus occurs weeks in advance of the actual breeding season, so that the male arrives on the breeding grounds with the testes fully developed. A similar sequence results in the enlargement of the female reproductive organs, development of eggs in the ovaries, formation of the brood patch, and so on.

Enlarged testes secrete greater amounts of male hormones that may brighten skin (not feather) colours and stimulate singing and courtship behaviour. During copulation, the male mounts the female from behind. Both sexes hold their tails to the side and turn back the feathers around the cloaca (the common opening of the bird's alimentary canal and excretory and reproductive systems), so that the swollen lips of the male's and female's cloacae can come into contact. In some birds, such as geese, ducks, and game birds, there is a grooved, erectile penis inside the male's cloaca that guides the sperm, which have been stored in a nearby sac, into the female. In passerines, there is no penis, and copulation amounts to a brief 'cloacal kiss' during which the sperm are transferred.

Once transferred, the sperm remain for a while at the lower end of the oviduct, and then swim to the upper end of that duct to fertilize the egg. A single copulation is usually sufficient to fertilize the eggs laid over a period of about a week. In some birds the sperm remain viable for much longer — turkeys have been reported to lay fertile eggs more than two months after copulation. This is one reason there is considerable variation among species in the frequency of copulations.

Goshawks may copulate as many as 500 to 600 times per clutch of eggs, while the Skylark copulates but once. The reason for the difference appears to be related to the chances that other males will manage to copulate with the

Short-toed Eagle

Circaetus gallicus

ATLAS 89; PMH 73; PER 90; HFP 72; HPCW 53; NESTS 98; BWP2:96

		$\bigcirc$ 1 1 brood	SA1		
	BLDS: ♂♀	INCU: ♀			
3–7m	Monogamy	45–47	FLDG: ♂♀ 70–75		Ground glean

Breeding habitat Wide range of open country from rocky hillsides to coastal plains with an abundance of reptilian prey.

Displays ♂ carries snake or other reptile and passes it to ♀ in flight; both birds soar above nest calling.

Nesting Solitary and territorial, nest is small pile of twigs lined with greenery in tree. Built by ♀ from material from ♂ who brings the material in his beak. Egg white, 74mm. ♂ brings food to young, but normally only ♀ feeds them.

Diet Mainly snakes and some lizards, other vertebrates. Tends to avoid venomous species of snakes, though will take them. Patrols ground, frequently hovering, will sometimes stalk prey on ground.

Winters Migrates to Africa and India, via the Strait of Gibraltar and the Bosporus.

Conservation Marked decline in the north and west of range with many local extinctions. Occurs across S Europe, N Africa, S and C Asia, to India. See p. 528.

Essays Raptors at Sea Crossings, p. 93; Eyes Like a Hawk, p. 89; Conservation of Raptors, p. 103; Raptor Hunting, p. 113; Size and Sex in Raptors, p. 99; Migration, p. 377; Differential Migration, p. 323.

Refs Brown and Amadon 1968.

Marsh Harrier

Circus aeruginosus

ATLAS 101; PMH 74; PER 94; HFP 86; HPCW 53; NESTS 106; BWP2:105

		$\bigcirc$ 4–5 (3–8) 1 brood	SA1		
	BLDS: ♀	INCU: ♀			
	Monogamy	31–38	FLDG: ♀ 35–40		
	(Polygyny)			Sm mammals	

Breeding habitat Reedy marshes or well-vegetated margins of lakes and slow-moving rivers.

Displays Territorial displays include high circling above nest by ♂. ♂s sometimes fly with quick, jerky wing beats, and calling. ♂s make mock attacks on ♀s, with birds rolling over and presenting talons, and fast flight aerobatics. ♂ courtship-feeds ♀ in mid-air.

Nesting Solitary or in loose colonies. Nest is mound of reeds and twigs. Eggs bluish-white, 50mm, hatch asynchronously and older chicks may kill younger ones. Polygynous ♂s usually oldest birds who may supply food to the young of several mates. Young birds pairing early in the year may loose ♀s to older ♂s. Young stay with ♀ for some weeks after fledging and may be passed food in mid-air. Birds first breed at 2–3 years.

Diet Mainly marsh-dwelling vertebrates, mammals, and especially birds (sometimes adults sitting on nests, or young). Quarters open areas, flying low, quickly dropping to snatch prey with talons.

Winters Some resident populations, others migratory to Africa and India; no concentrations at short sea crossings.

Conservation Has declined in west and central Europe with local extinctions following marsh drainage and persecution. Now has scattered and fragmented range in SW Europe and N Africa, though more common throughout Asia. Has recolonized areas (like UK) following aggressive conservation efforts. See p. 528.

Essays Polygyny, p. 265; Raptor Hunting, p. 113; Wetland Conservation, p. 145; Raptors at Sea Crossings, p. 93.

Refs Brown and Amadon 1968; Marchant et al. 1990.

female in a 'monogamous' pair. In birds of prey and many colonial species, males must spend long periods away from females and therefore cannot guard their mates from other males. It is in those species that multiple matings seem to occur, as the male attempts to dilute any other male's semen that the female may have acquired in his absence.

In most terrestrial species, copulation takes place either on the ground, on a tree limb, or on some other perch. Some aquatic birds (phalaropes, ducks) copulate primarily in the water. Swifts may copulate in mid-air. The female solicits the male when some 20–30 m high by holding her wings in a stiff V over her back, and glides downward with the male in pursuit. This is followed by slow flight in which the male gently lands on her back and copulates during a shallow, descending glide.

If copulation is observed in the field, the habitat, time of day, position used, duration, and any other associated behaviour should be recorded, since information on this behaviour is needed for most species.

SEE: Monogamy, p. 335; Breeding Season, p. 293; Brood Patches, p. 3; Courtship Feeding, p. 223; Sleeping Sentries and Mate-guarding, p. 73. REF.: Birkhead, 1988.

Eyes Like a Hawk

BIRDS and people are 'sight animals'. For both, the eyes are the dominant sense organs, vastly more important than our inferior olfactory equipment. The reasons for our sensory similarity to birds can be found in human evolutionary history. At one point the ancestors of *Homo sapiens* were small, tree-dwelling primates. When leaping from limb to limb and snatching up insect prey with the hands, sharp, binocular vision was very useful; those of our forebears that tried instead to smell the location of a branch on which to land were unlikely to survive to reproduce. And since in the breezy treetops odours quickly dissipate, they do not provide good cues for detecting food, enemies, or mates. Birds, flying from perch to perch higher and faster than our primate forebears leapt from branch to branch, naturally also evolved sight as their major device for orienting to the world.

Most birds have binocular vision. It is especially well developed in predators that must precisely estimate ever-changing distances to moving prey. Their eyes tend to be rotated toward the front of the head, so that their visual fields overlap to some degree. This trend is most pronounced in owls, whose eyes are almost as completely overlapping in field as ours. Small birds that are likely to be prey for raptors tend to have their eyes set on the sides of the head, permitting them to watch for danger in all directions. At the opposite extreme from the owls are the woodcocks, mud probers with eyes set high and back on the head, out of the way of vegetation and splattering mud and

Hen Harrier

Circus cyaneus

ATLAS 101; PMH 74; PER 96; HFP 86; HPCW 53; NESTS 106; BWP2:116

BLDS: ♀
Monogamy
Polygyny

4–6 (7–12)
1 brood
INCU: ♀
29–31

FLDG: ♂♀
32–42

Sm mammals

Breeding habitat Wide range of open habitats, moorland, young conifer plantations.

Displays Has a variety of high circling flights and flight displays similar to other harriers. Also has deeply undulating flights and alternating steep dives with steep climbs. In courtship-feeding ♂ passes food to ♀ in flight.

Nesting Often loosely colonial, though area around nest is defended. Nest is of sticks and grasses on ground. Eggs bluish-white, 46mm, hatch asynchronously. ♂ brings food to nesting ♀. Old ♂s have up to 5 ♀s; younger ♂s monogamous; number of ♀s per ♂ does not alter her breeding success.

Diet Birds (adults and young) and small rodents, especially voles. Quarters low over ground quickly pouncing on unsuspecting prey. May fly along forest edges.

Winters Resident in W, but migratory in N and E, wintering throughout S and W Europe, often in open farmlands or marshes.

Conservation Formerly marked decreases in many areas due to persecution, but has recolonized some areas following protection (mainland Scotland, N England, Wales). Has fragmented population in Europe, but is widely distributed in Asia, N and S America. See p. 528.

Essays Polygyny, p. 265; Eyes Like a Hawk, p. 89; Conservation of Raptors, p. 103; Raptor Hunting, p. 113; Size and Sex in Raptors, p. 99; Wing Shapes and Flight, p. 269; Mobbing, p. 261; Pellets, p. 257; Eye Colour and Development, p. 85.

Refs Brown and Amadon 1968; Marchant et al. 1990.

Pallid Harrier

Circus macrourus

ATLAS 101; PMH 74; PER 96; HFP 86; HPCW 54; NESTS 107; BWP2:126

Platform
BLDS: ♀,♂♀
Monogamy

4–5 (3–6)
1 brood
INCU: ♀
29–30

FLDG: ♂♀
35–45

Birds

Breeding habitat Open areas; uses drier steppe country in E than does Hen Harrier.

Displays Poorly known, but similar to other harriers.

Nesting Nest of grass on ground in tall vegetation. Eggs bluish-white, 45mm, hatch asynchronously. ♂ brings food to ♀.

Diet Mammals and birds; hunting method similar to Hen Harrier.

Winters Migrates to Africa and India.

Conservation Locally common from E Europe into C Asia, but numbers not well known. See p. 528.

Essays Eyes Like a Hawk, p. 89; Conservation of Raptors, p. 103; Raptor Hunting, p. 113; Size and Sex in Raptors, p. 99; Wing Shapes and Flight, p. 269; Mobbing, p. 261; Pellets, p. 257.

Refs Brown and Amadon 1968.

in a position to look out for predators. In fact, the Woodcock has better binocular vision to the rear than to the front!

Waders, waterfowl, pigeons, and other birds that have minimal binocular vision seem to depend on differences in apparent motion between close and distant objects for much of their depth perception. When a bird's eye is moving, closer objects appear to move at a faster rate than do distant objects — a phenomenon familiar from the way roadside telephone poles seen from the window of a moving car appear to pass more rapidly than the distant landscape. Presumably to enhance this distance-measuring method while walking, waders and waterfowl habitually bob their heads up and down, and pigeons move theirs back and forth. Even birds with relatively good binocular vision may use apparent motion to aid them in estimating distance; perched New Guinea kingfishers often 'post' up and down on their legs before diving after prey. To see how this works, move your head with one eye closed and note the relative motion of close and distant objects.

Raptors that must see prey at great distances and seed eaters that must pick tiny objects off the ground have eyes designed for high 'visual acuity', the capacity to make fine discriminations. There is, in fact, evidence that hawks can distinguish their prey at something like two or three times the distance that a human being can detect the same creature. One way that birds have attained such a high degree of acuity is by having relatively large eyes. A human eye weighs less than 1 per cent of the weight of the head, whereas a Starling's eye accounts for some 15 per cent of its head weight. Golden Eagles have eyes larger than those of a human being, and Ostrich eyes are the largest of any land animal, roughly five times as large as human eyes. But more than size alone appears to account for the astonishing performance of the eyes of hawks. Evolution has arranged the structure of their eyes so that each eye functions very much like a telescope. The eye has a somewhat flattened lens placed rather far from the retina, giving it a long 'focal length', which produces a large image. A large pupil and highly curved cornea admit plenty of light to keep the image on the retina bright.

Visual acuity in birds is also enhanced by the structure of the retina itself, which has tightly packed receptors and possesses other adaptations for producing a fine-grained image. Most of those receptors are the type called 'cones'. 'Rods', the receptors of the retina that are specialized to function in dim light, are relatively rare. Thus daytime acuity is, in part, achieved at the expense of night vision — a small price to pay for birds that are inactive at night anyway. In those relatively few species that are nocturnal, such as owls, rods predominate.

Acuity is only one dimension in which bird and human eyes differ. For instance, many birds can see the individual flashes of a fluorescent light bulb that is flickering 60 times per second. This provides sensitivity to rapid movements that can be critical for avoiding objects or catching prey in high-speed flight. The human eye is mis-focused underwater, which is why we must create an air pocket with a mask in order to see well when we dive. As another example, diving birds can change the shape of their lens dramatically so as to retain clear vision when they enter the water.

Montagu's Harrier
Circus pygargus

ATLAS 102; PMH 75; PER 96; HFP 86; HPCW 54; NESTS 107; BWP2:132

  |

	BLDS: ♀ Monogamy Polygyny	○/◉ 4–5 (3–10) 1 brood INCU: ♀ 28–29(27–30)	SA1 FLDG: ♂♀ 35–40		Sm mammals

Breeding habitat Open country with bushes and trees, often in river valleys or near lakes.

Displays Similar to other harriers; ♂ has downward spiralling flight with wings and tail spread.

Nesting Usually solitary. Nest is of twigs and grasses, on ground in thick vegetation. Eggs bluish-white, sometimes with streaks, hatch asynchronously. Larger chicks may kill smaller ones. Fed by ♀, but ♂ also brings food. First breeds at 2–3 years.

Some ♂s are bigamous.

Diet Young and adult birds, small mammals, other vertebrates, and insects taken on ground.

Winters In Africa and India, usually away from wetland areas.

Conservation Widespread declines, and now has fragmented population in Europe, into C Asia.

Essays Raptors at Sea Crossings, p. 93; Polygyny, p. 265; Differential Migration, p. 323.

Refs Brown and Amadon 1968.

Dark Chanting Goshawk
Melierax metabates

ATLAS 91; PMH 244; PER -; HFP 74; HPCW 54; NESTS 100; BWP2:144

  |

3–7m	BLDS: ♂♀ Monogamy	○ 1 (2) 1 brood INCU: ♀, ♂♀ ?	SA1 FLDG: ? ?		Insects	Ground glean

Breeding habitat Woodland, scrub, or more open country.

Displays Poorly known, but include high, circling flight like other birds of prey, and an undulating display flight. Pairs may chant at each other from perches.

Nesting Solitary. Nest is of twigs, mud, lined with debris. Eggs bluish-white, 53mm; if two eggs, second hatches after first.

Diet Reptiles and other small vertebrates, also large insects, caught

after rapid stoop or on ground while walking.

Winters Resident.

Conservation Little is known about the small population in Morocco; species occurs widely in Africa.

Essays Eyes Like a Hawk, p. 89; Conservation of Raptors, p. 103; Raptor Hunting, p. 113; Size and Sex in Raptors, p. 99; Wing Shapes and Flight, p. 269; Mobbing, p. 261; Pellets, p. 257; Raptor Hunting, p. 113.

Refs Brown and Amadon 1968.

Considering the frequent evolution of gaudy coloured plumage, it is not surprising that most if not all birds have colour vision, and that colour perception is often obvious in bird behaviour. One can watch a hummingbird moving from red flower to red flower; bowerbirds show colour preferences when decorating their bowers. Just how refined that colour vision may be has proven difficult to determine. However, the diversity of visual pigments found in birds' eyes, and the presence of an array of brightly coloured oil droplets inside the cones, suggest that avian colour perception may surpass our own. There is also evidence that some birds' eyes are sensitive to ultraviolet light. In hummingbirds the adaptive significance of this is clear, since some flowers from which they drink nectar have patterns visible in the ultraviolet end of the light spectrum. Why pigeons have the ability to see ultraviolet remains a mystery. Equally surprising is their recently discovered ability to detect the plane of polarized light. This probably serves them well in homing.

SEE: Raptor Hunting, p. 113; The Colour of Birds, p. 137; How Owls Hunt in the Dark, p. 251; Bird-Brained, p. 385; What Do Birds Hear?, p. 255; The Avian Sense of Smell, p. 13. REFS: Goldsmith, 1980; Snyder and Miller, 1978; Waldvogel, 1990.

Raptors at Sea Crossings

WHERE the crossing of inhospitable habitat, like the sea, cannot be avoided, migrants often concentrate at points that funnel into the shortest available crossing. Thus each autumn the Straits of Gibraltar, the Bosporus, and the Falsterbo Peninsula in Sweden witness spectacular concentrations of birds, especially of larger, soaring species such as raptors and storks. Raptors making regular passage over Gibraltar, for example, include thousands of Honey Buzzards and Black Kites, hundreds of Booted and Short-toed Eagles, Common Buzzards, and Sparrowhawks, and smaller numbers of Common and Lesser Kestrels, Egyptian Vultures, Montagu's and Marsh Harriers, and Ospreys. All of these species are seen also as regular spring migrants following the reverse route over Gibraltar.

Although the overwater journey at these sites is less than 25 km, the decision to cross appears not to be taken lightly, as large numbers of birds can typically be seen soaring and milling about before attempting to cross. The decision by an individual to cross or not is probably influenced by several factors including prior experience with that particular water crossing, physiological condition, weather (wind, visibility, rain), and time of arrival at the crossing relative to whether the bird already has been in flight for several hours or has just taken off.

Other routes commonly used by many raptors entail overwater crossings in excess of 200 km as the birds island-hop through the Mediterranean. These

Goshawk
Accipiter gentilis

ATLAS 90; PMH 75; PER 96; HFP 74; HPCW 55; NESTS 99; BWP2:148

  2–3 (1–5)
1 brood
BLDS: ♂♀   INCU: ♂♀, ♀
10–20m   Monogamy   35–38

SA1
FLDG: ♂♀
See below   Sm mammals   Low patrol

Breeding habitat Forest, particularly conifers, though may feed out over open country.
Displays High circling by one or both birds with vertical plunges, and slow flapping. ♀ appears first at nest and initiates aerial displays; calls frequently from perches. Pairs may duet.
Nesting Solitary. Nest is of twigs and branches in tree, lined with some green vegetation. Eggs bluish-white, 59mm, eggs hatch within 2–3 days of each other. Fed by ♀, but ♂ brings food. Smaller ♂s take 35–36 days to fledge, while larger ♀s about five days longer. Fed by parents for about another month.
Diet Birds and mammals up to size of Capercaillie and hares. Surprises prey

after short, highly manoeuvrable flights, on ground or in air.
Winters Mainly resident, but arctic populations may move southwards.
Conservation Declined in the last century due to persecution (UK populations gone by 1880s) and in this century due to heavy metal and pesticide pollution. In UK current (introduced) population is increasing slowly, though still persecuted. Widely distributed in Europe, N Asia, N America. See p. 528.
Essays Size and Sex in Raptors, p. 99; Copulation, p. 87; Conservation of Raptors, p. 103; Irruptions, p. 491.
Refs Brown and Amadon 1968; Marchant et al. 1990.

Sparrowhawk
Accipiter nisus

ATLAS 90; PMH 76; PER 96; HFP 74; HPCW 55; NESTS 98; BWP2:158

  4–6 (3–7)
1 brood
BLDS: ♂♀   INCU: ♀
6–12m   Monogamy   33–35

SA1
FLDG: ♂♀
24–30
See below   Low patrol

Breeding habitat A variety of woodlands, but may hunt outside them, especially along hedgerows
Displays Has high circling flight above nesting areas, and an undulating flight of flapping descents and upward glides. Like Goshawk, pairs have cartwheeling displays and perching, while calling.
Nesting Solitary. Nest is pile of twigs in fork of tree. Eggs bluish-white with red-brown blotches, 40mm, hatch almost synchronously. Until young are about 3 weeks old, all food brought to them is from ♂, though ♀ does all the feeding. ♂s fledge before ♀s. Adults continue to feed young for several weeks after fledging.
Diet Almost exclusively birds taken by surprise, following low flight close to cover. Waits on a perch, then may seize prey in air or from their perches.

Winters Resident except in N where populations migrate S, as far as India for Asiatic populations.
Conservation Declined severely when persecuted by gamekeepers and others. Declines in the 50s and 60s due to pesticides, and it almost became extinct in S and E England, with similar declines in other areas of W Europe. Has come back following protection, probably to former levels. Widespread in Europe and Asia.
Essays Size and Sex in Raptors, p. 99; Pesticides and Birds, p. 115; Dominance Hierarchies, p. 131; Parental Care, p. 171; Raptor Hunting, p. 113; Wing Shapes and Flight, p. 269.
Refs Brown and Amadon 1968; Marchant et al. 1990; Newton 1985 is a book about this species.

include flights from Greece and Turkey south via Crete and other nearby islands to Cyprus and on to North Africa (e.g. Montagu's Harrier, Red-footed and Saker Falcons), and passage from Italy to north Africa via Sicily and Malta (e.g. Osprey, Honey Buzzard, Black Kite, Red-footed Falcon, and Hobby). Perhaps the longest overwater journey undertaken by a European raptor is that of Merlins moving from Iceland to Great Britain via the Faeroe Islands. These birds must cover distances of 450–800 km before making landfall.

SEE: Migration, p. 377; Orientation and Navigation, p. 503; Wader Migration and Conservation, p. 167; Differential Migration, p. 323; Irruptions, p. 491; Wintering and Conservation, p. 409; Why Some Species Migrate at Night, p. 351. REFS: Gauthreaux, 1982; Kerlinger, 1989; Mead, 1983.

Birds on Borders

IT is generally agreed that nothing is more critical to protecting birds than preserving their habitat. And perhaps nowhere is the need for international cooperation in providing habitat protection more evident than in Europe where the borders dividing the countries also divide a number of areas very critical to birds. Currently 12 sets of national parks protect portions of these habitats and are of particular interest to birdwatchers.

Half of the paired (or in some cases clustered) border parks are found in Western Europe. The German–Netherlands–Danish border crosses tidal mud and sand flats along the shallow coast. This habitat is protected by Germany's Wattenmeer National Park, the Netherlands' Waddenzee State Nature Reserves, and Denmark's Vadehavet Wildlife Reserves. It is the staging area for 1 000 000 migratory waterfowl. Along the German–Luxembourg border, west of Frankfurt, the plateaux, gorges, meadows, and pasturelands of the river-threaded Germano–Luxembourg Nature Park are home to birds of prey, wildfowl, and herons. The Belgium–Luxembourg border is divided by the Sure River. The Belgium–Luxembourg Nature Park protects breeding Black Storks and large numbers of migrating cranes inhabiting the area's river valleys, gorges, and lake. At a site along the Franco–German border west of Heidelberg is the Pfalzerwald Nature Park. Its 'other half' — the Vosges du Nord Regional Nature Park — is located near Strasbourg. Within these two parks more than 130 forest-, peat bog-, heathland-, meadow- and cliff-dwelling birds are protected. On the Swiss–Italian border, the Swiss National Park (near Grisons) and the Stelvio National Park (in the Italian Alps) support more than 100 forest and alpine birds. And, finally, on the Franco–Italian border, the Vanoise National Park (in the central Alps of France) and the Gran Paradiso National Park (near Aosta) host a wide variety of high mountain birds.

Levant Sparrowhawk

Accipiter brevipes

ATLAS 91; PMH 76; PER 96; HFP 74; HPCW 56; NESTS 99; BWP2:173

		4–5 (3) 1 brood INCU: ♀ ?30–35			
5–10m	BLDS: ?♀ Monogamy		FLDG: ♂♀		Insects

Breeding habitat Woodlands.

Displays Very little known.

Nesting Nest twigs lined with green leaves in tree. Eggs bluish-white, lightly marked, 40mm, hatch asynchronously. Young fed by ♀, though ♂ brings food.

Diet Mainly lizards and large insects. Feeds unlike other Accipiters. Uses low, searching flight (usually gliding), then stoops to the ground to pick off prey. Hunts in pairs during non-breeding season.

Winters Migrates across Bosporus, but wintering areas uncertain.

Conservation Very limited and poorly-known distribution in SE Europe and adjacent areas of Asia. See p. 529.

Essays Size and Sex in Raptors, p. 99; Eyes Like a Hawk, p. 89; Conservation of Raptors, p. 103; Raptor Hunting, p. 113; Wing Shapes and Flight, p. 269; Mobbing, p. 261; Pellets, p. 257.

Refs Brown and Amadon 1968.

Common Buzzard

Buteo buteo

ATLAS 92; PMH 76; PER 94; HFP 76; HPCW 57; NESTS 100; BWP2:177

		2–4 (1–6) 1 brood INCU: ♂♀ 33–38			
Cliff 3–25m	BLDS: ♂♀ Monogamy		FLDG: ♂♀ 50–55(48–62)	Carrion	High patrol

Breeding habitat Wide range of open habitats, mountains, coasts, farmland with interspersed woods.

Displays High circling flight, may involve one or both birds when one may follow the other closely. Birds may carry twigs, while circling. Also a variety of aerial manoeuvres.

Nesting Territorial. Nest is a large pile of twigs and branches, lined with green vegetation in a tree or on cliff. Eggs white, blotched with reddish-browns, 55mm, hatch asynchronously. Young fed by ♀, but ♂ brings food. First breed at 3 years.

Diet Various small vertebrates, chiefly mammals, sometimes scavenges. Will sit on perch then glide in on prey or soar then drop onto prey on ground. Also walks along ground for large insects.

Winters Resident in S and W Europe, migratory in NE and in Asia; birds winter as far as S Africa, India. Birds concentrate at narrow sea crossings on migration at Falsterbo, Bosporus, and Strait of Gibraltar.

Conservation Marked decreases where persecuted by gamekeepers, especially in the UK where noticeably absent from comparable habitats on the continent, in which it is still common. Pesticides and decline of rabbits also affect range. Widespread across Europe, N Asia.

Essays Raptors at Sea Crossings, p. 93; Raptor Hunting, p. 113; Size and Sex in Raptors, p. 99; Soaring, p. 79; Commensal Feeding, p. 27; Migration, p. 377; Differential Migration, p. 323.

Refs Brown and Amadon 1968; Tubbs 1974 is a book about this species.

In Central and Eastern Europe, birdwatchers will be interested in four sets of border parks.

On the Polish–Belorussian border, the Bialowieza National Park (east of Warsaw) and the Belovezhskaya Pushcha State Hunting Reserve (north of Brest) protect some 228 primeval forest-dwelling and wetland-dwelling (including those preferring peat bog and meadow) birds. The list of the parks' birds is impressive, ranging from Black Stork, most European owls (including Pygmy), and numerous birds of prey (including Spotted Eagles), to Three-toed Woodpeckers. On the Polish–Czechoslovakian border, the Pieniny and the Pieninsky National Parks host 100 woodland breeding birds. On the Austrian–German border the Unterer Inn/Hagenauer Bucht Nature Protection Area and Ramsar Site, and the Unterer Inn Nature Conservation Area straddle the Inn River and protect many islands, sandbanks, shallow bays, and inland deltas supporting more than 280 wetland bird species. And, on the Hungarian–Austrian border southeast of Vienna, the Lake Ferto Landscape Protection Area and the Neusiedlersee Landscape Protection Zone hold Lake Ferto, Europe's largest salt lake and home to 260 migrating and breeding bird species (but more about this below).

Then, in Southern Europe, an additional two pairs of border parks protect especially large numbers of birds.

On the Macedonia–Greece border the Galicia National Park and the Mikra Prespa National Park contain parts of inland lakes and lakeshores supporting such wetland birds as egrets, pelicans, and Spoonbills. And, on the Turkey–Greece border, the Gala Golu Proposed Reserve on the Melic River and the Evros Delta Reserve contain delta marshes, reedbeds, and lagoons, as well as interior hills, outcrops, and forests. A remarkable array of the area's wetland birds and the region's largest populations of birds of prey (including vultures and Golden, White-tailed Sea, and Imperial Eagles) are protected there.

Establishment of these 12 sets of European border parks has, of course, been a critical step in the efforts to maintain and increase avian populations. The next step appears to be the formation of East–West Transfrontier parks. For example, formation of the first East–West park, uniting 35 000 acres currently separated by the Hungarian–Austrian border is scheduled for 1995. The new park will help to control expanding agriculture, pesticide contamination, cattle grazing, fish farming, tourism, and hunting. As noted earlier, this area contains Europe's largest salt lake (which is its third largest lake). It is also Central Europe's largest bird sanctuary, home to more than 300 species of breeding or migrating birds including Spoonbills, Purple Herons, Great White Egrets, White Storks, Great Bustards, and numerous geese and wildfowl.

SEE: Birds and the Law, p. 521. REFS: Anon, 1990*a*; Krasinski, 1990; Lucas, 1990.

Long-legged Buzzard

Buteo rufinus

ATLAS 93; PMH 77; PER 94; HFP 76; HPCW 57; NESTS 101; BWP2:190

  3–4 (2–5) 1 brood SA1

	BLDS: ?	INCU: ?	FLDG: ♂♀		
	Monogamy	?	?	Sm verts	

Breeding habitat Dry, open country.
Displays Little known, but probably similar to other buzzards.
Nesting Solitary. Nest, on cliffs or rocks, is structure of twigs and branches. Eggs white, blotched with brown, 60mm.
Diet Small mammals, reptiles, and insects, found while soaring.
Winters Mainly resident, though central Asian populations move southwards to India, and birds winter in Africa.
Conservation Numbers not well known, though no obvious changes across range from N Africa, SE Europe into C Asia. See p. 528.
Essays Raptor Hunting, p. 113; Size and Sex in Raptors, p. 99; Soaring, p. 79; Commensal Feeding, p. 27.
Refs Brown and Amadon 1968.

Rough-legged Buzzard

Buteo lagopus

ATLAS 92; PMH 77; PER 94; HFP 76; HPCW 58; NESTS 100; BWP2:196

  3–4 (2–7) 1 brood SA1

	BLDS: ♂♀	INCU: ♀	FLDG: ♂♀		
Conif tree	Monogamy	28–31	39–43		Hov & pounce

Breeding habitat Open country at high latitudes, but also boreal forests.
Displays Poorly known, but includes high circling and other displays similar to other buzzards.
Nesting Solitary. Nest of twigs on cliff, in tree, or even on ground, with thick lining of grass in arctic areas. Same nest is used year after year. Eggs white, blotched with reddish-browns, 55mm, hatch asynchronously. Brood size varies according to the availability of small mammals, and if food is scarce older chicks may eat younger ones.
Diet Small mammals, following low patrols, but this species often hovers before swooping down to catch prey. Will also swoop down from perch.
Winters Migrates southwards to central Europe and Asia, birds concentrating at Falsterbo; often wintering in agricultural areas.
Conservation Numbers fluctuate according to availability of lemmings and voles, but relatively remote habitats make this species less vulnerable to humans than other buzzards. Widely distributed throughout N Europe, N Asia, N America.
Essays Raptors at Sea Crossings, p. 93; Size and Sex in Raptors, p. 99; Soaring, p. 79; Commensal Feeding, p. 27; Migration, p. 377; Differential Migration, p. 323; Irruptions, p. 491.
Refs Brown and Amadon 1968.

Carrying Eggs

WHILE parental transport of chicks has been documented in a number of species, egg carrying by birds is rare, and few instances have been recorded. Published photographs of a female North American Pileated Woodpecker (*Dryocopus pileatus*) show it retrieving eggs after the sudden collapse of the nest tree, and the accompanying report verifies that within 20 minutes the clutch had been relocated into a new site.

Egg-carrying, however, is not limited to salvage operations. North American Cliff Swallows (*Hirundo pyrrhonota*) may carry their eggs into the nests of other colony members where they will not be recognized as foreign. Systematic study of this form of brood parasitism (where eggs are carried to, rather than laid in, the nests of others) has been limited, and may well be found in other colonial breeders. There are also records from Idaho in the USA of Magpies moving eggs from one nest to another and then back again. It is intriguing that the behaviour is recorded from a species already known to tolerate foreign eggs, those of the parasitic Great Spotted Cuckoo.

Evidence of eggs being carried into or away from nests may indicate a strategy to improve upon the odds for a successful breeding season or simply amount to a quick meal. In either case, birdwatchers may find its occurrence worthy of note.

SEE: Transporting Young, p. 9; Nest Sites and Materials, p. 443; Eggs and Their Evolution, p. 317; Life in the Egg, p. 447; Brood Parasitism, p. 249. REFS: Brown and Brown, 1988; Trost and Webb, 1986; Truslow, 1967; Yom-Tov, 1975.

Size and Sex in Raptors

IN most birds, males are larger than females, but in some, including many birds of prey, the reverse is true. No one is certain why 'reversed sexual size dimorphism' occurs in raptors, but a number of interesting hypotheses have been advanced. All are based on a well-established correlation: size difference between the sexes is less pronounced in species that pursue sluggish prey

Lesser Spotted Eagle

Aquila pomarina

ATLAS 96; PMH 78; PER 90; HFP 80; HPCW 58; NESTS 103; BWP2:203

6–21 m

BLDS: ♂♀
Monogamy

2 (1–3)
1 brood
INCU: ♀
38–41

SA1
FLDG: ♂♀
58?

Swoops

Breeding habitat Mixed forest and open country, often near marshes, but in SE Europe often in dry woodlands.

Displays Similar to other birds of prey. Has high circling displays with flight rolls, much calling. Pairs have talon-touching.

Nesting Territorial. Nest is large structure of branches often lined with fresh vegetation. Eggs whitish, spotted brown, 64mm; first egg larger than second egg which hatches later, and smaller chick nearly always dies or is killed by sibling. Probably first breeds at 4 years, when birds attain adult plumage.

Diet Small vertebrates, especially mammals. Quarters ground with low gliding flight or drops onto prey from perch. In Africa will join with other predators in exploiting the nestlings of Red-billed Queleas.

Winters In Africa. Birds concentrate at the crossing on the Bosporus.

Conservation Considerable declines in the west of its range, with local extinctions. Has fragmented and isolated populations from eastern Europe to SW Asia, and also in N India; has a relatively small range and may be in considerable danger. See p. 528.

Essays Average Clutch Size, p. 31; Eyes Like a Hawk, p. 89; Conservation of Raptors, p. 103; Raptor Hunting, p. 113; Size and Sex in Raptors, p. 99; Wing Shapes and Flight, p. 269; Mobbing, p. 261; Pellets, p. 257; Migration, p. 377; Hatching Asynchrony and Brood Reduction, p. 507.

Refs Brown and Amadon 1968.

Spotted Eagle

Aquila clanga

ATLAS 96; PMH 78; PER 90; HFP 80; HPCW 64; NESTS 103; BWP2:211

Shrub
3–25m

BLDS: ♂♀
Monogamy

2 (1–3)
1 brood
INCU: ♀
42–44

SA1
FLDG: ♂♀
60–65

Carrion

Breeding habitat Open forest, usually near water.

Displays Poorly known, but probably similar to Lesser Spotted Eagle.

Nesting Territorial. Nest is pile of twigs and branches lined with green vegetation. Eggs greyish-white, unmarked or with brown splotches, 68mm. Second, smaller chick hatches later and nearly always dies. Probably breeds for first time at 4 years, when birds attain adult plumage.

Diet A variety of vertebrates, carrion, and large insects. Hunts on the wing,

and will take birds from water surface; also hunts insects by walking.

Winters Migrates southwards, principally to India; only small numbers cross Bosporus as most of range is to the east.

Conservation Little known about numbers; species has extensive range across Europe and Asia. See p. 528.

Essays Raptor Hunting, p. 113; Birds on Borders, p. 95; Hatching Asynchrony and Brood Reduction, p. 507; Migration, p. 377.

Refs Brown and Amadon 1968.

than in those that pursue birds. Vultures, whose prey are least agile of all, show little sexual size difference. Male mammal-hunting buzzards, such as the Common Buzzard, are somewhat smaller than females, whereas in bird-hunting accipiters and falcons, females may be half as heavy again as males.

One explanation for the females' larger size suggests that it protects them from aggressive males that are well equipped with sharp talons and beaks, and the killer instincts to go with them. According to this theory, over evolutionary time, females have preferred to mate with smaller, safer males. In fact, the female may have to be able to dominate the male for proper pair bonding to occur and for the male to remain in his key role as food provider to both female and young. Such a system would involve sexual selection for smaller size in males. Bird-hunting raptors are assumed to show aggression most suddenly, and to represent the greatest threat to their mates, and they are the ones exhibiting the greatest size difference.

In experimental pairings set up so that male American Kestrels (*Falco sparverius*) were the larger of the pair, Cornell University ornithologist Tom Cade found that the females did not suffer from an avian version of wife abuse. The size difference in kestrels was not very great, however, so this may not be a definitive test of the hypothesis. It seems that while sexual selection may play a role, there probably is more to it.

Another hypothesis proposes that the size differences allow the two sexes to hunt different prey and thus reduce competition for food. Competition is thought to be more severe among bird-hunting raptors than among other hawks, since their small agile prey are able to flee in three dimensions and are thus effectively scarcer than, say, carrion or ground-dwelling rodents. Indeed, there are data indicating that the hunting success of bird-chasing raptors is only about half that of raptors preying on mammals, and only a sixth that of raptors eating insects. Tom Cade has suggested that, for bird eaters, available food supply in the nesting territory can become limiting, making it adaptive for the male to specialize on small prey and for the female to specialize on large prey. The male feeds the female and young at the beginning of the nesting season; the female becomes an active hunter when the nestlings are larger, and the adults tend to partition the prey resource in their territory.

But if reducing intersexual competition for food is the reason for the size difference in raptors, why aren't males sometimes the larger sex? One possible reason is that females need to be larger because they must accumulate energy reserves in order to produce their eggs. Another possibility, based primarily on work with owls, is that females do not forage for a substantial period while incubating eggs and brooding young. They avoid the risks of the hunt during that time, but they must rely on the small male to feed the entire family, and larger size provides them with more fasting endurance. Small fleet prey, aerial or terrestrial, are more abundant than large sluggish prey, so that over time smaller male bird-eating raptors would be favoured over larger, less agile ones, because they would be better providers. For species that take more sluggish prey, however, small males would not be so advantageous,

Tawny Eagle

Aquila rapax

ATLAS 97; PMH 244; PER 308; HFP 80; HPCW 64; NESTS 104; BWP2:216

	2 (1–3) 1 brood		SA1		
BLDS: ♂♀	INCU: ♀		FLDG: ♂♀		
Monogamy	45		60–85	Carrion	

Breeding habitat Open country; cultivation and open scrub to savannah and semi-desert.

Displays Pairs have high circling display with diving and swooping.

Nesting Territorial. Nest twigs, lined with dry grass, straw, fur, on ground with good view of surrounding areas. Eggs white, sometimes marked with brown, 69mm. Second chick usually attacked and often killed by larger sibling.

Diet Opportunistic predator on vertebrates (often ground dwelling mammals), dropping down from soaring onto prey, or ambushing them near their burrows. Will rob nests of other birds of prey. Also carrion and locally abundant insects, such as locusts and termites.

Winters Resident in N Africa.

Conservation Tawny Eagle has only small, scattered, and declining populations in N Africa, though is widespread in Africa S of Sahara. The conspecific Steppe Eagle does not now reach the area of this guide, and has declined in the CIS following the extensive plowing of the steppes. Steppe Eagle is widely distributed across C Asia and India.

Essays Conservation of Raptors, p. 103; Raptor Hunting, p. 113; Size and Sex in Raptors, p. 99; Wing Shapes and Flight, p. 269; Mobbing, p. 261; Pellets, p. 257.

Refs Brown and Amadon 1968.

Imperial Eagle

Aquila heliaca

ATLAS 96; PMH 79; PER 92; HFP 78; HPCW 65; NESTS 103; BWP2:225

		2 (3) 1 brood		SA1	
	BLDS: ♂●	INCU: ♂♀		FLDG: ♂♀	
10–25m	Monogamy	43			Birds

Breeding habitat Open Mediterranean woodland, often near wetlands.

Displays Has high circling and mock attacks between pairs and presentation of talons, with occasional cartwheeling, like other birds of prey.

Nesting Nest is of twigs and branches in large tree (or shrubs if trees not available) with greenery added. Eggs whitish with a few brown marks, 73mm; hatch asynchronously, and older chick intimidates younger, though killing is less common in this species than in other eagles. ♂s help more in feeding young in this species than in other eagles. Family groups may remain together for much of year.

Diet Vertebrates, mainly mammals and birds taken on ground; some carrion.

Winters Spanish populations resident. Eastern populations largely migratory, with small numbers crossing at the Bosporus.

Conservation Distinctive subspecies in Spain and Portugal, critically endangered with less than 70 pairs, and threatened with habitat destruction and pesticides. Eastern subspecies has declined, with only fragmented, isolated populations outside of the CIS. Occurs across C Asia. See p. 528.

Essays Conservation of Raptors, p. 103; Birds on Borders, p. 95.

Refs Brown and Amadon 1968.

which might explain the relationship between prey speed and the male–female size discrepancy.

SEE: Sexual Selection, p. 149; Polyandry, p. 195; Raptor Hunting, p. 113. REFS: Cade, 1982; Jönsson, 1987; Korpimäki, 1986b; Lewin, 1985; Lundberg, 1986; Mueller and Meyer, 1985; Temeles, 1985.

Conservation of Raptors

IN some areas populations and species of raptors are threatened with extinction — more so than many other kinds of birds. There are five reasons. First, birds of prey are often directly persecuted by people who believe (usually erroneously) that these birds are a threat to livestock and, especially, wild game. This antiquated notion remains entrenched, and many farmers and keepers kill hawks and eagles, while some 'hunters' take potshots at them. This is often illegal, since most raptors are protected against wanton shooting, at least in the European Community. In the 1870s Henry Dresser wrote of the now extremely rare White-tailed Sea Eagle in the British Isles: 'Mr. Gray states that a keeper in Skye shot fifty-seven Eagles on a single estate, and another in West Ross-shire shot fifty-two in twelve years, besides taking numbers of both eggs and young. Captain Cameron . . . had seen as many as sixty-two Sea-Eagles killed in Skye; and, as Mr. Gray justly remarks, no species of Eagle could long survive such persecution.'

Second, a great many hawks, falcons, and owls are taken for an illegal taxidermy trade, mainly in Europe. Reportedly, though, thousands of Northern Goshawks are slaughtered and stuffed each year in China. This sort of activity is also part of an old tradition in which collecting for 'science' long played a role. Egg collecting apparently helped in the decimation of the Spanish race of the Imperial Eagle in Catalonia, for example, and was also involved in the decline of Ospreys.

Third, falcons are illegally trapped by smugglers lured by the enormous price that the birds will bring in the Middle East, where falconry is a high-prestige activity for the elite. The majority of falcons used by the Arabs are migrant Asian Sakers. Gyrfalcons, because of their long wings and large size, are especially prized. Members of the Middle Eastern royal families have reportedly paid up to $100 000 each for healthy specimens of these arctic raptors, of which perhaps only a few hundred pairs now live in Europe.

Fourth, raptors are generally rather long-lived birds and feed high on food chains, which makes them more susceptible than short-lived or plant-eating species to poisoning by pesticides and other pollutants. Poisons accumulate in organisms over time, and poisons become concentrated as they move up food chains. There is no question that toxic substances have had catastrophic impacts on the populations of some raptors. Peregrines, for instance, went

Golden Eagle

Aquila chrysaetos

ATLAS 95; PMH 79; PER 92; HFP 78; HPCW 65; NESTS 102; BWP2:234

| Conif tree | BLDS: ♂♀ Monogamy | ⊜/○ 2 (1–3) 1 brood INCU:♀, ♂♀ 43–45 | FLDG: ♂♀ SA1 | Birds | |

Breeding habitat Mountains, open plains; in Scandinavia, mainly forest.

Displays Tends not to perform aerial acrobatics of other species of eagle, though birds will circle together and carry twigs.

Nesting Territorial. Nest is large pile of twigs and branches, lined with grass and green vegetation. On cliff or in large tree. Eggs whitish, usually blotched with brown, 75mm, hatch asynchronously. Larger first chick may kill smaller sibling. Adults stay with young well after fledging. May mate for life, first breeding at 3–4 years.

Diet Mammals (especially rabbits and hares) and birds (especially grouse), taken on ground after striking with talons; also carrion. Locally, birds are the major prey.

Winters Mainly resident, but leaves most northerly parts of range.

Conservation Marked decrease in UK in the last century due to persecution; species became extinct in Wales, England, and Ireland, very rare in Scotland. Similar patterns of decline elsewhere, but species has wide range in Europe, Asia, N Africa, and N America. See p. 528.

Essays Pesticides and Birds, p. 115; Territoriality, p. 397; Ducking the Bird Laws, p. 523; Birds on Borders, p. 95; Hatching Asynchrony and Brood Reduction, p. 507.

Refs Brown and Amadon 1968; Marchant et al. 1990.

Verreaux's Eagle

Aquila verreauxi

ATLAS 96; PMH -; PER -; HFP 80; HPCW 66; NESTS -; BWP2:245

| Tree | BLDS: ♂♀ Monogamy | ○/⊜ 2 (1–3) 1 brood INCU: ♂♀ 43–46 | FLDG: ♂♀ SA1 84–99 | Birds | Hov & pounce |

Breeding habitat Remote mountainous regions.

Displays Like other birds of prey. Has high circling and mock attacks between pairs and presentation of talons, with occasional cartwheeling. Birds may perch while calling loudly.

Nesting Solitary. Nest is of branches and twigs, with added greenery on cliff (or large tree if available). Eggs white, sometimes with small red markings, 81mm; older chick usually kills younger one. Adults stay with young several months after fledging.

Diet Mammals, especially hyraxes, swooping in after low searching flight to catch prey on ground.

Winters Resident.

Conservation In area of this guide, only in Judean desert, where there may be sporadic nesting attempts. Species occurs widely in Africa.

Essays Eyes Like a Hawk, p. 89; Conservation of Raptors, p. 103; Raptor Hunting, p. 113; Size and Sex in Raptors, p. 99; Wing Shapes and Flight, p. 269; Mobbing, p. 261; Pellets, p. 257; Hatching Asynchrony and Brood Reduction, p. 507.

Refs Gargett 1993 is a book about this species.

into catastrophic decline in Europe and were eliminated from much of North America through the large-scale use of DDT and its relatives, which began shortly after World War II. In the United States Peregrines had been exterminated east of the Mississippi by 1964, and continued to decline sharply in the West and North. Pesticides also have contributed to the decimation of Merlin populations in Great Britain. Infertility combined with destruction of moorland habitat by ploughing for crops and establishment of pine plantations had reduced them to about 600 pairs in 1983. Since then there has probably been a further decline.

Laws have been promulgated to limit the use of persistent pesticides that threaten raptors. Restrictions on pesticides have led to a substantial recovery of Peregrines in Britain, and some recovery (or at least halt of decline) in western Europe in general. The application of DDT has been largely banned in the United States since 1972, although it is a contaminant in dicofol (the main ingredient of Kelthane), a related chlorinated hydrocarbon pesticide, which is legally used. (There may also be illegal use of DDT itself.) Determined efforts to re-establish Peregrines in the eastern United States are now beginning to show results.

Finally, raptors, especially large ones, often suffer from habitat destruction, which makes areas with sufficient space for home ranges or suitable nesting sites scarce. Birds of prey need especially large home ranges and, often, this means large blocks of forest. Spanish Imperial Eagle populations declined rapidly as forests were cleared in the seventeenth, eighteenth, and nineteenth centuries. Habitat destruction, of course, is the overriding problem for tropical forest raptors. Sometimes habitat modification is enough to severely damage populations of birds of prey. In Britain, intensification of farming combined with climate change has made it more difficult for Barn Owls to find enough small rodents, and their populations declined nearly 70 per cent between 1932 and 1985.

Laws to protect raptors from the depredations of hunters have been effective in most European nations. For example, in Denmark, the Kestrel was protected by legislation around 1930, and showed an abrupt increase in survival. Its population rebounded even further after all birds of prey were protected in 1967, presumably because this reduced the number of Kestrels that were still being shot illegally. In the United States raptor protection is also becoming more effective.

In addition to legal protection, steps can be taken to help preserve raptor populations in deteriorating habitats. For example, in North America provision of artificial nesting sites has led to an increase in Osprey populations and shows potential for doing the same for Bald Eagles. In one ingenious programme, Osprey nest poles were dropped like darts from helicopters into coastal salt marshes. Another helpful step toward protecting many large raptors, as we are often reminded through magazine and television advertisements, has been providing insulated perches on the tops of poles carrying high-voltage power lines. In Scotland, in contrast, Ospreys have been making a comeback since the 1950s without the provision of artificial nest sites. Apparently a growing Scandinavian population (rebounding due to increased

Booted Eagle

Hieraaëtus pennatus

ATLAS 95; PMH 80; PER 92; HFP 88; HPCW 66; NESTS 102; BWP2:251

 Cliff 6–16m	 BLDS: ?♂♀ Monogamy	⊙/◯ 2 (1) 1 brood INCU: ♀ 36–38 ?	SA1 FLDG: ♂♀ 50–63	 Sm verts	 Aer pursuit

Breeding habitat Open Mediterranean woodland.

Displays As other birds of prey; has high circling above nest, steep descents with steep climbs, sometimes looping around. Pairs swoop, flight roll, and present talons.

Nesting Territorial. Nest of twigs and branches, lined with greenery, in tree or on cliffs. Eggs white, sometimes marked with brown, 55mm. Younger chick nearly always dies and is eaten by older.

Diet Small to medium-sized birds, lizards, and mammals, sometimes insects. Soars above open areas, hitting prey on ground, or pursues prey through forest; regularly hunts in twos (which may be mated pairs) in some areas.

Winters In Africa and India; birds concentrate at short sea-crossings at Bosporus and Strait of Gilbraltar.

Conservation Has declined in France and breeds only sporadically throughout C Europe; larger populations in SW Europe and in N Africa and in E apparently stable. See p. 528.

Essays Raptor Hunting, p. 113; Migration, p. 377; Hatching Asynchrony and Brood Reduction, p. 507; Raptors at Sea Crossings, p. 93; Differential Migration, p. 323.

Refs Brown and Amadon 1968.

Bonelli's Eagle

Hieraaëtus fasciatus

ATLAS 95; PMH 80; PER 92; HFP 78; HPCW 66; NESTS 101; BWP2:258

 Decid tree 10–40m	 BLDS: ♂♀ Monogamy	 2 (1–3) 1 brood INCU: ♂♀ 37–40	SA1 FLDG: ♂♀ 60–65	 Birds	 Aer pursuit

Breeding habitat Open, dry areas, including forests, often in mountains.

Displays Similar to other birds of prey; has high circling above nest, steep descents with steep climbs. Pairs swoop, flight roll, and may exchange branches.

Nesting Territorial. Nest is large structure of branches on cliff or in tree. Eggs white with a few darker marks, 69mm, hatch asynchronously. Generally only one young reared, because older sibling attacks younger one, but parents may help second chick and successfully fledge it. Young may accompany parents for at least two months.

Diet Medium-sized mammals, less often reptiles, stooping to catch prey on ground after soaring. Sometimes catches birds in flight. Sometimes feeds in pairs.

Winters Resident, but moves to lower and often wetter areas than in summer.

Conservation Has declined in most of the W part of range and has scattered, fragmentary range around Mediterranean. Occurs widely, however, in Africa and Asia. See p. 528.

Essays Eyes Like a Hawk, p. 89; Conservation of Raptors, p. 103; Raptor Hunting, p. 113; Size and Sex in Raptors, p. 99; Wing Shapes and Flight, p. 269; Mobbing, p. 261; Pellets, p. 257; Hatching Asynchrony and Brood Reduction, p. 507; Eye Colour and Development, p. 85.

Refs Brown and Amadon 1968.

protection) supplied migrants, and strict protection in Scotland has managed to reduce shooting and the stealing of eggs by collectors to a level that no longer prevents population growth.

Legal protection against shooting, capturing, and poisoning, habitat improvement, and re-establishment programmes all help preserve birds of prey, but in the long run these measures alone will not be enough. Without public education about raptors' aesthetic and direct economic value, laws are likely to contain too many loopholes and will be enforced with insufficient vigour. As with the entire extinction problem, long-term solutions almost certainly will depend on changing attitudes toward our fellow creatures, and reduction of the appropriation of Earth's resources by *Homo sapiens*. Until then, habitat destruction will continue to accelerate the loss of species — both spectacular ones that attract our interest and more obscure ones on which our favourites (and we) often depend.

SEE: Birds and the Law, p. 521; Wildlife and the Law, p. 520; Pesticides and Birds, p. 115; Birds and Agriculture, p. 367; Botulism, p. 59. REFS: Cade, 1982; Gonzalez *et al.*, 1989; Noer and Secher, 1983; Poole, 1989; Robbins, 1985; Shawyer, 1987; Sibley and Ahlquist, 1985; Temple, 1978; Vitousek *et al.*, 1986.

Coloniality

WHY do some birds, but not others, nest in tightly packed colonies? About one avian species in eight is a colonial nester, either with its own kind or in mixed-species aggregations. The habit is widespread taxonomically; African weavers, relatives of House Sparrows, do it, and so do penguins and gulls. Whether colonial nesting evolves in a species depends on the balance between the advantages and disadvantages of the behaviour from the viewpoint of the individuals involved. Social interactions related to foraging seem to be one major reason for the maintenance of coloniality in species with unpredictable food supplies that are patchy but locally abundant.

In birds that exploit resources that are variable in space and time, natural selection does not favour individual territories for resource control. Instead coloniality may have developed because it allows less-adept birds to follow more-successful foragers when they leave the colony to feed, and perhaps also because it provides some protection against predation.

For example, North American Cliff Swallows (*Hirundo pyrrhonota*) that have been unsuccessful in finding food, return to the colony and follow a successful forager to a food source. Most seabirds that nest together also forage together, suggesting that they too can benefit from each others' good fortune on the hunt. Even more impressive is the behaviour of colonially nesting Ospreys, where birds not only get information about the success of returning foragers, but discriminate among the kinds of fishes they are

Osprey

Pandion haliaetus

ATLAS 86; PMH 81; PER 90; HFP 70; HPCW 67; NESTS 92; BWP2:265

 Cliff | BLDS: ♂♀ Monogamy | 2–3 (1–4) 1 brood INCU: ♂♥ 37 (34–40) | SA1 FLDG: ♂♀ 53 (49–57) | |

Breeding habitat Near fresh, brackish, or salt water, often with large trees or cliffs for nests.

Displays Similar to other birds of prey; has high circling above nest, also steep descents with steep climbs with ♂ displaying fish or branch in its talons. Mating ceremony at nest follows presentation of fish.

Nesting Solitary, but in favourable areas nests may be quite close together. Nest is large pile of twigs and branches in tree, or on cliff. Eggs white or creamy, heavily blotched with dark browns, 62mm, hatch asynchronously. Fed by ♀, while ♂ hunts. Unlike eagles, younger chicks often survive to fledge.

Diet Fish, caught in talons after shallow swoop, followed by plunge with wings half folded and feet forward. Hovers, and often bird swoops diagonally downward, stops, hovers at lower height, swoops again, and so on; final dive may be from only a quarter of height of initial hover. Fish is manoeuvred, sometimes with difficulty, to face line of flight as bird flies up to a tree, where it will eat fish.

Winters Migrates to Africa and India.

Conservation In last century lost from much of European range, because of persecution. Has recolonized some areas (e.g. Scotland) following protection, and building of artificial nest sites. Is one of the most widely distributed species of bird. See p. 528.

Essays Raptors at Sea Crossings, p. 93; Pesticides and Birds, p. 115; Communal Roosting, p. 81; Coloniality, p. 107; Conservation of Raptors, p. 103; Raptor Hunting, p. 113; Ducking the Bird Laws, p. 523; Sleeping Sentries and Mate-guarding, p. 73.

Refs Brown and Amadon 1968; Marchant et al. 1990. Poole 1989, is a book about this species.

Lesser Kestrel

Falco naumanni

ATLAS 107; PMH 81; PER 98; HFP 94; HPCW 67; NESTS 114; BWP2:282

 | BLDS: – Monogamy | 3–5 (2–8) 1 brood INCU: ♂♥ 28–29 | 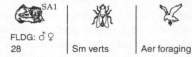 SA1 FLDG: ♂♀ 28 | Sm verts | Aer foraging

Breeding habitat Open, dry country around Mediterranean. Often nesting on buildings, so may be found in towns and villages.

Displays See Kestrel. After selecting nest site, ♂s will fly among the many other kestrels above the colony, trailing in its talons some large prey, such as a lizard, to attract ♀ to site. ♂s courtship-feed ♀s.

Nesting Colonial. Nest is a slight depression with no material and typically in tall building, or a cliff. Eggs buff-white, speckled or blotched with reddish-brown, 35mm, hatch synchronously. Young stay with parents at least until the migration.

Diet Mainly large insects, often caught on the wing as well as the ground. Also takes a variety of small vertebrates, especially lizards. Often hunts in loose groups; will also walk along ground.

Winters Migrates to Africa, often flocking where there are concentrations of prey.

Conservation Major declines in some areas, and a sporadic breeder in others. Very sensitive to the use of pesticides. Occurs around Mediterranean and across C Asia. See p. 528.

Essays Raptors at Sea Crossings, p. 93; Coloniality, p. 107; Raptor Hunting, p. 113.

Refs Brown and Amadon 1968.

carrying. Other colony members tend to depart and start fishing when a forager returns with a fish of a schooling species, and to fly in the direction from which the successful bird returned. In addition, when fishing has been bad, returning Ospreys often signal success at finding a school with an undulating display, thus actively participating in the exchange of information. This seemingly altruistic behaviour is probably explicable by the tendency of male Ospreys to nest near their parents, so that colony members are likely to be related.

Some birds, however, nest colonially and forage alone; others forage in flocks and nest alone. Yet these exceptions do not necessarily make the 'information-centre' hypothesis less likely. Herons, which rely on stealth and generally forage alone, still apparently learn a great deal about the productivity of remote feeding sites from other birds in their breeding colonies. Furthermore, established hunters might be less successful if accompanied to the feeding grounds by clumsy novices. Flock-feeding ducks do not breed colonially, presumably because their ground nests would be highly vulnerable to predators if grouped in colonies. But the ducks do come together daily in communal 'loafing areas' — and information can be exchanged there, rather than at a nesting colony.

The 'information-centre' hypothesis gains plausibility when we consider the occurrence of colonial nesting in species that appear to have little need for mutual predator defence, such as many Old World vultures and (before its decline) the California Condor. Closely related pairs of species, in which one is colonial and one is not, offer further support. The Lesser Kestrel breeds in colonies, while the closely related Kestrel, whose range partly overlaps the Lesser's, is usually a solitary breeder. It seems unlikely that the Lesser Kestrel cannot find safe places to nest where it feeds, and instead travels considerable distances to gain further security by becoming a member of a colony. The reason for the difference is probably related to diets rather than predator pressures. The Lesser Kestrel feeds mostly on insects, and presumably can learn from other colony members where locusts or other suitable prey are abundant. The Kestrel, on the other hand, preys largely on vertebrates, and its success may well be predicated on intimate knowledge of a limited territory.

Under the 'information-centre' hypothesis, reduced danger of predation is only a secondary benefit of coloniality. While increased numbers do increase chances of detecting the approach of a predator, beyond a colony size of a few hundred individuals the advantage of adding more sentries is vanishingly small. If predator detection were the major advantage of colonial breeding, why should some colonies have thousands of individuals? One possibility is that it leads to 'predator saturation'. Eggs and nestlings represent a large food resource, but they are present for only a short time. That time may be too brief for some predators to build or maintain populations large enough to take full advantage of the resource. On the other hand, large colonies sometimes expose their members to predation, since some predators will be attracted to vulnerable colonies and kill many, or even all, of the individuals in the colony.

The avoidance of predation does seem to be the major reason for colonial-

Kestrel
Falco tinnunculus

ATLAS 106; PMH 82; PER 98; HFP 94; HPCW 67; NESTS 114; BWP2:289

		3–6 (1–9) 1 brood	 SA1		
Decid tree	BLDS: ♂♀ Monogamy	INCU: ♀ 27–29	FLDG: ♂♀ 27–32	Birds	Aer pursuit

Breeding habitat Open country and open forests in a wide variety of habitats.

Displays Pairs circle and chase each other with dives and mock attacks. ♂ may fly with jerky wing-beats, with intermittent glides, or with shimmering flight of shallow, fast wing-beats. Birds begin to display, and courtship-feed, perhaps 2 months before eggs are laid.

Nesting Usually a solitary breeder. Nest is a scrape with no material where possible; elsewhere of twigs and grass. Nest placed in fork of, or hole in, tree, or on cliff. Often uses man-made structures. Eggs whitish but heavily marked with reddish-brown, 39mm, hatch asynchronously. ♀ cares for young while ♂ hunts and brings food. Survival very dependent on food supply. Smaller ♂s fledge generally two days before larger ♀s.

Diet Mammals (mainly voles) and some birds; Kestrel numbers may reflect vole densities, but species occurs in Ireland where voles are absent. Has distinctive hovering flight, swooping down, often in series of levels, before catching prey on the ground. In hover, head remains remarkably fixed in space, while body and wings are constantly adjusting to the wind. Has ability to feed in very poor light, and may feed by moonlight.

Winters Resident in S and W; in winter, numbers augmented from migrants in N and E Europe.

Conservation A major decline in Finland since the 1960s. Sensitive to pesticide use. Widespread across Europe, Africa, and Asia.

Essays Pesticides and Birds, p. 115; Coloniality, p. 107; Conservation of Raptors, p. 103.

Refs Brown and Amadon 1968; Village 1990 is a book about this species.

Red-footed Falcon
Falco vespertinus

ATLAS 106; PMH 82; PER 98; HFP 94; HPCW 68; NESTS 114; BWP2:302

	See below	3–4 (2–6) 1 brood	 SA1		
13–20m	BLDS: – Monogamy	INCU: ♂♀ 22–23 (27)	FLDG: ♂♀ 27–30	Sm mammals	Hawks

Breeding habitat Open country with woods.

Displays Poorly known, but probably similar to Kestrel and Lesser Kestrel.

Nesting Colonial. Uses former nest of crow, rooks, or magpie, and does not add material. Eggs buff, variably marked with brown, 37mm, hatch asynchronously. Young fed by ♀, ♂ brings food.

Diet Insects, taken from ground after hovering and dropping onto or near prey. Sometimes hawks for insects on wing. Young fed mainly small mammals.

Winters Migrates to southern Africa, gregarious both in winter and on migration.

Conservation Numbers not well known. Occurs from E Europe (breeds only sporadically in Czech Republic) into NC Asia.

Essays Ducking the Bird Laws, p. 523; Raptors at Sea Crossings, p. 93.

Refs Brown and Amadon 1968.

ity in at least some species whose prey is more uniformly or predictably distributed. For example, gaining information about food supplies seems unlikely to be an important reason for the formation of Sand Martin aggregations. These birds do not forage in groups, 10-day-old young weigh less in large colonies than in small, and in times of hunger, survival of young is lower in large than in small colonies. There is, however, evidence for the anti-predator hypothesis in this case. Predators are sometimes deterred by mobs of martins, and mobs are bigger in the larger colonies. Also, central nests suffer less from predation than do peripheral nests, and larger colonies have proportionately more central nests.

The predator hypothesis is also given some support by the demise of the bird that was the all-time champion colonial nester. The North American Passenger Pigeon once nested in colonies of billions of birds covering many square kilometres. When its numbers were reduced to the point at which large colonies could no longer form, it declined to extinction in spite of the presence of abundant habitat and food and the absence of further human molestation. In large colonies, the birds presumably saturated local predators; nests of scattered survivors simply may have been too vulnerable to predation. Indeed, the Passenger Pigeon may have evolved the need for the presence of large numbers before it would be stimulated to breed.

It is perhaps unrealistic to expect any clearcut resolution of the information vs. predation argument. Nevertheless there may be a tendency for young birds in a colony to benefit most from acquiring information, while older birds gain more through protection from predation. Older, more experienced birds are almost always better able to find food than inexperienced individuals. More experienced individuals, however, would suffer more competition for the food they find if they were followed by colony mates to the feeding grounds. But as they are more dominant, the older birds can acquire the safest nesting sites in the centre of the colony. Younger birds, in contrast, may accept a higher risk of losing their eggs and young at the periphery of the colony, in exchange for enhancement of their feeding success by the presence of more experienced birds for them to follow.

SEE: Geometry of the Selfish Colony, p. 15; Flock Defence, p. 257; Crèches, p. 45; Communal Roosting, p. 81; Mixed-species Flocking, p. 429; Mobbing, p. 261; Disease and Parasitism, p. 315. REFS: Blockstein and Tordoff, 1985; Brown 1986; Brown and Brown, 1986; Elgar and Harvey, 1987; Götmark, 1990; Greene, 1987; Hoogland and Sherman, 1976; Hunt et al., 1986; Siegel-Causey and Kharitonov, 1990; van Vessem and Draulans, 1986; Ward and Zahavi, 1973; Weatherhead, 1985; Wittenberger and Hunt, 1985.

Merlin

Falco columbarius

ATLAS 106; PMH 82; PER 98; HFP 94; HPCW 68; NESTS 111; BWP2:308

 Conif tree | BLDS: ♀ Monogamy |  5–6 (2–7) 1 brood INCU: ♂♀ 28–32 | SA1 FLDG: ♂♀ 25–32 | | Low patrol

Breeding habitat Wide range of open country, especially hilly moorland, in N Europe.

Displays Rather inconspicuous, ♂ has shimmering wing flight, like Kestrel.

Nesting Solitary and territorial. Nest is a scrape on the ground lined with a little vegetation. Sometimes nests in trees or a cliff. Eggs buffish, heavily blotched with reds and browns, 40mm, usually hatch synchronously.

Diet Small birds. Flies low, along the ground, surprising prey, often making prey fly before hitting it either on ground or sometimes in air. Sometimes hunts in pairs.

Winters Migrates to S and W Europe, wintering in open habitats including farmland and coast.

Conservation In UK, probably long-term decline; decreases also in Sweden, Finland. Like most other birds of prey, is sensitive to human disturbance. Occurs widely across N Europe, N Asia, N America. See p. 528.

Essays Raptors at Sea Crossings, p. 93; Piracy, p. 213; Conservation of Raptors, p. 103; Ducking the Bird Laws, p. 523.

Refs Brown and Amadon 1968.

Hobby

Falco subbuteo

ATLAS 105; PMH 83; PER 98; HFP 94; HPCW 69; NESTS 111; BWP2:316

 Conif tree 6–32m | See below BLDS: – Monogamy | 3 (2–4) 1 brood INCU: ♀ 28–31 | SA1 FLDG: ♂♀ 28–34 | Insects |

Breeding habitat Open country close to woodland, widespread throughout Europe and Asia.

Displays ♂ has a variety of fast flight displays, diving and calling at ♀ on perch, or both may have fast pursuit flights.

Nesting Solitary and territorial, usually. Uses the former nest of another bird (often crows) and does not add material. Eggs pale brown, spotted with reddish-browns, 42mm, hatch almost synchronously. Young fed by ♀, ♂ hunts. Accompany adults for several weeks after fledging.

Diet Birds (especially high-flying swallows and martins) and insects, sometimes bats and other small

vertebrates. Hunts in open, often high, taking prey on the wing, following short stoop (birds), and snatching insects which will then be eaten in flight. Often active in the evening where birds may be taken near roosts. Prey are attacked from below from where their silhouettes may be conspicuous against the sky.

Winters Migrates to S Africa and India.

Conservation Marked decrease in W Europe (but not UK, where increasing) but stable in most areas and widely distributed. Sensitive to human persecution. Occurs widely across Europe and Asia.

Essays Diet And Nutrition, p. 493; Raptor Hunting, p. 113.

Refs Brown and Amadon 1968; Marchant et al. 1990.

Raptor Hunting

ONE of the most spectacular sights in the world of birds is a stooping Peregrine killing another bird. The Peregrine plunges steeply downward, wings partially closed, at speeds that approach 400 kph. It was long thought that falcons and other raptors struck with their feet clenched like a fist. High-speed cinematographic studies, however, have shown that they strike their prey from above with all four toes fully extended. The Peregrine's victim is often ripped by the falcon's talons, producing a shower of feathers. Usually the prey is picked up off the ground afterward, although occasionally the falcon will stoop again and gather the tumbling bird before it falls to the ground.

Peregrines use other modes of hunting as well, sometimes diving past their prey and then zooming up from beneath to snatch it from behind and below, or simply catching a small bird from above with their talons. Sometimes they will patrol low over the ground like a Marsh Harrier attempting to flush game birds. The hunting success of Peregrines can vary widely with location, season, and even sex, as American ornithologist Tom Cade showed with an interesting comparison. One breeding male in the eastern United States, hunting Blue Jays (*Cyanocitta cristata*) almost exclusively, caught 93 per cent of his targets one season. A breeding female in Australia was successful only 31 per cent of the time, but she captured mostly coots which were more than five times as heavy as the Blue Jays. Considering that the female probably weighed half again as much as the male, and analysing the energy costs and benefits of both hunting patterns, Cade concluded that it took the male 49 kilocalories (kcal, what dieters normally just call a 'calorie') to deliver 1000 kcal of prey to the eyrie, while the female expended just 43 kcal to get

A Merlin stoops on a Dunlin, killing it with a slashing blow from its open feet.

Eleonora's Falcon

Falco eleonorae

ATLAS 105; PMH 83; PER 98; HFP 92; HPCW 69; NESTS 110; BWP2:327

		2–3 (1–5) 1 brood	^{SA1}		
BLDS: – Monogamy		INCU: ♀ 28	FLDG: ♂♀ ?35–40	Birds	Aer pursuit

Breeding habitat A limited number of rocky islets in Mediterranean.

Displays ♂s advertise by calling loudly, displaying prey items in flight, and fast downward glides followed by quick upward swoop. Plunge and swoops typical of pair's display.

Nesting Colonial. Has unusual and specialized breeding season, timing nesting to coincide with the autumn migration of birds. Nest a scrape with no material on cliff ledge on or steep slope with boulders and cover. Eggs off-white, blotched with pinkish-browns, 42mm, hatch asynchronously. Young fed by ♀, ♂ hunts.

Diet Large insects and small birds. Prey caught on the wing, often in early morning or late evening, but also by moonlight. Will also hawk for insects. When catching migrant birds, will face into the wind, hover, and wait for migrants to pass, then stoop at and chase them. 100 or more birds may hunt gregariously, forming a barrier 1000m high and several km long to migrants.

Winters Migrates eastward out of Mediterranean to E Africa and Madagascar. Winter habits not well known.

Conservation World population may number about 4500 pairs though colonies are often remote and poorly known. See p. 528.

Essays Hormones and Nest Building, p. 329.

Refs Brown and Amadon 1968; Walter 1979 is a book about this species.

Sooty Falcon

Falco concolor

ATLAS 104; PMH 244; PER -; HFP 92; HPCW 69; NESTS 110; BWP2:334

		2–3 1 brood	^{SA1}		
Ground	BLDS: – Monogamy	INCU: ♂♀ 27–28	FLDG: ♂♀ 21–35	Birds	Aer foraging

Breeding habitat Cliffs, above wadis, in deserts.

Displays Unknown.

Nesting Timed to exploit the autumn migration of birds across the Sahara, eggs are laid in mid to late July (in Israel, at least), during the hottest time of year. Nest is a shallow, unlined scrape, high on a cliff ledge or in old Brown-necked Raven nest. Eggs whitish with sparse reddish markings, 40mm. ♂ brings food to ♀, sometimes passing the food to her in mid-air. Chases Brown-necked Ravens from nest area – these birds may prey upon the falcon's young.

Diet Flying insects, but during breeding season mostly migrant birds. Takes birds up to the size of sandgrouse, but typically aerial feeders such as swifts, swallows, and bee-eaters taken in mid-air. Locally specializes on bats. Diet includes terrestrial lizards and rodents.

Winters In Madagascar.

Conservation Occurs from NW Africa into Israel. Numbers poorly known, but wintering numbers indicate that it is more abundant that Eleonora's Falcon. Considered not uncommon in S Israel.

Essays Eyes Like a Hawk, p. 89; Conservation of Raptors, p. 103; Raptor Hunting, p. 113; Size and Sex in Raptors, p. 99; Wing Shapes and Flight, p. 269; Mobbing, p. 261; Pellets, p. 257.

Refs Brown and Amadon 1968; Paz 1987.

the same job done. The female is more efficient, but is limited in the amount of time she can hunt because of her duties at the nest. The somewhat less-efficient male probably delivered more nourishment to the young because he could spend more time hunting.

As a group, raptors exhibit an extraordinary variety of hunting techniques. Aside from owls (which are sometimes considered raptors) almost all are diurnal hunters, but a few like the Hobby will pounce on mice in the moon-light. Some, like the Peregrine, hunt at high speed. The Sparrowhawk, for example, often flashes through relatively thick woodland, manoeuvring skil-fully and often snatching passerines right from their perches. Others, like Kestrels, Black-winged Kites, and Rough-legged Buzzards, often hover when hunting, and then drop steeply down on their targets. And still others, in-cluding Common Buzzards and Booted Eagles, often soar as they watch for prey on the ground. But most hunting by raptors probably is done from perches with a commanding view from which the bird can scan the surround-ing terrain with its telescope-like vision, and from which it can glide rapidly to gather in its prey. Whichever technique is used, most prey of raptors are killed by the talons of the contracting foot being driven into their bodies; if required, the hooked bill is used to give a *coup de grâce*. The exceptions are falcons, which ordinarily kill by biting into the neck of victims not dispatched in mid-air. (Owls also bite the necks of their prey.)

Of course, there are some birds of prey (in addition to falcons) that employ rather specialized hunting techniques. Perched or hovering Ospreys plunge into water to grab living fish; American Snail (*Rostrhamus sociabilis*) and Hook-billed (*Chondrohierax uncinatus*) Kites course around like harriers in pursuit of their less-than-agile preferred food: snails.

Birds of prey can be significant causes of mortality in populations of other birds. For example, about one-fifth of the Redshank and Ringed Plover overwintering in Scotland appear to fall prey to raptors. In Wytham Wood near Oxford, England, up to one third of fledgling tits may be eaten by Sparrowhawks.

SEE: Eyes Like a Hawk, p. 89; How Owls Hunt in the Dark, p. 251; Size and Sex in Raptors, p. 99. REFS: Brown and Amadon, 1968; Cade, 1982; Goslow, 1971; Perrins and Geer, 1980; Ratcliffe, 1980; Rudolph, 1982; Whitfield, 1985.

Pesticides and Birds

BIRDS played a major role in creating awareness of pollution problems. In-deed, many people consider the modern environmental movement to have started with the 1962 publication in the United States of Rachel Carson's classic *Silent spring*, which described the results of the misuse of DDT and

Lanner Falcon
Falco biarmicus

ATLAS 104; PMH 84; PER 100; HFP 90; HPCW 70; NESTS 109; BWP2:338

	See below		SA1		
	BLDS: –	3–4 (2)			
	Monogamy	1 brood			
		INCU: ♂ ♀	FLDG: ♂ ♀		
Decid tree		32–35	44–46	Sm verts	

Breeding habitat Low, rocky mountains to deserts.

Displays Pairs have high circling and fast, aerobatic flight displays with birds stooping at each other.

Nesting Solitary and territorial. Uses old nest of crows or other birds of prey, usually on a cliff, sometimes in a tree. Does not add material. Eggs white, heavily overlaid with brownish blotching, 51mm, hatch asynchronously. ♀ feeds while ♂ hunts. Young remain with parents for several weeks after fledging.

Diet Birds up to doves and sandgrouse in size, but also small vertebrates and large insects. Catches prey on the ground following a stoop. Often hunts in pairs.

Winters Resident.

Conservation Almost gone from Europe; a popular bird with falconers, and vulnerable to illegal taking of young. Widespread in Africa. See p. 528.

Refs Brown and Amadon 1968. Cade 1982 is a book about falcons.

Saker Falcon
Falco cherrug

ATLAS 103; PMH 84; PER 100; HFP 90; HPCW 70; NESTS 109; BWP2:344

	See below		SA1		
	BLDS: –	3–5 (2–6)			
Decid tree	Monogamy	1 brood			
15–20m		INCU: ♂ ♀	FLDG: ♂ ♀		
		28–30	40–45		

Breeding habitat Open country, grasslands, with some trees.

Displays Not well known, but high circling and aerial mock fights similar to other large falcons.

Nesting Solitary and territorial. Uses nest of other birds of prey, on cliff or in tree. Does not add material. Eggs off-white, heavily spotted reddish-browns, 54mm, hatch asynchronously. Young cared for at first by ♀, ♂ brings food. Young stay with adults for several weeks.

Diet Small mammals, also birds taken on ground following low, searching flight.

Winters Some resident, many migrate to SE Europe, Africa, and India.

Conservation Little information on numbers. Local in E Europe and across C Asia.

Essays Conservation of Raptors, p. 103; Eyes Like a Hawk, p. 89; Raptor Hunting, p. 113; Size and Sex in Raptors, p. 99; Wing Shapes and Flight, p. 269; Mobbing, p. 261; Pellets, p. 257.

Refs Brown and Amadon 1968.

other pesticides. In the fable that began her book, Carson wrote: 'It was a spring without voices. On the mornings that had once throbbed with the dawn chorus of robins, catbirds, doves, jays, wrens, and scores of other bird voices there was now no sound; only silence lay over the fields and woods and marsh.'

Her concern was well-founded. The use of synthetic organic pesticides escalated dramatically after World War II. In 1950 there were just 15 compounds on the British Ministry of Agriculture's List of Approved Products for Farmers. In 1960 there were 47 chemicals on the list; in 1970, 163; and in 1980, 198. Organochlorine pesticides, which are acutely toxic, were killing large numbers of birds in Europe and North America in the 1950s, alerting some scientists to the dangers pesticides posed to avian communities. It was not, however, until the impacts of the chlorinated hydrocarbon DDT and its relatives became evident late in the 1950s and early in the 1960s that public attention was drawn to the problem.

The potentially lethal impact of DDT on birds was first noted in the late 1950s when spraying to control the beetles that carry Dutch elm disease led to a slaughter of American Robins (*Turdus migratorius*) in Michigan and elsewhere in the United States. Researchers discovered that earthworms were accumulating the persistent pesticide and that the robins eating them were being poisoned. Other birds fell victim, too. Gradually, thanks in no small part to Carson's book, gigantic 'broadcast spray' programmes were brought under control.

DDT, its breakdown products, other chlorinated hydrocarbon pesticides, and non-pesticide chlorinated hydrocarbons such as PCBs, pose particularly insidious threats to birds, both terrestrial and aquatic. Because these poisons are persistent they tend to concentrate as they move through the feeding sequences in communities that ecologists call 'food chains'. For example, in most marine communities, the living weight (biomass) of fish-eating birds is less than that of the fishes they eat. However, because chlorinated hydrocarbons accumulate in fatty tissues, when a tonne of contaminated fishes is turned into 90 kilograms of seabirds, most of the DDT from the numerous fishes ends up in a relatively few birds. As a result, the birds have a higher level of contamination per kilogram than the fishes. If Peregrine Falcons feed on the seabirds, the concentration becomes higher still. With several concentrating steps in the food chain below the level of fishes (for instance, tiny aquatic plants, crustacea, small fishes), very slight environmental contamination can be turned into a heavy pesticide load in birds at the top of the food chain. In one estuary on New York's Long Island, concentrations of less than a tenth of a part per million (ppm) of DDT in aquatic plants and plankton resulted in concentrations of 3–25 ppm in gulls, terns, cormorants, mergansers, herons, and ospreys.

'Bioconcentration' of pesticides in birds high on food chains occurs not only because there is usually reduced biomass at each step in those chains, but also because predatory birds tend to live a long time. They may take in only a little DDT per day, but they keep most of what they get, and they live many days. Large raptors may survive for more than two decades.

Gyrfalcon
Falco rusticolus

ATLAS 103; PMH 81; PER 100; HFP 90; HPCW -; NESTS 108; BWP2:350

 See below

BLDS: –
Monogamy

3–4 (2–6)
1 brood
IN: ♀, ♂♀
35 (34–36)

SA1
FLDG: ♂♀
46–49

Breeding habitat Arctic tundra, often along sea coast.
Displays Flies around nest site, calling and often carrying prey, with birds diving at each other.
Nesting Solitary and territorial. Uses nest of other bird of prey or raven on cliff ledge. No material added. Eggs buff, spotted with red, 59mm, hatch asynchronously. Egg numbers depend on the availability of prey. At first, ♀ feeds young, ♂ hunts.
Diet Birds, often grouse, ducks, and wading birds in tundra habitats and gulls and auks from sea cliffs. Generally flushes prey, gains height, and catches prey in stoop.
Winters Resident, but individuals move southwards from most northerly parts of range.
Conservation Marked declines where persecuted and where eggs are taken illegally; widespread in remote arctic areas of Europe, Asia, and N America.
Essays Conservation of Raptors, p. 103; Bird Droppings, p. 485.
Refs Brown and Amadon 1968.

Peregrine Falcon
Falco peregrinus

ATLAS 104; PMH 85; PER 100; HFP 92; HPCW 71; NESTS 109; BWP2:361

 See below

BLDS: –
Monogamy

3–4 (2–6)
1 brood
INCU: ♂♀
28–29 per egg

SA1
FLDG: ♂♀
35–42

Breeding habitat In Europe, particularly mountains, sea cliffs or other open habitats. Sometimes uses buildings in cities.
Displays Display flights over nest similar to other birds of prey, with high circling, mock fights, calling, and aerobatics between pairs.
Nesting Territorial. On cliffs or sometimes buildings. Does not build nest, but will use nest of other species such as crows or buzzards. Eggs whitish, heavily marked with reddish-browns, 55mm, hatch asynchronously. ♂ feeds ♀ on nest.
Diet Birds taken on wing in open, following spectacular stoop from above. When nesting in cities uses domestic pigeons as prey.
Winters Resident in south and western mountainous areas, northern populations migrate to southern and western Europe.
Conservation Marked declines with local extinctions. The decline of this species following extensive pesticide use (and partial recovery since) both in Europe and North America provided important clues to just how dangerous pesticide application was to species at the top of food chains. Not only were adults poisoned directly, but nesting birds often failed to hatch eggs, because the egg shells thinned (and so were easily broken) when the ♀s were poisoned. The species is recovering well from this former decline and has worldwide distribution. See p. 528.
Essays Pesticides and Birds, p. 115; Conservation of Raptors, p. 103; Diet And Nutrition, p. 493; Piracy, p. 213; Raptor Hunting, p. 113; How Fast and High Do Birds Fly?, p. 63.
Refs Brown and Amadon 1968; Marchant et al. 1990; Ratcliffe 1993 is a book about this species.

The insidious aspect of this phenomenon is that large concentrations of chlorinated hydrocarbons often do not kill the bird outright. Rather, DDT and its relatives alter the bird's calcium metabolism in a way that results in thin eggshells. In the USA, heavily DDT-infested Brown Pelicans and Bald Eagles tended to find omelettes in their nests, since the eggshells are unable to support the weight of the incubating bird. Shell-thinning resulted in the decimation of Brown Pelican populations in much of North America and the extermination of Peregrine Falcons in the eastern United States and south-eastern Canada. Shell-thinning caused lesser declines in populations of Ospreys, Golden and Bald Eagles, and White Pelicans, among others.

Similar declines in Peregrines, Sparrowhawks, and Kestrels took place in the British Isles, but the culprit there appears to have been acute dieldrin poisoning. Grey Heron populations suffered breeding failures on the Continent, but were not significantly affected in Britain. Differences in pesticide practices from nation to nation apparently were responsible for these varying patterns. Fortunately, the causes of the failures were identified in time. The use of DDT was banned almost totally in the United States in 1972, and restrictions have been placed on it and related compounds in Britain and Europe.

Some reduced bird populations started to recover quickly thereafter, with species as different as Ospreys and American Robins returning to the pre-DDT levels of breeding success in a decade or less. Furthermore, attempts to re-establish the Peregrine in the eastern United States using captive-reared birds show considerable signs of success. Peregrines, Kestrels, Sparrow-hawks, and Golden Eagles have recovered nicely in Britain.

Unfortunately, however, DDT still persist in the environment. It occurs as a contaminant in other compounds, and is picked up by migratory birds in the tropics, where its use is still largely unrestricted. DDT and other pesticides continue to hang as a heavy shadow over many bird populations, and many worry that as the end of the century approaches, the once hopeful trend may be reversing.

Pesticides other than chlorinated hydrocarbons also threaten bird populations. Organophosphorus pesticides such as parathion are powerful poisons even though they break down rather rapidly in the environment. And all insecticides, to the degree that they actually reduce insect populations, reduce the food supply of insectivorous birds. In fruit-growing areas of southern Swabia (Germany), Great Tit nestlings suffer from pesticide-induced starvation. This, of course, damages the natural pest-control service those birds supply and deprives people of many glimpses of beauty.

When it was published, *Silent spring* was attacked viciously by the pesticide industry and by narrowly trained entomologists, but its scientific foundation has stood the test of time. Misuse of pesticides is now widely recognized as threatening not only bird communities but human communities as well.

SEE: Hatching, p. 487; Wintering and Conservation, p. 409; Conservation of Raptors, p. 103. REFS: Beaver, 1980; Bonney, 1986; Carson, 1962; Ehrlich et al., 1975; Gooders, 1983; Mattes et al., 1980; Newton et al., 1982; Nygård, 1983; Spitzer et al., 1978; Wiemeyer et al., 1989.

Barbary Falcon

Falco pelegrinoides

ATLAS 104; PMH 244; PER -; HFP 92; HPCW 71; NESTS 110; BWP2:378

 See below

BLDS: –
Monogamy

 3 (2–5)
1 brood
INCU: ?
?

 SA1
FLDG: ?♂ ♀
?

Breeding habitat In desert and semi-desert areas with cliffs.

Displays Probably like Peregrine Falcon.

Nesting Uses old nest of another species, on cliff. Does not add material. Eggs white to buff, heavily speckled with deep red-brown, 51mm.

Diet Birds; taken in much the same way as Peregrine Falcon.

Winters Mainly resident.

Conservation A little-known species with a fragmented range from N Africa into SW Asia.

Essays Eyes Like a Hawk, p. 89; Conservation of Raptors, p. 103; Raptor Hunting, p. 113; Size and Sex in Raptors, p. 99; Wing Shapes and Flight, p. 269; Mobbing, p. 261; Pellets, p. 257.

Refs Brown and Amadon 1968.

Hazel Grouse

Bonasa bonasia

ATLAS 109; PMH 85; PER -; HFP 96; HPCW -; NESTS 116; BWP2:385

BLDS: ♀
Monogamy

 6–10 (11–15)
1 brood
INCU: ♀
25 (23–27)

 P3
FLDG: ♀
See below | Fruits

Breeding habitat In coniferous or mixed forests.

Displays ♂s are solitary, and display by rapidly beating wings while on ground, calling with high whistle. ♀, adopting low stance, approaches ♂, and ♂ circles ♀ with wings drooping before mating.

Nesting Well-concealed nest is on ground; lined with plant material. Eggs yellowish or buff, usually spotted with reddish-brown, 45mm, hatch synchronously. Young leave nest with ♀ after a day and remain with ♀ for about 3 months. The young of this species, like those of most game birds, can fly

short distances within a week or two of hatching. The young still take several weeks to attain full adult size.

Diet A variety of plant material taken from near the ground in summer, but from trees in winter. Small chicks take mostly insects.

Winters Resident.

Conservation Some retreat from the western part of range, but widespread across Europe and Asia. See p. 528.

Essays Promiscuity, p. 127; Leks, p. 123; Territoriality, p. 397; Precocial and Altricial Young, p. 401; Wing Shapes and Flight, p. 269.

Incubation Time

HOW much time different species actually spend sitting on the eggs during incubation is even more variable than who does the sitting. Individual bouts of incubation by many small passerines such as wrens may last less than ten minutes; an albatross, in contrast, may sit on its eggs continuously for weeks at a stretch. Where only one parent incubates, it usually spends about two-thirds to three-quarters of the daytime hours on the eggs, and the remainder feeding. Flycatchers and others that hunt flying insects spend only slightly over half their time on the nest. Small birds have high metabolic rates, and stoking their fast-burning fires exhausts fat reserves rapidly. They could not survive even a small part of a normal albatross incubation session.

The constancy of incubation often is genetically controlled and adapted to the habitat. It may have a profound effect on the ability of different species to colonize new areas or adjust to climatic change. For example, two related species, the Starling and the South Asian Crested Myna, were both introduced into North America in the late 1800s. The species have very similar breeding habits, but the former has spread over virtually the entire continent, while the latter has remained restricted to the vicinity of Vancouver, British Columbia, where it was introduced. One hypothesis to explain the differing success of these two close relatives is that the myna's incubation constancy is genetically attuned to its subtropical homeland. It sits on its eggs for only about half of the day, which would be adequate in a warm climate but is suboptimal in British Columbia. The Starling, in contrast, incubates for almost three-quarters of the daylight hours. Although both lay clutches of 5 eggs, the Starling successfully rears an average of 3.5 young per clutch; the myna manages to fledge an average of 2. This relatively low reproductive rate may account for the myna's limited success in Vancouver, compared with the explosive spread of the Starling.

Since, in general, birds do not begin incubating until the clutch is complete, 'incubation time' is defined as the period from the laying of the last egg of the clutch until that egg hatches (or, if individual eggs can't be identified, from the last egg laid to the first egg hatched). It is one more aspect of incubation that varies a great deal. Incubation time is roughly correlated with the weight of the egg. The eggs of small songbirds generally hatch in about 11 days, those of the Royal Albatross in about 80 days.

More information on incubation, based on careful, long-term observations of nests, is needed for many species of European birds. Data to be gathered include who incubates (and if both parents do, how the load is shared), the proportion of time the eggs are covered in different kinds of weather, egg turning frequency, and elapsed time from laying to hatching.

SEE: Incubation: Controlling Egg Temperatures, p. 273; Hatching Asynchrony and Brood Reduction, p. 507; Who Incubates?, p. 285. REF.: White and Kinney, 1974.

Red / Willow Grouse

Lagopus lagopus

ATLAS 108; PMH 86; PER 100; HFP 96; HPCW -; NESTS 115; BWP2:391

 | | 6–11 (4–17) 1 brood INCU: ♀ 19–25 |  FLDG: ♂♀ See below

BLDS: ♀
Monogamy

Breeding habitat Heather moorland in UK, tundra, dwarf willow, and birch forests elsewhere.

Displays Courting ♂s call and strut, with red wattles over eyes swollen, head thrown back, tail raised and spread, and wings drooped. ♂s also call in flight.

Nesting Territorial. Nest is scrape on ground in thick cover; lined with grasses. Eggs yellowish, blotched with dark brown, 46mm, hatch synchronously. Young leave nest when dry. Independent at about 8 weeks, but can fly when much younger.

Diet Heather, willows, birch, berries when available; chicks take insects.

Winters Moves to lower elevations avoiding deep snow cover. Often in flocks.

Conservation Populations fluctuate and there have been declines in some areas following reduced game management, loss of moors to forests. Species has wide distribution across N Europe, N Asia, N America. See p. 530.

Notes Some populations in UK cycle in numbers every 6–7 years, while other populations do not.

Essays Leks, p. 123; Monogamy, p. 335; Disease and Parasitism, p. 315; Swallowing Stones, p. 135; Promiscuity, p. 127; Territoriality, p. 397; Avian Snowshoes, p. 123.

Refs Marchant et al. 1990; Hudson 1986 is a book about this species

Ptarmigan

Lagopus mutus

ATLAS 107; PMH 86; PER 100; HFP 96; HPCW -; NESTS 116; BWP2:406

 | | 5–8 (3–12) 1 brood INCU: ♀ 21–23(20–26) | FLDG: ♂♀ See below | Fruits |

BLDS: ♂♀
Monogamy

Breeding habitat Open rocky mountainsides at high altitude and tundra down to sea level.

Displays Very similar to Red Grouse.

Nesting Nest is scrape on ground, barely lined with grasses. May make many scrapes before choosing one. Eggs red when fresh fading to buff with many dark blotches, 44mm, hatch synchronously. Young leave within a day, capable of some flight at 10–15 days, and become independent at about 3 months.

Diet Birch and willow buds, twigs, and berries when available; small chicks feed on insects.

Winters Resident; often in flocks.

Conservation No major changes in range across N Europe (isolated populations in the Alps, Pyrenees), N Asia, N America.

Notes Numbers cycle in abundance with 10-year period.

This species illustrates how changing climate affects bird distributions. Why should a species be found in such separate locations, when most of the individuals are resident? After the last glaciation, tundras were more widespread. As the climate warmed, tundras moved up in latitude and elevation, 'stranding' this species on mountain tops in central Europe. Some of these isolated populations are endangered: see p. 529.

Essays Feet, p. 289; Diet And Nutrition, p. 493; Hormones and Nest-Building, p. 329; Commensal Feeding, p. 27; Nest Lining, p. 439; Promiscuity, p. 127; Leks, p. 123; Territoriality, p. 397; Avian Snowshoes, p. 123.

Avian Snowshoes

MANY northern birds must at least occasionally traverse snow on foot, but of these, only Ptarmigan and Willow Grouse possess structures to facilitate walking on snow. In winter, most grouse acquire a fringe of scales along each toe that enlarges the surface area of the foot. Ptarmigan and Willow Grouse have gone further to increase their foot surface area: in winter plumage, they develop highly modified dense feathering that covers both surfaces of their feet, and their claws become significantly longer. It is likely that winter foot feathering also provides thermal insulation, although its effectiveness has not been measured. Experiments with feathered and plucked Willow Grouse feet in soft snow, however, clearly demonstrate that foot feathering aids walking for these birds in much the same way as snowshoes support people. The feathers increase the bearing surface of the foot by about 400 per cent and reduce the depth that the foot sinks in snow by roughly 50 per cent.

SEE:Temperature Regulation and Behaviour, p. 163; Feet, p. 289. REF.: Hohn, 1977.

Leks

THE mating system of some species of birds involves males displaying communally at a traditional site (one used year after year). Such a traditional site is known as a 'lek' or, sometimes, an 'arena'. Males of certain members of the grouse family (Black Grouse, Capercaillie), Ruffs, Great Snipe, and Great Bustards compete for mates at leks. During their displays, grouse call repeatedly (often with a 'popping', 'rattling', or 'bubbling' sound) while carrying out a ritualized dance. Females approach the lek, choose and mate with a male from the displaying group, and then leave to nest and rear the young alone.

Up to 200 male Black Grouse may hold territories on a lek (largely in the Commonwealth of Independent States; groups of 10–40 are more common in western Europe), with the males near the centre normally mating with the most females. In general a male's success at attracting females is highly correlated with his position on the lek, which in turn is largely determined by his place in a complex male dominance hierarchy. This leads to relatively few males siring most of the young; central males may get 85–98 per cent of copulations (although some non-lekking 'soloist' males may be quite successful). Male Capercaillie have a modified lek system, making use of leks, transient arenas, or just responding to the presence of a female. There may be

Black Grouse
Tetrao tetrix

ATLAS 109; PMH 87; PER 102; HFP 98; HPCW -; NESTS 117; BWP2:416

		6–11 (4–15) 1 brood	P3		
Shrub	BLDS: ♀	INCU: ♀	FLDG: ♀	Fruits	
0–6m	Polygyny	25–27	See below		

Breeding habitat Open birch and pine woods, and broken woods near moorland.

Displays ♂s form leks in autumn and spring at traditional lekking areas in open places. ♂s fan and cock lyre-shaped tails with white under-tail coverts spread out vertically; from the front, the coverts appear as a circle. ♂s defend places in the lek. They hiss and call and have a wide variety of complex displays, including fighting with other ♂s, in order to attract the ♀s that come by and inspect them. ♂s centrally placed in lek are apparently those that are most successful in mating. ♀s solicit ♂s by crouching.

Nesting ♂ plays no part. Nest is scrape lined with grasses on ground in cover; sometimes in shrubs above the ground in old nest of other species. Eggs creamy, spotted with reddish browns, 51mm, hatch synchronously. Large numbers of eggs may be nests of two ♀s. Young are capable of flight at 10–14 days and independent at about 12 weeks.

Diet Birch and pine needles, berries when available; chicks take insects.

Winters Resident, often in loose flocks.

Conservation In W, marked decreases from the last century due to habitat changes and intense hunting. Widely distributed across Europe and Asia, however. See p. 528.

Essays Promiscuity, p. 127; Leks, p. 123; Territoriality, p. 397; Visual Displays, p. 33.

Refs Marchant et al. 1990.

Capercaillie
Tetrao urogallus

ATLAS 108; PMH 87; PER 102; HFP 98; HPCW -; NESTS 118; BWP2:433

		7–11 (5–16) 1 brood	P3		
	BLDS: ♀	INCU: ♀	FLDG: ♀	Fruits	
	Polygyny	24–26	See below		

Breeding habitat Mainly forests, especially coniferous, prefers old forests but also uses plantations.

Displays ♂s have complex displays on traditional, communal display areas. On these areas, individual birds are more widely dispersed than on typical leks. Song involves a variety of tapping, popping, gurgling sounds on the ground or in trees. Visual displays involve head and tail held vertical, tail spread, and wings drooping by side. ♂s commonly fight. ♀s may approach ♂s in small groups encouraging the ♂s by calling.

Nesting Nest is shallow scrape lined with vegetation. Eggs pale yellowish with a few brown streaks, 57mm, hatch synchronously. Young can fly at 2–3 weeks and are independent at 2–3 months.

Diet Needles of pine and other conifers, berries when available; insects important for chicks.

Winters Resident, some in flocks.

Conservation Extinctions following deforestation in Scotland (where it was later reintroduced) and other areas. Recently, Scottish population has declined to 2000 birds. Occurs in isolated populations in montane areas of S Europe and across N Europe, N Asia. See p. 528.

Essays Promiscuity, p. 127; Leks, p. 123; Territoriality, p. 397.

Refs Marchant et al. 1990.

temporary polygynous pair-bonds, but as in more typical lekking species a few males do most of the mating.

Not all species of grouse establish leks. Male Hazel Grouse and the North American Spruce, Blue, and Ruffed Grouse (*Dendrogapus canadensis, D. obscurus,* and *Bonasia umbellus* respectively) display at dispersed sites, although, as in lekking species, the females do not remain with the males after mating. In contrast, Willow Grouse remain paired for much of the year, and males may help rear the young. American behaviourists Jack Bradbury and Sandra Vehrencamp have developed a model which indicates that the size of female home ranges (areas visited in the course of normal activities) is a major factor in determining whether or not males form leks. Where home ranges are larger there are more places where several overlap, and it is the existence of those female 'hotspots' that stimulate the evolution of lekking.

The grouse mating systems also seem to be determined in part by habitat. Lekking species tend to live in open country; species with males that display in isolation tend to be forest dwellers. Natural selection may not have favoured the evolution of leks in northern forest habitats that give predators an opportunity to approach leks with little chance of detection. Also, female home ranges are smaller in forests than in open country. In the tropics, however, many groups of birds (e.g. cotingas, manakins, hermit humming-birds) display at leks within the forest.

The system in Ruffs is similar to that in grouse, ordinarily with 5–20 males holding territories on the lek. There are normally two types of males. 'Independents' either hold or will hold territories on the lek, display aggressively, and have dark display plumage, primarily the ruff of neck feathers. 'Satellites', who generally do not display, have light display plumage, are more or less tolerated by the independents, and mate opportunistically. The independent males go through a wide variety of displays, featuring the showy ruff of feathers around their necks, and do battle with each other, but are silent. As in the grouse, a few males monopolize most of the females (although the relative success of independent and satellite males is not known with precision and has been the topic of interesting evolutionary speculation). On one lek in Holland, one male participated in 52 of 100 observed copulations.

Such male 'hotshots' stand out even more on some tropical leks. For instance, one of eight lekking males of the Lesser Bird of Paradise performed 24 out of 25 copulations. Such data have led American ornithologists Bruce Beehler and Mercedes Foster to question the common assumption that female choice is the essence of lek behaviour, and to focus more on interactions among males that lead one to achieve such dominance. The issue is still under active discussion, and it seems likely that the degree to which male–male interactions as opposed to female choice contribute to mating patterns will vary from species to species.

Hundreds of Great Snipe males once gathered on leks in the late afternoon, but now numbers on the same leks are more often in the range of 10–20. Unlike most lekking species there is no sexual dimorphism in Great Snipes, but males use complex vocalizations and exposure of white tail

Caspian Snowcock

Tetraogallus caspius

ATLAS 110; PMH -; PER -; HFP 100; HPCW 72; NESTS 120; BWP2:449

 |

BLDS: ♀

?

(6–9)
1 brood
INCU: ♀?
28?

FLDG: ♀?
See below

Breeding habitat Tree line to below permanent snow, with rocky outcrops.

Displays Poorly known.

Nesting Nest is shallow scrape on ground in open. Eggs buffish with red splotches, 66mm, hatch synchronously. Capable of flight at 2–3 weeks, while still not fully grown.

Diet Roots and grasses.

Winters Moves to lower elevations.

Conservation Range poorly known but very limited. Occurs in local, isolated mountains in SW Asia.

Essays Leks, p. 123; Territoriality, p. 397; Precocial and Altricial Young, p. 401; Wing Shapes and Flight, p. 269.

Chukar Partridge

Alectoris chukar

ATLAS 113; PMH 88; PER 104; HFP 102; HPCW 73; NESTS 122; BWP2:452

BLDS: ♀
Monogamy

8–15 (16–20)
1 brood
INCU: ♀
22–24

FLDG: ♀
See below

Breeding habitat Stony open ground in dry Mediterranean habitats.

Displays ♂s display by tilting heads away from rival, turning sideways to expose brightly marked flanks. Rivals mutually circle each other, and will also attack if these displays fail. ♀s approach ♂s displaying in this way and solicit by crouching.

Nesting Nest is scrape sparsely lined on ground sheltered by rock. Eggs pale cream with red-brown speckles, 39mm, hatch synchronously. Young looked

after by ♀; not certain whether ♂s ever look after a clutch (compare with other partidges). Young can fly at 7–10 days and become full size at about 7 weeks.

Diet Grass seeds; chicks take insects.

Winters Resident; in flocks.

Conservation Has decreased where heavily hunted, but common and widespread in much of Asia, and introduced widely in N America.

Essays Precocial and Altricial Young, p. 401; Wing Shapes and Flight, p. 269.

feathers in night-time displays. Great Bustards have a less well-defined lek system, with only some of the males territorial.

Many birds, such as cranes, have spectacular displays and elaborate courtship dances. These birds are not lekking, however, because the males do not attempt to attract females by displaying competitively and repeatedly at traditional sites season after season, and because males and females form pair bonds rather than mating promiscuously.

SEE: Polygyny, p. 265; Monogamy, p. 335; Promiscuity, p. 127; Territoriality, p. 397; Dominance Hierarchies, p. 131; Visual Displays, p. 33. REFS: Avery and Sherwood, 1982; Beehler and Foster, 1988; Bradbury and Gibson, 1983; Krebs and Harvey, 1988; Lewin, 1988; Payne, 1984; van Rhijn, 1983; Wiley, 1978.

Promiscuity

SOME species of birds do not form pair bonds, but instead consort only briefly — for minutes or hours. The male's investment in offspring is limited to sperm, and the female raises the young alone. Male hummingbirds, for instance, court females for a short time, mate, and then resume their quest for other females. Males of many grouse species and some waders display on leks (mating grounds used each year) to attract females that depart immediately after mating. The males may subsequently mate with additional females. Such mating systems, in which no pair bond is formed, are termed promiscuous. Presumably promiscuous mating systems can evolve only where the advantage of the male remaining with the female to help in raising the young is negligible.

SEE: Monogamy, p. 335; Polygyny, p. 265; Leks, p. 123; Polyandry, p. 195; Cooperative Breeding, p. 275; Parental Care, p. 171.

Rock Partridge

Alectoris graeca

ATLAS 112; PMH 88; PER 104; HFP 102; HPCW -; NESTS 122; BWP2:458

BLDS: ♀	8–14?(6–21)	FLDG: ♀
Monogamy	1 (2) broods	See below
	IN: see below	Seeds
	24–26	

Breeding habitat Open stony hillsides, sometimes to high elevations.

Displays Has head-tilting, side-showing and circling displays like Chukar.

Nesting Territorial. Nest sheltered by plants or rocks; sparsely lined. Eggs pale cream speckled with reddish-brown, 41mm, hatch synchronously. Occurrence of second clutch uncertain; some evidence that ♀s lay two clutches with the ♂ incubating the second one. Young can fly at 7–10 days, become full-sized at about 7 weeks.

Diet Plants; chicks take insects.

Winters Resident; in flocks.

Conservation Declining in limited range, in SE Europe because of intense hunting. See p. 529.

Essays Precocial and Altricial Young, p. 401; Wing Shapes and Flight, p. 269.

Red-legged Partridge

Alectoris rufa

ATLAS 113; PMH 88; PER 104; HFP 102; HPCW -; NESTS 121; BWP2:463

BLDS: ♂	10–16 (7–20)	FLDG: ♂♀
Monogamy	1–2 broods	See below
	INCU: ♂♀	Greens
	23–24	

Breeding habitat Open ground including agricultural areas, from Mediterranean to Britain (where introduced).

Displays Has head-tilting, side-showing and circling displays like Chukar. Extends and droops wing on side away from rival. ♂s courtship-feed mates.

Nesting Territorial. Nest is built by ♂, who may make several. Nest is concealed within vegetation; slight lining of grass. Eggs pale cream with red or brown markings, 40mm, hatch synchronously. There may be two simultaneous broods with ♀ looking after one, the ♂ the other. If one brood, both birds attend it. Young capable of flight at about 10 days, and become full size at about 7 weeks. Some suggestion that ♀s lay clutches for more than one ♂.

Diet Seeds and other plant material, taken by digging with bill; chicks take insects.

Winters Resident; in flocks.

Conservation Seems to have declined where hunted, but has been successfully introduced to a number of areas (UK in 1790). Perhaps 3/4 million birds released in UK each year. Limited range in S and W Europe.

Refs Marchant et al. 1990.

Hesperornis *and Other Missing Links*

IN the interim between *Archaeopteryx* and living birds there are relatively few fossil, 'missing links' that cast light on the origins of birds. From early Cretaceous deposits laid down in Spain and elsewhere about 100 million years ago have come several birds assigned to the Enantiornithes ('other

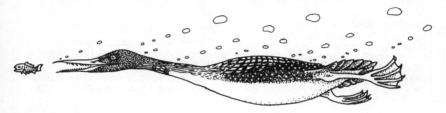

Like a primitive cormorant, an extinct Hesperornis *pursues a fish through the ocean (some 70 million years ago).* Hesperornis *had teeth like* Archaeopteryx, *which presumably were used to grip slippery prey, much as the serrations in the bill of a merganser are used today.*

birds'). These forms show their own peculiarities and may not be direct links between *Archaeopteryx* and modern birds. Also fascinating are specimens of Odontornithes ('toothed birds') from the late Cretaceous period, some 70 million years ago. They include fossils of two marine birds, the gull- or tern-like *Ichthyornis*, which had a deep sternum indicating powerful flight muscles, and the cormorant-like, flightless, *Hesperornis*. The latter retained *Archaeopteryx*-style teeth, presumably used (like the serrations in a merganser's bill) for gripping fishes; it is not clear whether *Ichthyornis* had teeth or not. Also still to be resolved is whether *Hesperornis* was 'secondarily' flightless (i.e. had winged ancestors) or was part of an avian line that never evolved flight.

Over the past 50 million years birds have left many fossils. They are most interesting for showing us kinds of birds that have gone extinct — such as *Diatryma*, a 2 m tall American flightless predator with an impressive hooked bill; the huge elephant birds of Madagascar that stood as much as 3 m tall and may have weighed 450 kg; and the equally gigantic moas of New Zealand.

SEE: Feathered Dinosaurs, p. 299; Natural Selection, p. 297; Bills, p. 391. REFS: Cracraft, 1986, 1988; Martin, 1983; Sanz *et al.*, 1988.

Barbary Partridge

Alectoris barbara

ATLAS 113; PMH 89; PER 146; HFP 102; HPCW 73; NESTS 122; BWP2:469

		10–14 (8–18) 1 brood	P3		
BLDS: ?		INCU: ?	FLDG: ♂♀		
Monogamy		?	See below		

Breeding habitat Rocky hillsides, barren or with scrub or dry forest.

Displays Like other patridges, has head-tilting, side-showing, and circling displays but apparently does not droop wings.

Nesting Nest is scrape on ground, under shelter of bushes; little lining. Eggs pale cream with fine red speckles, 41mm, hatch synchronously. Uncertain whether there are simultaneous broods (see Red-legged Partridge). Young probably similar to other Partridges in their ability to fly when very small, but taking several additional weeks to attain full size.

Diet Little known; young leaves are apparently important; chicks may take insects.

Winters Resident.

Conservation Decreased where heavily hunted, introduced into other areas. See p. 529.

Essays Precocial and Altricial Young, p. 401; Wing Shapes and Flight, p. 269.

Sand Partridge

Ammoperdix heyi

ATLAS 115; PMH -; PER -; HFP 104; HPCW 75; NESTS 126; BWP2:476

		5–7 1 brood	P3		
BLDS: ?		INCU: ?	FLDG: ?		
Monogamy?		?	?	Insects	

Breeding habitat Steep slopes, with rocks and little vegetation in desert areas, usually near some water.

Displays Not known, apparently.

Nesting Nest is scrape on ground, usually unlined, or lined with a little grass and stems. Eggs light buff, 37mm.

Diet Plant material and insects.

Winters Resident. Sometimes in small groups.

Conservation Limited and poorly-known distribution in Arabia, Egypt, and extreme SE of the area covered by this guide.

Essays Precocial and Altricial Young, p. 401; Wing Shapes and Flight, p. 269.

Dominance Hierarchies

IT all started with hens. Norwegian scientist Thorleif Schjelderup-Ebbe wondered how peace was kept in their flocks, and conducted a series of experiments to find out. He discovered that things were tranquil only in established flocks, in which each hen knew its place. And the hens learned their places in fights over chicken feed. Once a hen had been bested in a squabble, it henceforth would defer to the victor. Each hen knew whom it could dominate, and by whom it would be dominated. A 'peck order' was thus established in the flock and functioned to maintain social stability. The hens could recognize many other hens and could remember their relative dominance status. One hen demonstrated the ability to recognize 27 other individuals belonging to four different flocks. As you would expect, the birds at the top of the peck order benefited both by increased access to food and by avoidance of injuries (even bullies can get hurt in fights). The birds at the bottom, while having to wait until those higher up had eaten their fill, at least were not subjected to continuous fights that they were likely to lose.

Dominance hierarchies in pigeons are less rigid than those studied by Schjelderup-Ebbe, for an interesting reason. The ability of a bird to obtain food in a competitive situation depends not just on its own fighting ability, but that of its mate as well. For instance, when there is only room for one individual to feed, its mate (either sex) will 'patrol', driving off other birds so its partner can feed in peace. Thus a pigeon's position in the hierarchy will change with the degree of support provided by its mate. Passerines show similar dominance hierarchies. Dominant Great Tits, for example, are most successful at obtaining food at a feeder, and have to wait less time before feeding.

In all but polyandrous species of birds (those where one female mates with more than one male), males are normally dominant over females. That is especially true in the early stages of pair formation, although in some buntings and other finches and in some gulls, a reversal of dominance, with the male becoming subordinate, reportedly occurs after the pair bond is established. In experiments, females have been able to assume higher ranks in dominance hierarchies after receiving injections of male hormones or having their feathers dyed to resemble male plumage. Results of such experiments varied from species to species; doses of male hormone increased the social status of female Chaffinches and Japanese Quail (*Coturnix japonica*), but not of Starlings. Dyeing breast feathers of female Chaffinches red (like those of males) also increased their social status.

It is usually assumed that a high position in a dominance hierarchy increases the chances of survival and also increases reproductive output, and this is sometimes the case. In species where males display on leks, the dominant male generally holds the best territory on the lek and successfully

Black Francolin
Francolinus francolinus

ATLAS 114; PMH 89; PER -; HFP 104; HPCW 76; NESTS 127; BWP2:479

BLDS: ? Monogamy	8–12 (7–18) 1 brood INCU: ♀ 18–19	FLDG: ♂♀ ?	Insects	Foliage glean

Breeding habitat Tall dry scrub and forests, usually near water.

Displays Not well known. Most conspicuous displays are by ♂s which sing cricket-like song from exposed perches. In courtship, ♂ circles ♀, with head back, tail spread, and wings dragging on ground.

Nesting Nest is scrape on ground, usually unlined or lined with a little grass and stems. Eggs light brown or yellowish-olive, sometimes with white spots, 42mm, hatch asynchronously,

apparently – unlike most other game birds.

Diet Seeds and insects.

Winters Resident.

Conservation Has declined in W of range (formerly widespread in Greece) and became extinct in Europe. Occurs across to India and introduced into a number of places worldwide including Italy, where once native.

Essays Precocial and Altricial Young, p. 401; Wing Shapes and Flight, p. 269.

Double-spurred Francolin
Francolinus bicalcaratus

ATLAS 114; PMH -; PER -; HFP 104; HPCW 76; NESTS 128; BWP2:483

 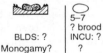 

BLDS: ? Monogamy?	5–7 ? brood INCU: ? ?	FLDG: ? ?		

Breeding habitat Open woodlands, palm groves, usually in river valleys.

Displays Not well known.

Nesting Nest well concealed in thick cover lined with vegetation and feathers. Eggs sandy-coloured, sometimes with sparse white spots, 42mm.

Diet Seeds, berries, leaves, and insects.

Winters Resident.

Conservation Very local in Morocco (once more common). More widespread in W Africa.

Essays Precocial and Altricial Young, p. 401; Wing Shapes and Flight, p. 269.

copulates with the greatest number of females. In monogamous species, however, it is not clear that dominant individuals have a better chance of survival than subordinates.

One study indicating this was done on juvenile Song Sparrows (*Melospiza melodia*) on an island near Victoria, British Columbia, Canada. It showed that dominance relationships at millet-provisioned feeders during summer were reflected in chances for surviving the subsequent winter and establishing a territory the following spring. In two consecutive years, dominant males showed 35 and 22 per cent better survival than subordinate males. For dominant females the equivalent figures were 32 and 33 per cent. The effects on successful settlement of territories were similar for both sexes — dominant individuals were more likely to settle into territories than subordinates.

A correlation between dominance and survival also could be inferred from studies of wintering Norwegian Willow Tits in which dominant adults largely excluded subordinate juveniles from the upper half of trees, where the risk of being caught by Sparrowhawks or small owls was lower.

The Song Sparrow study showed that sex and age were the major determinants of dominance. Males more frequently dominated females than vice versa, winning about 60 per cent of their encounters with females at the feeders. Among juveniles, time since hatching had a strong effect on the success of encounters, even when only 24 days separated the oldest juvenile from the youngest. In contrast, no effect of body size on dominance was detected; a small bird was as likely to dominate a larger one as the reverse. Overall, it appeared that after sex and age, previous experience in encounters was the most important factor in achieving dominance. Thus, early nesting would appear to be the best reproductive strategy for Song Sparrows: young produced early in the season will gain the most experience and are the most likely to survive to reproduce. But if nesting is started too early, offspring may be killed by food shortage or late winter storms. Undoubtedly, there is a fine ecological line between reaping the advantages of early nesting and suffering the consequences of premature breeding.

It has been suggested that in many circumstances being dominant is no more advantageous than being subordinate. For example, a dominant male may obtain a territory that is more resource-rich than that of a subordinate, but it may have to spend much more energy to protect it. Therefore, costs and benefits may more or less balance one another at each level in a dominance hierarchy, and evolution may favour the maintenance of the hierarchy itself. If those near the top were always the most successful at surviving and reproducing, that could lead to the disappearance of differences in dominance. Such a situation in which selection leads to the coexistence of several different modes of behaviour has been called by British evolutionist John Maynard Smith a 'mixed evolutionarily stable strategy'. Thus what started with hens has become a major topic of interest to evolutionary ecologists.

SEE: Bird Badges, p. 433; Natural Selection, p. 297; Visual Displays, p. 33; Leks, p. 123. REFS: Arcese and Smith, 1985; De Laet, 1985; Hughes, 1987; Lefebvre and Henderson, 1986; Roper, 1986.

Partridge

Perdix perdix

ATLAS 111; PMH 89; PER 104; HFP 102; HPCW 77; NESTS 123; BWP2:486

  ◯ 10–20 (4–29) 1 brood
BLDS: ♀   INCU: ♀
Monogamy   23–25

P3 FLDG: ♂♀ See below   Seeds

Breeding habitat   Wide range of open country including farmland.

Displays   ♂s threaten with upright display, tail jerked. Often much chasing during winter flocks, including ♀s who compete with each other to establish dominance. ♀ often initiates courtship, directing her beak at the barred flanks of the ♂.

Nesting   Territorial. Nest is scrape lined with grass, concealed within vegetation. Eggs buff to brown, 36mm, hatch synchronously. Young capable of flight at 15 days, and reach adult size at about 15 weeks.

Diet   Plants, particularly green leaves, grain and other seeds; small chicks take insects.

Winters   Resident; in flocks.

Conservation   Has declined dramatically in UK and much of Europe following changes in agricultural practices that led to increased mortality of young (which feed on insects). Also declines in other areas, but bird is widespread in Europe, extends into Asia, and has been widely introduced into N America. See p. 529.

Essays   Birds and Agriculture, p. 365; Distraction Displays, p. 175.

Refs   Marchant et al. 1990; Potts 1986 is a book on this species, its decline and the habitat changes that have affected this and other farmland species.

Common Quail

Coturnix coturnix

ATLAS 110; PMH 90; PER 104; HFP 104; HPCW 77; NESTS 127; BWP2:496

   8–13 (7–18) 1 (2) broods
BLDS: ♀   INCU: ♀
Monogamy   17–20
Polygyny

P3 FLDG : ♀ See below   Insects

Breeding habitat   Grassy meadows, corn fields, avoids marshes.

Displays   Highly secretive species and very little known. ♂s arrive on breeding areas first, and attract ♀s by calling in upright posture. ♂s are aggressively territorial and there can be intense fighting between them. ♀ calls and ♂ approaches, circling, dropping one wing.

Nesting   Territorial. Nest is lightly lined with vegetation; in thick cover. Eggs creamy or yellow, marked with very dark brown, 30mm, hatch synchronously. Young fledge at 19 days, but can get off ground at about 11 days. Some ♂s are polygynous, but breeding system is not well known.

Diet   Seeds and insects, taken by scratching ground with beak and feet.

Winters   In Africa and India. Migrates in small flocks.

Conservation   Large fluctuations in western edge of range, and perhaps elsewhere, make general picture unclear, but probably has declined considerably in N. Has wide range in Europe, Asia, and Africa.

Essays   Birds and Agriculture, p. 365.

Swallowing Stones

THE gizzard, a muscular section of the stomach lined with horny plates or ridges, may be characterized as the teeth and jaws of some birds. Within it, grain, acorns, nuts, mussels, and similar hard-shelled materials that have been swallowed whole are rotated every 20 to 30 seconds and crushed. The gizzard can be extraordinarily effective; within 24 hours of ingestion, a turkey can flatten objects that withstand enormous pressure per square centimetre (30 kg/cm^2). The grinding action of the gizzard is often aided by swallowed sand, grit, or a few pebbles. In Ostriches, grit may include stones up to 2.5 cm in diameter.

In the era when diets were commonly investigated by examining stomach contents recovered from dissected birds, detailed lists of gizzard contents were possible, if not always enlightening. Gilbert White, writing in 1770 reported:

Many times have I had the curiosity to open the stomachs of *woodcocks* and *snipes*; but nothing ever occurred that helped to explain to me what their subsistence might be: all that I could ever find was a soft mucus, among which lay many pellucid small gravels.

and, with reference to 'Land' Rails (i.e. Corncrakes),

... the gizzard thick & strong, & filled with many shell-snails, some whole, & many ground to pieces thro' the attrition which is occasioned by the muscular force & motion of that intestine. We saw no gravels among the food: perhaps the shell-snails might perform the functions of gravels or pebbles, & might grind one another.

Today's surveys, however, are often derived from observations of foraging birds. Direct observations have allowed us to verify that the accumulation of grinding aids is more than a bonus swallowed along with food. Granivorous birds are often seen swallowing selected stones, and Willow Grouse have been observed to migrate when deep snow covers their grit supply. The minerals of some grinding materials may provide necessary supplements, especially at certain times of the year. During egg laying, for example, females may actively seek sources of calcium. Ornithologists have speculated that, as in the case of the Common Pheasant, availability of calcium-rich grit may limit the breeding range of some species.

The size of the gizzard and the characteristics of the grinding aids vary depending on diet and available materials. If the composition of the diet changes during the year, so may the quantity or coarseness of the grinding aids. Also, when preferred grinding materials are scarce, others may be substituted: the indigestible heads of beetles, hard seeds, or fruit pits can be used to crush subsequent meals.

Grinding aids are rather coarse in herbivores (finches, gallinaceous birds, wildfowl, etc.) and in those insectivores, such as nightjars, that consume hard-bodied beetles. The gizzards of frugivores (fruit-eaters), nectarivores (nectar-eaters), and birds taking soft-bodied insects may be very reduced and hold at most only fine sand. In birds of prey, and a few other species including

Common Pheasant

Phasianus colchicus

ATLAS 114; PMH 90; PER 102; HFP 106; HPCW 78; NESTS 123; BWP2:504

		○ 7–17 1 brood	P3		
BLDS: ♀		INCU: ♀	FLDG: ♀		
Polygyny		7–15	23–28		
Monogamy			See below	Insects	Foliage glean

Breeding habitat Mainly wooded country, but commonly moves out of woodland to feed. In native range, valleys and river bottoms in mountainous and semi-arid habitats.

Displays ♂s have 'crowing' display, call from prominent perch, with wings flapping. ♂ circles ♀ and droops wings towards her.

Nesting Territorial. Nest is usually unlined in thick cover. Eggs light greenish or olive, 45mm, hatch synchronously. Young can fly at about 12 days, become independent at 10–12 weeks. ♂s may mate with 2 or (many) more ♀s. ♀ will lay her eggs in nest of other pheasants and, sometimes, in the nest of other birds.

Diet A variety of plant parts and invertebrates, taken by scratching the ground or digging with beak. Young chicks take mainly insects.

Winters Resident; in flocks.

Conservation Widely introduced in Europe and to N America (UK in 14th century). In UK, perhaps 10 million birds released and shot each year. Introduced in Finland about 1900, birds were vulnerable to cold winters, though now seem somewhat adapted to them. Pheasant introductions include a variety of recognizable subspecies, including birds with and without white neck bands, more or less white on the wing, or birds that are darkly coloured. Occurs across Europe, C and E Asia.

Essays Sexual Selection, p. 149; Population Dynamics, p. 515; Swallowing Stones, p. 135.

Refs Marchant et al. 1990.

Helmeted Guineafowl

Numida meleagris

ATLAS 116; PMH- ; PER -; HFP 100; HPCW 78; NESTS 121; BWP2:523

		○ 8–12 1 brood?	? ◐P3		
BLDS: ♀ ?		INCU:♀ ?			
Monogamy		24–25	FLDG:♀ (♂?)	Insects	

Breeding habitat Woody or bushy ravines, into savannas, grasslands, and agricultural land.

Displays Poorly known; birds often fight in flocks.

Nesting Nest is unlined or sparsely lined with vegetation in thick cover. Eggs creamy-buff, 49mm, hatch synchronously. Unusually large clutches may indicate bigamous ♂s, but mating system is thought to be monogamous, usually.

Diet Plant parts and insects.

Winters Resident; in flocks.

Conservation While widespread in Africa, now has very limited range and extremely small numbers in Morocco.

Essays Precocial and Altricial Young, p. 401; Wing Shapes and Flight, p. 269.

kingfishers and herons, the gizzard accumulates and consolidates indigestible portions of prey items into pellets and retains them until they are regurgitated. The gizzard is credited with permitting more diversified diets by releasing the nutrients from well-sealed seeds or armoured animals. By ingesting fairly coarse grit, the Greater Flamingo is able to digest snails filtered from mud, freeing it from competition with the sand-ingesting Lesser Flamingo, whose diet is limited to algae and diatoms. Some birds have special digestive problems that are not solved in the gizzard. Grebes, which ingest sharp, potentially harmful fish bones, habitually swallow their own feathers. The feather balls found in their stomachs are thought to embed dangerous bone tips. Leaf-eating South American Hoatzins (*Opisthocomus hoazin*) use their oesophagus and crop to ferment their fibrous diet before it reaches the gizzard.

Today, swallowing stones has a maladaptive side effect for many aquatic birds that select spent ammunition in the form of lead pellets as grinding aids. Hunters and conservationists have been in search of replacement ammunition made of steel or other non-toxic materials and substitutes are now widely employed. Lead anglers' weights posed a similar problem. In some British river systems, for example, Mute Swan populations were severely harmed in the mid-1980s. In the English Midlands more than half of the Mute Swans tested were found to have died from lead poisoning. A similar proportion was found on the River Thames. Since a 1987 ban on the sale of lead angling weights, there has been a welcome reduction in lead poisoning.

Aquatic birds will continue swallowing grinding materials; the question is whether they will continue to poison themselves by swallowing lead. The extent and seriousness of lead pellet ingestion may be managed to some degree by keeping water levels too deep for dabbling and by supplying alternative sources of grit. In France, experiments in a grit-deficient area of the Carmargue demonstrated that providing grit can reduce the incidence of pellet ingestion. In addition, Mallards provided with calcium-rich grit show overall lower mortality from lead ingestion. Dietary calcium, if present in adequate quantities, apparently can reduce the absorption of lead through the gastrointestinal tract.

SEE: Flamingo Feeding, p. 37; Pellets, p. 257; Diet and Nutrition, p. 493; Metabolism, p. 281. REFS: Barrentin, 1980; Jenkinson and Mengel, 1970; Mudge, 1983; Perrins and Middleton, 1985; Rundel, 1982; Sanderson and Bellrose, 1986; White, 1789.

The Colour of Birds

BIRDS are, hands down, the most colourful terrestrial vertebrates — only insects and coral reef fishes rival them among animals. Birds, like butterflies and moths, have two basic sources of colour. The more common is pigments,

Andalusian Hemipode

Turnix sylvatica

ATLAS 116; PMH 91; PER 104; HFP 110; HPCW 78; NESTS 130; BWP2:529

  4 (3–5) brood? INCU: ♂ 12–14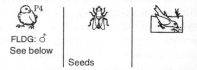

		4 (3–5) brood? INCU: ♂ 12–14			Seeds
BLDS: ♂♀ Monogamy Polyandry?			FLDG: ♂ See below		

Breeding habitat Range of open country with scrub. Isolated populations, in area covered by this guide, frequent palmetto scrub.

Displays Not well known, but unusual in that ♀ is larger and brighter and takes the lead during courtship. ♀'s call accompanies her body swelling up and shrinking down ('pumping') to attract ♂.

Nesting Nest is scrape lined with grasses, in thick cover. Eggs buff with black and reddish speckles, 26mm, hatch synchronously. Young fly first at about two weeks, become independent at 18–20 days and fully grown at about 1 month. ♀ courtship and pattern of incubation suggest polyandry, with ♀ laying more than one clutch for different ♂s to rear. The highly secretive habits make the situation uncertain, however.

Diet Insects and seeds.

Winters Resident.

Conservation Widespread in Africa and India, but very local, isolated, and fragmented range in area, probably indicates earlier, more extensive distribution. Once bred in Sicily. Very secretive habits has prevented accurate assessent of numbers. See p. 528.

Notes Hemipodes, or button quails as they are also known, are not related to the quails and pheasants. They were once placed in the order Gruiformes, (the order that contains the cranes, rails, and bustards), but modern DNA analyses suggest they belong to an order of their own.

Essays Birds and Agriculture, p. 365; Polyandry, p. 195.

Refs Sibley and Monroe 1990.

Water Rail

Rallus aquaticus

ATLAS 120; PMH 91; PER 106; HFP 114; HPCW 79; NESTS 131; BWP2: 537

		6–11 (5–16) 2 broods INCU: ♂♀			
Ground	BLDS: ♂♀ Monogamy	19–22	FLDG: ♂♀ 20–30	Greens	Surface dips

Breeding habitat Marshes with thick vegetation.

Displays Vocal (and more often seen than heard). Calls at night. Rivals may charge at each other, with neck forward and head lowered (sometimes mated pairs do this towards rival).

Nesting Nest is made of reeds, aquatic plants; on or near water in thick cover. Eggs creamy white, with reddish-brown spots, 36mm, hatch synchronously. Young brooded on nest by one parent while other brings food.

Diet Aquatic insects, with some plant matter, and sometimes small

vertebrates. Wades (sometimes swims) in shallow water, taking items near surface.

Winters Resident in W and S, migrates from C and E Europe to SW, and to Iraq and India.

Conservation Expansion in NW; elsewhere obvious increases in numbers. Range covers much of Europe across Asia.

Essays Thin as a Rail, p. 141; Wetland Conservation, p. 145.

Refs Marchant et al. 1990; Ripley 1977 is a book on all the rails and crakes of the world.

which are chemical compounds located in the feathers or skin. Pigments absorb some wavelengths of light and reflect others; it is the reflected light that reaches our eyes. The colour we perceive is a function of the wavelength of the light stimulating the receptors of our retinas. In the visual part of the electromagnetic spectrum, we see the shortest wavelengths as 'violet' and the longest as 'red'. Thus a Yellow Wagtail has pigment in its breast feathers that absorbs all the wavelengths except the ones that, when they enter our visual system, register as yellow. When no light is reflected we see black; when all wavelengths are reflected we see white.

Blue and iridescent colours in feathers are never produced by pigments, however. They are 'structural colours'. Blues are produced by minute particles in the feather that are smaller in diameter than the wavelength of red light. These particles are able to influence only shorter wavelengths, which appear blue, and are 'scattered' — reflected in all directions. Thus structural blue colours remain the same when they are viewed at different angles in reflected light. If, however, they are viewed by transmitted light (that is, with the feather between the light source and the observer), the blue disappears.

Iridescent colours are produced by differential reflection of wavelengths from highly modified barbules of the feathers that are rotated so that a flat surface faces the incoming light. The detailed structure of the barbule reflects some wavelengths and absorbs others, and the reflected wavelength changes with the angle of reflection. The structural colour is registered by the eye in response to the reflected wavelengths and changes with the angle formed by the light, the reflecting surface, and the eye.

Just as bird songs did not evolve to please the human ear, bird colours did not evolve to delight our eyes. The most spectacular colours typically function to impress members of the same species. The classic example is the tail of the peacock, but the brilliant colours of the breeding male Golden Oriole or male Rock Thrush illustrate the same phenomenon. Non-demonstrative colours commonly help a bird avoid predation. The camouflage of an eider female on her nest is an example of such cryptic coloration.

Many inconspicuous birds exhibit what is known as 'countershading'; they are darkest along the back, and gradually become lighter down the sides until the belly is pure white. Countershading tends to eliminate a sharply defined shadow, since the bird absorbs the most light above, where the light is brightest, and reflects the most light below, where the light is dimmest. The vast majority of shorebirds are countershaded, although the division between darker back and lighter belly may be rather sharp, for example in the Kentish Plover.

'Disruptive' coloration — the use of striking patterns to break up the outline of the bird — is another technique for avoiding detection. Ringed Plovers, for example, are very difficult to see in some circumstances. The extreme in cryptic coloration, of course, is found among those birds that simply take on the colour of the background against which they live. Ptarmigans in their pure white winter plumage are the classic example.

Birds often use colours to identify themselves to other members of their flock and thus help to hold it together. Examples include the colour patterns

Spotted Crake

Porzana porzana

ATLAS 120; PMH 92; PER 106; HFP 114; HPCW 79; NESTS 131; BWP2:545

  8–12 (6–15) 2 broods INCU: ♂♀ 18–19 per egg

| Floating | BLDS: ♂♀ Monogamy | INCU: ♂♀ 18–19 per egg | FLDG: ♂♀ > 25? | Greens |

Breeding habitat Thick vegetation in extensive marshes.

Displays Not well known. Calling ♂s attract ♀s and birds may duet. ♀ approaches ♂ and then 'escapes', leading to a courtship chase until she allows ♂ to catch up.

Nesting Territorial. Nest is a thick cup of reeds, sedges, etc. in dense cover, near water. Eggs olive-brown, covered with reddish-brown and grey spots, 34mm, hatch asynchronously, but all young leave nest at same time.

Diet Aquatic invertebrates and plants, picked up on or near water, while bird remains in close cover.

Winters In Africa and India.

Conservation Secretive habits prevent an accurate assessment of numbers. Like many obligate marsh nesters species is vulnerable to wetland drainage, and occurs sporadically at edge of its range in S and W. Occurs across Europe into adjacent areas of Asia. See p. 528.

Essays Thin as a Rail, p. 141; Wetland Conservation, p. 145.

Refs Ripley 1977.

Little Crake

Porzana parva

ATLAS 121; PMH 92; PER 106; HFP 114; HPCW 79; NESTS 132; BWP2:555

  7–9 (4–11) 1 (–2) broods INCU: ♂♀ 15–17 per egg

| Ground | BLDS:♂(♀?) Monogamy | INCU: ♂♀ 15–17 per egg | FLDG: ♂♀ 45–50 | Greens | Surface dips |

Breeding habitat Thick marshy vegetation, especially reeds, slightly wetter habitats than Spotted Crake.

Displays Very little known.

Nesting Territorial. Nest is small cup of sedges or other plant material, in thick cover above or near water. Eggs buff, spotted and blotched brown, 30mm, hatch asynchronously. Takes from 21–23 days for complete clutch to hatch.

Diet Similar to Spotted Crake, but more aquatic habits means that it will also feed while swimming, like Water Rail.

Winters Mainly in Africa.

Conservation Secretive habits means that numbers are difficult to assess. Like many obligate marsh nesters is vulnerable to wetland drainage, and occurs sporadically at edge of its range in S and W. Also, uses rice paddies and fish ponds in C and E Europe. Occurs across Europe into adjacent areas of Asia. See p. 528.

Essays Thin as a Rail, p. 141.

Refs Ripley 1977.

Disruptive coloration. The alternating pattern of white and black on the head and neck break up the outline of the Ringed Plover and make it more difficult to see against a variegated background than a bird that is uniformly light or dark.

revealed in flight by shorebirds such as Turnstones and Black-tailed Godwit. Colours found in the mouths of gaping chicks may function to stimulate parental feeding. Other colours may direct the feeding movements of the young, as does the red spot on the lower mandible of Herring, Lesser Black-backed, and other gulls, which encourage the young to solicit food.

Some colours are apparently produced incidentally by pigments deposited for other reasons. For instance, the tips of the outer wing feathers are subjected to more wear than those nearer the base of the wing. And feathers containing pigments are more resistant to wear than those without. That is thought to be the reason that the wingtips of many mostly white birds, such as many gulls, terns, pelicans, and gannets, are dark.

SEE: Feathers, p. 363; Moulting, p. 373; Eclipse Plumage, p. 53; Bird Badges, p. 433; Black and White Plumage, p. 7; Visual Displays, p. 33. REFS: Baker and Parker, 1979; Butcher and Rohwer, 1990.

Thin as a Rail

WHY, since rails and crakes tend to be widely distributed, are the two species breeding in Britain and the Continent often absent from life lists of bird-watchers? Granted, Baillon's, Spotted, and Little Crakes are protected (they are listed in Annex I of the Birds Directive, see p. 528), but their populations are not exceptionally sparse, and the Water Rail is abundant enough to be hunted legally in Europe. Apparently the reason lies not in their numbers, but in their behaviour. These birds are so secretive that they move about unnoticed, slipping into wetland vegetation without causing much of a ripple. In situations where other wetland birds take flight and depart emitting

Baillon's Crake

Porzana pusilla

ATLAS 120; PMH 89; PER 106; HFP 114; HPCW 80; NESTS 132; BWP2:562

		6–8 (4–11) 1 (2?) broods			
	BLDS: ♂♀?	INCU: ♂♀	FLDG: ♂♀		
Ground	Monogamy	14–16 per egg			Surface dips

Breeding habitat Thick vegetation in marshes and ponds. Very similar in habitats to Little Crake, apparently preferring denser, shorter vegetation.

Displays Very little known.

Nesting Nest is small cup of leaves and other plant material, in thick cover above or near water. Eggs yellow buff, streaked and spotted with brown, 29mm, hatch asynchronously. Takes from 17–20 days for complete clutch to hatch.

Diet Similar to Spotted Crake, but more aquatic habits means that it more often feeds while swimming, like Water Rail.

Winters Migration routes are poorly known. Birds winter in India, but there are records of migrants in the Sahara, suggesting Africa as a destination for European birds.

Conservation Secretive habits means that numbers are not well known. Like many obligate marsh nesters, is vulnerable to wetland drainage, and occurs sporadically at edge of its range in S and W. Range extends across Asia to Japan, and to Africa and Australia. See p. 528.

Essays Thin as a Rail, p. 141; Wetland Conservation, p. 145.

Refs Ripley 1977.

Corncrake

Crex crex

ATLAS 119; PMH 93; PER 106; HFP 114; HPCW 80; NESTS 132; BWP2:570

		8–12 (6–14) 1 (2?) broods			
	BLDS: ♀?	INCU: ♀	FLDG: ♀, ♂♀		
	Monogamy	16–19	34–38	Greens	Foliage glean

Breeding habitat Moist meadows; formerly agricultural fields, but mechanized mowing has led to a decline (See Below).

Displays Calling ♂s often approach other rivals and call at each other at close range. If the intruder is not discouraged by this, then the birds will fight.

Nesting Territorial. Nest is a cup of leaves or grasses in thick cover. Eggs pale greenish or brownish, spotted with reddish-browns and greys, 37mm, hatch synchronously.

Diet Invertebrates, green plants, and seeds, and possibly small vertebrates, picked off ground or plants.

Winters Migrates to Africa.

Conservation Sharp declines in W followed mechanization of agriculture, particularly the cutting of meadows earlier in the season, and reduced plant and insect diversity. Has been lost from England, and 90 per cent of UK population is now on islands off Scotland. Now sporadic and local in W, but species occurs across Europe into Asia. See p. 528.

Essays Thin as a Rail, p. 141; Birds and Agriculture, p. 365; Listing Birds in Danger, p. 526.

Refs Ripley 1977; Marchant et al. 1990.

harsh calls, rails and crakes often move silently. As Audubon wrote of Clapper Rails (a North American *Rallus*, similar to the Water Rail) in his *Birds of America* (1842):

On the least appearance of danger, they lower the head, stretch out the neck, and move off with incomparable speed, always in perfect silence . . . they have a power of compressing their body to such a degree as frequently to force a passage between two stems so close that one could hardly believe it possible for them to squeeze themselves through.

Unlike highly visible, skittering waders that run and pause in pursuit of the tide-line, deliberately stepping, cryptically coloured rails and crakes are usually hard to spot. On the rare occasions when they are in the open, rails tend to act as though they cannot be seen. Such apparent indifference to discovery is sometimes mistaken for boldness, but more likely indicates that they do not recognize a human being 20 metres away as a potential threat. Even their fibrous, domed nests fade into the grass. Their generally elusive behaviour causes difficulty for conservationists trying to census populations and learn enough about their ecology to implement effective management practices.

Mystery long surrounded the calls of these birds and, for a while, voices of some species were misdescribed and misattributed. Calls are limited mostly to the breeding season (although the Water Rail is conspicuously vocal during winter), and positive identification of their vocalizations awaited the success-ful use of tape-recordings to attract the birds within visual range. Other than their unseen acoustic advertisements, tell-tale evidence of the presence of rails consists of little more than their tracks, pelleted remains of meals, and splattered white droppings.

Their disappearing acts also work in water. Although normally buoyant, some species readily submerge, dive when pressed, and speed their paddling by using wings underwater. In fact, their main non-human predators are predatory fish that feed on their young.

Elusive rails and crakes may also use a tail-jerk display to confuse observers. During the display, the tail is cocked upward and the head (which usually bobs with each footfall) is frozen still. This posture is thought by some to permit a steady view of the foraging area while allowing the head to be mistaken for the tail.

Many birdwatchers search for these 'feathered mice' at dawn or dusk when the birds may come forth to bathe and preen at the water's edge. But it would not be surprising if searching for these furtive creatures proves ever more frustrating. The disappearance of a rail seen ambling amid the marsh grasses may be illusory, but the disappearance of high-quality rail habitat is not.

SEE: Wetland Conservation; p. 145; Birds and the Law, p. 521; Birds and Agriculture, p. 367; Pellets, p. 257. REFS: Audubon, 1842; Bollinger and Bowes, 1973; Meanley, 1985; Reynard and Harty, 1968; Ripley, 1977.

Moorhen

Gallinula chloropus

ATLAS 119; PMH 93; PER 108; HFP 116; HPCW 81; NESTS 133; BWP2:578

 Floating	 BLDS: ♂♀ Monogamy	5–9 (2–13) 2–(3) broods INCU: ♂♀ 21–22	 FLDG: ♂♀ 40–50	Aq inverts	Dabbles

Breeding habitat A wide variety of freshwater habitats with fringing vegetation.

Displays Chases off rivals by running after intruder with head down and flapping wings. Rivals may display by raising and spreading tail, arching wings, and lowering head and neck. Rivals may also face each other standing upright. There may be extensive fights. Mated pairs have bowing, bill-dipping, and mutual preening displays, as well as chases.

Nesting Territorial. Nest, in vegetation on ground near water or floating in water, is mass of vegetation with cup lined with grass. Occasionally in bushes. Eggs light brown, spotted with dark reddish-brown or black, 43mm, hatch synchronously. Young are looked after by both parents and young of early broods sometimes help their parents care for their siblings in later broods. See essay on Cooperative Breeding, p. 275.

Diet A variety of plant and invertebrate food taken while swimming, by dipping head under water, up-ending, or while walking on land or aquatic vegetation.

Winters Resident in S and W where waters do not freeze, leaves N and E. Often in loose flocks.

Conservation Has spread northwards in Europe and has a worldwide distribution.

Notes Birds using small, shallow, water bodies are particularly vulnerable to hard winters.

Essays Nest Sites and Materials, p. 443; Transporting Young, p. 9.

Purple Gallinule

Porphyrio porphyrio

ATLAS 119; PMH 94; PER 106; HFP 116; HPCW 81; NESTS 133; BWP2:592

	 BLDS: ♂♀ Monogamy	3–5 (2–7) 1 brood (2?) INCU: ♂♀ 22–25	 FLDG: ♂♀ > 60?	 Ground glean

Breeding habitat Swamps with reedy edges, to narrow or sheltered lakes, or slow-moving rivers.

Displays Rivals in erect posture will flick tails or adopt hunched position with head down. In courtship, displays are similar to Moorhen's with bowing, courtship feeding, and mutual preening.

Nesting Nest is platform of aquatic plants above water. Eggs pale buff, spotted with reddish-brown or grey, 55mm, hatch synchronously. European gallinules are apparently territorial and monogamous, but elsewhere in range birds are cooperative breeders (that is, several birds help at the nest, or help defend territory). The additional birds may include young of previous years, or several ♀s laying in one nest.

Diet Mainly plants, but will take a variety of insects and small vertebrates. Powerful bill and feet allow birds to climb into vegetation to get at seed heads or to pull up vegetation to eat soft roots.

Winters Resident; often in loose flocks.

Conservation European populations are small, isolated and threatened by marsh drainage, but species has wide distribution across Africa, S Asia to Australia and New Zealand. See p. 528.

Essays Wetland Conservation, p. 145; Cooperative Breeding, p. 275.

Wetland Conservation

THE disappearance of British wetlands, swamps, and fens has been closely followed by the disappearance of birds. Drainage began in earnest in the seventeenth century, and as the habitat disappeared, so numbers of Black Terns, Ruffs, Avocets, Savi's Warblers, cranes, Spoonbills, Black-tailed Godwits, Marsh Harriers, and Bearded Tits dwindled. But it wasn't until the Second World War that changes in agricultural practices accelerated wetland losses to unprecedented rates. Acreage of grazing marsh in north Kent, for example, has been halved from some 15 000 hectares to less than 8000. Since the 1970s Dunlin populations have been halved, and since the 1980s Redshank numbers have dropped by 25 per cent. The trend is not yet slowing. In a survey of 123 estuaries recently reported by Philip Rothwell, fully 80 are at risk — if not from the development of marinas and industry or the expansion of ports, then from pollution, barrages, and land reclamation projects. These sites are important to some two million geese, swans, ducks, and waders that rely on wetlands in the winter. Many other birds depend upon wetland staging grounds during migration.

Efforts to halt British wetland loss have been as unprecedented as the damage. In 1965, for example, the Duke of Edinburgh launched Enterprise Neptune, a campaign to protect 900 miles of coasts of England and Wales. It reached its 500-mile mark in 1988 and, at current costs of £15 a foot, needs £31 million to protect the remaining 400 miles. Nineteen years after the inception of Enterprise Neptune, an area on the Hampshire coast close to the mouth of the Beaulieu River was declared the first bird sanctuary under the Wildlife and Countryside Act. The area includes Gull Island and Warren Shore Island. Access to the former is forbidden year-round and the latter is closed to the public during the breeding season March 1 to July 31. Offences against the birds carry fines of up to £1000.

Through the protection of areas of outstanding natural beauty, some 4000 sites of Special Scientific Interest, and the efforts of volunteer conservation organizations, there is hope for the remaining wetlands of England and Wales. Indeed, one of the world's best-known centres for the study of wetland species, the Wildfowl and Wetlands Trust, has been in operation at Slimbridge, Gloucestershire, for more than forty years. Public support for habitat conservation, in general, has been accelerating, and the Royal Society for Nature Conservation, the umbrella body representing 46 associated nature conservation trusts, has acquired more than 120 000 acres in some 1600 nature reserves. The public is increasingly sensitive to the degradation of the wetlands that remain. The filling in of two hectares of reedbed near Weymouth, which put at risk breeding Bearded Tits and Cetti's Warblers in 1985, kept Lodmoor, Dorset, under media scrutiny. Nonetheless, protected

Coot
Fulica atra

ATLAS 118; PMH 94; PER 108; HFP 116; HPCW 82; NESTS 134; BWP2:599

	6–10 (1–13) 1–2 broods			
BLDS: ♂♀ Monogamy	INCU: ♂♀ 21–24	FLDG: ♂♀ 55–60	Aq inverts	Ground glean

Breeding habitat A variety of open, but vegetation-fringed lakes and rivers
Displays Generally similar to Moorhen. Rivals patter across water, flapping wings, with head down, or swim at each other with heads down, wings arched, and tails raised and fanned. Pairs have bowing, mutual preening, and courtship chases.
Nesting Territorial. Nest is pile of dead vegetation usually hidden in reeds. Eggs light brown, finely spotted with dark brown or black, 53mm, hatch asynchronously. Young stay with parents until fledged.
Diet Mainly plants, but some aquatic insects. Uses a variety of feeding methods, including picking from surface of water, from vegetation near water, up-ending, diving, or moving onto land to graze. More likely to be in open water and to dive than Moorhen.
Winters Resident in W, moves onto more open water. Migratory in east towards S and W. Usually in flocks.
Conservation Has moved N in last century; has benefited from man-made waters. Sharp declines after severe winters in N. Is widely distributed across Europe, Asia, and Australia.
Essays Piracy, p. 213; Feet, p. 289; Transporting Young, p. 9; Wetland Conservation, p. 145.

Crested Coot
Fulica cristata

ATLAS 118; PMH 94; PER 108; HFP 116; HPCW 82; NESTS 134; BWP2:612

	5–7 (4–11) 1 brood?			
BLDS: ♂♀ Monogamy	INCU: ♂♀ 18–20 (–22)	FLDG: ♂♀ ?	Aq inverts	Ground glean

Breeding habitat Vegetated marsh and lake edges; very similar to Coot.
Displays Where known, similar to Coot.
Nesting Nest is pile of dead vegetation hidden in reeds, over water. Eggs pale grey with fine reddish to dark brown speckling, 54mm.
Diet Like Coot and feeds in similar ways.
Winters Resident, in flocks.
Conservation Threatened with imminent extinction in Europe, with numbers falling to under a dozen in the 1970s. Local, isolated populations in Morocco. Main range of the species is in Africa S of the Sahara, Madagascar. See p. 528.
Notes Differences in ecology and behaviour from Coot are not well described.
Essays Listing Birds in Danger, p. 526; Wetland Conservation, p. 145.

land always remains somewhat at risk, and inquiry into how well (or badly) management is progressing must be pursued without fail.

The draining of swamps, fens, and wetlands on the Continent has also displaced many species, including Dalmatian and White Pelicans, Great White Egrets, Pygmy Cormorants, Spoonbills, Glossy Ibises, and Ruddy Shelducks. The largest remaining areas of primeval marshlands are centred in the southeastern countries. Although to some degree protected, these areas, too, remain under threat. Even the species-rich reserves at the mouth of the Danube in Romania are compromised by large-scale reed exploitation.

Preventing drainage of remaining wetlands is not sufficient to guard today's mix of wetland species. Many birds are sensitive to disturbance from even the most well-intended nature enthusiast. The mere presence of anglers, for example, is enough to reduce the nesting success of wetland birds. After angling was prohibited on the Austrian side of the Lower Inn River, a 'Ramsar' site (see Wildlife and the Law, p. 520), water bird populations increased markedly. Unfortunately, threats from water sports are not limited to the breeding season. There is a growing tendency for canoeists and anglers (using boats) to pursue their sports in winter. Counts made in Germany's Ermatinger Becken/Bodensee indicate that during 1986–1987 boats made up just over one-third of the disturbance factors but were responsible for two-thirds of the disturbances to wetland birds. When flocks of a thousand or more were driven to the air, the triggers, nine times out of ten, were boats. Such disturbances affect the distribution of bay birds, and have encouraged up to 40 per cent of the water birds to leave.

Further studies are needed to identify and then confirm apparent trends. Long-term surveys help to verify whether short-term local population changes accurately reflect regional changes among flyway migrants and wintering species. They are critical to wetland bird conservation. An 18-year survey (1966–84) on Coots and Mute Swans in Southern Bavaria, for example, showed a 16 per cent decline in the former, and a 35 per cent increase in the latter per decade, with wide, sometimes opposing, short-term fluctuations. Similarly, local European studies of the Little Grebe confirm negative trends in breeding populations due to habitat loss, even though dramatic fluctuations are clearly evident. In addition to long-term regional censusing, experimental management techniques will help to determine the effectiveness of policy decisions aimed at protecting the growing network of British and Continental wetland reserves. For example, manipulation of the flood water levels on the nature reserve at Elmley on the Isle of Sheppey suggested the possibility of dramatically increasing the numbers of breeding and winter wildfowl. By maintaining appropriate water levels, the 300 Wigeons, 800 Redshanks, 10 Snipes, and 20 Shovelers in 1974/75 increased to 22 000 (a 70-fold increase), 2345, 160, and 423 respectively in 1984/85.

Efforts to recover strategic wetlands in Britain and the Continent are mirrored around the world. In the United States, for example, where more than half the wetland acreage present at the time of settlement is already gone, work is under way in many areas to halt further losses and reclaim

Common Crane

Grus grus

ATLAS 117; PMH 95; PER 108; HFP 110; HPCW 82; NESTS 128; BWP2:618

BLDS: ♂♀ Monogamy	2 (1–3) 1 brood INCU: ♂♀ 30 (28–31)	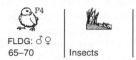 FLDG: ♂♀ 65–70	Insects

Breeding habitat Small swamps, pools, and lakes, within boreal to deciduous woodlands.

Displays Cranes are famous for their dancing displays, which occur throughout year, but mainly in the spring. Starting with a single bird, dances spread throughout the flock. Birds run around with wings beating, suddenly stopping, bowing, and leaping into the air. In courtship, ♂s call to attract ♀s. Pairs call together with bills pointed skywards and wing plumes erect.

Nesting Nest is large mound of vegetation on or near shallow water. Eggs buff to grey or brown, blotched and streaked with reddish-browns, 94mm, hatch asynchronously. Young stay with parents on migration. Age of first breeding uncertain; birds probably pair for life.

Diet A variety of plant material, including roots, seeds, and fruits, also invertebrates and small vertebrates.

Winters In large flocks on large lakes and open fields in traditional areas, in S Europe, N Africa, to Middle East and India. Birds also stop over on traditional resting sites.

Conservation Historical declines in west, once breeding in Britain, Ireland, Spain, Germany. Nesting areas are vulnerable to drainage and disturbance, as are wintering sites and migratory stopovers. Occurs across N Europe, N Asia, SW Asia. See p. 528.

Essays Flock Defence, p. 257; Leks, p. 123; The Avian Sense of Smell, p. 13; Birds on Borders, p. 95; Wetland Conservation, p. 145.

Refs Johnsgard 1983 is a book about this and other species of crane.

Demoiselle Crane

Anthropoides virgo

ATLAS 117; PMH 95; PER 308; HFP 110; HPCW 83 ; NESTS 130; BWP2:631

BLDS: ♂♀? Monogamy	2 (1–3) 1 brood INCU: ♂♀ 27–29	FLDG: ♂♀ 55–60	Insects	

Breeding habitat Open country, grassland, steppes with access to water.

Displays Dance displays and pairs calling together, similar to Common Crane.

Nesting Nest has little or no lining; on ground, usually near water. Eggs pale buff to grey, with dark brown spots, 83mm, hatch synchronously. Young probably stay with adults on migration, breed at 2 years, and probably mate for life.

Diet Mainly plant material (especially grass seeds) and will damage cereal crops on occasion. Will also eat insects and a variety of small vertebrates.

Winters In flocks; in Africa and India in similar habitats (and sometimes with) Common Crane.

Conservation Extinctions in west of range, and Moroccan population extinct or very close to it. Occurs across CIS where status is uncertain.

Essays Flock Defence, p. 257; Leks, p. 123; The Avian Sense of Smell, p. 13; Birds on Borders, p. 95; Wetland Conservation, p. 145.

Refs Johnsgard 1983.

what is not already permanently damaged. On a global scale, however, wetland restoration and conservation is just beginning.

SEE: Wildlife and the Law, p. 520; Birds and Agriculture, p. 365; Birds on Borders, p. 95; Birds and Global Warming, p. 311; The Bewick's of Slimbridge, p. 39. REFS: Bezzel and Engler, 1985; Bezzel and Hashmi, 1989; Howe, 1987; Pain, 1990a,b; Reichholf, 1988; Schneider, 1987; Whitlock, 1981.

Sexual Selection

IT was Charles Darwin who originally proposed that the so-called secondary sexual characteristics of male animals — such as the elaborate tails of Peacocks, the showy neck feathers of Ruffs, the bright plumage of many other birds, and even deep voices in men — evolved because females preferred to mate with individuals that had those features. Sexual selection can be thought of as two special kinds of natural selection, as described below. Natural selection occurs when some individuals out-reproduce others, and those that have more offspring differ genetically from those that have fewer.

In one kind of sexual selection, intra-sexual selection, members of one sex create a reproductive differential among themselves by competing for opportunities to mate. The winners out-reproduce the others, and natural selection occurs if the characteristics that determine winning are, at least in part, inherited. In the other kind of sexual selection, members of one sex create a reproductive differential in the other sex by preferring some individuals as mates. If the ones they prefer are genetically different from the ones they shun, then natural selection is occurring.

In birds, the first form of sexual selection occurs in two main ways. Firstly males can compete among themselves for the resources needed by breeding females. For example male Indian Honeyguides (*Indicator xanthonotus*) defend bees' nests, the wax from which females eat at the start of the breeding season. Secondly, and more commonly, males compete among themselves for territories, as is obvious when those territories are on leks (traditional mating grounds). Males that manage to acquire the best territories on a lek (the dominant males) are known to get more chances to mate with females. In some species of grouse and other such lekking birds, this form of sexual selection combines with the second form, because once males establish their positions on the lek the females then choose among them.

That second type of sexual selection, inter-sexual selection, in which one sex chooses among potential mates of the opposite sex, appears to be the most common type among birds. As evidence that such selection is widespread, consider the reversal of normal sexual differences in the ornamentation of some polyandrous birds. There, the male must choose among females, which, in turn, must be as alluring as possible. Consequently in polyandrous

Little Bustard
Tetrax tetrax

ATLAS 121; PMH 96; PER -; HFP 112; HPCW 83; NESTS 136; BWP2:638

BLDS: ♀	3–4 (2–6) 1 (2?) broods INCU: ♀
Monogamy Polygyny	20–22

FLDG: ♀
25–30

Breeding habitat Open regions with low vegetation, including grassy pastures and crops.

Displays ♂s advertise with snorting call, a quick turn of the head, exposing distinctive black and white neck markings. There is also foot-stomping, and a short leap while flapping wings to show distinctive markings. Displays may be communal in late winter.

Nesting Territorial, but territories are clustered. Nest unlined scrape in low vegetation. Eggs greenish-olive to olive-brown, with heavy brown longitudinal streaks, 52mm, hatch synchronously. Role of ♂s in care of young uncertain or variable. ♀s breed in

their first year, ♂s in their second. Up to 3♀s per territory in some areas.

Diet Plants, invertebrates, and (rarely) small vertebrates. Young chicks fed mainly insects.

Winters Resident in S, migrates to southern part of range in N; in flocks, sometimes large ones.

Conservation Following considerable decline, species now has fragmented and isolated populations around Mediterranean, N to France, eastwards to Asia. Vulnerable to hunting, and habitat loss to agriculture. See p. 528.

Essays Birds and Agriculture, p. 365; Ducking the Bird Laws, p. 523.

Houbara Bustard
Chlamydotis undulata

ATLAS 122; PMH 96; PER -; HFP 112; HPCW 83; NESTS 136; BWP2:649

BLDS: ♀	2–3 (4–5) 1 brood INCU: ♀
Monogamy?	28

FLDG: ♀
35? | Insects

Breeding habitat Arid plains, sandy or stony semi-desert, well away from humans.

Displays Towards rivals, raises and fans tail, draws neck and head over body. Towards mate, raises long crown feathers, erects neck feathers, draws head and neck backwards, and continues to expand neck feathers until these completely cover head.

Nesting Territorial. Nest is shallow unlined hollow in shade of low bush. Eggs light olive-brown streaked and spotted with red-browns and greys, 62mm, hatching synchronously or asynchronously. Mainly fed by ♀, though

sometimes ♂ may help. May first breed at two years.

Diet Plants, insects, and small vertebrates; young chicks take insects. May be largely independent of water, though will drink from pools when possible.

Winters In flocks. Resident in N Africa, migrates to Persian Gulf from Asia.

Conservation Poorly known, but rare or extinct in many areas where it once occurred. Species has isolated and fragmented distribution across N Africa through the Middle East into CIS Asia. Particularly vulnerable to hunting. See p. 528.

Essays Ducking the Bird Laws, p. 523.

species the *female* is ordinarily more colourful — it is her secondary sexual characteristics that are enhanced. This fooled even John James Audubon and John Gould, who confused the sexes when labelling their paintings of phalaropes. Female phalaropes compete for the dull-coloured males, and the latter incubate the eggs and tend the young.

There is evidence that female birds of some species (e.g. Wrens, Collared Flycatchers, American Red-winged Blackbirds, *Agelaius phoeniceus*) tend to choose as mates those males holding the most desirable territories. In contrast, there is less evidence that females preferentially select males with different degrees of ornamentation. One of the most interesting studies, by Swedish ornithologist Malte Andersson, involved Long-tailed Widowbirds living in a grassland on a plateau in Kenya. Males of this polygynous 15 cm weaver (a distant relative of the House Sparrow) are black with red and buff on their shoulders and have tails about 40 cm long. The tails are prominently exhibited as the male flies slowly in aerial display over his territory. This can be seen from a kilometre away. The females, in contrast, have short tails and are inconspicuous.

Nine matched foursomes of territorial widowbird males were captured and randomly given the following treatments. One of each set had his tail cut about 15 cm from the base, and the feathers removed were then glued to the corresponding feathers of another male, thus extending that bird's tail by some 25 cm. A small piece of each feather was glued back on the tail of the donor, so that the male whose tail was shortened was subjected to the same series of operations, including gluing, as the male whose tail was lengthened. A third male had his tail cut, but the feathers were then glued back so that the tail was not noticeably shortened. The fourth bird was only banded. Thus the last two birds served as experimental 'controls' whose appearance had not been changed, but which had been subjected to capture, handling, and (in one) cutting and gluing. To test whether the manipulations had affected the behaviour of the males, numbers of display flights and territorial encounters were counted for periods both before and after capture and release. No significant differences in rates of flight or encounter were found.

The mating success of the males was measured by counting the number of nests containing eggs or young in each male's territory. Before the start of the experiment the males showed no significant differences in mating success. But after the large differences in tail length were artificially created, great differentials appeared in the number of new active nests in each territory. The males whose tails were lengthened acquired the most new mates (as indicated by new nests), outnumbering those of both of the controls and the males whose tails were shortened. The latter had the smallest number of new active nests. The females, therefore, preferred to mate with the males having the longest tails.

Subsequently, in similar experiments, Anders Møller manipulated tail-length in Swallows, which unlike the widowbirds are monogamous. He found that males with lengthened tails were able to obtain mates earlier and to father second clutches more frequently; they fledged more than twice as many young in a single season than did males with their tails artificially

Great Bustard

Otis tarda

ATLAS 121; PMH 97; PER 108; HFP 112; HPCW 84; NESTS 135; BWP2:659

BLDS: ♀
Polygyny

2–3 (1–4)
1 brood
INCU: ♀
21–28

FLDG: ♀
30–35

Breeding habitat Open grasslands; also including agricultural land.

Displays ♂s have traditional communal display grounds. Extraordinary display starts by raising tail to show white under-tail coverts. Then bird raises tail almost to head, inflates neck pouches to display bare skin patch, and erects neck feathers; by now bird has fluffed up to look like a white balloon. This posture held for up to several minutes. Bird can quickly revert to former self. ♀s approach dominant ♂s and incite displays prior to mating.

Nesting Gregarious; often around display grounds, but also away from them. Nest is shallow hollow in vegetation. Eggs olive-green, to grey, blotched with browns, 80mm, hatch

asynchronously. ♂s first breed at 5 years, ♀s at 3.

Diet Plants, insects, and small vertebrates; young chicks take insects. Walks slowly forward pecking or jabbing downwards.

Winters Resident in W; migrates to Turkey and SW Asia from eastern populations. In flocks.

Conservation A marked decrease, this species once bred across W Europe. Small and very isolated populations occur from Spain to Asia. Species is often hunted and vulnerable to habitat losses because it needs large areas of grasslands, which are often converted to farmland. See p. 528.

Essays Leks, p. 123; Birds and Agriculture, p. 365; Birds on Borders, p. 95.

Painted Snipe

Rostratula benghalensis

ATLAS 141; PMH -; PER -; HFP 140; HPCW 85; NESTS 167; BWP3:10

BLDS: ♂
Polyandry

4 (2–3)
? brood
INCU: ♂
19

FLDG: ♂
?

Seeds

Breeding habitat Marshy areas surrounded by lush vegetation, with muddy margins or areas of water weeds.

Displays Species is polyandrous and it is the brighter coloured ♀s that call, defend territories, and initiate displays to deter other ♀s and to attract ♂s. Skulking habits make observations of behaviour difficult. ♀s call from the ground, and also in low flight (somewhat like Woodcock). ♀s display towards rivals by facing them and spreading their wings; will fight aggressively. Towards ♂, ♀s use spread-wing display, call, and they also preen ♂.

Nesting ♀s may mate with 2–4 ♂s each year. Nest is cup lined with plant

material, on ground in thick cover. Eggs light buff with marks of dark brown, 36mm, probably hatch synchronously. ♀s find new mate after eggs are laid. ♀s probably breed at 2 years, ♂s at 1.

Diet Aquatic invertebrates, seeds, taken by probing mud or by sweeping bill side to side in water; crepuscular, possibly nocturnal.

Winters Resident.

Conservation Only in Egypt in the area covered by this guide; no apparent changes in numbers. Widely distributed across Africa, S Asia to Australia.

Essays Polyandry, p. 195; Precocial and Altricial Young, p. 401.

shortened. In addition, females preferred males with artificially enhanced tails as partners in extra-pair copulations. Under natural conditions Møller found that males arriving first on the breeding grounds tended to have more success at winning mates. Thus sexual selection for ornamentation appears to operate in monogamous as well as polygamous species.

One might ask why the tails of male widowbirds or Swallows have not evolved even greater length. The obvious answer is that natural selection counters sexual selection. Male widowbirds in breeding plumage already look like aircraft towing banners, and dragging their lengthy ornament around must make them much more susceptible to predators. Møller discovered one of the costs of long tails in Swallows: birds with experimentally lengthened tails captured smaller, less profitable prey and showed signs of dietary deficiency in their plumage. Sexual ornaments do not, however, necessarily reduce the chances of an individual surviving. In Common Pheasants, the length of spurs on the legs of the males is a good indicator of whether or not an individual will survive the winter. Experimental manipulation of spur length has also shown that long spurs are attractive to females.

The widowbird, Swallow, and pheasant studies required considerable manipulation of birds in a natural environment that was especially favourable for making observations. Evidence for female choice of mates has also been accumulated without such intervention in the course of a 30-year study of Arctic Skuas on Fair Isle off the northern tip of Scotland. These skuas are 'polymorphic' — individuals of dark, light, and intermediate colour phases occur in the same populations. Detailed studies by population biologist Peter O'Donald of Cambridge University and his colleagues indicate that females prefer to mate with males of the dark and intermediate phases, and as a result those males breed earlier than light-phase males. Earlier breeders tend to be more successful breeders, so the females' choices increase the fitness of the dark males. O'Donald concludes that the Fair Isle population remains polymorphic (rather than gradually becoming composed entirely of dark individuals) because light individuals are favoured by selection farther north, and 'light genes' are continuously brought into the population by immigrants from the north.

Further work is required to determine the details of female choice in birds, and to settle many issues related to sexual selection. The effort required will be considerable, and suitable systems may be difficult to find, but the results should cast important light on the evolutionary origin of many physical and behavioural avian characteristics.

We know remarkably little about the origins of sexual selection. Why, for example, do female widowbirds prefer long-tailed males? Possibly females choose such males because the ability to grow and display long tails reflects their overall genetic 'quality' as mates — and the females are thus choosing a superior father for their offspring (as, apparently, do female pheasants). Or the choice may have no present adaptive basis, but merely be the result of an evolutionary sequence that began for another reason. For instance, perhaps the ancestors of Long-tailed Widowbirds once lived together with a

Oystercatcher

Haematopus ostralegus

ATLAS 122; PMH 97; PER 110; HFP 118; HPCW 86; NESTS 137; BWP3:17

 |  | 3 (1–4)
1 brood | | |
--- | --- | --- | --- | --- | ---
| BLDS: ♂♀
Monogamy | INCU: ♂♀
24–27 | | FLDG: ♂♀
28–32 | Earthworms

Breeding habitat Near seashore, but also inland, generally following rivers.

Displays Pairs defend territories against rivals; both birds (but especially the ♂), stretch neck forward, point bill downwards, hunch back, and call very loudly, sometimes with accelerating peeping. This is a common and conspicuous display at territory boundaries, sometimes involving 4 birds. Both pairs may also fly along boundaries calling loudly.

Nesting Territorial. Nest is on ground and has little lining. Eggs yellowish or greyish with dark spots and blotches, 57mm, hatch synchronously. Unlike most other waders, the specialized feeding habits mean the young may remain with the parents for weeks to be fed and shown how to feed. See essay on Precocial and Altricial Young, p. 401. First breeds at about 4 years.

Diet Mainly molluscs, especially cockles and mussels, but earthworms inland. Walks forward probing the mud or ground for cockles and worms. Has two techniques for opening bivalves. The first is to hammer the shell, until it breaks, the second is to split open the shell by repeatedly stabbing the open parts of the seam between the two valves. See essay.

Winters Migratory, moving to coastal areas in winter as far south as equatorial Africa; in flocks.

Conservation Increases throughout region, with several inland regions colonized. Occurs in Europe and N Asia.

Essays Bills, p. 391; Oystercatchers and Oysters, p. 155; Parental Care, p. 171; Birds and Agriculture, p. 365; Empty Shells, p. 199; Wader Displays, p. 181.

Refs Marchant et al. 1990.

Black-winged Stilt

Himantopus himantopus

ATLAS 129; PMH 97; PER 110; HFP 118; HPCW 86; NESTS 138; BWP3:36

 | | 4 (3–5)
1 brood | | |
--- | --- | --- | --- | --- | ---
| BLDS: ♂♀?
Monogamy | INCU: ♂♀
22–25 | | FLDG: ♂♀
28–32 | Surface dips

Breeding habitat A broad range of shallow, still waters from fresh to brackish to hyper-saline, in lakes, rivers, and estuaries.

Displays Both birds defend territory, with bolt upright posture or bobbing, and birds often fly at rivals with head down and legs trailing below, rather than behind. Courtship includes head-bobs, and preening.

Nesting Usually colonial. Nest is often in exposed site on mud, surrounded by water, or can be hidden in short vegetation. May be a simple scrape or a pile of vegetation. Eggs pale buff with blackish spots or blotches, 44mm, hatch

synchronously.

Diet Mainly insects and other aquatic invertebrates picked from surface or under the water; birds will wade to their bellies and submerge head and neck.

Winters Migrate to Africa; in flocks.

Conservation Nesting habits make the species locally vulnerable to disturbance and predation. Widely distributed worldwide, with no major declines in Europe, but often has fragmented and isolated distribution imposed by habitat requirements. Some distinctive subspecies (outside of Europe) are endangered. See p. 529.

Essays Wader Feeding, p. 187.

population of near relatives whose males had slightly shorter tails. The somewhat longer tails of males of the 'pre-Long-tailed' Widowbirds were the easiest way for females to recognize mates of their own species. Such a cue could have led to a preference for long tails that became integrated into the behavioural responses of females. Although we are inclined to think the first scenario is correct, and that tail-length is a reflection of genetic quality, the data in hand do not eliminate the second possibility.

Behavioural ecologists W. D. Hamilton and M. Zuk have proposed that a male possessing bright and elaborate plumage and able to put on prolonged displays (including long, complex, and variable songs) is showing outward signs of his freedom from parasites and disease. That resistance could have a genetic component, in which case the male would be a very desirable mate. Support for this notion has been found in correlations between parasite infection and bright male coloration in both European and North American species, and in experimental work showing that artificially infected Red Jungle Fowl (*Gallus gallus*) had less bright colours than uninfected birds (while parasite load did not affect traits like bill size and body weight). It has recently been shown, however, that there is no relationship between song quality and parasite infection. Future tests of the controversial Hamilton–Zuk hypothesis could include seeing whether the most decorative males and the most elaborate displays are found in areas where pathogens and parasites pose the greatest threats to avian populations.

SEE: Natural Selection, p. 297; Leks, p. 123; Polyandry, p. 195; Polygyny, p. 265; Monogamy, p. 335; Dominance Hierarchies, p. 131. REFS: Andersson, 1982; Catchpole, 1987; Hamilton and Zuk, 1982; Møller, 1988b, 1989b, 1990; O'Donald, 1983. Payne, 1984; Pomiankowski, 1989a, 1989b; Read, 1987; Read and Weary, 1990; Schantz et al. 1989.

Oystercatchers and Oysters

ANYONE who has tried to open cockles and mussels or other bivalves can empathize with the challenge facing Oystercatchers, for they often subsist in large part on those and other molluscs. Bivalves have powerful 'adductor' muscles that hold the two shells together; prying them open is no easy task for us, even with the aid of a stout, sharp knife. Yet Oystercatchers, birds a mere 45 cm long, accomplish the feat quickly (often in under 30 seconds) and apparently with ridiculous ease.

How they do it has been elucidated by careful studies of the Oystercatcher (one of six similar species in the worldwide oystercatcher family). The trick, in part, lies in having the right tool — a long, stout bill with mandibles that are triangular in cross section and reinforced so that they do not bend easily. But the success of the Oystercatcher depends mainly upon use of one of two

Avocet
Recurvirostra avosetta

ATLAS 129; PMH 98; PER 110; HFP 118; HPCW 86; NESTS 139; BWP3:48

	BLDS: – Monogamy	3–4 (2–5) 1 brood INCU: ♂♀ 23–25 (20–28)	P2 FLDG: ♂♀ 35–42		 See below

Breeding habitat Shallow, usually brackish or saline, still waters.

Displays Displays against rivals with upright posture and head bobbing. Pairs have bowing courtship display, and birds may dip bill in water and preen repeatedly, moving very close to each other. ♂ may walk to and fro behind ♀ as they preen, before mating.

Nesting Colonial, nest is a shallow scrape on mud-flats lined with vegetation. Eggs pale buff, spotted with black, 50mm, hatch nearly synchronously. First breeds at 2 years.

Diet Aquatic invertebrates taken by either picking from water or mud or sweeping bill side to side through water. Will wade up to their bellies and sometimes feed communally in long lines.

Winters Similar to breeding season but more coastal areas and estuaries; in flocks.

Conservation Became extinct in UK and elsewhere in the last century. Has now recolonized those areas thanks to protection. Has fragmented distribution across Europe, C Asia, and Africa S of Sahara. See p. 528.

Essays Bills, p. 391; Wader Feeding, p. 187; Commensal Feeding, p. 27; Wetland Conservation, p. 145.

Refs Marchant et al. 1990.

Stone Curlew
Burhinus oedicnemus

ATLAS 142; PMH 98; PER 110; HFP 142; HPCW 87; NESTS 165; BWP3:67

	BLDS: ♂♀? Monogamy	2 (1–3) 1 (2) broods INCU: ♂♀ 24–26 (27)	P2 FLDG: ♂♀ 36–42	 Sm verts	 Ground glean

Breeding habitat Open stony fields, chalky grasslands, open heaths, and dry, saline lakes or estuaries.

Displays Have group displays in which several neighbouring pairs assemble to call, jump, and charge at each other. Typical threat is bolt upright posture with tail fanned and wings held folded but away from body. When pairs greet, both arch necks with bills pointing downwards. When threatened by predators (especially on nest) birds lie flattened with neck and head outstretched.

Nesting Nest is deep scrape on bare ground. Eggs pale buff, spotted or blotched with dark browns, 54mm, second egg usually hatches within 1 day of the first. Probably 3 years old when first breeds.

Diet Invertebrates and small vertebrates; mainly crepuscular or nocturnal.

Winters S populations resident, N ones migrate to S Europe and N Africa. In flocks.

Conservation Marked declines in UK and other areas following habitat loss: increased cultivation of marginal land, forestation of heaths, growth of shrubs following loss of rabbits. UK population over 2000 in 1930s, down to 250 now. Species is locally common and has large, if fragmented range across Europe, N Africa, and Asia. See p. 528.

Essays Birds and Agriculture, p. 365.

Refs Marchant et al. 1990.

learned techniques. Oystercatchers are either stabbers or hammerers. Stabbers sneak up on open molluscs and plunge their bills between the shells, severing the adductors before the bivalve can 'clam up'. The meat is then neatly chiselled away from each shell, shaken free, and eaten. Hammerers, in contrast, loosen the bivalve from its moorings and then shatter one shell with a rapid series of well-directed, short, powerful blows. The bill is then inserted through the hole, the adductors are cut, the shells pried apart, and the mollusc removed and devoured.

Young Oystercatchers mostly learn the techniques by observing their parents, who feed them for variable periods, often continuing beyond fledging. In fact, adults and young may associate for up to a year. During this period, the offspring gradually refine their skills as stabbers or hammerers, and learn to take other prey including crabs, marine worms, and, when feeding inland, earthworms and (to a lesser degree) a variety of insects. When Oystercatchers eat large crabs, they turn the victim on its back, kill it with a stab through the centre of the nervous system, and then demolish the shell by hammering. Presumably worms are detected by extremely sensitive nerve endings at the bill tip. These sensory receptors are thought to be specialized to respond to vibrations (similar receptors are found on the bills of other waders that probe for prey).

The diet of an individual Oystercatcher depends not just on what it observed its parents doing but on its age, the form of its bill (which grows rapidly and thus can change shape rapidly), the availability of various kinds of food, what other Oystercatchers of the same population are eating, and the prior experience of the individual. Bills of individual wintering birds may be pointed, blunt, or chisel-shaped. Each shape is adapted to a different way of finding food and handling prey. When individuals in experiments were forced to alter the way they fed, they suffered some loss of efficiency until their bills grew into a new shape. We don't know, however, just how important is each factor governing diet; clearly a great deal is still to be learned about Oystercatcher feeding.

SEE: Wader Feeding, p. 187; Parental Care, p. 171; Bills, p. 391. REFS: Heppleston, 1971; Hulscher, 1985; Norton-Griffiths, 1967; Safriel, 1985; Sutherland, 1987; Swennen *et al.*, 1983; Tinbergen and Norton-Griffiths, 1964.

Origin of Flight

THERE is an ongoing argument about the evolution and behaviour of the famous fossil *Archaeopteryx*, which combined characteristics of both birds and reptiles. Some palaeontologists, notably John Ostrom of Yale University, believe that it was a ground dweller, racing after insects and clapping its

Senegal Thick-knee

Burhinus senegalensis

ATLAS 143; PMH -; PER -; HFP 142; HPCW 87; NESTS 166; BWP3:80

 | | 2
1 brood |
BLDS: ♂♀?
Monogamy? | | INCU: ?
? | FLDG: ♂♀?
? | Sm verts | Ground glean

Breeding habitat Open stony fields, grasslands, but avoids deserts; often near rivers.

Displays Not well known, but may be similar to Stone Curlew. Like that species, when threatened by predators (especially on nest) birds lie flattened with neck and head outstretched.

Nesting Territorial. Nest is scrape on bare ground. Eggs pale buff to brown, lightly marked brown, 49mm.

Diet Invertebrates and small vertebrates; mainly crepuscular or nocturnal, sometimes feeding in small groups.

Winters Resident. Often in small groups.

Conservation Species is locally common in Nile valley and has large, if fragmented range across Africa.

Cream-coloured Courser

Cursorius cursor

ATLAS 144; PMH 99; PER 113; HFP 142; HPCW 89; NESTS 167; BWP3:91

 | | 2 (3)
1 (2?) broods |
BLDS: ?
Monogamy? | | INCU: ♂♀
? | FLDG: ♂♀
? |

Breeding habitat Desert areas usually with sparse vegetation, dunes, stony deserts.

Displays Not well known. ♂ has display flight with rapid wing beats and calling. In most extreme deserts, during hottest part of day, uses shade of bushes or telephone poles if available, running from shade to shade if disturbed.

Nesting Often nests in small groups opportunistically following rains. Nest is usually unlined, on bare ground in the open. Eggs creamy or pale buff with fine brown spots, 35mm. Young remain with parents until at least fledging. Young can feed themselves by the time they fledge.

Diet Insects, caught usually after short chases on foot.

Winters Resident or disperses to nearby desert areas; usually in small flocks.

Conservation Numbers are little known; species may be threatened with local extinction on Atlantic islands off N Africa. Occurs widely across N Africa, Arabian peninsula to Iran. See p. 528.

Essays Temperature Regulation and Behaviour, p. 163.

feathered forelimbs together like nets to trap its prey. Its feathers, like mammalian hair, may have originally evolved from reptilian scales as a general insulating body covering. Those individuals able to speed their pursuit (or escape predators) by employing their feather nets to glide down slopes or to extend leaps over obstacles would have left more offspring than slower individuals, and natural selection would have opened the road to more skilful flight. There are birds today, including the Greater Coucal, a close relative of cuckoos that lives in south-east Asia, that fly reluctantly and clumsily (much as did *Archaeopteryx* in this view), indicating that 'partial flight' is a viable mode of locomotion.

A more classic view is that the immediate ancestors of *Archaeopteryx* were arboreal, and gradually enlarged scales into feathers to help cushion falls. Eventually they evolved primitive wings in order to glide between trees. In this scenario, gliding gradually evolved into flapping flight, and off the first birds went. A problem with this arboreal scenario is that the ancestors of *Archaeopteryx* were certainly bipedal, and today all reptiles and mammals that live in trees are quadrupedal, and able to hang on with all four feet.

Recently a team of physical and biological scientists, Gerald Caple, Russel Balda, and William Willis, developed a mathematical/physical model of the evolution of flight. It postulates a bipedal insectivore that jumps after its prey evolving into an animal able not only to fly but eventually to land with precision on a tree branch. They agree with Ostrom that a runner, rather than a glider, was ancestral to the birds; gliding quadrupeds would have to make too many unlikely transitions to be plausible bird ancestors. On the other hand, they could not envision how 'insect nets' could develop into functional wings.

On the basis of their model, the team concluded that movements of forelimbs in a jumping animal would have been a great advantage in controlling its orientation, which, in turn, would have added to its rate of success at capturing aerial prey such as insects. Furthermore, those movements would be similar to those required for both control and propulsion during powered flight, so that no novel nerve–muscle pathways would have to evolve, as would be the case with the transition from glider to flyer. The model predicts rapid evolution of powered flight, and that feathers near the end of the wing would have developed before those near the base, since small lift-developing surfaces (essentially winglets) far from the body's centre of gravity would have been most efficient at providing control. This prediction might eventually be supported if a transitional fossil with well-developed primaries and poorly developed secondaries should be discovered.

Needless to say, we may never have answers to all the puzzles of the origins of flight, but evolutionists are agreed that *Archaeopteryx* was either an ancestor of modern birds or a rather close relative of such an ancestor. The nearly identical nature of the feathers of *Archaeopteryx* and modern birds, both in their structural details and in their division into primaries and secondaries, shows this. It is extremely unlikely that such similar organs evolved twice independently.

SEE: Feathered Dinosaurs?, p. 299; How Do Birds Fly?, p. 217; Adaptations for Flight, p. 511; Natural Selection, p. 297. REFS: Caple *et al.*, 1983; Martin 1983; Ostrom, 1979.

Collared Pratincole

Glareola pratincola

ATLAS 143; PMH 99; PER 112; HFP 142; HPCW 89; NESTS 166; BWP3:99

 | | | |

BLDS: ♂♀
Monogamy

3 (2–4)
1 brood
INCU: ♂♀
17–19

FLDG: ♂♀
25–30

Ground glean

Breeding habitat Open areas: dried mud-flats on edge of marshes, dry grasslands, semi-desert.

Displays Has display flight over colony with stiff exaggerated wing-beats. Calls in flight or on ground. Birds defend nest sites within colony, raising tails and spreading wings. When pairs meet have bowing display rather like Stone Curlew, with necks arched and bills pointed downwards.

Nesting Colonial. Nest is on ground in open, often near water, consists of scrape with almost no material. Eggs creamy with dark brown to black markings, 32mm, hatch asynchronously.

Adults regurgitate food to young for up to a week. Young leave nest within 2–3 days, and may remain with adults until after fledging.

Diet Large insects caught on wing. While feeding, pratincoles resemble large swallows. Will also run along ground to catch insects.

Winters In Africa; in flocks.

Conservation Widely but sporadically distributed across southern Europe, Africa, and SW Asia. Some suggestions of increase in N of range but some severe local declines. See p. 529.

Essays Precocial and Altricial Young, p. 401; Wing Shapes and Flight, p. 269.

Black-winged Pratincole

Glareola nordmanni

ATLAS 144; PMH 99; PER 113; HFP 142; HPCW 89; NESTS 166; BWP3:108

 |

BLDS: ♂♀
Monogamy

4 (3–5)
1 brood
INCU: ?
?

FLDG: ♂♀
?

Ground glean

Breeding habitat Open steppe often near water, or salt-flats.

Displays Not well known, probably similar to Collared Pratincole.

Nesting Colonial. Nest is shallow scrape in bare ground, with a sparse lining of vegetation. Eggs olive with black markings, 32mm. Young are fed by ther parents for the first few days.

Diet Probably similar to that of the Collared Pratincole. Feeds early

morning and before dark, often on swarming insects. Will run along ground after prey.

Winters In Africa.

Conservation Limited range in SW CIS, central Asia. Decreasing due to CIS policy of converting steppes to agriculture.

Essays Wader Displays, p. 181; Precocial and Altricial Young, p. 401; Wing Shapes and Flight, p. 269; Birds and Agriculture, p. 365.

Colour of Eggs

BIRD eggs show an enormous diversity of colours. Some bird groups that are considered relatively 'primitive', such as cormorants and pelicans, are thought to have retained the pale, uniform white or bluish colour typical of their reptilian ancestors. In more 'advanced' groups, unmarked white eggs are found mostly among some cavity-nesting species where there is no need for the eggs to be camouflaged. (Indeed white eggs may be more visible to the parents and therefore less at risk from accidental clumsiness.) Other cavity nesters, such as certain tits, have spotted eggs, presumably an indication that they once nested in the open. Pale eggs are also common among some duck species that cover their eggs with nesting materials when they have a break from incubating, or among those species such as doves, owls, and herons that start incubating as soon as the first egg is laid and never leave them exposed.

Seabird species that nest in gigantic colonies tend to have eggs that are extremely variable in both colour and markings. Their colours, like all egg colours, are from pigments produced by glands in the female's oviduct. As the egg moves down that tube the colours are squeezed out on to the shell. As the ecologist Bernd Heinrich put it: '. . . the motion of the egg affects the colour patterns. It is as if innumerable brushes hold still while the canvas moves. If the egg remains still there are spots, and if it moves while the glands continue secreting, then lines and scrawls result.'

Chester Reed, an early American egg collector, assumed that guillemots (*Uria* spp.) didn't know whose egg they were attending when they returned to their colony, but actually the variability of designs produced by the oviduct 'brushes' permits individuals to recognize their own 'painting'. Experiments have shown that guillemots learn the pattern of their own egg and will reject others. If its egg becomes gradually discoloured with guano, the guillemot will continually adjust the image of the 'proper' egg and will reject an unstained egg of its own basic pattern. Thus the birds are not genetically programmed to recognize their own egg pattern, but rather learn the pattern of the egg they've laid and then continually update its image.

In most birds, however, the colours of the eggs in one way or another help with their concealment, as anyone who has sought brown Arctic Tern eggs against a pebbly background can testify.

SEE: Brood Parasitism, p. 249; Incubation: Controlling Egg Temperatures, p. 273; Variation in Clutch Sizes, p. 55; Empty Shells, p. 199; Life in the Egg, p. 447. REFS: Heinrich, 1986; Lack, 1958.

Little Ringed Plover

Charadrius dubius

ATLAS 124; PMH 100; PER 112; HFP 120; HPCW 90; NESTS 141; BWP3:114

BLDS: ♂	4 (3–5) 1–2 broods INCU: ♂♀ 24–25(22–28)	FLDG: ♂♀ 25–27 (24–29)	Aq inverts
Monogamy			

Breeding habitat Open sandy or gravelly areas beside shallow freshwater, including rivers and gravel pits.

Displays Vigorously defends territory. Runs towards rivals in hunched position, calling. ♂s attract mates with song flights above territory (see Ringed Plover below). Like many ground nesting waders has a variety of displays designed to lure predators away from nest. These may involve bird moving about conspicuously, apparently feeding, wagging tail, or bobbing, or flying around intruder. Other displays suggest that the bird is injured.

Nesting Nest is a shallow scrape often on shingle bank, sometimes lined with small stones. Several scrapes are built by the ♂ and the ♀ picks one during courtship. Eggs pale brownish or buff, variously marked with dark browns,

30mm, hatch synchronously. ♀ may leave young with ♂ and then lay another clutch. Adults stay with young 1 or more weeks after fledging.

Diet Insects, other small invertebrates in wet ground or in shallow water. Foot-trembles (see Ringed Plover below).

Winters In Africa and S and E Asia, in similar habitats to those used in summer; usually solitary, though sometimes in small flocks.

Conservation Has increased in some areas (still increasing in UK) because birds can use artificial habitats like gravel pits. Very widely distributed across Europe and Asia into N Africa.

Essays Distraction Displays, p. 175; Wader Displays, p. 181.

Refs Marchant et al. 1990.

Ringed Plover

Charadrius hiaticula

ATLAS 123; PMH 100; PER 112; HFP 120; HPCW 90; NESTS 140; BWP3:129

BLDS: ♂	3–4 (2–5) 2–(3) broods INCU: ♂♀ 23–25	FLDG: ♂♀ 24	
Monogamy			

Breeding habitat Mainly coastal, shingle shores but also river banks inland, or near pools in arctic tundra.

Displays Similar to Little Ringed Plover. Song flight of ♂ over territory has unusually slow, flapping wing-beats, a 'butterfly' flight. Has distraction display.

Nesting Territorial. Nest shallow scrape in open, often on shingle bank lined with small stones or some plant material. Eggs greyish to buff, variously marked blackish, 35mm, hatch synchronously. Young remain with parents until fledging.

Diet Invertebrates, including marine worms, crustaceans, molluscs, and insects (inland). Runs, stops, and pecks. Will use foot-trembling: stands on one

foot and vibrates the surface, with other foot. Try this yourself; the firm sand becomes liquid and easier to penetrate.

Winters On coastlines, on mud-flats as well as sandy shores, and up rivers; locally in Europe, south to southern Africa. Most northerly breeding populations winter furthest south, while some UK birds are resident.

Conservation Local increases (UK) and decreases, in Finland, (because of seashore disturbance). Species is widely distributed from E arctic Canada, to Europe, to W Siberia.

Essays The Colour of Birds, p. 137; Raptor Hunting, p. 113; Empty Shells, p. 199; Wader Feeding, p. 187; Wader Migration and Conservation, p. 167.

Refs Marchant et al. 1990.

Temperature Regulation and Behaviour

THE ability to maintain a high and constant body temperature enables birds to exploit a remarkable range of habitats — tropical, temperate, and polar. This achievement is not without cost, however. The 'expense' of metabolic heat production must be repaid by taking in sufficient energy to balance what has been expended, and mechanisms must be available to shed excess heat when necessary. If the environmental temperature falls, birds raise their metabolic rate to prevent their internal temperature from falling as well. In contrast, if the environmental temperature becomes too hot, birds must mobilize water to lose heat through evaporative cooling (as we do when we perspire) and avoid death from overheating. Since birds have no sweat glands, water must be evaporated from the respiratory tract by panting, or in non-passerines by rapidly vibrating the upper throat and floor of the mouth ('gular flutter').

To minimize the energy cost of temperature regulation ('thermoregulation'), birds use a variety of morphological and behavioural traits to adjust their rates of heat loss and heat gain. Unfeathered (uninsulated) body surfaces serve as important sites for heat exchange with the environment. When heat-stressed, therefore, some birds, such as American Black Vultures (*Coragyps atratus*), excrete onto their unfeathered legs to increase heat loss by evaporation.

When it is cold, unfeathered legs become avenues for potential heat loss. To minimize such loss, the arteries and veins in the legs of many birds lie in contact with each other and function as a countercurrent heat exchange system to retain heat. Arterial blood leaves the bird's core (trunk) at body temperature, while venous blood in the bird's foot is quite cool. As the cool blood returns toward the core, heat moves by conductance from the warm arteries into the cool veins. Thus, arterial blood reaching the feet is already cool and venous blood reaching the core has already been warmed. By constricting the blood vessels in its feet, a bird may further decrease heat loss by reducing the amount of blood flow to its feet. Thus while the core temperature of a duck or gull standing on ice may be 40°C, its feet may be only slightly above freezing.

Behaviour also can play a significant role in reducing the amount of heat lost from unfeathered surfaces. By standing on one leg and tucking the other among its breast feathers, a duck or gull on ice reduces by half the amount of unfeathered limb surface area exposed; by sitting down and thus covering both legs, heat loss from the limbs is minimized. In cold weather, buntings and other finches foraging on the ground frequently drop down and cover their legs and feet with their breast feathers while pausing in their search for food. Similarly, Starlings and Blackbirds alternately cover one or the other leg with plumage under such conditions. On cold or windy days, waders often can be seen resting with their beaks tucked away among their feathers,

Kittlitz's Plover
Charadrius pecuarius

ATLAS 124; PMH -; PER -; HFP 121; HPCW 92; NESTS 142; BWP3:146

BLDS: ♂♀ Monogamy	2 (1) 1–2 broods INCU: ♂♀ 23–26 (–28)	FLDG: ♂♀ 25?	Aq inverts		

Breeding habitat Inland on dry open ground, often along sandy river banks or lake edges; sometimes coastal.

Displays Like Ringed and Little Ringed Plover, birds chase each other with breast feathers fluffed, calling.

Nesting Territorial or in small groups. Nest is shallow scrape in open, near water, unlined or lined with small stones or vegetation. Eggs buff with black lines and streaks, 32mm, hatch synchronously. Young remain with parents until fledging.

Diet Invertebrates, particularly insects and molluscs (inland). In addition to usual run, stop, and peck method, also uses foot to vibrate the surface (see Ringed Plover).

Winters Resident; sometimes in small groups.

Conservation Locally common in Egypt; occurs locally across Africa.

Essays Precocial and Altricial Young, p. 401; Wing Shapes and Flight, p. 269; Wader Displays, p. 181.

Kentish Plover
Charadrius alexandrinus

ATLAS 124; PMH 101; PER 112; HFP 120; HPCW 91; NESTS 142; BWP3:153

BLDS: ♂ Monogamy	3 (2–4) 1 (2) broods INCU: ♂♀ 24–27 (23–29)	FLDG: ♂♀ 27–31	

Breeding habitat Mainly coastal, but inland along sandy streams, saline lagoons.

Displays Similar to Ringed Plover, but also has an upright threat posture with breast feathers fluffed and head tucked in; alternates this posture with running at rivals. Has distraction display at nest.

Nesting Nest is shallow scrape in open, near water, lined with small stones. ♂ builds several scrapes from which ♀ chooses one. Eggs buff with black spots and streaks, 33mm, hatch synchronously; young remain with parents until fledging.

Diet Invertebrates, including crustaceans, molluscs, and insects (inland). Runs, stops, and pecks; also

uses foot to vibrate the surface (see Ringed Plover).

Winters Mainly coastal, from S Europe to Africa, eastern populations to shores of Indian Ocean.

Conservation Declines in N and W of Europe (where species is at edge of range); beach nesting areas are particularly vulnerable to disturbance. Has been lost as UK breeder. Widely distributed worldwide: occurs in N and S America, Europe, N Africa, and across to Japan.

Essays The Colour of Birds, p. 137; Wader Feeding, p. 187; Distraction Displays, p. 175; Wader Migration and Conservation, p. 167.

Refs Sharrock 1976.

Behavioural thermoregulation. Waders retract legs and place heads beneath wings to retard heat loss. Left to right: Oystercatchers, Little Stint, Sanderling, Temminck's Stint.

sometimes in combination with standing on one leg or sitting. And, of course, birds can further enhance their effective insulation by fluffing out their feathers to increase the thickness of their 'coat'.

In cooler weather, rather than increasing their metabolic rate, birds can save energy by using environmental heat to raise their body temperature passively. Darters, for example, do this by sunning with wings spread, while many small- and medium-sized species, especially passerines, assume sunning postures in which they squat or sit with their feathers slightly erected and wings drooped. Usually the bird is oriented so its back is fully exposed to the sun's direct rays. Interestingly, some grebes that sunbathe in this way have either back feathers with black bases or black-pigmented skin on their back, both of which presumably facilitate heat absorption.

Behavioural thermoregulation can also help shed excess heat. Gulls, for example, usually nest in open habitats with little or no available shade and often face problems of overheating. Nesting Herring Gulls will rotate 180° to constantly face the sun on hot, windless days. Radiative heat gain is thus reduced by minimizing the surface area exposed to direct solar radiation and by allowing the gulls to present only their most reflective plumage (white head, neck, and breast) to direct sunlight. Gulls and coots will stand to expose their unfeathered legs and feet to prevent overheating — or better still, stand in water and generate evaporative cooling.

Gull chicks lack thermoregulatory ability until they are several days old and face acute problems of overheating. In many shadeless gull colonies, chicks avoid heat stress by standing in the shade provided by their parents. In 1773, Gilbert White described adult warblers nesting in the vines on the wall of his house in the heat of summer 'hover[ing] over the nest all the hotter hours, while with the wings expanded, and mouths gaping for breath, they screened off the heat from their suffering offspring'. At the opposite climatic

Greater Sandplover

Charadrius leschenaultii

ATLAS 125; PMH 101; PER-; HFP 120; HPCW 92; NESTS 142; BWP3:170

BLDS: ♂♀?
Monogamy?

3 (2–4)
1 brood?
INCU: ♂♀
?

P2

FLDG: ♂♀
?

Summer:
Insects
Winter:
Aq inverts

Breeding habitat Open, arid, semi-desert, and dry grasslands, often saline flats.

Displays Poorly known; has song-flight on breeding grounds.

Nesting Nest is a scrape, unlined or sparsely lined with vegetation, on ground in open. Eggs buffish or brownish-yellow, tinged green, spotted blackish-brown, 39mm, hatch synchronously.

Diet Insects, especially beetles, using typical plover peck, run, and, stop method. In winter, various shore invertebrates.

Winters Coastal, around Indian Ocean to eastern Pacific; in flocks.

Conservation Very small numbers in SW Asia, common across C Asia.

Essays Wader Displays, p. 181; Precocial and Altricial Young, p. 401; Wing Shapes and Flight, p. 269.

Dotterel

Charadrius morinellus

ATLAS 126; PMH 102; PER 112; HFP 122; HPCW 93; NESTS 146; BWP3:183

BLDS: ♂♀
Monogamy
Polyandry

2–3 (1–4)
See below
INCU: ♂ (♀)
24–28(23–30)

P2

FLDG:♂ (♀)
25–30

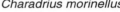

Breeding habitat Tundra, often stony mountainous areas.

Displays Birds may begin to form pairs on spring migration. ♀s initiate the displays, trying to lure ♂ into joint display flight, with erratic 'butterfly' flight similar to Ringed Plover.

Nesting Nest shallow hollow on open ground. Eggs greyish to buffish, heavily marked with brown or black, 41mm, hatch within 1 day of each other. ♂s do most of the incubation and caring for the young, though ♀s may help. Sometimes ♀s seek out another mate (or two), being serially polyandrous. Such ♀s often take a greater share in rearing young of their second brood than those with only one mate.

Diet Insects and other invertebrates.

Winters Open ground, and arid areas in N Africa; often stops at traditional areas en route; in small flocks.

Conservation A widespread decline in the UK during the last century due to persecution. Now thought to be increasing, though this could be because of better surveys. There are isolated small populations across W and C Europe; main range is from Scandinavia across arctic Asia. See p. 528.

Essays Birds and the Law, p. 521; Wader Displays, p. 181; Polyandry, p. 195.

Refs Marchant et al. 1990; Nethersole-Thompson 1973 is a book about this species.

extreme, Willow Grouse chicks must reduce the length of foraging bouts in order to return to their mother for brooding as their body temperature drops in the cold of northern Europe.

Many birds have evolved the ability to maintain their body temperature at lower levels during periods of inactivity, often in response to food deprivation. This turning down of the thermostat (known as 'regulated hypothermia' or 'torpor') achieves significant energy savings in species ranging from passerines to raptors. For example, House Martins from eleven days old and into adulthood are able to enter torpor when deprived of food at low ambient temperatures, and drop their body temperature to as little as 26°C with a metabolic rate that is only 10–20 per cent of their normal level. Even in the presence of abundant food supplies, Willow Tits regularly enter nocturnal hypothermia and lower their body temperature to 33°C. Hummingbirds, swifts, and nightjars enter a state of torpor in which body temperature may drop by 20 degrees or more for several hours during the night. The Common Poorwill of North America (*Phalaenoptilus nuttallii*), can sustain a regulated torpor continuously for several days during extremely inclement weather. Although the energy savings are great in birds that enter torpor, they face increased danger of predation because they are unable to respond quickly. There is also a substantial metabolic cost incurred by arousal from torpor that demands immediate payback in food intake. Nevertheless, recent studies indicate that the ability to enter shallow torpor for short periods may be much more widespread among birds than previously believed.

Try to keep thermoregulatory needs in mind when you are watching birds. Indeed, temperature-regulating actions of waders and gulls are among the most readily observed and interpreted of bird behaviours.

SEE: Metabolism, p. 281; Black and White Plumage, p. 7; Spread-wing Postures, p. 17; Winter Feeding by Redpolls and Crossbills, p. 489; Feet, p. 289; Bird Droppings, p. 485.
REFS: Bech and Reinertsen, 1989; Brent *et al.*, 1985; Heller, 1989; Larochelle *et al.*, 1982; Löhrl, 1986; Lustick *et al.*, 1978; Midtgard, 1989; Pedersen and Steen, 1979; Prinzinger and Siedle, 1988; Reinertsen and Haftorn, 1986; Walsberg, 1983; White, 1789.

Wader Migration and Conservation

COASTAL areas of western Europe and western Africa provide wintering habitat for the millions of waders that breed in the vast region bounded by Ellesmere Island, Canada, on the west and by Siberia on the east. As a group, waders undertake some of the most spectacular long-distance migrations of any land birds. For birds wintering in southern Africa, each journey may

Golden Plover

Pluvialis apricaria

ATLAS 125; PMH 103; PER 114; HFP 122; HPCW 93; NESTS 143; BWP3:201

		P2			
BLDS: ♂♀	4 (2–5)				
Monogamy	1 brood	FLDG: ♂♀			
	INCU: ♂♀	25–33			
	28–31				

Breeding habitat Open moorland and tundra.

Displays Birds begin to display in spring flocks, calling to each other from upright posture and holding wings vertically to show white linings. Birds run after each other, in hunched position. ♂ has song flight.

Nesting Nest, in low vegetation, is a shallow scrape lined with moss and other vegetation. ♂ makes a number of scrapes and ♀ chooses one of them. Eggs buff to yellowish or olive, various blackish markings, 52mm, usually hatch synchronously. Sometimes brood is divided; each group looked after by a different parent.

Diet Insects, particularly beetles, and other invertebrates (earthworms); some berries and seeds. Uses typical plover feeding method of alternating short runs with probing.

Winters Fields, pastures, in large flocks, in S and W Europe to N Africa.

Conservation Decreases in S populations, due to habitat loss and disturbance of moorland areas, but widely distributed from Iceland into arctic Asia. See p. 529.

Essays Mixed-species Flocking, p. 429; Wader Displays, p. 181; Distraction Displays, p. 175.

Refs Marchant et al. 1990.

Grey Plover

Pluvialis squatarola

ATLAS 126; PMH 103; PER 114; HFP 122; HPCW 94; NESTS 143; BWP3:216

		P2	Summer: Insects	
BLDS: ♂♀	4 (3)		Winter:	
Monogamy	1 brood	FLDG: ♂♀	Aq inverts	
	INCU: ♂♀	35–40		
	26–27			

Breeding habitat Lowland tundra around Arctic Ocean.

Displays Similar to other plovers. Song flights may start while on migration. Birds also run at territorial rivals, or walk parallel to them in a hunched position.

Nesting Territorial. Nest is shallow scrape, in open with little lining. Eggs grey or buff, blotched and spotted with dark browns, often mainly around widest part, 52mm, hatch within 2 days of each other. Young cared for by ♂ in later stages, when ♀ leaves. Thought to breed first at 2–3 years.

Diet Insects on breeding grounds, marine worms, crustaceans, and

molluscs in winter. Feeds in typical plover manner, running or walking alternating with stops and pecking.

Winters Coastal mud-flats and sandy beaches worldwide. Often territorial along beaches in winter, birds can be seen evenly spaced along shorelines.

Conservation Breeds in remote areas, widely throughout arctic Asia, N America, and in limited area of Europe. Wintering numbers in UK increasing.

Essays Wader Feeding, p. 187; Wader Displays, p. 181; Distraction Displays, p. 175; Wader Migration and Conservation, p. 167; Spacing of Wintering Waders, p. 179.

cover nearly 13 000 kilometres. Some fly at altitudes exceeding 3500 metres and achieve cruising speeds approaching 80 kph.

Many birds cover a much shorter annual circuit by travelling south from their high-latitude breeding grounds but remaining in Europe. Although Lapwing and Snipe winter inland, Oystercatcher, Ringed Plover, Grey Plover, Knot, Sanderling, Dunlin, Bar-tailed Godwit, Curlew, Redshank, and Turnstone move to the milder climates found along the coasts and estuaries of western Europe and Britain. The most important site for migratory waders in continental Europe is the Wadden Sea, a shallow coastal area comprising some 8000 square kilometres set behind a long chain of barrier islands stretching from western Denmark (the Vadehavet) through northern Germany (the Wattenmeer) to the Netherlands (the Waddenzee). Indeed, many of the islands themselves serve as important breeding sites or as high-tide roosts for migrants. The Danish portion of the Wadden Sea assumes particular importance during migration, as it is a crucial locale for replenishment of fat reserves after the first leg of the migrants' southward journey. Similarly, in the spring it serves as the last area in which birds flying north can forage before making the final portion of their migration to the breeding grounds.

The Wadden Sea is faced with multiple threats to its future as critically important wader habitat. Proposed draining and reclamation of large areas will result in enormous tidal habitat losses. Pollution from increased industrialization, oil terminals, and undersea oil exploitation poses a major threat to the integrity of this fragile environment. In addition, there is increasing pressure from recreational activities and the facilities (such as boat harbours and airfields) to support them. Spurred in part by increased coastal development, intensive cooperative studies of wader movements across political boundaries have been undertaken in the past several years in an effort to understand better the pattern of habitat utilization by waders outside the breeding season. These studies have revealed a complex network of sites on which particular species or races are inextricably dependent. Observations of marked birds have established the existence of considerable within-season movement among sites in the Wadden Sea and between coastal Europe and British estuaries. Even within Britain, there is constant fluctuation throughout the winter in both the numbers and origins of birds found on any given British estuary. In addition to the numerous small estuaries of the British coastline, the Wash in the east and the Ribble Estuary and Morecambe Bay in the northwest appear to be particularly important wintering sites.

Although British estuaries, the Wadden Sea, and coastal sites in France, Spain, and Portugal provide critical wintering habitat, more waders winter in northwest Africa than in the whole of Europe. Important wintering areas are found on the Atlantic coast of Morocco and along the West African coast, especially in Mauritania, Senegal, and Guinea-Bissau. At least 3 million waders spend the winter in West Africa south of the Sahara. The tremendous importance of some of these sites is illustrated by the recent finding that perhaps as many as 30 per cent of the more than 7 million waders that migrate through the eastern Atlantic flyway each year use the Banc d'Arguin in Mauritania. These numbers include large proportions of the total flyway

Spur-winged Plover

Hoplopterus spinosus

ATLAS 127; PMH 104; PER 114; HFP 124; HPCW 94; NESTS 147; BWP3:227

BLDS: ♂	4 (3–5)	P2	
Monogamy	1–2(3) broods	FLDG: ♂♀	
	INCU: ♂♀	35+ ?	
	22–24		

Breeding habitat   Open habitats by marshes, often salt marshes

Displays   Towards rivals, has upright posture, sometimes with wings spread to show black-and-white pattern, alternating with running at rival in hunched position. Courtship involves ♂s circling ♀s.

Nesting   Territorial. Nest is a scrape with some plant lining, in open near water. ♂ makes several scrapes from which ♀ chooses one. Eggs whitish to yellowish, heavily marked with black, 40mm, hatch synchronously.

Diet   Insects, caught after short, fast walk; sometimes other invertebrates.

Winters   Mainly resident, N populations migrate southwards.

Conservation   Breeds locally in Europe, more common in Africa. See p. 529.

Essays   Incubation: Controlling Egg Temperatures, p. 273.

Sociable Plover

Hoplopterus gregarius

ATLAS 128; PMH 104; PER -; HFP 124; HPCW 95; NESTS 148; BWP3:240

BLDS: ?	4 (3–5)	P2	
Monogamy	1 brood	FLDG: ♂♀	
	INCU: ♂♀?	35–40	
	25		

Breeding habitat   Open steppe usually near water, sometimes on dried mud.

Displays   Very little known. Apparently there is a group display by up to 10 ♂s in open, flat areas, with aggressive displays and fights.

Nesting   Nest a scrape with sparse grass lining in open. Eggs yellowish-buff to olive, spotted and streaked black, 46mm, hatch synchronously.

Diet   Insects, especially beetles, locusts, and insect larvae. Feeds like other plovers.

Winters   In Africa and India in grasslands and agricultural fields; in flocks.

Conservation   Probably no longer breeds in area of this guide, though apparently more widespread in the last century. Vulnerable to conversion of steppe to agriculture.

Essays   Birds and Agriculture, p. 365; Precocial and Altricial Young, p. 401; Wing Shapes and Flight, p. 269.

population of Ringed Plover, Kentish Plover, Knot, Curlew Sandpiper, Bar-tailed Godwit, and Whimbrel. By comparison, the number of waders travelling all the way to southern Africa is quite small.

Thus the picture that has emerged indicates that many wader populations are comprised of individuals that depend on more than one area in the non-breeding season. This dependence may involve a sequence of sites required each year for migration staging, for moult, and then for varying portions of the winter. In some cases, an additional set of alternative sites is required during periods when unfavourable climatic conditions force birds from their usual wintering areas.

The convergence of immense numbers at key locations along their migration route places the long-term survival of even abundant species in jeopardy. By providing plentiful food resources that enable the birds quickly to replenish their energy reserves, each of these spots is critical for successful migration. Hence, a few crucial staging areas may underpin the entire migration system of several wader species. Such enormous concentrations dependent upon a few widely spaced locales severely undermines the usual link between a species' abundance and its immunity to extinction.

See: Spacing of Wintering Waders, p. 179; Wader Feeding, p. 187; Sandpipers, Social Systems, and Territoriality, p. 189; Birds and the Law, p. 521; Migration, p. 377; Wintering Site Tenacity, p. 409; Timing of Migration, p. 405. Refs: Evans *et al.*, 1984; Myers, *et al.*, 1987; Pienkowski and Evans, 1984.

Parental Care

The eggs of most egg-laying reptiles hatch long after the parents have abandoned them; a few lizards and snakes guard their eggs, and pythons even incubate theirs for a while. The young of those female snakes that carry their eggs inside the body until they hatch also receive no parental care. In fact, among reptiles only crocodiles and their relatives tend both eggs and hatchlings. In contrast, nearly all birds provide extended care for their offspring. The exceptions are brood parasites, which foist the responsibility on to other species, and some megapodes, turkey-sized birds of the southwest Pacific.

Most megapodes scratch together a mound (sometimes astonishingly large) of vegetation or sand and lay their eggs inside. The heat for incubation is provided by decay of the vegetation, the sun, or (occasionally) volcanic activity. Some megapodes tend the mound, opening and closing it to regulate the incubation temperature; others desert it entirely. A few megapodes do not build mounds, but simply lay their eggs in warm spots on sand or between rocks and cover them with leaves.

Patterns of care in precocial birds (those with young ready to leave the nest almost immediately after hatching) vary a great deal. The major parental

Lapwing

Vanellus vanellus

ATLAS 127; PMH 105; PER 114; HFP 124; HPCW 96; NESTS 146; BWP3:250

Saucer	4 (2–5)	P2		
BLDS: ♂♀	1 brood			
Monogamy	INCU: ♂♀	FLDG: ♂♀		
Polygyny	28 (24–34)	35–40(29–42)		

Breeding habitat Farm land and short grassy areas, salt marshes.

Displays ♂s have hunched run at rivals (see other plovers). Aerial displays with birds swooping at rivals are most conspicuous display. Song flight is varied, including slow, butterfly-like flapping, steep dives and climbs, rolling from side to side, and other acrobatics.

Nesting Territorial. Nest is a scrape sometimes extensively lined with vegetation, in open. ♂ makes several scrapes, from which the ♀ chooses one. Eggs pale buff to brown, heavily marked blackish, 47mm, hatch within a day of each other. Some ♂s are polygamous, with several ♀s nesting in their territories.

Diet Insects and earthworms; picked from surface or with short probe; will feed during moonlit nights. Uses foot-trembling (see Ringed Plover).

Winters In habitats similar to those used during breeding season. Resident in S and W, birds are joined there by migrants from C and N Europe and Asia. If cold spells are severe, large movements of birds from the continent may be observed. Often in large flocks.

Conservation Formerly suffered declines from egg collecting. Increasing range in N. Common and widespread across Europe and Asia.

Notes Yellow Wagtails and Meadow Pipits may nest near Lapwings, because they defend area against predators.

Essays Birds and Agriculture, p. 365; Indeterminate Egg Layers, p. 437; Wader Displays, p. 181; Commensal Feeding, p. 27; Migration, p. 377.

Refs Marchant et al. 1990.

Sanderling

Calidris alba

ATLAS 133; PMH 106; PER 114; HFP 128; HPCW 97; NESTS 150; BWP3:282

		P2	Summer: Insects	
BLDS: ♀?	4 (3)		Winter:	
Monogamy	1 (2) broods	FLDG: ♂♀	Aq inverts	
Polygyny	IN: see below	17		
	24–27 (31)			Probes

Breeding habitat Arctic tundra at high latitudes; near water.

Displays ♂s have song flight over territory with fluttering flight and glides; birds may briefly hover. Has ground chases at rivals (like some plovers).

Nesting Nest is in small hollow in stony ground, often lined with willow leaves. Eggs olive-green with a few dark spots, 35mm, hatch synchronously. Many birds are monogamous and pair shares duties. Some ♂s may mate with two ♀s consecutively. Sometimes two ♀s share the same nest. Some ♀s lay two clutches and each parent looks after one.

Diet In breeding season, insects and some plant material. In winter, probes sand, often running after receding waves, for small invertebrates.

Winters Sandy shores almost worldwide; in flocks.

Conservation Has a very tiny population within area covered by this book (Spitsbergen). Breeds in remote areas. Wintering populations indicate that this is an abundant species.

Essays Polygyny, p. 265; Sandpipers, Social Systems, and Territoriality, p. 189; Wader Feeding, p. 187; Wader Displays, p. 181; Wader Migration and Conservation, p. 167; Spacing of Wintering Waders, p. 179.

duties for most are to keep the young safe from predators and to watch over them as they feed. In many, however, the adults also help instruct the chicks in what's good to eat, how to find it, and how to handle it. Oystercatchers first present food to their young and then train them to find it for themselves. The latter is a long process. Some Oystercatchers specialize in opening mussels and other bivalve molluscs, a difficult task that can be accomplished in less than a minute by an experienced individual, but one that requires many months to learn.

The young of most birds (including all passerines), are altricial (born naked, blind, and helpless) and require much more care and feeding than precocial young. One or both parents must bring food to altricial young until they are ready to leave the nest, and in most species the offspring are fed by the parents for a while after fledging. Most passerines are monogamous, and usually both parents help in rearing the young. When the young are newly hatched the male often does more of the food gathering and the female more of the brooding — covering the young to keep them warm (or to shield them from sun or rain) and protecting them from predators. Frequently, the male also feeds the female, and she in turn may pass food on to her helpless chicks. In cooperative breeders, such as Bee-eaters, help with feeding young may be received from birds whose own nests have failed.

In polygynous species (where one male mates with more than one female), the male's parental role usually is reduced in both precocial and altricial birds. Polyandrous species (one female mates with more than one male) are nearly all precocial, and the burden of caring for the offspring either falls exclusively on the males or is shared.

Generally parent birds feed their offspring a diet similar to their own, but during the breeding season the diet of the adults (and thus of the young) shifts toward higher-protein foods. Many passerine birds that during the winter subsist mainly on vegetable foods eat insects and feed them to their young during the breeding season. There is a tendency for the adults to consume the smaller insects themselves and, for the sake of efficiency, to carry larger ones back to the nest.

Other parents swallow the food as they forage and then regurgitate it for the young when they return to the nest. Some birds, notably pigeons, produce a special 'crop milk', which is also regurgitated for the young. Petrels regurgitate an oil for their young along with half-digested food from which the oil is derived. Raptors usually carry their prey back to the nest and tear it into bite-sized chunks for their chicks.

The feeding instinct in parental birds is very strong, and feeding behaviour is usually elicited by feeding calls and gaping on the part of the chicks. When a bird's own brood is destroyed, it may transfer its attention to the young of others; observations of birds feeding the young of other parents of the same species, and even of other species, are quite common. In the United States, one Northern Cardinal (*Cardinalis cardinalis*) was even observed to have adopted a school of gaping goldfish at a pond where the fish were accustomed to begging from people!

Presumably, the length of time that adults will care for their young is

Little Stint
Calidris minuta

ATLAS 132; PMH 107; PER 116; HFP 126; HPCW 97; NESTS 150; BWP3:303

BLDS: ?
See below

4 (3)
2 broods
IN: see below
20–21

P2
FL: see below
?

Summer:
Insects
Winter:
Aq inverts

Breeding habitat Marshes, tundra above about 65°N.

Displays Both sexes have song flights, sometimes together, with ascents followed by spiralling descents. Also sing on ground.

Nesting Nest is shallow cup lined with vegetation in open, usually near water. Eggs pale greenish or buffish with brown spotting, 29mm, hatch synchronously. Mating system is not fully understood: some ♀s lay two clutches leaving the first for the ♂ to look after.

Diet Insects, particularly flies on breeding grounds, and molluscs,

crustaceans in winter. Picks and does not probe.

Winters Mud-flats, salt and freshwater marshes from Mediterranean to Africa and India; in flocks.

Conservation Remote breeding areas, means counts of breeding populations are difficult. Occurs widely from Norway (where only a few tens of pairs nest) to arctic Asia.

Essays Polyandry, p. 195; Sandpipers, Social Systems, and Territoriality, p. 189; Wader Feeding, p. 187; Wader Displays, p. 181.

Temminck's Stint
Calidris temminckii

ATLAS 132; PMH 107; PER 116; HFP 126; HPCW 97; NESTS 150; BWP3:311

BLDS: ?
See below

4 (2–3)
1–3 broods
IN: see below
21–22

P2
FL: see below
15–18

Breeding habitat Open tundra near coast, rivers, or lakes.

Displays ♂s sing in flight, while circling, and on the ground (the latter while wing-fluttering). Rivals also run parallel along ground.

Nesting Nest is cup lined with grass in open. Eggs pale greenish to buffish with dark brown spots, 28mm, hatch synchronously. Mating system is polygamous by both sexes – each ♀ laying two clutches (sometimes a third) in quick succession with the ♀ parent looking after the last clutch (see Little Stint). However, a ♂ courts all the ♀s that enter his territory and sometimes

two ♀s use same nest within one territory.

Diet Insects, aquatic invertebrates picked from surface; does not probe.

Winters Saline mud-flats and often freshwater marshes from Africa to SE Asia; in flocks.

Conservation Numbers fluctuate, but generally breeds in remote areas and populations are not easily surveyed. Occurs across arctic from UK to CIS Asia.

Essays Who Incubates?, p. 285; Polyandry, p. 195; Sandpipers, Social Systems, and Territoriality, p. 189; Wader Feeding, p. 187; Wader Displays, p. 181.

determined by several factors. In most cases, the longer the care, the better the chances that the young will survive to maturity. Counterbalancing prolonged dependence in the 'calculations' of evolution, however, are the possibility of the parents rearing a second brood and the physical cost of extended care. These factors affect the probability of the adults being able to survive migration or wintering to breed again the next season. As far as possible, evolution will favour the strategy that maximizes the reproductive output of an individual *over its entire lifetime*; this may limit the amount of care given to any one set of offspring. There is, in fact, often a conflict between the evolutionary interests of parents and young, it being best for the parents to cease care before it is best for the young to be on their own. Sparrowhawks, for instance, stop feeding their young at least three weeks before the young will cease to hang around the nest and accept food; they basically force the young to become independent by withdrawing feeding. This apparent parent-offspring conflict is not restricted to birds (as some of us well know) and is one of the more interesting topics in sociobiology.

SEE: Precocial and Altricial Young, p. 401; Incubation: Controlling Egg Temperatures, p. 273; Oystercatchers and Oysters, p. 155; Monogamy, p. 335; Polygyny, p. 265; Polyandry, p. 195; Cooperative Breeding, p. 275; Crèches, p. 45; Bird Milk, p. 243. REFS: Hussell, 1988; Stamps *et al.*, 1985; Trivers, 1974.

Distraction Displays

SOME nesting birds make themselves as conspicuous as possible when approached by a predator. Rather than attempting to cover their nests, eggs, or young, these birds deliberately attract the attention of the intruder, usually behaving in an exaggerated manner. As Gilbert White, writing of hens, described in 1773:

Thus an hen, just become a mother, is no longer that placid bird she used to be, but with feathers standing on end, wings hovering, and clocking note, she runs about like one possessed. Dams will throw themselves in the way of the greatest danger in order to avert it from their progeny.

Birds may use other tactics, including feigning an injury, exhaustion, or illness to divert a predator from the nest or young. Again, as White observed, 'Thus a partridge will tumble along before a sportsman in order to draw away the dogs from her helpless covey'. Birds may also feign attacks.

Broken-wing displays are most easily provoked and most realistic in waders, waterfowl, and other species with ground nests. They typically involve spreading and dragging a wing or tail, while slowly fluttering away from the nest or young, and may include calling or the flashing of brightly contrasting feathers.

Purple Sandpiper

Calidris maritima

ATLAS 133; PMH 110; PER 116; HFP 128; HPCW 98; NESTS 150; BWP3:345

BLDS: ♂	4 (3) 1 brood INCU: ♂♀	
Monogamy	21–22	

 FLDG: ♂
?

Breeding habitat Coasts, upland tundra, and along streams.

Displays Has display flight, circling above territory with rapid shallow wing-beats, while singing. On ground ♂ lifts one wing vertically exposing white underside to rival.

Nesting Territorial. ♂ makes several scrapes; ♀ chooses one. Nest is a hollow lined with vegetation; in the open. Eggs pale buff to olive, variously marked with brown, 37mm, hatch within a day of each other. ♀ departs at or before eggs hatch and leaves ♂ to care for the young.

Diet Mainly feeds on insects on inland sites, in summer. In winter, picks molluscs and a variety of invertebrates from wave-swept rocks, running quickly to catch items as waves retreat and to avoid waves when they come in. Also finds prey by turning over seaweed and small rocks.

Winters On rocky, seaweed-covered shores, from Spain northwards, in areas free from ice; in small flocks.

Conservation No obvious changes in numbers, breeds from N America to Europe and a small part of arctic Asia.

Essays Sandpipers, Social Systems, and Territoriality, p. 189; Distraction Displays, p. 175; Wader Displays, p. 181.

Dunlin

Calidris alpina

ATLAS 131; PMH 110; PER 116; HFP 126; HPCW 98; NESTS 149; BWP3:356

BLDS: ♂♀	3–4 (2–6) 1 brood INCU: ♂♀	
Monogamy	21–22(20–24)	

	Summer: Insects Winter: Aq inverts	
FLDG: ♂♀ 19–21		Ground glean

Breeding habitat Moorland, tundra, coastal marshes, rivers, and shores.

Displays In song flight, ♂ ascends quickly then circles over territory with shallow fast wing-beats. Also sings on ground. Towards rival also has wing-lift display (see Purple Sandpiper above).

Nesting Nest is shallow cup concealed in grass tussock, made by both birds during displays. Eggs pale buffish or greenish, variously marked with dark or red browns, 34mm, hatch synchronously. ♂ remains with brood longer than does ♀.

Diet Pecks for insects on breeding grounds. In winter, rapidly probes mud for marine worms, molluscs, or other invertebrates; usually wades into shallow water, up to belly, and may immerse head.

Winters Mud-flats, salt-marshes, often in large flocks, from UK south to Africa and to SE Asia.

Conservation Has declined locally in NW Europe following habitat losses (such as conifer planting in Scotland) but still abundant and widely distributed across N America, Europe, Asia.

Essays Flock Defence, p. 257; Sandpipers, Social Systems, and Territoriality, p. 189; Wader Feeding, p. 187; Distraction Displays, p. 175; Wader Displays, p. 181; Wader Migration and Conservation, p. 167.

Refs Marchant et al. 1990.

Distraction display. A Little Ringed Plover feigns injury to lure a predator away from its nest.

Some displays give the impression of a small running mammal. In the 'rodent-run' display of the tundra-nesting Purple Sandpiper, the bird drags its wings (creating the illusion of a second pair of legs), erects its feathers (providing some resemblance to fur), and 'squeals' while dodging invisible barriers.

Effectively leading a predator away from the nest would be favoured strongly by natural selection, but how these stylized antics evolved remains controversial among behavioural ecologists. Some conclude that distraction displays are a product of the conflicting desires of the parent to approach the predator aggressively, to return to the nest, or to retreat. Others suggest that they evolved directly as a defence against particular predators, with more stylized sequences found in species that have had longer association with heavy predation. In either case, fear is a prerequisite; tame birds cannot be induced to perform distraction displays, and demonstrations may be reduced or impossible to elicit if the bird is repeatedly subjected to nondamaging intrusions.

Experimenters have measured how close to the nest an intruder can approach before a distraction display is elicited and how far from the nest the parent moves before performing. Interestingly, the most conspicuous and therefore most risky distraction displays occur at different stages in precocial and altricial species. Once precocial young hatch, they are soon able to fend for themselves. Parental defence at this point may be crucial in aiding them to reach independence. It may be worth the parent risking its life in defence of its young because the benefit of doing so is greater than that achieved by abandoning the young to their fate and beginning a new nesting attempt in whatever remains of the season. In altricial young the comparable point — when the young have a sporting chance of independent existence — is reached later, near fledging. In these species this is generally the period of most vigorous distraction displays.

SEE: Visual Displays, p. 33; Precocial and Altricial Young, p. 401; Mobbing, p. 261; Duck Displays, p. 47; Wader Displays, p. 181; Altruism, p. 245; Gulls Are Attracted to Their Predators, p. 203; Bird-brained, p. 385; Parental Care, p. 171. REFS: Armstrong, 1949; Barash, 1975; Hinde, 1954a, b; White, 1789.

Broad-billed Sandpiper

Limicola falcinellus

ATLAS 131; PMH 111; PER 116; HFP 126; HPCW 98; NESTS 149; BWP3:372

BLDS: ♂	4 (3) 1 brood INCU: ♂♀	FLDG: ●♀
Monogamy	21	?

Seeds | Ground glean

Breeding habitat Arctic bogs.

Displays Has song flights that may last up to an hour; parachuting glides are followed by descents with wings held above body, followed by ascents with rapidly beating wings, and intermittent fluttering of the wings.

Nesting Territorial. ♂ makes 2–3 nests; ♀ chooses one. Nest is lined with vegetation; in tussock in wet area. Eggs pale buff to grey, speckled or blotched with browns, 32mm, hatch synchronously. ♂ cares for older chicks.

Diet Pecks at surface for freshwater insects on breeding grounds and pecks or probes for various invertebrates on mud-flats in winter.

Winters Freshwater marshes and mud-flats around Indian Ocean to Australia; in small flocks.

Conservation No obvious changes in numbers, but species has a limited and possibly fragmented range from Norway into Russian arctic. Appears to be much less numerous than most wading birds, with Finnish population, for example, numbering 10 000 pairs or less.

Ruff

Philomachus pugnax

ATLAS 136; PMH 112; PER 116; HFP 132; HPCW 98; NESTS 157; BWP3:385

BLDS: ♀	4 (2–3) 1 brood INCU: ♀	FLDG: ♀
Polygyny	20–23	25–28

Greens | Ground glean

Breeding habitat Marshlands or wet meadows.

Displays See notes below.

Nesting Nest is scrape lined with grass, concealed in marshy vegetation. Eggs olive, heavily and variously marked with dark brown, 44mm, hatch synchronously.

Diet Mainly invertebrates, some plants. Walks in dry area or wades into shallow water probing with beak.

Winters Mainly inland marshes, but also coastal marshes, from UK south to S Africa, east to India.

Conservation Considerable decreases in Europe, with many local extinctions, due to habitat drainage. Recolonized the UK, but formerly much more widespread. Species occurs widely across northern Europe and Asia. See p. 529.

Notes ♀s are much smaller than the ♂s which, in summer, have the elaborate feather ruffs which give the species its name. A complete range of colours is possible, but the feather ruffs and head tufts tend to be one of two colours: (1) black to dark brown, and (2) ochre to white. From 5 to 20 (up to 50) ♂s display on the leks, where the ♀s visit and select their mates. The two colour forms use different tactics on the leks. Birds with tufts of colour phase (1) tend to be resident on a given lek and hold fixed display sites, while other birds try to establish display sites on several leks. Birds with tufts of colour phase (2) tend not to hold fixed display sites and try to obtain matings opportunistically. They often perform coordinated displays towards ♀. The different mating tactics all pay off, but some individual birds are very much more successful than others.

Essays Leks, p. 123; Polygyny, p. 265; Sandpipers, Social Systems, and Territoriality, p. 189; Wetland Conservation, p. 145.

Refs van Rhijn 1991 is a book about this species.

Spacing of Wintering Waders

GROUPS of waders feeding in coastal areas and along the margins of inland lakes and rivers are a familiar sight to most European birdwatchers. Such scenes are common during migration and, in many places, throughout the winter as well. The spacing systems found among wintering waders cover the spectrum from individual feeding territories to large, tightly integrated foraging flocks.

At one extreme of the territoriality-flocking continuum are a few species that are usually observed as isolated individuals and only rarely seen in small groups. At the opposite extreme are species such as Knots (*Calidris canutus*) that are virtually always in moderate-to-large cohesive flocks. Most waders, however, fall somewhere in between, and many exhibit varying 'spacing behaviours' depending upon location, time of day, and density of food resources.

Behaviours involved in defence of a feeding site often differ markedly from those seen in defence of a breeding territory. The extensive vocalizations and aerial displays typical of the breeding season are replaced by conspicuous visual displays performed on the ground.

Like breeding territories, some feeding territories tend to have well-defined boundaries, and are occupied continuously for weeks or even months. But here again, a continuum exists from rather stable territories to those defended for only a few hours or a few days. Grey Plovers exhibit both extremes, although individual birds are apparently faithful to a single spacing strategy. In England, studies of colour-marked first-year birds reveal that they compete for feeding territories among themselves and with adult birds. Birds that successfully secure a feeding territory will defend it for up to six months and return to the very same territory in successive winters. The majority of wintering birds remain non-territorial, however, although some will defend feeding sites for short periods ranging from a few hours to a few days in a single winter.

Some birds defend 'portable' territories with boundaries that shift as food resources fluctuate (e.g. sand-dwelling invertebrates in the wave-wash zone along a beach, whose abundance varies as the tide rises or falls). An extreme example is a Sanderling defending an area around a foraging Black Turnstone (*Arenaria melanocephala*, a very close relative of the Turnstone) along the Pacific coast of North America. As the Black Turnstone flips through beach litter, the Sanderling forages in the newly exposed substrate (an example of 'commensal feeding', in which the Sanderling benefits without interfering with the Black Turnstone). When the Black Turnstone moves along the beach, the Sanderling follows, essentially defending a moving territory centred on the Black Turnstone.

Most of the evidence gathered from migration and wintering field studies indicates that non-breeding (wintering) territoriality is primarily resource-

Jack Snipe

Lymnocryptes minimus

ATLAS 141; PMH 112; PER 118; HFP 140; HPCW 98; NESTS 164; BWP3:403

		4 (3) 1 (2?) broods			
BLDS: ♂♀?	INCU: ♀?		FLDG: ?		
Monogamy	17–24		?	Seeds	

Breeding habitat Wet, marshy ground, and bogs among boreal forests.

Displays ♂ (possible also ♀) has display flight, with steep climb, fast wing-beats, followed by steep dive and shorter climb. In final dive, bird looks as though it will crash into ground.

Nesting Nest is lined with vegetation; sometimes in hummock, usually near water. Eggs olive to brown, with much dark brown blotching and speckling, 39mm, hatch synchronously.

Diet Mainly aquatic insects, but also other invertebrates and seeds, taken by probing with long beak; probably crepuscular or nocturnal.

Winters Freshwater marshes UK S to Africa, E to India and SE Asia; usually solitary.

Conservation Outside Scandinavia (where no obvious changes), the numbers of this species are not well known, because of the difficulties of counting them. Widely distributed across N Europe and Asia.

Common Snipe

Gallinago gallinago

ATLAS 139; PMH 113; PER 118; HFP 140; HPCW 99; NESTS 163; BWP3:409

		4 (2–5) 1 (2?) broods	
BLDS: ♀	INCU: ♀		FLDG: ♂♀
See below	18–20		

Breeding habitat A wide range of wet areas.

Displays Has conspicuous 'drumming' flight, where ♂ flies high then has steep dive with wings beating and tail widely fanned, with the outer feathers on each side separate from the rest. It is the vibrations of these feathers that produce the drumming sound. Bird then climbs and repeats display.

Nesting ♂ tries to mate with any ♀ on his territory and ♀ may be attended by more than one ♂. Nest is scrape concealed in clump of vegetation. Eggs olive to light brown, with dark brown blotches, 39mm, hatch synchronously. Parents divide brood between them, and each looks after one group.

Diet Aquatic invertebrates, mainly insects, captured by probing mud deeply, sometimes while walking, but also taken from a semicircle while standing still.

Winters As in breeding season, in a wide range of wet areas; leaves marshes that freeze. Some populations are resident.

Conservation Abundant and very widely distributed worldwide but has suffered declines in many areas where marshes drained.

Essays Wader Displays, p. 181; Wetland Conservation, p. 145; Nonvocal Sounds, p. 263.

Refs Marchant et al. 1990.

based, appearing and disappearing in response to changes in resource abundance and density. Territoriality is most common at intermediate food densities and in places where, or at times when, the risk of predation on the territory-holder is low. When food is scarce, territoriality disappears because the amount of food within a defensible area is simply insufficient to meet the energy needs of the territory-holder. Similarly, when food is superabundant, territoriality disappears, in part because the energy cost of trying to keep out invading birds attracted to the rich food supply is too great. Likewise, the size of individual territories also shows plasticity that depends on the density of prey.

Whether or not wintering waders are territorial is sensitive also to the risk territory-holders run of being eaten by falcons. Small solitary waders have been shown to be more susceptible to falcon predation than those in flocks. Flexibility is clearly a key feature of spacing systems exhibited by non-breeding waders.

Territorial defence in wintering waders shows striking parallels with defence of feeding territories by sunbirds. Central to both groups is the nature of their food resources. Only spatially clumped, energy-rich, and temporally renewable types of food can be defended — features shared by such disparate types of food as nectar produced by flowers and invertebrates whose availability shifts with the tides.

SEE: Wader Feeding, p. 187; Wader Displays, p. 181; Wader Migration and Conservation, p. 167; Territoriality, p. 397; Wintering Site Tenacity, p. 409; Sandpipers, Social Systems, and Territoriality, p. 189; Commensal Feeding, p. 27. REFS: Evans *et al.*, 1984; Myers, 1984; Myers *et al.*, 1979; Townshend, 1985.

Wader Displays

WADER displays are extremely varied and often complex. Above all, the meaning of both displays and calls appears to depend upon the ecological and social contexts in which they are given. During winter, waders are often found in flocks in estuarine mud flats and other open habitats. When breeding they usually nest on the ground, most often in the open. Thus highly visible, they are especially suitable subjects for studies of avian visual communication. Indeed, plumage colour and pattern are perhaps the simplest bases of wader communication, and in the breeding season frequently suffice to signal a bird's sex.

While their acoustic communication is not as well studied as that of passerines, waders also signal extensively using sound. Wader vocalizations tend to match the context of their open habitats. Loud, low-frequency, repeated sounds are used during aerial displays as territorial signals and to attract mates. Oystercatchers and others, for example, have evolved loud, piercing calls that carry over the crashing surf of rocky coasts. Such sounds

Great Snipe

Gallinago media

ATLAS 140; PMH 113; PER 118; HFP 140; HPCW 99; NESTS 162; BWP3:423

 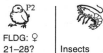

BLDS: ♂	4 (3–5) 1 (2?) broods INCU: ♀	FLDG: ♀	
Polygyny	22–24	21–28?	Insects

Breeding habitat Wet tundra and open marshes, wet ground within forests.

Displays ♂s have traditional communal display ground (lek) in open wet areas where typically 12–16 ♂s gather towards dusk. As night falls, birds begin to jump up, sometimes in unison, fluttering their wings, displaying conspicuous white tail feathers. Birds tend to face the centre of the lek, calling and producing drumming sound on ground. ♀s approach ♂s at lek at night.

Nesting Nest is lined with grass and concealed in thick cover. Eggs pale buff to greyish, blotched dark brown at the larger end, 43mm. Little known about nesting habits.

Diet Earthworms and insects, feeding method probably similar to Snipe, but apparently avoids wetter areas.

Winters In Africa usually in marshes, but also drier ground.

Conservation Retreated from western part of range in last century, perhaps due to habitat losses and hunting. Occurs from NE Europe into adjacent parts of Asia. See p. 529.

Notes Unlike other lekking species (Ruff, for example), the sexes are essentially identical in size and plumage. If anything, the ♀s are slightly larger than the ♂s.

Essays Leks, p. 123.

Woodcock

Scolopax rusticola

ATLAS 139; PMH 114; PER 118; HFP 140; HPCW 101; NESTS 159; BWP3:444

BLDS: ♀	4 (2–5) 1 (2?) broods INCU: ♀	FLDG: ♀	
Polygyny	21–24	15–20	Earthworms

Breeding habitat Large woodlands with ground cover.

Displays At dawn and dusk, song flight of ♂s (called roding): birds fly above forest and along edges of openings, with slow wing-beats (looks somewhat like an owl), and gives unusual call. ♀ flies up to join ♂, they land, and mate.

Nesting Nest is lined with dead leaves, well hidden in low cover. Eggs buff to brownish, spotted and blotched darker, hatch synchronously. ♂ stays with ♀ only long enough to improve his chances of paternity, then continues with roding display to attract another ♀.

Diet Insects and earthworms, picked up from surface, from under litter, or when probing wet ground.

Winters Resident in much of UK, migrates S and W from central and northern Europe; occurs in a wide range of wooded habitats.

Conservation Some local declines, but has spread and increased in UK and other western parts of range in the last 100 years or so. Widely distributed across Europe and Asia.

Essays Eyes Like a Hawk, p. 89; Polygyny, p. 265; Swallowing Stones, p. 135; Transporting Young, p. 9; Migration, p. 377.

Refs Marchant et al. 1990.

will remain recognizable over greater distances than more complex, high-frequency songs. They are less attenuated by distance and their repetitious nature helps to differentiate them from background noise. Exchanges between parents and offspring at the nest and other kinds of short-distance acoustic communication are not, of course, subject to the same constraints. The sounds produced by waders vary greatly, both from individual to individual and in the same individual in different situations. For instance, many species of calidridine sandpipers (members of the tribe Calidridini, which includes the smallest sandpipers) produce two distinct types of call: a trill lasting almost a second, and a much shortened, frequency-modulated call. Edward H. Miller, who has studied acoustic communication in waders extensively, reports that one male North American Least Sandpiper (*Calidris minutilla*) rarely trilled, while another male almost never gave the short call. Furthermore, the mix of trills and short calls uttered by a single sandpiper would change as the individual changed its direction of flight toward or away from an intruder.

Waders also communicate with a wide range of visual displays, some aerial, some on the ground. Aerial displays are especially suited to communication in open habitats, since the display can be viewed without obstruction over relatively long distances (woodland birds make much less use of aerial displays). The aerial display of the Lapwing has been studied in great detail. The male Lapwing starts a typical display sequence with 'butterfly flight' (slow, deep wingbeats), followed by a zigzag flight in which the body is rotated from side to side around its long axis. During the latter phase, the bird produces a humming sound with its specially modified outer primary feathers. Then the Lapwing flies low and soundlessly with slow, shallow wingbeats, finishing that phase with a steep climb. At the end of the climb there is a period of straight flight during which two distinct 'motifs' of its song are sung, and a third started. The third motif is finished during a steep bank and vertical dive. The bird may then repeat some of the earlier display components.

Other waders have similar components in their aerial displays. As examples, Oystercatchers may perform butterfly flights, Solitary Sandpipers (*Tringa solitaria*) do low display flights, and Common Snipe include dives in their high display flights. Aerial displays are very diverse, with variation in height, direction (straight, circling, undulating, etc.), wingbeat amplitude (shallow, deep), wingbeat frequency (rapid to glide), patterns of plumage display (especially tails or wings spread or flashed), calling during flight, and post-landing behaviour (deliberately exaggerated wing-folding, strutting). Descent from flight displays, with the frequent production of non-vocal sounds, is thought to convey a great deal of information about the signaller's change of behaviour.

As previously mentioned, the problem with interpreting wader aerial displays is that they are used in a wide variety of situations. For example, the Lapwing display may occur in response to predators, when a male returns to its territory, in response to other males, in response to females, and 'spontaneously' (when there is no obvious triggering stimulus). Furthermore, the precise form of the display varies with the stage of the breeding cycle, the time of day, the weather, and the audience.

Black-tailed Godwit

Limosa limosa

ATLAS 138; PMH 114; PER 118; HFP 138; HPCW 101; NESTS 158; BWP3:458

BLDS: ♂
Monogamy

3–4 (5)
1 brood
INCU: ♂ ♀
22–24

P2
FLDG: ♂ ♀
25–30 (35)

Breeding habitat Wet uplands and damp meadows.

Displays ♂s display to rivals by crouching or by pointing head downward, bending legs, and ruffling feathers, or by moving head even lower and pointing rear upwards; there is often much fighting between rivals. ♂s attract ♀s by acrobatic display flight while calling.

Nesting Territorial, within loosely dispersed colonies. Nest is scrape lined with grass more or less concealed in short vegetation. ♂ builds several scrapes; ♀ chooses one. Eggs olive to brown, heavily blotched dark brown, 47mm, hatch synchronously.

Diet Probes, often rapidly, for aquatic invertebrates while wading in shallow water. Head is often completely submerged.

Winters Usually coastal marshes and estuaries, also freshwater marshes; from Europe and S to Africa, India, and N Australia; in flocks.

Conservation In this century has increased in NW, colonizing or recolonizing grazed meadows. Species is vulnerable to habitat drainage and over much of W Europe breeding populations are small and fragmented. (Holland has a large population, however.) Isolated populations across Asia. The Icelandic population is an isolated, distinct subspecies; it is common.

Essays The Colour of Birds, p. 137; Wader Displays, p. 181; Wetland Conservation, p. 145.

Refs Marchant et al. 1990.

Bar-tailed Godwit

Limosa lapponica

ATLAS 138; PMH 115; PER 118; HFP 138; HPCW 101; NESTS 159; BWP3:473

BLDS: ♂ ♀ ?
Monogamy

3–4 (2)
1 brood
INCU: ♣ ♀
20–21

P2
FLDG: ♂ ♀
?

Breeding habitat Marshy tundra.

Displays Very little known because breeding areas are so remote.

Nesting Perhaps territorial. Nest is scrape lined with vegetation more or less in open. Eggs olive to greenish, variably spotted with dark brown, 54mm, hatch synchronously.

Diet Probes for aquatic invertebrates in moderately shallow water, sometimes with head under water. Takes insects on

breeding grounds and marine worms, molluscs, and crustaceans in winter.

Winters Mainly coastal; estuaries from UK to Africa to Australia; in flocks.

Conservation Declines in Finland in early part of this century from egg hunting. Common and widespread nesting from Scandinavia across Asia to Alaska, but breeding areas are remote and birds are difficult to census.

Essays Wader Feeding, p. 187; Wader Migration and Conservation, p. 167.

Context seems to play a similar role in giving meaning to the ground displays of waders. For instance, five different displays used by Black-tailed Godwits in aggressive encounters have been studied in detail. They include two 'upright' displays in which the legs are stretched, one with the back plumage smooth or slightly ruffled, the other with it ruffled. In each case, the wings, tail, and bill are in different positions. The non-upright displays are 'forward' (body almost horizontal, legs not stretched, neck extended, plumage very ruffled, bill usually down); 'crouch' (body horizontal, legs deeply bent, neck withdrawn, plumage ruffled or smoothed, bill in various positions); and 'tilt' (body slanted forward with breast near ground, legs deeply bent, neck withdrawn, plumage smooth, bill forward).

Analysis of these five displays and their variations revealed no simple association with attack or retreat behaviour. Neither was any component of the displays (e.g. ruffling of plumage, lowering of bill) clearly a sign of attack or retreat. Again it appears that details of the context in which the displays occur (rather than the attack-retreat dichotomy) are required for their interpretation. Indeed, attacking Black-tailed Godwits within two metres of their opponents showed a different array of displays from those of godwits separated by four metres or more.

Often the same general elements are used in both aggressive and sexual displays, so that their interpretation depends entirely on the audience or the stage of the breeding cycle. Male Least Sandpipers use a forward tilt, elevated tail, and wing-up display when approaching other individuals of either sex. Courtship displays are differentiated from antagonistic ones only by being more slowly paced and more stereotyped (showing less variation). Male Killdeer (*Charadrius vociferus*), a North American plover which has been found more than thirty times in Europe, may do a 'forward-tipped, neck-extended' display during which the legs are often kicked backward (scraping) when defending their territories against other males, when advertising for mates, during nest building, and as a pre-copulatory display.

Certain kinds of display show constancy of context not only within but also between species. For example, Little Ringed Plovers, among many others, all show a similar threat posture in which the body is kept horizontal, the flank feathers are spread over the closed wings, and the head withdrawn, giving the individual a flattened appearance.

To make sense of communication in waders, careful notes should be made of the detailed form of the communication itself as well as of the context in which it occurs. Keep records of the physical environment (season, time of day, weather, illumination, background noise, etc.), the state of the communicating bird itself (sex, maturity, breeding condition, activity before, during, and after communicating—feeding, flying, nest-building, resting, etc.), and the identity of birds of the same species, other bird species, or other animals to whom the communication might be directed (for instance, conspecifics of the same or opposite sex, individuals of closely related species that might compete for resources, potential predators). Pay particular attention to subtle movements, such as bobbing of the head, a slight change in the angle at which the body is held, or an extension of the wings before they are

Whimbrel

Numenius phaeopus

ATLAS 138; PMH 107; PER 120; HFP 138; HPCW 101; NESTS 158; BWP3:484

 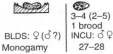

		3–4 (2–5) 1 brood	P2		
BLDS: ♀(♂?)	INCU: ♂♀		FLDG: ♂♀		
Monogamy	27–28		35–40	Insects	Probes

Breeding habitat Moorland and tundra, sometimes fairly wet, also bogs within boreal forest.

Displays ♂s have song flight over territory, steep climbs alternate with the birds descending, without flapping, and with wings held stiffly. ♂s court ♀ with tail fanned to expose white rump. (In some subspecies white is reduced or absent, however.) Birds may sing on ground together.

Nesting Territorial. Nest is sparsely lined and in open. Eggs greenish to buffish, blotched with dark brown, 58mm, hatch synchronously. Become independent of parents at fledging and breed when 2 years old.

Diet Aquatic invertebrates taken from the surface or with short probe. On shores, follows retreating tide.

Winters Mainly coastal on mud-flats and also coral reef flats, almost worldwide south of about 30°N; in flocks.

Conservation No great changes in numbers and species (with distinct subspecies) occurs across Arctic. Many nesting populations are located in remote areas where censuing is very difficult. Has recovered in Scotland from lows in 1930s and 40s, but is still vulnerable to land use changes.

Refs Marchant et al. 1990.

Curlew

Numenius arquata

ATLAS 137; PMH 116; PER 120; HFP 138; HPCW 102; NESTS 157; BWP3:500

		4 (2–5) 1 brood	P2	Summer: Insects Winter:	
BLDS: ♂	INCU: ♂♀		FLDG: ♂♀	Aq inverts	
Monogamy	27–29		32–38		Probes

Breeding habitat Moorland, freshwater marshes, wet fields, or meadows along rivers.

Displays ♂ has song flight with steep ascents and downward glides (like Whimbrel) with wings in shallow V. Sometimes several birds involved. ♂'s threat displays similar to those of Black-tailed Godwit, with legs bent, bill pointed down, and rear up.

Nesting Territorial. Nest is shallow hollow on ground, often well concealed in vegetation, but sometimes exposed, lined with plant material. Several built by ♂; ♀ chooses one. Eggs greenish to brownish, variously marked with browns, 68mm, hatch synchronously.

Diet Mainly invertebrates, berries, and seeds on breeding grounds. Aquatic invertebrates in winter. Takes prey from surface or from probing (usually shallow probes) into mud, for marine worms, or grass tussocks for insects.

Winters Mainly coastal mud-flats, estuaries throughout Europe, Africa, and Asia; in flocks.

Conservation Ability to use man-made habitats has certainly helped species, but local decreases can be attributed to wetland drainage and, in the past, hunting. Nests widely across Europe and Asia.

Essays Drinking, p. 313; Sandpipers, Social Systems, and Territoriality, p. 189; Birds and Agriculture, p. 365; Wader Feeding, p. 187; Wetland Conservation, p. 145; Wader Migration and Conservation, p. 167.

Refs Marchant et al. 1990.

folded after landing. These may seem insignificant, but they may carry important messages for other birds.

SEE: Visual Displays, p. 33; Duck Displays, p. 47; Environmental Acoustics, p. 327; Spacing of Wintering Waders, p. 179; Observing and Recording Bird Biology, p. xxxiii; Gull Displays, p. 205. REF.: Miller, 1984.

Wader Feeding

TRYING to watch warblers feeding can be a neck-and-patience-straining exercise, as Robert MacArthur found in the course of his North American classic study of how these small insect-eaters divide their food resources. Such 'resource partitioning' by birds can be observed in much greater comfort, however, while seated behind a spotting scope (perhaps in a shelter) watching waders forage in an estuary.

In such a situation you might see an Avocet. Its upcurved bill seems less strange when you notice how it is used as a scythe, by swinging it back and forth in the water, stirring the bottom and snatching up insects and small crustaceans thus exposed. Nearby a Black-winged Stilt might stalk its victims in water 15 cm deep or more, a habitat inaccessible to the stubby-legged Temminck's Stints snatching invertebrates from the surface of an adjacent mud flat. On the same flat a Curlew might use its 23 cm, curved, forceps-like bill to probe the burrow of a large marine worm, while a Dunlin uses its short beak to feel for smaller worms or insect larvae just below the mud's surface, and a Kentish Plover collects prey from the surface, hunting by sight alone (since the pattering feet of a flock would warn sensitive prey to withdraw into their burrows). In general the size of prey taken by waders increases with body size, but not with bill length.

Although crowded together at high tide, waders begin to sort themselves out into preferred feeding habitats as the tide recedes. Little Stints remain on drier, algae-covered mud, picking food from the surface; beyond them, Knots and Dunlins concentrate on probing bare, wet mud. Farther out, the long-legged Bar-tailed Godwits wade while probing the mud beneath shallow water. On sandy, wave-washed beaches Sanderlings dash nimbly back and forth at the very edge of the ebb and flow, probing the sand for tiny shrimp-like crustaceans.

Turnstones, as their name suggests, fill their bellies in quite a different way — they turn over rocks, shells, and even seaweed to expose concealed prey, and sometimes dig deeply into sand. Oystercatchers, similarly well named, can extract a mussel's meat from between its shells, but that's a story for another essay.

Wader foraging behaviour can alter markedly as environmental conditions change. For instance, Grey and Ringed Plovers in England feed more on large prey items when the weather is warm, winds die down, and the substrate is

Spotted Redshank

Tringa erythropus

ATLAS 134; PMH 116; PER 120; HFP 130; HPCW 103; NESTS 154; BWP3:517

  | 4 (3)
1 brood
BLDS: ♂♀ INCU: ♂ (♀?)
Monogamy 23? | FLDG:♂(♀?)
? |
Ground glean

Breeding habitat   Bogs or near rivers in boreal forest.

Displays   Not well known. Has song flight.

Nesting   Nest is shallow hollow lined with vegetation, often in open. Eggs greenish or olive, blotched or spotted blackish-brown, 47mm, hatch synchronously. ♂s take greater share of nest chores, ♀s may not help at all or leave as early as a week before hatching, though some leave after hatching.

Diet   Aquatic invertebrates, obtained by picking or probing. Will wade up to belly or even swim, immersing head and neck and up-ending.

Winters   Freshwater marshes, mud-flats, estuaries; from the UK to Africa to SE Asia; sometimes in flocks.

Conservation   No obvious changes, but most of the breeding range is remote; occurs across European and Asiatic boreal forest.

Essays   Who Incubates?, p. 285; Sandpipers, Social Systems, and Territoriality, p. 189.

Redshank

Tringa totanus

ATLAS 134; PMH 117; PER 120; HFP 130; HPCW 103; NESTS 153; BWP3:525

  |  4 (3–5)
1 brood
BLDS: ♀ INCU: ♂♀
Monogamy 24 (22–29) | FLDG:♂♀,♂♀
25–35 | Probes

Breeding habitat   A wide variety of inland wet meadows, marshes, and coastal wetlands.

Displays   On the ground ♂s chase and try to mate with any ♀ in early stages of displays. Display flight by continuously calling ♂s alternates ascents with shallow, jerky wing-beats and downward glides. This attracts ♀s who fly up to follow ♂s. On landing, ♂s lift wings vertically.

Nesting   Loosely colonial in some populations. Nest is in shallow hollow, often in tussock or other cover, lined with grass. Eggs cream to buff, spotted and blotched with reddish-brown 45mm, hatch synchronously.

Diet   Invertebrates; insects on breeding grounds, marine worms, crustaceans, and molluscs in winter. Pecks at prey on surface of mud, or uses shallow probes into wet mud.

Winters   Mainly coastal marshes; in Europe, Asia, and Africa. In loose flocks.

Conservation   Declines following wetland drainage in many areas. Common and widely distributed across Europe and Asia, but local in SW and into N Africa.

Essays   Raptor Hunting, p. 113; Wader Displays, p. 181; Sandpipers, Social Systems, and Territoriality, p. 189; Wetland Conservation, p. 145; Wader Migration and Conservation, p. 167; Breeding Site Tenacity, p. 219.

Refs   Marchant et al. 1990.

Left: Oystercatcher opening mussels. Centre: Turnstone foraging on items beneath rocks. Right, bottom to top: Ringed Plover (searches surface); probing species that forage at different depths — Sanderling, Knot, Greenshank, Bar-tailed Godwit, Curlew.

wet, all of which make these prey more active. When large prey are not as available the birds concentrate their feeding on smaller species.

In a single year, one Oystercatcher can consume more than 150 kg of mussel meat. Indeed, each day many waders take in about a third of their weight in food. When you see huge mixed-species flocks of waders feeding in estuaries, you can view it as a tribute to the great biological productivity of those environments.

SEE: Oystercatchers and Oysters, p. 155; Spacing of Wintering Waders, p. 179; Hartley's Titmice and MacArthur's Warblers, p. 425. REFS: Burger and Olla, 1984; Evans *et al.*, 1984; Lifjeld, 1984; Pienkowski, 1983; Wander, 1985.

Sandpipers, Social Systems, and Territoriality

STUDIES of breeding sandpipers in different arctic and subarctic habitats have shown how differences in mating systems and territoriality may be related to ecological factors such as the distribution and abundance of food resources

Marsh Sandpiper

Tringa stagnatilis

ATLAS 135; PMH 117; PER 120; HFP 130; HPCW 103; NESTS 155; BWP3:540

BLDS: ?
Monogamy

4 (5)
1 brood
INCU: ♂♀
?

FLDG: ♂♀
?

Breeding habitat Edges of lakes and marshes, almost always by fresh water.

Displays Not well known; has up-and-down display flight and ground chases like other members of the genus *Tringa*.

Nesting Solitary, but sometimes in scattered colonies. Nest is scrape with sparse grass lining in low vegetation. Eggs pale to buff, variously marked with reddish- and blackish-browns, 39mm, hatch synchronously.

Diet Aquatic invertebrates; feeds very actively, running erratically with quick jabs with its beak to pick up items on surface. These habits often quickly distinguish this species at a distance from other feeding waders. Regularly wades up to its belly.

Winters Freshwater and marine marshes; in flocks with other waders.

Conservation Numbers across CIS not well known, sporadic breeder outside CIS, and sensitive to wetland drainage.

Essays Who Incubates?, p. 285; Sandpipers, Social Systems, and Territoriality, p. 189.

Greenshank

Tringa nebularia

ATLAS 135; PMH 118; PER 120; HFP 130; HPCW 103; NESTS 155; BWP3:547

BLDS: ♂
Monogamy

3–4 (1–5)
1 brood
INCU: ♂♀
23–26

FLDG: ♂♀
25–31

Breeding habitat Moorland and tundra, often near forest or open areas within boreal forests, near water.

Displays ♂ has ascending-descending display flight like other members of its genus. ♀s rise up to join ♂s, who then pursue them.

Nesting Nest is scrape in open or in woodland clearings, lined with vegetation; ♂ makes several scrapes from which ♀ chooses one. Eggs pale cream to buff, variously and heavily marked with reddish-brown, 51mm, hatch synchronously. Birds first breed at two years.

Diet Aquatic invertebrates and small fish; walks or wades up to belly, picking or lunging at prey; occasionally swims and up-ends.

Winters Freshwater marshes and estuaries, from UK to S Africa to Australia; in small flocks and with other waders.

Conservation Common and widespread across northern Europe and Asia, with no great changes in numbers.

Essays Wader Displays, p. 181; Breeding Site Tenacity, p. 219.

Refs Nethersole-Thompson and Nethersole-Thompson (1979) is a book about this species; Marchant et al. 1990.

and the need to avoid predators. For instance, in northern Alaska where food is relatively scarce and unpredictable, monogamous Dunlins establish territories sufficiently large to provide the pair with enough food to carry it through the leanest of years. This keeps densities of breeding populations low; when male Dunlins holding territories were removed experimentally, other males promptly replaced them. The replacements apparently had either been non-territorial or occupied inferior locations. In contrast, in southern Alaska where the longer growing season provides a more predictable and abundant food supply, Dunlin territories are smaller and the population density higher. In both situations, however, Dunlin nests are well spaced because of male aggressiveness.

Experimental evidence shows that wide spacing of nests in gull colonies reduces nest predation, and this line of reasoning may apply to sandpipers also. Since foxes, weasels, gulls, and skuas prey heavily on sandpiper nests, one result of such spacing may be higher nesting success. The pair bond of Dunlins allows one adult to incubate while the other forages. In addition to limiting egg predation, the presence of both parents on the territory reduces egg chilling, which otherwise would delay the chicks' hatching and could reduce their chances of survival.

Some monogamous species, such as the Western Sandpiper (*Calidris mauri*), do not defend feeding territories. The Western's nesting habitat is patchily distributed but located close to abundant food. Western Sandpipers nest in 'islands' of shrubby vegetation on the tundra that provide some protection from predators, but they feed outside of their territories. Monogamous, territorial social systems like those of the Dunlin and Western Sandpiper are also found in a variety of other waders including the Knot (*Calidris canutus*), Redshank, Surfbird (*Aphriza virgata*), and the Purple, Terek, Semipalmated (*Calidris pusilla*), Least (*C. minutilla*), Baird's (*C. bairdii*), Rock (*C. ptilocnemis*), and Stilt (*C. himantopis*) Sandpipers.

Other species of sandpipers exhibit a variety of non-monogamous mating systems. Sanderlings, Temminck's Stints, and Little Stints are serially polyandrous: a female lays two or three clutches, which are normally fathered by more than one male and cared for by the males; alternatively, she lays two clutches — one male incubates one clutch while she incubates a second one. White-rumped (*Calidris fuscicollis*), Curlew, and Sharp-tailed (*C. acuminata*) Sandpipers are polygynous. Those males displaying on the best territories may have more than one mate, but do not assist in incubation. Pectoral Sandpipers (*Calidris melanotos*), Buff-breasted Sandpipers (*Tryngites subruficollis*), and Ruffs are promiscuous. Males display vigorously (the Buff-breasted Sandpipers and Ruffs on leks) but play no part in incubation. Female Pectoral Sandpipers, although they nest within the territory of a male, may mate with several males in close succession before the clutch is complete.

This second group of sandpipers shows much more variation in territorial strategies and reproductive effort than do the monogamous species. They are more 'opportunistic', adapting their strategies to local conditions, especially the temporary availability of abundant food. For instance, instead of being conservative like Dunlins and setting up a territory that will contain enough

Green Sandpiper

Tringa ochropus

ATLAS 136; PMH 119; PER 122; HFP 132; HPCW 103; NESTS 157; BWP3:569

 See below

BLDS: ?
Monogamy

 4 (2–3)
1 brood
INCU: ♂♀
20–23?

P2
FLDG: ♂♀
28?

 Surface dips

Breeding habitat Bogs or rivers in northern forests.

Displays Has an ascending then descending song flight like other species of this genus. ♀ flies up to join ♂.

Nesting Nest is usually up in a tree in an old nest of pigeon, thrush, or squirrel. Eggs cream, streaked and speckled with red or dark browns, 39mm, hatch synchronously. ♀ leaves before young fledge.

Diet Aquatic invertebrates, mainly insects, picked from surface of shallow water while wading up to belly or while swimming. Will duck head and neck under water. Also stirs up mud with feet.

Winters A variety of marshes, mainly fresh water from UK south to Africa and to SE Asia; usually solitary.

Conservation Perhaps some local declines in W but common and widespread across N and E Europe, as far south as Ukraine and across Asia.

Wood Sandpiper

Tringa glareola

ATLAS 136; PMH 119; PER 122; HFP 132; HPCW 103; NESTS 156; BWP3:577

See below

 See below
BLDS: ?
Monogamy

4 (3)
1 brood
INCU: ♂♀
22–23

P2
FLDG: ♂♀
30?

 Ground glean

Breeding habitat Bogs and marshes in northern forests.

Displays Not well known, but similar to other waders in this genus.

Nesting Birds may pair on migration. Nest is cup lined with vegetation, in ground, in cover, or in old nest (see Green Sandpiper). Eggs pale greenish or buff, variously marked with dark browns, 38mm, hatch synchronously. Young cared for mostly by ♂, as ♀ leaves soon after hatching.

Diet Insects and other aquatic invertebrates; probes, picks prey from surface, or sweeps with bill. Wades into water up to belly, sometimes immersing head and neck. •

Winters Broad range of fresh waters, lakes, streams; some on estuaries; Africa, SE Asia to Australia; in small flocks.

Conservation A sporadic breeder in western part of range (e.g. UK), with declines following habitat loss. Common and widespread across northern Europe and Asia. See p. 529.

Essays Who Incubates?, p. 285; Sandpipers, Social Systems, and Territoriality, p. 189.

food in any circumstances, Pectoral Sandpipers acquire fat reserves during their northward migration that permit them to ride out periods of food shortage. Like the White-rumped Sandpiper, they may breed at very high densities, in which case males may hold small (rather than their usual large) territories, since a continuous food supply is assured. Rather than guarding their nest to avoid predation, Pectorals keep the nest hidden, and incubation by only one adult reduces tell-tale traffic to and from the nest. Single adult incubation may also help to conserve food supplies for that adult and the young, since a second adult will not be depleting resources near the nest.

Opportunistic arctic breeders accept the increased hazards of nesting in highly productive locations such as lowland marshes. They get a rich harvest of insects in exchange, but risk increased predation associated with more closely spaced nests and flooding by summer rains (water runs off the tundra very rapidly because it cannot soak into the ground, which is frozen just below the surface).

The various mating systems offer different advantages, and those advantages accrue differentially to the two sexes. The females of polyandrous species are freed from the necessity of incubating the first clutch, so their reproductive output is increased. Polygynous males with good territories may greatly increase their reproductive output, gaining more benefit than the two or more females sharing the territory. This may generate an evolutionary pressure toward a lek system that frees the female, once mated, from any constraints inherent in the male's territorial needs. The best territory for a displaying male may not be the best one for a female to use for nesting and rearing her young. Females in promiscuous species are free to optimize their choice of nest sites.

Several of the sandpiper species usually considered monogamous are occasionally polygamous (polygynous or polyandrous) and show other tendencies toward more opportunistic strategies, such as communal feeding away from the territory while maintaining a monogamous pair bond. Also, they will re-nest if the first clutch is lost, suggesting a possible evolutionary stepping-stone to the strategy of the male rearing the first clutch and the female the second, which in turn could open the door to polyandry.

We have simplified the account here, and more research is needed to confirm various aspects of sandpiper social systems, but as you can see, different members of this structurally rather uniform group of birds have developed very different ways of reproducing successfully in northern environments.

SEE: Monogamy, p. 335; Polygyny, p. 265; Polyandry, p. 195; Leks, p. 123; Territoriality, p. 397; Wader Displays, p. 181. REFS: Myers, 1985; Myers *et al.*, 1987; Pitelka *et al.*, 1974; Tinbergen *et al.*, 1967.

Terek Sandpiper

Xenus cinereus

ATLAS 134; PMH 120; PER 122; HFP 130; HPCW 104; NESTS 153; BWP3:587

BLDS: ? Monogamy	4 (2–5) 1 brood INCU: ♂♀? 23–24?	FLDG: ♂♀ ?		Seeds	Ground glean

Breeding habitat Streams and marshes in boreal forests or tundra; in Finland, along shore of Baltic.

Displays Not well known.

Nesting Nest is lined with vegetation in open or short vegetation. Eggs cream or buff, variously marked with dark browns, 38mm, hatch synchronously.

Diet Aquatic insects and seeds on breeding grounds. Takes mud-flat invertebrates in winter, walking along with head down and probing exposed mud or picking from surface. Sometimes extracts long marine worms, which it washes in pools before eating.

Winters Coastal mud-flats from W Africa to India to Australia.

Conservation Numbers not well known, but in E wintering numbers indicate species is common; occurs across CIS.

Essays Who Incubates?, p. 285; Sandpipers, Social Systems, and Territoriality, p. 189.

Common Sandpiper

Actitis hypoleucos

ATLAS 135; PMH 120; PER 122; HFP 132; HPCW 104; NESTS 156; BWP3:594

Saucer BLDS: ♂♀ Monogamy	4 (3–5) 1 brood INCU: ♂♀ 21–22	FLDG: ♂♀ 26–28		

Breeding habitat Edges of lakes, rivers, and streams, particularly in hilly areas where water flow is rapid.

Displays In ground chases, birds run after each other with heads down. Threats also include wing-lifting, where one or both wings are lifted vertically for a few seconds to expose white underlinings towards intruder. Spreads and tilts tail towards rival. Over water, display flights are in tight circles, with birds alternating fast shallow wing-beats with gliding.

Nesting Territorial. Nest varies from flimsy to substantial and is lined with vegetation; placed in thick cover, close to water. Both sexes make scrapes and the ♀ chooses one and builds nest. Eggs buff or pale cream, finely and variously marked with red-browns, 36mm, hatch synchronously. Brood may be split and each half reared by one parent.

Diet Insects and other aquatic invertebrates, picked off ground or from between stones.

Winters A wide variety of freshwater habitats as well as coastal areas, from Europe S to Africa, India, and to Australia; usually solitary.

Conservation Some local decreases in W, but species is common and widespread across Europe and Asia.

Essays Wader Displays, p. 181.

Polyandry

THE mating of one female with more than one male while each male mates with only one female is known as polyandry (literally, 'many males'). It is a rare mating system, occurring in less than one per cent of all bird species, and is found mostly in waders. Polyandry is often accompanied by a reversal of sexual roles in which males perform all or most parental duties and females compete for mates. The common pattern of sexual dimorphism is often reversed in polyandrous birds: the female is often larger and more colourful than the male. This reversal confused early biologists and led Audubon to mislabel males and females in all his phalarope plates, and caused Gould to reverse male and female in his Grey Phalarope plate.

Two types of polyandry have been documented: simultaneous polyandry and sequential polyandry. The Dunnock often shows simultaneous polyandry in which two males associate with the same female in the same breeding territory. One male is dominant over the other, but the subordinate male often manages to mate with the female despite strenuous efforts of the dominant male to prevent it. If subordinate males manage to mate, they then help to feed the young. If they don't mate, they don't help.

In another form of simultaneous polyandry, each female holds a large territory containing the smaller nesting territories of two or more males who care for the eggs and tend the young. Northern Jacanas (*Jacana spinosa*, a New World 'lily-trotter') characteristically practise this form of polyandry. Females may mate with all of their consorts in one day and provide each male with help in defending his territory. A female will not copulate with a mate while their eggs are being incubated or during the first six weeks of the life of the chicks. If a clutch is lost, she will quickly copulate with the broodless male and lay a new batch of eggs within a few days.

A variation on the preceding theme is 'cooperative simultaneous polyandry', in which more than one male mates with a single female and the single clutch of mixed parentage is reared cooperatively by the female and her several mates. This arrangement occurs in Galápagos Hawks (*Buteo galapagoensis*), some populations of North American Harris' Hawks (*Parabuteo unicinctus*), (occasionally) in Acorn Woodpecker (*Melanerpes formicivorus*) groups, and (in the form of trios) has recently appeared as a common mating system in threatened populations of Bearded Vultures in the Pyrenees. In the last, shortage of prime territories for males may have made the behaviour advantageous, improving the reproductive output of all participants.

In sequential polyandry (the most typical form of this mating system), a female mates with a male, lays eggs, and then terminates the relationship with that male, leaving him to incubate the eggs while she goes off to repeat this sequence with another male. Red-necked and Grey Phalaropes are examples of sequentially polyandrous species. A possible evolutionary

Turnstone
Arenaria interpres

ATLAS 130; PMH 121; PER 122; HFP 122; HPCW 104; NESTS 148; BWP3:613

BLDS: ♀	4 (2–3) 1 brood	
Monogamy	INCU: ♂♥,♂♀	FLDG: ♂♀
	22–24 (27)	19–21

Breeding habitat Rocky coasts and estuaries, sometimes inland on rock-strewn tundra.

Displays Like other waders, has ground chases, with head down and feathers ruffled and wing-lifting displays. ♂ has display flight over territory, flying with deep, slow wing-beats. Often calls from exposed perch.

Nesting Nest is lined with leaves, on ground in open, often with a view of surrounding area. Eggs olive or pale green, heavily blotched blackish-brown, 41mm, hatch synchronously. ♀s leave before ♂s, who stay with young until they fledge.

Diet Insects and other aquatic invertebrates, carrion. Flips over seaweed, stones, flotsam, and probes into crevices.

Winters Rocky, seaweed-covered shores, and mud-flats, almost worldwide; in flocks.

Conservation Some local decreases, especially in S, but common and widespread across N Europe, Asia, and N America.

Essays The Colour of Birds, p. 137; Spacing of Wintering Waders, p. 179; Wader Feeding, p. 187; Wader Migration and Conservation, p. 167.

Red-necked Phalarope
Phalaropus lobatus

ATLAS 142; PMH 121; PER 124; HFP 128; HPCW 104; NESTS 152; BWP3:629

BLDS: ♂♀	4 (3) 1–2 broods	
Monogamy	INCU: ♂	FLDG: ♂
Polyandry	17–21	20?
		Ground glean

Breeding habitat Freshwater marshes, pools in tundra or northern edge of boreal forests.

Displays ♀ is more brightly coloured, initiates the displays. If ♂ is attracted, ♀ may swim around him and attempt to get him to follow her; she guards ♂ against other ♀s.

Nesting Nest is in grass tussock or in open close to water, lined with vegetation. Both sexes build scrapes, ♀ chooses one. Eggs greenish to buff, spotted and blotched darker, 30mm, hatch synchronously. ♀s may lay two clutches if ♂s are available to look after them. ♂s will attempt to mate with more than one ♀.

Diet Aquatic invertebrates picked from surface of water or floating vegetation (including seaweed), or from just beneath surface, sometimes up-ending, while swimming. Also wades, and walks over floating seaweed if firm enough. Like Grey Phalarope also spins on the water, swimming in a tight circle every second or so. Spinning is thought to bring prey to surface.

Winters In tropical seas, often far from shore where productivity is high (such as upwellings); usually in large flocks. Migrates overland and sometimes encountered in large flocks near breeding grounds, in early autumn or later, south on saline lakes.

Conservation Local declines but widespread and common around Arctic Ocean. See p. 529.

Essays Copulation, p. 87; Who Incubates?, p. 285; Polyandry, p. 195; Sexual Selection, p. 149; Differential Migration, p. 323.

precursor of sequential polyandry is found in Temminck's Stint, Little Stint, and Sanderling. In these species, each female lays a clutch of eggs that is incubated by the male, followed by a second clutch that she incubates herself. These two-clutch systems can be envisioned as a step toward the sort of sequential polyandry seen in the American Spotted Sandpiper (*Actitis macularia*), but females of that species never incubate a clutch alone unless their mate is killed, even when resources are abundant. A two-clutch system is seen in captive Red-legged Partridge, but it is suspected that females of this species may lay clutches for several males in the wild.

Sometimes polyandry and polygyny exist side-by-side. Tengmalm's Owl is often polygynous, but biandry (one female mated to two males) is also known for this species, in which the male does most of the caring for the young.

There is an interesting sidelight to the story of polyandry in birds. In polygynous mammals (one male mating with several females) such as lions and gorillas, infanticide can occur when a new male takes over a harem. By killing the young of the previous harem ruler, the new male presumably brings females back into heat. This gives him a chance to increase his own reproductive contributions and, perhaps, to reduce use of resources by unrelated offspring. Similar behaviour, in which males induce females to breed sooner by killing their chicks, almost certainly occurs in House Sparrows and swallows. In Northern Jacanas, field experiments indicate that females taking over the territories of other females often practise infanticide, destroying the offspring of previous females. The males attempt to defend their broods (which represent their genes, and those of the old, but not the new, female), just as lionesses attempt to defend their cubs from infanticidal male lions taking over a pride. This behaviour in jacanas is the first known example of infanticide being used as a reproductive strategy by female birds.

SEE: Monogamy, p. 335; Polygyny, p. 265; Cooperative Breeding, p. 275; Leks, p. 123; Natural Selection, p. 297; Sandpipers, Social Systems, and Territoriality, p. 189. REFS: Davies, 1983; Emlen *et al.*, 1989; Erckmann, 1983; Heredia and Luke, 1990; Oring, 1982, 1986; Reynolds, 1987; Solheim, 1983; Veiga, 1990.

Adoption in Gulls and Other Birds

IT is quite unusual for birds to adopt chicks, but intraspecific adoption has been reported in a number of gulls and Great Grey Owls, and Herring Gull chicks have been adopted by Lesser Black-backed Gulls. Attempts have been made to explain intraspecific adoption on the basis of kin-selection — adoptive parents promoting their own genes by adopting chicks of relatives. That may be the explanation for the owls, where sibling owls can eventually settle to breed rather close to each other. Such philopatry would increase the chance

Grey Phalarope

Phalaropus fulicarius

ATLAS 141; PMH 122; PER 124; HFP 128; HPCW 104; NESTS 152; BWP3:640

BLDS: ♂●♀	4 (3) 1 (–2) broods INCU: ♂ 18–20
Monogamy Polyandry	

P2		
FLDG: ♂ 16–18		Ground glean

Breeding habitat Arctic tundra near ocean, or freshwater pools; much more marine than Red-necked Phalarope.

Displays Like Red-necked Phalarope, ♀ initiates displays and fights other ♀s. ♀ has display flight, circling above ground, with slow wing-beats, attempts to entice ♂ to join her. ♀ follows ♂ and birds swim close together as part of their courtship display.

Nesting Nest is in open or short vegetation, is shallow hollow lined with grass. Both sexes make scrapes, ♀ chooses one and ♂ finishes nest. Eggs greenish to buff, variously marked darker, 30mm, hatch synchronously. ♀ abandons nest with eggs for ♂ to look after and will seek another mate if available. ♂s will attempt mating with any ♀, and ♀s guard mates.

Diet Diet and foraging mode, like Red-necked Phalarope.

Winters In productive tropical seas like Red-necked Phalarope; although wintering areas are generally different, both species occur on passage together at sea.

Conservation Remote, northern breeding areas mean that numbers are poorly known. There are only small populations in the area covered by this guide – less than 100 pairs in Iceland, for example. On the basis of winter flocks is known to be widespread and common around Arctic Ocean.

Essays Who Incubates?, p. 285; Polyandry, p. 195; Differential Migration, p. 323.

Pomarine Skua

Stercorarius pomarinus

ATLAS 146; PMH 123; PER 124; HFP 144; HPCW 104; NESTS 169; BWP3:653

BLDS: ♂♀	2 (1–3) 1 brood INCU: ♂♀ 25–27 per egg
Monogamy	

SP	Summer: Sm mammals Winter: Fish	
FLDG: ♂♀ 31–32 (37)		Aer pursuit

Breeding habitat Arctic tundra on coast, up rivers, or near lakes.

Displays Both sexes defend territory with slow flapping flights or active chases, sometimes for long periods. On ground, birds have 'long' call with wings partly spread, neck arched, and head down. In mating ceremony birds face each other and vibrate wings. Has courtship-feeding. Like other Skuas vigorously attacks intruders near nest.

Nesting Territorial. Nest has little or no material; on ground, in open. Eggs olive to brown, blotched darker, 64mm, hatch asynchronously. Young fed by regurgitation and stay with adults for at least a couple of weeks after fledging.

Diet Lemmings in breeding season; in winter, fish caught by surface dipping, or stolen from other sea-birds after chase, or carrion. Will also kill birds and is capable of powerful, agile chases.

Winters At sea, often far from shore almost worldwide in productive areas (upwellings, for example); occasionally seen inshore.

Conservation Because of remote nesting areas, populations are difficult to census. Nests widely around Arctic Ocean. Breeding numbers and success probably fluctuate with the availability of small mammal prey.

Essays Piracy, p. 213.

of adopting related young but the degree of relatedness among gull neighbours, and the high price of adoption (as indicated by the prevalence of hatching asymmetry and brood reduction) argues against this hypothesis for these birds. And, of course, it cannot explain interspecific adoption.

Instead it appears that selection pressure on the chicks has produced a behaviour reminiscent of brood parasitism. Faced with inadequate parental care, chicks 'run away' and attempt to insert themselves into the brood of another pair of adults. The chicks parasitize the foster parents, taking advantage of the adults' low discriminatory powers that may have evolved to prevent killing of the parents' own chicks by mistake, and by behaving in ways that will not elicit aggressive responses from the prospective foster parents. Chicks almost always attempt to join broods where they will be at least as old as the oldest resident chick — and about 50 per cent of adoptions may lead to the death of a resident.

SEE: Brood Parasitism, p. 249; Hatching Asynchrony and Brood Reduction, p. 507; Altruism, p. 245. REFS: Bull and Henjum, 1987; Hébert, 1988; Holley, 1984.

Empty Shells

BIRDS appear to have an aversion to empty eggshells. Upon discovery, shells are typically picked up with the bill, flown from the nest, and dropped at some distance. Grebes thrust their eggshells under the water, releasing them far from the nest. Adult hawks usually eat the shells. Many birds with precocial young desert both nest and eggshells, herding their chicks elsewhere. These devices for distancing chicks from the remains of their eggs attracted the attention of the pioneer ethologist Niko Tinbergen, who studied the shell-disposal behaviour of Black-headed Gulls.

Black-headed Gulls normally fly away with the eggshell within a couple of hours after a chick hatches; sometimes they carry it off within minutes. Tinbergen hypothesized that the bright white lining of the shell would attract predators to the nest. But there are risks involved in shell disposal. When the gull leaves to dispose of the shell, the chicks and any remaining eggs are exposed for up to ten seconds, more than enough time for a winged predator to zoom in, grab one of them, and depart.

Tinbergen tested his hypothesis in several ways. In an area patrolled by predators, he distributed a mix of gull eggs, some unmodified and some painted white. The results were unambiguous: although both kinds of eggs were found and eaten, the white ones were discovered more frequently. Then he and his co-workers put out two sets of unmodified gull eggs, some alone and some accompanied by empty eggshells placed about 10 cm away. The eggs were covered with a few grass straws to help camouflage them, and those with the shells nearby were covered a little better than the lone eggs.

Arctic Skua
Stercorarius parasiticus

ATLAS 146; PMH 123; PER 124; HFP 144; HPCW 105; NESTS 168; BWP3:662

| | BLDS: ♂♀ Monogamy | 2 (1–3) 1 brood INCU: ♂♀ 25–28 | FLDG: ♂♀ 25–30 | Summer: Sm mammals Winter: Fish | Aer pursuit |

Breeding habitat Arctic tundra, moorland, usually near sea, but inland in Iceland and elsewhere; often near freshwater pools.

Displays Similar to Pomarine Skua. Has communal bathing places – small pools where birds come to preen when not on nest.

Nesting Territorial; sometimes in small colonies. Nest is shallow scrape on ground in open, ♂ selects site and ♀ builds. Eggs greenish to brown, spotted with darker brown, 57mm, hatch asynchronously. Young fed by both parents until some weeks after fledging. Birds probably pair for life.

Diet In breeding areas, small mammals and birds (taken on ground or in flight); steals eggs of other birds; also takes insects and berries. In winter (and breeding, if possible) steals fish from auks, terns, and small gulls. Commonly attacks Arctic Terns, hitting them, grabbing fish from tern's beak or (if dropped) before it falls to ocean. Also takes fish directly.

Winters Like Pomarine Skua; at sea. More common along coasts on migration than other skuas.

Conservation Population is difficult to census, but common and widely distributed around Arctic Ocean.

Notes Comes in dark and light colour phases (and also intermediate). The lighter phase tends to breed at a younger age (3–4 years) than darker phases (4–5 years). In some populations, there is a tendency for birds to mate with a different colour phase, rather than its own.

Essays Piracy, p. 213; Population Dynamics, p. 515; Sexual Selection, p. 149.

Refs O'Donald 1983 is a book about this species. Furness 1987 is a book about skuas.

Long-tailed Skua
Stercorarius longicaudus

ATLAS 146; PMH 124; PER 124; HFP 144; HPCW 105; NESTS 169; BWP3:675

| | BLDS: ♀ Monogamy | 2 (1–3?) 1 brood INCU: ♂♀ 23–25 per egg | FLDG: ♂♀ 24–26 (22–27) | Summer: Sm mammals Winter: Fish? | Aer pursuit |

Breeding habitat Arctic tundra or mountain tundra.

Displays Like other skuas; has acrobatic courtship flights.

Nesting In small colonies or solitary, nest is in very shallow hollow on ground and is usually unlined. Eggs brown or olive, blotched darker, 55mm, hatch asynchronously. Clutch size is larger, egg size is greater in good rodent years. No eggs at all may be laid in bad years. Parents stay with young for a few weeks after fledging.

Diet Like Arctic Skua, but less likely to steal from terns. Hunts lemmings by hovering and then swooping in for kill. In winter feeding habits almost unknown.

Winters Like other skuas, at sea. Uncommon inshore.

Conservation Difficult to census, but widely distributed around Arctic Ocean. Breeding numbers strongly dependent on supply of small mammals.

Essays Piracy, p. 213.

Again, the results were clear: even though they were better camouflaged, eggs near shells were three times more likely than lone eggs to be found and eaten by gulls and crows.

Further experiments showed that the farther from an intact egg the eggshell was placed, the safer the intact egg. And the gulls, when presented with variously coloured but otherwise identical eggshell 'dummies' (bent strips of metal), were most likely to remove from their nests those resembling real eggshells. There was a lesser tendency to dispose of dummies with very conspicuous colours like red or blue, and *no* tendency to remove green dummies that blended well with the surrounding grass. Colour, not shape, proved to be the crucial clue eliciting shell disposal. These two experiments reinforced the idea that eggshell removal improved protection from predators. The experiment with dummies indicated, in addition, that evolution had produced in the gulls a response that reduced the conspicuousness of the nest not only through removal of shells and other prominent objects, but through maintenance of vegetation that might help camouflage eggs and young.

Tinbergen went on to discover a great deal about how gulls differentiate between an egg, a half-hatched chick, and an empty eggshell. To determine whether the thin edge of a broken shell was the main characteristic telling the adult that it was not an egg, he did a series of tests using modified eggs: blown eggs with the shell intact but empty, blown eggs with additional flanges of broken eggshell glued to them, eggshells open and filled with either plaster or cotton wool, and eggshells open and filled with lead weighing as much as a chick. His results showed that it is the weight of the chick that apparently prevents the gulls from disposing of a hatching egg with a thin edge before the chick is free. If a gull started to pick up a shell containing a lead weight in it, it stopped immediately. Not a single 'chick-weighted' shell was removed from the nest.

The gulls' shell-disposal behaviour seems to be grounded in both instinct and learning. First-time breeders remove shells experimentally placed in their nests even before they have laid their first egg, presumably an act programmed into their genes. But birds that have been given dummy eggs of unnatural colours (including black) to incubate, preferentially remove dummy shells of the same colour. Such preferential association seems to be a learned response that 'fine-tunes' their instinctive egg-removal reaction.

Tinbergen observed that Oystercatchers and Ringed Plovers removed eggshells from their nests much more rapidly than did the gulls. He concluded that the slowness of the gulls was related to their colonial nesting habits. Some Black-headed Gulls will gulp down their neighbours' pipped eggs or freshly hatched chicks. Apparently it pays parent gulls to stay with the chicks until they are dry and fluffy, in order to prevent cannibal gulls from attacking them. Oystercatchers and plovers, being solitary nesters, do not run the same risk by leaving the nest early to dispose of shells.

SEE: Gull Development, p. 203; Hatching, p. 487; Parental Care, p. 171; Bird-brained, p. 385. REF: Tinbergen, 1953.

Great Skua

Stercorarius skua

ATLAS 145; PMH 124; PER 124; HFP 144; HPCW 105; NESTS 168; BWP3:686

 / ◯
2 (1)
1 brood
BLDS: ♂♀   INCU: ♂♀
Monogamy   29 (26–32)

 SP

FLDG: ♂♀
44 (40–51)

| Sum: Birds |
| Sm mammals |
| Wint: Fish |

Aer pursuit

Breeding habitat Open moorland and tundra, usually near sea, and typically near sea-bird colonies.

Displays Wing-raising threat display on ground while calling is a common display. Rivals walk around each other in circles. Has courtship-feeding.

Nesting Colonial. Nest is shallow scrape on ground in open. Eggs olive, grey or brown, usually variously marked with dark browns, sometimes unmarked, 71mm, hatch asynchronously. Young guarded by ♀, ♂ brings most of food. Parents look after young for up to 3 weeks after fledging. Probably mates for life.

Diet Takes young and adult sea-birds, some rabbits, carrion. In winter, fish, obtained directly by dropping to surface or by piracy; also takes offal, following fishing boats.

Winters At sea.

Conservation Northern subspecies has very limited range. While sensitive to human disturbance, has increased in range, spreading to UK and other areas outside of Iceland in this century. Increase due to protection and perhaps increased availability of fish offal.

Notes There are southern hemisphere subspecies.

Essays Piracy, p. 213; Parent–Chick Recognition in Colonial Nesters, p. 227.

Refs Furness 1987.

Great Black-headed Gull

Larus ichthyaetus

ATLAS 148; PMH 125; PER -; HFP 146; HPCW 106; NESTS 171; BWP3:705

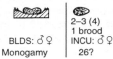
2–3 (4)
1 brood
BLDS: ♂♀   INCU: ♂♀
Monogamy   26?

SP

FLDG: ♂♀,♂♀●
?

Many

See below

Breeding habitat Lakes, rivers, and deltas.

Displays Immediate nest area defended against neighbours, but behaviour little known. See essay on Gull Displays, p. 205.

Nesting Colonial. Nest is unlined or with sparse vegetation, on ground, in open. Eggs creamy or olive green, boldly and variously marked with brown, 78mm, hatch asynchronously.

Diet Omnivorous, taking fish and terrestrial animals, including small mammals and locally abundant large insects (sometimes taken on wing); scavenges. Like other gulls, uses a wide variety of feeding methods.

Winters On coasts of Black Sea, Caspian Sea, and Indian Ocean.

Conservation Scattered breeding populations across CIS steppes, locally common but numbers not well known.

Essays Coloniality, p. 107; Courtship Feeding, p. 223; Adoption in Gulls and Other Birds, p. 197; Gull Development, p. 203; Gulls Are Attracted to their Predators, p. 203; Piracy, p. 213.

Gulls Are Attracted to their Predators

WHEN a weasel, fox, or other mammalian predator enters a breeding colony of gulls, numerous birds gather in the air above the intruder, making it very conspicuous. Gulls come from a considerable distance and circle or hover over the predator for quite a while, sometimes even landing in its vicinity before returning to their territories. With the exception of those whose nests are immediately threatened, the gulls show little inclination to attack. Instead they appear nervous and ready to flee.

Experiments using models of predators show that breeding Herring and Lesser Black-backed Gulls are more attracted to models that have a dead gull placed close to them than they are to the models alone. Furthermore, once gulls have seen a predator model with a dead gull, they are more attracted to it if experimenters place it within the colony again on the same day, even without the dead gull. Indeed, there is some evidence that the heightened reaction to the predator lasts at least a day after it is seen with the dead bird. This heightened reaction is specific to the predator model seen with the corpse; there is no increased reaction to a model of a different predator subsequently presented in the same place. After seeing a predator model with a dead gull, the live gulls alight farther from the model on subsequent encounters. They remain attracted, but are more cautious.

The results indicate that the attraction of the gulls to their enemies is a method of learning about them. Apparently they can generalize — they draw conclusions about the predator after another gull has had a lethal encounter with it. This is a beneficial reaction, since mammalian predators such as weasels and foxes may engage in 'surplus killing' (dispatching more victims than they can consume). Also these hunters can specialize for a period of time on one group of prey. An animal that has killed one gull may be more likely to kill others; individual foxes have been observed habitually killing gulls in breeding colonies. It requires little imagination, then, to see the potential adaptive advantage for gulls of investigating predators.

SEE: Natural Selection, p. 297; Flock Defence, p. 257; Bird-brained, p. 385; Coloniality, p. 107; Distraction Displays, p. 175. REF.: Kruuk, 1976.

Gull Development

GULL chicks are semi-precocial: they hatch covered with down, with their eyes open, and able to walk; but unlike fully precocial chicks, they remain in or near the nest for the first two or three weeks. For the next several weeks they

Mediterranean Gull

Larus melanocephalus

ATLAS 149; PMH 125; PER 126; HFP 148; HPCW 106; NESTS 172; BWP3:712

  3 (2)
1 brood
BLDS: ♂♀? INCU: ♂♀
Monogamy 23–25

 SP
FLDG: ♂♀
35–40 Fish

Many

See below

Breeding habitat Mainly coastal lagoons and estuaries, large inland lakes.

Displays See essay on Gull Displays, p. 205.

Nesting Colonial; sometimes in very large colonies. Nest is on ground; lined with grass and feathers. Eggs pale yellowish or buff, variously marked with dark browns or black, 54mm, hatch synchronously. First breeds at 2–3 years.

Diet Both terrestrial and aquatic insects in breeding season, taken on the wing or picked up from ground; fish and molluscs at other times; uses surface dipping, surface diving, and up-ending; scavenges at rubbish dumps and at sea for fish offal.

Winters Coastal, mainly around Mediterranean, but also N to UK, Baltic; in flocks.

Conservation A gull with a relatively restricted distribution breeding in local, fragmented populations; evidence points to an increase, with new breeding areas colonized in W. See p. 528

Essays Gull Development, p. 203; Migration, p. 377; Parent–Chick Recognition in Colonial Nesters, p. 227.

Little Gull

Larus minutus

ATLAS 148; PMH 126; PER 126; HFP 148; HPCW 107; NESTS 172; BWP3:730

 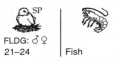 2–3 (1–5)
Platform 1 brood
BLDS: ♂♀ INCU: ♂♀
Floating Monogamy 23–25

 SP
FLDG: ♂♀
21–24 Fish Surface dips

Breeding habitat Freshwater marshes, lakes, rivers.

Displays See essay on Gull Displays, p. 205.

Nesting Nests colonially, sometimes with other gulls; on ground, in vegetation near to or on water; nest is hollow lined with vegetation, can be quite large if on water. Eggs olive-brown to buff, spotted and blotched darker brown, 42mm, hatch asynchronously. First breeds at 2–3 years.

Diet In breeding season aquatic insects; has tern-like foraging technique, flying into wind with bill pointed downward, dropping to surface to pick up prey. Will land on water and submerge head to get prey. Also takes fish.

Winters Coastal on muddy and sandy beaches, widely across area covered by this guide; in flocks where common.

Conservation Breeds sporadically well outside its main range across the CIS (as far as N America).

Essays Gull Development, p. 203.

hide in nearby vegetation (when available) until they fledge. Both adults feed the chicks regurgitated meals at least until fledging and, in some species (such as the Herring Gull), for a considerable post-fledging period. To elicit the adult's feeding response, Herring Gull chicks peck at a 'target' on the adult's lower mandible, a contrasting red spot.

When juvenile gulls are fledged they do not look like their parents, but instead have a distinctive streaked brown plumage. As the birds mature, the patterns of the plumage change, and these changes differ among gull species. Generally the process takes longer in larger species. Black-headed and some Common and Little Gulls develop adult plumage and breed when they are two years old. Others do not reproduce until they are three (some Common, Little, Herring, and Mediterranean Gulls) or four years old (i.e. Herring, Greater and Lesser Black-backed Gulls, and Kittiwake). The largest gulls, such as the Herring and the Black-backs, may take five years or more to reach maturity.

Adults of some species have different breeding and winter plumages; thus, to identify gulls one must often differentiate among five or more colour patterns within a species. In addition, gulls sometimes hybridize.

SEE: Precocial and Altricial Young, p. 401; The Colour of Birds, p. 137; Black and White Plumage, p. 7; Eye Colour and Development, p. 85; Hybridization, p. 461. REFS: Grant, 1986; Tinbergen, 1953.

Gull Displays

GULLS are highly gregarious, staunchly territorial, and in some cases ruthlessly cannibalistic. They have evolved intricate patterns of communication to get what they want and keep what they have. Loud, strong-billed, long-winged, and web-footed, their signals include calling, posturing, and ritualized movements that are easy for birdwatchers to observe and relatively easy to interpret — especially when the birds are on their breeding grounds. On the one hand, many gull displays are ceremonial and many of these ceremonies are similar among species; indeed, interbreeding may be common (Herring Gulls, for example, hybridize with Lesser Black-backed, Glaucous-winged, and Great Black-backed Gulls.). On the other hand, however, the intensity of displays varies, some gull species have evolved more postures and movements than others, and many displays are used to convey different signals when used in different contexts. It may be helpful to note that, in general, the angle of a gull's body and bill and the position of its wings and neck provide important clues for interpreting gull communication.

Even brief overviews of gull behaviour (such as this one) commonly feature a discussion of the Herring Gull whose displays were described by Niko Tinbergen more than 30 years ago. Tinbergen identified eight of the

Sabine's Gull

Larus sabini

ATLAS 148; PMH 127; PER 126; HFP 148; HPCW 107; NESTS 173; BWP3:739

		3 (2) 1 brood			Many
	BLDS: ?	INCU: ♂♀	FLDG: ♂♀		See below
	Monogamy	23–25	?	Fish	

Breeding habitat Pools and marshes in northern tundra, usually near ocean.

Displays See essay on Gull Displays, p. 205.

Nesting Nests colonially, often with Arctic Tern. Nest is shallow cup; in open, with little or no lining. Eggs olive buff, blotched with darker browns, 44mm, hatch asynchronously.

Diet Aquatic insects in breeding season; invertebrates and small fish in winter; like other gulls, opportunistic in use of prey. Also like other gulls, uses a variety of feeding methods, including plunging, dipping to water surface from flight, up-ending in water. Walks across mud to pick up prey.

Winters At sea, south of the equator in W Africa or western S America; sometimes in flocks.

Conservation Difficult to census, because of remote arctic breeding grounds; occurs locally around Arctic Ocean.

Essays Coloniality, p. 107; Courtship Feeding, p. 223; Adoption in Gulls and Other Birds, p. 197; Gull Development, p. 203; Gulls Are Attracted to their Predators, p. 203; Piracy, p. 213.

Black-headed Gull

Larus ridibundus

ATLAS 148; PMH 127; PER 126; HFP 148; HPCW 107; NESTS 171; BWP3:749

		2–3 (1–4) 1 brood			Many
	Platform BLDS: ♂♀	INCU: ♂♀	FLDG: ♂♀		See below
Floating	Monogamy	23–26	35?	Aq inverts	

Breeding habitat A wide variety of marshes, lakes and rivers; inland and coastal.

Displays See essay on Gull Displays, p. 205.

Nesting Nests colonially; on ground, in open or in vegetation. Nest varies from shallow scrape to large pile, if in wet area. ♂ may select site, both birds adding material. Eggs pale greenish to brownish or grey blotched with darker browns, 52mm, hatching either synchronously or asynchronously. Usually first breeds at 2 years.

Diet Insects and earthworms, but like other gulls highly opportunistic. Uses a variety of feeding methods, including plunging, dipping to water surface from flight, swimming on surface, and up-ending. Walks across fields, shallow water, and mud, picking up prey.

Winters Widespread, both inland, near water but commonly on open fields, and along coast. From N America S to Africa and to SE Asia; in large flocks.

Conservation A dramatic increase in range. First bred Finland in 1864, now common up to 70°N. Has colonized Iceland, Greenland, and N America this century. Species is common and widespread across Europe and Asia.

Essays Gull Development, p. 203; Habitat Selection, p. 423; Indeterminate Egg Layers, p. 437; Mixed-species Flocking, p. 429; Piracy, p. 213; Empty Shells, p. 199; Feeding Birds, p. 357.

most common calls, most of which are associated with characteristic visual displays. The (1) *Call-Note*, used year-round, which often elicits a return call, probably helps to inform gulls of the presence of other gulls. The (2) *Charge Call* is a loud, modified (staccato) Call-Note which is used when a gull intends to attack. The (3) *Trumpeting Call*, used year-round, but heightened in spring, is given as a challenge in antagonistic interactions or as part of pair-bonding. In the Herring Gull this is a three-phase call beginning with one or two notes uttered while the head is held forward, high notes uttered with the head pointed downward, and culminating with loud screams and body shakes as the head is jerked upward and the neck is stretched. The (4) *Mew Call* is a long, plaintive note uttered with the neck forward or downward and the gape held wide. It is used in numerous contexts including interactions between antagonists, mates, and parents and chicks (especially when chicks are hungry or cold). During (5) *Choking* the gull produces a peculiar sound while bobbing (as though out of breath). This call, too, is used in various contexts including interactions between antagonists, nest-building, and courtship feeding. The (6) *Alarm Call* is a rhythmic cry which indicates flight rather than attack, but may be alternated with a Charge Call when the bird is fully confronted. The (7) *Begging Call* is elicited during pair bonding, uttered prior to copulation, and used by chicks in need. Finally, the (8) *Copulation Note* is the only call unique to the male. Tinbergen ranked the character of this call between Choking and Alarm Call.

Gulls are colonial. While on their breeding grounds territorial disputes are commonplace and signals tend to be strident as males and pairs defend their patch. Even the use of a wide variety of signals, however, may fail to prevent all-out fighting. When an intruder appears, the territory holder declares possession of the site with a *Trumpet Call* (which may be joined by the call of neighbours). Should the intruder fail to retreat, a more emphatic demonstration follows. During the *Upright Threat* (also called the Aggressive Upright Posture, and performed by Mediterranean, Slender-billed, Audouin's, Common (but rarely in boundary disputes), Lesser Black-backed, Herring, Little, Sabine's, Glaucous, Great Black-backed, Black-headed, and Ivory Gulls) the male walks toward the opponent with his neck stiffly tensed and stretched forward and upward, head pointed downward, wings slightly lifted, wrists pushed aggressively forward, and eyes partially closed. Then, increasing his pace as the charge intensifies, he lifts his wings. To signal his intent to give way the intruder may assume the *Anxiety Posture* (also called the Anxiety [or Intimidated] Upright Posture and performed by Mediterranean, Audouin's, Common, Lesser Black-backed, Herring, Little, Glaucous, Great Black-backed, and Black-headed Gulls). The deferring gull stretches his neck forward and upwards, holding his head horizontally or slightly elevated, eyes open but facing away from his opponent, feathers flattened toward his body and wings readied for flight.

If, however, a charge fails to drive off the intruder, it may be followed by a *Display Run* as the gull assumes the Upright Posture and steps toward the intruder while uttering a Long Call, or moves about with legs bent in a measured Strutting or Stomping. The defender may also switch to the *Grass*

Slender-billed Gull

Larus genei

ATLAS 152; PMH 128; PER 126; HFP 146; HPCW 109; NESTS 170; BWP3:773

		2–3 (1)
		1 brood
BLDS: ?	INCU: ♂♀	
Monogamy	22	

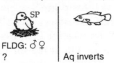

		Many
SP		See below
FLDG: ♂♀		
?	Aq inverts	

Breeding habitat Fresh and brackish lakes, often near tern colonies.

Displays See essay on Gull Displays, p. 205.

Nesting Colonial. Nest is lined with plants, seaweed, and other material, on ground in open. Eggs creamy-white, variously marked with dark browns, 54mm, hatch synchronously.

Diet Fish, aquatic invertebrates; like other gulls highly opportunistic. Uses a variety of feeding methods, including plunging, dipping to water surface

from flight, swimming on surface, and up-ending.

Winters Coastal, often estuaries, in Mediterranean to Indian Ocean; in flocks.

Conservation Has very local and fragmented breeding distribution in Europe, N Africa, more common in CIS, especially Black and Caspian Seas, Iraq. See p. 528.

Essays Coloniality, p. 107; Courtship Feeding, p. 223; Adoption in Gulls and Other Birds, p. 197; Gull Development, p. 203; Gulls Are Attracted to their Predators, p. 203; Piracy, p. 213.

Audouin's Gull

Larus audouinii

ATLAS 152; PMH 128; PER 128; HFP 146; HPCW 109; NESTS 170; BWP3:780

		2–3 (1)
		? brood
BLDS: ♂♀?	INCU: ♂♀	
Monogamy	26–33	

	Many
SP	See below
FLDG: ♂♀	
35–40?	

Breeding habitat Uninhabited, rocky Mediterranean islands.

Displays See essay on Gull Displays, p. 205.

Nesting In small colonies or alone; nest is among rocks, lined with vegetation, seaweed, or debris. Eggs olive-buff with dark spots and blotches, 64mm, hatch within two days of each other.

Diet Mainly fish, caught after dipping to surface from low flight, but like other

gulls highly opportunistic and can use a variety of feeding methods.

Winters Coastal Mediterranean; in small flocks.

Conservation A rare gull, nesting in only a few, scattered colonies, sometimes in small numbers. Changes in numbers not well known. See p. 528.

Essays Coloniality, p. 107; Courtship Feeding, p. 223; Adoption in Gulls and Other Birds, p. 197; Gull Development, p. 203; Gulls Are Attracted to their Predators, p. 203; Piracy, p. 213.

Pulling display. Grass Pulling (performed by Mediterranean, Herring, Glaucous, Great Black-backed, and, rarely, Black-headed Gulls) is a bluff-fight and is also often used between contentious neighbouring pairs. Males assume an Upright Threat Posture and move to within a foot of one another. One bird briskly pecks at the ground, ripping off vegetation which may be momentarily held in the bill or tossed aside with a jerking motion. This sequence may be repeated by one or both males and may be followed by intermittent, vigorous hacking of the ground, as one of the gulls darts with wings flashing while attempting to uproot firmly secured grass or grasp or tear off a portion of the vegetation held in the other's bill. (Tinbergen likened Grass Pulling by gulls to table-pounding by people.) Serious *Fighting*, although rare, may ensue in Kittiwake and in Mediterranean, Audouin's, Common, Lesser Black-backed, Herring, Little, Sabine's (sometimes in flight), Glaucous (only in colonies), Great Black-backed (rarely), Black-headed, and Ivory Gulls.

Fighting varies among gull species, but generally one of the males rushes in, attempting to grasp the opponent with his bill; once engaged, the pair lean backward, as if Grass Pulling, spreading their wings and delivering loud wing-blows. Pulling may be sustained and carry the entangled pair some distance. (Kittiwakes falling from a cliff may continue fighting in the water, while Ivory Gulls falling from a cliff ledge separate midair, one in pursuit of the other.) Generally, fights that escalate beyond tumbling and chasing may result in feather loss and bleeding. In an effort to dominate, each male attempts to get on top of his opponent, while pecking or striking with his wings. Females are less demonstrative but may also jab with their bills, engage in Grass Pulling or charge intruders.

To defend a potential nest site, the pair either rushes the intruders while Choking, or they remain at the site, lower their breasts, bend their legs, and point their heads downward, rhythmically jerking their heads as if to peck the ground while calling at a matching tempo and sometimes moving their legs in a scraping motion. This sequence may be mirrored by the intruding pair (or pairs). When the bluff fails, males may end up Fighting. Antagonistic displays may also include aerial manoeuvres. In the *Swoop and Soar* display (seen in Slender-billed, Black-headed, and Little Gulls) the gull dives toward the opponent with exaggerated wing-beats while uttering Long Calls. Other displays that may be used in antagonistic interactions include *Ground-Oblique* (often performed while uttering the Trumpet Call), *Lower Oblique, Alarm*, and *Looking Down* postures, and *Defensive-gaping* or a *Gaping-jab*.

Gulls are usually monogamous and sexual behaviour is typically initiated by the female. Perhaps not surprisingly, the same behaviour that deters competing males (such as the Trumpeting Call) also attracts females. During pair bonding the female walks toward her potential mate with her neck drawn in and her head and body held forward. Since she is an intruder until the male decides otherwise, she continuously displays appeasement by moving her head in a tossing motion while quietly and rhythmically calling. If the approach is permitted, she circles the male who may change his stance and stretch to exaggerate his size as if alerting himself to the likely intrusion

Common Gull

Larus canus

ATLAS 152; PMH 129; PER 126; HFP 152; HPCW 109; NESTS 175; BWP3:790

					Many
	Platform	3 (2–5)			See below
Decid tree	BLDS: ♂♀	1 brood	FLDG: ♂♀		
0–10m	Monogamy	INCU: ♂♀ 22–28	35?	Aq inverts	

Breeding habitat Inland, moorland lakes and rivers, and coastal on rocky islands, or sand dunes.

Displays See essay on Gull Displays, p. 205.

Nesting Usually colonial. Nest varies from simple scrape to well-built nest of vegetation or seaweed in various sites from ground to low tree. Eggs greenish to olive, variably marked with dark browns, 58mm, usually hatch asynchronously. Larger clutches can be the result of two ♀s using the same nest; some ♂s are bigamous and all three birds defend nest site. First breeds at 2–4 years.

Diet Terrestrial and aquatic invertebrates, fish; walks across ground to find earthworms and insects; like other gulls is highly opportunistic in use of prey. On water uses a variety of feeding methods, including plunging, dipping to water surface from flight, swimming on surface, and up-ending.

Winters Widespread, on coasts and inland on farmland; in flocks.

Conservation Increasing in numbers and in range, occurs across northern Europe, Asia, and western N America (where it is called the Mew Gull).

Essays Gull Development, p. 203; Habitat Selection, p. 423; Piracy, p. 213; Feeding Birds, p. 357.

Lesser Black-backed Gull

Larus fuscus

ATLAS 151; PMH 130; PER 128; HFP 150; HPCW 109; NESTS 73; BWP3:801

					Many
		3 (1–2)			See below
	BLDS: ♂♀	1 brood	FLDG: ♂♀		
	Monogamy	INCU: ♂♀ 24–27	30–40?		

Breeding habitat Usually coastal islands or dunes, some inland on moorland.

Displays See essay on Gull Displays, p. 205.

Nesting Nest is a pile of seaweed or vegetation, in cover, or on cliff ledge. Eggs olive to dark brown, heavily blotched darker, 67mm, hatch within a day or so of each other. Usually first breeds at 4 years.

Diet Like other gulls highly opportunistic, often taking fish at sea and a wide variety of animal prey on land. Uses a variety of feeding methods,

including plunging, dipping to water surface from flight. Walks across fields. Scavenges extensively and obtains food by pirating other gulls.

Winters Widely on both coastal and inland lakes and rivers, in western Europe, Mediterranean, Africa.

Conservation Common, increasing in numbers and range, and widespread across N Europe and Asia.

Essays Adoption in Gulls and Other Birds, p. 197; Gull Development, p. 203; Gulls Are Attracted to their Predators, p. 203; Hybridization, p. 461; Feeding Birds, p. 357.

of an opponent. The male may stretch his neck forward uttering a Mew Call and the pair may then perform nest-building movements or appear to engage in the Choking display. Alternatively, the male may partially stretch his neck, turning and twisting it, which leads the female to *Head-toss* intensely and peck at his bill or grasp it in an attempt to stimulate *Courtship Feeding*.

During Courtship Feeding the male regurgitates. Regurgitation signals acceptance by the male, but pair bonding requires time. Courtship Feeding may take place two or three times daily for several weeks. (In those instances when pecking fails to incite Courtship Feeding, the female faces the danger of attack. If grabbed, she will not fight back.) During copulation the female displays Head-tossing and Begging, and the male responds with Courtship Feeding and Head-tossing and Begging of his own. Aerial heterosexual behaviour is not common but a display flight ending with a *Parachute Descent* while giving a Long Call has been described for Audouin's. Other heterosexual displays involved in pair bonding may include: *Looking Down, Facing-away, Aggressive Upright Posture and Long Call, Hunched Posture, Head-flagging, Allopreening,* and, unique among Kittiwakes, *Upright Choking*.

Nest-building ceremonies generally involve bouts of Choking. Tinbergen noted that during nest-building ceremonies Herring Gulls drop bits of vegetation on a selected site. The female may then sit, arrange the material in a circle and peck at the male's bill and neck, or the pair, while facing each other, may move with necks outstretched, bodies forward, Mewing and then Courtship Feeding. Nest relief ceremonies may include adding nesting material, Mewing, Choking, Head-tossing, Facing Away, Food Transfer, or aerial displays. In some species the ceremony is minimal. That of the Little Gull, for example, involves only an exchange of Long Calls.

Parent–chick communication is essential to keep chicks fed and out of harm's way. Gull chicks instinctively peck at the bills of their parents, especially at the contrasting spot on the bill of those species (e.g. Herring and Glaucous Gulls) that possess one. Pecking prompts the adult to regurgitate a meal, and the chicks quickly learn to beg. During Begging (or appeasement displays), chicks may assume a Hunched Posture with Head Pumping and calling. When chicks are not hungry, even Mewing by the adult willing to regurgitate may fail to interest them. Chicks quickly learn the calls of their parents and discover that an Alarm Call means to look out and that a Mew Call indicates the danger has passed. Chicks also learn not to stray; those that leave the territory may be considered strangers even by their own parents and, as in the Mediterranean Gull, killed by their parents or other adult gulls and eaten. In some cases, however, adoption may occur (Common, Herring, and Sabine's Gulls), and in others (Slender-billed Gull), young gulls form crèches while still being fed by adults.

Whether involved in a noisy boundary dispute, a bout of Courtship Feeding, or cowering to appease another bird, gulls provide birdwatchers with a fascinating array of behaviours to observe and interpret as individuals establish and maintain their position within the colony. Thus, what on first impression is a mass of cantankerous, cacophonous birds packed into a noisy

Herring Gull
Larus argentatus

ATLAS 151; PMH 130; PER 128; HFP 150; HPCW 109; NESTS 173; BWP3:815

					Many
		3 (2–4) 1 brood			See below
	BLDS: ♂ ♀	I: ♂ ♀, ♂ ♀	FLDG: ♂ ♀		
Ground	Monogamy	28–30 (26–32)	35–40		

Breeding habitat   In W, mainly coastal, using rocky coasts, buildings; also on inland lakes and rivers.

Displays   See essay on Gull Displays, p. 205.

Nesting   Nest, on ground, cliff ledges, or buildings, is large pile of vegetation. Eggs pale greenish to brown, spotted and blotched with darker browns, 70mm, hatch within two days of each other. First breeds at 3 years or later.

Diet   Highly opportunistic. Uses a variety of feeding methods, including plunging, dipping to water surface from flight, swimming on surface, and up-ending. Walks across fields, shallow water, and mud picking up prey; often feeds on refuse in dumps. May crack large molluscs by dropping them from heights. Several attempts may be needed. Will paddle feet to soften sand and make prey more accessible.

Winters   Widespread across area covered by this guide to Indian and Pacific Oceans; coastal, inland at dumps and agricultural fields; in large flocks.

Conservation   Common, widespread, increasing in numbers and range, in Europe, Asia, N America.

Essays   Adoption in Gulls and Other Birds, p. 197; Gull Development, p. 203; Gulls Are Attracted to their Predators, p. 203; Hybridization, p. 461; Seabird Nesting Sites, p. 233; Empty Shells, p. 199; Temperature Regulation and Behaviour, p. 163; Feeding Birds, p. 357; Nest Evolution, p. 345; Nest Sites and Materials, p. 443; Parent–Chick Recognition in Colonial Nesters, p. 227.

Refs   Tinbergen's 1953 book, The Herring Gull's World, is a classic study in animal behaviour.

Glaucous Gull
Larus hyperboreus

ATLAS 150; PMH 131; PER 128; HFP 150; HPCW 110; NESTS 174; BWP3:840

					Many
		3 (2–4) 1 brood			See below
	BLDS: ♂ ♀	INCU: ♂ ♀	FLDG: ♂ ♀		
Ground	Monogamy	27–28	?		

Breeding habitat   Coastal in arctic on rocky cliffs and shores.

Displays   See essay on Gull Displays p. 205.

Nesting   Nest is an often substantial pile of vegetation or seaweed, on cliff or ground. Eggs pale brown to olive, blotched and spotted darker, 77mm. Hatch synchronously.

Diet   Highly opportunistic. In breeding season, searches sea-bird colonies taking eggs and young. Takes marine invertebrates from shoreline, fish from

oceans, and scavenges extensively. Pirates prey from other birds.

Winters   Coastal in arctic waters if free of ice and S to UK, eastern N America.

Conservation   Has decreased in Iceland, but increased elsewhere; is locally abundant and widespread around Arctic ocean.

Notes   Sometimes hybridizes with Herring Gull.

Essays   Piracy, p. 213; Hybridization, p. 461.

mob, is to the practiced eye an integrated community whose turf is meticulously subdivided and jealously tended.

SEE: Parent–Chick Recognition in Colonial Nesters, p. 227; Gull Development, p. 203; Coloniality, p. 107; Territoriality, p. 397; Crèches, p. 45. REFS: Costello, 1971; Cramp and Simmons, 1982; Tinbergen, 1953; Tinbergen and Falkus, 1970.

Piracy

EVOLUTION pays no attention to the commandment 'Thou shalt not steal'. Birds steal from each other just about anything that is not nailed down. They purloin mates, nesting material, eggs, and prey. The term 'piracy', however, is generally restricted to the harassment of one bird by another in order to force the first to give up food. In scientific jargon, such piracy is referred to as 'kleptoparasitism'.

Skuas are classic avian pirates that attack other birds in mid-air and make them relinquish their food. As the British ornithologist Henry Dresser wrote more than a century ago, 'they gain their livelihood chiefly by levying blackmail on their weaker neighbours.' Gulls themselves also pirate food from other birds, including terns, alcids, waders, and other gulls. Black-headed Gulls in southern Spain have been observed to show clear preferences in attacking victims, especially harassing Black-tailed Godwits. Furthermore the gulls used different attack patterns on different species of victims. Curlews may attack conspecifics for prey, while themselves being victimized by gulls. Overall, the curlews and probably other kleptoparasites will perform such behaviour whenever it is more profitable (in terms of food energy gained) to steal rather than forage.

A Pomarine Skua harries a Herring Gull.

Great Black-backed Gull
Larus marinus

ATLAS 150; PMH 131; PER 128; HFP 150; HPCW 110; NESTS 174; BWP3:849

BLDS: ♂♀
Monogamy

2–3 (1–5)
1 brood
INCU: ♂♀
27–28

 SP

FLDG: ♂♀
55–60

Many

See below

Breeding habitat Mainly rocky coasts and islands, also islands in lakes.

Displays See essay on Gull Displays p. 205.

Nesting Nest is often bulky pile of vegetation or seaweed. Egg pale buff to olive-brown, blotched dark browns, 77mm, hatch asynchronously. Breeds first at 4–5 years.

Diet Highly opportunistic. In breeding season searches sea-bird colonies (including Manx Shearwaters, Puffins) taking eggs, young, and adults (sometimes on wing). Will swallow birds to the size of Common Terns whole. Takes marine invertebrates from shorelines, fish from oceans, and scavenges extensively, also pirates prey of other birds.

Winters Widespread in N Atlantic; sometimes inland.

Conservation Common, widespread, and spreading its range around N Atlantic.

Essays Gull Development, p. 203; Habitat Selection, p. 423; Feeding Birds, p. 357.

Kittiwake
Rissa tridactyla

ATLAS 153; PMH 132; PER 126; HFP 152; HPCW 110; NESTS 175; BWP3:863

BLDS: ♂♀
Monogamy

2 (1–3)
1 brood
INCU: ♂♀
25–32

SP

FLDG: ♂♀
35–54

Aq inverts

Surface dips

Breeding habitat Coastal; nests on cliffs, occasionally on buildings.

Displays See essay on Gull Displays, p. 205.

Nesting Colonial. Nest is pile of seaweed and mud cemented to cliff. Eggs grey to pale brown, variably spotted and blotched dark browns, 57mm, hatch synchronously. Has been the subject of a detailed study of breeding success and age. Older pairs do better than younger birds and birds often mate for life. Divorces are more common in inexperienced breeders. Young ♀s lay smaller clutches.

Diet Nearly always from the ocean, dipping to the surface from flight or surface diving. May fly low over water, then make short, fast, angled dive to surface. Takes fish and planktonic invertebrates, particularly shrimp from highly productive upwellings.

Winters At sea, often far from shore in the N Atlantic, N Pacific.

Conservation Common, increasing in numbers and range; widely distributed in N Atlantic, N Pacifc.

Essays Gull Development, p. 203; Seabird Nesting Sites, p. 233; ; Parent–Chick Recognition in Colonial Nesters, p. 227; Breeding Site Tenacity, p. 219.

The victims of pirates may have food snatched from their bills, may be forced to regurgitate, or, if pursued by skuas, may occasionally become prey themselves. Skuas obtain much of their food in this way, as do frigatebirds. The latter are lightly built to permit aerobatic flight, and possess feathers that are not very resistant to wetting. They get their food on the wing and thus lean heavily on boobies and other tropical seabirds to fish for them. At the extreme, the Common Gulls at the Cork city dump reportedly have given up foraging for themselves and subsist entirely on food pirated from Black-headed Gulls.

Piracy is also commonly practised by some raptors. In one unusual case, a Sparrowhawk had its food snatched by a Merlin, which, in turn was robbed by a Honey Buzzard, which lost it to a Peregrine. North American Turkey Vultures (*Cathartes aura*) are known to force nestling Great Blue Herons (*Ardea herodias*) to regurgitate their last meal, which is scooped up and later fed to the vultures' own chicks. Raptors, however, get the tables turned on them occasionally, sometimes being forced to give up their catch to birds such as crows and magpies. Apparently this behaviour on the part of the passerine pirates is derived from mobbing.

Interestingly, dabbling ducks, including American Wigeons (*Anas americana*) and Gadwalls, often pirate aquatic vegetation from coots. The latter can dive deeper, and thus the ducks can dine on pond weeds that ordinarily grow beyond their reach. They also may save energy in some circumstances by pirating rather than dabbling, since American Coots (*Fulica americana*) have been observed simply to drop their food plants immediately upon surfacing when approached by a pirate. Although coots can be quite aggressive, they seldom attack the pirates, perhaps because the extensive preening required after agonistic interactions would consume too much time that could be more profitably spent feeding. Coots can be pirates as well as victims; groups of two to five juvenile coots have been known to snatch aquatic vegetation from the bills of diving ducks and swans.

But most groups of birds do not practice piracy. It is rare in songbirds (shrikes attacking wheatears being notable exceptions, as are Blackbirds which steal snails from other thrushes after the snails' shells have been cracked) and not recorded in pigeons, doves, or gallinaceous birds. Apparently piracy is a behaviour that evolves under rather special ecological circumstances. Most birds seem to have great success collecting their own food, rather than running the risks of stealing it from others. But in some circumstances, for example in times of food shortage or when there is an abundance of birds feeding on large, visible food items, piracy will pay — if the potential parasite is strong and agile enough to steal, and if it does not face too much competition from other kleptoparasites.

SEE: Natural Selection, p. 297; Commensal Feeding, p. 27. REFS: Amat and Aguilera, 1990; Amat and Soriguer, 1984; Barnard, 1984*a,b*; Brockman and Barnard, 1979; Dresser, 1871–81; Ens *et al.*, 1990; Ryan, 1981; Tye, 1984.

Ivory Gull

Pagophila eburnea

ATLAS 153; PMH 132; PER 128; HFP 152; HPCW -; NESTS 176; BWP3:875

  | 1–2 (3)
1 brood
INCU: ♂ ♀
24–25?

BLDS: ♂ ♀
Monogamy

Cliff

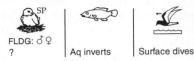

FLDG: ♂ ♀
? | Aq inverts | Surface dives

Breeding habitat Islands in the high arctic, on cliffs or barren ground.

Displays See essay on Gull Displays, p. 205.

Nesting Colonial. Nest is on cliff or flat ground; large pile of seaweed. Eggs olive or buff, spotted and blotched darker, 60mm, hatch synchronously.

Diet Fish, planktonic invertebrates, and carrion. Dips to water surface from flight, surface dives, and often scavenges behind seals and polar bears.

Winters Edge of pack ice.

Conservation Population numbers are not well known; colonies are local and remote; has declined in Spitsbergen.

Essays Coloniality, p. 107; Courtship Feeding, p. 223; Adoption in Gulls and Other Birds, p. 197; Gull Development, p. 203; Gulls Are Attracted to their Predators, p. 203; Piracy, p. 213.

Gull-billed Tern

Gelochelidon nilotica

ATLAS 153; PMH 133; PER 130; HFP 158; HPCW 111; NESTS 177; BWP4:6

 | 1–3 (4)
1 brood
INCU: ♂ ♀
22–23

BLDS: ♂ ♀
Monogamy

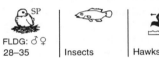

FLDG: ♂ ♀
28–35 | Insects | Hawks

Breeding habitat Salt marshes, estuaries, and freshwater lakes, rivers.

Displays Early in nesting, ♂s fly up from ground, may carry food, and call repeatedly. This encourages small group of other birds to fly and join leader as they all fly over colony. As season progresses, courtship displays become more restricted to near nest site. Between pairs, a landing bird may stretch neck upwards, then point bill skyward; birds may also flag heads, turning their heads from side to side.

Nesting Colonial. Nest is shallow depression in sand with little or no lining. Eggs off-white to cream, various markings of dark browns, 49mm, hatch asynchronously. Young stay with parents after fledging and may leave on migration with them.

Diet Flies upwind, dipping to surface of water to pick up fish. Uses similar technique to catch large invertebrates and small vertebrates on land. Also hawks for insects over land.

Winters Both coasts and inland waters, widespread but mainly Mediterranean S to Africa and SE Asia to Australia. N American populations to similar latitudes. Often in small flocks.

Conservation Recent declines in some parts of Europe, following habitat losses, but species is widely distributed in northern hemisphere. See p. 529.

Essays Courtship Feeding, p. 223; Visual Displays, p. 33; Monogamy, p. 335; Precocial and Altricial Young, p. 401; Preening, p. 349.

How Do Birds Fly?

HOLD a strip of paper lengthways and blow along the top of it and you will see in action the physical principle that governs the flight of both birds and aeroplanes: the higher the velocity of air passing over a surface, the lower the pressure on that surface. Wings are shaped in a manner that causes the air to move more rapidly over their upper surfaces than beneath their lower ones. As you can see in the diagram, the flow splits at the leading edge of the wing and rejoins at the trailing edge. The air moving over the top travels a greater distance to get past the wing than does air going under the bottom of the wing, and therefore the 'over' air must move faster to 'catch up' with the 'under'. This difference in speed, according to the principle first enunciated in 1738 by Swiss physicist Daniel Bernoulli, reduces the pressure on the upper wing surface. You can think of the upper air thinning out as it races to cover a greater distance in the same time as the air going under the wing. The lower pressure can be thought of as sucking the wing upward, creating lift which counters the downward pull of gravity — just as blowing over the top of the strip of paper causes it to rise against the force of gravity that is pulling it downward. That is a simplified description of how much of the lift of a

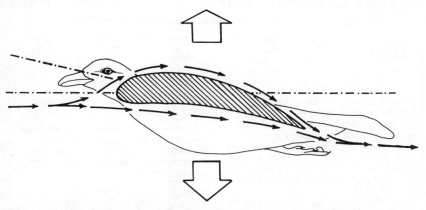

Diagram of gull in flight. Upper bold arrow: lift. Lower bold arrow: gravity. Thin arrows indicate airflow over wing — note the longer route over the top of wing, necessitating higher speed of airflow which generates lift. Long, lower dot-dash line: axis of airflow. Upper, shorter dot-dash line: axis of wing. The angle between the dot-dash lines is the angle of attack.

wing is generated; the details we'll leave to mathematical aerodynamicists. It will suffice here to note that a bird or an aeroplane will remain airborne at a given altitude when its lift is equal to its weight.

Caspian Tern

Sterna caspia

ATLAS 154; PMH 133; PER 130; HFP 158; HPCW 111; NESTS 178; BWP4:17

BLDS: ♂♀
Monogamy

2–3 (1)
1 brood
INCU: ♂●
20–22

FLDG: ♂♀
30–35

Breeding habitat   Coastal on sheltered islands, lagoons, estuaries (also inland on large lakes in areas outside those covered by this guide).

Displays   In aerial courtship, pairs fly together high over nesting area while calling; in ground courtship, ♂ approaches ♀ with fish in his beak. During early stages of nesting, ♂ may bring in fish, calling at some distance from nest; ♀ apparently recognizes ♂'s call, begs, and is passed the fish as the ♂ flies low over her.

Nesting   Usually colonial. Nest is unlined shallow scrape in open. Eggs pale cream, finely marked with dark browns and blacks, 64mm, hatch over two days or less. Adults will stay with young for several months. First breeds at 3 years.

Diet   Chiefly fish. Flies over water with bill pointed downwards; dives into the water, taking off and swallowing fish in flight.

Winters   In coastal waters, widely from Mediterranean southwards; often singly or in small flocks.

Conservation   Local decreases and increases in Europe, species is widely distributed almost worldwide, though distribution is fragmented. See p. 529.

Essays   Courtship Feeding, p. 223; Visual Displays, p. 33; Monogamy, p. 335; Precocial and Altricial Young, p. 401; Preening, p. 349.

Lesser Crested Tern

Sterna bengalensis

ATLAS 154; PMH 134; PER -; HFP 158; HPCW 112; NESTS 178; BWP4:42

BLDS: ?
Monogamy

1 (2)
1 brood
INCU: ♂♀
21–26

FLDG: ♀
32–35

Aq inverts

Breeding habitat   Sea coasts; beaches or among dunes.

Displays   Similar to Sandwich Tern.

Nesting   Nest is a shallow scrape, usually unlined; in the open. Eggs white or buffish; variably marked with blackish, 52mm. When there are two young, each parent may look after one; young may form crèches.

Diet   Mainly fish taken by plunge-diving, sometimes into the surf; also aquatic invertebrates.

Winters   Coastal waters; in flocks, and with other terns.

Conservation   Very small number nest in Mediterranean; scattered colonies from Africa through Indian Ocean to Australia; numbers not well known, but locally common.

Essays   Courtship Feeding, p. 223; Visual Displays, p. 33; Monogamy, p. 335; Precocial and Altricial Young, p. 401; Preening, p. 349; Crèches, p. 45.

The angle at which the wing meets the airflow is known as the 'angle of attack'. As that angle is increased, the bird is able to fly at a slower speed. If the angle of attack is increased too much, however, the smooth flow of the air over the wing's upper surface is disrupted, lift is lost, and the wing is said to 'stall'. Both birds and aeroplanes tend to increase the angle of attack and then stall their wings in the process of slowing down and landing.

The feathers of the inner portion of the wing remain close together, making an airfoil similar to that of an aeroplane's wing. On the leading edge, however, is a structure called the 'alula' (a few feathers protruding from the bird's 'thumb'), which forms a slot that helps to smooth the airflow at high angles of attack. The alula, like similar slots on the wings of many aeroplanes, helps to maintain lift at lower airspeeds.

During gliding, forward motion is due to the gradual descent of the birds (relative to the air) under the pull of gravity. During flapping flight, the wings produce the forward thrust which moves the bird forward. It is this forward motion that generates the lift to counteract gravity and so enables the bird to follow a horizontal course. The primary feathers, the large feathers at the further end of the wing, play a crucial role in flapping flight. During the downstroke the wing moves down relative to the body and forward relative to the air. The overall lift generated points forward and upward, providing respectively thrust to move the bird forward and vertical lift to counteract gravity. The wings are often folded near the body on the upstroke (during which the wings also move backward), and the primaries are separated from each other to reduce air resistance. The primaries also twist in their orientation so that they can still provide some thrust on the upstroke, while the secondaries continue to provide lift (they also contribute to propulsion).

SEE: Wing Shapes and Flight, p. 269; Soaring, p. 79; Skimming: Why Birds Fly Low Over Water, p. 67; How Fast and High Do Birds Fly?, p. 63. REFS: Pennycuick, 1975, 1989; Rayner, 1988; Rüppell, 1977.

Breeding Site Tenacity

THE tendency to return each season to the same nest site or breeding colony is known as 'site tenacity', 'site fidelity', or 'philopatry'. For example individual seabirds tend to return to the same colony site and often to the same nest site within the colony over many years. Individual Fulmars studied in the Orkney Islands have been breeding at the same colony for some 40 years. In general site tenacity increases with age of the bird. It is a behaviour not restricted to seabirds, for it also occurs to varying degrees in a wide variety of species including Goldeneye, Greenshank, Common Swift, Sand Martin, Swallow, Willow Warbler, and Chaffinch.

Ornithologists think the major advantage of returning to an established

Sandwich Tern
Sterna sandvicensis

ATLAS 155; PMH 134; PER 130; HFP 158; HPCW 113; NESTS 179; BWP4:48

BLDS: ♂♀	1–2 (3)	FLDG: ♂♀
Monogamy	1 brood	28–30
	INCU: ♂♀	
	21–29	

Breeding habitat Two distinct habitats; in W, on islands off exposed coasts; in E on islands in Black and Caspian Seas.

Displays Courtship begins in winter and only young breeders arrive at nesting grounds unpaired. ♂s have display flight circling high above ground, carrying fish and calling to attract one or more ♀s; bird may glide with wings in high V. Following this display, ♂, when joined on ground by ♀, offers fish to her. ♂ adopts a hunched, low position, ♀ with wings partly open, with neck stretched upwards. ♀ accepts fish, and both birds adopt more upright posture, walking around each other, flagging heads from side to side.

Nesting Nests colonially often close to other terns and gulls. Nest scrape is usually unlined, in open. Eggs off-white to cream, variably marked with brown, grey, and black, 51mm, hatch asynchronously. Sometimes young form into crèches. First breeds at 3 years.

Diet Fish, caught by plunge-diving, after flying overhead or hovering briefly. In winter in Africa, studies of feeding success show that older birds caught nearly 50 per cent more fish per hour than first-year birds.

Winters Coastally; Eurasian birds to S Africa, Indian Ocean; in flocks.

Conservation Numbers fluctuate widely, as some breeding sites are forsaken and others colonized. Scattered colonies across Europe, N and S America. See p. 529.

Essays Crèches, p. 45; Breeding Site Tenacity, p. 219.

Roseate Tern
Sterna dougallii

ATLAS 156; PMH 134; PER 130; HFP 160; HPCW 113; NESTS 181; BWP4:62

BLDS: ♂♀	1–2 (4)	FLDG: ♂♀	Skims
Monogamy	1 brood	27–30 (22–)	
	INCU: ♂♀		
	21–26		

Breeding habitat Coastal islands and beaches.

Displays Similar to Common Tern.

Nesting Colonial; often with Common and Arctic Terns. Nest is a scrape on sand or shingle, often concealed under vegetation or rocks; usually has no lining. Eggs pale cream to buff, variously marked dark brown, 43mm, hatch asynchronously. Young remain with parents for several weeks after fledging. First breeds at 3 years.

Diet Fish, caught after plunge-diving from flight or, sometimes from a hover. Also shallow dips to surface. Sometimes pirates fish from other terns in flight.

Winters Coastal in warm oceans, almost worldwide.

Conservation Though distributed world-wide, colonies are often small, isolated, and vulnerable; UK and Ireland are main breeding sites in area covered by this guide. Species declined in the last century but with protection, population has recovered from near extinction in this century. There are recent declines and species is considered endangered in N America. See p. 529.

Essays Courtship Feeding, p. 223; Monogamy, p. 335; Precocial and Altricial Young, p. 401; Preening, p. 349.

breeding site is that the bird's familiarity with the area reduces its susceptibility to predation and other adverse conditions. Studies have shown that sex and age of the nesting bird, prior reproductive success at the particular site, and physical stability of the nest site are all important factors affecting the strength of site tenacity.

For most site-tenacious species, birds that rear young successfully are more likely to return to the nest site the following year than are unsuccessful breeders. A finer discrimination is made by North American Black Skimmers (*Rynchops niger*), which are more likely to abandon a colony site following predation than following flooding. Presumably future failures as a result of predation are more predictable than those resulting from flooding.

In northwest Scotland, the Nethersole-Thompson family has studied a population of Greenshanks continuously since 1964. Their studies demonstrate that up to 91 percent of ringed males and 80 per cent of females return to the area to breed in successive years, and up to nearly a third of the nests were re-used in consecutive breeding seasons. Among males, breeding-site fidelity was markedly stronger in older, previously successful individuals.

The degree of predictability or physical stability of the nest site strongly influences the evolution of site tenacity. This is demonstrated by cliff-nesting species such as Kittiwakes and other gulls, and by many alcids, which return repeatedly to the same sites (cliffs tend to be there year after year). At the opposite extreme are nest sites on open sand or mud beaches, river sandbars, salt marshes, and the banks of water-courses, all subject to periodic inundation. Since the sites themselves are ephemeral, species nesting in these places, such as Redshanks and Sandwich Terns, exhibit little site tenacity. Swallows and Sand Martins provide another good example of well-developed versus poorly developed site tenacity in related species that select very different sorts of nest sites. Buildings stand for many years; sand banks are prone to erosion.

The repeated use of a nest or colony site is due to the behavioural choice of the individual bird. Specific sites, however, may be used over time by a succession of individuals, each of whom recognizes that site as a quality nest location. Such features include physical stability, protection from predators and inclement weather, and association with a rich food supply. Of course, scarcity of other suitable nest sites in an area may also promote site tenacity.

Occupation of 'traditional' nesting locations and roosts over many generations will often occur in species exhibiting site tenacity. A stretch of chalk cliff near Hunstanton, Norfolk, England, was first mentioned as occupied by Peregrines in 1604 and the eyrie was not deserted until about 1820. Interestingly, a number of traditional Peregrine sites abandoned during the population crash of the 1960s have now been reoccupied as the population has expanded again. Presumably today's Peregrines discern the same merits in these sites as did their forebears.

SEE: Habitat Selection, p. 423; Wintering Site Tenacity, p. 409; Coloniality, p. 107; Seabird Nesting Sites, p. 233. REFS: Dobkin *et al.*, 1986; Lawn, 1982; McNicholl, 1975; Mikkonen, 1983; Ratcliffe, 1980; Thompson *et al.*, 1988.

Common Tern
Sterna hirundo

ATLAS 156; PMH 135; PER 130; HFP 160; HPCW 113; NESTS 179; BWP4:71

		2–3 (1) 1 brood			
BLDS: ♂♀	INCU: ♂♀	FLDG: ♂♀			
Monogamy	21–22	22–28 (–33)	Aq inverts	Skims	

Breeding habitat Islands, quiet shore lines, both coastal and inland on lakes.

Displays ♂ has jerky, bouncy flight high over colony, often calling and carrying fish, to entice ♀ to join. Wings may be held in high V as pair flies together. When ♀ joins ♂ on nesting territory, birds walk around each other calling; ♂ may present ♀ with a fish.

Nesting Colonial. Nest is a shallow scrape on shingle, often in open, sometimes among vegetation. Eggs cream to light brown, variably marked dark browns or black, 41mm, hatch asynchronously. Young dependent on parents for several weeks after fledging, when birds leave colony. First breeding 3–4 years.

Diet Fish, sometimes crustaceans, taken by plunging into ocean following level flight or, often, after hovering. High winds and choppy water reduce feeding success and then birds must seek quieter waters. Sometimes returns to nest with several fish in beak at one time. Also feeds by dipping to water surface from flight. Some individuals pirate fish from other terns.

Winters Coastal, mainly warm oceans almost worldwide; in flocks.

Conservation Vulnerable to disturbance. There are local declines, but the species has recovered from persecution of last century and is common and widespread in northern hemisphere. See p. 529.

Essays Courtship Feeding, p. 223; How Long Can Birds Live?, p. 497; Parent–Chick Recognition in Colonial Nesters, p. 227; Breeding Site Tenacity, p. 219.

Refs Hume 1993 is a book about this species.

Arctic Tern
Sterna paradisaea

ATLAS 155; PMH 135; PER 130; HFP 160; HPCW 113; NESTS 181; BWP4:87

		2 (1–3) 1 brood			
BLDS: ♂♀	INCU: ♂♀	FLDG: ♂♀			
Monogamy	20–24	21–24	Aq inverts	Skims	

Breeding habitat Coastal islands, inland rivers, mainly in the arctic, N to pack ice, S to UK.

Displays Like those of Common Tern.

Nesting Colonial; often mixed in with Common Terns in S. Nest is shallow scrape on shingle, sand, often unlined. Eggs buff to brown, variably marked dark browns, 41mm, hatch synchronously. Young remain with parents for several weeks after fledging. Usually first breeds at 4 years.

Diet Similar to that of Common Tern.

Winters Probably the most remarkable of all migrants. Atlantic populations (including those of N America, Greenland) move along the coast of Europe, around W Africa, southwards. Winters in the highly productive waters off the Antarctic pack ice. Makes the round trip each year, although young birds may remain in equatorial waters. Oldest ringed bird was 34 years old; at about 32 000 km per round trip, it would have flown over nearly a million km during migration alone, probably more. In flocks.

Conservation Common and widespread around Arctic Ocean, may be some retreat from the most southerly colonies. See p. 529.

Essays Colour of Eggs, p. 161; Wildlife and the Law, p. 520.

Courtship Feeding

DURING the breeding season you may have watched one adult bird feed another. Whether it occurs when pairs are first getting established or some-time later after incubation has begun, this behaviour is known as 'courtship feeding'. In most species males present solid or regurgitated food to the soliciting female. In species in which the females do the courting, the roles may be reversed.

Courtship feeding is frequently seen in terns. For instance, in an effort to lure females to his territory in the nesting area, a male Common Tern carries a fish around the breeding colony and displays it to prospective mates. After a pair bond is formed, during the 'honeymoon period' the male tern actually feeds the female, and soon thereafter they begin to copulate. During the following five to ten days, both sexes feed themselves, but the male also frequently feeds the increasingly dependent female. For the few days prior to egg-laying the female is fed almost exclusively by the male, but this activity declines rapidly as the second and third eggs are laid.

It is generally thought that courtship feeding serves more than a ceremonial or pair-bonding function, as it provides the female with consider-able nutritional benefit and the number of eggs and total clutch weight are partly determined by the female's nutritional status. Measurements suggest that the total weight of a Common Tern's clutch is correlated with the amount of food the male delivers, especially during the honeymoon. Male Common Terns in one Massachusetts (USA) colony were unable to deliver as much food to their mates as males in a second colony. In the colony where the males were less successful, the females laid fewer and lighter eggs.

If the female's nutritional status is so critical to her reproductive output, why does she gradually stop feeding herself prior to egg-laying? The prob-able answer is that she has become too heavy to hunt efficiently. Before laying her three-egg clutch a female Common Tern weighs half again as much as she does when not breeding. Terns forage by cruising at low speed and making precise dives at fishes. A female's additional weight would increase the energy requirements of flight, and perhaps make controlled dives too difficult.

This does not mean that improving the female's nutrition is the only function of courtship feeding. In gulls, it is also an important inducement to copulation (as it may be in the Common Tern). It may also serve to facilitate the formation of the pair bond and reduce aggression between the male and female. Still, when a male warbler, crossbill, tit, or tern is seen feeding a female, it seems apparent that he is increasing his own reproductive success by keeping her fit and healthy.

SEE: Average Clutch Size, p. 31; Visual Displays, p. 33; Gull Displays, p. 205; Variation in Clutch Sizes, p. 55. REFS: Nisbet, 1977; Tasker and Mills, 1981.

Little Tern
Sterna albifrons

ATLAS 156; PMH 137; PER 132; HFP 160; HPCW 115; NESTS 182; BWP4:120

  1–3 (4)
1 brood?

BLD: ♀,♂♀? INCU: ♀
Monogamy   18–21

 SP
FLDG: ♂♀
19–21(15–18) | Aq inverts | Skims

Breeding habitat In W, mainly coastal, on shingle and sandy beaches; in E and elsewhere up rivers in comparable places.

Displays Like those of other terns.

Nesting Colonial. Nest is usually a bare scrape on shingle, in open, usually with no lining. Eggs off-white to greenish or buff, variably marked darker, 32mm, hatch synchronously. Young remain with parents until and perhaps during migration. First breeds at two years.

Diet Small fish and crustaceans. Often hovers before plunging into water; also

takes insects in low flight over water.

Winters On coasts of warm oceans, widely; usually inshore in sheltered waters, but some records from productive oceans far offshore. In flocks.

Conservation Widespread, worldwide, but beach nesting habits make it very vulnerable to human disturbance and colonies near coastal resorts often need strict protection. See p. 529.

Essays Courtship Feeding, p. 223; Visual Displays, p. 33; Monogamy, p. 335; Precocial and Altricial Young, p. 401; Preening, p. 349.

Whiskered Tern
Chlidonias hybrida

ATLAS 158; PMH 137; PER 132; HFP 162; HPCW 115; NESTS 184; BWP4:133

  2–3 (4?)
1 brood

BLDS: ♂♀ INCU: ♂♀,♂♀
Monogamy   18–20?

 SP
FLDG: ♂♀
23? | Fish | Skims

Breeding habitat Inland waters, usually lakes, productive and fringed with vegetation. Will use man-made waters.

Displays Has aerial display flights over colony like other terns. After pairing, ♂ brings food, lands, adopts erect posture, ♀ bows towards him almost touching bill to ground.

Nesting Colonial. Has floating nest of vegetation, anchored to water plants. Eggs pale blue to greenish, spotted or blotched blackish-brown, 39mm, hatch synchronously.

Diet Usually insects, also fish and amphibians, taken from plunge-diving

from near water, often hovering first. Also dips to water surface from flight, or takes insects in air over water or marsh.

Winters Africa, India, SE Asia, Australia; in similar waters to breeding, but also sheltered coastal habitats. In flocks.

Conservation Has scattered breeding populations widely across Europe, Asia, Africa, and Australia. Locally abundant. See p. 529.

Essays Courtship Feeding, p. 223; Visual Displays, p. 33; Monogamy, p. 335; Precocial and Altricial Young, p. 401; Preening, p. 349.

Birds and Oil

A recurring sight on television news programmes is dedicated naturalists attempting to save birds that have had their feathers contaminated with oil discharged into oceans, bays, or rivers. When oil tankers clean their tanks or have accidents, marine birds, such as divers, grebes, murres, puffins, Razorbills, auklets, gulls, and ducks, are placed in jeopardy. Many birds may smell fresh oil and flee the area of a spill; unfortunately, many others cannot.

For a short time after oil is released into the water, it may contain toxins that can be inhaled and ingested by oiled birds in the process of preening and can cause pneumonia, kidney and liver damage, and other problems. Experiments with Black Guillemots indicate that swallowing even very small amounts of oil can lead to considerable physiological stress, interfere with adult foraging, and reduce the growth rates of young. A little oil on eggs during the first half of incubation can prove toxic to the developing embryo inside.

Even after the toxins have dissolved or evaporated, many hazards remain. The relatively inert oil mats the plumage, reducing its insulating and buoying properties. The soiled birds, swimming continually in an attempt to remain warm and afloat, eventually succumb to exhaustion. The oil may also depress populations of the birds' prey, leading to starvation, or birds may be poisoned by ingesting contaminated food.

Oiled birds rescued before they enter the last stages of distress can be saved by careful feeding, warming, and washing with detergent. Treatment is a time-consuming process, but records indicate that up to two out of every three oiled birds may be saved. Such statements can be misleading, however, in several ways. For example, volunteers are unlikely to rescue more than a small fraction of the affected birds after a major spill. At best their attempts may help to preserve a rare species in the path of a spill. In addition, volunteers usually are mobilized only in the face of major disasters. The constant attrition that accompanies low-level, chronic oceanic oil pollution generally is neglected. Also largely neglected are the deaths of many birds annually in oil collection ponds in oil facilities. Deaths there surpass even the large numbers that perish in major oil spills.

The degree to which chronic oil contamination of the sea contributes to long-term declines of Razorbill, Guillemot, and Puffin populations in the North Atlantic, is controversial; oil pollution probably has been one factor among many. About 3.5 million tons of oil — about a tenth of a per cent of the amount pumped from the ground annually — is spilled or released by tankers into the oceans each year along with untreated waste water. This spillage will decrease, we hope, since seagoing nations have been instituting ever more stringent measures to eliminate the problem at its source and have imposed

Black Tern
Chlidonias niger

ATLAS 157; PMH 137; PER 132; HFP 162; HPCW 116; NESTS 183; BWP4:143

Scrape	2–3 (4)	 SP		
BLDS: ♂♀	1 brood INCU: ♂♀	FLDG: ♂♀		
Monogamy	21–22	19–25?	Fish	Dives

Breeding habitat Normally productive freshwater marshes and ponds, but sometimes brackish marshes.

Displays Aerial courtship includes flights high over colony, calling. ♀ comes up to join ♂. On landing near nest site both birds adopt and upright posture. On ground there is courtship-feeding, ♀ giving a begging call.

Nesting Colonial. Floating nest of vegetation is a small platform of reeds anchored to water plants or in marsh vegetation. Eggs cream to light brown with heavy blackish-brown spotting, 35mm, hatch usually within about a day of each other. Young may become independent of parents within a couple of weeks or less (this is shorter than other species of terns).

Diet Insects and other aquatic invertebrates, fish, and amphibians. From flight, dips to surface of water or marsh vegetation to catch prey, less commonly, plunge-dives; also takes insects in flight.

Winters Coastal lagoons and estuaries; sometimes well offshore on migration; in flocks. European birds and possibly Asian birds winter in tropical W Africa; occurs in very large numbers in the Netherlands on migration.

Conservation Has decreased in Europe, especially W, no longer breeds in UK due to habitat losses. Has wide range in CIS and N America. See p. 529.

Essays Wetland Conservation, p. 145.

Refs Sharrock 1976.

White-winged Black Tern
Chlidonias leucopterus

ATLAS 158; PMH 138; PER 132; HFP 162; HPCW 116; NESTS 184; BWP4:155

	2–3 (4)	SP		
BLDS: ♂♀?	1 brood INCU: ♂♀	FLDG: ♂♀		
Monogamy	18–22	24–25?	Fish	Aer foraging

Breeding habitat Freshwater marshes, sometimes alkaline lakes, surrounded by vegetation.

Displays Not well known but similar to those of Black Tern.

Nesting Colonial. Nest is floating pile of water weeds, anchored to other plants. Eggs cream to light brown, heavily blotched and spotted blackish-brown, 35mm, hatch asynchronously. First breeds at 2 years.

Diet Similar to that of Black Tern.

Winters Africa and SE Asia, mainly inland on rivers and marshes, but some on coastal wetlands; in flocks.

Conservation May have declined in W from habitat losses. Breeds only sporadically or in small numbers outside of extensive range in CIS and China.

Essays Courtship Feeding, p. 223; Visual Displays, p. 33; Monogamy, p. 335; Precocial and Altricial Young, p. 401; Preening, p. 349.

strict sanctions against those who deliberately inject oil into the oceans. Furthermore, superior methods of containing accidental spills when they occur are being developed, although the Exxon Valdez disaster in Alaska left considerable doubt about their effective deployment. And, of course, the use of oil spills as a weapon, as happened in the Gulf War of 1991, poses a gigantic threat to avian populations.

Ironically, the birds themselves may help us control the problem. Petroleum residues ingested at sea have been detected in the stomach oil of storm-petrels. These and other tubenoses forage at the surface (where pollutants are concentrated), feed intermittently over large areas, digest oils slowly, and regurgitate samples of the oil readily. Therefore, it has been suggested that the Procellariiformes could become part of an oceanic pollution monitoring system.

SEE: Pesticides and Birds, p. 115; Population Dynamics, p. 515. REFS: Boersma, 1986; Nettleship and Birkhead, 1985.

Parent–Chick Recognition in Colonial Nesters

IN spite of the apparent chaos of seabird nesting colonies, returning adults almost invariably manage to locate and feed only their own offspring, indicating either that some form of parental recognition of chicks (or vice versa) exists, or that parents use the precise position of the chick as the clue to its identity. The timing and development of recognition, as well as whether it is accomplished by parent or chick or both, have been explored in selected species of shearwaters, penguins, gulls, terns, alcids, and swallows. These studies have all shown that recognition develops only in species in which circumstances, such as the young wandering away from the nest or being gathered in communal groups ('crèches') for feeding, could lead to confusion. The onset of recognition coincides with the time when young of different broods begin to mingle. Where such intermixing does not occur (such as in Manx Shearwaters that nest individually in isolated burrows), researchers have found no evidence of recognition between parents and their chicks (the parents *do*, however, recognize their burrows or nest sites).

Guillemot

Uria aalge

	No nest	🥚/◯ 1 1 brood	SP		
	BLDS: –	INCU: ♂♀	FLDG: ♂♀		
Ground	Monogamy	28–37	See below		

Breeding habitat Rocky coasts; on cliffs or on islands among boulders.

Displays Threat to rivals on nesting ledges involves pointing bill, spreading wings, and sometimes fighting. Pair formation probably takes place in 'clubs' — the flocks of birds resting on the water away from the colony. Courtship displays include bill-fencing and bowing, and 'sky-pointing' with bill; mutual preening.

Nesting Colonial, in very dense groups on cliff ledges, flat tops of stacks; no nest. Eggs highly varied, white to blue to reddish, variously spotted and blotched darker, sometimes unmarked, 82mm. Young enter the sea at about 20 days, but probably cannot fly for several weeks afterwards; are fed by the ♂s at sea for a few weeks. Age of first breeding, 5 years. Colonies tend to breed synchronously, and birds laying outside main period are more likely to lose eggs and young to aerial predators, such as gulls.

Diet Fish caught from surface dives

from 20m to possibly 60m below surface of water. Often feed in loose flocks.

Winters Coastally, N Atlantic and N Pacific.

Conservation 19th century hunting was stopped by one of the first bird protection laws in UK. In this century there have been declines in the size of colonies in S, dramatic declines in N Norway (perhaps due to human over-fishing), but local increases elsewhere. Vulnerable to oil spills, especially in S, where most spills have occurred. Common across N Atlantic, N Pacific. See p. 528.

Essays Birds and Oil, p. 225; Swimming and Underwater Flight, p. 61; Eggs and their Evolution, p. 317; Sleeping Sentries and Mate-guarding, p. 73; Parent–Chick Recognition in Colonial Nesters, p. 227.

Refs Nettleship and Birkhead 1985 is an edited volume about this and other species of auks.

Brünnich's Guillemot

Uria lomvia

	No nest	🥚 1 1 brood	SP		
	BLDS: –	INCU: ♂♀	FLDG: ♂♀		
	Monogamy	30–35	See below		

Breeding habitat Like Guillemot, but more northerly.

Displays Similar to Guillemot, but no sky-pointing and less bill-fencing.

Nesting Breeds colonially in vast groups on cliff ledges, no nest. Eggs highly varied, like those of Guillemot, 79mm. Young leave ledges for sea before they can fully fly at about 15–30 days. At sea, young are cared for by ♂ for several weeks afterwards.

Diet Similar to Guillemot.

Winters At sea, again more northerly than Guillemot; N Atlantic and N Pacific.

Conservation Harvested for food in Greenland and subject to massive mortality from fishing nets; there have been severe declines in the western Atlantic. No such declines reported in area of this guide. Breeding colonies are often vast.

Essays Seabird Nesting Sites, p. 233; Birds and the Law, p. 521.

Many investigations have employed the technique of exchanging broods at different ages to determine whether recognition exists and when it occurs. Among gulls and terns, the age at which recognition develops is related to the timing of young leaving the vicinity of the nest. For example, in the ground-nesting Sooty Tern (*Sterna fuscata*), adults reject strange chicks that are more than four days old. The tree-nesting Brown Noddy (*Anous stolidus*) does not discriminate between its own and strange chicks until about 14 days, which is the age when young leave the nest. Kittiwakes nest on cliff ledges, and young do not mix until they fledge; adults do not discriminate between their own and other chicks. In contrast, ground-nesting Herring Gulls reject foreign chicks beginning at about five days, but in cliff-nesting populations, where young leave the nest later, adults will still accept transfer chicks that are one to two weeks old. Franklin's Gulls (*Larus pipixcan*), with widely spaced floating nests, do not discriminate among chicks less than one to two weeks old.

Development of recognition has been most thoroughly studied in the Laughing Gull (*Larus atricilla*), a North American species that occasionally appears as a transatlantic vagrant along coastal areas of Britain, Ireland, and western Europe. Chicks remain close to the nest for three or four days, and although they begin to recognize their parents' calls at one to three days, their discriminatory ability becomes much sharper at five to six days. Learning occurs in stages as the young gulls are exposed to different adult calls. Adults identify their chicks by the response that their calls elicit, rather than by the calls of the chicks. Similarly, Ring-billed Gulls (*Larus delawarensis*) do not recognize their chicks by vocalizations, but distinguish them instead by their appearance.

In species with altricial or spatially-confined young, the timing of recognition is also correlated with the potential for confusion with young from different broods. Adult Guillemots nesting on crowded cliff ledges can recognize their own chicks shortly after hatching; the chicks learn their parents' calls while still in the egg! For most altricial species, the critical time requiring discrimination comes at fledging. Young of the colonial Sand Martin begin to fledge at 18–19 days. Until then, parents need simply return to the correct burrow to ensure that they are feeding their own young. Experiments confirm that exchanged chicks are readily accepted until they reach 15 days of age, when their begging calls are replaced by brood-specific 'signature' calls that the adults use to discriminate between their own and other young.

Why is the development of parent–offspring recognition delayed until shortly before it is required? The likely answer is that there is an evolutionary cost involved in recognition prior to the onset of chick mobility. Not only would earlier recognition be superfluous for the purpose of rejecting alien chicks, it could even lead to evicting one's own chick by mistake.

SEE: Vocal Functions, p. 413; Vocal Development, p. 479; Coloniality, p. 107; Crèches, p. 45. REFS: Beecher *et al.*, 1981; Beer, 1979; Falls, 1982.

Razorbill
Alca torda

ATLAS 159; PMH 139; PER 134; HFP 164; HPCW 117; NESTS 185; BWP4:195

| Ground | No nest Crevice BLDS: – Monogamy | 1 (2) 1 brood INCU: ♂♀ 32–39 | SP FLDG: ♂♀ 14–24 | Aq inverts | |

Breeding habitat Coastal cliffs and islands.

Displays Pairing probably occurs on sea and other resting areas near colony. Courtship includes sky-pointing, bill-fencing, bowing, and mutual preening.

Nesting Colonial. Nest site is variable. Some lay egg on ledges like Guillemot, others in crevices among boulders or in rabbit burrows; builds no nest. Eggs varied, whitish to brown, variably marked blackish-brown, 75mm. After young leaves nest it is cared for by the ♂ at sea.

Diet Mainly fish, also marine invertebrates, caught in much more shallow surface dives than used by both guillemots, typically 2–5m.

Winters At sea, S to N Africa.

Conservation Local increases and decreases; like Guillemot, vulnerable to oil spills.

Essays Birds and Oil, p. 225; The Northern Penguin, p. 231; Seabird Nesting Sites, p. 233.

Great Auk
Pinguinus impennis

Extinct: not covered by field guides; BWP4: 207

| | No nest BLDS: – Monogamy | 1 1 brood INCU: ♂♀ 39–45? | SP FLDG: ♂♀ | |

Breeding habitat Small rocky islands.

Displays Courtship probably involved head-shaking and bobbing, with open, yellow mouth (see Black Guillemot).

Nested Colonial. Egg laid on bare ground. Eggs dirty white to yellowish buff, marked with black and brown, 124mm.

Diet Mostly fish, squid and other invertebrates. Possibly foraged to depths of 70m or more.

Wintered At sea, S to Carolinas (USA) and UK.

Conservation Extinct since 1844 when last known pair was collected. Once occurred from Newfoundland to Scotland and Norway, declined due to severe hunting pressure (killed for food and oil) and then, as it became rare, adults and eggs were taken for museum specimens.

Essays The Northern Penguin, p. 231.

Notes Species was flightless.

The Northern Penguin

FEW people realize that the original 'penguin' bred in the Northern Hemisphere. The designation was first applied to the extinct flightless bird now known as the Great Auk or Garefowl, as its latinized generic name, *Pinguinus*, attests. This diving fish-hunter stood some 75 cm tall, and was widely distributed in the North Atlantic. The Great Auk was swift and agile in the water, but clumsy and vulnerable on land. It was so common on the Newfoundland Banks that in the 1767 edition of *The English Pilot* their presence was listed as a clue to seamen that they were near the Banks. Great Auk breeding colonies on offshore islands served as butcher shops for seamen; the birds could be herded right across gangplanks and on to boats. They disappeared from Britain around 1760; soon thereafter their value increased as they were slaughtered for their feathers in addition to their meat. Their eggs were collected and their chicks were used for fish food. Audubon reported early in the nineteenth century: 'When I was in Labrador, many of the fishermen assured me that the "Penguin", as they name this bird, breeds on a low rocky island to the south-east of Newfoundland, where they destroy great numbers of the young for bait'.

As human exploitation increased from the middle of the sixteenth century, numbers of the Great Auk decreased. Mother Nature may have pitched in with some bad luck. The 'Little Ice Age', which began around the thirteenth century and lasted to about the middle of the last century, may have made life difficult for these large alcids, surrounding many of their best breeding islands with ice, giving polar bears access to their colonies, and perhaps reducing supplies of fish upon which the auks depended. As a final blow from nature, in 1830 one of the breeding sites, the rocky island of Geirfuglasker off Iceland, disappeared in a volcanic eruption. Presumably, however, some of the breeding birds from Geirfuglasker simply moved to the adjacent

Great Auks.

Black Guillemot
Cepphus grylle

ATLAS 160; PMH 140; PER 134; HFP 164; HPCW -; NESTS 186; BWP4:208

  1–2 (3?) 1 brood
BLDS: – INCU: ♂♀ 23–40
Cliff Monogamy

 SP
FLDG: ♂♀ 31–51

 Aq inverts

Breeding habitat Rocky coasts.

Displays Threat display involves hunching up and opening mouth to show red gape. In mating displays, birds have upright posture, strutting walk, with high stepping that shows off their bright red feet. Pairs have head-bobbing displays.

Nesting In small colonies; lays eggs among boulders and rocks and in holes; no nest. Eggs whitish to buff or pale blue-green, spotted and blotched dark browns and black, 59mm, hatch

synchronously. Parents apparently do not accompany young to sea. First breeds at 2–4 years.

Diet Fish and crustaceans, caught in shallow dives to 10m or less.

Winters At sea from UK north to pack-ice; in small flocks or often solitary.

Conservation Numbers thought to be more or less constant; occurs widely in N Atlantic and around Arctic Ocean.

Essays Birds and Oil, p. 225; Seabird Nesting Sites, p. 233.

Little Auk
Alle alle

ATLAS 160; PMH 140; PER 134; HFP 164; HPCW -; NESTS 187; BWP4:219

 No nest
BLDS: – INCU: ♂ ♀ 28–31
Cliff Monogamy

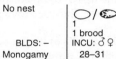 1 1 brood

 SP
FLDG: ♂ ♀ 23–30

Breeding habitat Sea cliffs and rocky slopes near ocean, most common in the High Arctic.

Displays Much displaying takes place at the 'clubs' where the birds rest on the sea (see Guillemot). Mating displays have head-wagging and bowing between birds; birds also 'sky-point' with bills.

Nesting Breeds in vast colonies, on cliffs or among boulders. No nest. Cliffs may be covered in snow when eggs are laid – or even when young hatch. Eggs very light bluish-green, unmarked or with

darker spotting and scrawls, 49mm. Role of parents at and after fledging time, not certain (cf. other Auks).

Diet Planktonic crustaceans.

Winters Cold, N Atlantic waters, S to UK, N to ice; in small flocks.

Conservation Some colonies in the 100 000s. Some retreat in range is apparent in the S, perhaps due to climate changes.

Essays Skimming: Why Birds Fly Low over Water, p. 67.

island of Eldey. So this large, and thus presumably always relatively scarce (compared to abundant guillemots, Razorbills, etc.) alcid appears to have been in ecological trouble and suffering population declines just at the time people increased exploitation.

The Great Auk never got a chance to respond, as some of its relatives have, to recent amelioration of climatic conditions in the North Atlantic. In June of 1844 the last two individuals known to be taken by human beings were captured by Icelanders on Eldey. They were turned over to a dealer, and the fate of their skins is not known, although some of their internal organs are preserved in the University of Copenhagen's Museum of Zoology.

The last reported sighting of the Northern Penguin was off Newfoundland, Canada, in 1852. Around 1880 Henry Dresser wrote in his classic *Birds of Europe* '. . . it has at one time been by no means a very rare bird in the extreme north-western portion of the Western Palearctic Region, there can be scarcely any doubt that it is now altogether extinct'. He was, sadly, correct. Now only the name penguin lives on, transferred to the ecologically similar but unrelated birds of the Antarctic and southern oceans. Outside that isolated continent, flightless birds have proved highly vulnerable to human-caused extinction. Perhaps, then, it is not surprising that Europe's flightless bird, the Great Auk, was among the first to go.

SEE: Listing Birds in Danger, p. 526. REFS: Audubon, 1844; Bengtson, 1984; Dresser, 1871–81; Halliday, 1978.

Seabird Nesting Sites

SEABIRDS — species spending most of their time at sea — breed along the entire western seaboard of Eurasia. They nest from southern Spain, the home of the Yellow-legged Herring Gull, to Spitsbergen and Arctic Russia, where Ivory Gulls breed close to pack ice. Species differ characteristically from each other in their foraging behaviour and the type of prey they catch. Because safe nest sites free of land predators are often in short supply, many species may nest together on the same offshore island. Nevertheless they usually select different nesting sites. For example, in the Shetland Islands of northern Britain, Black Guillemots nest among boulders just above the shoreline. Razorbills lay their eggs in crevices scattered throughout the cliff and Guillemots nest in dense groups on wider ledges. Kittiwakes build a substantial nest on tiny, rocky projections on the cliff. The much larger Shags require larger rocky ledges on which to place their nests of sticks and seaweed. Puffins and Manx Shearwaters nest in burrows in the soil, the former usually near to the cliff edge and the latter often inland on flatter ground. Herring and Common Gulls, Arctic and Great Skuas, and Common and Arctic Terns all nest in the open on flat ground. The terns nest in densely packed colonies enabling them

Puffin

Fratercula arctica

ATLAS 160; PMH 140; PER 134; HFP 164; HPCW 117; NESTS 186; BWP4:231

		○/❀			
		1 (2?)	SP		
	Crevice	1 brood			
	BLDS: ♂♀	INCU: ♀ (♂♀)	FLDG: ♂♀		
Cliff	Monogamy	36–45	?	Aq inverts	

Breeding habitat Coastal islands and cliffs.

Displays Threat displays include leaning forward with bill open and sky-pointing with bill. Most courtship takes place offshore in rafts of birds; includes head-flicking and mutual billing.

Nesting Colonial; adds some plant material to a burrow or lays egg in crevices on cliff. Eggs white, usually unmarked, sometimes marked brown, 63mm. Young deserted by parents sometimes before, often at, fledging. First breeds at 5 years.

Diet Fish and crustaceans taken in shallow dives (up to 15m deep). Many fish may be carried, crosswise in bill, to young in nest.

Winters Pelagic, from Mediterranean N to pack-ice in Atlantic; usually solitary.

Conservation Some local declines, in N Norway perhaps due to commerical over-fishing. An abundant species in the N Atlantic and into Arctic Ocean.

Essays Bills, p. 391; Birds and Oil, p. 225; Seabird Nesting Sites, p. 233; Swimming and Underwater Flight, p. 61.

Refs Boag and Alexander 1986, and Harris 1984 are books about this species.

Crowned Sandgrouse

Pterocles coronatus

ATLAS 161; PMH -; PER -; HFP 167; HPCW 118; NESTS 188; BWP4:249

		(2–3)	P3		
		1 brood?			
	BLDS: ♀	INCU: ♂♀	FLDG: ♂♀		
	Monogamy	?	?		

Breeding habitat Rocky desert and hillsides with only very sparse vegetation.

Displays Not well known.

Nesting Nest is an unlined scrape on ground, in open. Eggs cream, variously marked light brown, 39mm.

Diet Seeds, picked off ground.

Winters Resident or nomadic, birds moving out of driest areas when conditions become too extreme; often in flocks.

Conservation The numbers of this species are not well known, but probably fluctuate with rainfall like other sandgrouse. Locally common across N Africa, Arabia, into SW Asia.

Notes See Spotted Sandgrouse.

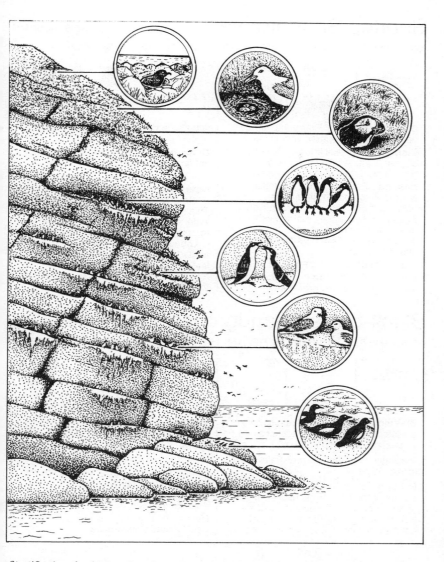

Stratification of seabird nesting sites typically found along the northwest coast of Europe. Bottom to top: Black Guillemots, Kittiwakes, Razorbills, Guillemots, Puffin, Herring Gull, Storm Petrel.

to 'gang-up' and chase away any of the larger gulls and skuas. The tiny 25 gram Storm Petrel nests in small crevices, often in boulder scree.

Sometimes differences in preferred nest sites are subtle. On the island of St George in the Pribilofs between Alaska and eastern Siberia familiar (Black-legged) Kittiwakes and rarer Red-legged Kittiwakes (*Rissa brevirostris*) nest in

Spotted Sandgrouse

Pterocles senegallus

ATLAS 161; PMH 249; PER -; HFP 166; HPCW 118; NESTS 188; BWP4:253

  |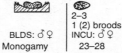

2–3
1 brood?
BLDS: ♀   INCU: ♂♀
Monogamy   29–31

FLDG: ♂♀
?

Breeding habitat Rocky and sandy desert, with only sparse vegetation.

Displays Not well known. Pairs have a display flight. Adults feign injury to lure ground predators away from young.

Nesting Perhaps loosely colonial. Nest is a scrape on ground, in open, sometimes in a natural hollow. Eggs pale buff, lightly marked light brown or red-brown, 41mm, hatch asynchronously. Each parent may look after one young.

Diet Seeds, picked off ground.

Winters Resident or nomadic, birds moving out of driest areas when conditions too extreme; often in flocks.

Conservation Numbers not known, but fluctuate with rainfall.

Notes Sandgrouse have a number of remarkable adaptations to deserts. This species may nest up to 10km from water; birds visit water holes early in the morning and sometimes in the evening. ♂s bring water to the young (who are tended by the ♀). ♂s wet their belly feathers, which soak up water, then return to young, who then pass feathers though bill to squeeze out water.

Black-bellied Sandgrouse

Pterocles orientalis

ATLAS 162; PMH 141; PER 136; HFP 168; HPCW 119; NESTS 189; BWP4:263

2–3
1 (2) broods
BLDS: ♂♀   INCU: ♂♀
Monogamy   23–28

FLDG: ♂♀
?

Foliage glean

Breeding habitat Salt flats, flat dry grassy plains, with other scattered vegetation, agricultural areas.

Displays Not well known. Pairs have display flight.

Nesting Solitary. Nest is a shallow scrape on ground. Eggs usually cream or buff, well and variously marked with browns and greys, 48mm, timing of hatching not known. ♂ brings water to young (see Spotted Sandgrouse).

Diet Seeds; taken from ground or plants. Young may also feed on insects.

Winters Resident; in flocks.

Conservation Population size not well known; some local decreases. Occurs from Iberia, across N Africa into SW Asia. See p. 529.

Notes Will fly long distances to water. See Spotted Sandgrouse.

close proximity. Both use narrow nesting ledges, but the Red-legged prefers those beneath overhanging rocks.

The quality of the nest site may be important for breeding success. During a study of the Shag, there was a period of exceptionally high mortality following which the survivors moved to better quality nest sites, and so increased their breeding success. Hence the survivors must have been able to recognize some of the qualities of a good site.

Although nest sites tend to differ between species, there is some overlap in preferences and, where this happens, competition for sites occurs. Fulmars, whose numbers have increased markedly in western Europe this century, use sites similar to those chosen by Razorbills, and battles for a site may result. Similarly, Puffins and Manx Shearwaters may compete for nesting burrows; their fights may result in the loss of the egg which will not be replaced that season.

Cliffs where several species of seabirds nest together are some of the best places to observe habitat selection in action. Additional quantitative analyses of differences between sites, and at the same site from season to season, would be most informative.

SEE: Habitat Selection, p. 423; Coloniality, p. 107. REFS: Squibb and Hunt, 1983; Threlfall, 1985.

Salt Glands

SEAWATER has about three times the salt content of the body fluids of birds. How then do birds such as albatrosses, which spend months at sea, survive without freshwater to drink? The answer has been elucidated in the past few decades.

Marine species possess enlarged nasal glands, known as salt glands, to regulate the salt content of the blood. Nasal glands are found above or in front of the eyes of all birds. Those in land birds are normally inactive. Ocean birds drink seawater, and the glands remove salt from the blood, producing a concentrated waste fluid that has a salt content of about 5 per cent (compared to about 3.5 per cent in seawater). The salty solution either dribbles out of the bill or, in petrels, is blown forcibly from the nostrils. With the aid of the salt glands, the normal salt content of the body fluids can be rapidly restored after a seawater drink. Although avian physiologists have investigated the operation of the salt glands in detail in cormorants, among others, and have uncovered some clues to their remarkable efficiency at removing salt from the blood, the functioning of the glands is still not entirely understood.

Interestingly, Mallard ducklings experimentally exposed to high concentrations of salt in their drinking water developed larger salt glands than ducklings given less salty water. Apparently in species that may be exposed

Pin-tailed Sandgrouse

Pterocles alchata

ATLAS 162; PMH 141; PER 136; HFP 168; HPCW 120; NESTS 188; BWP4:269

		3 (2) 1 (2?) broods	P3		
BLDS: –		INCU: ♂♀	FLDG: ♂♀		
Monogamy		19–23	?		Foliage glean

Breeding habitat Dry, open country from rocky hills to dried-out salt marshes, to agricultural areas.

Displays Threat displays involve pecking from low posture, calling, and fighting. Have courtship flights in which small groups of birds fly high and erratically. On ground birds walk stiff-legged with tails down and spread.

Nesting Sometimes in loose colonies. Nest is unlined scrape on ground often in natural hollow. Eggs cream to buff, variably marker darker, 47mm. ♂ brings

water to young; young may become independent as early as 10 days.

Diet Seeds; taken from ground or plants. Young fed on very small seeds.

Winters Resident and nomadic in area covered by this guide; migrates out of Asian breeding grounds, to the S. Sometimes in very large flocks.

Conservation Population numbers are not well known and fluctuate. Nests from Iberia and N Africa to SW Asia. See p. 529.

Pallas's Sandgrouse

Syrrhaptes paradoxus

ATLAS 162; PMH 142; PER 136; HFP 168; HPCW 120; NESTS 190; BWP4:277

		2–3 (4) 2 (3?) broods	P3		
BLDS: –		INCU: ♂♀	FLDG: ♂♀		
Monogamy		28?	?	Greens	Foliage glean

Breeding habitat Normally arid steppe, but avoids harsh deserts.

Displays Not well known, but includes pursuit flights (see other Sandgrouse).

Nesting In loose colonies. Nest is scrape on ground, in open; usually no material. Eggs cream to buff variously marked dark brown; 43mm, hatch asynchronously.

Diet Seeds and green shoots, picked from ground or from plants.

Winters Wide range of open areas; resident or some southward movement.

Conservation Population numbers poorly known, but very erratic.

Notes Perhaps the most spectacular irruptive bird species. Normally nests no closer than the Caspian Sea (and so outside the area covered by this guide). However, in 1863, 1888, and 1908 birds nested across Europe, as far west as UK, and reached Ireland, Spain, and N to the Arctic. In 1888, these flocks arrived in the west in late April. A few stayed and survived until 1889.

Essays Irruptions, p. 491.

to water of different salinities, the glands are able to respond to the differing needs of individuals.

Birds are not the only organisms that have evolved glands for the excretion of salt. The famous marine iguanas of the Galápagos Islands periodically snort sprays of salt from their nostrils, and some turtles, bony fishes, and sharks also have the glands, which are located in body areas as different as the rectum and the gills.

SEE: Drinking, p. 313; Bird Droppings, p. 485; Metabolism, p. 281.

Coevolution

WHEN organisms that are ecologically intimate — for example, predators and prey, or hosts and parasites — influence each other's evolution, we say that 'coevolution' is occurring. Birds are often important actors in coevolutionary systems. For example, predation by birds largely drives the coevolution of model and mimetic butterflies. Some butterflies have evolved the ability to store poisonous chemicals from the food plants they eat as caterpillars, thus becoming distasteful. This reduces their chances of being eaten, since birds, once they have tried to devour such butterflies, will avoid attacking them in the future. Meanwhile, other butterflies have gradually evolved colour patterns that mimic those of the distasteful butterflies (called 'models'). This is disadvantageous for the models: if the mimics become common then most of the butterflies with the model's colour pattern taste good, not bad, and the birds may resume attacking the models. Being tasted and spat out by a bird is a most dangerous experience for a butterfly. Therefore, mimicry presumably leads to a 'coevolutionary race' — the tasty mimics evolving toward the colour patterns of the distasteful models, and the models evolving away from the converging mimics. The birds may also be under selection for better powers of discrimination. Individuals that can tell the mimetic butterflies from the models will gain more nourishment at less cost in time and effort.

Birds, presumably, are directly involved in coevolutionary relationships not just with their prey, but also with competitors, predators, pathogens, and brood parasites. In some cases there is a convergence between members of mixed species feeding flocks, a phenomenon called 'social mimicry'. Mimics may gain food by copying other species in the flock, but may have evolved the resemblance to avoid aggression from stronger flock members that are being forced to share their food. Other possibilities are that similar appearance makes communication between the participating species easier, or that it makes the flock more confusing to predators.

The relationship of seed-hoarding North American Clark's Nutcrackers (*Nucifraga columbiana*) and Pinyon Jays (*Gymnorhinus cyanocephalus*) with whitebark and pinyon pines is a relatively well-studied example of coevolu-

Rock Dove
Columba livia

ATLAS 163; PMH 142; PER 136; HFP 170; HPCW 121; NESTS 191; BWP4:285

BLDS: ♂♀
Monogamy

2 (1)
5 + broods
INCU: ♀
16–19

FLDG: ♂♀
35–37

Greens

Breeding habitat Naturally on rocky cliffs, either inland, or, commonly, on coasts. Has long been domesticated, however, and feral populations occur almost worldwide in human settlements, including large cities.

Displays ♂ has display flight with slow deep flaps, occasional wing-claps, and a glide with wings up and tail spread. Courtship has ♂ flying to ♀, then bowing while spreading tail, ruffling head and neck feathers, calling. Pair may mutually preen; there is courtship feeding.

Nesting Loosely colonial. Nest in crevice in cave or ledge on cliff or building is a cup of vegetation. Eggs white, 39mm, hatch asynchronously. The remarkably high number of broods per year is the result of nesting almost

year round – even in places as far N as the UK.

Diet Seeds, sometimes greenery, and feral populations take a wide variety of foods from humans. Young fed crop milk, a rich secretion from the adults' crops.

Winters Resident; in flocks.

Conservation This is an abundant and widespread species that has been introduced widely in the last two centuries.

Essays Dominance Hierarchies, p. 131; Communal Roosting, p. 81; Visual Displays, p. 33; Drinking, p. 313; Feeding Birds, p. 357; Nest Sites and Materials, p. 443; Bird Milk, p. 243, Commensal Feeding, p. 27.

Refs Goodwin 1983 is a book about this and other species of doves and pigeons.

Stock Dove
Columba oenas

ATLAS 164; PMH 143; PER 136; HFP 170; HPCW 121; NESTS 191; BWP4:298

BLDS: ♂♀
Monogamy

2 (1)
2–5 broods
INCU: ♂♀
16–18

FLDG: ♂♀
20–30

Foliage glean

Breeding habitat Wide range of open country, especially agricultural areas near woodland

Displays ♂'s display flight resembles that of Rock Dove. ♂s attract ♀s by calling and then have bowing display like Rock Dove. If ♀ departs, she is pursued by ♂, whose displays are repeated.

Nesting Nest is often in hole in tree or cliff with small amounts of vegetation added; also mass of twigs in branches of tree. Eggs white, 38mm, hatch asynchronously. May compete with Jackdaws for nest holes.

Diet A variety of plant parts, but mainly seeds, taken from the ground. Young fed

crop milk (see Rock Dove, and essay, p. 243).

Winters Resident in W and S, migrates to those areas from E and N; in flocks.

Conservation Has expanded range in W, especially the UK, where once confined to S and E. Some local declines perhaps due to use of pesticide-coated seeds in agricultural areas. Occurs widely across Europe, into Asia.

Essays Monogamy, p. 335; Declines in Forest Birds: Europe and America, p. 339; Visual Displays, p. 33; Drinking, p. 313; Gilbert White, p. 271; Bird Milk, p. 243.

Refs Goodwin 1983; Marchant et al. 1990.

tion; and the evolution of long sickle-shaped bills in some Latin American hummingbirds and some African and Asian sunbirds that match the long, sharply curved flowers from which they sip nectar (and which they pollinate) is another. Hermit hummingbirds and the curved flowers of the genus *Heliconia* (seen increasingly as horticultural cut flowers) provide widespread and conspicuous examples of the latter phenomenon throughout the lowland moist forests of Central and South America.

Many fruit-eating birds, especially in tropical rain forests, are coevolving with the plants whose fruits they eat. While the birds get nourishment, the plants get their digestion-resistant seeds dispersed by regurgitation or passed along with the birds' droppings. Many characteristics of plants have evolved to facilitate dispersal, and the behaviour and diets of birds have responded to those changes. In particular, the plants have evolved conspicuously coloured, relatively odourless fleshy fruits to attract the avian dispersers of their seeds. They are coevolving in response to the finely honed visual systems of the birds; plant species coevolving with colour-blind mammalian seed-dispersers have, in contrast, dull-coloured but smelly fruits. Often, as with laurels, the bird-dispersed plants have evolved fruits with giant seeds covered by a thin, highly nutritious layer of flesh. This forces the bird to swallow the fruit whole, since it is difficult or impossible just to nip off the flesh. In response, birds that are specialized frugivores (that is, they do not take other kinds of food) have evolved both bills with wide gapes (so they can swallow the fruit whole) and digestive tracts that can rapidly dissolve the flesh from the large impervious seed, which then can be regurgitated.

Temperate regions are the home of birds whose dependence on fruit is generally more seasonal. In autumn elderberries turn black and haws turn red to signal their ripeness to, for example, Blackcaps fattening before migration and various thrushes.

The most dramatic examples of avian coevolution are probably those involving brood parasites, such as cuckoos, and their hosts. In many cases the parasites have evolved eggs that closely mimic those of the host, and young with characteristics that encourage the hosts to feed them. In response, some hosts have developed the ability to discriminate between their own and parasitic eggs, and various methods of destroying the latter.

Many examples of coevolution in response to competition between bird species can be inferred from studies of dietary habits and bill structures in various guilds of birds. Here, as in coevolution of birds with their predators and the other cases mentioned, direct evidence of coevolution is lacking. It is lacking for the same reason that there are very few cases of plain old single-population evolution actually being observed in nature. The process occurs over hundreds or thousands of generations, and extraordinary circumstances are required for evolution to be 'caught in the act'.

SEE: Natural Selection, p. 297; Hoarding Food, p. 453; Bird Guilds, p. 77; Brood Parasitism, p. 249. REFS: Barnard 1982, 1984*a,b*; Diamond, 1984; Dobkin, 1984; Ehrlich, 1970; Ehrlich and Ehrlich, 1973; Futuyma and Slatkin, 1983; Moynihan, 1960, 1981; Snow and Snow, 1988; Thompson, 1982; Wheelwright, 1988; Willson, 1986.

Wood Pigeon

Columba palumbus

ATLAS 165; PMH 143; PER 136; HFP 170; HPCW 122; NESTS 191; BWP4:311

Shrub	BLDS: ♂♀	1–(3)
3–5m	Monogamy	1–2 broods
		INCU: ♂♀
		17

FLDG: ♂♀	Seeds	Ground glean
20–35		

Breeding habitat A wide range of habitats, primarily farmland near woods, also towns.

Displays Has display flight, with quick ascent, wing-claps at apex, and then more shallow gliding descent. ♀ approaches ♂ when he gives this display. When pairs meet, ♂ spreads and raises tail, bows, and calls.

Nesting Territorial. Nest is a flimsy platform of twigs usually above ground in tree or other vegetation. Eggs white, 41mm, hatch synchronously.

Diet Green plant parts, seeds, berries, etc. Feeds while walking along ground. Young fed crop milk.

Winters Resident in S and W, migrates to those areas from N and E; exploits agricultural fields and occurs in large flocks.

Conservation Abundant, widespread, and increasing (especially in N). May be increasing its use of urban habitats. Occurs throughout Europe into Asia and N Africa.

Essays Visual Displays, p. 33; Dominance Hierarchies, p. 131; Drinking, p. 313; Feeding Birds, p. 357; Gilbert White, p. 271; Bird Milk, p. 243.

Refs Goodwin 1983; Marchant et al. 1990; Murton 1965 is a book about this species.

Collared Dove

Streptopelia decaocto

ATLAS 166; PMH 143; PER 134; HFP 172; HPCW 123; NESTS 195; BWP4:340

Shrub	BLDS: ♂♀	2 (1)
2–16m	Monogamy	3–6 broods
		INCU: ♂♀
		14–18

FLDG: ♂♀		
17 (15–19)		

Breeding habitat Originally dry open forest; now suburban areas and around farms.

Displays In display flight, ♂ ascends quickly, wing-claps at apex, then glides down, circling, with tail and wings spread. Towards mate has bowing display like other doves.

Nesting Territorial. Nest in tree or bush is a flimsy platform of twigs. Eggs white, 31mm, hatching interval variable. Breeds almost year round.

Diet Agricultural grains, seeds, and fruits, taken on the ground. Young given crop milk.

Winters Resident; in flocks.

Conservation Perhaps the most remarkable range change of a European

bird in this century, this species was restricted to SE Europe and Asia until the 1930s, when the species moved westward. The reasons for this sudden shift are not well understood; the species is a successful human commensal, but such habitats were available for centuries prior to 1930. First bred in the UK in 1955. Has reached the extremities of Europe, has bred in Iceland, occurs above the Arctic Circle in Norway, and in Spain. Vulnerable to cold winters in N. Is now spreading N in Florida, USA.

Essays Drinking, p. 313; Feeding Birds, p. 357; Bird Milk, p. 243; Commensal Feeding, p. 27.

Refs Goodwin 1983; Marchant et al. 1990.

Bird Milk

LIKE mammals, the young of some birds are fed on special secretions from a parent. Unlike mammals, however, both sexes produce it. The best known of these secretions is the 'crop milk' that pigeons and doves feed to squabs. The milk is produced by a sloughing of fluid-filled cells from the lining of the crop, a thin-walled, sac-like food-storage chamber that projects outward from the bottom of the oesophagus. Crops are presumably devices for permitting birds to gather and store food rapidly, minimizing the time that they are exposed to predators. Crops tend to be especially well developed in pigeons and gallinaceous birds.

Crop milk is extremely nutritious. In one study, domestic chicks given feed containing pigeon crop milk were 16 per cent heavier at the end of the experiment than chicks that did not receive the supplement. The pigeon milk, which contains more protein and fat than does cow or human milk, is the exclusive food of the nestlings for several days after hatching, and both adults continue feeding it to the squabs for more than two weeks. The young pigeons are not fed insects as are the chicks of many seed-eating birds; instead, the crop milk provides the critical ration of protein.

The milk of Greater Flamingos contains much more fat and much less protein than does pigeon milk, and its production is not localized in a crop, but involves glands lining the entire upper digestive tract. Interestingly, the milk contains an abundance of red and white blood cells, which under the microscope can be seen migrating like amoebas through the surface of the glands. Young flamingos feed exclusively on this milk for about two months, while the special filter-feeding apparatus that they will later employ for foraging develops.

Emperor Penguin chicks may also be fed 'milk' in some circumstances. For two months of the Antarctic winter, fasting while the female is out at sea feeding, each male incubates a single egg on his feet, covering it with a fold of abdominal skin. If the female has not returned with food by the time the chick hatches, the male feeds it for a few days on milk, a rich crop secretion. After its brief diet of milk, the chick will be fed by regurgitation. Its food is fish and squid caught by the male and female at sea.

Thus three very different groups of birds have evolved the capacity to produce milk as solutions to very different problems: the need for protein and fat in the pigeons, which feed very little animal material to the squabs; the need for liquid food consumption during the development of the specialized feeding apparatus of the flamingos (which would make any other form of food difficult for the chicks to ingest); and the need for a convenient food supplement by penguins when breeding on the barren Antarctic ice shelf.

SEE: Flamingo Feeding, p. 37; Brood Patches, p. 3. REFS: Hedge, 1973; Lang, 1963.

Turtle Dove

Streptopelia turtur

ATLAS 166; PMH 144; PER 134; HFP 172; HPCW 124; NESTS 195; BWP4:353

| Decid tree 1–10m | BLDS: ♂♀ Monogamy | 1–2 2– 3 broods INCU: ♂♀ 13–14 (16) | FLDG: ♂♀ 20? | Fruit | |

Breeding habitat Woodland edges and parkland, or farmland with scattered trees.

Displays Has display flights and courtship displays similar to other doves.

Nesting Nest is a flimsy platform of small twigs with scanty lining of roots, plants, tree, or bush. Eggs white, 30mm, hatch synchronously. Young fed crop milk.

Diet Seeds, grains, and fruits taken on the ground.

Winters Migrates to Africa S of Sahara, apparently including even those populations that occur in the far east of the range in Asia.

Conservation Common and widespread across Europe, N Africa, and W Asia; local increases in NW, decline in UK.

Essays Drinking, p. 313; Birds and the Law, p. 521; Ducking the Bird Laws, p. 523; Bird Milk, p. 243.

Refs Goodwin 1983; Marchant et al. 1990.

Laughing Dove

Streptopelia senegalensis

ATLAS 167; PMH 144; PER- ; HFP 172; HPCW 126; NESTS 195; BWP4:366

| 1–5m | BLDS: ♂♀ Monogamy | 2 (1) 2 (3?) broods INCU: ♀ 12–14 |  FLDG: ♂♀ 14–17 | Insects | |

Breeding habitat Around cultivation and habitation, often more urban in its habitat than Collared Dove.

Displays Has display flights and courtship displays similar to other doves.

Nesting Nest is a flimsy platform of small twigs and plant stems. Eggs white, 27mm, hatch asynchronously?

Diet Mainly seeds, but some insects, taken from the ground.

Winters Resident; often in small flocks.

Conservation Widely distributed in Africa, SW Asia, and India; isolated populations in the Middle East and Turkey were perhaps introduced there.

Essays Flock Defence, p. 257; Drinking, p. 313; Bird Milk, p. 243.

Refs Goodwin 1983; Long 1981

Altruism

SOME bird behaviour can be interpreted as altruistic—as when one bird seems to put itself at risk to help another. A classic example is the bird in a flock that spots a predator and gives an alarm call, alerting the rest of the group. Another is the bird that joins in mobbing a hawk, perhaps teaching juveniles that the hawk is an enemy. Why doesn't the first bird keep quiet and keep to the far side of the flock, rather than risk attracting the attention of the predator by calling? What evolutionary explanation could there be for a bird spending its time and energy (and perhaps getting injured or killed) to teach others about the danger of hawks? After all, the rule in natural selection is to leave as many offspring as possible, and self-sacrifice rarely seems a route to reproductive success. Intuitively, one would expect strong selection *against* altruistic behaviour, making its evolution unlikely.

How, then, does behaviour that appears altruistic evolve? There are two ways. One is when the so-called altruistic actions actually turn out to be selfish. For instance, the 'altruistic' alarm call could be ventriloquial, preventing the predator from locating the caller. By scaring the rest of the flock into flight, the caller may be manipulating the other birds into rising from the grass, thereby calling themselves to the attention of the predator. The caller, presumably having seen the predator first, may be improving its chances to get away in the ensuing confusion—at the expense of its unprepared colleagues.

Indeed, Great Tits giving 'alarm' calls are sometimes anything but altruistic. For example, they may give false alarm calls when a flock of sparrows is monopolizing a food resource or when another Great Tit is competing for the same food. By manipulating the other birds with the calls, they obtain more food for themselves.

Similarly, a small bird mobbing a hawk may not be truly altruistic; it may be protecting itself. Perhaps it is safer to keep the enemy close and in view and try to drive it away, than to wonder where the hawk is and what it is doing.

The second way such behaviour could evolve works even if the actions are truly altruistic from the viewpoint of immediate individual survival (there is evidence in mammals that some alarm calls are altruistic in this sense). Altruism of that sort can be favoured by natural selection if the individual or individuals helped are relatives of the altruist. The most obvious case is when a parent sacrifices its life to help its offspring, in the process increasing the chances that the parent's genes are well represented in the breeders of the next generation. The act is directly altruistic but evolutionarily selfish. Altruism toward more distant relatives can also be favoured through a form of natural selection called 'kin selection'. In this case, the altruist is helping to pass on, not the genes it has provided (as it does when aiding its offspring), but genes that are identical with its own but are carried by its kin.

Namaqua Dove

Oena capensis

ATLAS 167; PMH -; PER- ; HFP 172; HPCW 126; NESTS 196; BWP4:374

0.5–2m	BLDS: ♂♀ Monogamy	(2–3) 2–3 broods INCU: ♂♀ 13–16	FLDG: ♂♀ 11–12 (–16)	Insects

Breeding habitat Open, dry areas, savannas, and also settlements.
Displays ♂ has circular display flights, following ♀. Has bowing display, lowering head and raising tail.
Nesting Nest is a platform of small twigs and plant stems. Eggs cream, 27mm.
Diet Mainly seeds, but some insects, taken from the ground; walks or runs quickly.

Winters Mainly resident, though makes local movements to exploit rains. Often in small groups, sometimes in large flocks.

Conservation First found breeding in Israel, in 1961, increasing records since then; is widely distributed in Africa.

Essays Drinking, p. 313; Bird Milk, p. 243; Walking vs. Hopping, p. 375.

Refs Goodwin 1983; Long 1981.

Ring-necked Parakeet

Psittacula krameri

ATLAS 169; PMH 145; PER 138; HFP 190; HPCW 127; NESTS 196; BWP4:379

	BLDS: – Monogamy	3–4 (2–6) 1 brood? INCU: ♀ 22–24 (21–28)	FLDG: ♂♀ 40–45	Fruit	Foliage glean

Breeding habitat In native range, in open woodland and often near villages and towns; where introduced, suburban habitats.
Displays Threat display involves head-bobbing and ♀s vigorously defend nest hole. In courtship ♂s have a slow walk, with head up, and a bow. ♀ may spread wings slightly and sway. ♂ then preens ♀, and may adopt vertical position with one foot lifted.
Nesting Nest is in tree hole (such as an old woodpecker hole); adds no material. Eggs white, 31mm, hatch asynchronously. ♂ feeds ♀ when she is incubating. First breeds at 2–3 years.
Diet Seeds, fruit; often found at bird feeders in the UK – which may explain how they can cope with its cold winters.

Winters Resident; in flocks.

Conservation Introduced into W Europe, including the UK in 1969, where may be increasing. In Nile Delta introduced in the early 20th century, and numbers several hundred birds. In Israel, introduced populations have been found in a number of locations since the 1960s. This species is native to India, SW Asia, and Africa, where it can be a serious agricultural pest.

Essays Disease and Parasitism, p. 315; Ducking the Bird Laws, p. 523; Feathers, p. 363; Monogamy, p. 335; Precocial and Altricial Young, p. 401; The Avian Sense of Smell, p. 13.

Refs Forshaw 1978; Marchant et al. 1990; Paz 1987.

For instance, half of a hatchling's genes are duplicates of genes of the father, passed on through the sperm; the other half come from the mother, passed on through the egg. Parents each share 50 per cent of their genes with their offspring. Brothers and sisters also share half of each other's genes on average, as can be seen from the following example: A mother bird can be thought of as having two versions of each of her thousands of kinds of genes, but only one of the two goes into each egg. Suppose the two kinds of her 'A' gene are A^1 and A^2. Each nestling has a 50 per cent chance of getting A^1, and a 50 per cent chance of getting A^2. What, then, are the chances of two nestlings from the same clutch both getting A^1 or both getting A^2 from their mother? This problem is analogous to the probability that two people, each flipping a coin, will both get the same result. That will occur half of the time, since the possible outcomes are HT (John gets a head and Anne a tail), HH (both get heads), TH (John a tail and Anne a head), and TT (both tails). The chance of one offspring getting A^1 and the other A^1, or of one offspring getting A^2 and the other A^2, is the same as getting either HH or TT — that is, 50 per cent.

The same reasoning applies not just to 'A' genes but to all the kinds of genes in both the mother and the father, so that half of the genes of one sibling are identical with those found in the other sibling. Thus a brother and sister have the same 'genetic relatedness' as a parent and child. By similar reasoning it can be shown that grandparents and grandchildren share a quarter of their genes with each other, first cousins an eighth of their genes, and so on. From an evolutionary perspective, then, natural selection could favour a bird sacrificing its life to save two of its siblings — unless in the process that bird was giving up the chance to fledge more than two offspring of its own (two siblings or two offspring represent identical genetic 'contributions' for an individual). On the other hand, a bird should not sacrifice itself to save one first cousin unless it 'knew' it would have no additional offspring and its death would not jeopardize either its own young or siblings.

Of course, neither birds nor people keep precise track of relatives and make conscious decisions about the probability that a given act will promote a certain proportion of genes identical with their own. Nevertheless, there is considerable evidence that kin selection can cause directly altruistic behaviours to evolve. All that is required is for the altruist to help close relatives more than non-relatives and for the risk to the altruist to be relatively small. This is commonly seen among cooperatively breeding birds, such as the Bee-eater (*Merops apiaster*), where some individuals forgo the opportunity of breeding in a given year when the probability of breeding success is low, and instead help to rear their brothers and sisters. The probability of the altruists breeding successfully in the following year presumably will be greater or, at least, no worse.

SEE: Natural Selection, p. 297; Cooperative Breeding, p. 275; Flock Defence, p. 257; Mobbing, p. 261. REFS: Emlen and Wrege, 1988; Krebs and Davies, 1984; Møller, 1988*a*.

Great Spotted Cuckoo
Clamator glandarius

ATLAS 168; PMH 145; PER 138; HFP 174; HPCW 128; NESTS 196; BWP4:391

Nest of other species	up to 18 –	A	
BLDS: – Monogamy	INCU: – (host) 12–14(11–15)	FLDG:–(host) 20–26	Ground glean

Breeding habitat Open woodland.
Displays ♂ and ♀ establish joint territory. ♂ has dove-like display flight, ascending quickly, then gliding downward with tail spread. ♂ courtship-feeds ♀.
Nesting Parasitic; lays in nests of corvids, especially Magpies, and other medium-sized birds. Up to 75 per cent of Magpie nests may be parasitized in some areas. ♀ watches intended host carefully and quietly. ♂ may help in luring host away from nest, so that ♀ can slip in and lay her egg (sometimes more than one) and damage the host's eggs. (The host then removes the dead eggs.) Eggs pale greenish-blue, spotted brown, mimicking host's eggs, 32mm. Cuckoo's young usually hatches first (at 13 days,

compared with about 18 days for the Magpie). Cuckoo thus fledges first, and may either kill the host's young directly or indirectly by demanding a greater proportion of the food and attention. Sometimes two ♀s lay in one nest, and if so, the young of the second cuckoo survive less often than the first.
Diet Lepidopteran larvae (caterpillars), particularly those that are normally protected by hairs (which the bird first removes); also other insects, taken on the ground or in bushes.
Winters In Africa.
Conservation Apparently increasing in Europe. Occurs from S Europe to Africa, Turkey, and Middle East.
Essays See list for Cuckoo below.

Cuckoo
Cuculus canorus

ATLAS 168; PMH 146; PER 138; HFP 174; HPCW 129; NESTS 197; BWP4:402

Nest of other species	/○ up to 25 –	A	
BLDS: – See below	INCU: –(host) 11–13	FLDG:–(host) 17–21	

Breeding habitat Ranges widely over woodlands, reed-beds, farmland, and grasslands.
Displays Courtship involves ♂ bowing and opening wings and raising fanned tail.
Nesting Lays eggs in nests of over 100 species of small birds. Mating system not clear, but ♂s court every ♀ and ♀s may mate with several different ♂s. In some areas ♂s overlap in their home ranges. ♀s possibly defend areas in which they lay eggs. ♀ locates host nest, by finding out which parts of the host territories are most closely defended, then destroys eggs and sometimes small young in host nest. Eggs variable in colour and pattern, matching host's, 22mm. When young cuckoos hatch, they eject host's eggs and young from nest. (Sometimes also

smaller cuckoos laid in same nest.) With larger hosts, sometimes host young and cuckoo survive. Young fed sometimes for several weeks after they leave nest.
Diet Lepidopteran larvae (caterpillars), particularly those that are normally protected by hairs (which may be eliminated later as pellets), also other insects, picked off bushes, trunks, and ground. ♀s thought to eat eggs of intended hosts.
Winters Africa S of Sahara, SE Asia.
Conservation Possible decreases, but difficult to count. Common throughout Europe and Asia.
Essays Brood Parasitism, p. 249; Colour of Eggs, p. 161; Mobbing, p. 261; Coevolution, p. 239.
Refs Wyllie 1981 is a book about this species.

Brood Parasitism

SOME species of birds thrive not by carefully rearing their own young, but by pawning that task off on adults of other species. This habit has been most thoroughly studied in the Cuckoo. Female Cuckoos lay their eggs only in the nests of other species of birds. A Cuckoo egg usually closely mimics the eggs of the host one or two of whose eggs is often removed by the Cuckoo. The host may recognize the foreign egg and abandon the nest, or it may incubate and hatch it.

Shortly after hatching, the young Cuckoo, using a scoop-like depression on its back, instinctively shoves over the edge of the nest any solid object that it contacts. With the disappearance of their eggs or rightful young, the foster parents are free to devote all of their care to the young Cuckoo. Frequently this is an awesome task, since the Cuckoo chick often grows much larger than the host adults long before it can care for itself. One of the tragicomic scenes in nature is a pair of small foster parents working like Sisyphus to keep up with the voracious appetite of an outsized young Cuckoo.

Interestingly, different females within a population of Cuckoos often parasitize different host species. Some Cuckoos may specialize in parasitizing the nests of Garden Warblers; others of the same population may lay in the nests of Reed Warblers, and yet others may lay in nests of Pied Wagtails. The eggs of each female usually closely mimic those of the host selected and the mimetic patterns are genetically determined. If the hosts discriminate against badly-matching Cuckoo eggs (see below) and if young female Cuckoos generally parasitize the same host as raised them, the mimicry between Cuckoo and host eggs would be maintained. Host preferences may well be learned by young female Cuckoos as they are raised by their foster parents.

Some host species are much more likely to reject Cuckoo eggs (by desertion of the nest or, in larger-billed species, often by ejection of the Cuckoo egg) than others. There is considerable evidence that differences in the probability of rejection are due to various Cuckoo-host pairs having progressed to different stages of their coevolutionary races. Relatively recently parasitized populations or species presumably have not yet had time to evolve the ability to discriminate between their eggs and those of the Cuckoo. Magpies in a population isolated from Great Spotted Cuckoos do not reject cuckoo eggs when they are experimentally placed in Magpie nests. In contrast, Magpies from populations that have a long evolutionary history with the cuckoos reject more than three quarters of both mimetic and non-mimetic cuckoo eggs (nearly 100 per cent of the non-mimetic eggs were identified and rejected). In a locality where Great Spotted Cuckoos had parasitized Magpies for less than 40 years, Magpies rejected some eggs, especially non-mimetic ones. Similarly, bird species which for one reason or another (e.g. unsuitable diet) are not

Senegal Coucal

Centropus senegalensis

ATLAS 169; PMH -; PER -; HFP 175; HPCW 129; NESTS 198; BWP4:427

	BLDS: ?	(3–5) 1 brood? IN: ♂ (♂♀?)
0.5–4.0m	Monogamy?	18–19

FLDG: ?		
18–20	Sm verts	

Breeding habitat   Dry grasslands with trees, to dry forests. Sometimes on edge of marshes.

Displays   Pairs often duet when calling to defend territory. Displays not well known.

Nesting   Probably territorial. Nest is large sphere. Eggs white, 34mm, hatch asynchronously.

Diet   Large insects and small vertebrates, usually taken on ground. Large prey hammered on ground until dead.

Winters   Resident.

Conservation   Local in Nile delta, widespread in Africa S of Sahara.

Notes   Coucals are related to, but in a different family from, cuckoos.

Essays   Origin of Flight, p. 157.

Barn Owl

Tyto alba

ATLAS 169; PMH 147; PER 138; HFP 176; HPCW 130; NESTS 199; BWP4:432

		◯ 4–7 (2–14) 1–2 broods
	Crevice	
Cliff	BLDS: –	INCU: ♀
	Monogamy	30–31

FLDG: ♂♀	
50–55	

Breeding habitat   Mostly open agricultural land, open land with scattered trees.

Displays   ♂s have rather erratic display flight over territory, repeatedly calling. In early courtship, ♂ flies close behind ♀, sometimes hovering in front of her, and may show her potential nest sites. Courtship feeding may start a month before egg laying. Pairs may preen each other even outside of breeding season.

Nesting   Territorial. Nest in barn, church tower, etc. or large holes in trees, cliffs; no material added. Eggs white, 40mm; clutch sizes and number of broods dependent on availability of food; hatch asynchronously. ♂ brings food to ♀. Small young often fail to get enough food, die, and are eaten by their older siblings. Young are dependent on parents for another few weeks.

Diet   Most commonly voles (except in Ireland where voles absent!), mice, and other small vertebrates. Hunts in low patrol, dropping to ground to catch prey, after hovering. As with other owls, rejected pellets provide unusual opportunities to study diet. Nocturnal, and able to locate prey strictly by sound.

Winters   Resident. Irruptive when small mammal populations crash.

Conservation   Has declined in W perhaps due to loss of nest sites; one of the world's most widely distributed species, strangely missing from most of the CIS and China, but found nearly everywhere else.

Essays   How Owls Hunt in the Dark, p. 251; Feet, p. 289; Hoarding Food, p. 453; Mobbing, p. 261; Pellets, p. 257; Precocial and Altricial Young, p. 401; Wing Shapes and Flight, p. 269; The Avian Sense of Smell, p. 13; Monogamy, p. 335; Hatching Asynchrony and Brood Reduction, p. 507.

Refs   Marchant et al. 1990; Bunn et al. 1982 and Shawyer 1987 are books about this species. Mikkola 1983 is a book about this and other species of European owls.

satisfactory Cuckoo hosts do not ordinarily reject Cuckoo eggs experimentally placed in their nests.

Cuckoo-host relationships appear to change through time for non-evolutionary reasons as well, including changes in population sizes of both Cuckoos and their victims. For example, in recent decades the rate of parasitization of Reed Warblers in Britain has more than doubled, while rates on other hosts have decreased. The decreases are probably due to a general decline in Cuckoo populations for reasons unrelated to their hosts, possibly as a result of reductions in food supply or increased mortality on their wintering grounds. The explanation for the heavier use of Reed Warbler nests could be that Cuckoos of the type or gens parasitizing the warblers are now more reproductively successful than those of other gentes, and are increasing even while Cuckoos as a whole have dropped to some 60 per cent of their previous population size.

There are some 127 members of the cuckoo family worldwide. Only about 40 per cent of these species are brood parasites; the rest care for their own eggs and young. But of some 80 bird species worldwide that are *obligate* brood parasites (that cannot raise their own young), 50 are Old World cuckoos. Western Hemisphere cuckoos belong to a different subfamily and can nest on their own.

Brood parasitism is much less common in other groups of birds. It is found in about one per cent of bird species, including members of such diverse groups as ducks, weavers, whydahs, and cowbirds. Interestingly, because of habitat changes within the last 150 years, American Brown-headed Cowbirds (which are obligate parasites), now have access to many new hosts. These generally show higher levels of parasitization than Cuckoo hosts. Both cowbird–host and Cuckoo–host coevolutionary interactions are now being subject to intensive scrutiny by ornithologists.

Brood parasitism is not restricted to females of one species laying eggs in the nests of other species. Females of a wide variety of birds, including ducks and swallows, sometimes lay eggs in the nests of other females of their own species. This behaviour is examined in other essays.

SEE: Parasitized Ducks, p. 67; Coevolution, p. 239; Monogamy, p. 335. REFS: Brooke and Davies, 1988; Davies and Brooke, 1989a, 1989b; Davies et al., 1989; Gärtner, 1982; von Haartman, 1981; Harvey and Partridge, 1988; Heinrich, 1986; Marchant et al., 1990; Moknes and Røskaft, 1987, 1988; Payne, 1977; Rohwer and Spaw, 1988; Wickler, 1968.

How Owls Hunt in the Dark

NOCTURNAL owls are formidable, silent hunters. Their silence on the wing derives from the structural modification of their primary flight feathers, a trait shared by nearly all owls. The forward edge of the feather is serrated rather than smooth, which disrupts the flow of air over the wing in flight and

Scops Owl

Otus scops

ATLAS 172; PMH 147; PER 138; HFP 178; HPCW 132; NESTS 201; BWP4:454

		○ 4–5 (3–7) 1 brood	SA2		
	BLDS: –	INCU: ♀	FLDG: ♂♀		
	Monogamy	24–25	21–29	Sm verts	Hawks

Breeding habitat Wooded, open country.

Displays Like many owls, when disturbed, raises head and sleeks body into tall thin vertical position, remaining still and well camouflaged. Main territorial defence achieved by long periods of monotonous calling. This attracts ♀ and both birds may duet.

Nesting Territorial. Nests in tree hole, building, or old bird nest; no material added. Eggs white, 31mm, hatch asynchronously.

Diet Insects and small vertebrates; nocturnal. May fly down from perch to ground or catch insects while on the wing.

Winters Africa, S of Sahara, most southerly European populations resident.

Conservation Decreases in the NW of range, but widely distributed across S and E Europe into Asia and N Africa.

Essays Feet, p. 289; Hoarding Food, p. 453; Mobbing, p. 261; How Owls Hunt in the Dark, p. 251; Pellets, p. 257; Precocial and Altricial Young, p. 401; Wing Shapes and Flight, p. 269; The Avian Sense of Smell, p. 13; Monogamy, p. 335; Hatching Asynchrony and Brood Reduction, p. 507.

Refs Mikkola 1983.

Eagle Owl

Bubo bubo

ATLAS 171; PMH 147; PER 140; HFP 176; HPCW 132; NESTS 199; BWP4:466

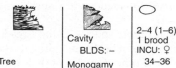 

		○ 2–4 (1–6) 1 brood	SA2		
	Cavity	INCU: ♀			
	BLDS: –	34–36	FLDG: ♂♀		
Tree	Monogamy		50–60	Birds	

Breeding habitat Areas away from human habitation across a wide range of habitats, from northern forests to rocky outcrops in deserts.

Displays ♂ defends territory and attracts ♀ by calling; pairs duet.

Nesting Territorial. Nests in small cave or large hole in tree; no material added. Eggs white, 60mm, hatch asynchronously. First breeds at 2–3 years.

Diet Mammals, commonly hares and rabbits, but up to the size of deer fawns, and birds commonly up to the size of ducks, and even as large as herons. Nocturnal. Takes birds including adults, and sometimes birds of prey, from nests.

Winters Resident.

Conservation Widely distributed across Europe, Asia, and N Africa. Is conspicuously absent from, and has declined in, heavily populated areas. Vulnerable to direct persecution, species has recovered locally where protected. See p. 528.

Essays Feet, p. 289; Hoarding Food, p. 453; Mobbing, p. 261; How Owls Hunt in the Dark, p. 251; Pellets, p. 257; Precocial and Altricial Young, p. 401; Wing Shapes and Flight, p. 269; The Avian Sense of Smell, p. 13; Monogamy, p. 335; Birds and the Law, p. 521; Hatching Asynchrony and Brood Reduction, p. 507.

Refs Mikkola 1983.

eliminates the vortex noise created by airflow over a smooth surface. Thus equipped, owls arrive upon their prey without a sound.

Owls, especially those that hunt at night, are able to locate even faint sounds with remarkable accuracy. The best studied of these nocturnal predators is the Barn Owl. Extensive experiments conducted by neurobiologists Mark Konishi and Eric Knudsen in totally darkened, soundproofed rooms unequivocally demonstrated that Barn Owls can locate and capture prey by sound alone. The Barn Owl's sensitive hearing is enhanced by its facial ruff, a concave surface of stiff dark-tipped feathers. The ruff functions as a reflector, channelling sounds into the ears. Once a sound is detected, the owl orients toward it and accurately pinpoints its location both horizontally and vertically to within 1.5 degrees.

The cue used to determine whether a sound comes from the right, from the left, or from straight ahead is the difference in time that it takes for the sound to reach each ear. When the sound source is dead ahead, no time differential occurs. Another cue, the difference in the intensity of sound received by each ear, is used to locate a sound vertically. Barn Owls (*Tyto* species), along with owls of at least eight other genera, have asymmetrical openings to their ears — as shown in the accompanying figure. A sound coming from above will seem slightly louder in the ear with the higher opening; if a sound is equally loud in both ears then the source must be at eye level.

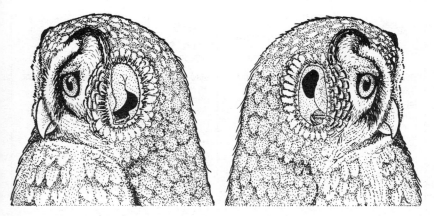

An owl's head with feathers pulled back to expose the asymmetry of its ears.

The owls' ears are linked to specialized cells contained within a discrete region of the midbrain. Each cell is sensitive to a unique combination of time and intensity differentials and responds only to sound issuing from one small area in space. The Barn Owl's brain thus contains a 'neural map' of auditory space. So armed, it is little wonder that the successful Barn Owl is arguably the most widespread bird species on Earth.

Highly refined auditory systems are not the only reason that some owls

Brown Fish Owl

Ketupa zeylonensis

ATLAS 171; PMH -; PER -; HFP 176; HPCW 133; NESTS 200; BWP4:481

		1–2 (3) 1 brood?	SA2		
	BLDS: ?	INCU: ♀(♂?)	FLDG: ?		
	?	35?	?	Fish	Swoops

Breeding habitat Wooded, often rocky habitats near water.

Displays Very little known.

Nesting Territorial. Nests in hole in tree or cliff ledge; little or no lining added. Eggs white, 58mm.

Diet Aquatic invertebrates especially freshwater crabs, and vertebrates, including fish, frogs, and sometimes birds and mammals. Nocturnal, feeds by flying low over water and snatching prey from surface. Feet covered with wart-like and spiny projections that help to grasp slippery prey.

Winters Resident.

Conservation Extremely rare and local in the isolated population in the Middle East, more widespread in India and SE Asia. May have declined in Israel due to the use of poisons to control rodents.

Essays Feet, p. 289; Hoarding Food, p. 453; Mobbing, p. 261; How Owls Hunt in the Dark, p. 251; Pellets, p. 257; Precocial and Altricial Young, p. 401; Wing Shapes and Flight, p. 269; The Avian Sense of Smell, p. 13; Monogamy, p. 335; Hatching Asynchrony and Brood Reduction, p. 507.

Refs Paz 1987.

Snowy Owl

Nyctea scandiaca

ATLAS 171; PMH 148; PER 140; HFP 176; HPCW 134; NESTS 199; BWP4:485

		3–9 (2–14) 1 (0) brood	SA2		
	BLDS: –	INCU: ♀	FLDG: ♂♀		
	Monogamy	30–33	43–50	Birds	Swoops

Breeding habitat Mountain and arctic tundra.

Displays In territorial display, ♂ bows forward, lifts tail, and calls. ♂ has undulating display flight, flying up, then dropping with wings held in high V, sometimes carries prey. ♂ feeds lemming to ♀ in courtship.

Nesting Territorial. Nest is a scrape on ground, usually on small prominence, little or no material added. Eggs white, 57mm, hatch asynchronously. ♂ brings food to ♀. Whether the birds attempt to nest or not, the number of eggs laid, and how many young survive, all depend on the availability of food. Some ♂s are bigamous.

Diet Mainly lemmings and voles, but also other mammals and birds. Hunts mainly in low light, but also in the daytime during the northern summer;

also feeds at night. Flies low over ground or, where possible, locates prey from perch, or while hovering.

Winters Retreats from most northern part of range and is generally nomadic, sometimes well S of normal winter range.

Conservation Breeding numbers fluctuate widely with the availability of small mammals. Perhaps some decline in numbers. Occurs across the arctic. See p. 528.

Essays Bird Droppings, p. 485; Feet, p. 289; Hoarding Food, p. 453; Mobbing, p. 261; How Owls Hunt in the Dark, p. 251; Pellets, p. 257; Precocial and Altricial Young, p. 401; Wing Shapes and Flight, p. 269; The Avian Sense of Smell, p. 13; Monogamy, p. 335; Irruptions, p. 491; Hatching Asynchrony and Brood Reduction, p. 507.

Refs Mikkola 1983.

can hunt successfully in the dark. Owl sensory abilities are often coupled with remarkably sedentary habits. Research by David Dobkin on Barred Owls (*Strix varia*) in New Jersey and studies of Tawny Owls in England reveal that individual birds hold hunting territories in which they operate night after night for many years. Familiarity with the environment, especially with such things as the heights of favourite perches above the ground, seems essential for successful hunting. Hearing helps to compensate for the difficulty of seeing at night, but intimate knowledge of the habitat completes the job.

SEE: What Do Birds Hear?, below; Raptor Hunting, p. 255; Size and Sex in Raptors, p. 99; Breeding Site Tenacity, p. 219; Pellets, p. 257. REFS: Fay and Feng, 1987; Knudsen, 1980; Konishi, 1983; Martin, 1986.

What Do Birds Hear?

THE rich acoustic complexity of the vocalizations of many songbirds has long implied, at the very least, that the birds are able to perceive the diversity of such sounds. Widespread vocal learning and the faithful reproduction of complicated songs among the songbirds indicates that birds can indeed hear what others are 'saying'. One wonders, however, just how much of the detailed acoustic and temporal complexity seen in a sonagram (a visual representation of a sound) actually is perceived by the birds.

The ability of birds to discriminate between sounds of different frequencies and degrees of loudness appears to be no better than that of humans. As a group, birds are most sensitive to sounds in the frequency range of one to five kilohertz (kHz; a thousand cycles per second), with an absolute upper limit (except for owls) of about 10 kHz. Even birds that use echolocation for manoeuvring in the dark (Oilbirds and cave swiftlets) rely primarily on sounds in the two to five kHz range, in contrast to bats, which use ultrasonic frequencies.

The hearing abilities of fewer than 20 avian species have been tested rigorously under controlled laboratory conditions, but the results appear to indicate that all species can hear the vocalizations of all the other species, as well as their own. The avian ear appears to be capable of separating sounds that are as close together as two to three thousandths of a second, which is comparable to or somewhat better than what can be seen in a sonagram.

SEE: Sonagrams: Seeing Bird Songs, p. 307; How Owls Hunt in the Dark, p. 251; Bird Voices, p. 475; Environmental Acoustics, p. 327; Eyes Like a Hawk, p. 89; The Avian Sense of Smell, p. 13. REFS: Dooling, 1982; Gillis, 1990.

Hawk Owl

Surnia ulula

ATLAS 174; PMH 148; PER 140; HFP 180; HPCW -; NESTS 202; BWP4:496

| | | 6–10 (3–13) 1 brood INCU: ♀ 25–30 | | SA2 FLDG: ♂♀ 25–35 | Birds | Low patrol |

BLDS: –
Monogamy

Breeding habitat Openings in northern conifer and birch forests.

Displays When alarmed may adopt sleek vertical posture (see Scops Owl). Has habit of raising and lowering tail. ♂ has display flight, also calls from perch. Pairs duet. Courtship-feeding.

Nesting Territorial. Nests in tree hole or old bird's nest; no material added. Eggs white, 40mm, hatch asynchronously. Clutch size is larger in good vole years.

Diet Voles, sometimes other small vertebrates, especially birds. Diurnal. Swoops down from perch, sometimes from low flight.

Winters Nomadic, irrupting beyond breeding range in some years. Irrupting birds mainly juveniles.

Conservation The numbers of breeding birds fluctuate with prey availability. Occurs across northern boreal forests of Europe, Asia, and N America.

Essays Feet, p. 289; Hoarding Food, p. 453; Mobbing, p. 261; How Owls Hunt in the Dark, p. 251; Pellets, p. 257; Precocial and Altricial Young, p. 401; Wing Shapes and Flight, p. 269; The Avian Sense of Smell, p. 13; Monogamy, p. 335; Hatching Asynchrony and Brood Reduction, p. 507; Irruptions, p. 491.

Refs Mikkola 1983.

Pygmy Owl

Glaucidium passerinum

ATLAS 173; PMH 148; PER 140; HFP 180; HPCW -; NESTS 202; BWP4:505

| | | 4–7 (3–10) 1 brood INCU: ♀ 28 | | SA2 FLDG: ♂♀ 27–34 | Birds | Aer pursuit |

BLDS: –
Monogamy

Breeding habitat Usually conifer forests, both northern and montane.

Displays When disturbed has sleek vertical posture (see Scops Owl). ♂ calls from perch. Shows ♀ possible nest holes. There is courtship-feeding.

Nesting Territorial. Nests in tree hole, often that of woodpecker; no material is added. Eggs white, 29mm, hatch synchronously. ♂ brings food to his mate.

Diet Voles, other small mammals, birds up to the size of crossbills. Often feeds at dawn and dusk. Captures mammals by swooping down from open perch, and

captures birds from branches after short flight from perch, or in mid-air. This species is locally an important predator of small birds, particularly the Goldcrest and some tits, that feed on the exposed outer branches of trees.

Winters Resident; northern populations irruptive when vole numbers crash.

Conservation Has declined in Germany. Occurs across Europe and Asia. See p. 528.

Essays Hoarding Food, p. 453; Birds on Borders, p. 95; Irruptions, p. 491; Courtship Feeding, p. 223.

Refs Mikkola 1983.

Pellets

OWLS do exactly what children are warned against — they swallow their food whole, or nearly so. When they eat a small vertebrate, they digest all but the bones and fur or feathers. They regurgitate those remains in the form of a hard, felted or feathered pellet — sometimes one victim per pellet, sometimes a dozen or more. Where owls feed on insects, each regurgitated pellet contains the indigestible parts of the exoskeletons of numerous individuals.

Regurgitating indigestible portions of food in the form of pellets is also common in raptors and gulls, and has been recorded in many other groups of birds, including flycatchers, corvids, herons, sandpipers, kingfishers, rails, and even honeyeaters (primarily Australian birds that supplement their nectar/fruit diets with insects).

Pellets, especially those of birds like owls that swallow their prey whole, provide ornithologists with records of what the birds are eating at various times and in various places. The hard pellets last a long time in dry climates and can be collected in numbers near roosts. If the skulls and teeth are dissected from the pellet the identity of rodent prey can be determined easily. The pellets of raptors such as eagles and hawks are less useful, since they tear much of the flesh from their victims, and do not swallow the bones.

SEE: Diet and Nutrition, p. 493; Swallowing Stones, p. 135.

Flock Defence

ONE of the advantages that animals may obtain by grouping is a better chance of avoiding predators. Assuming a predator generally will attack the closest individual, a bird can reduce its 'domain of danger', the area in which it can be the closest prey to a predator, by joining a flock. Where there is cover, of course, hiding rather than flocking may be a more effective predator defence strategy.

Simply reducing the domain of danger may not be enough to cause the evolution of flocking behaviour, even in open country. Flocking may, in fact, backfire. The flock may be so conspicuous or represent so much potential food that it attracts predators that might otherwise miss or ignore a lone bird. However, there are other possible advantages of flocking. For instance, in

Little Owl

Athene noctua

ATLAS 173; PMH 149; PER 142; HFP 180; HPCW 134; NESTS 202; BWP4:514

BLDS: –
Monogamy

2–5 (1–7)
1 brood
INCU: ♀
27–28 (23–35)

SA2
FLDG: ♀
30–35

Sm verts

Aer foraging

Breeding habitat Diverse open areas with trees, woodland edges, and into steppe and deserts.

Displays When disturbed has sleek vertical posture (see Scops Owl). ♂s call from perches. Pairs mutually preen for extended periods.

Nesting Territorial. Nests in hole in tree or rocks, or in ground (e.g. in a rabbit burrow); no material added. Eggs white, 36mm, hatch over varying intervals of time. ♂ brings food to incubating ♀. Young may be fed by parents for several weeks after fledging.

Diet Insects (especially beetles), small mammals, and birds, taken after swooping down from perch. Nocturnal. Also takes insects on wing.

Winters Resident.

Conservation Introduced into the UK in 1870s and spread rapidly, though vulnerable to cold winters. Decreases in numbers in much of central Europe, perhaps due to pesticide use. Widely distributed across Europe, Asia, and N Africa.

Essays Birds and Agriculture, p. 365.

Refs Mikkola 1983; Marchant et al. 1990.

Tawny Owl

Strix aluco

ATLAS 174; PMH 149; PER 140; HFP 182; HPCW 134; NESTS 203; BWP4:526

< 12m

BLDS: –
Monogamy

2–5 (1–6)
1 brood
INCU: ♀
28–30

SA2
FLDG: ♂♀
32–37

Sm verts

Low patrol

Breeding habitat Mainly deciduous woodland, farmland, parks, and towns.

Displays ♂s call from perches and will attack rival intruders. May have display flight about territory. There is courtship-feeding and mutual preening.

Nesting Territorial. Usually nests in tree hole; no material added. Eggs white, 47mm, hatch asynchronously. ♂ brings food to incubating ♀. Number of eggs laid depends on food supply. Breeds when one year old and usually mates for life.

Diet Mammals (mice and voles) and a wide range of other vertebrates and insects; nocturnal. Swoops down from perch, but also hunts in flight. Birds,

taken at their roosts, often very important prey item in towns.

Winters Resident.

Conservation Spread N and NE in last century. Common and widespread across Europe, parts of Asia, and N Africa.

Notes Absent in Ireland, where voles are not native. Sometimes aggressively attack humans who come close to nest.

Essays Courtship Feeding, p. 223; Hartley's Titmice and MacArthur's Warblers, p. 425; How Owls Hunt in the Dark, p. 251; Hatching Asynchrony and Brood Reduction, p. 507.

Refs Mikkola 1983; Marchant et al. 1990.

some situations being in a flock may reduce the amount of time each bird must spend watching for predators, and thus increase the amount of time it has for feeding or other activities. Suppose a certain bird must spend half of its time feeding in order to survive, and can watch for predators the other half. A cat might sneak up on the bird by moving only when the bird was busy feeding. If two birds forage together, and they feed and look out at random, one bird or the other will be looking out three-fourths of the time. A little arithmetic shows that ten birds feeding together will have at least one individual watching for predators 99.9 per cent of the time.

This bit of theory is supported by results from an interesting experiment with Laughing Doves. Experimenters used bait to attract natural flocks of the doves and then 'flew' a model hawk down a slanting wire toward them. The entire procedure was filmed, and the reactions of the birds analysed in slow motion. When flock sizes were between 4 and 15 birds, the size of the flock and the speed with which individuals became aware of the hawk and fled were directly related: the more birds, the quicker the reaction. Flocks of less than 4, however, reacted even faster than flocks of 4 to 15, but because they were always skittish and had many 'false alarms', they did not feed well. In contrast, flocks of more than 15 birds had slower reaction times, often because they were engrossed in battles over the food.

Similar results have been obtained from observations of falcons attacking wintering waders on a California estuary. The risk to the waders was high when solitary birds were the prey or when large flocks were attacked. Waders were less likely to be captured when flocks of intermediate size were the targets. Birds seem to recognize that flock size is related to their security. Willow Tits, Dunlin, and Cranes have been shown to spend more time feeding and less time watching in large flocks than in small flocks (but Dunlin did not reduce vigilance in large flocks if they were preening, probably because it tended to obscure their vision more than feeding did).

So, at least over an intermediate range of flock sizes, the notion that more eyes are better than fewer seems to hold. Within that intermediate range, larger flocks may detect predators more easily. Furthermore, flock members may reduce their chances of being eaten once the predator is detected. The sudden flight of large numbers of birds, or their simultaneous calls, may temporarily bewilder a predator and allow the entire flock to escape. It may also be more difficult for a predator to pick a victim from a wheeling flock than to catch a lone individual. This phenomenon is well known to the duck hunter who blasts away at an entire flock and does not hit a single bird. Thus the Laughing Doves in the larger flocks may still be safer in those flocks than they would be feeding alone.

Finally, flocks of birds may turn the tables on predators. Starling flocks, for example, have been observed to attack their attackers and force them into water or on to the ground.

SEE: Mobbing, p. 261; Geometry of the Selfish Colony, p. 15; Mixed-species Flocking, p. 429; Altruism, p. 245. REFS: Alonso *et al.*, 1987; Hamilton, 1971; Hogstad, 1988a; Myers, 1984; Redpath, 1988; Siegfried and Underhill, 1975.

Hume's Tawny Owl

Strix butleri

ATLAS 175; PMH - ; PER -; HFP 183; HPCW 135; NESTS 203; BWP4:547

SA2		

	$\bigcirc$ 5 1 brood?			
BLDS: –	INCU: ?	FLDG: ?	Sm verts	Swoops
Monogamy?	32–36	35–37		

Breeding habitat Sometimes in dry forests, but usually in wadis with cliffs, close to water.

Displays Not well known.

Nesting Territorial. Nest is probably in rock crevices.

Diet Mammals, particularly gerbils and jerboas. Also birds, lizards, and insects. Has low, wavering flight when hunting, or swoops down from perch.

Winters Resident.

Conservation Range and population size poorly known, but locally common in area of limited extent in Israel, Egypt, parts of Arabian peninsula.

Essays Feet, p. 289; Hoarding Food, p. 453; Mobbing, p. 261; How Owls Hunt in the Dark, p. 251; Pellets, p. 257; Precocial and Altricial Young, p. 401; Wing Shapes and Flight, p. 269; The Avian Sense of Smell, p. 13; Monogamy, p. 335; Hatching Asynchrony and Brood Reduction, p. 507.

Refs Mikkola 1983; Paz 1987.

Ural Owl

Strix uralensis

ATLAS 175; PMH 150; PER 140; HFP 182; HPCW -; NESTS 204; BWP4:550

 SA2		

3–16m	See below	$\bigcirc$ 2–4 (2–7) 1 (0) broods			
	BLDS: –	INCU: $\female$	FLDG: $\male\female$	Birds	Low patrol
	Monogamy	27–34	40?		

Breeding habitat Open woodland, especially northern conifers, but also deciduous.

Displays Similar to Tawny Owl.

Nesting Nests in tree hole, nest box, old nest of bird of prey or crow; no material added. Eggs white, 50mm, hatch asynchronously. Whether bird nests at all, and, if so how many eggs are laid, depends on rodent food supply (typically 2 eggs in bad years, to 4 in good ones). Young remain with adults for about 3 months after fledging. First breed at 3–4 years, if food supply is good, later if not. Usually mate for life.

Diet Small mammals and birds taken after swooping down from perch, but also in flight. Will take mammals under snow by plunge diving into it. Mainly nocturnal, but will feed in the daytime.

Winters Resident.

Conservation Not well known, perhaps increasing where provided with nest boxes; occurs across Europe and Asia.

Essays Hartley's Titmice and MacArthur's Warblers, p. 425; Hoarding Food, p. 453; Mobbing, p. 261; How Owls Hunt in the Dark, p. 251; Pellets, p. 257; Precocial and Altricial Young, p. 401; Wing Shapes and Flight, p. 269; The Avian Sense of Smell, p. 13; Monogamy, p. 335; Hatching Asynchrony and Brood Reduction, p. 507.

Refs Mikkola 1983.

Mobbing

IT is not uncommon to see a group of Swallows or choughs chasing a hawk or eagle, or a group of Blackbirds fluttering and calling around a perched owl. Such 'mobbing' behaviour is probably the most frequently observed overt anti-predator strategy. Nevertheless, the exact purpose of such noisy group demonstrations remains a matter of some debate.

Mobbing tends to occur most intensely on the breeding grounds. Presumably migrants have less reason to mob, perhaps because they would be leaving the vicinity of the predator anyway. Mobbing may thus function to divert the predator from areas where there are nests or fledglings, or simply to confuse and annoy the predator in the hope of getting it to move away.

This 'move-along' hypothesis, first put forth by E. Curio, a specialist in the biology of predation from Ruhr University in Germany, is supported by the research of American ornithologist Douglas Shedd. Shedd has shown that Black-capped Chickadees (*Parus atricapillus*) will respond to predators in autumn and winter, even in January with the temperature 40 below zero. The chickadees, which remain in residence all year long, still find it profitable to mob in winter. Migratory North American Robins (*Turdus migratorius*), in contrast, sometimes approached a stuffed screech-owl and audio tape combination outside the breeding season, but never mobbed.

Careful experiments have shown that birds can learn from each other which predators to mob (indeed, one bird in an experiment was taught by another to 'mob' a many-coloured plastic bottle, although the mobbing was halfhearted). Therefore one function of mobbing may be educational—to teach young birds the identity of the enemy. Another may be to alert other birds to the presence of the predator, either getting them to join in the mobbing or protecting them, since a predator is less able to sneak up on an alert victim. The original mobber may benefit directly by the predator being moved along, or indirectly if the protected birds are its kin.

Much is lacking in our understanding of mobbing. There are accounts of predators killing mobbing birds, and the behaviour of mobbers indicates that danger increases with proximity. Great Tits with nestlings, for example, use a variety of techniques to mitigate the risk as they approach their enemies. Their movements are complex, and change with proximity to the predator. Tits also increase their rate of calling as they approach, either to add to the confusion of the predator, or to impress the predator with their vigour. Calling requires great energy, and thus its high rate may persuade the predator that it would be a waste of energy to attempt to capture the tit.

Predators don't turn on their tormenters and snatch up one or two of the mobbing birds, apparently because the mobbers' actions make it very difficult to catch them. If mobbers frequently did perish in the attempt to harass their

Great Grey Owl

Strix nebulosa

ATLAS 175; PMH 150; PER 140; HFP 182; HPCW -; NESTS 203; BWP4:561

 | See below |  3–6 (1–9) 1 (0) brood |  SA2 | |
--- | --- | --- | --- | --- | ---
| | BLDS: – | INCU: ♀ | FLDG: ♀ | |
| | Monogamy | 28–30 (36) | 60–65 | | Hov & pounce

Breeding habitat A wide range of habitats in northern coniferous forests.

Displays When disturbed has sleek vertical posture (see Scops Owl). ♂s call from perch to defend territory and attract mates. Has flight display, similar to Snowy Owl, with ♂ carrying food. Courtship-feeding and mutual preening. Aggressively defends nest against humans.

Nesting Territorial. Nests usually in old nest of bird of prey, but also in top of broken tree stump, or on the ground; no material added. Eggs white, 53mm, hatch asynchronously. ♂ brings food to incubating ♀. Whether bird nests and, if so, how many eggs are laid, depends on food supply. Adults feed young for several weeks after fledging. Breeds when one year old, and often changes mate from year to year.

Diet Voles, other small mammals, and birds; feeds at dusk or in daytime, swooping down from perch. Sometimes hovers. Can take prey from beneath snow surface, diving into snow head first. More specialized on small mammals than the other species in this genus.

Winters Resident or nomadic, especially in some winters.

Conservation Occurs across boreal forests of Europe, Asia, and N America. Breeding numbers depend on small mammal food supply and fluctuate considerably.

Essays Feet, p. 289; Hoarding Food, p. 453; Mobbing, p. 261; How Owls Hunt in the Dark, p. 251; Pellets, p. 257; Precocial and Altricial Young, p. 401; Wing Shapes and Flight, p. 269; Hartley's Titmice and MacArthur's Warblers, p. 425; Monogamy, p. 335; Hatching Asynchrony and Brood Reduction, p. 507.

Refs Mikkola 1983.

Long-eared Owl

Asio otus

ATLAS 171; PMH 150; PER 142; HFP 178; HPCW 135; NESTS 200; BWP4:572

 | See below Scrape | 3–5 (1–6) 1 (2?) broods | SA2 | |
--- | --- | --- | --- | --- | ---
Ground | BLDS: ♀ | INCU: ♀ | FLDG: ♂♀ | |
| Monogamy | 25–30 | 30+ | Birds | Swoops

Breeding habitat Wide range of woodland, mainly conifers.

Displays When disturbed has sleek vertical posture, with ear-tufts erect (see Scops Owl). ♂s call from perch to defend territories. Has erratic display flight, with glides and occasional wing-claps. There is courtship-feeding and mutual preening.

Nesting Territorial. Usually nests in old crow's nest, sometimes scrape on ground; little or no material added. Eggs white, 40mm, hatch asynchronously. ♂ brings food to incubating ♀. Young remain with adults for several weeks after leaving nest.

Diet Voles and mice, other small mammals, and birds; nocturnal. Uses slow, low patrol over open ground, or hunts from perch.

Winters Northern populations migratory; southern ones resident.

Conservation Local declines (not in UK) but widely distributed across N Europe, Asia, and N America.

Essays Hatching Asynchrony and Brood Reduction, p. 507; Nonvocal Sounds, p. 263.

Refs Mikkola 1983; Marchant et al. 1990.

enemies, presumably mobbing would quickly disappear; that it persists suggests that surprise is an essential element in raptor hunting.

SEE: Altruism, p. 245; Flock Defence, p. 257; Eyes Like a Hawk, p. 89. REFS: Curio *et al.*, 1978; Curio and Regelmann, 1985; Shedd, 1985.

Nonvocal Sounds

WHEN we think of bird sounds, song is usually the first thing that comes to mind. But many birds have found other ways of generating acoustical signals to serve functions usually accomplished by songs and calls. Some bird sounds used in territorial and courtship displays are produced with bills, feet, wings, or tails. Many songbirds can snap their bills audibly, but otherwise the use of such sounds in displays is limited primarily to species with poor singing abilities and occurs infrequently among the passerines.

Both White and Black Storks incorporate bill clattering and bill tapping in their mating displays; in the White Stork it specifically serves as a sign of recognition between members of a pair. Bill snapping is performed by most owls as a defensive threat display. One of the most familiar uses of bills to produce auditory displays occurs in Great Spotted, Lesser Spotted, and Three-toed Woodpeckers. Both sexes engage in loud rhythmical drumming by striking their bills against a hollow or dried branch or even on metal gutters, stovepipes, and drainpipes of buildings. Drumming functions much as song does to proclaim territorial boundaries and to attract mates. Both sexes of the Great Spotted Woodpecker also drum as part of their pre-copulatory display and can pound away at rates that exceed 20 blows per second and produce a signal that is audible up to a kilometre away.

By altering the spacing of wing or tail feathers and causing them to vibrate, birds can create a variety of whistling, rattling, buzzing, or other sounds as air passes through those feathers in flight. These sounds are evident in the courtship flight displays of both Common and Great Snipe. The 'drumming' produced by Common Snipe in flight results from vibration of the outer pair of tail feathers (rectrices) which are physically separated from the remaining tail feathers when the tail is fanned out. These outermost rectrices differ structurally from the other rectrices in several characteristics, most notably by their relative stiffness.

Sharp clapping sounds also can be made by the two wings or their carpal bones actually striking each other, and occur in the display flights of African Flappet Larks (*Mirafra cinnamomea*) Short-eared and Long-eared Owls, Wood Pigeon, Common Swift, and Nightjar. Both male and female Nightjars wing-clap and females have been recorded doing so beyond the mating season when flying in the company of their offspring.

SEE: Visual Displays, p. 33; What Do Birds Hear?, p. 255; Vocal Functions, p. 413; Environmental Acoustics, p. 327; Bills, p. 391; Feathers, p. 363.

Short-eared Owl
Asio flammeus

ATLAS 171; PMH 151; PER 142; HFP 178; HPCW 135; NESTS 200; BWP4:588

 | | | |

BLDS: ♀	INCU: ♀		FLDG: ♂♀		
Monogamy	24–28		24–27	Birds	Hov & pounce

4–8 (–16)
1 (2) broods

SA2

Breeding habitat Open country, tundra, marshes, young conifer plantations.

Displays Raises ear tufts when disturbed. ♂ patrols territory with display flight, sometimes fights to eject intruder. Towards ♀ has lengthy aerial display with wing-claps, ascending circling flight, then holds wings in V, and stoops.

Nesting Nest is scrape on ground, lined with vegetation, in thick cover. Eggs white, 40mm, hatch asynchronously. Number of eggs laid depends on numbers of voles. Large numbers of eggs may be of two ♀s using same nest. Young depend on parents for several weeks after leaving nest.

Diet Mainly voles, but also other small mammals, and birds; feeds day and night, with low patrol over ground, often hovering before pouncing on prey. Will also search from perch.

Winters Largely migratory though some populations are resident. Moves into agricultural fields, salt marshes, steppes and even deserts, widely across Europe, S Asia, Africa, south of the Sahara, and N America.

Conservation Widespread across N Europe, Asia, N America, and also in S America. Some local increases and decreases. Numbers dependent on the availability of small mammals, and consequently bird densities fluctuate widely. Benefits from early stages of moorland afforestation. See p. 528.

Essays Population Dynamics, p. 515; Hatching Asynchrony and Brood Reduction, p. 507; Nonvocal Sounds, p. 263.

Refs Mikkola 1983; Marchant et al. 1990.

Marsh Owl
Asio capensis

ATLAS 172; PMH 249; PER -; HFP 178; HPCW 135; NESTS 201; BWP4:601

 | | |

BLDS: ?	INCU: ♀(♂?)	?	FLDG: ♂♀		
Monogamy?	28?		?	Sm mammals	Hov & pounce

2–3 (5)
1 (2?) broods

SA2

Breeding habitat Large areas of wet grasslands or marshland.

Displays Has display flight somewhat similar to that of Short-eared Owl.

Nesting Territorial. Nest is shallow, unlined hollow, in cover on ground. Eggs white, 40mm, hatch asynchronously.

Diet Insects, small mammals, and birds. Feeds like Short-eared Owl.

Winters Resident.

Conservation Very local in area covered by this guide; more widespread in Africa.

Essays Feet, p. 289; Hoarding Food, p. 453; Mobbing, p. 261; How Owls Hunt in the Dark, p. 251; Pellets, p. 257; Precocial and Altricial Young, p. 401; Wing Shapes and Flight, p. 269; The Avian Sense of Smell, p. 13; Monogamy, p. 335; Hatching Asynchrony and Brood Reduction, p. 507.

Polygyny

POLYGYNY, where one male mates with more than one female while each female mates with only one male, is thought to be the fundamental mating system of animals. The reason is straightforward. By definition, the sex that produces the larger reproductive cells (eggs) is the female, and the one that produces the smaller (sperm) is the male. Males therefore make a smaller investment in the embryos that result from the fusion of egg and sperm cells. The difference is especially pronounced in birds, since the sperm is microscopic and the egg (relatively) gigantic. The male thus puts proportionately little energy into any single embryo, while the female has a great stake in each one, since she can produce relatively few eggs in her lifetime. Females must therefore exercise care in choosing the fathers of their limited number of young. It would seem, in contrast, that male birds should be much less choosy and attempt to have as many mates as possible A male that mates with a weak or otherwise unfit female loses a small part of his reproductive potential; a female making a similar mistake may sacrifice all or almost all of hers.

Most birds, however, are monogamous. Apparently both parents must help to rear the young if the adults are to have much chance of leaving any genes to posterity. None the less in Europe almost 40 per cent of 122 well-studied species of passerines are polygynous, with roughly half of those being regular polygynists. Under what circumstances, then, does polygyny occur? One idea is that polygyny is likely when males hold territories that vary greatly in the quality of resources. Females will tend to choose superior males — by inference those that have high-quality territories. When those males already have mates, females have a choice. They can either select a male that holds an inferior territory, or they can become the second mate of one of the superior males. If the difference between high- and low-quality territories is great enough, the latter strategy will be better. Little or no aid from a male holding a resource-rich territory will yield a better chance of producing surviving offspring than the full cooperation of a male with an inferior territory. The male with a superior territory will benefit by increased reproduction, as will the second female.

Sometimes that is precisely what is found. In Japan, Great Reed Warbler females often chose to become second mates of males that had settled early in prime territories. And those females were as reproductively successful as females that settled as the sole mates of late-arriving males. Other studies of North American Red-winged and Yellow-headed Blackbirds (*Agelaius phoenicius* and *Xanthocephalus xanthocephalus*), Dickcissels (*Spiza americana*), Indigo Buntings (*Passerina cyanea*), and Lark Buntings (*Calamospiza melanocorys*) also show relationships between various aspects of territory quality and the likelihood that a male holding a given territory will have more than one mate. But

Tengmalm's Owl

Aegolius funereus

ATLAS 174; PMH 151; PER 142; HFP 180; HPCW 136; NESTS 202; BWP4:606

BLDS: –
Monogamy
See below

4–7 (1–10)
1 (2?) broods
INCU: ♀
25–32

 SA2

FLDG: ♂♀
28–36

Birds

Breeding habitat Northern and montane forests of conifer and birch.

Displays Has sleek, vertical posture when disturbed (see Scops Owl). ♂ calls from perch; after attracting ♀, shows her potential nest holes. Pairs do not mutually preen, but there is courtship-feeding.

Nesting Territorial. Nest is in tree holes, often those of woodpeckers (especially Black Woodpecker); no material added. Eggs white, 33mm, hatch asynchronously. ♂ brings food to incubating ♀ and for about 6 days prior to laying, a period in which the ♀ remains in the nest hole. Clutch size dependent on vole supply. While usually monogamous, may also be polygynous. In good vole years, about 15 per cent of ♂s that have already established one territory will establish a second territory while the first mates are incubating. ♀s in these second territories rear about

half the number of young as those ♀s in the first territory a ♂ establishes. The ♂ feeds his second mate as well as his first while she is laying, but tends to neglect her later. However, some ♀s abandon their young about 3 weeks after hatching, leave them in the care of the ♂ and start a new brood with a new mate.

Diet Voles, mice, and small birds. Nocturnal, though will feed in daytime. Hunts from perch, swooping down on prey. Will cache food in winter, when dead prey remain frozen.

Winters Resident, irruptive following vole crashes.

Conservation Apparently increasing. Widely distributed across Europe, Asia, and N America. See p. 528.

Essays Hoarding Food, p. 453; Polyandry, p. 195; Polygyny, p. 265; Irruptions, p. 491.

Refs Mikkola 1983.

Nubian Nightjar

Caprimulgus nubicus

ATLAS 177; PMH -; PER -; HFP 184; HPCW 136; NESTS 205; BWP4:617

 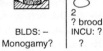

BLDS: –
Monogamy?

2
? brood
INCU: ?
?

 SP

FLDG: ?
?

Breeding habitat Dry scrubland and semi-desert, avoiding the very dry areas used by Egyptian Nightjar; usually near water.

Displays Very little known; has wing-clapping, like other Nightjars.

Nesting Territorial. Nest on ground in open. Eggs white with light markings, 25mm.

Diet Insects, particularly moths and beetles, taken at night or dusk, often near water.

Winters Probably resident.

Conservation Locally common in Israel, but considered rare in Egypt. Has a poorly-known range S into E Africa.

Essays Bills, p. 391.

in other cases such relationships have not been found, and it is not clear how capable females are of assessing the quality of territories. Thus the role of variation of male territory quality in promoting polygyny is still debated.

In Europe there are numerous polygynous species, including Bitterns, Hen, Montagu's, and probably Marsh Harriers, Tengmalm's Owls, Woodcock, Wrens, Pied and Collared Flycatchers, Cetti's, Fan-tailed, and Great Reed Warblers, and Blue and Penduline Tits. The systems in Great Reed and Cetti's Warblers seem similar to that in Marsh Wrens, with those males holding the more desirable territories having more mates. In Hen Harriers, polygyny may simply permit more females to breed once males have become sufficiently dense to saturate an area's carrying capacity (as determined by the territorial interactions of the males), or when males are scarce for other reasons. The degree of polygyny also seems related to the distribution of breeding habitat and prey availability.

The situation in Tengmalm's Owls is especially interesting in that while males seem to profit from bigamous associations, females do not. It has been suggested that the males are polyterritorial (hold two spatially separated territories) and deceive the females into thinking they are in monogamous relationships! Polyterritoriality is found in roughly a third of European polygynous species and has been most thoroughly studied in Scandinavian populations of Pied Flycatchers. Males first lure a female to a nest hole, and having started a family with her, begin singing at a distant hole to attract another mate. After copulation, the male then returns to the first female and helps her rear her young, leaving the second female to fend for herself or giving her only minimal help. In Swedish populations studied by Rauno Alatalo, Arne Lundberg, and their colleagues, secondary females generally fledged less than two-thirds as many young as the primary female, and the fledglings were smaller and lighter.

The inferior reproductive performance of the second female has led Alatalo and Lundberg to conclude that she was deceived by the male at the time of mating; she expected the male's aid in raising the brood, but did not get it. But G. Stenmark and his colleagues found that secondary females in Norwegian populations of Pied Flycatchers suffered a much smaller reduction in reproductive success. They suggest that females are not deceived by the males, but mate with them because this is a superior strategy to spending energy searching for an unmated male and risking not reproducing at all. Differences were also found in the behaviour of mated and unmated males, suggesting that observant females should be able to discriminate between them. On the other hand, widowed females do appear to attempt to entrap males into helping them care for their offspring. By soliciting copulations they may lead the males to conclude that they have made a reproductive contribution to a recently laid clutch, and thus induce them to give aid.

Hans Temrin and S. Jakobsson found that in polyterritorial Wood Warblers secondary females sometimes had more success than primary females, mostly because early nests were subject to more nest predation and the secondaries sometimes had exclusive help from males whose first brood had been destroyed. They found evidence that secondary females were making

Nightjar

Caprimulgus europaeus

ATLAS 176; PMH 152; PER 142; HFP 184; HPCW 138; NESTS 204; BWP4:620

BLDS: – Monogamy	2 (3) 1–2 broods INCU: ♂♀ 17–19

FLDG: ♂♀
16–17

Breeding habitat Open areas bordering on woods, large woodland glades, intro drier areas, including semi-desert.

Displays ♂s sing from perch, soon after dark and through night. Pursues rival with wing-clapping. In courtship flight, ♂ has slow, butterfly-like flight, with wing-claps and glides. With wings help up and tail spread (showing white wing markings), chases ♀. Has distraction display when predators approach nest.

Nesting Territorial. Nest is shallow, unlined scrape on ground. Eggs well camouflaged, off-white to cream, variously marked with grey and dark brown, 32mm, hatch asynchronously. Young dependent on adults for about two weeks after fledging.

Diet Insects, particularly moths and beetles, taken at night, flying low over vegetation or through open forest. Catches prey on wing. Large mouth with

fringing rictal bristles is not used as a trawl and kept opened continuously, but opened to form a trap when prey are about to be captured. Sometimes flies out from perch to capture prey.

Winters Africa, south of the Sahara in a wide range of habitats from edges and clearings in wet forest to *Acacia* savannas.

Conservation Has decreased in NW and possibly elsewhere. In UK, continued fragmentation of heaths, downs, and increasing forestry plantations (used only when trees are small) are perhaps major causes. Occurs widely throughout region to C Asia. See p. 528.

Essays Bills, p. 391; Wing Shapes and Flight, p. 269; Distraction Displays, p. 175; Temperature Regulation and Behaviour, p. 163; Nonvocal Sounds, p. 263.

Refs Marchant et al. 1990.

Red-necked Nightjar

Caprimulgus ruficollis

ATLAS 176; PMH 152; PER 142; HFP 184; HPCW 138; NESTS 205; BWP4:636

BLDS: – Monogamy?	2 1–2 broods? INCU: ? ?

FLDG: ♂♀
?

Breeding habitat Dry woodland or scrub.

Displays Not well known, but has wing-clapping and nocturnal singing like Nightjar.

Nesting Sometimes in loose neighbourhood groups. Nest is shallow scrape on ground. Eggs greyish-white, variously marked yellow-brown, 32mm. ♂ alone looks after young if ♀ starts second clutch.

Diet Like Nightjar; in S Spain commonly feeds over water or small ponds.

Winters Probably W Africa S of the Sahara; range not known with any certainty.

Conservation Has very limited range in Iberia and N Africa; locally common.

Essays Feathers, p. 363; The Avian Sense of Smell, p. 13; Nest Sanitation, p. 75; Swallowing Stones, p. 135.

the best of options available to them when they arrived on the breeding grounds; these females sometimes rejected single males on inferior territories in favour of bigamous relationships. The question of whether polyterritoriality involves deception is thus complex, and remains unsettled. We have only scratched the surface of the discussion here. Polygyny is not always associated with territoriality. Certain seed-eating savanna species of African weavers (relatives of House Sparrows) have superabundant resources and the males are not territorial, presumably because defending an area does not increase their access to food. The females apparently do not need help from males to raise the young, and the weavers nest in colonies, minimizing the need for a partner in nest defence. The female is thus free to choose any male to father her offspring, regardless of his other attachments. Here, as in most situations where males are territorial, polygyny is related to the availability of resources — in this case their superabundance rather than their uneven distribution.

SEE: Monogamy, p. 335; Polyandry, p. 195; Promiscuity, p. 127; Natural Selection, p. 297; Territoriality, p. 397; Cooperative Breeding, p. 275; Leks, p. 123. REFS: Alatalo *et al.*, 1981; Alatalo and Lundberg, 1984; Balfour and Cadbury, 1979; Bibby, 1982; Borowiec and Lontkowski, 1988; Dhondt, 1987; Emlen and Oring, 1977; Ezaki, 1990; Gjershaug *et al.*, 1989; Lenington, 1983; Møller, 1986; Orians, 1967; Oring, 1982; Picozzi, 1984a, 1984b; Simmons *et al.*, 1987; Slagsvold, 1986; Stenmark *et al.*, 1988; Temrin *et al.*, 1984; Temrin and Arak, 1989; Temrin and Jakobsson, 1988; Ueda, 1986; Verner and Willson, 1966.

Wing Shapes and Flight

ONE can tell a great deal about how a bird lives just from its wing shape. Most passerines, doves, woodpeckers, and gallinaceous birds have wings that taper down more or less to a point at their outer tip. Those wings have a low aspect ratio (they are short relative to their width), designed for rapid take-off and swift twisting flight, but not for sustained high speed. At each wingtip a spiralling vortex is formed as air spills from the high-pressure area under the wing into the low-pressure area over it. Narrowing the tips reduces the area subject to the drag-inducing formation of vortices. Tapered, low-aspect-ratio wings are found on birds that must be fast and agile in order to outmanoeuvre both their prey and their predators.

Slots between feathers at the tip of the wing lower the speed at which air flowing over the wingtip can cause enough turbulence to initiate a 'stall' (reducing lift so that the bird starts descending). Slots thus aid low-speed manoeuvring and are better developed in small, agile birds such as warblers than in less-active species such as House Sparrows. They are also prominent features on the wings of crows and their relatives.

Egyptian Nightjar

Caprimulgus aegyptius

ATLAS 177; PMH 152; PER -; HFP 184; HPCW 138; NESTS 205; BWP4:641

| | BLDS: –
Monogamy? | 2 (1)
2 broods?
INCU: ♂♀
? | FLDG: ♂♀
? |

Breeding habitat Deserts, usually with adjacent rivers or lakes.

Displays Not well known; apparently like those of the Nightjar.

Nesting Nest is shallow, unlined scrape on ground. Eggs white or creamy, mottled with pale olive-brown and grey, 32mm, hatch asynchronously.

Diet Like that of the Nightjar; frequently forages over water.

Winters In Africa, southern fringes of Sahara.

Conservation Not well known. Scarce and local in Egypt. Occurs from NW Africa to SW Asia.

Essays Feathers, p. 363; The Avian Sense of Smell, p. 13; Nest Sanitation, p. 75; Swallowing Stones, p. 135.

Common Swift

Apus apus

ATLAS 178; PMH 153; PER 144; HFP 186; HPCW 139; NESTS 206; BWP4:657

| Decid tree | BLDS: ♂♀
Monogamy | 2–3 (1–4)
1 brood
INCU: ♂♀
18–27 | FLDG: ♂♀
37–56 |

Breeding habitat Almost ubiquitous, nesting on cliffs, buildings, or in hollow trees.

Displays Residents defend nest sites against prospective users, fighting if need be. Pairs court at nest site and mutually preen. Mating can occur on nest or in air. Pairs chase each other. ♀ (probably) indicates willingness to mate by holding wings fixed in high V, calling, gliding downwards, with wings flat. ♂ joins her with his wings held up. Birds may glide downwards or flap as much as they can, before separating. Also has 'screaming display' with one bird joined by others flying over colony calling loudly.

Nesting Colonial. Nest is usually in roof of building, less often in tree hole; vegetation gathered on wing and feathers are glued together with saliva. Eggs white, 25mm, hatch within a day or so of each other. Fledging period is

variable because bad weather delays the nestlings' growth. Pairs for life.

Diet Windborne insects and spiders, taken in flight, from near ground or over water to high in the sky.

Winters Africa, S of Sahara; in flocks.

Conservation Common and widespread. Occurs across nearly all of Europe, into N Africa and C Asia.

Notes In unusually cold weather, large numbers of birds may huddle together for warmth on cliff ledges etc.

Essays Copulation, p. 87; Feet, p. 289; Metabolism, p. 281; Wing Shapes and Flight, p. 269; Temperature Regulation and Behaviour, p. 163; Nest Sites and Materials, p. 443; Nonvocal Sounds, p. 263; Breeding Site Tenacity, p. 219.

Refs Lack's 1956 book, Swifts in a Tower, is a classic in natural history. Marchant et al. 1990.

Top: albatross. Bottom, left to right: falcon, pheasant, passerine.

Flat, rather high-aspect-ratio wings (long relative to their width) lacking slots are found in falcons, swallows, plovers, and other specialists in high-speed flight. In contrast, hawks that soar in open country have lower-aspect-ratio wings; Sparrowhawks and owls that hunt in woodlands and must be able to turn rapidly have an even lower aspect ratio. Wings that are more cambered (arched in cross section) with low aspect ratio and well-developed slots, characterize vultures and other soaring land birds, while extremely high-aspect-ratio wings characterize albatrosses and other oceanic 'slope soarers'.

As one might suspect, birds and insectivorous bats with similar feeding habits have similar wing shapes. For instance, Hobbies, swallows, and swifts that aerially capture insects in the open tend to have higher aspect ratios than warblers and flycatchers that forage near vegetation. Bats that forage near vegetation have the superior manoeuvrability provided by low aspect ratios and wing loadings; those that feed in the open have wings shaped more like those of swallows.

SEE: How Do Birds Fly?, p. 217; Soaring, p. 79; How Fast and High Do Birds Fly?, p. 63; Flying in V-Formation, p. 43. REFS: Norberg, 1986; Rayner, 1988.

Gilbert White

THE *Natural History of Selborne* by Gilbert White (1720–93), is thought to be the fourth most printed book in the English language, and stands alone among nature books featuring birds. Much of its success lies in the Oxford-trained author's decision to avoid the affected language of his predecessors. White's notion that any naturalist intimately acquainted with the local environment is better prepared to advance knowledge than one attempting to grasp the

Pallid Swift

Apus pallidus

ATLAS 178; PMH 153; PER 144; HFP 186; HPCW 139; NESTS 206; BWP4:670

BLDS: ? Monogamy	2–3 (1–4) 1 (2?) broods INCU: ♂♀ 18–24	FLDG: ♂♀ 42–50

Breeding habitat   Lowland, often coastal Mediterranean areas.

Displays   Little known. Apparently, nesting colonies defend their feeding territories against other colonies of the same species and of other swifts.

Nesting   Colonial. Nests are usually on buildings or cliffs and consist of vegetation and feathers, glued with saliva. Eggs white, 25mm, hatch asynchronously.

Diet   Like that of the Common Swift. Feeds at lower elevations and apparently in denser flocks than Common Swift.

Winters   Africa, S of Sahara, but not well known; in flocks.

Conservation   The population size is not well known; locally common and widely distributed in S Europe, N Africa, and SW Asia.

Essays   Copulation, p. 87; Feet, p. 289.

Refs   Lack 1956.

Alpine Swift

Apus melba

ATLAS 179; PMH 154; PER 144; HFP 186; HPCW 139; NESTS 206; BWP4:678

BLDS: ♂♀ Monogamy	3 (1–4) 1 brood INCU: ♂♀ 17–23	FLDG: ♂♀ 45–55

Breeding habitat   Wide variety of areas including mountains, and into grasslands.

Displays   Has screaming display like that of the Common Swift. Mating occurs both on nest and in the air, like Common Swift.

Nesting   Colonial. Nest is a saucer of vegetation collected on wing and feathers, fixed with saliva to wall or in hole. Eggs white, 30mm, hatch synchronously. First breeds at 2–3 years. Pair uses same nest site each year.

Diet   Sometimes flies to great heights above the ground, catching insects. Will feed at night around lights.

Winters   Africa, S of Sahara; Indian birds resident. In flocks.

Conservation   Population size is variable and very sensitive to bad weather. Some increase in range in C Europe. Occurs around Mediterranean through SW Asian grasslands, into India and Africa.

Notes   Birds huddle together in cold weather: see Common Swift, p. 270.

Essays   Copulation, p. 87; Feet, p. 289.

Refs   Lack 1956.

wider world prompted many to follow his lead. Unlike other 18th-century naturalists such as Joseph Banks and Thomas Pennant who travelled afar to collect specimens, White, a clergyman, confined himself to Selborne, Hampshire, in southern England.

A contemporary of Linnaeus, and writing when much of bird identification was accomplished with the aid of a gun, White took more notes than specimens and recorded observations of many of Selborne's 120 or so bird species. He had a particular interest in their 'life and conversation', and in the nature of migration. (At the time, a number of migrants were thought to hibernate rather than depart for the winter.)

For birdwatchers interested in learning which species were to be seen in the countryside 50 miles south of 18th-century London, and for students of history tracking changes in attitudes toward wildlife, no writer of the period recorded the birdlife of pre-industrial England in a more readable style:

I have consulted a sportsman, now in his seventy-eighth year, who tells me that fifty or sixty years back, when the beechen woods were much more extensive than at present, the number of wood-pigeons was astonishing; that he has often killed near twenty in a day; and that with a long wild-fowl piece he has shot seven or eight at a time on the wing as they came wheeling over his head. . .

Reverend White provided an incomparable service; his *History* is second to none.

SEE: Classifying Birds, p. 3. REFS: Strebeigh, 1988; White, 1789.

Incubation: Controlling Egg Temperatures

FOR an egg to develop normally, it must be exposed for a considerable length of time to warm temperatures — a few degrees below the normal 40°C avian body temperature. Indeed, the ideal incubation temperature for many birds' eggs is about human body temperature, 37°C. Almost all birds create the required temperature by sitting on the eggs and incubating them, often transferring heat via a temporarily bare area of abdominal skin called the 'brood patch'. A few birds, like penguins, pelicans, and gannets, transfer heat through their webbed feet. A unique form of incubation is found in the turkey-like megapodes of Australasia, the East Indies, and some Western Pacific islands. Some megapodes heat their eggs in a large mound of decaying vegetation, which they have scratched together. By opening and closing the mound as needed, the birds carefully regulate the heat of decomposition, which takes the place of the parental body heat used in normal incubation. One megapode species uses not decomposing vegetation but volcanically-heated soil to warm the eggs.

White-rumped Swift

Apus caffer

ATLAS 179; PMH 154; PER 144; HFP 186; HPCW 140; NESTS 207; BWP4:687

 | See below

BLDS: ?
Monogamy | 2 (1–3)
? brood
INCU: ♂♀
20–26 | 

FLDG: ♂♀
35–53 | |

Breeding habitat Formerly caves and cliffs, now buildings and bridges.

Displays Has communal screaming display (see Common Swift). Otherwise not well known, but similar to those of the Common Swift.

Nesting Colonial. Takes over nests of swallows, especially Red-rumped; lines them with feathers. Eggs white, 23mm, hatch asynchronously. Has three broods per year in parts of Africa; number of broods in Europe is not recorded.

Diet Like that of other swifts.

Winters Wintering areas of European birds not known; African birds winter in flocks.

Conservation Has apparently colonized Spain and Morocco since the 1960s; major range is Africa S of Sahara. See p. 529.

Essays Copulation, p. 87; Feet, p. 289.

Refs Lack 1956.

Little Swift

Apus affinis

ATLAS 180; PMH 154; PER -; HFP 186; HPCW 140; NESTS 207; BWP4:692

 | See below
BLDS: ♂♀
Monogamy | 2–3 (4)
2 broods?
INCU: ♂♀
18–26 | 

FLDG: ♂♀
33–49 | |

Breeding habitat Widespread, often in and near towns, cliffs.

Displays Has screaming displays (see Common Swift), apparently sometimes in the presence of other species of swift. Also displays with wings held in V, fixed or with very shallow fast beats.

Nesting Colonial. Nest is a sphere of vegetation and feathers stuck together with saliva and fastened with saliva to building or cliff. Also uses old nests of Red-rumped Swallow. Eggs white, 23mm, hatch asynchronously.

Diet Insects caught in mid-air.

Winters Mostly resident; most northerly populations migratory; in flocks.

Conservation Widely distributed across Africa, India, and S Asia; probably increasing.

Essays Copulation, p. 87; Feet, p. 289.

Refs Lack 1956.

The embryo inside the egg is also very sensitive to high temperatures, so that in some situations eggs must be protected from the sun. Ducks with open nests, for example, will pull downy feathers (originally plucked to form their brood patches) over the nest to cover the eggs when they leave it, providing shade if the weather is hot and helping to retard heat loss when it is cold. Open-nesting ducks usually have camouflage down that does not reveal the nest's location; hole-nesting ducks have white down. Other species may stand over the nest and shade the eggs when temperatures rise. Little Ringed and Spur-winged Plovers and some other waders soak their belly feathers and use them to wet the eggs before shading, thus helping to cool the developing embryos by evaporative heat loss.

Embryos are less sensitive to cold than to heat, particularly before incubation has started. Mallard eggs have been known to crack by freezing and still hatch successfully. Eggs cool when incubation is interrupted, but this is not usually harmful, and few birds incubate continuously. Instead egg temperature is regulated in response to changes in the temperature of the environment by varying the length of time that a parent bird sits on them or the tightness of the 'sit'. In general it appears that the goal is to keep the egg temperature above the level (25–27 °C) at which embryonic development ceases. In one study, female American House Wrens (*Troglodytes aedon*), which incubate without help from the males, sat on their eggs for periods averaging 14 minutes when the temperature was 15 °C, but an average of 7.5 minutes when it rose to 30 °C.

Many birds apparently sense egg temperature with receptors in their brood patches, which help them to regulate their attentiveness (time spent incubating) more accurately. Since the embryo itself increasingly generates heat as it develops, periods of attentiveness should generally decline as incubation progresses. Attentiveness is also influenced by the insulating properties of a particular nest.

Eggs are also turned periodically — from about once every eight minutes in some passerines to once an hour by Mallards. The turning presumably helps to warm the eggs more evenly, and to prevent embryonic membranes from sticking to the shell.

SEE: Who Incubates? p. 285; Incubation Time, p. 121; Life in the Egg, p. 447. REFS: Haftorn, 1988; Schardien and Jackson, 1979; White and Kinney, 1974.

Cooperative Breeding

'COOPERATIVE' or 'communal' breeding occurs when more than two birds of the same species provide care in rearing the young from one nest. Less than three per cent (approximately 220) of bird species worldwide are known to be cooperative breeders. There are two types of cooperative arrangements: species in which non-breeders ('helpers-at-the-nest' or 'auxiliaries') help

White-breasted Kingfisher
Halcyon smyrnensis

ATLAS 181; PMH 249; PER -; HFP 190; HPCW 141; NESTS 210; BWP4:701

	BLDS: ♂♀	5–6 (4–7)
	Cooperative?	? brood
		INCU: ♂♀
		?

FLDG: ♂♀	
18–20	Sm verts

Breeding habitat Wide range of aquatic habitats, from coastal swamps to fresh water; not necessarily near water, and may be found in forests and gardens.

Displays Sings for long periods on perch. May sit with wings open to display white markings.

Nesting Territorial. Nests in an excavated tunnel 60–150cm long in bank. Eggs white, 29mm. May have helpers at the nest: see Pied Kingfisher; Cooperative Breeding essay, p. 275.

Diet Insects, fish, amphibians, and reptiles, and other small vertebrates. Swoops down from a perch to take prey on ground. Like the majority of kingfishers worldwide, this species does not feed primarily on fish.

Winters Resident.

Conservation Locally common in few locations in which it occurs in the area covered by this guide; occurs across SW Asia into India and SE Asia.

Essays Feet, p. 289; Pellets, p. 257; Swimming and Underwater Flight, p. 61; Nest Evolution, p. 345; Swallowing Stones, p. 135.

Common Kingfisher
Alcedo atthis

ATLAS 180; PMH 154; PER 146; HFP 190; HPCW 142; NESTS 210; BWP4:711

	BLDS: ♂♀	6–7 (4–8)
	Monogamy	1–2 (6) broods
1–2m	Polygyny	INCU: ♂♀
		19–20

FLDG:♂♀,♀
23–27

Breeding habitat Close to water, generally sheltered streams, but also lakes and sometimes coastal waters.

Displays ♂s actively defend territories, with upright posture, bill moved slowly from side to side, or hunching forward, calling. Sometimes flicks wings open. Will often chase intruders out. Courtship has aerial chases with birds calling, which may lead to inspection of possible nesting sites or excavations. There is courtship-feeding.

Nesting Territorial. Nests in a burrow in a bank, 30–90 cm long. Eggs white, 23mm, hatch synchronously. Some ♂s are polygynous. Sometimes broods overlap, with ♀ incubating later brood while ♂ feeds earlier brood or seeks new mate. In such cases ♂s may have up to 6 broods a year.

Diet Fish, sometimes aquatic invertebrates, caught by diving from a perch or after hovering over water. Dives reach a depth of 1m below water, with the aid of the wings to swim downward.

Winters Resident in S and W, migratory elsewhere.

Conservation Vulnerable to hard winters: became locally extinct in N after 1962/63 winter. Also vulnerable to water pollution and disturbance from human leisure activities. Species is widely distributed across Europe and Asia and into N Africa. See p. 528.

Essays Feet, p. 289; Pellets, p. 257; Swimming and Underwater Flight, p. 61; Nest Evolution, p. 345; Swallowing Stones, p. 135.

Refs Marchant et al. 1990; Boag 1982 is a book about this species.

protect and rear the young of others, and species in which there is some degree of shared parentage of offspring. In the latter case, cooperative breeders may exhibit shared maternity, shared paternity, or both. Among the cooperative breeders in the region covered by this handbook are the Moorhen, Long-tailed Tit, Bee-eater, Arabian Babbler, and Dunnock, but each differs from the others in the details of its breeding biology.

Helpers in Moorhens are the young of a monogamous pair's first brood of the season, and often aid in the care of subsequent broods and defence of the parental territory. These juvenile helpers range from four to ten weeks of age and occasionally share in egg incubation and nest repair duties, in addition to helping brood and feed their younger siblings. Helpers do not remain in the breeding territory beyond the end of the breeding season. As in Moorhens, young of first broods of House Martins and Swallows also help to rear their siblings in later broods produced in the same season.

In Bee-eaters, helpers are sexually mature birds that have failed in their own breeding attempt for that season. Studies in France indicate that about 25 per cent of Bee-eater nests that successfully hatch chicks have one to four helpers aiding in feeding the chicks. Breeding adults (two years old or older) are more likely than breeding one-year olds to have helpers; in several cases where known, the helpers are close relatives of at least one member of the breeding pair. As the season progresses, failed breeders switch from renesting attempts to helping behaviour. Both intraspecific nest parasitism ('egg dumping' by one or more females into the nest of another female) and low levels of extra-pair copulations have been documented in studies of this species which raise the possibility that helpers may contribute genetically at some nests, as has been documented for the related White-fronted Bee-eater (*Merops bullockoides*) of Africa.

As in the Bee-eater, auxiliaries in Long-tailed Tits are apparently failed adult breeders. Potential helpers are attracted to join a successful pair by a conspicuous hover display performed by the parent birds each time they bring food to the nest. One or two helpers per nest usually appear during the latter part of the nestling period, and often contribute as much as either parent in feeding the nestlings and fledglings. Although it seems unlikely that these helpers make a direct genetic contribution to the offspring they help rear, they nevertheless may be genetically related to them.

From long-term studies in Israel, we know that the Arabian Babbler differs markedly from the cooperative breeders in Europe. Birds live in communal groups of 2 to 22 on year-round territories defended by each group. In the arid habitat where this species occurs, all suitable territories are filled. Approximately 5 to 10 per cent of the population are floaters without group membership; such birds occasionally survive to join a group or coalesce with other floaters to form a new group and occupy a vacant territory, but such formation appears to be very rare in undisturbed habitat and most floaters perish. Territories are stable over many years and are passed through the male lineage from parent to offspring. Males may spend their entire lives in their natal territories, whereas females must disperse and join another (often nearby) group in order to breed.

Pied Kingfisher
Ceryle rudis

ATLAS 181; PMH 250; PER -; HFP 190; HPCW 142; NESTS 210; BWP4:723

	4–5 (1–7) 1 (2?) broods		
BLDS: ♂♀	INCU: ♂♀	FLDG: ♂♀	
Cooperative	15?	23–26	Sm verts

Breeding habitat By still, fresh, or salt water from deserts to open country.

Displays Defence against rivals includes a wing-spread threat posture, to show white wing markings. Courtship display often involves several birds flying through the colony calling.

Nesting Often colonial. Nests in a tunnel 60–250cm long in bank; cavity is unlined. Eggs white, 29mm, hatch asynchronously. Young are dependent on parents for several weeks after fledging. One of the few species in this book that is a cooperative breeder; that is, the adults have helpers at the nest. See essay, p. 275. Helpers are generally young ♂s – sons of the nesting pair. They feed the nesting ♀ and her young and defend the nest. ♀s may be in short supply because they suffer high levels of predation while on the nest. Nests with helpers fledge more young than those without. Can breed at 1 year, but some ♂s help instead.

Diet Fish, sometimes amphibians or invertebrates. Dives after hovering or plunges from perch.

Winters Resident. Sometimes in loose flocks.

Conservation Local in area, but distributed widely in Africa, India, and SE Asia.

Essays Feet, p. 289; Pellets, p. 257; Swimming and Underwater Flight, p. 61; Nest Evolution, p. 345; Swallowing Stones, p. 135; Cooperative Breeding, p. 275.

Refs Brown 1987 is a book about cooperative breeding in birds.

Little Green Bee-eater
Merops orientalis

ATLAS 182; PMH -; PER -; HFP 189; HPCW 143; NESTS 211; BWP4:734

	3–6 (–8) 1 brood?	?		
BLDS: ♂♀	INCU: ♂♀	FLDG: ?		
Monogamy	?	?		

Breeding habitat Arid areas, including agricultural fields, often near water, along river banks; also coastal.

Displays Little known, but similar to Bee-eater.

Nesting Sometimes solitary, but also in loose colonies. Nests in a tunnel 0.5–2.0m long running into a bank or into the ground; unlined. Eggs white, 20mm, hatch asynchronously. Apparently does not have helpers at the nest.

Diet Insects, taken on the wing. From perch or ground sallies out to catch prey, hammering large prey against perch to kill them.

Winters Resident; often in small flocks.

Conservation Occurs along Nile Valley and in Israel, where may be increasing locally. Locally common across Africa, SW Asia into India and SE Asia.

Essays Altruism, p. 245; Parental Care, p. 171; Nest Evolution, p. 345; Hatching Asynchrony and Brood Reduction, p. 507.

Refs Fry 1984 is a book about this and other species of Bee-eater.

Generally there is only one babbler nest in a territory, but usually two (and up to as many as four) females may lay eggs in the nest and all adult males (maximum of three) may copulate with each breeding female. Unlike the 'cooperative' breeders that they appear to be, female babblers engage in behaviours that increase the probability of their own eggs being the successful ones in the communal clutch. The most effective of these behaviours is the tossing of other females' eggs from the nest, but it is unclear just how frequently this occurs. All group members older than a few months help feed the nestlings. Joint clutches may number up to 13 eggs, but no more than six young are fledged successfully. Although joint clutches do not fledge more young than individual clutches, there is an advantage to living in a large group because small groups experience greater interference from neighbouring large groups and cannot successfully defend the higher quality territories.

Cooperative breeding arrangements in Dunnocks might be better described as 'uncooperative breeding'. Dunnocks exhibit the most variable breeding system of any European bird species. In a single population studied in Britain, breeding territories were occupied by monogamous pairs, polygynous males with two females, polyandrous females with two or three males, and polygynandrous arrangements of two males with several females! In multi-mate groups (where the requisite data exist), same-sex individuals were not close relatives. DNA fingerprinting has revealed shared male paternity of clutches but no intraspecific brood parasitism by females, so that maternity of the clutch is unambiguous.

Female Dunnocks defend their individual territories against each other, and males compete amongst themselves to defend one or more female territories. This within-sex competition constantly threatens the stability of monogamous pairs and leads to the multi-mate variations. In multi-male territories, the amount of feedings that a male supplies to the nestlings is determined by the amount of access that he had to the female during the mating period — a good predictor of his paternity! There are no helpers aside from parental birds.

Why has evolution produced cooperative breeding systems? Initial hypotheses were based on kin selection (seemingly 'selfless' behaviour like helping at the nest being favoured because it increases the reproductive success of relatives who are similar genetically to the helper) or on maximizing reproductive output. As more cooperatively breeding species have been examined worldwide, these explanations generally have not been supported. Instead, cooperative systems appear to arise when environmental constraints force birds into breeding groups because the opportunities for younger birds to breed independently are severely limited. Limitations may include a shortage of territory openings because higher quality habitats are saturated with established breeders; a shortage of sexual partners (generally females), indicated by the skewed sex ratios that are common in groups; and unpredictable availability of resources, which could make it too risky for individual pairs to commit themselves to reproduce in any given year. That cooperative breeding is a common strategy in arid and semi-arid portions of Africa and Australia lends strong support to this line of reasoning. Cooperative breeding may

Blue-cheeked Bee-eater

Merops superciliosus

ATLAS 182; PMH 155; PER -; HFP 188; HPCW 143; NESTS 211; BWP4:740

	BLDS: ♂♀ Monogamy	5–7 1 brood INCU: ♂♀ ?	FLDG: ?		

Breeding habitat Deserts and other arid areas near water; also coastal.

Displays Similar to those of the Bee-eater.

Nesting Often in loose colonies. Nests in a tunnel 1–3 m long running into a bank or the ground; cavity is unlined. Eggs white, 26mm. Does not apparently have helpers at the nest.

Diet Often feeds in flocks, taking insects, especially dragonflies, on the wing. From perch or ground sallies out to catch prey.

Winters Migrates to Africa S of the Sahara. Often in flocks.

Conservation Locally common with scattered populations in area covered by this guide; widespread, scattered populations across Africa, SW Asia.

Essays Altruism, p. 245; Parental Care, p. 171; Nest Evolution, p. 345.

Refs Fry 1984.

Bee-eater

Merops apiaster

ATLAS 182; PMH 155; PER 144; HFP 188; HPCW 144; NESTS 211; BWP4:748

Ground	BLDS: ♂♀ Cooperative	6–7 (4–9) 1 brood INCU: ♂♀ 20	FLDG: ♂♀ 20–33?		

Breeding habitat Open country with scattered trees and shrubs for perches, often near rivers whose banks provide nest sites.

Displays Courtship display has ♂ making short flight from perch, returning to ♀, who vibrates tail and opens wings. ♂ may bring insects and courtship-feed.

Nesting Colonial. Nest is usually in tunnels in sand banks, 70–200cm long, but also digs into ground; no lining. Eggs white, 26mm, hatch asynchronously—as many as 9 days apart. One of the unusual species in which there is cooperative breeding: there are helpers at the nest – usually young ♂s. About one quarter of the successful nests have helpers—see essay, p. 275.

Diet Flying insects, and, as its name suggests, often bees and other hymenoptera. Hunts from perch, sallying out to catch prey. May remove stings by rubbing them against perch, but birds certainly ingest some stings and are often stung.

Winters Migrates to Africa S of Sahara. In flocks.

Conservation Common and widespread across S and E Europe, C Asia, and N Africa.

Essays Altruism, p. 245; Parental Care, p. 171; Nest Evolution, p. 345; Ducking the Bird Laws, p. 523; Hatching Asynchrony and Brood Reduction, p. 507.

Refs Brown 1987; Fry 1984.

be viewed primarily as a means by which young adults put off the start of their own breeding in order to maximize their lifetime reproductive output, and in the process occasionally promote genes identical with their own via kin selection.

SEE: Natural Selection, p. 297; Altruism, p. 245; Population Dynamics, p. 515. REFS: Brown, 1987; Davies, 1990, 1992; Gibbons, 1987; Lessells and Avery, 1989; Lessells and Krebs, 1989; Petrie, 1986; Skutch, 1987; Stacey and Koenig, 1990; Zahavi, 1990.

Metabolism

THE physical and chemical processes that maintain a bird's life are called, collectively, its 'metabolism'. A flow of energy is required to run the metabolism of any organism, and ultimately the energy source for all birds is the sun. Green plants 'capture' the sun's energy in the process of photosynthesis, and birds then acquire it by eating plants or by eating other animals that eat plants. The energy is used to do the work of building tissues, contracting muscles, manufacturing eggs, processing information in the brain, and powering all the other activities of a living bird.

The entire metabolic process is run by biological catalysts known as enzymes. They are long, chain-like protein molecules that are twisted into characteristic three-dimensional shapes. Enzyme molecules function rather like templates to hold reacting molecules together in the proper position to speed their interactions. If your enzymes lose their shape ('denature'), they stop functioning, your metabolism ceases, and you're dead. Birds are no different. That's why boiling kills; it denatures enzymes.

To compare rates at which different animals use energy, scientists calculate the rate at which each animal consumes oxygen when at rest and under no stress either from temperature or other sources. That consumption is then used to calculate the basal metabolic rate, which is expressed as the number of kilocalories of energy used per kilogram of body weight, per hour. Small birds have proportionately larger surfaces (through which heat is lost) in relation to their mass of metabolizing tissue than do large birds. A Blue Tit can maintain the same body temperature as a Mute Swan because it has such a higher basal metabolism (i.e. uses proportionately more energy). Hummingbirds, with their tiny bodies and high levels of activity, have the highest metabolic rates of any animals — roughly a dozen times that of a pigeon and a hundred times that of an elephant. To maintain those rates, hummingbirds have to consume nearly their own weight in nectar daily. In fact, a warm-blooded animal can't be smaller than the smallest hummer or shrew. Further reduction in size would make it impossible for the creature to eat fast enough to maintain its body temperature.

The basal metabolic rates of non-passerine birds are very similar to those of some mammals. Passerines, for reasons that are not understood, tend to

Roller
Coracias garrulus

ATLAS 183; PMH 155; PER 146; HFP 188; HPCW 144; NESTS 212; BWP4:764

Bank | Burrow BLDS: ? Monogamy | 3–5 (2–7) 1 brood INCU: ♂♀ 17–20

FLDG: ♂♀ 25–30

Breeding habitat Open woodland but also grasslands with scattered trees and shrubs.

Displays Flight display: bird climbs steeply, dives steeply, sometimes somersaults, rolls side to side, while calling. Birds arrive on breeding grounds paired. Aerial chases may involve several birds. Pairs have bowing ceremony, mutual preening, and courtship-feeding.

Nesting Territorial. Usually nests in hole in tree, often that of a woodpecker; no lining is added. Sometimes digs

tunnel into banks. Eggs white, 35mm, hatch synchronously.

Diet Large insects, particularly beetles, grasshoppers, and crickets. Swoops to ground from perch.

Winters Africa, S of Sahara.

Conservation Has declined in W and C Europe, but is locally common across Europe, into N Africa, and into C Asia. See p. 529.

Essays Nest Evolution, p. 345; Courtship Feeding, p. 223; Visual Displays, p. 33.

Hoopoe
Upupa epops

ATLAS 184; PMH 156; PER 146; HFP 190; HPCW 145; NESTS 212; BWP4:786

1–5m | BLDS: ♂♀ Monogamy | 7–8 (4–12) 1 brood INCU: ♀ 15–16(14–20)

FLDG: ♀ 26–29 | Sm verts | Ground glean

Breeding habitat Open sandy ground in a variety of habitats, from semi-desert to grasslands to openings in forests.

Displays When giving well-known monotonous call, ♂ bows head, and inflates neck at each call. Birds display to rivals by erecting crests and spreading wings and tail, exposing prominent markings. Between pairs there are chases and courtship-feeding.

Nesting Territorial. Nests in a hole in tree, building, or ground; cavity may have no lining or be lined with vegetation. May excavate soft, rotten wood. Eggs yellowish to grey, or olive, 26mm, hatch asynchronously. ♂ feeds nesting ♀. Sometimes there are 2 broods per year

in the S. Fed by parents after fledging.

Diet Insects, mainly larvae and pupae, obtained while walking and probing the ground or flushed and pursued along ground. Sometimes takes small lizards.

Winters Resident in S, northern populations migrate, probably to S of Sahara.

Conservation Local declines, particularly in NW and C Europe, but common and widespread across much of Europe (not N), Asia, and Africa.

Notes DNA analyses suggest that Hoopoes belong in an order of their own and are not closely related to rollers and bee-eaters as was once thought. See Sibley and Monroe 1990.

have 30–70 per cent higher metabolic rates than either non-passerines or mammals of equal mass. When they are active, birds and mammals, of course, have metabolic rates well above their basal rates. Yet birds do not generally use more energy than mammals to get the same job done — indeed they often use less. Flying is faster and energetically cheaper than walking or running for comparably heavy animals. Overall, birds and mammals are metabolically very similar.

When hovering, hummingbirds are using energy at as much as eight times the resting rate. At the other extreme of their activity range, hummingbirds may become torpid at night — that is, they let their body temperature drop, often until it is close to that of the surrounding air. Many other birds, such as swifts, nightjars, and Willow Tits, can also lower their body temperature to save energy at night.

In cold weather, all non-torpid birds must operate at well above their basal metabolic rates in order to maintain their body temperatures. Small species, such as Willow and Siberian Tits that overwinter in temperate and subarctic areas, are at particular risk of freezing. They have proportionately large surface areas through which heat is lost and thus must eat continuously during short daylight hours to stoke their metabolic fires. If they do not, they will not reserve enough energy to see them through the long night, even if they maintain a lower body temperature. A wintering tit living at 40 degrees below freezing must spend on the order of 20 times as much time feeding per day as it would in the warmth of spring.

Birds have only slightly higher body temperatures than mammals; avian temperatures range from around the human level of 37°C (penguins) to 40° (most resting birds). But in general, the temperature ranges of the two groups, like their overall metabolisms, are remarkably similar, considering their different modes of life. Both have evolved to function at temperatures just below those at which the crucial protein enzymes begin to denature. Maintaining constant body temperature is thus not just a problem for birds trying to keep from chilling in cold weather; it is even more critical when the air temperature rises above that of the body. Birds must then avoid overheating and sudden death. The relatively large body surfaces of small birds absorb environmental heat (and lose cooling moisture) quickly, and this is one reason few songbirds are evident at midday during heat waves; they seek shade and become inactive. Soaring birds, in contrast, may take advantage of 'thermals' — rising packets of warm air — and avoid midday heat and the denaturation of their proteins in the cool air of higher altitudes.

Why do birds (and mammals) run these risks of maintaining a high, constant temperature, especially since it costs them to do so? A small bird must consume many times more food than an ectothermal ('cold blooded' — not generating a high body temperature metabolically) lizard of the same weight that warms to operating temperature in the sun and cools again at night. One obvious reason for the constancy of their temperatures is to allow birds and mammals to be active at night and during cold weather. They can penetrate areas and take on activities from which reptiles are barred. No lizard could feed alongside a Siberian Tit in winter. Another advantage to

Wryneck

Jynx torquilla

ATLAS 185; PMH 156; PER 146; HFP 196; HPCW 146; NESTS 215; BWP4:800

  7–10 (5–12) 1–2 (3) broods INCU: ♂♀ 11–14

3–6m	BLDS: – Monogamy	11–14	FLDG: ♂♀ 18–22 (25)		

Breeding habitat Open woodlands, usually deciduous.

Displays Towards rivals, bird ruffles head feathers, spreads tail, droops wings and points at intruder. Will sway head backwards and forwards. As part of showing potential nest site to mate, may drum in or near hole. When threatened at close range (such as when caught for ringing) will hiss and contort head and neck.

Nesting Territorial. Nests in a hole in tree, or bank, often taking over hole in use by other species; no lining added. Eggs white, 21mm, hatch synchronously. Parents remain with young for 1–2

weeks after fledging.

Diet Ants, also other insects. Breaks up ant nests, extracting insects with its long sticky tongue. May sit near ant trails picking up individuals as they pass by.

Winters Migrates to Africa, S of Sahara and to India and SE Asia; some birds resident and winter in southern Europe. Occurs in a wider variety of habitats, including those with only a few trees and shrubs.

Conservation Has declined most obviously in the UK, but also elsewhere in NW of range. However, widely distributed across Europe and Asia.

Essays Nest Lining, p. 439.

Grey-headed Woodpecker

Picus canus

ATLAS 190; PMH 157; PER 146; HFP 192; HPCW 147; NESTS 213; BWP4:813

  7–9 (4–11) 1 brood INCU: ♂♀ 14–15

2–20m	BLDS: ♂♀ Monogamy	14–15	FLDG: ♂♀ 24–28		Bark glean

Breeding habitat Open woodland, especially deciduous; more often in montane forest than is Green Woodpecker.

Displays Will remain motionless on far side of tree for long periods if disturbed. ♂ gives far-reaching call from perch; also drums on tree and has long flights around territory. Pairs climb trees with jerky movements and sway heads from side to side.

Nesting Territorial. Nests in hole drilled in tree; no lining added, but wood chips left in. Eggs white, 28mm, hatch synchronously. Young are independent

soon after fledging.

Diet Insects, especially ants, taken mainly on the ground where it probes with bill, sticking insects to its tongue. Also low in trees; rarely taps, instead searches rotten wood.

Winters Resident.

Conservation No obvious changes in range and population size; occurs widely across Europe and Asia. See p. 529.

Essays Bills, p. 391; Feathers, p. 363; Feet, p. 289; Hoarding Food, p. 453; Mixed-species Flocking, p. 429; Wing Shapes and Flight, p. 269; Nest Sites and Materials, p. 443.

constancy is that the thousands of temperature-sensitive reactions that compose the metabolism can be better coordinated if they are carried out in a relatively uniform thermal environment.

But why are temperatures of endotherms ('warm-blooded' animals), and ectotherms when they are active, so close to the point of overheating? High temperatures, besides increasing the rate of chemical reactions, permit important physical functions that depend on diffusion to go on more rapidly. Heat speeds the diffusion of transmitter chemicals in nerve connections; the hotter a bird can be, the more rapidly vital information can be processed and commands sent to the bird's muscles. This allows birds to react more quickly. So high operating temperatures have clear advantage for both avian predators and prey; and unlike lizards and other ectotherms, birds are not dependent on the sun's warmth to attain those temperatures. It has also been suggested that maintaining a constant high brain temperature aids memory and facilitates learning.

SEE: Temperature Regulation and Behaviour, p. 163; Drinking, p. 313; Spread-wing Postures, p. 17; Black and White Plumage, p. 7. REFS: Blem, 1990; Calder, 1974, 1984; Calder and King, 1974; Paynter, 1974.

Who Incubates?

WHICH parent incubates varies greatly among species, as we indicate in the species treatments. In most birds, parents share incubation. Cormorants, like many other birds that share the task, relieve each other regularly, twice a day. In other birds, including some sandpipers, pigeons, and doves, the female incubates at night while the male takes his turn during 'working hours' — about 9 am to 5 pm. Both sexes of most woodpeckers alternate during the day, but the male sits on the eggs at night. Starlings, on the other hand, share the task during the day, but the female alone incubates at night. In monogamous species in which both adults incubate the same clutch, the eggs usually are covered most of the time. That is the case in the Common Waxbill, an estrildid finch introduced into Europe from Africa, one of the most extreme examples of shared incubation: in this species the pair spends virtually full time sitting together on the clutch.

The female is the only incubator in many raptors, hummingbirds, many passerines, and most or all European polygynous species (those in which one male has more than one mate). Often the male is not without duties; he may feed the incubating female and stand watch from a nearby perch. Hornbills, usually black-and-white birds of the Old World tropics with brightly coloured bare parts and huge, downcurved bills, lay their eggs in cavities. The female (except for ground hornbills) then seals herself into the cavity with the eggs, using first mud and then faeces mixed with food remains (in some species the

Green Woodpecker

Picus viridis

ATLAS 190; PMH 157; PER 146; HFP 192; HPCW 147; NESTS 214; BWP4:824

1–5m	BLDS: ♂ ♀ Monogamy	5–7 (4–11) 1 brood INCU: ♂ ♀ 17–19 (15)	FLDG: ♂ ♀ 23–27		Bark glean

Breeding habitat Mainly deciduous woodland, but also a wide range of man-made open woods and parks.

Displays Gives far-reaching call with open bill from perch, rarely drums on tree. On ground or on trunk, rivals sway heads from side to side, or in circle pointing bills skyward. ♂ tries to attract ♀ to potential nest site; courtship includes mutual head-swaying and courtship-feeding.

Nesting Territorial. Nests in hole drilled in tree; no lining added. Eggs white, 32mm, hatch synchronously. Young remain with parents for several weeks after fledging.

Diet Ants taken on ground, sometimes on trees. Long tongue (can stick out 10cm) is coated with sticky saliva and can be inserted into or across ant nests to lick up prey. Will take other insects. Is not completely immune to ant attacks and removes ants from its plumage.

Winters Resident.

Conservation Some local decreases, but has spread in N (especially in the UK); widely distributed within Europe, though numbers decline markedly in very cold winters.

Essays Bills, p. 391; Feathers, p. 363; Feet, p. 289; Hoarding Food, p. 453; Mixed-species Flocking, p. 429; Wing Shapes and Flight, p. 269; Nest Sites and Materials, p. 443.

Refs Marchant et al. 1990.

Levaillant's Green Woodpecker

Picus vaillantii

ATLAS 191; PMH -; PER -; HFP -; HPCW 147; NESTS -; BWP4:837

Conif tree	BLDS: ? Monogamy?	6–7 (4–8) 1 brood? INCU: ?	FLDG: ? ?		

Breeding habitat Open, dry upland woodlands with oak, poplar, cedar, and pine.

Displays Little known, but probably very like those of the Green Woodpecker. Frequently drums on trees.

Nesting Nests in hole in tree. Eggs white, 30mm.

Diet Ants taken on ground; diet is probably very similar to that of Green Woodpecker.

Winters Resident.

Conservation Locally distributed in NW Africa.

Notes Considered a subspecies of Green Woodpecker by some authorities.

Essays Bills, p. 391; Feathers, p. 363; Feet, p. 289; Hoarding Food, p. 453; Mixed-species Flocking, p. 429; Wing Shapes and Flight, p. 269; Nest Sites and Materials, p. 443.

male helps), leaving only a narrow vertical slot through which the male passes her food. Males of some hornbill species feed the female throughout incubation and raising of the young; in others the female breaks out when the young are partially grown. The young then reseal the entrance and the female helps with the feeding chores. In most genera the female moults and becomes temporarily flightless during her confinement.

In polyandrous birds (those in which one female mates with more than one male), like jacanas and phalaropes, it is common for the male to be the sole incubator. Polyandry is relatively rare, though, and in only about 5 per cent of bird species do males do all the incubating. In certain polyandrous waders, such as Temminck's Stints and Spotted Sandpipers (*Actitis macularia*, a North American species, accidental in Europe), the female lays a series of clutches, each of which is incubated by a different male. The final clutch is incubated by the female herself.

In the remaining bird species the pattern is variable, with one or both sexes incubating according to circumstances. What controls the distribution of the incubation task is not thoroughly understood, but ecological factors such as distance to food supplies, climate, and predation pressures must all play roles. For example, seabirds that must travel long distances to feed, clearly cannot leave all of the incubation chores to a single parent.

SEE: Incubation: Controlling Egg Temperatures, p. 273; Incubation Time, p. 121; Polyandry, p. 195; Hatching Asynchrony and Brood Reduction, p. 507. REF.: White and Kinney, 1974.

Acid and Eggshells

ACID precipitation is one of our most serious environmental problems. Nitrogen oxides from car exhausts and industrial furnaces, and sulphur dioxide from the stacks of power plants burning fossil fuels provide the raw materials for acid being deposited over much of the planet. Acid precipitation has already virtually destroyed many lakes in Scandinavia and northeastern North America, and is thought to be a cause of forest damage in many parts of the Northern Hemisphere and, perhaps, in the rainforests of sub-Saharan Africa.

For years little was known about the impact of acid rain, snow, and fog on bird populations. As might be expected, the first effects appeared to have been mainly reductions of birds' food supplies, and occurred mostly in aquatic systems. Declines of divers that attempt to raise their young on fish-poor acidified lakes in North America have been reported, and acid precipitation is suspected of playing a role in the decline of the American Black Duck as well. In Britain, acidified sections of streams harbour few of the larval insects upon which Dippers feed, and breeding Dippers are correspondingly scarce in these sections.

Black Woodpecker

Dryocopus martius

NESTS 185; PMH 157; PER 148; HFP 192; HPCW 148; NESTS 213; BWP4:840

		$\bigcirc$ 4–6 (1–9) 1 brood		
Conif tree 4–25m	BLD: ♂♀,♂♀ Monogamy	INCU: ♂♀ 12–14	FL: ♂♀,♂♀ 24–28	Bark glean

Breeding habitat   Mature, old-growth forests, both deciduous and coniferous.
Displays   Gives far-reaching call from perch, also drums loudly on tree. On trunk, rivals move heads in circle pointing bills skyward, showing red crown patch. ♂ tries to attract ♀ to potential nest site. Mutual head-swaying.
Nesting   Territorial. Nests in hole drilled in tree; no lining added, though wood fragments may be left behind. Eggs white, 34mm, hatch synchronously.
Diet   Ants; has shorter tongue than Green Woodpecker, but feeds in similar way, often on ground. Also attacks rotten tree stumps with powerful bill, looking for ants and wood-boring beetle larvae. May drill holes in trees to tap the sugar-rich sap produced by the damage, returning at intervals, when the sap has accumulated.

Winters   Resident, but often in more open forests.

Conservation   Has increased range in W and occurs widely in Europe and Asia. See p. 529.

Essays   Island Biogeography, p. 303.

Great Spotted Woodpecker

Dendrocopos major

ATLAS 186; PMH 158; PER 148; HFP 194; HPCW 148; NESTS 214; BWP4:856

		$\bigcirc$ 4–7 (3–8) 1 brood		
3–5m	BLD: ♂♀,♂♀ Monogamy	INCU: ♂♀ 10–13	FLDG: ♂♀ 18–24	Birds	Foliage glean

Breeding habitat   Wide range of woodlands, including parks and gardens.

Displays   Drumming important in defining territory. ♂ attracts ♀ to potential nest hole, by drumming on tree and with fluttering display flight.

Nesting   Territorial. Nests in hole drilled in tree. Eggs white, 27mm, hatch synchronously. Young remain with parents for about a week after fledging.

Diet   Insects; climbs trees, head up, using stiff tail feathers as a prop, probing into cracks in bark. Will hack at rotten wood and chisel holes to get at wood-boring insects. Is also predatory on eggs and young of nesting birds in the summer. Conifer seeds important in winter; bird sets cone onto an anvil – a natural crack or one created by chiselling. Makes holes (rarely in UK) in rings around tree, to tap the sugar-rich sap produced. Returns at intervals to drink and reopen holes.

Winters   Resident; northern populations in conifers sometimes have large irruptions, when food supply fails.
Conservation   Has increased in NW, following declines in the last century; common and widespread over most of Europe and large parts of Asia; locally in N Africa.
Notes   Does not occur in Ireland, an area that is within the general range of this species and which surely provides the habitats for a species with such generalized habitat requirements. Islands often lack species for reasons to do with the low rate of colonization (which seems unlikely for this highly mobile species) and the high rate of species extinction of the small founder populations: see essay on Island Biogeography, p. 303.
Essays   Acid and Eggshells, p. 287; Bird-brained, p. 385; Feeding Birds, p. 357; Nonvocal Sounds, p. 263.
Refs   Marchant et al. 1990.

Now direct acid damage to breeding populations may have been detected in north European forests. In the Netherlands, resident Great Tits, Blue Tits, Coal Tits, Nuthatches, and Great Spotted Woodpeckers all have shown eggshell thinning in the 1980s, in contrast to migrant Pied Flycatchers (in which the females start laying soon after arrival). The decrease in eggshell quality, a function of insufficient calcium deposition, was related to soil types, being most severe in woods growing on poor sandy soils, but not detectable in woods occupying loam or clay soil. Uptake of calcium by trees is impaired by acidification of the poorer soils, and caterpillars (a major food source for the breeding birds) feeding on those trees also contain less calcium. It seems likely, then, that acid precipitation is having an impact on birds reminiscent of that seen from the overuse of chlorinated hydrocarbon pesticides.

SEE: Pesticides and Birds, p. 115; Birds and Global Warming, p. 311. REFS: Drent and Woldendorp, 1989; Hölzinger and Kroymann, 1984; Schreiber and Newman, 1988.

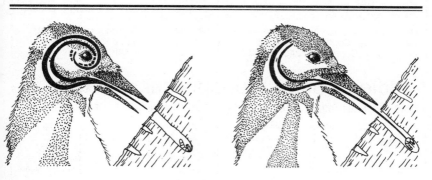

How woodpecker tongues work.
Great Spotted Woodpecker tongue retracted (left) and extended (right). The exceptionally long tongue wraps around the skull and is anchored at the base of the bill. It is extended by a complex system that includes very long hyoid (tongue-base) bones. The tips of such woodpecker tongues are barbed to help in extracting insects from holes, and the tongue is coated with sticky saliva which helps to retain the prey.

Feet

AVIAN feet, like bills, tell us a great deal about the taxonomic relationships, behaviour, and ecology of birds. More than half of the 9000 or more species of birds, for example, are passerines, birds characterized largely by the form of their feet. The Passeriformes, passerines or perching birds, have feet with four separate toes, three of them directed forward, and one (first, or inner, the homologue of our big toe) directed backward. All four passerine toes join

Syrian Woodpecker

Dendrocopos syriacus

ATLAS 187; PMH 158; PER 148; HFP 194; HPCW 149; NESTS 214; BWP4:874

		4–7 (3–8) 1 brood			
	BLDS: ♂♀	INCU: ♂♀	FLDG: ♂♀		
1–4m	Monogamy	9–14	17–25	Fruit	Foliage glean

Breeding habitat Overlaps with that of the Great Spotted Woodpecker, including a wide range of forests. More common in gardens and orchards and less common in large tracts of forest.

Displays Drumming important in defining territory. ♂ attracts ♀ to potential nest hole and birds may duet drum. Pairs have head-swaying display.

Nesting Territorial. Nests in hole drilled in tree; no lining. Eggs white, 25mm, hatch synchronously.

Diet Insects, taken in much the same way as Great Spotted Woodpecker, also seeds. Some populations feed mostly fruit to their young. Takes plant material throughout year. Also feeds on the ground.

Winters Resident.

Conservation Has spread in E Europe. First found in N Bulgaria and Yugoslavia in 1890s, in Austria, Rumania, Czech Republic in middle part of this century, spreading into Ukraine, and so on. Occurs in E Europe, Turkey, locally in the Middle East. See p. 529.

Essays Bills, p. 391; Feathers, p. 363; Feet, p. 289; Hoarding Food, p. 453; Mixed-species Flocking, p. 429; Wing Shapes and Flight, p. 269; Nest Sites and Materials, p. 443.

Middle Spotted Woodpecker

Dendrocopos medius

ATLAS 187; PMH 158; PER 148; HFP 194; HPCW 149; NESTS 214; BWP4:882

		4–7 (8) 1 brood			
	BLD: ♂♀,♂♀	INCU: ♀	FLDG: ♂♀		
1–5m	Monogamy	11–14	22–23		Foliage glean

Breeding habitat Mainly in deciduous forests, especially mixed hornbeam and oak.

Displays Defends territory with call, much less often by drumming. Towards ♀s ♂ has fluttering flight, aerial chases, and, on trunk, spreads wings.

Nesting Territorial. Nests in hole drilled in dead tree. Eggs white, 25mm. Young remain with parents for up to 2 weeks.

Diet Feeds on insects in trees much like Great Spotted Woodpecker, generally in rotten wood in dead trees.

Winters Resident.

Conservation Has declined, especially in N, because of forest losses and changing forest practices that leave less of the rotten wood the birds need for their nests. Occurs C and E Europe to Turkey, Iran. See p. 529.

the leg at the same level. Foot structure varies considerably among the other major taxonomic groups. Some swifts have all four toes pointing forward; kingfishers have the middle and outer toes fused for part of their length; woodpeckers have two toes pointed forward and two backward (except in the Three-toed Woodpecker and its close North American relative, the Black-backed Woodpecker, in which the first toe has been lost). The four toes of raptors are widely separated. Owls can turn their fourth (outer) toes either forward or backward. Many waterbirds and waders have three toes pointed forward and a hind toe which is often reduced greatly and joins the leg so far above the level of the other toes that it loses contact with the ground; the toes of some species are completely webbed (e.g. auks) and those of others are partially webbed or lobed (e.g. grebes).

These differences, of course, are related to the life-styles of the birds. The independent, extremely flexible toes of the passerines, along with the completely opposed first toe, are ideal for grasping perches. Swifts have strong claws for clinging to vertical surfaces. All the toes often point forward in dead

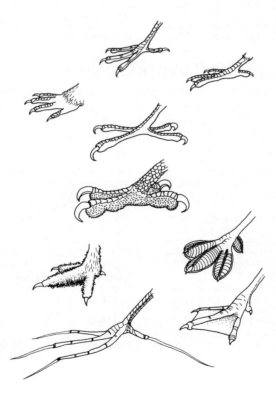

Top to bottom: passerine, kingfisher (right), swift (left), woodpecker, Osprey, grebe (right), Ptarmigan (left), jacana (left), duck.

White-backed Woodpecker
Dendrocopos leucotos

ATLAS 189; PMH 159; PER 148; HFP 196; HPCW 149; NESTS 215; BWP4:891

Conif tree 2–7m	BLDS: ♂♀ Monogamy	3–5 1 brood INCU: ♂♀ 10–11	FLDG: ♂♀ 24–28		Foliage glean

Breeding habitat Mainly in montane deciduous (sometimes coniferous) woodland. Prefers areas with many dead trees and so avoids plantations which have few dead trees. In pine forests on W coast of Norway.

Displays ♂ (less often ♀) drums. Rival ♂s adopt vertical posture on tree trunk, or have erratic pursuit flights. Displays like those of Great Spotted Woodpecker.

Nesting Territorial. Nests in hole drilled in rotten tree. Eggs white, 28mm.

Diet Insects, mainly wood-boring beetles; gleans seeds and fruit in winter. Often feeds in rotting, fallen logs and stumps. Pecks logs vigorously as if boring a hole. Extracts nuts from their shells by hammering in natural anvil (see Great Spotted Woodpecker, p. 288).

Winters Resident.

Conservation Has declined in Scandinavia and possibly elsewhere; vulnerable to forestry practices (see above). Small, fragmented populations outside of main range from E Europe across middle latitudes of Asia. See p. 529.

Essays Bills, p. 391; Feathers, p. 363; Feet, p. 289; Hoarding Food, p. 453; Mixed-species Flocking, p. 429; Wing Shapes and Flight, p. 269; Nest Sites and Materials, p. 443.

Lesser Spotted Woodpecker
Dendrocopos minor

ATLAS 189; PMH 159; PER 148; HFP 196; HPCW 150; NESTS 215; BWP4:901

2–8m	BLDS: ♂♀ Monogamy	4–6 (3–8) 1 brood INCU: ♂♀ 11–12	FLDG: ♂♀ 18–20		Foliage glean

Breeding habitat Wide range of woodlands, often moist or riverine, large gardens and parks, but tending to avoid conifers.

Displays ♂s, sometimes ♀s, drum; ♂s also have far-reaching call. Between rivals, there are aerial chases, and a gliding flight with wings held up. Has wing-spreading display when on tree. Pairs may duet drum.

Nesting Territorial. Nests in hole drilled in tree (often drilled into a branch rather than main trunk). Eggs white, 19mm, hatch synchronously.

Diet Insects, searching trunks, branches, and twigs that are generally smaller in diameter than used by other woodpeckers. Sometimes hawks for insects in flight.

Winters Resident; northern populations sometimes irruptive.

Conservation Local declines, marked in Finland; has colonized Denmark. Often not common, but very widely distributed across Europe and N Asia.

Essays Bills, p. 391; Feathers, p. 363; Feet, p. 289; Hoarding Food, p. 453; Mixed-species Flocking, p. 429; Wing Shapes and Flight, p. 269; Nest Sites and Materials, p. 443; Nonvocal Sounds, p. 263; Irruptions, p. 491.

Refs Marchant et al. 1990.

individuals, but in life the inner two actually work against the outer two in grasping the soft materials the swifts use in making their nests. The fused toes of kingfishers help in excavating nest tunnels; the opposing toes of woodpeckers aid in clinging to tree trunks.

Birds of prey have powerful feet, strong, sharp, highly curved claws and roughened pads on the undersides of their toes to help them readily grasp prey. The padded toes of fish-eating Osprey have spines to help hold on to slippery fishes. Birds that spend a lot of time walking tend to have flat feet with a reduced backward-pointing toe; and if, like waders, they often walk on soft surfaces, they may have some webbing between the toes (e.g. Semipalmated Sandpiper). Species that scratch a great deal (such as game birds) have blunt, thick claws attached to powerful legs. Ptarmigans, which walk on snow, have heavily feathered (highly insulated) feet that function as snowshoes. Ravens in the Arctic have up to six times thicker horny insulating soles than do tropical ravens. Birds with bare legs, especially those with webbed feet, have circulatory adaptations to help them avoid problems of heat loss from their extremities.

Birds that swim generally have webbing between their toes so that the feet can be used to paddle. Lobes, rather than webbing, are often found on the toes of birds, such as Coots, that divide their time between swimming and walking on mud. Jacanas, tropical relatives of the waders, have extremely long toes that spread their weight enough to permit them to walk on floating aquatic vegetation, including lily pads — giving them the common name 'lily trotters'.

SEE: Swimming and Underwater Flight, p. 61; Temperature Regulation and Behaviour, p. 163; 'Passerines' and 'Songbirds', p. 351; Avian Snowshoes, p. 123.

Breeding Season

EVOLUTION generally has adjusted the timing of avian breeding seasons to maximize the number of young produced. In the temperate, sub-arctic, and arctic zones, the overriding factor is the availability of food. Abundant nourishment is needed, not only by growing nestlings and juveniles, but also to meet increased energy demands of breeding adults. For females those increased demands include the energetic burden of producing eggs; males need additional energy to support vigorous displays and to defend territories. Generally one or both adults participate in constructing a nest, foraging for more than one individual (mate or chicks), and providing territorial defence or guarding young from predators.

For most birds the young hatch and grow when insects are abundant. In the arctic and sub-arctic, egg-laying is concentrated primarily in May and June to take advantage of the late June–early July flush of mosquitoes,

Three-toed Woodpecker

Picoides tridactylus

ATLAS 185; PMH 159; PER 148; HFP 196; HPCW -; NESTS 215; BWP4:913

1–10m	BLDS: ♂♀ Monogamy	3–5 (–7) 1 brood INCU: ♂♀ 11

FLDG: ♂♀ 22–25	Sap	

Breeding habitat Mainly thick northern forests, usually conifer or birch, with wet patches. Isolated populations in conifers in mountains of C Europe (see notes).

Displays ♂ (sometimes ♀) defends territory with drumming. Has head-swaying and wing-spreading displays like other woodpeckers.

Nesting Nest hole is drilled in dead tree; no lining, retains wood fragments. Eggs white, 25mm, hatch synchronously. Young remain with parents for several weeks.

Diet Insects, mainly wood-boring beetles. Also drills holes for sap (see Great Spotted Woodpecker).

Winters Resident.

Conservation Local declines, but widely distributed in boreal forests in Europe, Asia, and N America, with isolated populations in mountains elsewhere. See p. 529.

Notes Most woodpeckers have two toes pointing forward and two pointing backwards, an arrangement that gives them a good grip on the tree trunks. For reasons not well understood, this species has lost one of the back-pointing toes. See essay on feet, p. 289.

This species illustrates how changing climate affects bird distributions. Why should a species be found in such separate locations, when most of the individuals are resident, and use a habitat that is not continuous across Europe? After the last glaciation, as the climate warmed, boreal forests moved up in latitude and elevation, 'stranding' this species on mountain tops in central Europe.

Essays Declines in Forest Birds: Europe and America, p. 339; Birds on Borders, p. 95; Nonvocal Sounds, p. 263.

Bar-tailed Desert Lark

Ammomanes cincturus

ATLAS 198; PMH 250; PER -; HFP 200; HPCW 152; NESTS 219; BWP5:59

	BLDS: ? Monogamy	2–4 (–5) ? brood INCU: ? ?

FLDG: ? ?	Greens	Foliage glean

Breeding habitat Open stony or sandy desert.

Displays Not well known; ♂ has song-flights like Desert Lark, a wandering up and down flight with slow deep wing-beats, while singing.

Nesting Territorial. Nest is a saucer of dry plant material rimmed with small stones. Eggs white, with a few black, pale purple, and grey spots, 22mm.

Diet Seeds, other vegetation, and insects; runs rapidly, stopping to pick from surface or low plants.

Winters Resident; in flocks.

Conservation Distribution is not well known, occurs across Sahara, Arabia into SW Asia.

Essays Songbird Foraging, p. 417; Walking vs. Hopping, p. 375.

blackflies, butterflies, and other six-legged prey. The supply is rich near the pole, but the season is short, and birds must court, mate, and nest while there is still the risk of frigid storms. In fact, geese that nest in the arctic arrive on snow-covered breeding grounds in order to lay and start incubating as soon as nest sites are clear. The geese depend on reserves of body fat to sustain them in the initially food-poor environment.

In general, among passerines the number of broods raised annually decreases as the poles are approached. Widely distributed species in Europe that manage to rear only one brood at the northern edge of their ranges, may rear two or more at their southern limits. In temperate areas, many passerine species commonly re-nest if a clutch or brood is lost; in contrast, many non-passerines can produce only one brood. In some non-passerines, such as arctic-breeding geese, the reproductive organs begin to shrink as soon as the eggs are laid. These birds would have neither the energy reserves to lay replacement eggs if a clutch were lost, nor sufficient time to rear the young of a second clutch even if one could be produced. In fact, the young of arctic-breeding geese often do not have time to mature fully before winter conditions return, and seasons without successful breeding are common for species such as Brent, Barnacle, and Snow Geese (*Chen caerulescens*).

Although not the only factors, assured food supplies and accompanying benign weather are by far the two most common influences that affect the timing of avian breeding seasons. To find examples of other factors, however, we must look outside of Europe. For instance, the Clay-colored Robin (*Turdus grayi*) breeds in the dry season in Panama when food is relatively scarce, as fewer losses of eggs and young to predators more than compensate for the risk of starvation for the chicks.

In addition to weather, food availability, vulnerability to predation, and other such 'ultimate' causes favouring the evolution of breeding at a particular time, we must consider environmental changes that are 'proximate' triggers of breeding behaviour. The overwhelming majority of bird species living outside of the tropics sense the lengthening days as spring approaches and use this as the trigger to begin breeding. Day length, *per se*, has relatively little to do with breeding success, although, of course, long hours of daylight to forage — especially for time-constrained bird populations in the Far North — can be very important. But evolution seems to have latched on to day length as a 'timer' of activities, since it is a predictable signal that accurately forecasts future events.

If, for example, birds that breed in the arctic did not start to develop their reproductive organs until insects were abundant, the insects would be gone before the eggs hatched. The day-length cue for development occurs long before the insects emerge. Proximate factors (weather and associated abundance of food) also play important roles in initiating the springtime changes in reproductive physiology, and especially in fine-tuning responses to the cues already provided by day length. Dunnocks experimentally provided with abundant food will begin laying their eggs about two to three weeks earlier than birds without supplemented diets.

At least some birds also have 'biological calendars', internal timing devices

Desert Lark
Ammomanes deserti

ATLAS 198; PMH –; PER -; HFP 200; HPCW 152; NESTS 218; BWP5:65

 | BLDS: ♂♀ Monogamy | 1–5 1–2 broods INCU: ? ? | FLDG: ♂♀ ? | Greens

Breeding habitat Rocky, hilly areas in desert and semi-desert regions; avoids open desert flats.

Displays ♂ has undulating song flight with deep slow wing-beats between perches; also a steeply ascending flight; there are courtship chases between members of a pair.

Nesting Nest is a scrape lined with vegetation and edged with small stones in available cover. Eggs pinkish to greenish-white with reddish-brown and other dark spots, 20mm. Young leave the nest before they are able to fly and are fed by adults for several weeks.

Diet Seeds, green shoots, and insects, taken on ground or from low plants.

Winters Resident; sometimes in small flocks.

Conservation Population size is not well known, but widely distributed across Sahara to India.

Essays Drinking, p. 313; Temperature Regulation and Behaviour, p. 163.

Hoopoe Lark
Alaemon alaudipes

ATLAS 199; PMH 250; PER -; HFP 198; HPCW 153; NESTS 217; BWP5:74

 Ground | ? BLDS: ? ? | ? 1 Brood? INCU: ♀,♂● 14? | FLDG: ♂♀ ? | Ground glean

Breeding habitat Open flat sandy or mixed desert, desert grasslands.

Displays When disturbed has habit of running quickly away from intruder, rather like Cream-coloured Courser. ♂ has conspicuous song flight, flies up vertically, singing, with wings fluttering and tail open to show bold markings, then steeply descends, sometimes somersaulting towards ground. Courtship pursuits between pairs.

Nesting Nest is a saucer of twigs, lined with grass and soft material, in small shrub or on ground. Eggs white, to light buff variously marked reddish-brown, 24mm. Young remain with adults several weeks after fledging.

Diet Insects, snails; walks or runs then stops to dig prey from below surface.

Winters Resident.

Conservation Widespread and locally common across Sahara, Arabia, SW Asia.

that are independent of external environmental cues and tell them when it is time to breed. Consider experiments involving the Short-tailed Shearwater, a Southern Hemisphere species that 'winters' in the summer off the Pacific coast of North America but breeds on islands near Australia. Birds were kept in a laboratory for over a year and subjected to a constant light regime, 12 hours of light and 12 hours of darkness, for the entire period. In spite of this constancy, their reproductive organs developed and their feathers moulted at the same time as those of Short-tailed Shearwaters in the wild. The physiological basis for biological clocks and calendars — the mechanisms by which they function — remains one of the great mysteries of biology.

SEE: Hormones and Nest Building, p. 329; Metabolism, p. 281; Timing of Migration, p. 405; Variation in Clutch Sizes, p. 55. REFS: Davies and Lundberg, 1985; Marshall and Serventy, 1959; Morton, 1971.

Natural Selection

THE characteristics of birds result from evolutionary processes, the most important process being natural selection. Charles Darwin was the first to point out that just as stock owners shaped their herds by selecting which animals would be allowed to breed, so too nature shaped all organisms by 'selecting' the progenitors of the next generation. Darwin's thinking had been influenced by the great economist Thomas Malthus, who emphasized the capacity of people and other organisms to multiply their numbers much more rapidly than their means of subsistence. Darwin realized, therefore, that most individuals born of any species could not have survived long enough to reproduce. He concluded that those able to survive and reproduce had not been a random sample of those born, bur rather variants especially suited to their environments.

Darwin knew nothing about genetics; the work of Gregor Mendel remained undiscovered until early in the twentieth century, almost fifty years after the publication of *Origin of species*. We now know that variation among individuals is due to both environmental and hereditary factors. Inherited variation results from the joint action of mutation (changes in the genes themselves) and, in birds and all other sexually reproducing organisms, recombination. Basically, recombination is the reshuffling of genes that occurs during the process of sperm and egg production. Because of mutation and recombination, each individual bird is genetically unique — that is, each has a unique 'genotype'. Geneticists typically examine only a small portion of the genetic endowment of an individual, such as the two pairs of genes (out of many thousands) that cause a cock's comb to be single and large or pea-shaped and small. Thus one might speak of the 'single-comb' and 'pea-comb' genotypes.

In modern evolutionary genetics, natural selection is defined as the differential reproduction of genotypes (individuals of some genotypes have more

Dupont's Lark

Chersophilus duponti

ATLAS 199; PMH 160; PER 150; HFP 200; HPCW 153; NESTS 219; BWP5:82

BLDS: ?
Monogamy

3–4 (2–5)
1 (2?) brood
INCU: ?
?

FLDG: ?
?

Seeds

Breeding habitat   Dry grasslands or low shrub.

Displays   Has song flight, rising high into sky for long periods, like Skylark.

Nesting   Nests on ground sheltered by plant tussock or other cover; a scrape lined with vegetation. Eggs white to pinkish, heavily spotted red-brown, 24mm.

Diet   Insects and seeds, dug from surface of ground.

Winters   Resident, some dispersal; moves to cereal fields; flocks with other species of larks.

Conservation   Range and numbers not well known. Locally common but secretive habits make it difficult to count. In Spain and isolated areas of N Africa. See p. 528.

Notes   Probably named in honour of Léonard Dupont, by Vieillot, the ornithologist who first described the bird.

Thick-billed Lark

Rhamphocorys clotbey

ATLAS 192; PMH -; PER -; HFP 203; HPCW 154; NESTS 220; BWP5:87

BLDS: ?
?

3–5 (2–6)
1 brood?
INCU: ?
?

FLDG: ?
?

Insects

Foliage glean

Breeding habitat   Dry grasslands or desert edges with little vegetation.

Displays   Has erratic song flight, rising high into sky but little known about this and other displays.

Nesting   Territorial. Nest is on ground sheltered by bush, sometimes in open, lined with vegetation. Eggs white to pinkish, with fine red-brown spots, 26mm.

Diet   Seeds, other plant parts, and insects, dug from surface of ground, or removed from plants.

Winters   Resident, some nomadic dispersal; sometimes in large flocks.

Conservation   Range and population size not well known; occurs from Morocco to Arabia.

Essays   Songbird Foraging, p. 417; Walking vs. Hopping, p. 375.

offspring survive to breed in the next generation while individuals of other genotypes have fewer such offspring). Natural selection would be occurring if, in a population of jungle fowl (the wild progenitors of chickens), single-comb genotypes were reproductively more successful than pea-comb genotypes. Note that the emphasis is not on *survival* (as it was in Herbert Spencer's famous phrase 'survival of the fittest') but on *reproduction*. Thus while selection can occur because some individuals do not survive long enough to reproduce, sterile individuals also lack 'fitness' in an evolutionary sense, as do individuals unable to find mates. We emphasize that fitness here refers only to the reproductive success of a kind of individual — if big, handsome, male grouse madly displaying on a lek turn out to have fewer offspring than smaller, drab males that skulk in the bushes and waylay females, it is the wimpy males that are more fit.

Natural selection provides a context in which to view the physical and behavioural characteristics of birds. Whether it is the large size of a female Sparrowhawk in comparison with the male, the territorial behaviour of a Redshank, the bill shape of a Scottish Crossbill, or the coloniality of a Shag, a key question to ask is 'how did natural selection manage that'?

SEE: Selection in Nature, p. 471; Altruism, p. 245; Sexual Selection, p. 149; Coevolution, p. 239; Size and Sex in Raptors, p. 99; Geometry of the Selfish Colony, p. 15. REFS: Ehrlich, 1986*a*; Ehrlich and Roughgarden, 1987; Futuyma, 1987; Seger, 1987.

Feathered Dinosaurs?

FOR years biologists have half-jokingly referred to birds as 'feathered reptiles'. In part, it is a ploy to annoy bird lovers with the thought that the objects of their fancy are just singing lizards wrapped in stretched-out scales called 'feathers'. Yet the phrase reflects an important biological reality: birds are undeniably the modified descendants of reptiles, as their body structure and habit of laying eggs out of water clearly show.

The fossil record of ancient birds is not extensive. One probable reason is that birds have hollow light bones to aid flight, and those bones crush easily and tend to disintegrate before fossilization is complete. Also, probably few early birds lived in areas (such as swamps and estuaries) where fossils are readily preserved. The existence of several superb specimens of *Archaeopteryx* preserved in slate compensates for this paucity of fossils. Some 150 million years ago, at the end of the Jurassic period, *Archaeopteryx* was a denizen of warm swamps in what is now Bavaria in Germany.

Archaeopteryx makes an ideal 'missing link', showing characteristics intermediate between reptiles and birds. It had teeth like those of reptiles, but feathers almost identical with those of modern birds. Its long bony tail was reptilian, but had feathers attached to it. Its elongated forelimbs resembled those of modern birds, but had three movable clawed fingers, which presum-

Calandra Lark

Melanocorypha calandra

ATLAS 193; PMH 160; PER 150; HFP 202; HPCW 154; NESTS 219; BWP5:93

BLDS: ♂♀
Monogamy

4–5 (3–6)
2 broods
IN:♀(♂♀?)
12–16

FLDG: ♂♀
?

Probes

Breeding habitat Open grasslands, dry agricultural land.

Displays Sings from ground, low bush, or commonly in circling display flight, with slow deep wing-beats. Sometimes small groups of ♂s may sing at same time.

Nesting Territorial. Nest is on ground in cover of plants; a saucer lined with grasses. Eggs whitish to pale yellow, heavily and variously marked darker, 25mm.

Diet Insects in summer, seeds and shoots in winter; runs along ground picking items from surface; sometimes digs.

Winters Mainly resident; some migration in E. Often in large flocks.

Conservation Has decreased in Europe, but widely distributed across S Europe, N Africa, and SW Asia. See p. 528.

Essays Territoriality, p. 397.

Bimaculated Lark

Melanocorypha bimaculata

ATLAS 193; PMH 251; PER -; HFP 202; HPCW 154; NESTS 219; BWP5:103

BLDS: ♀
Monogamy

3–5 (6)
1 (2?) broods
INCU: ♀
12–13

FLDG: ♂♀
?

Foliage glean

Breeding habitat Mountain slopes in grasslands; fields.

Displays Has display flight like that of Calandra Lark. ♂s often seen chasing each other.

Nesting Territorial. Nests on ground in shelter of vegetation; a saucer lined with plant material. Eggs white or greyish, heavily spotted with buffish to reddish-brown, 24mm.

Diet Insects in summer (also fed to young), seeds in winter. Takes seeds from ground or from low plants.

Winters Resident, or migrates S to Arabia, India; in desert areas or agricultural fields. Often in large flocks.

Conservation Numbers not known; restricted to SW and central Asia.

Essays Flock Defence, p. 257.

ably were useful for climbing trees. (Chicks of the South American Hoatzin, the only living bird with clawed forelimbs, do use them in clambering through branches.) *Archaeopteryx* had other features that today are unique to birds, a 'wishbone' (furcula) formed by the fusion of the collarbones (clavicles) and two lobes on the bone that connects the jaw to the skull. But it lacked a robust, bony keel (part of the sternum) to which strong flight muscles could be attached. *Archaeopteryx* certainly could not fly as well as a modern bird, but it has been suggested that with the muscles of a reptile (which gram for gram are about twice as powerful as those of birds), *Archaeopteryx* could have flown 1.5–2 kilometres.

Recently a fossil bird some 135 million years old was discovered in China that shares many more morphological features with modern birds, including a sternum, a fused cluster of tail vertebrae to support tail feathers, and curved claws with an opposable first digit (to allow it to grasp branches). This fossil and others about 125 million years old from Spain and Mongolia suggest that early avian evolution was strongly and rapidly shaped by the requirements of flight.

Archaeopteryx tells us a great deal about what the distant ancestors of modern birds were like, but we run into controversy again when trying to trace *Archaeopteryx* back to its precise reptilian ancestors. One view, still held by some palaeontologists, suggests that about 200 million years ago its ancestral line split off from a group of reptiles, the thecodonts. Thecodonts are considered ancestral to crocodiles, dinosaurs, and pterosaurs (contemporaries of dinosaurs that could fly but were unrelated to birds). Some thecodonts resembled crocodiles or Komodo dragons, but two recently discoverd 200-million-year-old tit-sized thecodont fossils show interesting bird-like features. One has similarities in the skull and signs of feather-like structures; the other has clavicles fused into a furcula and also has elongated scales.

More recently, palaeontologist John Ostrom has concluded that instead of being derived from thecodonts, the birds are descended directly from a group of relatively small, agile, predatory dinosaurs called coelurosaurs. Some coelurosaurs were quite ostrich-like, and the forelimbs of others were constructed very much like those of *Archaeopteryx*.

The debate between these views impinges on another argument still raging in palaeontology — were the dinosaurs 'warm-blooded'? Some claim that the metabolism (the chemical and physical processes that maintain life) of dinosaurs was more like that of birds and mammals than reptiles. They credit the dinosaurs with evolving highly efficient circulatory systems, regulating their body temperature by generating their own heat, and being relatively smart. Others remain convinced that dinosaurs, like modern reptiles, were 'cold-blooded' creatures that regulated their temperature behaviourally, moving in and out of the sun, orienting at different angles to it, and becoming torpid when it was cold and sunless.

Some enthusiasts for the 'warm-blooded dinosaurs' theory have gone so far as to suggest that dinosaurs be moved out of the reptiles and classified with the birds. There is a certain charm to the notion that the dinosaurs did not disappear 65 million years ago, and that some can be found today visiting

White-winged Lark
Melanocorypha leucoptera

ATLAS 193; PMH 160; PER -; HFP 202; HPCW 155; NESTS 220; BWP5:109

  |

BLDS: ♀	5–6 (4–7)	FLDG: ♂♀
Monogamy?	1 (2?) brood	?
	INCU: ♀	
	12	

Breeding habitat Dry grasslands.

Displays Not well known. Has song flight above territory with slow deep wing-beats, or from low bush.

Nesting Territorial. Nest is saucer of grass on ground in cover. Eggs white to pale buff or greenish, variably spotted brownish, 23mm. Young leave nest before fledging and are fed by parents.

Diet Insects and seeds in the summer, seeds in the winter.

Winters Moves to areas S and W of breeding range into more mixed habitats. In flocks.

Conservation Numbers poorly known; has limited range in CIS and probably has declined due to 'virgin lands' policy of ploughing steppes.

Essays Birds and Agriculture, p. 365.

Black Lark
Melanocorypha yeltoniensis

ATLAS 194; PMH 161; PER -; HFP 202; HPCW 155; NESTS 220; BWP5:115

  |

BLDS: ♀	4–7 (8)	FLDG: ?	
Monogamy	1 (2?) brood	?	
Polygyny	INCU: ♀	Insects	Foliage glean
	15–16		

Breeding habitat Dry grasslands, often with shrubs, near water.

Displays ♂ sings on ground or low perch with wings dropped and tail raised. Wings may also be extended to front of bird and bird may run along ground while singing. Also has song flight, with such deep beats that wings may meet over back. ♂s chase each other when setting up territories.

Nesting Territorial. Nest is a saucer of dead grass on ground in cover. Eggs greyish to bluish-white marked buff, brown and grey, 26mm. Some ♂s are polygynous.

Diet Seeds and insects in the summer, seeds in the winter, dug from the snow. Also takes seeds on low plants.

Winters Resident or moves to areas S and W of breeding range, looking for areas of light snow; in nomadic flocks, sometimes large ones.

Conservation Not well known; probably has lost habitat with ploughing of the steppes and has relatively limited range in CIS.

Essays Birds and Agriculture, p. 365; Polygyny, p. 265; Black and White Plumage, p. 7.

our feeders or singing territorial songs in the local wood. This nomenclatural change would seem premature, however, especially since the name of the older group might catch on and, as palaeontologist Alan Charig has pointed out, prompt us to change some old proverbs. Do we really want to say 'a dinosaur in the hand is worth two in the bush', or 'dinosaurs of a feather flock together'?

SEE: *Hesperornis* and Other Missing Links, p. 129; How Do Birds Fly?, p. 217; Adaptations for Flight, p. 511; Origin of Flight, p. 157; Natural Selection, p. 297. REFS: Charig, 1979; Cracraft, 1986, 1988; Desmond, 1975; Hecht, 1990; Martin, 1983; Ostrom, 1979; Sanz *et al.*, 1988; Wellnhofer, 1988.

Island Biogeography

WHY do many more species of birds breed in Britain than on the island of Ireland? One answer is that Britain is larger than Ireland, and numbers of species ordinarily increase with available space. This does not, however, explain why so many species seem curiously absent from Ireland, or Britain, when they breed commonly in adjacent areas of continental Europe. Why, for example, does Ireland lack the three woodpecker species that breed widely in Britain? Why does the Crested Lark breed close to Calais but not above the white cliffs of Dover?

Two eminent ecologists, the late Robert MacArthur of Princeton University and E. O. Wilson of Harvard, in the 1960s developed a theory of 'island biogeography' to explain such uneven distributions. They proposed that the number of species on any island reflects a balance between the rate at which new species colonize it and the rate at which populations of established species become extinct. If a new volcanic island were to rise out of the ocean off the coast of a mainland inhabited by 100 species of birds, some birds would begin to immigrate across the gap and establish populations on the bird-free island as soon as enough plants, insects, and so forth had colonized the island to make it habitable. The rate at which these immigrant species could become established, however, would inevitably decline, for each species that successfully invaded the island would diminish by one the pool of possible future invaders (the same 100 species continue to live on the mainland, but those which have already become residents of the island can no longer be classed as potential invaders).

Equally, the rate at which species might become extinct on the island would be related to the number that have become residents. When an island is nearly empty, the extinction rate is necessarily low because few species are available to become extinct. Now the resources of an island are limited. Therefore, as the number of resident species increases so the average population of each species will tend to become smaller. This, and the very fact that there are more species, means that the rate at which species become extinct

Short-toed Lark

Calandrella brachydactyla

ATLAS 197; PMH 161; PER 150; HFP 200; HPCW 156; NESTS 218; BWP5:123

BLDS: ♀, ♂ ♥
Monogamy?

3–5 (6)
2 broods
INCU: ♂ ♥
13

 A
FLDG: ♂ ♀
12–13

Insects

Foliage glean

Breeding habitat A wide variety of dry open country, also salt marshes with *Salicornia*.

Displays ♂ has song flight over territory. Ascends, sings while wandering over territory, glides down to ground, then ascends again, repeating these up-and-down movements for some time. ♂s chase each other from territories.

Nesting Territorial. Nests on ground, usually in shelter; nest is a cup of grasses lined with finer material. Eggs whitish or buff, variously marked with greys and dark browns, 20mm, hatch synchronously. Young leave nest 3 days before fledging.

Diet Insects and seeds in the summer (young fed insects), seeds in winter. Taken from the ground or low plants; sometimes digs.

Winters Migrates to Africa S of the Sahara in dry grasslands. Often in large flocks.

Conservation Local decreases (e.g. France) but often common from S Europe, N Africa, and throughout SW and C Asia. See p. 528.

Essays Songbird Foraging, p. 417; Walking vs. Hopping, p. 375.

Lesser Short-toed Lark

Calandrella rufescens

ATLAS 198; PMH 161; PER 150; HFP 200; HPCW 157; NESTS 218; BWP5:135

BLDS: ♀
Monogamy

3–4 (5)
2 broods
INCU: ♀, ♂ ♥
?

 A
FLDG: ♂ ♀
?

Foliage glean

Breeding habitat Dry open country and salt marshes; overlaps with Short-toed Lark, but also in drier habitats.

Displays ♂s sing in flight or from low perch. Has song flight with alternating fluttering ascents and gliding descents.

Nesting Territorial. Nest is saucer of vegetation on ground in cover. Eggs white to light brown, variously marked darker brown, 20mm. Young leave nest before they are able to fly.

Diet Insects in summer and seeds in winter; feeds like Short-toed Lark; also flies from ground to catch insects on wing.

Winters Resident (W) or migrates southward (E), wintering in semi-desert areas. Often in large flocks.

Conservation Numbers not well known; often common from S Europe, N Africa across middle latitudes of Asia.

Essays Walking vs. Hopping, p. 375.

increases as the number of residents increases. The rate at which additional species will establish populations will be high when the island is relatively empty, and the rate at which resident populations go extinct will be high when the island is relatively full. Thus, there must be a point between 0 and 100 species (the number on the mainland) where the two rates are equal — where input from immigration balances output from extinction. That equilibrium number of species would be expected to remain constant as long as the factors determining the two rates did not change. But the exact species present *should* change continuously as some species go extinct and others invade (including some that have previously gone extinct), so that there is a steady *turnover* in the composition of the fauna.

That is the essence of the MacArthur–Wilson equilibrium theory of island biogeography. How well does it explain what we actually observe in nature? One famous 'test' of the theory was provided in 1883 by the catastrophic volcanic explosion that devastated the island of Krakatoa, located between the islands of Sumatra and Java. The flora and fauna of its remnant (and of two adjacent islands) were completely exterminated, yet within 25 years (1908) thirteen species of birds had recolonized what was left of the island. By 1919–21 twenty-eight bird species were present, and by 1932–34, twenty-nine. Between the explosion and 1934, thirty-four species actually became established, but five of them went extinct. By 1951–52 thirty-three species were present, and by 1984–85, thirty-five species. During this half century (1934–85), a further fourteen species had become established, and eight had become extinct. As the theory predicted, the rate of increase declined as more and more species colonized the island. In addition, as equilibrium was approached there was some turnover. The number in the cast remained roughly the same while some of the actors were gradually replaced.

The theory predicts other things, too. For instance, everything else being equal, distant islands will have lower immigration rates than those close to a mainland, and equilibrium will occur with fewer species on distant islands. Close islands will have high immigration rates and support more species. By similar reasoning, large islands, with their lower extinction rates, will have more species than small ones — again everything else being equal (which it frequently is not, for larger islands often have a greater variety of habitats and more species for that reason alone).

Island biogeographic theory has been applied to many kinds of problems, including forecasting faunal changes caused by fragmenting previously continuous habitat. For instance, in much of Europe only patches of the once-great deciduous forest remain, and many species of songbirds are disappearing from those patches. One reason for the decline in birds, according to the theory, is that fragmentation leads to both lower immigration rates (gaps between fragments are not crossed easily) and higher extinction rates (less area supports fewer species).

Long-term studies of a bird community in an oak wood in Surrey, England, support the view that isolation can influence the avifauna of habitat islands. A rough equilibrium number of 32 breeding species was found in that community, with a turnover of three additions and three extinctions annually. It

Crested Lark
Galerida cristata

ATLAS 195; PMH 162; PER 150; HFP 204; HPCW 158; NESTS 222; BWP5:145

		3–5 (7) 2 (3?) broods		
BLDS: ♀	INCU: ♀, ♂●	FLDG: ♂♀		
Monogamy	11–13	15–18		Foliage glean

Breeding habitat Dry, open ground, agricultural fields, often near towns.

Displays ♂ sings from ground, perch, or in flight. In song flight, rises to high above ground with fluttering, hovering flight or meanders over territory. Flights last about 5 minutes. ♂ chases rivals on ground or in low flight off territory. In courtship ♂ lifts tail and crest, dances around ♀.

Nesting Territorial. Nest is a saucer of grass; on ground in cover. Eggs off-white to buff, with fine grey and brown spots, 23mm, hatch within 2 days of each other; young leave nest several days before they can fly.

Diet Insects (especially beetles) and seeds in the summer, mainly seeds in the winter. Taken from surface or dug from ground (also dung). Sometimes hawks for flying insects. Young fed insects.

Winters Mainly resident; northern populations move south. In small groups.

Conservation Has decreased in the N, but common and widespread across Europe, N Africa, and parts of Asia.

Notes Does not breed in the UK or on many Mediterranean islands that are within the general range of this species and which surely provide the habitats for a species with such generalized habitat requirements. Islands often lack species for reasons to do with the low rate of colonization and the high rate of species extinction of the small founder populations: see essay on Island Biogeography, p. 303.

Thekla Lark
Galerida theklae

ATLAS 196; PMH 162; PER 150; HFP 204; HPCW 159; NESTS 223; BWP5:163

		3–4 (2–7) 2 broods	
BLDS: ?	INCU: ♀	FLDG: ?	
Monogamy	?	15?	

Breeding habitat Like that of Crested Lark, but rather more common on hillsides and bushy areas.

Displays ♂s sing from ground, perch, or in flight. Song flights like that of Crested Lark, and last for about 5 minutes.

Nesting Territorial. Nest is a saucer of grass; on ground in cover. Eggs grey to buff, with fine grey and brown spotting; 23mm. Young leave nest up to a week before they can fly.

Diet Mainly insects in summer and seeds in winter; does not dig, but probes under stones, flipping small ones aside. Young fed insects.

Winters Resident. Not usually in flocks.

Conservation Locally common in Spain and N Africa. See p. 528.

was projected that if the wood were as thoroughly isolated as an oceanic island, it would maintain only five species over an extended period — two species of tits, the Wren, the Robin, and Blackbird. Similar results are found for islands like Bardsey and Skokholm that house bird observatories. Counts of breeding birds over several decades show that many species colonize the island only to become locally extinct later. Indeed, this turnover in species is obvious in the breeding birds of Britain, although at a much lower rate.

Island biogeographic theory can be a great help in understanding the effects of habitat fragmentation. It does not, however, address other factors that can greatly influence which birds reside in a fragment. Some of these include whether nest-robbing species are present in such abundance that they could prevent certain invaders from establishing themselves, whether the fragment is large enough to contain a territory of the size required by some members of the pool of potential residents, or whether other critical habitat requirements of species in that pool can be satisfied. To take an extreme example of the latter, a grass-covered, treeless habitat in Belgium would not be colonized by Black Woodpeckers, even if it were large and Black Woodpeckers were found in adjacent woodlands.

Island, biogeographic theory is now more than a quarter century old, and has come under attack for its shortcomings. But that's how it should be. Ecological theory is designed to help us think about the real world, but it is not a substitute for an intimate knowledge of nature's ways.

SEE: Declines in Forest Birds: Europe and America, p. 339; Habitat Selection, p. 423.
REFS: Butcher et al., 1981; MacArthur and Wilson, 1967; Rusterholz and Howe, 1979; Schoener and Spiller, 1987; Williamson, 1981, 1989.

Sonagrams: Seeing Bird Songs

TWO people attempting to describe a Skylark's song may conjure up two entirely different sound images. Both would agree that it undulates in pitch and includes some whistle-like phrases, some trills, and some buzzes. But such a verbal description is most unsatisfying to anyone who has never heard the song. It is equally unsatisfactory for the ornithologist wishing to examine questions of individual repertoire size and variation, the amount of song and syllable sharing among individuals, the existence of dialects, or the degree of geographic variation in songs among populations. With the development of the sound spectrograph or sonagraph, it became possible for the first time to approach these questions in an objective and quantitative manner, which has resulted in an impressive number of studies over the past thirty years. This work was facilitated by the development of high-quality portable tape

Woodlark

Lullula arborea

ATLAS 195; PMH 162; PER 152; HFP 204; HPCW 159; NESTS 220; BWP5:173

  3–4 (2–6) 2 (3) broods INCU: ♀ 12–15 BLDS: ♂♀ Monogamy FLDG: ♂♀ 10–13   Foliage glean

Breeding habitat Fields, grasslands with at least a few trees, or openings in or near woods. In UK also burnt heathland.

Displays ♂ sings in flight or from tree. In song flight, bird circles or hovers with fluttering wings, for about 2 minutes; unmated birds may sing for much longer periods.

Nesting Territorial. Nest is a deep cup on ground, lined with finer material including hair; often in cover of bush. Several early stages of nests built by both birds; final nest finished by ♀. Eggs off-white, with brown to grey spotting and blotching, 22mm, hatch synchronously. Young leave nest a few days before they can fly. Young remain with parents into autumn. First brood stays nearby while parents rear second clutch.

Diet Insects in summer (also given to the young) and seeds in winter. Picks up food on ground or from low plants, also digs.

Winters More open areas than in summer; S and W populations resident, others migrate to these areas. In small flocks.

Conservation Has declined in NW and C, but widely distributed across much of Europe, into Turkey and N Africa. See p. 529.

Essays Declines in Forest Birds: Europe and America, p. 339; Hormones and Nest Building, p. 329; Vocal Functions, p. 413.

Refs Marchant et al. 1990.

Skylark

Alauda arvensis

ATLAS 194; PMH 163; PER 150; HFP 204; HPCW 160; NESTS 221; BWP5:188

  3–5 (2–7) 2–3 (4) broods INCU: ♀ 11 BLDS: ♀ Monogamy FLDG: ♂♀ 18–20 Insects   Foliage glean

Breeding habitat A very wide range of open ground, meadows, agricultural fields.

Displays Has familiar song flight, ascending with fluttering wings high in the sky. Flights frequently last for less than 5 minutes, though a small percentage sing for much longer. Birds vigorously defend territories against rivals, fighting with them in air or chasing them off. In courtship, ♂ adopts erect posture and hops in front of ♀.

Nesting Territorial. Nest on ground, in open or in available cover, saucer of grass, lined with finer material. Eggs whitish, heavily spotted with browns, 23mm, hatch synchronously. Young leave nest about 10 days before fledging.

Diet Insects and seeds (summer), seeds (winter). Picks from ground or low plants; sometimes digs.

Winters Resident in SW, migrates to these areas from N and E. In flocks.

Conservation Widespread declines since 1980, in UK, Scandinavia, C Europe, as a consequence of changing farming practices. Species is still abundant throughout Europe, much of Asia, and locally in N Africa.

Notes When Merlins attack singing birds, those that continue to sing vigorously (perhaps showing how fit they are and so how difficult to catch they will be) are less likely to be killed than those that stop singing.

Essays Copulation, p. 87; Birds and Agriculture, p. 365; Territoriality, p. 397; Sonagrams: Seeing Bird Songs, p. 307; Vocal Copying, p. 383.

Refs Marchant et al. 1990.

recorders used in conjunction with microphones mounted in parabolic reflectors or with very sensitive directional microphones.

The sonagraph produces on paper a graphic picture (a 'sonagram') of sound, showing frequency (measured in kilohertz — thousands of cycles per second) on the vertical axis and time (in seconds) on the horizontal axis. Thus displayed, complex songs can be separated objectively into their constituent components, as shown in the sonagram (below) of a portion of Skylark song. The song begins with a series of trills ascending in pitch, followed by a relatively long tone, then a trill composed of separable, repeated syllables, and note-complex, both of which descend in pitch. This is followed by a series of ascending short notes, a long descending whistle, and a terminating buzzy trill of essentially continuous syllables.

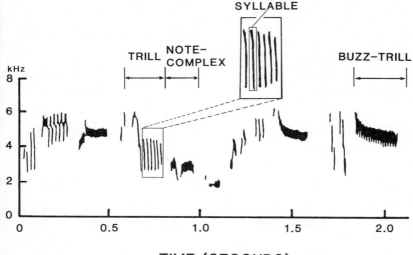

Sonagram composite of Skylark song.

Although the sonagraph was a major advance in the study of bird vocalizations, its utility was somewhat limited by the slow and laborious process of sonagram production, with each sonagram limited to only two and a half seconds of recording. These limitations have been overcome by a new generation of modern frequency spectrum analysers that display sonagrams instantaneously on a visual display unit, and selectively print 'hard copy' that can exceed 10 seconds of continuous sound. Literally thousands of songs now can be scanned and analysed in a relatively short time.

SEE: What Do Birds Hear?, p. 255; Bird Voices, p. 475; Vocal Copying, p. 383; Vocal Dialects, p. 477; Vocal Functions, p. 413.

Shore Lark

Eremophila alpestris

ATLAS 200; PMH 163; PER 152; HFP 198; HPCW 160; NESTS 216; BWP5:210

BLDS: ♀	2–4 (5)	FLDG: ♂♀	
Monogamy	1 (2) broods	16–18	Foliage glean
	INCU: ♀		
	10–11		

Breeding habitat Two populations; one in dry arctic tundra, in Scandinavia and Russia; the second on mountain tops in Morocco, eastern Europe, and eastward.

Displays Sings on ground or in flight. Ascends, sometimes silently, to high in the sky, alternating a fluttering flight with gliding, singing continuously. Flights may last less than 5 minutes, but longer in some areas. ♂ chases rivals on the ground.

Nesting Territorial. Nest is on ground in cover; a saucer of grass, lined with finer material. Eggs off-white, heavily spotted buff to brown, finely lined with black and brown, 23mm. Two broods in lower latitudes, one in higher; hatch synchronously. Young leave the nest about a week before fledging.

Diet Insects in summer (and fed to young), but also some seeds; seeds in winter. Taken from ground or low plants.

Winters Northern populations move S; often coastal on shingle beaches, salt marshes, agricultural land; southern populations resident. In flocks.

Conservation Marked declines in Finland and Scandinavia since the 1970s, for reasons not understood; but very widely distributed mainly in arctic N America, Europe, Asia; also montane E Europe through Asia; grasslands in N America.

Notes This species illustrates how changing climate affects bird distributions. Why should a species be found in such separate locations? After the last glaciation, as the climate warmed, tundra moved up in latitude and elevation, 'stranding' some populations of this species on mountain tops in the S and E.

Temminck's Horned Lark

Eremophila bilopha

ATLAS 200; PMH -; PER -; HFP 199; HPCW 161; NESTS 216; BWP5:225

BLDS: ?	2–4	FLDG: ?	
Monogamy?	1 brood?	16–17?	Insects	Foliage glean
	INCU: ?		
	?		

Breeding habitat Dry grasslands, desert shrub, to edges of desert in lowlands (compare these habitats with those occupied by Shore Lark in N Africa).

Displays Not well known, but similar to those of Shore Lark. Song given on ground or in flight, but bird does not rise high into the air. ♂ raises black 'horns' on head, ruffles feathers, drops wings, and spreads tail at ♀.

Nesting Territorial? Nest is on ground in cover; saucer of grass, lined with finer material. Eggs off-white, heavily spotted buff to brown, finely lined with black and brown, 22mm.

Diet Seeds and insects; taken from ground or low plants.

Winters Resident; in flocks.

Conservation Locally common across N Africa into Middle East and Arabia.

Essays Songbird Foraging, p. 417; Walking vs. Hopping, p. 375.

Birds and Global Warming

As the human population explodes and more and more people struggle for affluence, the burden of so-called 'greenhouse gases' in the atmosphere is increasing steadily. There is a growing consensus among scientists that this will lead to a global warming, and that, in turn, will result in substantial climatic change. The odds are perhaps 50–50 that change will occur with unprecedented rapidity, and have severe deleterious effects on natural ecosystems — to say nothing of agriculture and all human enterprises carried out on lowlying land near the sea, which will be inundated.

Bird communities will not escape the consequences of this warming, although it is very difficult to predict specific impacts because climatic models cannot provide very precise local predictions. In many temperate areas, for instance, climate bands may shift too rapidly for forests to 'keep up'. Climate may warm as much as 2–5°C in the next century, and each degree of rise could result in a shift in the range of tree species of about 100–150 km. In the American state of Michigan the endangered Kirtland's Warbler (*Dendroica kirtlandii*) can only breed in young stands of jack pine on sandy soils. Computer models indicate that, in a few decades, the jack pines may vanish from those soils and lead to the extinction of the warbler.

If atmospheric scientists are correct, Kirtland's Warbler will be just the tip of the iceberg. Many alpine and arctic bird populations may also disappear with their habitats. For example, birds such as the Ptarmigan on Scottish mountains will die out as their limited habitat changes to that found today lower down the mountainsides. As they are isolated, the birds have nowhere higher in altitude or further north to move to. Many boreal species may also find their habitats dwindling.

But it is not just birds of cold climates that will suffer. As the seas rise, waders may find their mudflats flooded at a greater rate than the rate at which new ones develop further inland. Also, many arid areas in Africa may become still drier, which could lead to the loss of migrant species. Some species, such as the Sand Martin and Whitethroat, have declined in Europe following droughts in the Sahel. These birds need to find good food supplies south of the Sahara after their long desert crossing in autumn, or to fatten up for their return journey in spring. When the Sahel is dry many fail to return. Prolonged or more serious droughts threaten disaster for these species.

Those concerned with bird conservation would do well to press their governments to take strong steps to slow the flow of greenhouse gases into the atmosphere.

SEE: Acid and Eggshells, p. 287; Listing Birds in Danger, p. 526. REFS: Botkin *et al.*, 1991; Ehrlich and Ehrlich, 1990, 1991; Ehrlich *et al.* 1992; Marchant *et al.*, 1990; Schneider, 1989.

Brown-throated Sand Martin
Riparia paludicola

ATLAS 203; PMH -; PER -; HFP 207; HPCW 161; NESTS 226; BWP5:231

1–3m	BLDS: ♂♀ Monogamy?	3–4 1 brood? INCU: ♂♀ 12?	

FLDG: ?
20?

Breeding habitat Much the same as that of the Sand Martin – needs sandy banks for its nest, so commonly found near rivers, lakes, etc. Generally breeds S of Sand Martin but ranges of two species overlap.

Displays Not well known; this species may mate in the air as well as on the ground.

Nesting Moroccan population breeds in the winter. Nests colonially, excavating a hole in a sandy bank, up to 1m deep, lining it with feathers and grass. Eggs white, 17mm.

Diet Small insects caught in the air.

Winters Resident; in flocks, outside of breeding season.

Conservation Widely, if locally distributed across Africa, N India, and SE Asia.

Notes Also called Plain Sand Martin.

Essays Disease and Parasitism, p. 315; Mobbing, p. 261; Wing Shapes and Flight, p. 269; Coloniality, p. 107; Nest Sanitation, p. 75; Nest Sites and Materials, p. 443.

Sand Martin
Riparia riparia

ATLAS 203; PMH 148; PER 152; HFP 206; HPCW 161; NESTS 226; BWP5:235

2–4m	BLDS: ♂♀ Monogamy	4–6 (2–7) 2 broods INCU: ♂♀ 14–15	

FLDG: ♂♀
18–26

Breeding habitat Needs sandy banks for its nest, so commonly found near rivers, lakes, gravel pits.

Displays ♂ first occupies old hole or digs shallow hole; at hole, he advertises by singing, ruffling plumage, and vibrating wings. ♀s prospect, looking for suitable holes. There is much calling when birds are choosing sites. Pairs defend burrow vigorously, fighting if necessary.

Nesting Nests colonially, excavating a hole in a sandy bank, up to 1m deep, lined with feathers and vegetation. Eggs white, 18mm, hatch synchronously. More young survive in longer burrows and when pairs nest in synchrony with other pairs in the colony. Only one brood in N.

Diet Small insects caught in the air. Often forages over water, but also open areas over land.

Winters European populations: Africa, S of Sahara, in a wide range of habitats, but usually near water. In flocks. Migration of UK population is well known due to an intensive ringing effort. Birds cross the English Channel to avoid long sea crossing, follow the coast of France, and skirt Pyrenees. Some move across to Mediterranean coast while others cross Spain. Birds travel in flocks, perhaps using traditional routes, and roost at night, usually in reed-beds.

Conservation UK population suffered approximately a 75 per cent decline in 1968–9 (other NW populations similar), probably due to drought in Sahelian wintering grounds. E European populations winter in E Africa where drought was less severe. Species is common and widely distributed across Europe, Asia, and N America.

Notes Birds bathe by flying low over water and dipping into it.

Essays Birds and Global Warming, p. 311; Sleeping Sentries and Mate-guarding, p. 73; Nest Evolution, p. 345; Parent–Chick Recognition in Colonial Nesters, p. 227; Population Dynamics, p. 515; Breeding Site Tenacity, p. 219.

Refs Marchant et al. 1990.

Drinking

As for all living things, water is essential to the survival of birds. All birds lose water to their environment by evaporation from the moist lining of the lungs as they breathe, and although they lack specialized sweat glands, birds also lose water through the skin. Water is also lost when waste products are excreted. The rate of water loss depends primarily on weather, body size, and activity. In hot, dry conditions water loss is high, as birds cool themselves by panting to speed evaporation from the lungs. Like heat loss, it is higher in smaller birds because of their greater surface area in relation to volume. Water loss is also influenced by how much a bird flies as opposed to rests, the time of day it is active, whether it is actively defending a territory, and so forth.

Most birds drink to make up for the loss, and do so by dipping the bill and then tipping the head back to let the water run down into the throat to be swallowed. This dipping-tipping routine may explain the apparent 'sky-pointing' behaviour in long-billed species such as Curlews. Many small birds use dewdrops as a source of water. Pelicans sometimes drink by holding their beaks open in the rain. Fulmars, doves, and pigeons drink more like horses, immersing the bill and sucking up the water. During the winter, many northern species consume snow as a source of water.

Not all land birds need to drink water, however. Hummingbirds, with their largely liquid diet of nectar, normally face a problem of flooding rather than dehydration. Because they must process so much nectar to get the sugar they require they must void huge quantities of urine — the equivalent of 40 gallons per day for a human being! Birds of arid areas may either go very long periods without drinking or never drink at all. They manage this in part by manufacturing water, as we all do, in the process of 'burning' their food (cellular respiration). They also obtain water from their food (even dry seeds contain some), and they conserve water by being active at the coolest times of the day.

The main function of a bird's kidneys is to remove from the blood the nitrogen-containing wastes formed during the breakdown of proteins — and to do so while maintaining the proper balance of water, salts, and other materials in the body. Birds adapted to arid environments can remove these wastes while passing very little water in the urine.

Most mammals excrete these wastes largely in the form of urea, a rather poisonous compound that must be diluted with considerable water. Birds excrete uric acid, which does not dissolve easily in water, is relatively non-toxic, and can be voided nearly dry. Birds, however, must use much more energy to produce the uric acid than mammals do to produce urea. Thus they pay a price for their efficient water retention. Like birds, reptiles excrete uric acid and also pay a high energetic price. Presumably the excretion of uric acid

African Rock Martin / Pale Crag Martin

Ptyonoprogne fuligula

ATLAS 201; PMH -; PER -; HFP 206; HPCW 162; NESTS 225; BWP5:248

3–15m	BLDS: ♂♀ Monogamy?	2–3 1–3 broods INCU: ♂♀ 16–18	FLDG: ♂♀ 15 (–30)	

Breeding habitat Sides of rocky valleys and ravines, also buildings. Habitat differences from Crag Martin are not obvious, but generally occurs to the S of that species.

Displays Poorly known.

Nesting Solitary or colonial. Nest is half cup of mud adhered to the cliff surface, lined with plant material and feathers. Eggs white with black and grey spots, 19mm.

Diet Small insects taken in flight, as birds forage over cliff faces or nearby rivers. Glides frequently.

Winters Resident, often wintering near lakes or marshes and readily exploits insects disturbed by grass fires. In flocks.

Conservation Occurs widely, if locally, across Africa and SW Asia.

Notes Many field guides call this species the Pale Crag Martin, separating it from African Rock Martin. Cramp (1988) groups the two 'species' together.

Essays Disease and Parasitism, p. 315; Mobbing, p. 261; Wing Shapes and Flight, p. 269; Coloniality, p. 107; Nest Sanitation, p. 75; Nest Sites and Materials, p. 443.

Crag Martin

Ptyonoprogne rupestris

ATLAS 201; PMH 164; PER -; HFP 206; HPCW 162; NESTS 225; BWP5:254

	BLDS: ♂♀ Monogamy?	3–5 (1) 2 broods INCU: ♀ (♂♀) 13–17	FLDG: ♂♀ 24–27	

Breeding habitat Sides of rocky valleys and ravines, near water. Rarely nests on buildings.

Displays Defends nest site by diving at intruder, calling. Courtship involves noisy chases.

Nesting Solitary or small loose colonies. Nest is half cup of mud adhered to cliff surface, lined with plant material and feathers. Eggs white with a few red and grey spots, 20mm,

hatch synchronously. Young depend on parents for 1–3 weeks after fledging.

Diet Small insects taken in flight as birds forage over cliff faces or nearby rivers.

Winters Resident in S, migratory in N, moving to N Africa, often wintering near lakes or marshes. In flocks.

Conservation No consistent changes in range. Occurs around Mediterranean and across Asia.

originally evolved in both groups to permit the laying of terrestrial eggs. Fish and amphibian eggs can pass water-soluble nitrogen compounds, ammonia and urea, into the water in which they are bathed. Reptile and bird embryos must store their nitrogenous wastes inside the egg, and to avoid poisoning themselves, manufacture uric acid. With vast new terrestrial environments thus opened to reptiles and their avian descendants, the energetic cost of uric acid production by the embryo proved a bargain. Evolution then simply co-opted its 'invention' for adult birds and reptiles as well.

SEE: Salt Glands, p. 237; Bird Droppings, p. 485; Temperature Regulation and Behaviour, p. 163; Metabolism, p. 281; Eggs and Their Evolution, p. 317.

Disease and Parasitism

MANY organisms obtain energy and nutrients by feeding on birds, some by killing them outright, others by gradually extracting nourishment from them. Those animals big enough to kill and devour a bird all at once are called predators, and those small enough to live on or in birds indefinitely are called parasites. Parasites may or may not have a sufficient impact on a bird to make it sick. When a bird's tenants are microorganisms — protozoans, bacteria, fungi, viruses, or rickettsiae (tiny bacteria-like organisms) that cause diseases — we call them pathogens.

There is a great variety of avian diseases. Birds get malaria (caused by close relatives of the protozoans that cause human malaria), aspergillosis (a fungal infection), tuberculosis (highly contagious but not the same bacterium that causes human tuberculosis), avian cholera (bacterial), Newcastle disease (viral), fowl plague (viral), avian pox (viral), avian influenza (viral), and hundreds of other infections. People cannot catch most avian diseases, but birds can serve as hosts of pathogens that cause serious human illnesses. The rickettsia that causes psittacosis is sometimes contracted by people from pets in the parrot family (Psittacidae), but the disease name is misleading, as the pathogen has been found in at least 140 species of 17 orders of birds. Psittacosis may be fatal in people. Outbreaks of many avian diseases (tuberculosis, fowl plague) can be attributed to contact between free-flying birds and domestic or feral waterfowl.

Birds can serve as reservoirs for encephalitis viruses that are carried by mosquitoes to human beings. The birds usually do not suffer heavily from mosquito-transmitted viruses, but there are exceptions. The mosquito species *Culex pipiens*, accidentally introduced into the Hawaiian Islands in 1826, was an agent (vector) for transmitting the avian pox virus, malarial protozoans, and other pathogens. Many lowland species of the wonderful Hawaiian

Swallow

Hirundo rustica

ATLAS 201; PMH 164; PER 152; HFP 206; HPCW 163; NESTS 224; BWP5:262

2–5m

BLDS: ♂♀
Monogamy
Polygyny

4–5 (2–7)
2–3 broods
INCU: ♀ (♂♀)
11–19

A

FLDG: ♂♀
19 (18–23)

Ground glean

Breeding habitat Widespread, though avoids forests. Often around farms or edges of settlements where adjacent pastures provide areas to forage.

Displays ♂ sings in flight or on perch near nest to attract ♀, pecks at potential nest site. Pairs defend the nest site vigorously, singing and adopting threat posture with heads forward and plumage smoothed, or use chases and fighting. Both birds will fight intruders, but ♂s are more often aggressive.

Nesting Solitary; only occasionally in small colonies. Nests in buildings, rarely in caves; an open cup of mud adhered to a beam or the wall, lined with feathers. Eggs white, spotted with red, 20mm, hatch synchronously. Young depend on parents for a few weeks. Some ♂s are polygynous, particularly where birds are colonial. Young of first brood may sometimes help raising young of later broods. See Cooperative Breeding essay, p. 275.

Diet Small insects taken on the wing. Sometimes picks up insects from ground.

Winters European populations to Africa S of Sahara. In a range of open habitats. A very few birds winter in S Europe. In large flocks.

Conservation Declines in several N areas (perhaps because of winter rainfall changes) but common and an unusually widespread species, found across Europe, Asia, and N America.

Essays Communal Roosting, p. 81; Birds and Agriculture, p. 365; Monogamy, p. 335; Parasitized Ducks, p. 67; Sleeping Sentries and Mate-guarding, p. 73; Sexual Selection, p. 149; Polygyny, p. 265; Breeding Site Tenacity, p. 219.

Refs Marchant et al. 1990.

Red-rumped Swallow

Hirundo daurica

ATLAS 201; PMH 165; PER 152; HFP 206; HPCW 163; NESTS 225; BWP5:278

2–5 m

BLDS: ♂♀
Monogamy

4–5 (2–7)
2 broods
INCU: ♂♀
14–15(13–16)

A

FLDG: ♂♀
22–26 (–29)

Foliage glean

Breeding habitat Wide range of open country with access to cliffs, caves, buildings, bridges.

Displays ♂ defends nest site, calling and chasing away intruders. Near potential nest sites ♂ has display flight, around or with ♀.

Nesting Solitary or in very small colonies; defends nest site. Nest is of mud secured beneath horizontal surface, completely enclosed with extended spout for entrance, and lined with feathers. Eggs white, sometimes with fine red to brown spots, 20mm, hatch synchronously.

Diet Small insects taken in air. Sometimes takes insects off plants.

Winters In open grasslands, in Africa S of Sahara, though European birds cannot be distinguished from the resident populations there. In flocks.

Conservation Has been spreading N. Occurs widely, if sometimes locally, across S Europe, S Asia, and Africa.

Essays Disease and Parasitism, p. 315; Mobbing, p. 261; Wing Shapes and Flight, p. 269; Coloniality, p. 107; Nest Sanitation, p. 75; Nest Sites and Materials, p. 443.

honeyeaters apparently were susceptible to the pathogens and the diseases may have been responsible for their extinction; highland forms were spared because the mosquito could not survive at altitudes above 600 metres.

Birds are dined upon by a great variety of parasites. Chewing bird-lice (Mallophaga) invade plumage and live on accumulated 'dandruff', on blood, or on other fluids. Fleas, louse flies (Hippoboscidae), small bugs (Hemiptera, relatives of bedbugs), ticks, and mites suck blood. Internally, birds host roundworms, tapeworms, flukes and so on, which live either in the digestive tract or in the blood vessels. Little is known about the impact of parasites on the dynamics of natural populations of birds, but there are indications that it can be considerable, especially in populations of colonially nesting species, and the topic is getting increasing attention. In one study of seabird colonies on islands off the coast of Peru, outbreaks of tick infestations were found to be associated with both the buildup of guano deposits and the occurrence of El Niño. This warming of coastal waters makes anchovies unavailable for breeding birds, making them malnourished and thus susceptible to parasites and pathogens.

A somewhat similar example comes from the work of biologists Charles and Mary Brown of Yale University in the United States who found that the number of 'swallow bugs' (bedbug-like parasites) per nest went up as the size of Cliff Swallow (*Hirundo pyrrhonota*) colonies increased. In addition, the weight of ten-day-old chicks declined as the number of bugs per nestling rose. By fumigating some nests and leaving others infested, they showed that the bugs also increased fledgling mortality in large colonies but not in small ones. In response to the threat of the parasites, the swallows apparently construct new nests (rather than re-use old ones) in large colonies more frequently than in the less heavily infested small colonies. The swallows may also switch sites in alternate years, leaving their parasites to starve in empty nests in the meantime.

Parasites also can produce strange secondary effects on birds. For instance, incubating Red Grouse, parasitized by the nematode worm *Trichostrongylus teruis*, apparently give off more odour and may thus be more readily found by mammalian predators!

SEE: Coevolution, p. 239; Coloniality, p. 107; Nest Sites and Materials, p. 443; Nest Sanitation, p. 75; Starlings, p. 463; Bird Droppings, p. 485. REFS: Brown and Brown, 1986; Hudson and Rands, 1988; Loye and Zuk, 1991; Moss and Camin, 1970.

Eggs and their Evolution

FEMALES of all vertebrates produce eggs, but the reptiles 'invented' the eggshell, a device that could keep the egg from drying out and allow reproduction away from water (or, at least, from extremely moist environments).

House Martin
Delichon urbica

ATLAS 203; PMH 165; PER 154; HFP 206; HPCW 164; NESTS 226; BWP5:287

| 3–50m | BLDS: ♂♀ Monogamy | ○/🥚 3–5 (1–7) 2 broods INCU: ♂♀ 14–16(11–19) | FLDG: ♂♀ 22–32 (–40) | | |

Breeding habitat Open country, especially a round settlements or cliffs.

Displays Defends nest site vigorously. Before pairing ♂ sits on unfinished nest, ruffling feathers and calling at intruders. ♂ follows ♀s prospecting for nest.

Nesting Often in small colonies. Nest usually adhered to building wall, sometimes on cliffs; constructed of mud, tends to be completely enclosed except for small entrance lined with feathers. Birds will attempt to steal nesting materials from neighbours. Eggs white, sometimes with fine red spots, 19mm, hatch synchronously. Young may roost on nest for a few days after fledging. Only one brood in N. Where 2 broods, young of first brood may help raising second brood. See Cooperative Breeding essay, p. 275.

Diet Small insects taken in flight.

Winters Africa, S of Sahara, S to South Africa. Birds feed in flocks, perhaps at high elevations and high in the air.

Conservation Some local declines, but common and widespread across Europe, N Africa, and Asia.

Essays Nest Sites and Materials, p. 443.

Tawny Pipit
Anthus campestris

ATLAS 205; PMH 166; PER 156; HFP 210; HPCW 165; NESTS 229; BWP5:313

  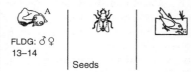

| | BLDS: ♂♀ Monogamy Polygyny | 🥚 4–5 (3–6) 1 (2) broods INCU: ♀ (♂♀) 12 (11–13) | FLDG: ♂♀ 13–14 | Seeds |

Breeding habitat Open country such as grasslands, semi-desert, sandy heaths, and dunes.

Displays ♂ has aerial song flight, also given from prominent perch. Has steep ascent with fluttering flight, and usually steep, rapid descent. This often causes other ♂s to sing, and there can be fights and chases. Courtship involves rapid, erratic chases.

Nesting Territorial. Nest, hidden on ground, is a cup of grass lined with finer plant material and hair. Eggs whitish, heavily blotched and spotted brown, 21mm, hatch synchronously. Young remain with parents for about a month. Occasionally polygynous.

Diet Insects; also seeds in winter. Uses a run, stop, and peck method.

Winters Africa, S of Sahara, Arabia, India. Sometimes in small groups.

Conservation Has declined in N and NW of range, but is locally common across Europe, N Africa, into central Asia. See p. 529.

Essays Walking vs. Hopping, p. 375.

With the exceptions of the platypus and echidna, mammals provide the developing embryo with a suitable environment within the mother. The other major group of reptile descendants, the birds, not only have continued the reptilian tradition, but have evolved eggshells of an improved design in a wide variety of sizes, shapes, colours, thicknesses, and textures.

Bird eggs are virtually self-contained life-support systems. All they require for the embryo to develop properly are warmth and oxygen. Oxygen diffuses into the egg through microscopic holes between the calcium carbonate crystals that compose the eggshell. There are not many of these pores — for example, they make up only about 0.02 per cent of the surface of a duck egg. Carbon dioxide and water vapour diffuse outward through the same pores. Birds can lay their eggs in even drier environments than reptiles because water is one of the by-products when the fatty yolk is broken down to provide energy for the developing embryo. Reptile eggs primarily use protein rather than fat as a source of energy and do not produce as much 'metabolic water'.

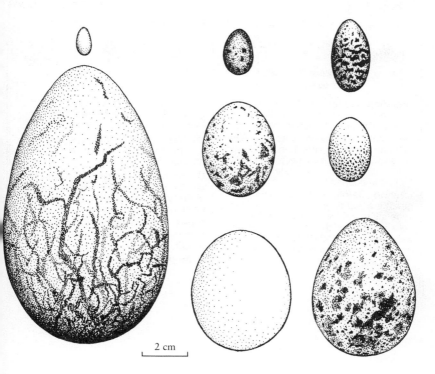

Left-hand column: Ruby-throated Hummingbird (Archilochus colubris), Great Auk (extinct). Middle column: Pied Wheatear, Black Kite, Brown Fish Owl. Right-hand column: Nightjar, Mistle Thrush, Curlew.

Eggs and their Evolution   319

Long-billed Pipit

Anthus similis

ATLAS 205; PMH -; PER -; HFP211; HPCW 165; NESTS 229; BWP5:331

  3 (2–5)
2 broods?

BLDS: ?
Monogamy?

INCU: ?
13–14

FLDG: ?
14?

Breeding habitat Dry, often rocky hillsides.

Displays ♂ displays from ground, perch, and in flight. Bird ascends, circles, then glides down, after remaining in flight for several minutes.

Nesting Nests on ground in shelter or rock or other cover; a cup of grass lined with finer vegetation. Eggs whitish, with heavy dark brown markings, 22mm.

Diet Mainly insects, also some plant material. Walks or runs along ground pecking at prey.

Winters Resident or short migration to S of breeding range. Sometimes in small flocks.

Conservation Occurs locally across Africa, SW Asia.

Tree Pipit

Anthus trivialis

ATLAS 206; PMH 167; PER 154; HFP 208; HPCW 166; NESTS 227; BWP5:344

  2–6 (–8)
1–2 (3) broods

BLDS: ♀
Monogamy

INCU: ♀
12–14

 A

FLDG: ♂♀
12–14

Foliage glean

Breeding habitat A wide variety of open ground near trees, avoiding both continuous forest and open grasslands.

Displays ♂ sings from tree tops, flies up at an angle, singing, then glides with wings and tail spread back to perch. ♂s chase each other, and ♂ chases ♀ to ground in courtship.

Nesting Territorial. Nest is hidden on ground; a cup of grass, lined with finer vegetation and hair. Eggs variable in colour, being bluish, pinkish, or brownish, with darker spots and blotches; some are unmarked, 20mm, hatch within 2 days of each other.

Diet Insects, taken usually from the ground, but sometimes from trees. Some plant material taken in winter.

Winters S of Sahara in open habitats with trees, though is more widespread on migration.

Conservation Some local decreases and increases, but common across most of Europe N of Mediterranean, and N central Asia.

Notes Only rarely breeds in Ireland – see essay on Island Biogeography, p. 303.

Refs Marchant et al. 1990.

The proportion of yolk differs between altricial and precocial birds. The former, which hatch so undeveloped that they require significant parental feeding (and thus need less stored energy), generally have eggs that contain about 25 per cent yolk. Precocial birds, which can walk and feed themselves shortly after hatching, have eggs with about 40 per cent yolk (67 per cent in megapodes, inhabitants of Australia and Pacific islands which upon hatching are virtually ready to fly). Interestingly, in spite of this difference, and although bird eggs range in weight from about a quarter of a gram (small hummingbird) to a kilogram and a half (Ostrich), all bird eggs lose water amounting to about 15 per cent of their original weight during incubation. Water loss is probably strictly controlled to keep the water content of the developing chick's tissues constant even though metabolic water is continually being produced.

Small birds tend to lay *proportionately* large eggs; the egg of a wren weighs about 13 per cent of the wren's weight, while an Ostrich egg weighs less than 2 per cent of an adult's weight. As might be expected, the eggs of precocial birds tend to be heavier in proportion to body weight than those of altricial birds. The parents must 'invest' more in the egg to give the chick the energy and materials required for more advanced development within the confines of the shell.

Although most are 'egg-shaped', some eggs, such as those of owls, are nearly spherical. Fast-flying, highly streamlined birds such as swifts and hummingbirds tend to lay long, elliptical eggs, while those of auks, guillemots, and waders are more pointed at the narrow end. This shape appears to be especially advantageous for birds that nest on bare ground or cliffs because, when disturbed, pointy eggs tend to roll in circles, rather than away from the 'nest' (and possibly over the cliff). Such eggs also can be packed closely with the pointy ends inward, helping adults to cover them efficiently during incubation.

Bird eggs vary enormously in colour, and there is also variation in the surface texture of eggs — for instance, those of many ducks are greasy and water-repellent. Shells vary in thickness, too. Those of some brood parasites are thickened or even double-layered, which helps prevent cracking when they're dropped into a host's nest. And shells may be subject to thinning and weakening by environmental pollutants that interfere with the bird's calcium metabolism.

Why have birds not 'advanced' beyond egg-laying and started to bear their young alive like mammals? People have claimed that viviparity (live-bearing) is incompatible with flight, but bats disprove that hypothesis. American biologists Daniel Blackburn of Vanderbilt University and Howard Evans of Cornell University point out that the evolutionary path to viviparity usually involved retaining eggs for longer and longer periods until they finally hatch within the female's body. Blackburn and Evans argue that egg retention would offer little advantage to birds, and several disadvantages. Among the latter are a loss of productivity — since females obviously could not retain many eggs until they hatched — and probably increased risk to the mother associated with the added burden of weight. In addition, in many species,

Meadow Pipit

Anthus pratensis

ATLAS 204; PMH 167; PER 154; HFP 208; HPCW 166; NESTS 227; BWP5:365

BLDS: ♀
Monogamy
Polygyny

3–5 (2–6)
2 broods
INCU: ♀
13 (11–15)

FLDG: ♂♀
10–14

Seeds

Breeding habitat A wide variety of open habitats including moorland, meadows, forest clearings.

Displays ♂ song flight has fluttering angled ascent followed by gliding descent with wings and tail raised. ♂ chases ♀s with shallow wing-beats; on ground he lowers wings and raises tail, sometimes presenting nesting material. ♂ will feed ♀ near nest.

Nesting Territorial. Nest is hidden on ground, often in grass tussock; a cup of grass lined with finer plant material and hair. Eggs variable; brownish or greyish, spotted with grey, brown, or black, 19mm, hatch within 2 days

of one another. Young remain with parents for about 2 weeks. Occasionally polygynous. One brood in N.

Diet Insects and other invertebrates picked from ground; in addition seeds in the winter.

Winters Resident in W, migratory in Iceland, and N and E of range, moving to a wide range of open country in S and W Europe and N Africa. Sometimes in flocks.

Conservation An abundant species across N Europe.

Essays Birds and Agriculture, p. 365; Habitat Selection, p. 423; Polygyny, p. 265.

Red-throated Pipit

Anthus cervinus

ATLAS 204; PMH 168; PER 156; HFP 208; HPCW 166; NESTS 228; BWP5:380

BLDS: ♂♀
Monogamy

5–6 (2–7)
1 brood
INCU: ♀
10–14

FLDG: ♂♀
11–15

Seeds

Breeding habitat Tundra, typically on damp ground, often with small bushes.

Displays ♂ sings mainly in flight. Ascends at angle, with fluttering wing-beats, then glides, sometimes circling, on open wings, before descending with wings and tail spread. ♂s chase and fight each other. Threat postures include head raised to show red throat. ♂ courts ♀, chasing her with shallow wing-beats, spreading tail to show white outer feathers. ♂ will feed ♀ near nest.

Nesting Territorial. Nest is on ground; a concealed cup of grass, built by ♀ into hollow created by ♂. Eggs variable,

olive, grey, or buffish, variously marked with greys and browns, 19mm, usually hatch over a period of 2 days.

Diet Insects, sometimes seeds; picked or probed from ground.

Winters Some around Mediterranean but mainly Africa, S of Sahara (Asian populations to SE Asia), often in wet habitats, including fields, but a variety of other habitats. In small groups or flocks.

Conservation Locally common, but, at least in Scandinavia, numbers fluctuate greatly from year to year. Breeds across arctic from Norway through Asia to Alaska (locally).

Essays Walking vs. Hopping, p. 375.

the contribution of the male to the care of offspring would be lost, and it has been suggested recently that a female bird's body may be too hot for proper egg development. It seems likely, therefore, that evolving viviparity would be a step backward for birds — they are doing just fine laying eggs.

SEE: Incubation: Controlling Egg Temperatures, p. 273; Average Clutch Size, p. 31; Colour of Eggs, p. 137; Variation in Clutch Sizes, p. 55; Pesticides and Birds, p. 115; Empty Shells, p. 199. REFS: Anderson *et al.*, 1987; Blackburn and Evans, 1986; Carey, 1983; Diamond, 1982; Lewin, 1986.

Differential Migration

IN many bird species, males winter farther north than females or juveniles. Where females are larger than males (as in many birds of prey) or where dominance relationships between the sexes are reversed (as in polyandrous Spotted Sandpipers (*Actitis macularia*) and phalaropes), females often winter farther north. Three hypotheses have been advanced to explain this phenomenon of 'differential migration' in which males, females, and sometimes different age groups within each sex, winter at different latitudes. The body-size hypothesis suggests that larger birds have greater cold tolerance and enhanced ability to fast through periods of inclement weather, and therefore can better endure the rigours of winter. Hence, smaller individuals should migrate farther south. A second explanation is based on dominance relationships within a species. In general, smaller individuals are subordinate to larger ones and will lose out in competition; therefore they will be forced to migrate farther south. Third, the arrival-time hypothesis states that if members of one sex experience more intense competition for breeding resources, then individuals of that sex should benefit by early return to the breeding grounds. This can best be achieved by wintering as close as possible to breeding areas.

Unfortunately, because males are larger than females in most migratory species, and because older birds tend to dominate younger birds, it is often difficult to distinguish among these three hypotheses, which obviously are not mutually exclusive.

SEE: Migration, p. 377; Orientation and Navigation, p. 503; Wader Migration and Conservation, p. 167; Breeding Season, p. 293; Wintering Site Tenacity, p. 409; Breeding Site Tenacity, p. 219; Wintering and Conservation, p. 409; Why Some Species Migrate at Night, p. 351; Spacing of Wintering Waders, p. 179. REFS: Curry-Lindahl, 1981; Gauthreaux, 1982; Kerlinger, 1989; Ketterson and Nolan, 1983; Lovei, 1989; Myers, 1981.

Rock Pipit

Anthus petrosus

ATLAS 206; PMH 168; PER 154; HFP 210; HPCW 166; NESTS 228; BWP5:393

		3–5 (2–9) 2 broods		
	BLDS: ♀	INCU: ♀	FLDG: ?	
	Monogamy	14–15	16	
Cliff	Polygyny			Seeds

Breeding habitat Shores of rocky coasts, in NW Europe.

Displays ♂ sings on ground and in flight. ♂ ascends at an angle with fluttering flight, then descends at angle. ♂s aggressive and chases common. ♂ chases ♀ with shallow wing-beats, wings lowered, tail raised and fanned.

Nesting Territorial. Nest is in crevice among rocks, or hole in bank, lined with grass and seaweed. Eggs whitish, spotted with greys and browns, 21mm. In some populations, some ♂s are polygynous. One brood in N. Older ♀s lay larger clutches.

Diet Invertebrates (insects, crustaceans, worms, molluscs) from along shorelines, picking prey from among rocks and sea weed. Sometimes takes plant material.

Winters Many populations are resident, though N ones migrate S. May defend winter feeding territories, but also occurs in flocks.

Conservation Common and widespread in appropriate habitats in its limited range.

Notes This is one of two ecologically very different populations – Rock and Water Pipits, which have traditionally been considered the same species. We treat them separately because of their ecological distinctness and follow a recent decision (see Knox, A. 1988, *British Birds*, **81**, 206–11) which considers them to be two species.

Refs Marchant et al. 1990.

Water Pipit

Anthus spinoletta

ATLAS 206; PMH 168; PER 154; HFP 210; HPCW 166; NESTS 228; BWP5:393

		4–6 (–8) 2 broods		
	BLDS: ♀	INCU: ♀	FLDG: ♂♀	
	Monogamy	14–15	14–15	Seeds

Breeding habitat Mountainous areas above tree line in Europe (and a wider range of habitats elsewhere).

Displays ♂ sings from ground or in flight. Ascends at angle, with fluttering flight, then circles over territory, then glides downward. In threat display birds show off throat markings (see Red-throated Pipit). Courtship like that of Rock Pipit.

Nesting Territorial. Nest is well concealed in bank; cup of grass with a little lining of finer material. Eggs off-white, heavily spotted grey and brown, 21mm.

Diet Insects, some other invertebrates, and plant material including seeds.

Winters In lowland wet grasslands and marshes, from S and SW Europe, N Africa, and SW Asia. Often in small flocks.

Conservation Common and widespread; occurs widely across Asia and arctic and mountain regions of N America.

Notes See notes under Rock Pipit above.

Essays Commensal Feeding, p. 27.

Species and Speciation

SPECIES are distinctly different kinds of organisms. Birds of one species are, under most circumstances, incapable of interbreeding with individuals of other species. Indeed, the 'biological species concept' centres on this inability to hybridize successfully, and is what most biologists mean by 'distinctly different'. That concept works very well when two different kinds of birds live in the same area. For example, Willow Warblers and Chiffchaffs are clearly distinct kinds because their breeding ranges overlap, but they do not mate with one another. If they did, they might produce hybrid young, which in turn could 'backcross' to the parental types, and (eventually) this process could cause the two kinds of warblers to lose their distinctness.

On the other hand, when relatively similar populations have non-overlapping ranges, it is much more difficult to decide whether to classify them as different species. For example, the eastern populations of the Collared Flycatcher are considered by some to be a separate species, the Semi-collared Flycatcher. The forms intergrade, and most taxonomists now consider the Semi-collared to be a *subspecies* of the Collared Flycatcher. Subspecies are simply populations or sets of populations within a species that are sufficiently distinct that taxonomists have found it convenient to formally name them, but not distinct enough to prevent hybridization where two populations come into contact.

Judgements about whether two populations should be considered different species or just different subspecies may be very difficult to make. For instance, in some areas where populations of Hooded and Carrion Crows meet, they hybridize, but in other areas of overlap they do not. Although there is dispute most ornithologists consider the two forms as subspecies of the same species. In situations where differentiated but clearly closely related forms have separate geographic ranges, taxonomists often consider them to be separate species within a 'superspecies'.

These complications are a natural result of applying a hierarchical taxonomic system, developed a century before Darwin, to the results of a continuous evolutionary process. Geographic variation — birds showing different characteristics in different areas — is inevitable among the populations of all species with extensive breeding distributions. It is largely the result of populations responding to different pressures of natural selection in different habitats. If populations of a single bird species become geographically isolated, those different selection pressures may, given enough time, cause the populations to differentiate sufficiently to prevent interbreeding if contact is re-established. In nature, degrees of differentiation and varying abilities to hybridize fall along a continuum, so one finds what one would expect in an evolving avifauna: some populations intermediate between subspecies and species whose members will hybridize; populations (members of super-

Yellow Wagtail

Motacilla flava

ATLAS 209; PMH 169; PER 156; HFP 212; HPCW 166; NESTS 230; BWP5:413

BLDS: ♀ Monogamy	4–6 (3–8) 1 (2) broods INCU: ♂♀ 11–13	FLDG: ♂♀ 16		Hawks

Breeding habitat Damp meadows, fields, edges of lakes, marshes, rivers.
Displays Sings from perch or in flight. Starts from a perch, ascends at a steep angle, puffs out breast feathers, spreads tail, dangles legs and descends with fluttering flight. Repeats this display frequently. ♂ aggressively defends territory, facing rival, with tail depressed, wings dropped, pointing bill upwards, and puffing out breast feathers. Resident may hiss at intruder. ♂ adopts similar position in courting ♀. ♀ may solicit by raising tail and head.
Nesting Territorial. Nest is on ground in cover; a cup of grass lined with hair and other fine material. Eggs greyish-white to pale buff, heavily speckled with dark browns; 17mm, hatch synchronously.
Diet Small insects and other invertebrates, picked from ground while walking or running, or caught in flight after short chase.
Winters European populations winter in Africa S of Sahara in a wide variety of wet habitats; in flocks.

Conservation Some declines in W, but species is common and widespread across Europe, N Africa, Asia, and Alaska (locally). No obvious effect of the Sahelian drought.
Notes While in most species, the subspecies or races are hard to distinguish in the field, this species is characterized by a large number that are often easy to identify and occur in the different parts of its range. The UK yellow-headed race now breeds in SW Norway, Netherlands, and NW France, alongside (and not interbreeding with) the continental race. Thus, the two forms appear to behave as different species.

No longer breeds in Ireland regularly, two populations there having become extinct. Is also absent from the Åland Islands in the Baltic; see essay on Island Biogeography, p. 303.

Essays The Colour of Birds, p. 137; Declines in Forest Birds: Europe and America, p. 339; Habitat Selection, p. 423; Migration, p. 377.
Refs Marchant et al. 1990.

Citrine Wagtail

Motacilla citreola

ATLAS 210; PMH 169; PER -; HFP 212; HPCW 167; NESTS 231; BWP5:433

BLDS: ♀ Monogamy ?	4–6 (–7) 1–2 broods INCU: ♂♀ 14–15	FLDG: ♂♀ 13–15	Aq inverts	Hawks

Breeding habitat Marshes, lake edges, river banks, in arctic tundra, mountain meadows, and among forests and grasslands.
Displays In song flight, ♂ flies up from perch, hovers, drops at an angle. ♂s aggressively defend territories against rivals.
Nesting Territorial, though often territories are in loose groups. Nest is a cup of vegetation, lined with leaves, feathers, and hair, with more insulating material in colder areas. Eggs pale grey or buffish, with greyish-brown markings,

19mm. Young fed by parents after fledging.
Diet Insects and aquatic invertebrates, taken from ground or water surface, bird will also wade into shallow water and immerse head. Will also catch insects in air after brief flight.
Winters Mainly in India in a variety of wetlands; in flocks.
Conservation May be increasing range. Common and widespread in much of Asia, extending into Europe in the CIS.
Essays Songbird Foraging, p. 417.

species) that have differentiated to the point where they will not hybridize but have not yet regained full contact; and populations so distinct that they can be recognized as full species whether or not they occur together. As an example of the latter, the Cirl Bunting and the Yellow-breasted Buntings have separate distributions, but clearly are separate species.

Biologists differ on the details of both the definition of species and the mechanisms of speciation, and our treatment here is necessarily simplified. Changing views of the specific status of birds can be an annoyance, since they may result in new names for familiar birds. But changes reflect increased knowledge of the biology of the birds involved.

SEE: Classifying Birds, p. 3; Natural Selection, p. 297; Hybridization, p. 461. REFS: Futuyma, 1987; Zink and Remsen, 1986.

Environmental Acoustics

TWO people standing on opposite sides of a rushing stream and attempting to talk to one another are faced with a communication problem. If they shout loudly, their voices may carry above the noise of the water, depending on the distance between them, but their words may not be discernible. In transmitting their songs and calls, birds face similar challenges posed by such obvious problems as running water, wind, rain, physical barriers (rocks and vegetation), and more subtle influences on sound transmission such as humidity and temperature. Only recently have ornithologists begun to consider the role of the environment through which a vocalization must travel as a selective force in the evolution of songs and calls.

A sound travelling through air is attenuated and degraded by an array of environmental features. 'Attenuation', the progressive reduction of intensity (loudness), is frequency-dependent and determines the distance that a sound will carry. 'Degradation', a change in the pattern of frequency and intensity, is a problem where communication requires more than simple detection of the signal by the receiver. Especially in bird song, receivers must discriminate among signals with different acoustic structures.

The pioneering studies of ornithologists Claude Chapuis and Eugene Morton demonstrated that different habitats pose different problems for successful sound transmission. For instance, in general, the higher the frequency, the greater the attenuation due to absorption and scattering. Thus higher-frequency sounds are less satisfactory for communication in forests (where there is much vegetation to absorb and scatter sounds) than are lower-frequency sounds. Lower-frequency sounds are also less influenced by absorption and scattering by the ground, and so would tend to be the frequencies used by birds that generate their sound signals from close to the ground in both densely vegetated and open habitats.

Grey Wagtail

Motacilla cinerea

ATLAS 210; PMH 169; PER 156; HFP 212; HPCW 168; NESTS 230; BWP5:442

		A 4–6 (3–7) 1 (–2) broods	A	
	BLDS: ♀	INCU: ♂♀	.FLDG: ♂♀	Aq inverts	Hawks
	Monogamy	11–14	13–14(11–17)		

Breeding habitat Streams and rivers, usually fast flowing with rocks and boulders.

Displays ♂ sings from high perch, sometimes gliding down on open wings. Highly aggressive towards rivals, chasing them from territory. Threat posture involves pointing bill upwards to display black throat. ♂ courts ♀ with tail and bill raised. ♀ may solicit by raising her tail vertically, quivering wings, and her bill pointed upwards to show her white throat.

Nesting Territorial. Nest is in hole or crack in rocks or under bridge; a cup of moss and grass lined with softer material, to fit available space. Eggs off-white to buff, with grey to brown spotting, 19mm, hatch synchronously. Young remain with parents for about two weeks after fledging even when a second clutch is attempted.

Diet Insects taken from ground, in shallow water, or in air after short chase. Will also take small fish and amphibians.

Winters Resident in S and W, birds in E move to those regions, wintering in similar habitats to resident birds. Solitary or in small flocks.

Conservation Has increased range, though is vulnerable to hard winters in C and N that make its habitat inaccessible. Occurs in W and S Europe, SW Asia, and across much of N and C Asia.

Refs Marchant et al. 1990.

Pied/White Wagtail

Motacilla alba

ATLAS 209; PMH 170; PER 156; HFP 212; HPCW 168; NESTS 230; BWP5:454

Cliff	BLDS: ♂♀	(5–6) (3–8) 2 (3) broods	A	
	Monogamy	INCU: ♂♀	FLDG: ♂♀		Hawks
		11–16	11–16		

Breeding habitat A wide variety of open areas, sometimes near water; but also agricultural areas, large gardens, parks, etc.

Displays Song display not as obvious as other wagtails, given from a conspicuous perch. ♂s aggressively defend territories; threat and courtship postures, with bill and tail raised, similar to other wagtails.

Nesting Territorial. Nest is in a crevice or hole in bank, or wall of building, etc; sometimes a large cup of vegetation lined with softer material such as hair and feathers. Eggs whitish to grey, with fine darker spotting, 20mm, hatch synchronously.

Diet Small insects and other invertebrates, picked up from ground or surface of water, after walking or running after prey. Also makes short flights after prey.

Winters Resident in S and W, N populations migrate as far as Africa S of Sahara. In small flocks or in winter territories, depending on the food supply. Indeed, the choice is known to change quite rapidly as the food supply changes. Often roosts communally, with up to thousands of birds.

Conservation Some local increases and decreases. Vulnerable to cold winters: >60 per cent decline in UK in 1962–3. Abundant across almost all of Europe and most of Asia, and into N Africa.

Notes While in most species, the subspecies or races, are hard to distinguish, this species is characterized by a large number of often easy to identify races, which occur in the different parts of its range. The Pied Wagtail occurs mainly in the UK, the White Wagtail is on the continent.

Essays Brood Parasitism, p. 249.

Although both Chapuis and Morton found that birds of dense tropical forest habitats have songs with lower average frequencies than birds of adjacent open habitat, Morton found no differences in song frequencies between birds in similarly contrasting temperate habitats in North America. This apparent lack of difference may be explained by the fact that most North American forest species (in contrast to many tropical forest species) rarely sing from on or near the ground.

Recent studies have shown that the acoustic features of songs used by a species may be closely adapted to habitat characteristics to minimize information loss during singing. Ornithologist Jorma Sorjonen found that the penetration of songs of Thrush Nightingales breeding in dense shrubby habitats in Finland varied with the physical characteristics of individual song types, and that loud, well-penetrating, simple song types were more likely to be copied by territorial males. Experimental playback of local songs and of songs recorded from birds breeding in more open habitats in Russia demonstrated more effective penetration by the local song types. Morton found similar results in comparisons of Carolina Wren (*Thryothorus ludovicianus*) songs recorded and experimentally played back in two different habitats of the eastern United States. Whether other species show such close local adaptation in song charcteristics remains to be explored.

SEE: Sonagrams: Seeing Bird Songs, p. 307; Vocal Dialects, p. 477; Bird Voices, p. 475; What Do Birds Hear?, p. 255; Vocal Copying, p. 383. REFS: Chapuis, 1971; Gish and Morton, 1981; Morton, 1975; Sorjonen, 1983; Wiley and Richards, 1982.

Hormones and Nest Building

PASSERINES are dedicated builders and may make more than 1000 trips to carry construction materials to their nests in a very brief period. Physiologists and ornithologists have been piecing together how the complex practice of nest building is triggered by environmental factors and driven by hormones (chemical messengers).

Increased day length increases the springtime production of hormones involved in nest building. This solar trigger is most apparent in birds that live some distance from the equator, where seasonal change in day length is substantial. As the days lengthen the pituitary gland produces hormones that promote the enlargement of the gonads (ovaries and testes). Once enlarged, these organs release a flood of gonadal steroid hormones including (mainly in females) oestradiol and progesterone. In concert with environmental cues (such as the presence or absence of females or other males, bird song, or the time of day when food is available), this flood of hormones leads to courtship and mating and helps to activate nest-building behaviour and the onset of ovulation.

Yellow-vented Bulbul

Pycnonotus xanthopygos

ATLAS 211; PMH -; PER -; HFP 216; HPCW 169; NESTS 232; BWP5:479

 Shrub | BLDS: ? Monogamy | 3 (2–4) 2–3 broods INCU: ♂♀, ♀? 14? | A FLDG: ♂♀ 13–15 | | Foliage glean

Breeding habitat Gardens, suburbs, moist forest in Mediterranean habitats.

Displays ♂ sings from high perches. Threat display involves spreading tail and moving it up and down; rivals may face each other and point bills skyward, flicking wings. Pairs have greeting ceremony with fluttering wings and calling.

Nesting Territorial. Nest is a cup of vegetation, lined with finer material in bush. Eggs light blue or pinkish, heavily spotted with brown and greys, 24mm.

Diet Bulbuls are quite generalized in their feeding, taking fruit, seeds, nectar, and other plant material, and also insects, taken in flight and from ground or vegetation.

Winters Resident. Sometimes in large flocks, sometimes pairs (apparently siblings), which may defend winter territories and roost side by side.

Conservation Locally common in limited range from S Turkey to around Arabian peninsula.

Notes Sometimes considered a subspecies of the Common Bulbul (see below).

Common Bulbul

Pycnonotus barbatus

ATLAS 212; PMH –; PER -; HFP 216; HPCW 170; NESTS 232; BWP5:484

 Shrub | BLDS: ? Monogamy | 2–3 (–4) 1 brood? INCU: ♀ 12–14 | A FLDG: ♂♀ 12–14 | | Foliage glean

Breeding habitat Dry scrub or woodland in arid or semi-desert areas, also common in gardens.

Displays ♂s call from high perch. Displays not well known.

Nesting Territorial. Nest is a cup of grass and other vegetation, lined with hair; in tree or shrub. Eggs white to pinkish, with heavy reddish-brown spotting, 24mm.

Diet Fruit, insects, seeds, nectar. Insects caught on ground or through aerial hawking.

Winters Resident; in flocks.

Conservation Common and apparently increasing; occurs in NW Africa and Nile Valley and elsewhere in Africa.

The gonadal hormones also prompt the release of yet another chemical messenger, prolactin, which may induce brooding behaviour. The sequence prompting release of prolactin is typically reinforced in females by the sight of the egg and in males by the sight of the incubating female. Coming full circle then, as prolactin reaches a critical level it suppresses further release of hormones from the pituitary gland. No longer stimulated by pituitary hormones, the gonads (in birds that produce only one brood a year) begin to regress and residual sexual interest is rechannelled into parental behaviour. In species that produce more than one brood annually, such as the House Sparrow, Goldfinch, and Starling, the gonads do not regress between broods.

The hormone-driven changes in behaviour may be quite distinct. Studies have shown, for example, that males implanted with testosterone become more aggressive and increase the size of their territories. Similarly, a rise in testosterone initiates the moult of white plumage to conspicuous breeding plumage in Willow Grouse and inhibits moult in Ptarmigan, causing the males of both species to contrast more starkly with their backgrounds as they become more aggressive, and presumably more sought-after by females.

The transitions from courtship to nest building, to brooding and parenting are not always clear-cut. Since nest building requires a lower level of hormonal stimulation than does sexual behaviour, building may begin early in the courtship cycle or continue during incubation, and may account for some of the so-called dummy nests that are constructed and never used. Apparently, by responding to early hormonal signals, some birds incorporate portions of the nesting ritual into their pair-bonding displays.

In some cases increased day length may not be the only triggering mechanism. In a few species, such as Eleonora's Falcon of the Mediterranean, breeding occurs exclusively in the autumn, and the timing of broods coincides with the abundance of migrating prey. In others, late secretion of chemical messengers may occasionally influence birds to reinitiate some aspects of courtship. Called 'autumnal recrudescence', this partially reactivated post-season breeding behaviour is likely responsible for some incongruous interactions you may witness. More than 200 years ago, Gilbert White noted that:

Many birds which become silent about Midsummer reassume their notes again in September; as the thrush . . . woodlark, willow-wren, etc.; hence August is by much the most mute month, the spring, summer, and autumn through. Are birds induced to sing again because the temperament of autumn resembles that of spring?

Indeed, a 50-year-old survey of the British Isles by A. Morley identified 68 species showing a resurgence of breeding behaviour in autumn that occasionally led to additional broods.

Experimental evidence indicates that nest building may involve more than chemical clockwork, and that building simple nests is indeed instinctive. Construction of complex nests, however, improves over time as skills in choosing and preparing nest sites and materials are sharpened. For complex

Waxwing

Bombycilla garrulus

ATLAS 210; PMH 170; PER 156; HFP 216; HPCW 171; NESTS 231; BWP5:490

 3–15m | BLDS: ♂♀ Monogamy | 5–6 (4–7) 1 brood INCU: ♀ 14–15 | FLDG: ♂♀ 14–15 (–17) | Summer: Insects Winter: Fruit | Foliage glean

Breeding habitat Boreal spruce and pine forests.

Displays Not well known; in threat, bird sleeks body and adopts erect posture; courtship involves ruffling of feathers and raising crest and rump feathers. In courtship-feeding, food item may be passed backwards and forwards between pair.

Nesting Not certainly territorial and may nest in loose colonies. Nest in tree; cup of twigs and grass lined with finer material. Eggs pale blue, with some black spotting, 24mm.

Diet In summer, and on warm autumn days, insects caught by fly-catching from perches. Birds rise steeply then glide and circle around, rather like bee-eaters.

In winter fruit, usually hawthorns, and other plant material.

Winters Makes irruptive movements and often found in easily-approachable flocks in gardens, orchards and whereever a supply of fruit can be found. Moves S of breeding range in Europe, sometimes reaching far beyond normal range. Normally UK has a few records in each year but in 1965–6, there were many thousands.

Conservation Population size is not well known; breeds across N Europe, Asia, and N America.

Notes Has unusual ability to metabolize alcohol, present in the fermenting fruit.

Essays Songbird Foraging, p. 417; Irruptions, p. 491.

Dipper

Cinclus cinclus

ATLAS 274; PMH 171; PER 154; HFP 272; HPCW 171; NESTS 292; BWP5:510

 0–3m | BLDS: ♂♀ Monogamy | 4–5 (1–8) 1–2(3) broods INCU: ♀ 12–18 | FLDG: ♂♀ 20–24 | |

Breeding habitat Fast-flowing streams with plenty of rocks and boulders, generally in upland regions.

Displays Both sexes sing, and singing takes place throughout the year, sometimes from perch, sometimes in flight. Towards mate or rival, singing bird points bill skyward exposing white throat, ruffles plumage, spreads tail, and opens wings, quivering them. ♀ solicits by crouching and opening quivering wings.

Nesting Territorial. Nest usually overhangs water in crevice or on ledge, often under bridge; often a large domed mass of moss and grass, with a finer lining. Eggs white, 26mm, hatch synchronously. Young fed by parents (♂ only if there is a subsequent clutch) for about 2 weeks after fledging.

Diet Aquatic invertebrates, especially insects. Has remarkable feeding method of deliberately walking under water and then moving stones, capturing the exposed prey. Will dive into and swim under water, using its wings. See essay, opposite page.

Winters Mainly resident and winters in the far N if streams retain even some areas free from ice. Defends territory in winter. Some birds migrate S, however, and may be found on lowland streams.

Conservation Some local decreases, but has increased where rivers have been cleaned up; widely distributed in suitable habitat across Europe, N Africa, and C Asia.

Essays Acid and Eggshells, p. 287; Swimming and Underwater Flight, p. 61.

Refs Marchant et al. 1990.

construction the hormone-environment interaction can guide the building process, but perfection requires practice.

SEE: Breeding Season, p. 293; Nest Sites and Materials, p. 443; Migration, p. 377; Nest Lining, p. 439; Copulation, p. 87; Vocal Functions, p. 413; Courtship Feeding, p. 223. REFS: Bergerud and Gratson, 1988; Collias and Collias, 1984; Morley, 1943; Phillips, *et al.*, 1985; White, 1789.

Dipping

THE most unusual foraging strategy of any European songbird belongs to the aquatic Dipper. This bird is often seen flying rapidly along upland streams, perching on emergent rocks, wading in the water, and frequently disappearing beneath its surface. Although Dippers occasionally glean insects from streamside rocks or even flycatch, they extract most of their prey from the water. Often they wade along, heads beneath the surface, as they snap up prey. They also stride along the bottom completely submerged and 'fly' underwater using powerful beats of their wings as they search for food. Dipper plumage is very soft, dense, and difficult to saturate, and a white nictitating membrane (third eyelid) can be drawn across the eye to help keep it clear of dirt suspended in the water. Amazingly, these birds are able to forage on the bottom of streams in which the current is too fast and the water too deep for people to stand, and even feed under the ice of frozen streams.

Dippers are completely dependent on stream and river productivity, since even those prey captured out of water mostly have aquatic larvae. The abundance of larval caddisflies and stoneflies is a major determinant of Dipper abundance in Wales, and where acidification of streams has reduced aquatic insect populations, the Dippers have suffered. The food preferences

Wren
Troglodytes troglodytes

ATLAS 274; PMH 171; PER 158; HFP 272; HPCW 172; NESTS 291; BWP5:525

		○/◉ 5–8 (3–9) 2 broods	◁A		
BLDS: ♂ ♀ Monogamy Polygyny	INCU: ♀ 12–20	FLDG: ♂ ♀ 14–19			Foliage glean

Breeding habitat Needs thick cover but finds this in a wide variety of woods, gardens, agricultural land, and even on offshore islands.

Displays ♂s (sometimes ♀s) sing throughout year. Threaten with wings spread and quivered. In courtship ♂ flies after ♀ with tail fanned and fluttering flight.

Nesting Territorial. Nest is in thick cover near ground such as brambles, or in hole or crevice in bank; a domed mass of vegetation lined with feathers and hair. Many nests built by ♂ from which ♀ selects one and lines it. Eggs white, sometimes spotted with brown, 16mm, hatch within 3 days of each other. Mating system is variable. Island races are thought to be monogamous. But in W, about half the ♂s are serially polygynous with up to four ♀s, resulting in overlapping broods. Monogamous ♂s

help with rearing young, polygamous ♂s much less so, but may look after brood after it has fledged.

Diet Insects and spiders, taken from eaves, bark, crevices. Generally feeds on or near ground.

Winters Resident in the S and W, migrates S from N areas. Is particularly vulnerable to hard winters.

Conservation Abundant over much of Europe, into N Africa, across C Asia, and N America. In some years, may be the most abundant UK bird. (See Chaffinch and Blackbird.)

Notes There are a number of distinctive subspecies on small islands, such as the Outer Hebrides, Fair Isle, St. Kilda, Shetlands, Faeroes. See p. 529.

Essays Island Biogeography, p. 303; Monogamy, p. 335; Polygyny, p. 265; Sexual Selection, p. 149; Feeding Birds, p. 357; Nest Sites and Materials, p. 443.

Dunnock
Prunella modularis

ATLAS 216; PMH 172; PER 158; HFP 220; HPCW 172; NESTS 236; BWP5:548

Decid tree 0.5–3m	BLDS: ♀ See below	○/◉ 4–6 (3–7) 2 (3) broods INCU: ♀ 12–13	◁A FLDG: ♂ ♀ 11–12	Seeds	Foliage glean

Breeding habitat A wide variety of woods, hedges, gardens.

Displays ♂ chases ♀ for extended periods.

Nesting Nest is usually in deep cover, in bush etc. cup of twigs and other plant material, lined with hair, feathers, and other soft material. Eggs blue, sometimes with red spotting, 19mm, hatch synchronously. Has an unusually complicated social system which has only recently been discovered. ♂s and ♀s have independent home ranges, but up to 6 birds may overlap in one place. Breeding system is often monogamous, but may also involve a ♂ and two or more ♀s, two ♀s and one ♂, or two or

more ♂s plus two or more ♀s! ♀s gain from two or more ♂s because these ♂s may all feed their young, and this allows for larger clutches. ♂s try to remain with ♀ to ensure paternity and ♀ tries to lose such ♂s. See p. 337.

Diet Insects, plus seeds in the winter. Hops along the ground, in or near cover.

Winters Resident in S and W, migratory to SW from N and E.

Conservation Has increased in range and is abundant across much of W and N Europe.

Essays Polygyny, p. 265; Polyandry, p. 195; Cooperative Breeding, p. 275.

Refs Davies 1992 is a book about this species' peculiar social system.

of Dippers overlap those of trout, but the degree of competition between them has not been determined. However much competition may exist between the birds and the fishes, the need to preserve their habitat gives ornithologists common cause with anglers.

SEE: Swimming and Underwater Flight, p. 61; Acid and Eggshells, p. 287; Songbird Foraging, p. 417. REFS: Ormerod, 1985; Ormerod et al., 1985; Price and Bock, 1983.

Monogamy

AN estimated 90 per cent of all bird species are monogamous. Monogamy is defined as one male mating with one female and forming a 'pair bond'. The bond may form for the breeding season. The pair then separate for the non-breeding period. The following season the same pairbond may reform, depending in part, of course, on whether both pair members have survived. This is the habit of many seabirds (e.g. Manx Shearwater), waders (e.g. Dunlin), and passerines (e.g. Swallow). Alternatively the pair may remain bonded more or less closely throughout the year (e.g. Jackdaw, Sparrowhawk). This latter situation is expressed most dramatically in, for example, Bewick's Swans and Barnacle Geese where pairs migrate together between Arctic breeding grounds and British wintering haunts.

Presumably monogamy evolved in situations where young have a much better chance of surviving if both parents cooperate in rearing them. None the less, the amount of time and energy invested by monogamous male parents varies greatly. The male Willow Grouse serves only as a sentinel watching for danger. The male North American Eastern Bluebird (*Sialia sialis*, a thrush) provides a site for the rearing of young (by defending a territory containing a nest cavity), but experimental removal of males has shown that they are not essential for successful brood-rearing. In some monogamous species, the male defends a territory in which his mate collects the food required by the offspring, but does not himself feed the nestlings. But levels of male parental investment are even higher in most other passerines, where males also feed incubating females and/or help to feed the young. In herons, egrets, some woodpeckers, and others, males not only provide food for the young but share in incubation as well. And the ante is raised even further in such ground-nesting birds as geese, swans, gulls, terns, and waders in which males also commonly place themselves in danger by vigorously defending the nest and young from predators.

The traditional view of why more or less permanent monogamous bonds are formed is changing, as interest has begun to focus on the parentage of offspring reared by 'monogamous' pairs. Increasingly, ornithologists and behavioural ecologists have come to view monogamy as part of a 'mixed' reproductive strategy in which matings may occur outside the primary pair

Radde's Accentor

Prunella ocularis

ATLAS 216; PMH -; PER -; HFP 221; HPCW 174; NESTS 237; BWP5:560

BLDS: ?	3–4	
	1 brood?	
1m?	INCU: ?	
	?	

FLDG: ♂♀
?   Seeds

Breeding habitat Mountain slopes with rocks or bushes, at 2 000 to 3 000m.

Displays Very little known. ♂ sings from prominent perch.

Nesting Nest is a cup of grass, lined with finer material such as moss, hair. Eggs blue.

Diet Insects and seeds; forages along ground.

Winters Resident or makes short movements to S. Sometimes in small groups.

Conservation Local and not always common in limited range in E central Turkey, parts of Iran, and CIS.

Notes DNA analyses suggest that dunnocks and accentors belong in the same family as sparrows and wagtails.

Refs Sibley and Monroe 1990.

Alpine Accentor

Prunella collaris

ATLAS 217; PMH 172; PER 158; HFP 220; HPCW 174; NESTS 237; BWP5:574

	3–4(–6)	
BLDS: ?	2 broods	
Cooperative?	INCU: ♂♀	
	14–15 (11–)	

FLDG: ♂♀
16+ ?   Seeds

Breeding habitat Rocky mountain slopes, at high altitudes from above tree line to snow line.

Displays ♂ sings from perch, but also in flight, first rising steeply, hovering, then descending, and repeating the process. In courtship ♂ sings and hops around ♀.

Nesting Territorial. Nest is in a crevice in rocks or among boulders; a cup of grass, lined with moss, feathers, and hair. Eggs light blue, 23mm, hatch synchronously. May be a cooperative breeder (see essay), since extra birds are often seen at nests. The possibility,

however, that this species has the complicated mating systems of the Dunnock has not been ruled out.

Diet Insects and seeds taken as bird walks or hops along ground. Will make very short flights to catch insects in air. Typically feeds on edge of melting snow.

Winters Moves down lower; often in small groups, sometimes in flocks.

Conservation Little known about numbers; isolated populations on high mountains from Spain and N Africa across Europe and Asia to Japan.

Essays Cooperative Breeding, p. 275.

bond, but both members of the pair still contribute substantially only to the care and feeding of the young from their own nest. Some species are viewed as facultatively monogamous; that is, if released from certain environmental constraints, they would typically exhibit some other form of mating system such as polygyny (one male mating with more than one female) or promiscuity (mating without forming pair bonds). According to this view, for example, dabbling ducks are monogamous only because males are unable to monopolize more than one female. These ducks breed synchronously and their populations typically contain more males than females.

Three lines of evidence have contributed to the shift in viewpoint about the nature of monogamy. First, ecologist Yoram Yom-Tov showed intra-specific nest parasitism ('egg dumping' by females in nests other than their own) to be much more frequent than previously assumed. Consequently, females of birds as different as Goldeneyes, Moorhens, and Starlings may often incubate clutches containing one or more eggs laid by another female that may or may not have been sired by her mate. The parasitic female may be monogamous, but she is 'stealing' parental investment from another pair. Therefore the situation is not one in which mated pairs rear only their own offspring, as traditional use of the term monogamy has implied.

Second, a few recent studies employing new biochemical techniques of genetic analysis have allowed investigators to determine whether one or both members of a pair are the parents of all of the nestlings or fledglings they are rearing. Investigations of cooperatively breeding Acorn Woodpeckers (*Melanerpes formicivorus*), Collared and Pied Flycatchers (which are often polygynous) and 'monogamous' House Sparrows, Snow Geese (*Anser caerulescens*), and Reed Buntings demonstrate conclusively that clutches with mixed parentage (containing offspring of more than one female, more than one male, or both) are not infrequent, indicating some infidelity by either or both sexes and/or egg dumping by females.

A third line of evidence is observations of the frequency of attempted extra-pair copulations (EPCs) in many 'monogamous' bird species, such as the Magpie. A male of this species must be continuously vigilant when his mate is receptive — a few seconds of inattention and a rival male is likely to be mounting his mate. If, under these circumstances, a male thinks he has been cuckolded, he may desert his mate's first clutch of eggs and build a new nest in which she lays a second complete clutch.

Perhaps the ultimate in mate-guarding among birds is found in Dunnocks, which may have monogamous, polygynous, or polyandrous mating systems. Monogamous Dunnock males follow their mates closely to prevent EPCs. They also go through an elaborate display before copulation that includes pecking at the cloaca of the female. The female voluntarily exposes the cloaca and ejects sperm from a previous mating before the male copulates with her. The cloaca-pecking display is most intense in situations where EPCs are most probable.

Because few species have been investigated using biochemical techniques in conjunction with careful observation of pair behaviour and nest parasitism, the results of future analyses may lead to a further re-evaluation of the evolutionary significance of monogamy. At the moment it is perhaps best

Rufous Bush Robin

Cercotrichas galactotes

ATLAS 246; PMH 172; PER 160; HFP 254; HPCW 174; NESTS 274; BWP5:586

Decid tree
2–3m

BLDS: ♂♀
Monogamy

4–5 (2–6)
2 broods
INCU: ♀
13

A

FLDG: ♂♀
12–13(11–15) | Fruit

Probes

Breeding habitat Trees, scrub, open woodland, gardens, in drier areas around Mediterranean.

Displays ♂ sings from conspicuous perch or flies up then glides downward. On ground, bird threatens by spreading wings, spreading and raising conspicuously marked tail. Courtship is similar, except ♂ will turn away from ♀.

Nesting Territorial. Nest is in a shrub, cactus, or low tree; an untidy cup of twigs, grass, lined with softer material such as hair, feathers, or in some

locations, snake skin. Eggs whitish, heavily and variously marked with browns, 22mm, hatch synchronously?

Diet Insects taken on ground, earthworms from probing ground, will hover to take insects from vegetation. Also takes fruit.

Winters Migrates to Africa S of Sahara. Sometimes in small groups.

Conservation Locally common in S Europe, N Africa, into SW Asia and Africa S of Sahara.

Essays Nest Lining, p. 439.

Robin

Erithacus rubecula

ATLAS 255; PMH 173; PER 160; HFP 252; HPCW 175; NESTS 272; BWP5:596

Decid tree
0–5m

BLDS: ♀
Monogamy

4–6 (2–8)
2 (1–3) broods
INCU: ♀
13–15(12–21)

A

FLDG: ♂♀
12–14 (10–18) | Fruit

Ground glean

Breeding habitat A wide variety of woodlands, parks, gardens, etc.

Displays Both sexes sing from concealed perch, nearly all year long, though ♀s generally do not sing during breeding season. Birds threaten by fluffing breast and facing intruder; will fight intensely. ♂ courtship-feeds ♀, after nest is built.

Nesting Territorial. Nest is often in hole in bank, tree, or in building, is large cup of leaves, grass lined with finer material such as hair. Eggs whitish to very light blue, with orange-red spotting, 20mm, hatch synchronously. Clutch sizes are larger in the N, where there is often only one brood. ♂ will feed young when ♀ starts second brood. Some ♂s are bigamous.

Diet Insects, also fruit and seeds in winter. From perch will swoop down to catch prey on ground, returning to perch

or hopping along ground. Has familiar habit of waiting for gardeners to break soil and expose prey.

Winters Largely resident in S and W, migrates to those areas from N and E. Resident birds defend winter territories.

Conservation Some local decreases, but abundant across most of Europe into N Africa and parts of W Asia.

Essays Bird-brained, p. 385; Variation in Clutch Sizes, p. 55; Birds and Agriculture, p. 365; Visual Displays, p. 33; Island Biogeography, p. 303; Selection in Nature, p. 471; Songbird Foraging, p. 417; Commensal Feeding, p. 27; Feeding Birds, p. 357; Swallowing Stones, p. 135; Walking vs. Hopping, p. 375; Orientation and Navigation, p. 503.

Refs Lack's 1965 Life of the Robin is a classic study on the biology of a single species of bird.

simply to consider monogamy as a social pattern in which one male and one female associate during the breeding season, and not to make too many assumptions about fidelity or parentage.

SEE: Polygyny, p. 265; Polyandry, p. 195; Cooperative Breeding, p. 275; Promiscuity, p. 127; Leks, p. 123; Parasitized Ducks, p. 67; Sleeping Sentries and Mate-guarding, p. 73. REFS: Alatalo *et al.*, 1984, 1987; Birkhead, 1979, 1982, 1987, 1989; Burke and Bruford, 1987; Davies, 1983; Evans, 1988; Gowaty and Mock, 1985; Quinn *et al.*, 1987; Westneat *et al.*, 1990; Wetton *et al.*, 1987; Yom-Tov, 1980.

Declines in Forest Birds: Europe and America

IN Europe, dramatic declines in forest bird populations doubtless occurred long before there were birdwatchers to document them; most European forests were cleared for farming hundreds or thousands of years ago. The process still continues, and is being studied in Scandinavia where human disturbance is less severe than in most other parts of the continent. In northern Finland, for example, mechanized forestry has been destroying old growth and generally fragmenting the forest only since World War II. This has led to drops in populations of such forest-loving species as the Three-toed Woodpecker, Siberian Tit, Song Thrush, Redstart, Pied Flycatcher, Brambling, and crossbills, while edge species — the Yellow Wagtail, Whinchat, Redwing, and Garden Warbler — have thrived.

Since the 1970s there has been a decline in forest songbird populations over much of the eastern United States, as indicated by the Breeding Bird Survey and various more limited studies. The decline has not been uniform for all species; those that migrate long distances to tropical America have suffered more than residents or species that can overwinter in the southern United States. Nor has the decline been equal in all types of forest; the loss of species from woodlots and small forest tracts exceeds the loss from large stretches of forest.

One likely cause is the rapid destruction of the tropical forests where many migrants overwinter. This deforestation is probably responsible for the rapid decline of North American migrants such as Cape May and Worm-eating Warblers (*Dendroica tigrina* and *Helmitheros vermivorus*), Wood Thrushes (*Hylocichla mustelina*), and Northern Orioles (*Icterus galbula*).

Other factors in a post-World War II decline in migratory songbirds have to do with changes within temperate North America. They include increased cowbird (*Molothrus ater*) nest parasitism, loss and fragmentation of habitat, and increased nest predation in habitat patches. When Columbus landed in North America, cowbirds were confined largely to open country west of the Mississippi because the continuous forests of the eastern United States did

Thrush Nightingale

Luscinia luscinia

ATLAS 257; PMH 173; PER 160; HFP 254; HPCW 175; NESTS 273; BWP5:616

  |

	🍵	◯ 4–5 1 brood
	BLDS: ♀	INCU: ♀
	Monogamy	11–15

	🪰	
FLDG: ♂♀ 8–10	Fruit	Foliage glean

Breeding habitat Usually moist woodlands with thick undergrowth.

Displays ♂ sings from deep cover day and, commonly, night. Courting ♂ drops wings, raises and fans tail, chases ♀.

Nesting Territorial. Nest is in cover on ground, often against fallen branches; a cup of grass, lined with finer material on a pad of leaves. Eggs buff, olive or brown, 22mm.

Diet Insects, found by hopping along ground in leaf litter, also from vegetation; will take fruit.

Winters Africa S of Sahara in dense undergrowth. Defends winter territories.

Conservation Generally appears to be increasing; locally common from Scandinavia into C Asia.

Essays Interspecific Territoriality, p. 421; Walking vs. Hopping, p. 375; Vocal Dialects, p. 477; Environmental Acoustics, p. 327.

Nightingale

Luscinia megarhynchos

ATLAS 256; PMH 173; PER 160 ; HFP 254; HPCW 175; NESTS 273; BWP5:626

Shrub 0–0.5m	🍵 BLDS: ♀ Monogamy	◯ 4–5 (2–6) 2 broods INCU: ♀ 13

 FLDG: ♂♀ 11	🪰 Fruit	 Swoops

Breeding habitat Deciduous woodland with undergrowth, usually near water. In SW found in undergrowth in drier forests, such as pine. Found in drier habitats than Thrush Nightingale; their ranges barely overlap.

Displays ♂ sings often from deep cover during day and, commonly, night. In courtship ♂ sings, spreads wings, raises and spreads tail; ♀ crouches. Songs vary depending on the habitat: see essay on Environmental Acoustics, p. 327.

Nesting Territorial. Nest is in thick cover, on ground or low in undergrowth; a cup (sometimes a sphere) of leaves and grass, lined with finer material. Eggs bluish-grey to olive to brown, 21mm. ♂ may look after young while ♀ starts second clutch. Usually one brood in N.

Diet Insects taken from leaf litter, but will also drop to ground from perch like Robin. Takes fruit, particularly in early autumn.

Winters In Africa S of Sahara in areas with thick undergrowth. Defends winter territories and sings there.

Conservation Some long-term declines in W (especially UK), but locally common across S and SW Europe to N Africa and into SW Asia.

Essays Interspecific Territoriality, p. 421; Vocal Copying, p. 383.

Refs Marchant et al. 1990.

not provide suitable habitat for their ground feeding or social displays. As the forests were cleared, cowbirds extended their range, occupying most of the East but remaining rare until this century. Then increased winter food supply, especially the rising abundance of waste grain in southern rice fields, created a cowbird population explosion. The forest-dwelling tropical migrants — especially vireos, warblers, tanagers, thrushes, and flycatchers — proved very vulnerable to cowbird parasitism. That vulnerability is highest for birds nesting near the edge of wooded habitat and thus closest to the open country preferred by the cowbirds.

This provides one explanation for the much sharper decline of songbirds in forest fragments than in large areas of continuous forest: nest sites in a forest fragment are on average closer to open land than those in continuous forest because there is more 'edge' per unit area. In addition, there is evidence that fragmentation *per se*, with both reduction of total habitat area and increased isolation of habitat remnants, has strong negative effects on forest-dwelling long-distance migrants that need forest habitat, while often favouring short-range migrants and residents that do not have such strict habitat requirements.

Ecologist David Wilcove of the Wilderness Society in the USA tested the nest predation hypothesis experimentally by putting quail eggs in straw-coloured wicker baskets either on or above the ground, and placing large numbers of these pseudo-nests in forest patches of various sizes. He also constructed some artificial cavity nests to compare with the artificial cup nests. Wilcove found that predation was heavier in suburban woodlots (70 per cent) than in rural woodlots (48 per cent), and much higher in smaller forest fragments than in large continuous forests. In the continuous forests of the Great Smoky Mountains in the eastern United States, eggs were destroyed in only 2 per cent of the experimental nests.

The pseudo-nests were more conspicuous than normal nests, so Wilcove's field experiments cannot be used to determine actual predation rates, but they do strongly indicate that higher levels of nest predation are at least a partial explanation for the decline of migrant songbirds in forest fragments. Again, the increased proportion of forest edge in fragments is implicated; many important nest predators are most common along woodland borders. In addition Blue Jays and American Crows have benefited greatly from other human-induced changes in the landscape, such as increased suburbanization. High losses of songbird eggs in suburban areas are, however, doubtless due to the abundance there not just of nest-robbing birds, but of dogs, cats, rats, raccoons, and grey squirrels as well.

So it looks as if many factors may be contributing to the decline of American songbirds. Sadly, the prognosis is grim. Ornithologists think that cowbirds are likely to continue to increase, and the now-thriving nest predators are unlikely to decline. The loss of songbirds might be halted if conservation depended entirely on temperate-zone events, because habitat fragmentation in the United States and Canada could be stopped or its effects controlled. But the inexorable destruction of tropical rain forests shows no sign of abating. If it continues at current rates for another few decades, many North

Bluethroat

Luscinia svecica

ATLAS 256; PMH 174; PER 160; HFP 252; HPCW 175; NESTS 272; BWP5:645

BLD: ♀ (♂♀)	⬯	5–7 (8–9) 2 broods	⬯	🪰	🐦
Monogamy		INCU: ♀ 13–14	FLDG: ♂♀ 14	Fruit	Foliage glean

Breeding habitat In birch and willow woodland below tundra, woodlands with thick undergrowth, near rivers, drier upland areas in Spain.

Displays ♂ (sometimes ♀) sings from perch, or in flight, sometimes at night. Threat posture has bill pointed upwards and tail raised, exposing distinctive throat markings. Song often mimics those of other bird species as well as insects, frogs, etc.

Nesting Territorial. Nest on ground, in thick vegetation; cup of leaves and grass; lined with finer materials. Eggs pale greenish with indistinct reddish-brown markings, giving egg reddish colour,

19mm; hatch within 3 days of each other. Usually only one brood in N.

Diet Insects taken from leaf litter or from low vegetation. Also takes fruit.

Winters Most European populations to SW Europe and Africa, S of Sahara; in undergrowth near water, reed-beds. May defend winter territories.

Conservation Species has fragmented and local distribution across much of Europe; only rarely breeds UK. Locally common across N Europe, Asia, and Alaska (where very local). See p. 528.

Essays Vocal Copying, p. 383.

Red-flanked Bluetail

Tarsiger cyanurus

ATLAS 257; PMH 174; PER 160; HFP 252; HPCW 175; NESTS 271; BWP5:664

BLDS: ?	⬯	5–7 1 (2) broods	⬯	🪰	🐦
Monogamy		INCU: ♀ ?	FLDG: ? 15?	Fruit	Foliage glean

Breeding habitat Northern conifer and birch forests with thick undergrowth.

Displays Not well known. ♂ often sings from exposed perch.

Nesting Territorial. Nest is on ground in hole in log, roots, etc; a cup of moss and grass, lined with softer material. Eggs whitish, usually with light reddish-brown spotting, 18mm.

Diet Insects; feeds on ground but also low in vegetation, and by sallying from a perch. Also takes fruits.

Winters In SE Asia. Holds winter territories.

Conservation Range may have increased in 1970s, spreading into Finland, but recent sightings are fewer. Occurs across boreal forest of Russia to Japan, and in Himalayas.

American passerine species will become much rarer or even disappear. In Britain between one third and one half of the ancient broadleaved woodland was lost between World War II and the mid-1980s. Solid evidence linking this loss to any reduction in bird populations, even those of such woodland specialists as Hawfinch and Woodcock, is hard to come by. To some degree the loss of broadleaved woodland has been counterbalanced by the planting of conifers. Thus the overall proportion of Britain covered by woodland blocks greater than 0.25 ha has increased from 6.7 per cent in 1947 to 9.4 per cent in 1980. And the planting of conifers has almost certainly aided the spread of Siskins in Britain.

It seems likely that forest birds in Europe will soon enter a much more rapid decline in response to continuing forest damage from acid deposition and other air pollution. For instance, 60 per cent of 202 breeding species in Baden-Württemberg (southwest Germany) are dependent on forests, and those forests are suffering from 'Waldsterben' (forest death). Threatened species include Golden Orioles, Collared Flycatchers, Stock Doves and a variety of owls and woodpeckers that nest in tree holes. Especially affected are inhabitants of coniferous forest such as Goldcrests, Firecrests, Coal Tits, Nutcrackers, and Ring Ouzels.

Trans-Saharan migrants will suffer because of desertification in the Sahel (the southern fringes of the Sahara), and other destruction of wintering habitat in Africa will add to the burdens imposed by deterioration of their breeding habitat. It is not likely, however, that deforestation in sub-Saharan Africa will further depress European bird populations in the way loss of forests in Latin America is expected to reduce the North American avifauna. First, most of West Africa is already deforested, and second, relatively few migrant European birds are dependent on forest habitat for wintering (the Pied Flycatcher may be an important exception). Indeed, conversion of forests to savanna may help some species.

Whether future patterns of decline of forest birds in Europe will be similar to those in North America will only be known after more time has passed and further analysis is done. The best-studied avian communities in European forests are dominated by species not primarily restricted to forest interiors and are thus expected to be less sensitive to forest destruction (at least of forests in their breeding range). Two of the most abundant and sensitive groups of forest birds in North America, wood warblers (Parulinae) and vireos (Vireonidae), are absent from Europe.

SEE: Island Biogeography, p. 303; Brood Parasitism, p. 249; Wintering and Conservation, p. 409; Acid and Eggshells, p. 287. REFS: Askins et al., 1990; Böhning-Gaese, 1992; Brichetti and Di Capi, 1987; Brittingham and Temple, 1983; Dobkin, 1994; Gates and Geysel, 1978; Grimmett, 1987; von Haartman, 1978; Haila, 1988; Helle, 1985; Hölzinger and Kroymann, 1984; Lynch and Whigham, 1984; Marchant et al., 1990; Rich et al. 1994; Robbins et al., 1989; Schmidt and Einloft-Achenbach, 1984; Terborgh, 1980, 1989; Väisänen et al., 1986; Wilcove, 1985; Wilcove and Terborgh, 1984.

White-throated Robin
Irania gutturalis

ATLAS 258; PMH 252; PER -; HFP 254; HPCW 176; NESTS 274; BWP5:671

 Decid tree 0–0.5m | BLDS: ♀ Monogamy | 4–5 (3–) 1 brood? INCU: ♀, ♂● 13–15 | ? FLDG: ♂♀ 16–18? | Foliage glean

Breeding habitat Rocky slopes with scattered trees and shrubs, to well-vegetated upland grasslands.

Displays ♂ sings from exposed perch, dropping wings and raising tail, or in flight, gliding over territory, or flying with slow wing-beats.

Nesting Territorial. Nest is a cup of grass, twigs, etc. lined with softer material. Eggs pale greenish-blue with light reddish-brown markings, 21mm; hatch over 3 days. ♂ feeds ♀ on nest. Young fed by adults for about a month after fledging.

Diet Insects, found in the leaf litter on ground or gleaned from foliage.

Winters E Africa. Sings in winter and may have winter territories.

Conservation Locally common from Turkey to Afghanistan.

Black Redstart
Phoenicurus ochruros

ATLAS 254; PMH 175; PER 162; HFP 252; HPCW 176; NESTS 270; BWP5:683

 | BLDS: ♀ Monogamy | 4–6 (2–8) 2 (3) broods INCU: ♀ 13–17 |  FLDG: ♂♀ 12–19 | Fruit | Hawks

Breeding habitat Rocky cliffs and hillsides up to snow line. Uses 'man-made cliffs' and so occurs in gardens and on buildings over much of Europe; also nests on large buildings in town centres.

Displays ♂ sings from high, exposed perch. Singing ♂ chases ♀ in courtship, fanning tail and dropping wings when landing near ♀.

Nesting Territorial. Nest is on ledge or in cavity in cliff or man-made substitute; a cup of grass, moss, leaves, etc., lined with softer material. Eggs white, 19mm, hatch synchronously? Young fed by parents for 2–4 weeks after fledging, by ♂ if ♀ starts second clutch.

Diet Insects taken by hopping along ground, picking items off ground or foliage, or by probing, or after short flights to catch prey in air. Also takes fruit.

Winters Resident in S and W, N and E populations move SW and into N Africa.

Conservation Has increased range in N and NW, and is locally common across S and C Europe to N Africa, SW and C Asia.

Refs Marchant et al. 1990.

Nest Evolution

ORNITHOLOGISTS can only speculate on the origins of nest building. Egg-burying as seen in the megapodes could trace back to reptiles that laid eggs in excavated sites. The compost nest of the Great Crested Grebe (which generates some heat as it decays during use) might reflect similar roots. Alternatively, the minimal constructions of ground-nesting non-passerines might be an extension of courtship rituals that re-direct some of the tension between the pair into various 'displacement behaviours'. Stereotypic behaviour such as grass-pulling as seen in Herring Gulls may build up a pile of potential nesting material, or mate-circling in terns may scratch bare patches into the vegetation. Structural complexity increases from shallow scrapes or the use of ground-level natural cavities to digging short burrows like those of Sand Martins (50–90 cm deep) and puffins (100 cm) and eventually to excavating the longer tunnels of bee-eaters and kingfishers.

Most non-passerines prepare a nest, but some with precocial young simply lay their clutch on the ground, forgoing the benefit of shelter to keep eggs dry or the advantage of even a pad or rim to help keep eggs in place. In general, open-nesting birds can keep their eggs just as warm as those that place their nest within shelter. To compensate for the reduced insulation, however, they spend more time on the nest and place themselves at greater risk of predation. There is speculation that a shift from nesting on the ground to seeking elevated sites or moving breeding colonies to offshore islands paralleled the evolutionary diversification of mammalian predators.

Hole-nesting is thought by many to be the primitive situation in passerines, with shortages of sites leading to competition. Thomas Alerstam and Goran Hogstedt have suggested that among small, hole-nesting altricial birds, sheltered sites are favoured both by resident species (which get the first pick) and by species foraging in plain sight of predators that may follow them back to the nest. Even where there is an abundance of potential sites, predation may limit nesting density within the habitat. (Predators create a 'search image', making them more adept at finding certain nest types.) Shortages of natural cavities and the need to limit the density of nests within an area thus may have prompted passerines to move into marginal sites that required modification and led to the constructions we now see.

Determining the degree of nest-site competition, however, is difficult, even today. Most field studies have been limited to experiments that add and/or remove nest-boxes and then measure the subsequent increase or decrease in breeding populations. It is also possible to evaluate whether the increases or decreases affect other nesting species. Marion East and Christopher Perrins, for example, found that breeding densities of hole-nesting Blue and Great Tits in a broad-leaved temperate woodland affect the density of open-nesting warblers. And it is possible to determine whether

Redstart
Phoenicurus phoenicurus

ATLAS 253; PMH 175; PER 162; HFP 250; HPCW 177; NESTS 270; BWP5:695

	BLDS: ♀	5–7 (3–10) 2 broods INCU: ♀
1–3m	Monogamy	11–15

FLDG: ♂♀		
12–15	Fruit	Foliage glean

Breeding habitat A variety of woodlands, including open parklands with large trees, gardens. Also in open uplands with stone walls.

Displays ♂ usually sings from high exposed perch. In courtship, ♂ raises wings and fans tail. ♂ may sing in nesting hole to attract ♀ to it, or enter and exit hole repeatedly.

Nesting Territorial. Nests usually in a hole in trees, rocks, or buildings; will readily use nest boxes. Nest is a cup of moss, grass, etc. lined with softer material. Eggs light blue, 19mm, hatch usually within 2 days of each other. Clutch sizes larger in the N and smaller later in the year. Young fed by both parents for about two weeks after fledging or by ♂ if there is another clutch. Usually one brood in N.

Diet Insects taken on ground, gleaned from foliage or bark of trees. May swoop down from perch or take prey in flight. Also takes fruit.

Winters Africa, S of Sahara in Sahelian zone.

Conservation Although common across most of Europe, N and SW Asia, and into N Africa, population underwent an 80 per cent decline in UK during 1970s perhaps due to Sahelian drought. Has largely recovered in UK, but not on continent.

Notes Breeds only sporadically in Ireland – see essay on Island Biogeography, p. 303.

Essays Declines in Forest Birds: Europe and America, p. 339; Ducking the Bird Laws, p. 523; Wintering and Conservation, p. 409; Birds and Global Warming, p. 311; Vocal Copying, p. 383; Population Dynamics, p. 515.

Refs Marchant et al. 1990.

Moussier's Redstart
Phoenicurus moussieri

ATLAS 254; PMH 252; PER -; HFP 250; HPCW 177; NESTS 271; BWP5:708

	Cavity BLDS: ?	4–5 (3–6) 1 (2?) broods INCU: ?
	Monogamy	?

FLDG: ♂♀		
?	Fruit	Hawks

Breeding habitat Rocky ground, open areas, and forest clearings; to high elevations.

Displays Very little known; ♂ sings from perch.

Nesting Territorial. Nest is on ground or in hole in tree or rocks; a cup of vegetation lined with softer material. Eggs white or very light blue, 18mm.

Diet Insects picked from ground or by probing ground, or from short flights catching prey in air. Sometimes takes fruit.

Winters Resident or moves away from breeding areas.

Conservation Numbers not known; has limited range in N Africa.

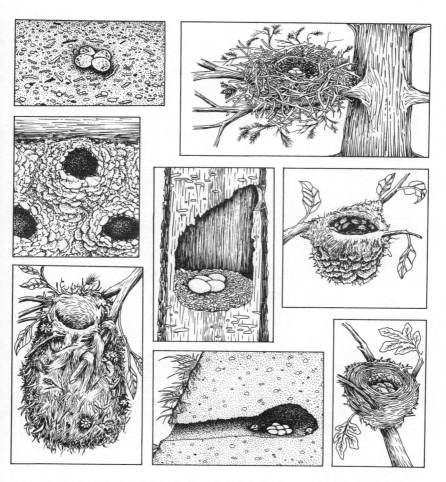

Examples of nests. Centre: woodpecker. Outer, clockwise from upper left: Ringed Plover, Common Buzzard, Goldcrest, finch, kingfisher, Penduline Tit, Cliff Swallow (Hirundo pyrrhonata).

predation in an area is the major source of total nest failure among hole-nesting species. Sven Nilsson, working in a deciduous and mixed deciduous/coniferous forest in Sweden, found that among Great, Marsh, and Blue Tits and Pied Flycatchers, it was. Even with these results, the evolutionary role of nest-hole competition remains speculative.

None the less, most ornithologists assume that along the evolutionary road from cavity nesting to open nesting, today's panoply of passerine nest types developed as birds that were unable to find satisfactory nest holes instead modified crevices that were originally unsuitable. With a continued shortage of sites, natural selection would favour tendencies to excavate com-

Blackstart
Cercomela melanura

ATLAS 254; PMH -; PER -; HFP 249; HPCW 178; NESTS 269; BWP5:718

BLDS: ?	3–4
?	1 brood?
	INCU: ?
	?

FLDG: ?♂♀		
?	Fruit	Foliage glean

Breeding habitat Dry rocky hillsides with scattered bushes, or rocky desert areas.

Displays Little known. ♂ sings from perch, courts ♀ with tail fanned and lowered wings.

Nesting Territorial. Nest is in hole in rocks; a cup of vegetation lined with finer material. Eggs off-white with red-brown spotting, 20mm.

Diet Insects taken after dropping to ground from perch, or by gleaning foliage, or in air after short chase.

Winters Resident.

Conservation Little known about numbers; locally common across southern edge of Sahara, into Sinai and Arabia.

Whinchat
Saxicola rubetra

ATLAS 244 ; PMH 175; PER 162; HFP 242; HPCW 178; NESTS 264; BWP5:722

BLDS: ♀	4–7 (2–)
Monogamy	1 (2) broods
	INCU: ♀
	12–13 (–15)

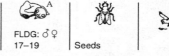

FLDG: ♂♀	
17–19	Seeds

Breeding habitat Open areas such as heaths, agricultural land, meadow, and young pine plantations.

Displays ♂ sings from exposed perch, sometimes in flight. Threatens with wings spread and tail opened, exposing conspicuous markings. ♀ opens and flutters wings.

Nesting Territorial. Nest is on ground, in thick cover; a cup of grass, leaves etc. lined with finer material. Eggs pale blue, often with few reddish spots, 19mm, hatch synchronously? Young cared for by parents for about a month after fledging.

Diet Insects, taken from ground after dropping from perch. Also takes seeds.

Winters Africa, S of Sahara in a wide range of open habitats. Locally, may defend territories.

Conservation Widespread and common across much of Europe and into W and SW Asia, but severe declines in numbers in many areas in W and C due to changing habitat. Overgrown, neglected fields are disappearing.

Essays Declines in Forest Birds: Europe and America, p. 339, Songbird Foraging, p. 417.

Refs Marchant et al. 1990.

partments in soil and decayed soft wood, chisel new holes in firm wood, or search for and assemble materials to augment otherwise marginal sites. In addition, larger species could readily take over tree holes occupied by smaller birds. Such secondary cavity nesting may be commensal (not placing the bird that constructed the nest at a disadvantage) or competitive. In the latter case, for example, by simply enlarging the entrance to the hole, larger birds could discourage smaller birds from using the cavity again.

The diversity of bird nests illustrates the variety of the structures that may provide satisfactory shelter for incubating eggs and rearing young. At the same time, the similarity of nests within a species, and often within a genus or larger group, indicates how highly stereotyped nest-building behaviour has become.

SEE: Nest Sites and Materials, p. 443; Nest Lining, p. 439; Nest Sanitation, p. 75; Hormones and Nest Building, p. 329; Disease and Parasitism, p. 315; Incubation: Controlling Egg Temperatures, p. 273; Cooperative Breeding, p. 275; Precocial and Altricial Young, p. 401; Selection in Nature, p. 471. REFS: Alerstam and Hogstedt, 1981, 1985; Collias and Collias, 1984; East and Perrins, 1986; Elkins, 1983; Fisk, 1978; Greenwood, 1985; Greig-Smith, 1986; Louther, 1977; Martin, 1988; Nilsson, 1984; O'Connor, 1984; Ricklefs, 1989; Wesolowski, 1983.

Preening

PREENING is a commonly observed behaviour involving the careful cleaning, rearrangement, and oiling of the feathers with the bill. Preening is essential in preserving those delicate structures so critical both for flight and for regulating body temperature. Most birds have a 'preen gland' on the rump at the base of the upper tail feathers. Ordinarily the bill is used to work oil squeezed from this gland into the feathers, and head scratching may be an attempt to distribute preen oil over the head, where the bill obviously cannot do the job. Many birds, however, oil the primary feathers directly by rubbing them over the preen gland. The oil apparently has several functions: to help keep the feathers flexible and waterproof and to inhibit the growth of fungi and bacteria.

In arctic Ross' Gulls (*Rhodostethia rosea*) and some other gulls and terns, the preen oil contains a pink colorant. The intensity of colour seems to depend on the diet and whether the bird is in breeding condition, and so the feathers become pink only in the breeding season. But in these species little colour shows above the neck, apparently because of the difficulty of spreading the oil on the head.

SEE: Feathers, p. 363; Temperature Regulation and Behaviour, p. 163; Head Scratching, p. 371. REFS: Grant, 1986; Simmons, 1987.

Stonechat

Saxicola torquata

ATLAS 245; PMH 176; PER 162; HFP 242; HPCW 179; NESTS 264; BWP5:737

		4–6 (2–7) 2–3 broods			
Shrub 0–1m	BLDS: ♀ Monogamy	INCU: ♀ 13–14	FLDG: ♂♀ 12–16	Fruit	Hawks

Breeding habitat A wide range of open land, especially heaths, moors.

Displays ♂ usually sings from exposed perch, often exposing conspicuous white wing coverts. Threat display includes wing-flicking. ♂ chases ♀, fanning and repeatedly raising and lowering tail when on ground near her.

Nesting Territorial. Nests low, in thick cover, especially gorse, often deep into bush with tunnel though the vegetation to reach it; a cup of grass and moss. Eggs off-white, with light reddish-brown spotting, 19mm, hatch synchronously? Migrant populations generally nest later and have 2 broods, resident populations nest earlier and have 3. Both parents feed young for several days after hatching, then ♂ may take over for about a week while ♀ starts new brood.

Diet Insects taken on ground, typically, after flying down from low perch and hopping for a few steps. Sometimes hawks, hovers, or gleans insects from foliage. Will take hairy caterpillars, running them through bill and beating them on ground first. Also takes fruits.

Winters Resident or moves to SW. Conservation Locally common across S and W Europe, absent from N, but other subspecies occur across much of temperate Asia to Arctic Circle, N Africa, and Africa S of Sahara. Vulnerable to hard winters in N and there are local declines, as heaths are converted to pastures.

Essays Birds and Agriculture, p. 365; Timing of Migration, p. 405.

Refs Marchant et al. 1990.

Isabelline Wheatear

Oenanthe isabellina

ATLAS 249; PMH 176; PER 162; HFP 244; HPCW 179; NESTS 266; BWP5:756

		5–6 (3–9) 2 broods			
	BLDS: ♀ Monogamy Polygyny	INCU: ♀ 12	FLDG: ♂♀ 15+		Swoops

Breeding habitat Open plains and grasslands with some shrubs and rocks, avoiding deserts, forests, and wetlands.

Displays ♂ sings from perch or in flight with conspicuously marked tail spread, ascends then glides or spirals downwards with wings also spread. ♂ courts ♀ at burrow by singing, raising tail, then entering it. During mating, ♂ dances backwards and forwards over ♀ in a sequence of up to 50 leaps, brushing ground with breast and beating wings against ground. In unique display, ♂ may roll from side to side near ♀.

Nesting Usually territorial. Nest is in a hole, typically that of a rodent, sometimes in natural hole; a cup of grass, lined with hair and other soft material. Eggs light blue, 22mm. Young

fed by parents for about 2 weeks after fledging. In some locations, a large proportion of ♂s may be polygynous, the first ♀ tries to exclude the second, until she starts to incubate her clutch. The second ♀ sometimes gets help from the ♂ in feeding the young in the nest.

Diet Insects caught on ground after quick pursuit or by dropping down from low perch.

Winters Africa S of Sahara, from W Africa to Arabia to India. In similar habitats to summer. Frequents recently burned areas. Holds winter territories.

Conservation May be expanding range in extreme SE of Europe; locally common across SW and C Asia.

Essays Polygyny, p. 265; Nest Evolution, p. 345.

'Passerines' and 'Songbirds'

PASSERINES are the perching birds, technically members of the order Passeriformes. Birds in this order are characterized by having four toes, three directed forward and one backward, all joining the foot at the same level. Orders are primary taxonomic subdivisions of classes. Birds compose the class Aves (we are in the class Mammalia; bees are in the class Insecta).

Roughly 60 per cent of the 9000 or so bird species are passerines, but they account for only about 40 per cent of the 160 families. Thus, this order makes up an extremely large fraction of bird diversity, and the families within it have a disproportionately high average number of species. Both facts indicate the great success of the passerine way of life: not only have a great many passerine species evolved, but the existence of so many similar species within families suggests a relatively low rate of extinction, a high rate of speciation, or both.

Because the diversity of passerine species is so extensive, and perhaps because they are the most familiar of birds, the class Aves is often conveniently divided simply into passerines and non-passerines. Within the Passeriformes, two groups which differ in the structure of the vocal apparatus are usually recognized: the Oscines and the Suboscines. None of the European passerine families are Suboscines; the most widespread group of Suboscines are probably the New World tyrant flycatchers (about 375 species), which are only superficially similar to European flycatchers. Others include ovenbirds, pittas, manakins, antbirds, and New Zealand wrens.

The Oscines, divided into about 50 families, are the 'songbirds'. This is the group of birds in which singing is most highy developed. The calls of some birds in other groups are quite musical, but it is in the Oscines that we perceive songs to reach their full beauty and complexity.

SEE: Feet, p. 289; Bird Voices, p. 475; Vocal Functions, p. 413; Species and Speciation, p. 325; Classifying Birds, p. 3.

Why Some Species Migrate at Night

THAT some migratory species characteristically travel at night while others fly during the day has long puzzled migration experts. Several hypotheses have been suggested to explain nocturnal migration: the need for migrants to forage during daylight to replenish depleted energy stores, the need to avoid

Wheatear
Oenanthe oenanthe

ATLAS 249; PMH 177; PER 162; HFP 244; HPCW 180; NESTS 265; BWP5:770

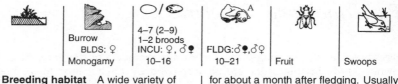

		○/⬬	A		
	Burrow	4–7 (2–9) 1–2 broods			
	BLDS: ♀	INCU: ♀, ♂♀	FLDG:♂♀,♂♀		
	Monogamy	10–16	10–21	Fruit	Swoops

Breeding habitat A wide variety of open habitats from tundra, mountain slopes, to steppes.

Displays ♂ sings from low perch, sometimes in flight. Threat display includes singing while tail is spread every few seconds or so, exposing conspicuous markings. May also bow towards intruder. Has a dancing display as bird jumps from side to side over intruder or mate. ♀ has greeting display holding body horizontally, opening and quivering wings.

Nesting Territorial. Nest is in a hole or burrow in ground, wall, or among rocks; a cup of grass and other vegetation, lined with softer material on a foundation of coarse material. Eggs very light blue sometimes with a few reddish spots, 21mm; large broods hatch over 3 or more days. Young remain with parents for about a month after fledging. Usually one brood in N.

Diet Insects. Bird chases prey along ground, drops on them from a perch, or catches them in mid-air. Will also probe ground. Also takes fruit.

Winters Africa S of Sahara, including (apparently) the arctic populations from E Canada and Greenland (which migrate through W Europe) and Alaskan populations (which go via Asia).

Conservation Some local decreases, in UK, W Europe and Russia. In UK needs short grass, maintained by grazing. Species does not readily exploit areas under crops. Common and occurs widely across Europe, N and C Asia, into N Africa, Alaska, and arctic N America.

Essays Bills, p. 391; Migration, p. 377; Birds and Agriculture, p. 365.

Refs Condor 1989 is a book about this species.

Pied Wheatear
Oenanthe pleschanka

ATLAS 250; PMH 177; PER 164; HFP 246; HPCW 181; NESTS 267; BWP5:792

		⬬	A		
		4–6 (3) 1 (2) broods			
	BLDS: ♀	INCU: ♀(?♂)	FLDG: ♂♀		
	Monogamy	13–14	13–14		Foliage glean

Breeding habitat Bare rocky hillsides or rocky patches within more mesic areas.

Displays ♂ sings from perch or in flight with steep ascent, hovering, then a glide downwards. Threat posture has bill pointed upwards, head tucked in, and tail spread. Has dancing courtship flight like that of Black-eared Wheatear.

Nesting Territorial. Nests in a hole in ground, rocks or buildings; a cup of grass lined with finer material. Eggs light blue with some red-brown spotting, 20mm.

Diet Bird takes insects on ground after dropping down from perch or taken from low foliage.

Winters Chooses similar habitats to summer, but will occupy drier agricultural land and even settlements. Attracted to burnt grasslands. Defends winter territories. In E Africa.

Conservation Locally abundant in isolated population in Cyprus, and from Bulgaria across central Asia to China.

Essays Black and White Plumage, p. 7; Birds and Agriculture, p. 365.

day-active predators, and the need to avoid atmospheric turbulence (a predictable consequence of the daily atmospheric cycle).

Ornithologists Paul Kerlinger and Frank Moore recently reviewed much of the literature relating to the timing of migrants' flight and analysed detailed meteorological data to predict the optimal altitude and time of day for migratory flight. They concluded that several characteristics of the night-time atmosphere create more favourable conditions for powered migrants (in contrast to soaring species). Taken together, the following factors promote a faster and energetically less expensive migration at night than at midday.

Compared to day, nocturnal temperatures are lower and relative humidities higher. These features respectively help prevent overheating and reduce the evaporative water loss (and risk of desiccation) of a flying migrant. In addition, cool air is denser than warm air, making it energetically less costly for a bird to generate lift. Wind patterns are also more advantageous at night: horizontal winds are slower so birds are not as likely to be blown off course, and night-time winds are less variable in direction owing to the absence of turbulence generated during the day by rising columns of warm air (thermals) that result from the sun's heating of the land surface. As a result, nocturnal migrants do not have to contend with turbulent air, thus alleviating the need for constant (and energetically expensive) adjustment of heading and air speed in order to maintain a straight and level track.

In general, birds that use powered flight (which includes virtually all songbirds) migrate at night or early in the morning. Typical of the data that have been gathered are the studies conducted by ornithologist Thomas Alerstam using radar observation in southern Sweden. He found that maximum numbers of thrushes, warblers, and wrens were on the move at around two hours past sunset and again after midnight.

In contrast, soaring migrants (such as storks and most raptors) fly at midday when thermals are readily available to carry them aloft. Relatively large, more powerful migrants like waterfowl and some waders are more likely to fly during daytime than are small passerines, especially in late autumn or early spring, when daytime temperatures are cooler and there is less turbulence. Endowed with their more substantial flight ability, ducks, geese, and many waders are also more likely than songbirds to fly at higher altitudes where winds are stronger.

Taken together, many studies of migrating birds support the idea that atmospheric structure has been a major selective force in the evolution of migratory flight times and flight altitudes. Very likely, the need to stop and feed during daylight hours and to avoid being seen by predators has added to the selection pressures favouring nocturnal migration.

SEE: Migration, p. 377; Orientation and Navigation, p. 503; How Fast and High Do Birds Fly?, p. 63; Wader Migration and Conservation, p. 167; Wintering and Conservation, p. 409; Adaptations for Flight, p. 511; Soaring, p. 79. REFS: Alerstam, 1981; Kerlinger, 1989; Kerlinger and Moore, 1989; Mead, 1983.

Black-eared Wheatear
Oenanthe hispanica

ATLAS 249; PMH 178; PER 164; HFP 244; HPCW 182; NESTS 267; BWP5:806

Cup	4–5 (6)	
BLDS: ♀	2 broods?	
Monogamy	INCU: ♀	
	13–14	

FLDG: ♂♀
11–12

Hawks

Breeding habitat Open habitats, usually with bushes and trees.

Displays Sings from perch or in fluttering flight over territory. Threat display has bill pointing skyward and tail spread. In courtship, ♂ has dancing flight, fast and low over ground in a figure-of-eight about 10m across above the ♀. In nest-showing display, perched ♂ opens wings and rotates entire body up and down.

Nesting Territorial. Nests in a rocky crevice or in thick vegetation; a grass cup lined with finer material such as hair. Eggs pale blue, some reddish-brown

spotting, 20mm, hatch synchronously. Young remain with parents for about 2 weeks after fledging.

Diet Bird takes insects from ground after dropping from low perch, while hawking, or while hopping along ground.

Winters In semi-desert and dry grasslands with scattered trees in Africa, S of Sahara. Holds winter territories.

Conservation Some local decreases, but locally common around Mediterranean to SW Asia.

Notes Absent from many Mediterranean islands – see essay on Island Biogeography, p. 303.

Desert Wheatear
Oenanthe deserti

ATLAS 250; PMH 179; PER -; HFP 244; HPCW 182; NESTS 266; BWP5:820

Burrow	4–5 (3–6)	
BLDS: ♀	1–2 broods	
Monogamy	INCU: ♀	
	13–14	

FLDG: ♂♀
13–18

Hawks

Breeding habitat Rocky or sandy desert with scattered shrubs, dry grasslands, or dry mountain sides. Despite its name, does not penetrate the barren desert areas used by White-crowned Black or Hooded Wheatears.

Displays ♂ sings from perch or in flight while circling over territory, with intermittent diving with tail spread. ♂ threatens by wagging or spreading tail. Towards rival or ♀ may fly up and down or in low loops around bird on ground.

Nesting Territorial. Nests in a hole in the ground, rocks, or in a rodent burrow;

a cup of vegetation lined with finer material, such as hair and feathers. Eggs light blue with reddish-brown spotting, 20mm.

Diet Bird takes insects from ground after dropping from low perch or by hawking. Sometimes chases prey along ground.

Winters Some resident, some S to Sahelian zone, eastwards to India, in dry plains to sandy deserts. Holds winter territories.

Conservation Locally common across N Africa and C Asia.

Bathing and Dusting

WHEN birds bathe in water or saturate themselves with dust they are actively maintaining their plumage. In well-watered areas bathing is most common; in arid regions dusting is more often observed. Experiments with quail show that frequent dusting helps to maintain an optimum amount of oil on the feathers. Excess plumage lipids, including preen oil, are absorbed by the dust and expelled along with dry skin and other debris. If quail are prevented from dusting, their feathers soon become oily and matted. Dusting may also help to discourage bird lice, but there is as yet no experimental evidence showing this to be the case.

Wrens and House Sparrows frequently follow a water bath with a dust bath (one reason to suspect an antiparasite function for dusting). Overall, the amount of time and effort birds put into bathing and dusting indicates how critical feather maintenance may be. Feathers are marvellous and intricate devices, but keeping them functional requires constant care.

A bird is considered to be bathing whenever it uses any of several stereotyped movements to wet its feathers. One pattern, wading, is commonly observed in birds with strong feet and broad, short, flexible wings. In a typical sequence a bird stands in the water, fluffs the feathers to expose skin between their bases, and rapidly flicks the wings in and out of the water. The breast is submerged and rolled vigorously back and forth, and then, as the front end emerges, the head is thrown back, forming a cup with the partially elevated wings and tail, and dousing the feathers of the back. Those feathers are erected so that the water reaches the skin, and then lowered, forcing the water between them. The sequence may be repeated, with the bird submerging farther in each cycle, until it is a mass of soaked, disarranged feathers. Variations on this theme can be seen in various species, including thrushes, jays, and tits.

Birds with weak feet, such as swifts and swallows, which spend most of their time flying, dip into the water in flight, thus getting their baths 'on the wing'. As the body is dipped, the tail is raised to direct a spray of water over the back, and the feathers are vibrated. Flycatchers dive repeatedly from their perches into water, and vireos (New World passerines that are rather warbler-like but with somewhat heavier bills) combine both wading and diving. They stand briefly and dip in the water between dives.

Many songbirds dart in and out of water, immersing and rolling briefly, before returning to dry land to flick their wings and vibrate their feathers before jumping in again. Some, such as the North American Wrentit (*Chamaea fasciata*), which live where water is scarce, wet their plumage with dew from vegetation.

For birds with stubby, weak legs not adapted to wading, bathing is passive. Most woodpeckers and nuthatches, for example, simply expose their feathers

Finsch's Wheatear

Oenanthe finschii

ATLAS 250; PMH -; PER -; HFP 246; HPCW 183; NESTS 268; BWP5:831

Burrow	5 (4–6)			
BLDS: ♀	1–2 broods			
Monogamy	INCU: ♀	FLDG: ♂♀		
	12–13	15–16		Swoops

Breeding habitat Rocky areas in plains and hillsides, with scattered shrubs.

Displays ♂ sings from perch or in flight circling over territory. ♂ threatens by crouching with bill pointed upwards, tail spread and flicked upwards. In courtship ♂ flies from perch to perch low over ♀, holding bill up and with tail spread. May also circle or fly loops over ♀.

Nesting Territorial. Nests in a hole in the ground, rocks, or burrow; a saucer of grass lined with finer plant material, wool, feathers, etc. Eggs pale blue with reddish-brown spotting. Has 2–3 broods in S of range.

Diet Insects, caught on ground after chase. Sometimes drops onto prey from low perch or hawks. See Spectacled Warbler, p. 396.

Winters Resident or moves S into Middle East, Iran. Holds winter territories.

Conservation Little known about population size in its range from Turkey to Afghanistan, adjacent parts of CIS.

Essays Black and White Plumage, p. 7.

Red-rumped Wheatear

Oenanthe moesta

ATLAS 251; PMH -; PER -; HFP 246; HPCW 183; NESTS 268; BWP5:841

	4–5			
BLDS: ♀	2 (3?) broods			
Monogamy	INCU: ♀	FLDG: ♂♀		
	?	?		Swoops

Breeding habitat Desert flats with scattered shrubs, often near salt pans, overlapping extensively in its habitats with Desert Wheatear.

Displays Not well known. Both sexes sing; ♂ sings from perch or in flight between perches, with tail fanned.

Nesting Territorial. Nests in a rodent burrow or other hole; a cup of vegetation lined with wool, feathers, and sometimes snake skin. Eggs pale blue to white with a few reddish-brown spots, 23mm.

Diet Catches insects after hopping along ground or by dropping from low perch.

Winters Resident; holds winter territories.

Conservation Locally common across N Africa to Jordan.

when it is drizzling. They have characteristic bathing ('showering') postures, extending their wings and spreading their tails.

The frequency of bathing by land birds typically is related to the weather. On a hot summer day tits may take five baths; in midwinter they still may bathe several times a week, often in snowmelt found in protected areas. Waterbirds and seabirds also bathe with stereotyped routines. Terns that spend most of their time flying bathe in the same way as swifts. Grebes, ducks, geese, and swans bathe either on the surface or while diving by opening their feathers and wings. Gulls and some rails bathe while wading.

After bathing, birds dry themselves using ritualized movements. Even swimming birds must force the surplus water from between their feathers to protect their insulating properties. Darters and cormorants, which often assume a characteristic sunbathing posture with drying wings spread, are, to varying degrees, also thermoregulating. Similarly, vultures adopt sunbathing postures to dry feathers and to thermoregulate. Songbirds shake themselves to throw off water by vibrating wings and tail and ruffling feathers. All birds normally follow bathing with preening.

For some species that live in areas where standing water is not readily available, dusting appears to substitute for water bathing. Birds create dust wallows by scraping the ground. They throw dust over their bodies and rub their heads in the wallow. The dust is first worked through the feathers and then shaken out. Wrens, sparrows, larks, bustards, bee-eaters, Hoopoes, game birds, and some raptors are among the European birds known to dust. As with water bathing, different species tend to have somewhat different dusting routines. Some birds both bathe and dust, as Gilbert White noted long ago in *The Natural History of Selborne*: 'House-sparrows are great *pulveratrices*, being seen grovelling and wallowing in dusty roads; and yet they are great washers'.

SEE: Preening, p. 349; Head Scratching, p. 371; Spread-wing Postures, p. 17; Anting, p. 469; Disease and Parasitism, p. 315; Temperature Regulation and Behaviour, p. 163.
REFS: Simmons, 1986; Slessers, 1970.

Feeding Birds

DISCARDS by people and industry can be an abundant source of nourishment for many opportunistic species of birds. Populations of crows, Starlings, House Sparrows, Great and Lesser Black-backed, Herring, Common, and Black-headed Gulls have increased greatly near garbage tips. Others profit from dumped refuse or offal released from fish-processing plants and from boats and ships in sea lanes; Fulmars, petrels, Herring, Great Black-backed, and other gulls may build enormous colonies. Chaffinches, Feral Pigeons, and House Sparrows have done well by human excess, and flocks

Red-tailed Wheatear
Oenanthe xanthoprymna

ATLAS 251; PMH -; PER -; HFP 244; HPCW 184; NESTS 266; BWP5:847

		 4–6 2 broods INCU: ♀ 13			
	BLDS: ♀ Monogamy		FLDG: ♂♀ ?		Swoops

Breeding habitat Usually barren, sometimes rocky uplands, locally to high elevation meadows.

Displays ♂ sings from perch or in slow flight over territory. Threat postures include bill pointed skywards and tail spread. Courtship includes a dancing flight of ♂, flying to and fro in low arcs over ♀ on ground. Before mating, ♂ sings to ♀, raising wings and lowering spread tail.

Nesting Territorial. Nests in a natural hole or burrow; a cup of plant material lined with finer material. Eggs pale blue to white, sometimes with reddish-brown spotting, 21mm.

Diet Bird catches insects while moving along ground, probing ground, or by dropping from low perch; also hawks

Winters Some resident; others to dry open country from E Africa, to Arabia and India. Holds winter territories.

Conservation Locally common in limited range from Turkey to Afghanistan.

Mourning Wheatear
Oenanthe lugens

ATLAS 250; PMH -; PER -; HFP 246; HPCW 186; NESTS 267; BWP5:858

		 4–5 (3–6) 1–2 broods INCU: ♀? ?			
	BLDS: ♀ Monogamy		FLDG: ♂♀ 15+		Ground glean

Breeding habitat Rocky hillsides and ravines.

Displays ♂ sings from perch or in flight with tail spread. Threat displays include flicking wings, bowing, and sometimes raising tail.

Nesting Territorial. Nests in a natural hole or burrow; a cup of plant material lined with finer material. Eggs pale blue with reddish-brown spotting, 21mm. Young may be dependent on parents for several weeks after fledging.

Diet Bird catches insects on ground after dropping from low perch or hopping along ground. Also hawks.

Winters Mainly resident, with some movements away from breeding habitats into more open areas. Holds winter territories.

Conservation Locally common, has fragmented range across N Africa into SW Asia and E Africa.

Essays Black and White Plumage, p. 7.

frequenting open-air cafes, railway stations, picnic places, litter baskets, and so forth, are commonplace. In North America, Red-winged Blackbirds (*Agelaius phoeniceus*) have expanded beyond their natural marshland habitat to cultivated areas where leftover grain is abundant and has allowed them to become the region's most numerous terrestrial bird.

Food *intentionally* provided for birds has also benefited many bird species, especially in hard weather. Severe weather has been drawing winter birds to human dwellings since foot traffic began exposing the ground beneath snow cover and farmers first spilled grain or left it out for domestic animals and poultry. Today, purposefully feeding wild birds is widespread, and is especially popular in Britain. Common garden-fed species include Blackbirds, Robins, Great, Blue, and Coal Tits, Starlings, Greenfinches, House Sparrows, Collared Doves, Song Thrushes, Dunnocks, Nuthatches, Chaffinches, and Great Spotted Woodpeckers. Many of the same group are also seen in gardens on the Continent. The 12 species most often found at European feeders include Great and Blue Tits, Blackbirds, House Sparrows, Robins, Chaffinches, Greenfinches, Magpies, Wrens, Dunnocks, Collared Doves, and Tree Sparrows, along with other species of tits, woodpeckers, doves, and Nuthatches as regular takers. Interestingly, on the Continent Starlings rank among the top dozen only in the Netherlands and Belgium.

Providing feed in large parks draws a somewhat different suite of winter birds, and may be important for a wide variety of city-tolerant species such as Mallards, Tufted Ducks and other waterfowl, Rock Doves and Wood Pigeons, Blackbirds, Starlings, and House Sparrows. Park populations of Coal and Great Tits, Robins, Chaffinches, and nuthatches have also increased in response to hand-outs.

The effect that these artificial resources may have on the survival, population stability, and migration patterns of birds is uncertain, but ornithologists guess that if hand-outs were to stop tomorrow, neither species extinctions nor major population declines would occur. Some recently enlarged ranges, however, would contract and detectable decreases in some regions would be likely if artificial feeding during winter were halted. Great Tits in northern Finland appear dependent on winter hand-outs, while those in western Europe and Britain can survive on natural food alone. British seed-eating tits tend to use well-established natural sites as long as possible, moving into gardens only when necessary. Yet, if southern-latitude tits experience even short snow- or ice-covered periods and supplemental food is insufficient, they suffer more from cold winters than do northern populations. Depleted populations, however, tend to re-establish themselves. During extreme cold spells, such as those of 1916–17, 1946–47, 1962–63, and 1978–79, many winter residents unable to find sufficient food before sunset failed to survive the night. None the less while Wrens, for example, decreased drastically during the 1963 cold spell, their numbers increased some 10-fold during the following decade.

In some circumstances, however, taking advantage of hand-outs may be a mistake for the birds. Feeding stations may attract weakened or sick individuals and promote the spread of avian diseases. In addition, many birds

Hooded Wheatear

Oenanthe monacha

ATLAS 249; PMH -; PER -; HFP 246; HPCW 187; NESTS 268; BWP5:867

		?
		?
		? broods
BLDS: ?	INCU: ?	
Monogamy?	?	

?		
FLDG: ?		
?	Seeds	Hawks

Breeding habitat Rocky desert wadis and ravines; a truly desert-adapted wheatear.

Displays Poorly known. ♂ sings from perch or in flight with tail spread.

Nesting Territorial. Nests in a hole. Eggs not described for certain.

Diet Bird takes insects on ground after dropping from low perch, or (more often than other wheatears) by hawking. Also takes seeds.

Winters Resident; holds winter territories.

Conservation Locally distributed from Nile Valley to Iran.

Essays Black and White Plumage, p. 7.

White-crowned Black Wheatear

Oenanthe leucopyga

ATLAS 252; PMH 253; PER -; HFP 248; HPCW 187; NESTS 268; BWP5:876

		3–5 (2–6)
		1–2 broods
BLDS: ♀, ♂♀	INCU: ♀	
Monogamy	14?	

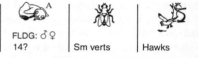

FLDG: ♂♀		
14?	Sm verts	Hawks

Breeding habitat Deserts; desert oases; a truly desert-adapted wheatear, often the only bird seen in some very dry areas.

Displays Sings from perch or in flight, gliding from one perch to another with wings and tail spread. In threat, has low bow, raising tail or pointing bill skywards (also used towards ♀). ♂ may fly over and around ♀ on ground.

Nesting Territorial. Nests in a natural hole in rocks; a cup of plant material lined with softer material such as wool or feathers. Eggs pale blue to white, with some reddish-brown spotting, 22mm. Second nest may be constructed before first brood is fledged. Young may remain with parents into winter.

Diet Diverse; catches insects in flight, on ground after dropping from perch, or pursues them along ground; also takes small lizards, fruits, and seeds.

Winters Resident. Holds winter territories.

Conservation Locally common across the Sahara and into Arabia.

Essays Black and White Plumage, p. 7.

will readily approach damp grain or bread contaminated with the mould *Aspergillus fumigatus*, which, if inhaled, can cause the potentially lethal infection, aspergillosis. Irregular feeding can be hazardous to birds that establish habitual foraging patterns; oversupply may attract undesirable species such as pigeons and Starlings which crowd out other birds. Feeding on the ground encourages predation by cats (Britain's 5 million house cats have been estimated to take well in excess of 20 million birds annually). Much more desirable from a birdwatcher's viewpoint, is that as the number of visitors increases, so does the number of bird-hunting raptors.

Hand-outs may cause other problems, as well. Beef suet brings many species of birds (including woodpeckers, nuthatches, titmice, wrens, thrushes, warblers, and Starlings) into gardens. Unfortunately, many feeders are kept stocked as spring advances. Sun-warmed suet not only may spoil at temperatures over 20°C but also tends to mat feathers, which can reduce insulation and waterproofing, inflame or infect feather follicles, and lead to a loss of facial feathers. In North America, a survey carried out in Iowa showed that more suet is taken by birds during May than during the rest of the year. Many Downy Woodpeckers (*Picoides pubescens*, the North American equivalent of the Lesser Spotted) that eat this warm suet become barefaced in the spring.

Today, in spite of the far-sighted efforts of many bird enthusiasts, the provision of supplemental food remains somewhat uneven. Increasing numbers of birdwatchers, however, are helping to determine the effectiveness of particular feeding techniques. In Britain, for example, the Garden Bird Feeding Survey, organized by the British Trust for Ornithology, has gathered data on the 100 or so species that frequent garden feeding stations. Weekly, 200 people across Britain watching designated stations count the number of birds feeding, while thousands of participants record which species are present at the feeders they are surveying. Among the findings is evidence that the variety and number of visitors depend not only upon the weather, but upon the abundance of the previous autumn's fruit and seed crop.

SEE: Commensal Feeding, p. 27; Disease and Parasitism, p. 315; Starlings, p. 463; Birds and Agriculture, p. 367; Declines in Forest Birds: Europe and America, p. 339.
REFS: Beecher, 1955; Churcher, and Lawton, 1989; De Graaf and Payne, 1975; Dunn, 1990; Goodwin, 1978; Kress, 1985; Leck, 1978; Orell, 1989; U.S. Fish and Wildlife Service and U.S. Bureau of the Census, 1980.

Black Wheatear
Oenanthe leucura

ATLAS 251; PMH 179; PER 162; HFP 248; HPCW 188; NESTS 269; BWP5:885

Ground

BLDS: ♂♀
Monogamy

3–5 (–6)
2 broods?
INCU: ♂♀
14–18 (–21)

FLDG: ♂♀
14–19

Fruit

Swoops

Breeding habitat Rocky areas including sea cliffs, mountain ravines, and hillsides.

Displays ♂ sings from perch, then ascends with fluttering wings, spreads tail, and glides to another perch. Often lands on special display ground where ♂ moves over small area raising and spreading tail. ♂ also carries small stones to nest hole as part of courtship.

Nesting Territorial. Nests in a crevice among rocks, in ground, walls, etc. Builds a platform (sometimes substantial) of small stones at sides of nest, which is a cup of grass with only a little lining. Eggs very pale blue with brown spotting concentrated at one end, 25mm.

Diet Catches insects by hopping along ground, swooping down to ground from low perch, or caught in air. Also takes fruit.

Winters Resident; in small groups which may be family parties.

Conservation Rare and decreasing in France, locally common southwards to NW Africa. See p. 529.

Rock Thrush
Monticola saxatilis

ATLAS 247; PMH 179; PER 164; HFP 242; HPCW 189; NESTS 265; BWP5:893

BLDS: ♀
Monogamy

4–5 (6)
1–2 broods
INCU: ♀
14–15

FL: ♂♀,♂♀
14–16

Fruit

Ground glean

Breeding habitat Rocky hillsides or ravines, usually with trees and shrubs, sometimes to high elevations.

Displays ♂ sings from perch or in flight, with tail spread, ascends steeply, flutters at greatest height, drops quickly with wings and tail spread, then may repeat process. In threat displays ♂ ruffles plumage and sings at rival. In courtship, ♂ moves neck and head from side to side, singing.

Nesting Territorial. Nests in a crevice or hole; a cup of grass, lined with finer material. Eggs pale blue, sometimes with a very few small brown spots, 26mm. Young remain with parents (often ♂) for about a month after fledging.

Diet Catches insects on ground after dropping from low perch, sometimes hops or runs along ground. Will hawk for insects, and take insects and fruit from plants.

Winters Africa S of Sahara (even those populations from E China). Holds winter territories.

Conservation Has declined over much of the N part of its range, but is locally common across S Europe, locally N Africa, and across Asia.

Essays The Colour of Birds, p. 137.

Feathers

BIRDS are *defined* by feathers. No bird lacks them, no other animal possesses them. Feathers are also a symbol of lightness. Therefore, a measure of their importance to birds is that, on average, they make up about 6 to 9 percent of a bird's weight. Birds produce them in very large numbers. Roughly between 1000 (hummingbirds) and 25 000 (swans) typical (or 'contour') feathers cover their bodies, supplemented by down and other specialized feather types.

As the figure shows, contour feathers have the familiar 'crow quill' form. The bare part of the shaft ('quill') is held in a socket ('follicle') in the skin. Each side of the rest of the shaft ('rachis') supports an intricate web of the 'vane'. The flat, flexible vane is one of nature's marvels. Under high magnification,

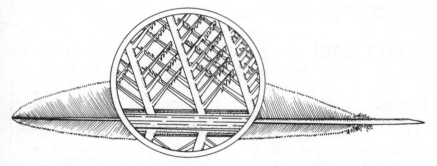

the numerous parallel 'barbs' of the vane, running diagonally outward from the rachis, look like feathers in miniature. The barbs have parallel 'barbules' running diagonally outward from their shafts — more than a million barbules per feather.

But under the high magnification of the electron microscope, the resemblance of barbs to feathers ends. The barbules on the side of each barb toward the feather tip are armed with minute hooks called barbials; those on the side toward the feather base (quill) have smooth ridges on their upper edges. The hooklets on the outer barbules of one barb attach it to the ridges on the inner barbules of the other. By this mechanism, the barbs and thus the entire feather, zip together into a functional unit, capable of resisting a rapidly moving airstream. Should the structure of the feather be disrupted by, say, an encounter with a twig, the bird can simply rejoin the barbs by drawing its beak over the feather during preening.

Down feathers, in contrast, have barbules without hooklets. Usually they lie beneath contour feathers, and provide the bird with insulation. Many contour feathers also have barbules lacking hooklets along the base of the shaft which provide a fluffy, insulating layer that lies close to the skin.

Blue Rock Thrush
Monticola solitarius

ATLAS 248; PMH 180; PER 164; HFP 242; HPCW 189; NESTS 265; BWP5:903

 1–5m	 BLDS: ♀ Monogamy	◯/◉ 4–5 (3–6) 1–2 broods INCU: ♀, ♂● 12–15	^A FLDG: ♂♀ 18?	 Sm verts	 Hawks

Breeding habitat Wide range of rocky habitats, including sea cliffs, quarries, mountain crags, and buildings.

Displays Sings from perch or in flight, like Rock Thrush. Threat display of crouching and ruffling feathers, singing. In courtship, ♂ has bowing display: first holds head and bill skywards, then almost touches bill to the ground.

Nesting Territorial. Nests in a crevice among rocks or wall; is a large shallow cup of vegetation lined with finer grass, feathers, etc. Eggs pale blue, sometimes with a few brownish spots, 28mm, probably hatch synchronously. Young remain with parents for about 2 weeks after fledging. Usually only one brood in N.

Diet Insects, sometimes lizards, taken on ground after bird drops from low perch. Will hawk for insects, and take insects and fruit from plants.

Winters Resident, though may move to lower elevations; Asian races migratory. ♂s and ♀s defend separate winter territories.

Conservation Some declines in N, but locally common across S Europe and N Africa across Asia to Japan.

Ring Ouzel
Turdus torquatus

ATLAS 261; PMH 181; PER 164; HFP 256; HPCW 190; NESTS 275; BWP5:939

 Shrub 0–5m	☕ Crevice BLDS: ♀ Monogamy	◉ 4 (3–6) 1–2 broods INCU: ♀, ♂● 12–14	^A FLDG: ♂♀ 14–16	Summer: Insects Winter: Fruit	 Foliage glean

Breeding habitat Open moorland with rocky areas, sometimes with trees, usually in uplands, less often to sea level. May need access to areas of short grass for feeding.

Displays ♂ sings from perch or in flight. ♂ chases rival ♂ along ground, raising tail and head to show white breast markings. Uses similar display towards ♀.

Nesting Territorial. Nest is usually near ground in cover with overhanging bank or in crevice; a cup of twigs, with mud plastering, thick lining of finer material. Eggs bluish-green, with reddish-brown blotches, 30mm, hatch synchronously. Young remain with adults for about 2 weeks after fledging.

Diet Insects and earthworms in summer; fruit in autumn and winter; takes food on ground or from trees.

Winters Around Mediterranean, particularly in N Africa, in dry hillsides. In flocks, often with other thrushes.

Conservation Has declined in UK, perhaps also Sweden, Iceland, probably due to disturbance; has local and highly fragmented distribution in upland areas in Europe and SW Asia.

Essays Declines in Forest Birds: Europe and America, p. 339.

Refs Marchant et al. 1990.

Next to the base of some contour feathers are simple, hair-like feathers called 'filoplumes', which are attached to special sensory receptors in the skin. When the feathers become ruffled, they disturb the filoplumes which in turn stimulate the receptors. Each receptor has a 'direct line' to the central nervous system, and provides the bird with exact information on feather disturbance, which can then be followed by appropriate preening. It also seems likely that the filoplumes, sensing changes in feather position caused by airflow over a flying bird, may play an important role in the sensory control of flight.

There are other kinds of specialized feathers. For instance, some birds — such as pigeons, hawks, herons, bitterns, and parrots — have 'powder down' feathers that produce, or disintegrate into, fine powder. These feathers may be concentrated in dense patches (herons) or scattered (hawks). The powder is distributed by preening and helps to waterproof and preserve other feathers. It may also give the feathers a metallic appearance. Powder down feathers tend to be abundant in birds, such as some pigeons and parrots, that lack preen glands.

Facial bristles are another kind of specialized feather. These feathers are concentrated around the mouths of flycatchers, swallows, nightjars, crows, and ravens and may function like the whiskers of a cat to amplify sensations of touch. When bristles cover the nostrils, as they do in some woodpeckers, they may help to filter out wood or other particles.

Feathers are raised, lowered, or rotated by muscles that attach to the walls of their sockets. This helps them to perform their functions — first and foremost flight, but also several others. Fluffing or sleeking the feathers varies the thickness of the feather-plus-air insulating layer and controls heat exchange with the environment, helping the bird to regulate its temperature. Feathers shield the bird from injury, sunburn, and rainfall. Tail feathers prop woodpeckers in position for their powerful pecking and act as a rudder for stiff-tailed White-headed Ducks swimming underwater. Colourful feathers are used in displays, and drab ones often provide camouflage. Feathers not only define birds, they are essential to their existence.

SEE: Moulting, p. 373; Preening, p. 349; Bathing and Dusting, p. 355; Anting, p. 469; Head Scratching, p. 371; Black and White Plumage, p. 7; Eclipse Plumage, p. 53; Temperature Regulation and Behaviour, p. 163. REF.: Necker, 1985.

Birds and Agriculture

CHANGING habitats, as comes about when land is developed for agriculture, may seriously affect bird populations. When tropical forests are cleared to create cropland or pasture (both of which often tend to degrade to useless-

Blackbird

Turdus merula

ATLAS 260; PMH 182; PER 164; HFP 256; HPCW 190; NESTS 275; BWP5:949

 Shrub
0–10m

 BLDS: ♀, ♂ ●
Monogamy

3–5 (2–6)
2–3 (5) broods
INCU: ♀
10–19

 FLDG: ♂♀
10–19

Fruit

Probes

Breeding habitat   Wide range of areas with trees, bushes, from deep forests to inner cities.

Displays   Sings from perch. Threat display has neck stretched upwards, bill raised slightly, and wings and tail lowered. Birds often chase each other on ground. ♂ courts ♀, stretching head forward, lowering and spreading tail, and raising rump feathers.

Nesting   Nests in a bush, tree, or in buildings; a large, untidy cup of vegetation, plastered inside with mud, lined with fine grass. Eggs greenish-blue, variously spotted red-brown; sometimes unmarked, 29mm, hatch within 2 days of each other. Young fed by parents for 2–3 weeks (by ♂ if ♀ is starting another clutch).

Diet   Takes insects and earthworms from ground, turning over leaf litter or probing soil; takes fruit (often in autumn or winter) from trees. Will take snails, but apparently lacks ability to extract large ones from shells (see Song Thrush); will steal extracted snails from that species.

Winters   Resident in S and W, migrates to those areas from N and E. Often in flocks, if unable to keep a winter territory.

Conservation   Abundant and increasing (colonizing islands) across most of Europe and parts of Asia. Perhaps the most abundant UK bird (see Chaffinch).

Essays   Declines in Forest Birds: Europe and America, p. 339; Birds and Agriculture, p. 365; Island Biogeography, p. 303; Mobbing, p. 261; Monogamy, p. 335; Piracy, p. 213; Songbird Foraging, p. 417; Birds and the Law, p. 521; Temperature Regulation and Behaviour, p. 163; Tool-using, p. 459; Ducking the Bird Laws, p. 523; Bird Droppings, p. 485; Feeding Birds, p. 357; Vocal Copying, p. 383.

Refs   Marchant et al. 1990.

Fieldfare

Turdus pilaris

ATLAS 259; PMH 183; PER 166; HFP 256; HPCW 191; NESTS 276; BWP5:977

 1–25m

 BLDS: ♀
Monogamy

 5–6 (3–7)
1–2 broods
INCU: ♀
10–13

 FLDG: ♂♀
11–15

 Fruit

Foliage glean

Breeding habitat   Birch, alder, and conifer woodlands, often on the edges or in openings, to high elevations and into settlements.

Displays   ♂ sings in flight with slow wing-beats. In threat display, ♂ crouches, ruffles feathers, shakes spread tail. In courtship ♂ follows ♀ with tail spread and lowered, bill pointing downward, and rump feathers raised.

Nesting   Often in small colonies; nests in a tree, usually where a branch meets the trunk; a cup of twigs and grass, with a mud lining filled with finer grasses. Eggs pale blue variously and variably marked with browns, 29mm, hatch asynchronously. Young remain with parents for about 2 weeks after fledging.

Diet   Takes invertebrates (insects, earthworms) from ground, turning over earth and stones, and fruits from trees in autumn and winter.

Winters   S populations resident, N ones move S and W, often in open fields near woods. In flocks, with other thrushes.

Conservation   Generally increasing, having recently colonized areas in the W (e.g. UK). Common and widespread across most of N and C Europe and much of N Asia.

Essays   Commensal Feeding, p. 27.

ness in a few years), forest bird populations are exterminated. When prairie farmers in North America drain wetlands for cultivation, duck populations nosedive.

In North America and Africa there were originally rather diverse communities of birds adapted to open lands, but the vast majority of birds in Britain and most of Europe were denizens of woodlands. Today's European farmland birds mostly rely on the more wooded parts of the agricultural landscape. In England, species most frequently found on farms are, in order of abundance, Blackbird (by far the commonest), Chaffinch, Dunnock, Robin, Wren, Skylark, Blue Tit, Song Thrush, Yellowhammer, Willow Warbler, Great Tit, Linnet, Greenfinch, and Starling. All but the Skylark and Yellowhammer are also abundant in woodlands — that is, the group consists mostly of woodland birds which can also use poor fragmented woodland.

As might be expected, bird diversity tends to be higher where small-scale farming combines crops than where large-scale mechanized farming devotes huge blocks of land to single crops. More information on the fascinating relationship between birds and farming in Great Britain can be found in a book by Raymond O'Connor and Michael Shrubb (1986).

For example, since World War II significant changes in the British agricultural landscape have included: conversion of woodland to cropland and alteration of heath and scrub (both only locally important); reduction of the amount of hedgerow; improved drainage of lowlying land; and escalating use of agricultural chemicals, including pesticides. None of these changes has been beneficial to the avifauna; all but the last result in loss of preferred habitat. For instance, loss of woodland tends to reduce food supplies, as birds make little use of cropland for feeding; insecticide spraying generally reduces the supply of insect food; and herbicides have destroyed many of the plants whose seeds once supported hordes of small songbirds. As Peter Lack of the British Trust for Ornithology put it: 'Winter flocks of finches are almost a thing of the past . . . Fifteen or 20 years ago, if you walked through farmland you would come across great flocks of finches — Linnets, Chaffinches, Goldfinches, Greenfinches, Reed Buntings, Yellowhammers and so on'. In contrast, some larger birds such as Magpies and Carrion Crows have been favoured by agricultural practices, and as nest predators, may have contributed to the decline of the smaller species.

Farming practices, including rotation patterns, can also have strong impacts on bird populations. For instance, regimes that lengthen the period that fields are allowed to lie fallow under grass, lucerne, or clover have apparently had a deleterious effect on Skylark populations, since the birds prefer to nest in young fallow fields. Lapwings, in contrast, are not so sensitive to changes in rotation schedules, but are strongly threatened by intensification of management, which increases crop densities. That makes it more difficult for adults to detect approaching nest predators, which they normally attack vigorously.

Recent changes in agricultural practices have affected avifaunas in continental Europe as well. Intensification of farming in northern Jutland led to an increase in the area permanently under barley, with a concomitant de-

Song Thrush

Turdus philomelos

ATLAS 260; PMH 183; PER 166; HFP 258; HPCW 191; NESTS 277; BWP5:989

 Shrub 0–8m | BLDS: ♀ Monogamy | 3–5 (2–6) 2–3 (4) broods INCU: ♀ 10–17 |  FLDG: ♂♀ 11–17 | Fruit | Foliage glean

Breeding habitat Wide range of mixed habitats with trees, bushes, and open areas including woodlands, farmlands, and gardens.

Displays ♂ sings from perch. In threat, birds crouch, lower and spread tail, and ruffle feathers. In courtship, ♂ holds bill open vertically, ruffles feathers, and runs near or around ♀.

Nesting Territorial. Nests in a bush or tree, often where branch joins trunk; a cup of twigs, and grass with thick mud lining. Eggs light blue with small brown or black spots or blotches, 27mm, hatch synchronously.

Diet Invertebrates (insects, earthworms, and snails); in addition fruit in autumn and winter. Searches leaf litter. Takes snails by banging them against a hard surface, such as a rock (an anvil), while holding the shell by its lip.

Winters Resident in S and W, migrates to those areas and N Africa from N and E. More movement when weather is unusually cold. Generally not in flocks, except on migration. Residents hold winter territories.

Conservation Some declines (steep in UK, where once was more common than Blackbird). Is abundant and generally increasing in N and W, found across most of Europe and parts of N and C Asia, SW Asia. Vulnerable to cold winters.

Essays Declines in Forest Birds: Europe and America, p. 339; Piracy, p. 213; Birds and Agriculture, p. 365; Selection in Nature, p. 471; Feeding Birds, p. 357; Nest Lining, p. 439; Tool-using, p. 459.

Refs Marchant et al. 1990.

Redwing

Turdus iliacus

ATLAS 259; PMH 184; PER 166; HFP 258; HPCW 191; NESTS 276; BWP5:1000

 Shrub 0–3m | BLDS: ♀ Monogamy | 4–6 (3–7) 2 broods INCU: ♀ 12–13 | FLDG: ♂♀ 8–13 | Fruit | Foliage glean

Breeding habitat Boreal forests of birch and conifers, to above tree line in willow scrub.

Displays ♂ sings from exposed perch. Surprisingly few displays other than singing and chasing off rivals.

Nesting Defends area close to nest, may feed outside this area. Nests in a tree, shrub, or in cover on ground; a cup of twigs and grass, plastered with mud and an inner lining of finer material. Eggs bluish-green, with extensive red-brown spotting, 26mm, usually hatch synchronously. Parents remain with young for about 2 weeks after fledging (♂ only, if ♀ is starting another clutch).

Diet Invertebrates (insects, earthworms, and snails), by running or hopping along ground; in addition takes fruit in autumn and winter.

Winters Most birds migrate S and W as far as N Africa. Often in open fields, with nearby hedges, but searches for bushes with berries. In flocks, with other thrushes.

Conservation Common and increasing (having recently colonized Scotland). Occurs from Iceland across Scandinavia to NE Asia.

Essays Declines in Forest Birds: Europe and America, p. 339; Vocal Dialects, p. 477; Vocal Copying, p. 383.

Refs Marchant et al. 1990.

crease in meadows and grasslands. Open land species such as Lapwings and Meadow Pipits have declined precipitously, and birds whose feeding is associated with grasslands, such as Starlings and Swallows have also decreased. The story in the Netherlands is also one of intensification altering grassland bird communities, to the detriment of most waders, with Ruffs being driven towards extinction outside of reserves. Mowing is done earlier in the year than previously and grazing cattle have higher population densities — and both are major factors in increasing the mortality of chicks. Some species tolerate this better than others, however, and Oystercatchers and Curlews are actually increasing in the Netherlands (although in England the latter are decreasing).

In Italy, bringing more land into cultivation has greatly decreased the area available to the avian inhabitants of steppes. The Little Bustard and the Andalusian Hemipode, for instance, were both exterminated in Sicily by that process before 1950. Corncrakes, Quail and Partridge have declined generally in western Europe as agriculture has been intensified, and the same has also reduced and fragmented populations of the Great Bustard. In the Soviet Union, the 'virgin lands' policy brought large areas of steppe under the plough. This, in turn, caused population declines of steppe birds such as the Black and White-winged Larks.

Destruction of orchards in southern Germany has had a deleterious impact on many species, including the Little Owl. All owl species are generally suffering from reduction in rodent populations associated with recent agricultural practices.

Birds, of course, may get revenge by eating some of the produce of farms. In Africa the Red-billed Quelea (*Quelea quelea*) sometimes is a serious agricultural pest, and in Scotland grazing by Greylag and Pink-footed Geese lowers cereal yields locally. But overall the damage done to farmers by birds is trivial compared to the worldwide impact of agriculture on bird populations.

SEE: Pesticides and Birds, p. 115; Declines in Forest Birds: Europe and America, p. 339. REFS: Baines, 1988; Beintema, 1988; Busche, 1989; Diehl, 1988; Dobkin, 1994; Ehrlich and Ehrlich, 1981; Folz, 1989; Hudson and Rands, 1988; Illner, 1988; Møller, 1983a; O'Connor and Shrubb, 1986; Patterson et al., 1989; Petretti, 1988; Potts, 1986.

Dawn Chorus

ALL birdwatchers are familiar with the dawn chorus, the burst of singing that starts just before daybreak in spring, continues as it becomes light, and then dies away. Bird species tend to join the chorus in a characteristic sequence. It has been suggested that the chorus occurs at dawn because of favourable conditions for transmitting sound, because foraging will be less profitable then

Mistle Thrush
Turdus viscivorus

ATLAS 258; PMH 184; PER 166; HFP 258; HPCW 191; NESTS 277; BWP5:1011

Conif tree 1–20m	BLDS: ♀ Monogamy	3–5(–6) 2 (–3) broods INCU: ♀ 12–15	FLDG: ♂♀ 12–15	Fruit	Foliage glean

Breeding habitat Originally open upland woodlands (open pine forests in Scandinavia), but spreading into lowland parklands and gardens.

Displays ♂ sings from high perch. ♂ courts ♀, chasing her around territory, spreading wings and tail when on ground, but unlike some other thrushes, does not raise rump feathers.

Nesting Territorial. Nest is usually high in fork of a tree, or against trunk; a cup of twigs, grass, with mud, with thick lining of finer grass or pine needles. Eggs light bluish-green spotted or blotched with reddish-brown, 30mm, hatch synchronously. Young remain with adults for about 2 weeks (with ♂ if ♀ begins another brood).

Diet Invertebrates (insects, earthworms, and snails), on ground; also fruit from trees and bushes in autumn and winter.

Winters Resident in S and W, moves to these areas from N and E; sometimes in small groups, but will also defend winter territories around berry bushes.

Conservation Generally increasing in N and W and locally common across most of Europe into W and C Asia, N Africa.

Essays Territoriality, p. 397.

Refs Marchant et al. 1990.

Cetti's Warbler
Cettia cetti

ATLAS 225; PMH 185; PER 166; HFP 226; HPCW 192; NESTS 244; BWP6:7

Reeds 0–1m	BLDS: ♀ Polygyny	4–5 (2–) 1–2 broods INCU: ♀ 16–17	FLDG: ♀ 14–16		

Breeding habitat Dense low vegetation, usually in marsh or near water.

Displays ♂ sings from top of tall grasses or often from dense vegetation; bird adopts upright posture with head thrown back and tail depressed. ♂ spends most of its time defending its territory; such defense lasts for much of the year.

Nesting Territorial. Nests in thick cover on or just above ground; a cup of leaves, grass, lined with finer material. Eggs bright brick-red to chestnut, 18mm. Adults remain with young for about a month after fledging. ♂s are about 30 per cent larger than ♀s and larger ♂s generally have more ♀s nesting in their territories (up to 4). ♀s of polygynous ♂s have larger clutches than ♀s that have monogamous ♂s as mates.

Diet Insects and other invertebrates (including aquatic species) taken on or near ground.

Winters Mainly resident, or moves S.

Conservation Increasing N, colonized coastal France in 1961, Holland in early 70s, UK in 1972; is locally common across S Europe, N Africa into Asia. Vulnerable to cold winters.

Notes Occurred in adjacent areas of continental Europe for some time before colonizing UK; see essay on Island Biogeography, p. 303.

Essays Polygyny, p. 265; Wetland Conservation, p. 145.

Refs Bibby 1982.

and so the 'costs' of singing are reduced, and because territorial intrusions are more likely to occur at that time.

Recent work on Great Tits by Ruth Mace at Oxford suggests the main function of the dawn chorus is to ensure that paired males are not cuckolded. The dawn peak of singing only occurs well after territories are established and pairs united. At high latitudes where foraging time is extended by long days, males roost later than more southern birds and still sing before dawn. But the duration of male song is longest when the females are most likely to be fertile. As the period of egg-laying approaches, songs get longer; after the last egg is laid songs decline in length. Furthermore females tend to lay eggs around dawn, and are thought to be most fertile for one or two hours after laying. Typically females emerge from their nest holes after having produced an egg, dart into cover with their mates, and copulate. The male's singing then declines dramatically.

Dawn is thus the time when females are most anxious to copulate, and present the greatest opportunity for neighbouring or even non-territorial males to mate with them. It is that period when mate-guarding by the male of the pair is most critical, and that guarding is signified by the territorial songs of the dawn chorus.

SEE: Monogamy, p. 335; Territoriality, p. 397; Copulation, p. 87; Environmental Acoustics, p. 327; Vocal Functions, p. 413; Sleeping Sentries and Mate-guarding, p. 73. REFS: Kacelnik and Krebs, 1982; Mace, 1987; McNamara et al., 1987.

Head Scratching

HEAD scratching is so essential to birds that even one-legged individuals will attempt it. As far as we can tell, it has several functions related to plumage maintenance. Since a preening bird cannot reach its head feathers with its beak, some species gather preen oil on the bill, scrape the bill with the foot, and then scratch the head. Head scratching may also remove moulted feathers. The area of the head most frequently scratched is near the ear, and it has been suggested that the behaviour is associated with pressure changes in the eustachian tubes. This, however, seems counterintuitive since claws are not inserted inside. But chronic ear scratching suggests that there may be another function in addition to spreading preen oil and cleaning. It could be removing ectoparasites (those that live on the outside of the host) and their eggs, something that is done with the bill on other parts of the body.

The motions used for head scratching are quite ritualized, and vary from species to species. Within a species the pattern of scratching is constant, and related species tend to scratch in similar ways. For example, sandpipers scratch their heads by directly raising a leg under the wing, whereas plovers

Fan-tailed Warbler

Cisticola juncidis

ATLAS 224; PMH 186; PER 166; HFP 226; HPCW 192; NESTS 244; BWP6:20

to 0.5m	BLDS: ♂♀ Polygyny	5–6 (4–7) 2 (3) broods INCU: ♀ 12–13?	FLDG: ♀ 14–15		

Breeding habitat Grasslands and other short vegetation, often wet meadows, including rice fields.

Displays Has jerky, undulating song flight, up to 30m, swooping down to ground and then up again with tail fanned.

Nesting Territorial. Nests in grass and rushes. Nest is long and pear-shaped with hole at top. Spiders' webs are wrapped around grass stems, and the cavity lined with soft plant material; the outside is made by the ♂, the inside by the ♀. Eggs are variably coloured from unmarked white, to whitish, with a variety of dark brown markings, 15mm. Social system is not well known within area covered by this guide, but elsewhere the birds are polygynous, with up to 5 ♀s per ♂.

Diet Insects, taken on or near ground.

Winters Resident; locally migratory.

Conservation Locally common from France southward into Africa, E to Japan. Increasing N into Holland, but vulnerable to hard winters and numbers fluctuate considerably.

Essays Polygyny, p. 265.

Graceful Warbler

Prinia gracilis

ATLAS 225; PMH -; PER -; HFP 226; HPCW 193; NESTS 245; BWP6:31

0.5–1.0m	BLDS: ♂♀ Monogamy	4–5 (2–) 2 (3) broods INCU: ♂♀ 11–13	FLDG: ♂♀ 12–13 (11–16)		Ground glean

Breeding habitat Low shrubs, sometimes near water, in dry regions.

Displays ♂ sings typically from a prominent perch with plumage ruffled, vibrating tail, or in a jerky, dancing display flight. Threatens using wing-snapping when perched or, more usually, when in flight.

Nesting Territorial. Nest is in grass or bushes; an untidy dome made of grass and spiders' webs, lined with softer material. Eggs whitish with fine brown spotting, 14mm, hatch asynchronously.

Young leave nest after about two weeks (before they can fly well). Looked after by ♂ if ♀ is starting another brood.

Diet Insects, taken in foliage or on ground.

Winters Resident; holds winter territories.

Conservation Locally common from Middle East southward into Africa, E into Asia.

Notes Also called Graceful Prinia.

Refs Paz 1987.

and the related Oystercatcher, Black-winged Stilt, and Avocet are all 'over-wing scratchers' — they scratch their heads by extending the leg *over* a drooped wing that is held close to the body.

An exceptional group in which the pattern of scratching does not follow taxonomic lines is the 40 North American wood warblers (the tribe Parulini of the Fringillidae). Seven species scratch directly and 31 others are overwing scratchers. The Black-and-white Warbler uses both methods while the habits of one species remain undetermined. Although all paruline species of the genus *Dendroica* belong to the overwing group, many other genera contain some species that are direct and others that are overwing scratchers. There is, however, an intriguing and as yet unexplained correlation between the ecology of the warblers and their scratching method. Species that dwell mostly on the ground tend to scratch under the wing; those that are primarily arboreal, over the wing. Perhaps underwing scratching helps to keep the wings of ground-dwelling birds clean.

SEE: Preening, p. 349; Bathing and Dusting, p. 355; Anting, p. 469; Disease and Parasitism, p. 315. REF.: Burtt and Hailman, 1978.

Moulting

BIRDS must spend a great deal of time caring for their feathers, since their lives depend on them. Preening, bathing, dusting, and other feather care operations, however, cannot prevent the feathers from wearing out. Because formed feathers (like our fingernails) are lifeless, horny structures, incapable of being repaired, worn feathers must be replaced. This process of replacement is termed moulting. The old, worn feathers are loosened in their follicles (sockets) by the growth of new intruding feathers, which eventually push them out. Moulting occurs in regular patterns over a bird's body. The adaptiveness of such patterns can be illustrated by arboreal woodpeckers, which retain the key inner pair of long tail feathers used in bracing and climbing until the outer feathers have been replaced. This is the reverse of the pattern found in most birds, which moult tail feathers from the centre of the tail first, and then progressively toward each side. The majority of adult birds moult once or twice a year, and the temporal pattern, not unexpectedly, is related to the wear rate on the feathers. Feathers of species that migrate enormous distances or live in thick brush, dodging among twigs and spines, wear more rapidly than those of non-migrants or those that live in open country. The former tend to moult twice a year, and the latter only once.

Moulting is timed to meet various needs. For example, resident temperate-zone birds require more insulating feathers in the winter than in the summer.

Scrub Warbler

Scotocerca inquieta

ATLAS 225; PMH -; PER -; HFP 226; HPCW 193; NESTS 246; BWP6:42

to 1m	BLDS: ♂♀ Monogamy?	3–4 (2–5) 1–2 broods INCU: ♂♀ 13–15	FLDG: ♂♀ 13–15 (11–)	Seeds	Ground glean

Breeding habitat Dry hillsides or deserts with scattered shrubs.

Displays Sings from close to ground or briefly from top of bush, or in flight, wagging tail.

Nesting Territorial. Nests near ground in shrub; a dome of twigs and grass with a softer lining of feathers and down, sometimes with two entrances. Eggs whitish with brown blotches and spots, 15mm. Clutches are smaller in desert areas than those near coast. Sometimes seen in small groups at breeding time.

Diet Insects, particularly grasshoppers taken from foliage or by digging into ground; seeds in the winter.

Winters Resident, sometimes in small groups.

Conservation Locally common across N Africa, Arabia, into SW Asia.

Essays Variation in Clutch Sizes, p. 55.

Refs Paz 1987.

Grasshopper Warbler

Locustella naevia

ATLAS 217; PMH 187; PER 168; HFP 222; HPCW 193; NESTS 237; BWP6:63

Reeds to 1m	BLDS: ♂♀ Monogamy	5–6 (3–7) 2 broods INCU: ♂♀ 12–15	FLDG: ♂♀ 10–12 (–15)		

Breeding habitat In dense low vegetation, wet or dry, including freshwater marshes and young conifer plantations.

Displays Sings, often for long periods, from low perch (sometimes an exposed one), day and night. When singing, body is held erect, head tilted up, and feathers ruffled.

Nesting Territorial. Nest is on ground or near it, in thick cover; a cup of grass on a base of leaves, often in a natural hollow, lined with softer material. Eggs pinkish-white, with extensive reddish-brown spotting, 18mm. Usually only one brood in N.

Diet Insects, taken from ground or low vegetation; sometimes in flight.

Winters Africa S of Sahara; habits not well known; solitary.

Conservation Population size fluctuates considerably; has increased range, but declined in the UK. Locally common across Europe into Asia.

Essays Why Some Species Migrate at Night, p. 351.

Refs Marchant et al. 1990.

The number is changed in the process of moulting; winter plumage may contain more than half again as many feathers as summer plumage. Since the feathers, which carry the colours of birds, are 'dead', a bird cannot totally change its colours without changing its feathers (although its appearance can change substantially just from wear). Therefore a male bird usually moults into his most colourful plumage prior to the breeding season. Moulting in most passerines takes from 5 to 12 weeks, but some raptors may require two years or more to completely replace their feathers. To offset the added energetic cost of producing new feathers, some female raptors (such as Osprey, Goshawk, and Peregrine Falcon) moult while incubating, a period of relative inactivity and low energetic expenditure.

Some aquatic birds, such as ducks, swans, divers, grebes, pelicans, and auks, are 'synchronous moulters' — they change their flight feathers all at once in a period as short as two weeks, but sometimes stretching over a month. During this period they cannot fly, and male ducks, in particular, often complete the process on secluded lakes in order to minimize their vulnerability to predators.

Why should synchronous moulters have evolved this seemingly risky process instead of undergoing a gradual moult like most birds? These birds tend to be heavy relative to their wing surfaces — they have high 'wing loadings'. The loss of only a few flight feathers would seriously compromise their flying ability, and so evolution has favoured being grounded for a 'quick overhaul' rather than a longer period of difficult flying.

SEE: Feathers, p. 363; Avian Snowshoes, p. 123; The Colour of Birds, p. 137; Preening, p. 349; Eclipse Plumage, p. 53; Metabolism, p. 281.

Walking vs. Hopping

A BIRD moving along a telephone wire rarely walks like a tightrope artist; instead, it will usually 'sidestep', 'switch-sidle', or 'hop'. Sidestepping (the way that people typically move along a ledge) involves alternately lifting each foot and moving it to the side while continuing to keep the same foot ahead. Switch-sidling consists of moving to the right or to the left by crossing one foot over the other. Hopping, is really jumping — moving both feet simultaneously.

When unconstrained by a narrow perch, many birds walk or run using the alternating strides typical of most bipeds. Others, particularly small, arboreally inclined species, usually hop. Why hopping is more common in smaller birds remains unclear. The evidence seems to point to economy of effort: short-legged birds move farther in a single hop than they do by taking

River Warbler
Locustella fluviatilis

ATLAS 219; PMH 187; PER 168; HFP 222; HPCW 194; NESTS 238; BWP6:77

 to 0.5m

 BLDS: ♂♀ Monogamy

5–6 (4–7) 1 brood INCU: ♀(♂?) 11–12

 FLDG: ♂♀ 14–16

 Ground glean

Breeding habitat A wide variety of low thick vegetation near fresh water, from marshes to both deciduous and coniferous forests. Common name is rather misleading.

Displays ♂ sings in thick cover (perhaps also from top of bush) with plumage ruffled; day or night.

Nesting Territorial. Nests on ground in thick cover; a cup of grass on base of leaves, lined with finer material. Eggs whitish with dark red and brown spotting, 20mm, hatch synchronously.

Diet Insects, taken from dense cover.

Winters E Africa, S of Sahara in a variety of habitats from reed-beds to woodland thickets. Solitary.

Conservation Has spread W and N into Scandinavia. Locally common from E Europe into Asia.

Refs Dementiev et al. 1968.

Savi's Warbler
Locustella luscinioides

ATLAS 218; PMH 187; PER 168; HFP 222; HPCW 194; NESTS 238; BWP6:89

 to 0.5m

 BLDS: ♂♀ Monogamy

4–5 (3–6) 1–2 broods INCU: ♂♀ 10–12(–14)

 FLDG: ♂♀ 11–15(–16)

Breeding habitat Reed-beds and other freshwater marshes.

Displays ♂ sings from top of reeds or from cover; day and night. May remain on its perch for hours. Sings upright, with tail down and head back.

Nesting Territorial. Nest is well hidden in base of reeds, near water level; a woven cup of grass lined with finer material. Eggs whitish with fine brown and grey spotting, 20mm

Diet Insects, spiders, snails; taken from low vegetation or water surface.

Winters Africa S of Sahara in thick, wet habitats.

Conservation Locally common and increasing NW. Lost from the UK in mid-19th century, recolonized in mid-20th. Vulnerable to wetland loss. From WC Europe across Asia.

Essays Wetland Conservation, p. 145.

several steps, whereas it is more economical for larger birds, with longer strides, to move one leg at a time.

Although birds of the same taxonomic groups often share a common pattern of ground locomotion, there are frequent exceptions. Most passerines hop, but *Locustella* warblers — Grasshopper, Pallas's Grasshopper (*L. certhiola*), Savi's, River, and Lanceolated (*L. lanceolata*) — are walkers. Even among *Locustella* species, walking styles vary. The Grasshopper, its name notwithstanding, has a deliberate step. The Lanceolated tends to creep. The gaits of Pallas's Grasshopper and Savi's are different again but similar to each other. Other passerines such as larks, pipits, and starlings typically stride. Diverse species, including Robins, Ravens, and Blackbirds, both hop and stride. Finches are typically hoppers. Whether a physically unconstrained bird hops or strides is not just a question of anatomy; speed also affects choice. When a bird is pressed, hopping may shift to running rather than hopping faster.

Leg length and behaviour are also associated with foraging style. Among ground-gleaners and waders, for example, species with shorter legs forage in shallower debris or water. Some ground-foragers, especially buntings, sparrows, and North American towhees (*Pipilo*) and juncos (*Junco*), are more likely than others to use a method of foraging called 'double-scratching' (essentially hopping in place to expose prey). But here, too, there is no simple division between birds that hop and those that stride or double-scratch. Some striders double-scratch and some hoppers do not. Similarly 'foot-quivering' (rapidly moving against the substrate without moving forward), which is commonly used by waders and gulls to bring invertebrates to the surface, has also been observed among ground-foraging *Catharus* thrushes. Here, however, the plasticity of leg motions is even more apparent. In some circumstances these thrushes use foot-quivering to flush prey, but it also serves as part of an aggressive display during intraspecific encounters.

SEE: Swimming and Underwater Flight, p. 61; Songbird Foraging, p. 417; Feet, p. 289; Visual Displays, p. 33; Avian Snowshoes, p. 123. REFS: Dagy, 1977; Hailman, 1973; Newell, 1989; Yong and Moore, 1990.

Migration

THE arrival of birds in the spring and their departure at the end of the breeding season is one of the most familiar aspects of European bird biology. Seasonal migration enables birds to avoid the physiological stresses of unfavourable climates and to exploit food supplies that are available for only limited periods each year. Thus, many species can breed at high latitudes during the

Moustached Warbler
Acrocephalus melanopogon

ATLAS 223; PMH 188; PER 168; HFP 226; HPCW 194; NESTS 242; BWP6:106

to 0.5m	BLDS: ♀ Monogamy?	3–4(–6) 1 brood INCU: ♂ ♀ 14–15

FLDG: ♂ ♀
12

Ground glean

Breeding habitat Freshwater marshes, especially reed-beds, lake edges, stream margins.

Displays ♂ usually sings from song perch or deep cover; no song flight.

Nesting Territorial. Nests over water, attached to plant stems; an untidy deep cup of vegetation, lined with softer material. Eggs whitish, with extensive fine light brown spotting, 18mm.

Diet Insects, spiders, snails; taken from low foliage or water surface.

Winters Resident or moves S within Europe, avoiding areas where water freezes.

Conservation Local around Mediterranean into Asia. See p. 529.

Aquatic Warbler
Acrocephalus paludicola

ATLAS 223; PMH 188; PER 168; HFP 226; HPCW 194; NESTS 243; BWP6:117

to 0.5m	BLDS: ♀ See below	4–6 (3–8) 1 brood INCU: ♀ 13–15

FLDG: ♀
13–14

Breeding habitat Marshes and tall grasses near fresh water.

Displays ♂ sings from perch, with head pointed upwards, head feathers ruffled, tail pointed downwards. Sometimes has short song flight; a rapid fluttering ascent to 30m, then down with tail fanned.

Nesting Territorial. Nest is near ground; a cup of grasses, spiders' web, lined with feathers. Eggs whitish with extensive, fine brown spotting, 17mm. Has an unusual mating system—or perhaps one overlooked in other species. All work at nest is done by ♀. ♂ spends most of his time displaying. Unlike most small birds where copulation lasts a few seconds, in this species it lasts nearly half an hour. The ♂ has unusually large testes and times his efforts (evenings) to maximize his chances of fertilizing the egg (laid next morning). Such effort may be necessary to ensure some success, but it is not completely successful. Using DNA fingerprinting, recent Polish studies found that only half the broods had a single father, the rest had from 2 to 4 fathers.

Diet Insects, gleaned from low in dense foliage.

Winters W Africa S of Sahara in reed-beds and moist grasslands.

Conservation Declining, probably due to wetland drainage. Locally common in E Europe, CIS. See p. 529.

Essays Polygyny, p. 265; Vocal Functions, p. 413.

Refs Dementiev et al. 1968.

brief but insect-rich arctic summer, and then fly south to the more hospitable climates of southwestern and Mediterranean Europe, or on to Africa. In all, some 185 species from Europe and Asia migrate regularly to tropical and southern Africa resulting in billions of birds moving across Europe into Africa each year. While northern birdwatchers may think of them as 'their' birds that go south for the winter, it may be more logical to think of them as southern species that make a relatively brief foray north to breed.

Seasonal migration presumably evolved as a means of increasing lifetime reproductive output. It permits exploitation of northern areas that either are more productive or provide less competition than the wintering grounds. Moreover, daylight periods in spring and summer are longer at higher latitudes, resulting in more hours per day in which birds can gather food.

Preparation for migration involves both physiological and behavioural changes. Physiological preparation includes the accumulation of fat to provide fuel for prolonged flight. Eurasian long-distance migrants typically undergo a pre-migratory fattening that increases their weight by 35–50 per cent. Not uncommonly, songbirds can lose 25–50 per cent of their body weight during overwater and trans-Saharan migration. Behavioural changes are especially prominent in nocturnal migrants, which alter their activity rhythms during darkness and begin to orient preferentially in the direction that they will soon fly.

Most long-distance migrants, especially smaller birds, fly at night; they may travel continuously or land daily around sunrise to rest and forage. When travelling over water or other unsuitable habitats, birds that normally stop each day may fly without a break for longer periods. For example, Sedge Warbler, Whitethroat, and Pied Flycatcher must fly 40–60 hours non-stop along a southwest–northeast axis for at least 2200–2500 kilometres across the Sahara. In spring migration, the Sedge Warbler appears to undergo a non-stop flight of 3500 kilometres from Uganda to the Middle East!

Recently, individuals of many songbird species that supposedly do not stop while migrating across deserts have been discovered in the Sahara and Sinai Deserts. Insects and fleshy fruits provided by desert oases may serve as important fuel for migrants that stop briefly en route to their wintering sites. It also appears that many songbirds headed for sub-Saharan Africa land within a few kilometres of the North African coast, where they replenish their fat stores before continuing on across the Sahara. Such resting areas in northern Africa may thus be quite important for European migrants and of great significance for the conservation of Europe's migratory songbird populations.

In contrast to long-distance migrants, species that move only relatively short distances within Europe usually travel during the day, generally spending only a few hours of the morning in migration. Aerial foragers such as swallows and swifts, however, do not stop by day. They simply feed in flight as they are migrating. Swallows, but not swifts, then usually settle to roost at night.

Most autumn migrants from western Europe fly southwesterly towards the Atlantic coast and the Mediterranean region before heading in a more

Sedge Warbler
Acrocephalus schoenobaenus

ATLAS 223; PMH 188; PER 168; HFP 226; HPCW 194; NESTS 243; BWP6:130

		5–6 (3–8)			
		1 (2) broods			
Reeds	BLDS: ♀	INCU: ♂♀	FLDG: ♂♀		
to 0.5m	Monogamy	13–15	13–14 (10–16)	Fruit	

Breeding habitat Generally near water in thick bushes, but also in thick vegetation away from water.

Displays ♂ sings on exposed perch and then may ascend at a steep angle, with fluttering wing-beats, slowly spiralling around, then gliding down with wings and tail spread. Will sing at night.

Nesting Territorial. Nest is on or above ground or over water; a deep cup of grasses, spiders' webs, woven to supporting plants, lined with finer material. Eggs pale, heavily and finely marked pale brown sometimes with thin black marks, 18mm.

Diet Insects, taken low in dense vegetation, sometimes in flight. Also feeds on berries in early autumn.

Winters Africa, S of Sahara in a variety of habitats, including reeds, grasses. May sing in winter.

Conservation Widespread and abundant across Europe into Asia, but declines in many areas in N and C. In Sweden and UK, a serious decline in last 20 years, because of Sahelian drought.

Essays Migration, p. 377; Wintering and Conservation, p. 409; Birds and Global Warming, p. 311; Vocal Copying, p. 383; Vocal Functions, p. 413; Why Some Species Migrate at Night, p. 351; Population Dynamics, p. 515.

Paddyfield Warbler
Acrocephalus agricola

ATLAS 221; PMH 189; PER -; HFP 224; HPCW 194; NESTS 270; BWP6:146

		3–6			
		1 (2) broods			
	BLDS: ♂♀	INCU: ♀	FLDG: ♂♀		
0.5–1 m	Monogamy?	12	?		

Breeding habitat Reeds and other vegetation near water, including saline lakes.

Displays Sings from near top of reeds, sometimes in flight.

Nesting Territorial. Nests among reeds; a tall cup bound to reeds, of grass, reeds lined with finer material. Eggs light olive to light brown with extensive light brown spotting and blotching, 17mm.

Diet Insects, taken from low vegetation or water surface; sometimes in mid-air.

Winters India and adjacent areas in grassy and marshy areas including rice paddies.

Conservation Locally common from Black Sea across C Asia.

Refs Ali and Ripley, 1987; Dementiev et al. 1968.

southerly direction to Africa. The pattern of long-distance migration to Africa is very complex, however, as many migrants fly nearly due south or even southeast over Europe before either crossing the Mediterranean or going around it via the Middle East. Almost every species that is broadly distributed across northern Europe shows a migratory divide that separates western populations into a southwest/south migratory route and eastern populations into a southeast/east route. The White Stork and Blackcap are good examples of such species which split into migratory fronts skirting the Mediterranean to west and to east.

Due to these patterns, particular concentrations of songbirds occur along the whole European west coast, the southwestern and eastern coasts of the Black Sea, through the narrow stretch of southern Italy to Sicily and on to Tunisia, over Malta, Cyprus, and along the easternmost coastal areas of the Mediterranean Basin, as shown in these schematic maps.

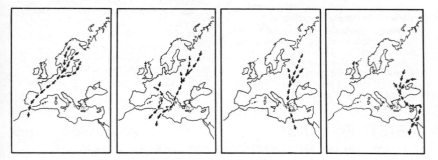

In general, populations of songbirds nesting in northern and eastern Europe are highly migratory, whereas populations in western Europe tend to be more sedentary. This phenomenon of 'partially migratory' species is exemplified by French populations of Robins which overwinter in France while German populations winter as far south as the Middle East and North Africa (although some birds, primarily males, remain in Germany through the winter). Partially migratory species include many European finches and thrushes, as well as Lapwing, Woodcock, and *Accipiter* hawks.

In terms of both number of species and number of individuals, Africa is more important as a wintering area for Eurasian migrants than is India or southeastern Asia. Approximately 135 species of songbirds are migrants to Africa of which nearly half are comprised of thrushes, warblers, swallows, pipits, and shrikes. Excluding waders, far more species of migrants winter north of the equator than in sub-equatorial Africa. Overall, the northern savannahs of West Africa and Sudan receive the majority of Eurasian migrants. The strong preference for savannah habitats may reflect the predominance of this biome in Africa today and its long and continuous availability over many tens of thousands of years. In contrast to the many species of North American migrants that use tropical rainforests, relatively few Eurasian species winter in such habitats; but the difficulty of detecting migrants in the rainforest canopy means that the full importance of tropical rainforests as wintering

Blyth's Reed Warbler
Acrocephalus dumetorum

ATLAS 222; PMH 189; PER 168; HFP 224; HPCW 195; NESTS 274; BWP6:155

to 1m	BLDS: ♂♀ Monogamy Polygyny	3–6 1 brood INCU: ♀(♂♀) 12–14	? FLDG: ♂♀,♀ 11–13	

Breeding habitat   Dense vegetation, less confined to water than is Reed Warbler, and may occur in grassy or herbaceous openings within deciduous or coniferous forest.

Displays   Sings, usually from dense cover, often for long periods day and night. Also sings in flight. ♂ courts ♀ by fanning tail, quivering wings, and chasing her through vegetation.

Nesting   Territorial. Nest is suspended from grasses; a tall cup of grasses and spiders' web, lined with finer material. Eggs whitish, variously spotted or blotched with olive, grey, or brown, 18mm. Extent of polygyny unclear; typically occurs in areas of high density.

Diet   Insects, spiders, and snails, taken in canopy, shrub, or herb layers. Tends to feed higher in the vegetation than others in genus.

Winters   In India and adjacent regions, in shrubs, grasses, trees. Possibly territorial.

Conservation   Local in E Europe, increasing, has spread into Baltic areas in the last 50 years; common across parts of C and SW Asia.

Essays   Hartley's Titmice and MacArthur's Warblers, p. 425; Why Some Species Migrate at Night, p. 351.

Refs   Ali and Ripley, 1987; Dementiev et al. 1968.

Marsh Warbler
Acrocephalus palustris

ATLAS 222; PMH 190; PER 170; HFP 224; HPCW 195; NESTS 269; BWP6:172

Reeds 0.5–3m	BLDS: ♀ Monogamy Polygyny	3–5(–6) 1 brood INCU: ♂♀ 12–14	FLDG: ♂♀ 10–11	

Breeding habitat   Thick vegetation; usually near water, but also drier, in gardens, parks, and up to subalpine meadows.

Displays   ♂ sings on top of bush, sometimes fans tail, jerking it to the side, or raises wings above back.

Nesting   Loosely colonial, though defends nesting area. Nest is suspended in tall herbs; a cup, sometimes deep, tightly woven around vertical supports, lined with finer material. Eggs whitish with brownish to olive spotting more distinct than spotting on eggs of Reed

Wabler, 19mm. Some ♂s establish a second territory, sometimes managing to attract a second ♀ to it.

Diet   Insects; also spiders, snails, taken from grass, shrubs, lower parts of trees.

Winters   E Africa S of Sahara in dense vegetation.

Conservation   Has declined severely in the UK to about 10 pairs, spread N into Sweden; locally common across Europe and into Asia.

Essays   Wetland Conservation, p. 145; Ducking the Bird Laws, p. 523; Vocal Copying, p. 383.

habitats is still largely unknown. The winter distribution of more than 40 species of Eurasian migrants in Africa is still not known in detail.

Several species undertake 'loop migrations' by following different routes in autumn and spring. The Pied Flycatcher, for example, flies to its winter areas in West Africa by way of southwestern Europe (especially through the Iberian Peninsula), but most of these birds return in spring along a more easterly route across northern Africa, Crete, and Italy. The evolutionary basis for loop migrations may be climatic, historical, or ecological.

Each species, subspecies, and even population, of long-distance migrant apparently has its own schedule of movement independent of external factors on the wintering grounds. In East Africa, ornithologist Kai Curry-Lindahl studied five subspecies of Yellow Wagtails that can be separated by plumage characteristics when wintering in mixed concentrations. He found that each migrates successively: the subspecies that breeds furthest south in Europe (and therefore with the shortest flight distance) departs first, while the most northerly-breeding subspecies is the last to leave the tropics.

SEE: Orientation and Navigation, p. 503; Wader Migration and Conservation, p. 167; Differential Migration, p. 323; Breeding Season, p. 293; Wintering Site Tenacity, p. 409; Breeding Site Tenacity, p. 219; Irruptions, p. 491; Wintering and Conservation, p. 409; Why Some Species Migrate at Night, p. 351; Spacing of Wintering Waders, p. 179; Raptors at Sea Crossings, p. 93. REFS: Bairlein, 1988; Curry-Lindahl, 1981; Gauthreaux, 1982; Kerlinger, 1989; Lovei, 1989; Mead, 1983; Safriel and Lavee, 1988.

Vocal Copying

MANY species of songbirds learn the specific song elements of their repertoires from one or more adult tutors, most often from the male parent. Such learning, for at least some species, is not confined to the period prior to sexual maturity. For example, territorial male Redwings listen to songs from adjacent territorial males and incorporate those songs into their repertoire. Generally, this type of vocal copying, where the individual copied (the model) is a member of the same species, is referred to as 'vocal imitation' and serves as the basic mechanism underlying the evolution of dialect systems (variation in songs among local populations).

There are, however, many examples of vocalizations that are characteristic of one species being copied by a second species. Such 'vocal mimicry' is well known in the Marsh Warbler, Skylark, Starling, Redstart, Bluethroat, Song Thrush, and Greenfinch. Species copied by the Marsh Warbler include African birds heard only on the warbler's wintering grounds, a well as European species. The function(s) of acquired alien sounds is still debated. Even the term 'vocal mimicry' is a source of dispute among ornithologists. In biology, mimicry generally connotes deception by the mimic directed toward some

Reed Warbler

Acrocephalus scirpaceus

ATLAS 221; PMH 190; PER 170; HFP 224; HPCW 196; NESTS 249; BWP6:193

Shrub	BLDS: ♀	3–5 (2–7) 1–2 broods INCU: ♂♀	FLDG: ♂♀	Fruit	
0.5–1.5m	Monogamy	9–12 (8–13)	10–12 (9–13)		

Breeding habitat   Mainly reed-beds, but also bushes near water.

Displays   ♂ sings from reeds or in flight; day and night – may sing 8–12 hours daily. Threat includes bill-snapping.

Nesting   Defends only small territory around nest. Nests often loosely colonially in reeds; a tall cup woven around vertical stems, of vegetation lined with finer material. Eggs greenish-white with olive green to grey spotting and blotching, 18mm.

Diet   Insects, spiders, snails, taken from reeds, other vegetation, while bird perches or hovers.
Winters   In Africa, S of Sahara in marshes, tall grasslands, thick vegetation.
Conservation   Common in reed-beds across Europe into C Asia. Spreading N and W, increasing in UK, and has bred in Ireland since 1981 (see essay on Island Biogeography, p. 303.).
Essays   Brood Parasitism, p. 249; Wintering Site Tenacity, p. 409.
Refs   Paz 1987; Marchant et al. 1990.

Clamorous Reed Warbler

Acrocephalus stentoreus

ATLAS 220; PMH -; PER -; HFP 224; HPCW 196; NESTS 242; BWP6:212

	BLDS: ♂♀ Monogamy	4 (3–6) 1 (2?) broods INCU: ♀	FLDG: ♂♀	
0.5–1m	Polygyny	13–14	11–13	

Breeding habitat   Mainly reed-beds, other vegetation (including crops) near water. In Israel, where this species and Great Reed Warbler overlap, occurs in Papyrus thickets, the Great Reed Warbler in reeds.
Displays   ♂ sings from exposed or concealed perch, day and night.
Nesting   Territorial. Nests in reed-beds; a tall cup suspended from vertical stems, made of reeds with a lining of finer material. Eggs, probably

like those of Great Reed Warbler, 22mm, hatch synchronously.
Diet   Insects, taken from surface of water or low in vegetation.
Winters   Resident (some other populations migrate).
Conservation   Locally common in Egypt, Middle East, and into S Asia and Australia. Has spread in Nile Valley following completion of Aswan dam.
Refs   Ali and Ripley 1987; Paz 1987.

signal-receiver, generally a predator or competitor. With most mimicked bird vocalizations, the true identity of the singer is quite clear because the mimic imparts some characteristic tonal quality, temporal pattern, or context of use that serves to differentiate it from the model's vocalizations. The human ear can detect these differences, and the model's more sensitive avian ear certainly would be expected to detect the rendition of a mimic. In short, in the vast majority of examples it is unlikely that anyone is fooled by vocal mimicry.

Why, then, are sounds of other species (as well as non-avian sounds such as the barking of dogs, screeching of machinery, or human whistling) sometimes incorporated into a bird's repertoire? The answer seems to be that selection has favoured a large and diverse repertoire in some species and that one way of increasing repertoire size and diversity is to incorporate sounds from the surrounding acoustic environment, even those not belonging to the bird's own species. Evidence from several studies indicates that an expanded repertoire may improve ability to attract a mate, intimidate rivals, and stimulate females. Experiments by ornithologist Clive Catchpole have demonstrated clearly that female Sedge Warblers and Great Reed Warblers respond more strongly (with copulatory-invitation displays) to larger repertoires when presented with a choice between small and large repertoires played to them in the laboratory. Experiments performed with female Great Tits yielded similar results. Parallel field studies found that polygynous male Great Reed Warblers with larger syllable repertoires attracted more females and produced more young. Similar studies with Great Tits found that males with larger repertoires were more likely to breed in successive years and more likely to produce offspring that survived to breed in the following year — two excellent measures of the singer's reproductive fitness.

Thus the effects of sexual selection tend to favour an increasingly large and diverse song repertoire within the limits imposed by the need for species recognition and by the capacity of the singer to memorize and produce sounds. The common, non-deceptive use of such vocalizations has been termed 'vocal appropriation' to eliminate the connotation of deceit implicit in the biological use of the term 'mimicry'.

SEE: Vocal Dialects, p. 477; Vocal Functions, p. 413; Vocal Development, p. 479; Territoriality, p. 397; Sexual Selection, p. 471; Bird Voices, p. 475; Polygyny, p. 265; Environmental Acoustics, p. 327. REFS: Baptista and Catchpole, 1989; Catchpole, 1987; Dobkin, 1979.

Bird-brained

To say the very least, birds do not have a reputation for great intelligence. Much of their behaviour is strictly stereotyped — males of many species will determinedly assault a stuffed male placed in their territory, seemingly

Great Reed Warbler
Acrocephalus arundinaceus

ATLAS 220; PMH 191; PER 170; HFP 224; HPCW 196; NESTS 274; BWP6:223

	BLDS: ♀ Monogamy Polygyny	3–6 1 (2) broods INCU: ♀ 14–15	A		
Shrub 0.5–1m			FLDG: ♂♀ 12–14		

Breeding habitat Reed-beds, sometimes other vegetation near open fresh-water.

Displays ♂ sings from tops of reeds; day and night.

Nesting Territorial, but like others in genus, tends to form loose colonies around good feeding areas. Nest is a tall cup, made of reeds etc. woven around supporting stems, and lined with finer material such as plant down, spiders' webs. Eggs greenish to bluish-white, distinctly blotched dark brown, 23mm. Brood hatches over 1–3 days. Older ♂s arrive earlier, have better territories (as judged by their greater breeding success), and have up to 3 mates.

Diet Emerging aquatic insects, spiders, snails, and some fruit, picked off marsh vegetation or sometimes in nearby trees.

Winters Africa S of Sahara in a variety of habitats including reed-beds, grasslands, and wet shrub and forest habitats.

Conservation Expanding N and W (expanding in Finland in the 1980s). Common across Europe,W and C Asia.

Notes Does not breed in the UK which is within the general range of this species and which surely provides the habitats for this species. (There are about 1000 breeding pairs in each of Belgium, Netherlands). Islands often lack species for reasons to do with the low rate of colonization and the high rate of species extinction: see essay on Island Biogeography, p. 303.

Essays Polygyny, p. 265; Vocal Copying, p. 383; Vocal Functions, p. 413; Wintering Site Tenacity, p. 409.

Olivaceous Warbler
Hippolais pallida

ATLAS 227; PMH 191; PER 170; HFP 228; HPCW 197; NESTS 248; BWP6:248

	BLD: ♂,♂♀? Monogamy	2–5 1–2 broods INCU: ♀ 11–13	A		
0.5–9m			FLDG: ♂♀ 11–15	Fruit	Hawks

Breeding habitat Open areas with trees and bushes, gardens, oases.

Displays ♂ sings from thick cover, sometimes from exposed perch or in flight when rises quicky and angles down to new perch.

Nesting Territorial, though often in loose groups. Nest is in low bushes; a cup of twigs, grasses, lined with finer material. Eggs whitish to pinkish with black spotting, 19mm.

Diet Insects, gleaned from upper foliage or caught in air. Will feed by

dropping to ground. Also feeds on fruit in the autumn.

Winters Africa S of Sahara in areas with scattered trees and shrubs; Nile Valley populations move S into Egypt, Sudan.

Conservation Locally common around Mediterranean into SW Asia. Spread recently into Hungary, Balkans.

Essays Hartley's Titmice and MacArthur's Warblers, p. 425.

Refs Dementiev et al. 1968; Paz 1987.

unable to recognize that the 'rival' poses no threat. Growing evidence indicates, however, that birds have been underestimated. It appears that they are more capable of learning and reasoning than had been assumed, and that they are, in fact, in the same intellectual league as most mammals.

One of the first bits of evidence from 'nature' on the ability of birds to learn was uncovered in the 1920s with the spreading habit of tits dipping into milk bottles left on doorsteps in Great Britain. The tits punctured foil tops and removed cardboard lids (or dissected lids layer by layer), and flocks were reported following milk carts and pilfering milk when carts were left unguarded. Other species of birds, even those less adept than tits at tearing things open (in nature, tits often tear bark while searching for insects), soon learned to follow this example, and by the end of World War II at least eleven species, including the Chaffinch, Robin, Starling, and Great Spotted Woodpecker, were performing the trick.

This behaviour had to spread by learning; there was not enough time for natural selection to produce the milk-robbing behaviour in tits and other birds. Similarly, by the middle of this century American Kestrels (*Falco sparverius*) were following slow trains in Mexico, catching small birds disturbed by the trains' passage. Trains had not been around long enough for the behaviour to evolve; it had to be learned.

There is a great deal of evidence that many birds learn by experience. For example, older birds are often more successful at both foraging and breeding than younger, less experienced individuals. Male bowerbirds (fascinating passerines found in New Guinea and Australia) often erect complex, decorated structures to woo their mates. Young males spend about two years improving their building skills, first constructing simple rudimentary bowers and gradually producing the complex structures of the breeding adult. The character of the bowers produced by a single species may show dramatic geographic variation. Ecologist Jared Diamond, who has studied these birds extensively in New Guinea, has suggested that the variation in bower styles may be culturally transmitted, just like styles in human art. Similarly, he notes that many juvenile birds in tropical rain forests spend months foraging with their parents, and there is evidence that they learn from them (and from other members of mixed-species foraging flocks) how to select appropriate food from a mix of poisonous items (fruit, insects) and non-poisonous items which often mimic the dangerous ones. Many juvenile birds in tropical forests die of starvation, and Diamond suggests that there is strong selection for learning ability in the birds of those forests.

Learning ability in birds has also been repeatedly demonstrated in laboratory experiments. Classic work by Jane Van Zandt Brower demonstrated that naive North American Blue Jays (*Cyanocitta cristata*), once they had tried to eat a distasteful monarch butterfly, learned immediately to avoid its black and orange colour pattern. They subsequently refused even to sample palatable viceroy butterflies, which closely resemble the monarchs. Indeed, the entire story of the evolution of mimicry in butterflies and other insects depends on the ability of birds to learn that certain colour or behaviour patterns are associated with unpleasant experiences—bad tastes or vomiting following

Booted Warbler

Hippolais caligata

ATLAS 228; PMH 192; PER -; HFP 228; HPCW 197; NESTS 248; BWP6:262

Shrub to 2.0m	BLDS: ♀ Monogamy?	4–6 (2–7) 1 brood INCU: ♂ ♀ 12–14 (11–)	FLDG: ♂ ♀ 13 (11–14)	Ground glean

Breeding habitat In open deciduous woodland, among low shrubs, tall herbage, farmlands with trees, often near water. Also birch woods in N.

Displays Sings from high perch or while moving from bush to bush; day and night.

Nesting Territorial, although where common, nests in loose groups. Nest is on or near ground in thick cover; a cup of plant stems, leaves, lined with finer material. Eggs light pinkish, with black or brown spotting, 16mm. Young remain with parents for 1–2 weeks.

Diet Insects; feeds low in foliage or hops along ground. Also flycatches.

Winters India and adjacent regions, around culitvation and areas with bushes; usually near water.

Conservation Locally common from E Europe into C Asia.

Essays Hartley's Titmice and MacArthur's Warblers, p. 425.

Refs Ali and Ripley 1987; Dementiev et al. 1968.

Upcher's Warbler

Hippolais languida

ATLAS 227; PMH - PER-; HFP 228; HPCW 198; NESTS 249; BWP6:272

0.5–2m	BLDS: ♂ ♀ Monogamy?	4–5 (3) 1–2 broods INCU: ? ?	FLDG: ? ?	

Breeding habitat Scattered bushes in arid regions, sometimes along water courses.

Displays Little known. ♂ sings from exposed perch, in upright position, with quivering tail, or in flight, fluttering up, gliding down on open, raised wings.

Nesting Territorial; may form loose groups, like others in genus. Nest is in bushes; a cup of plant stems, spiders' webs, lined with finer material. Eggs light pink, with black or brown spotting, 18mm.

Diet Insects, picked from trees, bushes, sometimes on ground. Tends to feed lower in the vegetation than does Olivaceous Warbler.

Winters In E Africa, in dry *Acacia* scrub.

Conservation Locally common in SW Asia.

Essays Hartley's Titmice and MacArthur's Warblers, p. 425.

Refs Dementiev et al. 1968.

ingestion (the emetic substance in monarchs is a heart poison). Furthermore, Blue Jays in cages adjacent to those in which Jays were fed edible butterflies were able to observe and learn from the other birds. When the observer jays were offered the same edible butterfly species, or an edible butterfly of a distinctly different species, they chose the species that they had already observed the other jays consume.

There is a large literature on pigeons, Canaries, and other caged birds learning to do such things as peck at keys in certain patterns, discriminate between symmetrical and asymmetrical figures, or recognize unique objects in a series (a screw in a group of aspirin tablets or an aspirin in a collection of screws) in order to gain food rewards. There is evidence that their basic mental processes share common features with ours. For example, pigeons learning sequences will memorize them more rapidly if they can divide the sequences into 'chunks' — much as we can remember 030-26-2905 more readily than 030262905.

There is also evidence that some birds have much higher intelligence than the sort involved in learning to open milk bottles, peck keys, and recognize unique objects. Anyone who has tried to hunt crows by parading first before their roosts carrying a broom handle until the crows do not flee, and then substituting a shotgun in an attempt to deceive the birds, has had a quick lesson in bird intelligence. Recently it has been shown in field experiments that Hooded Crows have the capacity to remember the sites of nests they robbed the previous year (presumably putting selection pressure on birds whose nests have been robbed to change their nest site for subsequent nesting attempts).

Parrots have a remarkable capacity to acquire language, and apparently considerable powers of association to go with it. One African Grey Parrot (*Psittacus erithacus*) has been trained to name over 40 items, and demonstrates the ability to grasp abstract ideas such as colour and shape. If it is shown a green square and asked 'what colour?' it usually says 'green'. If asked 'what shape?' it usually says 'square'. But parrots have long been recognized to be intelligent. More surprising is the recently discovered ability of pigeons to deal with problems whose solutions were once considered indications of insightful thinking in chimpanzees. Pigeons were taught to peck at a hanging banana while standing on a box placed right under it and, in a separate experiment, to push a box along the ground. Then they were presented with a banana hung too high for them to peck at, combined with a box at some distance from the banana. The pigeons solved the problem by combining their learned skills — they pushed the box under the banana, jumped on to it, and pecked away.

An even more stunning report of avian problem-solving, again by Hooded Crows, has come from Moscow University. A crow is presented with a row of caps, with some food hidden under the first cap. The crow is allowed to find the food by trial and error. Then the experiment is rerun, with the food under the second cap. After the crow finds it again, the next run has the food under the third cap, and so on. The experimenters claim that the bird soon learns the progression and uses it to find the food. If confirmed, this

Olive-tree Warbler

Hippolais olivetorum

ATLAS 226; PMH 192; PER 170; HFP 228; HPCW 198; NESTS 249; BWP6:280

Decid tree 1–3m	BLDS: ? Monogamy?	3–4 1 brood? INCU: ? ?

FLDG: ? ?	Fruit	Ground glean

Breeding habitat Trees (commonly oaks, olives) in dry areas.

Displays ♂ sings from concealed perch within canopy, day and night.

Nesting Territorial, in loose neighbourhood groups. Nest is in bush on fork of branch; a deep cup of grasses etc. Eggs pinkish-white, with black spotting, 22mm.

Diet Insects in canopy, sometimes on ground; also fruit in late summer.

Winters E Africa, S of Sahara in dry areas with scattered trees and shrubs, *Acacia* savanna.

Conservation Has restricted range in SE Europe. Expanding range in Bulgaria and Turkey. See p. 529.

Essays Hartley's Titmice and MacArthur's Warblers, p. 425.

Icterine Warbler

Hippolais icterina

ATLAS 226; PMH 192; PER 170; HFP 228; HPCW 199; NESTS 247; BWP6:286

Shrub 1–4m	BLDS: ♂♀ Monogamy	4–5 (2–7) 1 brood INCU: ♀ 13–15(12–16)

FLDG: ♂♀ 13–14(12–16)	Fruit	Hover & glean

Breeding habitat Open woodlands, parks, gardens; birch forest in N, oaks in S.

Displays ♂ sings from cover in tops of trees, moving through foliage; sometimes in flight between perches; sings day and night. Threat includes bill-snapping.

Nesting Territorial, in loose neighbourhood groups. Nest placed in fork of branches; a cup of grass and plant stems, bound with spiders' webs, lined with finer materials. Eggs, pale pink with fine black spotting, 18mm.

Diet Insects, in trees and bushes, taken while perched or hovering; berries in early autumn.

Winters Africa S of Sahara in dry open forest, gardens. Holds territories, sings.

Conservation Has increased in Sweden, Finland. Locally common across Europe into C Asia.

Notes Does not breed in the UK which is within the general range of this species and surely provides the habitats it needs. (There may be 50 000 birds in Holland and Belgium.) Islands often lack species for reasons to do with the low rate of colonization and the high rate of species extinction: see essay on Island Biogeography, p. 303.

Essays Hartley's Titmice and MacArthur's Warblers, p. 425.

experiment would mean that the bird has grasped a concept as complex as 'increase in number' or distance.

There is other impressive evidence of learned purposive behaviour in birds. A Rook appears to have figured out that by putting a plug in the drain hole of its aviary and tapping it firmly in place, it could help form a pool of water in which to bathe. The behaviour occurred most often on hot days when bathing was most desirable, so it was apparently not simply a version of the Rook's standard food-caching behaviour.

When we watch the behaviour of birds in nature we should be alert for evidence of them learning and acting intelligently to solve problems. They are clearly not automata, but we have yet to determine how often intelligence replaces instinct, and what differences in the capacity for thinking there may be between the various groups of birds.

SEE: Metabolism, p. 281; Tool-using, p. 459. REFS: Brower, 1958; Crocker, 1985; Diamond, 1982, 1986, 1987a; Kenyon, 1942; Sasvári, 1985; Sonerud and Fjeld, 1987; Terrace, 1987.

Bills

BIRDS pay a price for the advantages of flight. They must commit their forelimbs almost entirely to that enterprise. As a result the bill often must assume responsibility for diverse functions for which many mammals use their forelimbs — grasping, carrying, scratching, fighting, digging, and so forth.

The bill (or 'beak') consists of the upper and lower jaws (mandibles), ensheathed in a layer of toughened skin. The horny outer layer tends to be especially thick near the tip, where the most wear occurs. The edges of the bill may be sharpened for cutting, or serrated for grasping, but the edges of some bills, including those of ducks, are blunt and relatively soft except at the hardened tip. Ducks often must sort insects and seeds from murky water, and the edges of their bills are richly supplied with touch receptors that help ducks to detect their food.

In most birds the upper mandible is perforated by nostrils, although in some high-diving birds like Gannets the external nostrils are missing; Gannets avoid flooding by being 'mouth breathers' and keeping their mouths shut when they hit the ocean. Similarly the nostrils of woodpeckers are protected from being flooded with 'sawdust' either by feathers or by being reduced to narrow slits. In the marine Procellariiformes (albatrosses and their relatives) the nostrils are at the end of a tube (storm-petrels) or pair of tubes (albatrosses, shearwaters, and petrels) on top of the bill.

In most birds the horny sheath exfoliates (peels) and is continuously replenished from underneath. That covering grows about 0.4 mm per day in

Melodious Warbler

Hippolais polyglotta

ATLAS 226; PMH 193; PER 170; HFP 228; HPCW 199; NESTS 247; BWP6:299

Decid tree
0.5–6.0m

BLDS: ♀
Monogamy

4–5 (3–)
1 (2) broods
INCU: ♀
12–13 (14)

FLDG: ♂♀
11–13

Fruit

Breeding habitat Open woodland and bushes, often near water; generally avoids gardens.

Displays ♂ sings from tree tops or deep cover, sometimes in flight. Threat includes bill-snapping. Aggressive towards Icterine Warblers.

Nesting Territorial, with neighbourhood groups. Nest is often in forked branches of bush (less often in tree); a tall cup of stems, grasses, spiders' web, lined with finer material. Eggs, light pinkish with black spotting, 18mm.

Diet Insects, gleaned from trees or shrubs, or taken in flight; fruit in early autumn.

Winters In W Africa; in forests, clearings, and savannah.

Conservation Locally common in its restricted range in SW Europe and N Africa, has spread N and NE.

Essays Hartley's Titmice and MacArthur's Warblers, p. 425; Why Some Species Migrate at Night, p. 351.

Marmora's Warbler

Sylvia sarda

ATLAS 234; PMH 193; PER 172; HFP 234; HPCW 199; NESTS 256; BWP6:309

0.5–1.0m

BLDS: ♂♀
Monogamy

3–4 (2–5)
2 (3) broods
INCU: ♂♀
12–15

FLDG: ♂♀
11–12

Ground glean

Breeding habitat Low scrubby vegetation, maquis, on hillsides.

Displays Sings from conspicuous perch or in song flight: an ascent with fluttering wings to 7m, then a plunge into cover.

Nesting Territorial, pairs may remain together all year. Nest is near ground in low bush; a cup of twigs, with finer lining. Eggs whitish, with red, brown, and grey spotting, 17mm.

Diet Insects, taken from low vegetation or on ground.

Winters Resident, some move to N Africa. Sings in autumn and winter.

Conservation Islands in the W Mediteranean. No longer breeds on the island of Menorca having been replaced by Dartford Warbler. Between 1000 and 10 000 pairs in Corsica. See p. 529.

Notes The subtle differences in the habitats of warblers in this genus have been the subject of an intensive study by Cody. (See Cody 1985*b* and essay on Habitat Selection, p. 423.)

Essays Hartley's Titmice and MacArthur's Warblers, p. 425; Timing of Migration, p. 405.

oystercatchers, and permits the bill shape to change in response to the kind of prey being taken. Sometimes the sheath develops special protuberances that are used in courtship and subsequently shed. The large, eye-catching grooved bill of breeding Puffins returns to its smaller and duller appearance after the fancy scales peel away at the end of the reproductive season.

Bills are not used just for eating food, but also for catching it, prying up bark that conceals it, filtering it from water, killing it, carrying it, extracting it from shells or husks, cutting it up, and so on. Bills also serve for preening, plucking the brood patch, excavating, nest building, egg turning, defending, displaying, scratching, hatching, climbing, and more. Small wonder that bill size and shape are characteristics that vary enormously from species to species and among major groups. And small wonder that the adaptations of bills to these various functions have long fascinated ornithologists. In 1770 British naturalist Gilbert White was already speculating on the adaptive significance of bill length.

The most obvious adaptations of bills are those related to feeding. Birds that catch fishes with their bills must maintain a tenacious grip on slippery prey. Thus cormorants and pelicans have hooked upper bill tips, Smew, Red-breasted Mergansers, and Goosanders have serrated margins, and Puffins have a series of spines on the upper palate above the tongue. Most waders hunt by probing in mud and sand, and have long, slender, forceps-like bills for finding and grasping their prey. Avocets, however, tend to feed more at the water's surface and swing their upward-curved bills from side to side. Oystercatchers have especially stout bills designed for hammering and prying open recalcitrant molluscs.

Hummingbirds and many sunbirds also probe, and their fine bills are well designed for finding the nectar in deep tubes formed by the fusion of flower petals (corolla tubes). In tropical species the bills have coevolved with the size and shape of flowers of many plants. The straight 10-centimetre bill of the Sword-billed Hummingbird — the length of the bird's body and twice as long as the bill of any other hummer — permits it to drink nectar from (and pollin-ate) a passion flower with a corolla tube 11 centimetres deep. The almost semi-circular bills of sicklebill hummers fit exactly in the sharply curved corollas of *Heliconia* flowers (tropical American relatives of bananas).

Nightjars and their relatives have a wide-gaping bristle-fringed bill that acts as an aerial net, sweeping in insects during flight. Flycatchers also have large bristles that enlarge the effective gape; swifts and swallows, in turn, have very wide gapes but no larger bristles.

Used for hunting and excavating nest cavities in wood, the powerful bill of a woodpecker is shaped like a pickaxe, with a chisel-like point. The structure that supports the use of the bill is impressive: strong, grasping feet work in concert with stiff tail feathers to form a triangular brace and allow the bird to position itself for its strenuous pecking against trunks or branches. Its very long, sensitive 'tongue' (actually a complex extensible bone–muscle apparatus with a moderately short tongue on the end of it — see the illustration on p. 289) may wrap all the way around the bird's skull under the skin when it is retracted. When extended it is used to extract insects from holes and recesses.

Dartford Warbler
Sylvia undata

ATLAS 234; PMH 194; PER 172; HFP 234; HPCW 200; NESTS 256; BWP6:317

 | |
to 1m | BLDS: ♂♀ Monogamy | 3–4 (5–6) 2 (3?) broods INCU: ♂ ♀ 12–14 |  FLDG: ♂♀ 10–14 | Fruit

Breeding habitat Low, dry scrub (in the UK heather and gorse; in maquis in S Europe).

Displays ♂ sings from perch raising and lowering tail. In song flight, rises with fluttering wings to 7m, dances up and down, then descends.

Nesting Holds territories year-round. Nest is usually near ground, often in thick cover; a cup of vegetation lined with finer material. ♂ builds 'cock nests' – flimsy structures, which the ♀ inspects and then makes the choice of the final nest site. Eggs whitish, with fine brown and grey spotting, 17mm. Young remain with parents for 1–2 weeks after leaving nest.

Diet Insects, taken low in shrubs; also fruit in autumn.

Winters Resident; some disperse or move S.

Conservation Has limited range in SW Europe, N Africa; vulnerable to habitat loss and hard winters in N. In the UK declined to 11 pairs after 1962–3 winter; has now recovered to about 600 pairs. See p. 529.

Notes Was previously absent from the Balearic Islands, but colonized Minorca in 1975 and is now common there (see essay on Island Biogeography, p. 303).

Essays Habitat Selection, p. 423; Timing of Migration, p. 405.

Tristram's Warbler
Sylvia deserticola

ATLAS 234; PMH 254; PER - ; HFP 234; HPCW 200; NESTS 254; BWP6:329

 | |
1–1.5m | BLDS: ? Monogamy? | 3–5 1 brood INCU: ? 13? |  FLDG: ♂♀? 13–14?

Breeding habitat Low scattered shrubs (often *Cistus*), dry woodland, on hillsides.

Displays Sings from conspicuous perch or in flight, when it ascends, then descends with head and tail raised. Apparently, an excess of ♂s in some populations, leads to intense competition for ♀s, with ♂s chasing each other from bush to bush.

Nesting Territorial. Nest is in low

shrubs; a deep cup of coarse grass, lined with finer materials. Eggs whitish, with olive-brown and grey spotting, 16mm.

Diet Insects, taken while moving from twig to twig.

Winters Resident or moves S in N Africa, to lower, open habitats including desert fringes.

Conservation Local in limited range in N Africa.

Essays Habitat Selection, p. 423.

Left to right (and top to bottom): Fulmar, Crossbill, Greenfinch, Puffin, Carrion/Hooded Crow, Palestine Sunbird, Wheatear, Goosander, Nightjar, Gannet, Great Spotted Woodpecker, Peregrine Falcon.

Spectacled Warbler

Sylvia conspicillata

ATLAS 232; PMH 194; PER 172; HFP 234; HPCW 200; NESTS 255; BWP6:336

to 0.5m

BLDS: ♂♀
Monogamy

3–5 (6)
2 (3?) broods
INCU: ♂♀
12–13

FLDG: ♂♀
11–12

Fruit

Ground glean

Breeding habitat Open country, rocky hillsides, with low bushes, *Salicornia* salt flats.

Displays Sings from prominent perch or in song flight: rises quickly, without singing, then sings as it descends, rapidly beating spread wings. Sexual chases, with ♂ following ♀ around territory.

Nesting Territorial. Nest is near ground in thick cover; a cup of grass, lined with finer materials. Eggs whitish, with very fine olive-green spotting, 16mm.

Diet Insects, sometimes fruit. Feeds in small bushes, sometimes on ground. Locally, may follow Finsch's Wheatear, taking disturbed insects.

Winters Migrates to Africa from S Europe; resident in N Africa, Cyprus, Middle East. Holds territories year round where resident.

Conservation Locally common around W Mediterranean; isolated populations in E Mediterranean. Has declined in Malta.

Essays Habitat Selection, p. 423; Timing of Migration, p. 405.

Subalpine Warbler

Sylvia cantillans

ATLAS 232; PMH 194; PER 172; HFP 234; HPCW 200; NESTS 255; BWP6:346

Decid tree
0.5–1.5m

BLDS: ♂♀
Monogamy

3–4 (5)
2 broods
INCU: ♂♀
11–12

FLDG: ♂♀
11–12

Breeding habitat Edges of dry woodland, bushy areas with scattered trees.

Displays ♂ sings usually from cover, or song flight: flies up, descends with fluttering wing-beats, to new perch, singing all the time. May chase Blackcaps away from territory.

Nesting Territorial. Nest is in low bush, sometimes low tree; a cup of grasses, stems, lined with finer material. ♂ makes 'cock nests' – temporary nests that the ♀ inspects, selecting one as the final nest site. Eggs whitish, distinctly spotted red or light brown, grey, 16mm. ♂ may

look after first brood while ♀ incubates second.

Diet Insects, taken from shrubs and trees, typically near top, in contrast to similar species. Also fruit in early autumn.

Winters Africa, S edge of Sahara in dry scrub.

Conservation Locally common around Mediterranean, increasing range in SE.

Essays Habitat Selection, p. 423; Hartley's Titmice and MacArthur's Warblers, p. 425; Timing of Migration, p. 405.

Birds that glean foliage or bark for insects, such as warblers and treecreepers, tend to have slender bills that may or may not be downcurved. Those subsisting on seeds, such as sparrows, finches, and buntings, have short, stout bills adapted for cracking and husking seeds. The stout, crossed mandibles of crossbills have evolved to extract seeds from closed conifer cones. The Hawfinch has an extreme development of its jaw musculature and an arrangement of ridges on its palate and lower mandible that allow it to crack the pits of cherries and olives. Even relatively small differences in bill morphology found between the sexes in Wheatears, leading to different prey-carrying capacities, may well have significant consequences for foraging ecology.

The bills of omnivores like ravens have an intermediate shape between those of insectivores and those of seed-eaters. Thus a great deal can be surmised about birds' feeding habits simply from examination of their bills. One should always keep in mind, however, that bills do serve other functions — even though selection has obviously operated most strongly on their use in obtaining nourishment.

SEE: Flamingo Feeding, p. 37; Feet, p. 289; Oystercatchers and Oysters, p. 155; Selection in Nature, p. 471; Coevolution, p. 239. REFS: Benkman, 1988; Carlson and Moreno, 1983; Dobkin, 1984; Hulscher, 1985.

Territoriality

MANY birds attempt to exclude other birds from all or part of their 'home range', the area they occupy in the course of their normal daily activities. When they do, we say they are defending a 'territory'. This behaviour occurs predominantly during the breeding season and is directed towards members of the same species. In most cases territoriality appears to be an attempt to monopolize resources, especially food resources or nest sites, or to provide a site to which a mate can be attracted. But territoriality is also evident at other times of year; many species attempt to defend food resources in winter, or even when they are migrating. Some tits, for example, remain paired throughout the winter and defend territories either as pairs or as social groups consisting of a pair (rarely two pairs) and several juveniles. By spacing out the pairs, territoriality may also serve to reduce predation. Predators may hunt less diligently for a species that occurs at relatively low densities.

Some birds defend their entire home range. Others defend only their food supply, a place to mate, or the site of their nest. Mistle Thrushes regularly establish territories around fruit-bearing plants from autumn to early spring. Some tropical hummingbirds and sunbirds chase away other nectar-feeding

Ménétries' Warbler

Sylvia mystacea

ATLAS 231; PMH 254; PER -; HFP 232; HPCW 201; NESTS 263; BWP6:358

  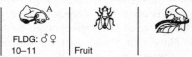

to 1m	BLDS: ♂♀ Monogamy?	4–5 1 (2) broods INCU: ♂♀ 11–13	FLDG: ♂♀ 10–11	Fruit	

Breeding habitat Scrub on rocky hillsides, tamarisk along water courses, gardens.

Displays ♂ sings from perch or in flight: flies up, hovers, circles, and descends.

Nesting Territorial. Nest is near ground, low in bush; a deep cup of vegetation, lined with finer material.

Eggs whitish with fine brown and grey spotting and blotching, 17mm.

Diet Insects taken from bushes; also fruit in autumn, seeds in winter.

Winters E Africa, S of Sahara, Arabia, in dry scrub, gardens.

Conservation Local in SW Asia.

Essays Habitat Selection, p. 423; Timing of Migration, p. 405.

Sardinian Warbler

Sylvia melanocephala

ATLAS 230; PMH 195; PER 172; HFP 232; HPCW 201; NESTS 254; BWP6:367

0.5–3m	BLDS: ♂♀ Monogamy	3–5 (6) 2 (3) broods IN: ♂♀, ♂♀ 13 (12–15)	FLDG: ♂♀ 11–12	Fruit	Ground glean

Breeding habitat Low undergrowth and scrub, maquis, on dry hillsides, and open pine and oak woodlands.

Displays ♂ sings from cover, or exposed perch, with body upright, wings, slightly lowered. In song flight, rises to 4m singing, then glides, still singing, to another bush. Highly aggressive towards rivals.

Nesting Territorial. Nest is near ground, low in bush; cup of vegetation lined with finer material Eggs whitish with fine brown and grey spottings, 18mm. ♂ makes 'cock nests' – temporary nests that the ♀ inspects, selecting the one in which to lay her eggs.

Diet Insects; in early autumn (and

locally, year-round) fruit. Feeds in low scrub, but also on ground, and when higher feeding *Sylvia* species absent, also in canopy.

Winters Resident, some S movement in N Africa into drier areas. Where resident, defends territories year-round.

Conservation Locally common around Mediterranean. Increasing in N, now common in Malta, where first recorded in 1874. Endemic race in Egypt may now be extinct.

Essays Habitat Selection, p. 423; Hartley's Titmice and MacArthur's Warblers, p. 425; Timing of Migration, p. 405.

Refs Paz 1987.

birds (and some butterflies) from favourite patches of nectar-bearing flowers. Sunbirds hold feeding territories if they can monopolize enough nectar to make the effort worthwhile, but not if there is so much nectar available that there is no energetic profit to be made by defending some of it.

On their leks (patches of ground traditionally used for communal mating displays), grouse, some sandpipers, and some other birds defend small territories. Most colonial-nesting seabirds simply defend the immediate vicinity of their nests — presumably to protect their nest sites and eggs and, at least in the case of some penguins, the pebbles from which the nest is constructed.

To minimize the amount of physical contact required to defend territories, animals have evolved 'keep-out' signals to warn away potentially intruding males. In many birds, of course, the most prominent signals are the songs of males. Far from being beautiful bits of music intended to enliven the human environment (as was long assumed), bird songs are, in large part, announcements of ownership and threats of possible violent defence of an area. If the aural warning is ineffective, the territory owner will often escalate activities to include visual displays, chases, and even combat. This territorial behaviour is typically quite stereotyped, and can usually be elicited experimentally with recorded songs or with stuffed specimens.

Territory size varies enormously from species to species, and even among individuals within species. Golden Eagles have territories of some 90 square kilometres; Willow Warbler territories in Swedish Lapland range from 500 to 1000 square metres, and some small flycatchers such as the Pied Flycatcher, may have very small territories, and effectively only defend the area around their nest site. Terns have territories of only a square metre or less in the immediate vicinity of the nest. Within a species territory size often varies in different habitats. In many parts of Europe the Great Tit inhabits both coniferous and broad-leaved deciduous woodland; the insect food consumed by the young is much more abundant in deciduous woodland. In these habitats the adults' territories may be smaller than one hectare, while in coniferous forests they are usually about five hectares.

Males of some species establish and hold more than one territory. Such 'polyterritoriality' is associated with polygyny, and is found in about a third of polygynous European passerines. It has been suggested that establishment of the second territory causes a second female to behave as she would if the male were monogomous, but this has been disputed. Similar behaviour is known, however, in one primate species.

SEE: Interspecific Territoriality, p. 421; Sandpipers, Social Systems, and Territoriality, p. 189; Population Dynamics, p. 515; Leks, p. 123; Spacing of Wintering Shorebirds, p. 179; Vocal Dialects, p. 477; Vocal Functions, p. 413. REFS: Alatalo *et al.*, 1981, 1982; Arvidsson and Klaesson, 1986; Gill and Wolf, 1975; Matthysen, 1990; Nice, 1964; Pedersen *et al.*, 1983; Slagsvold and Lifjeld, 1988; Snow and Snow, 1984; Temrin, *et al.* 1984.

Cyprus Warbler

Sylvia melanothorax

ATLAS 230; PMH -; PER 172; HFP 232; HPCW 201; NESTS 254; BWP6:382

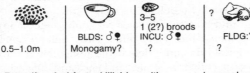

		3–5	?		
		1 (2?) broods		FLDG:?	
	BLDS: ♂♀	INCU: ♂♀			
0.5–1.0m	Monogamy?	?	?		Fruit

Breeding habitat Hillsides with shrubs, sometimes small trees; in lowlands in maquis (especially *Cistus*) forest edges.

Displays ♂ sings from elevated perch; in song flight, sings continuously from high perches, flying between them with deep and slow wing-beats, with occasional glides with wings held above body.

Nesting Territorial. Nest is low in bush; a cup of vegetation, lined with finer materials, bound by silk from spiders' webs. ♂ builds 'cock nests', ♀ selects one and completes it. Eggs whitish,

or pale greenish, with extensive fine reddish-brown spotting, 17mm.

Diet Insects, gleaned from vegetation, not ground.

Winters Mainly resident; though vacates high elevations. Some move through Israel, but do not appear to winter there. Residents sing for much of year (but not late in summer).

Conservation Found only in Cyprus, where it is locally common.

Notes Considered by some to be a race of the Sardinian Warbler.

Essays Habitat Selection, p. 423.

Rüppell's Warbler

Sylvia rüppelli

ATLAS 230; PMH 195; PER 172; HFP 232; HPCW 202; NESTS 254; BWP6:389

		4–5 (6)			
		1? brood		FLDG: ♂♀	
	BLDS: ?	INCU: ♂♀			
	Monogamy?	13		?	Fruit

Breeding habitat Dry, open, bushy country on hillsides, thorn scrub, ravines, open mountain woodlands.

Displays ♂ sings from elevated perch; in song flight, ascends to 15m, singing, then zigzags, finally descending with slow wing-beats, or with fully extended wings and spread tail.

Nesting Territorial. Nest is low in thorny bush in thick cover; a well-built cup of grass, etc., lined with finer

materials. Eggs whitish to pale green with fine reddish-brown spotting, 18mm.

Diet Insects; also fruit in autumn. Feeds mainly under cover, inside canopy of low bushes and trees.

Winters NE Africa in arid savannas, scrubby grasslands.

Conservation Locally common in very limited range in E Mediterranean. See p. 529.

Essays Habitat Selection, p. 423; Timing of Migration, p. 405.

Precocial and Altricial Young

'PRECOCIAL' and 'altricial', two words describing the degree of development in young birds at hatching, are good examples of useful scientific jargon. They save ornithologists from repeatedly using phrases when single words will do. A precocial bird is 'capable of moving around on its own soon after hatching'. The word comes from the same Latin root as 'precocious'. Altricial means 'incapable of moving around on its own soon after hatching'. It comes from a Latin root meaning 'to nourish' — a reference to the need for extensive parental care before fledging in altricial species. If you consult some of the literature we have cited, you may sometimes see the term 'nidifugous' used to describe precocial young that leave the nest immediately, and 'nidicolous' to describe young that remain in the nest. All nidifugous birds are precocial, but some nidicolous birds are precocial too — they remain in the nest even though capable of locomotion. These terms are less widely used than precocial and altricial, and we will not employ them outside of this essay.

Instead of a sharp dividing line between hatchlings that are precocial and those that are altricial, there is a gradient of precociality. In this guide, we recognize the following categories of young:

Precocial: Hatch covered with down, with eyes open, and leave the nest

Left: Sparrow hatchling (altricial — naked, blind and helpless on hatching). Right: Grouse hatchling (precocial 3 — downy, open-eyed, mobile on hatching, follows parents and is shown food).

Desert Warbler

Sylvia nana

ATLAS 231; PMH 195; PER -; HFP 234; HPCW 202; NESTS 255; BWP6:396

to 1m

BLDS: ♂?
Monogamy?

4–5 (–6)
1 (2?) broods
INCU: ♂♀
?

FLDG: ♂♀
?

Seeds

Ground glean

Breeding habitat Sandy or rocky desert, salt flats with scattered shrubs.

Displays ♂ sings from top of, or within, bush, or from ground, spreading and raising tail. Less often in short song flight from bush to bush. Sexual chases occur around territory.

Nesting Territorial. Nest is low in shrubs; a substantial cup of available vegetation lined with finer material. ♂ makes 'cock nests' – temporary nests which ♀ inspects, selecting the one in which to lay her eggs. Eggs white or light blue with distinct light brown and grey spotting and blotching, 16mm.

Diet Insects, also seeds, berries, taken from low scrub or by running along ground. May also follow wheatears, taking disturbed insects.

Winters Resident.

Conservation In NW Africa and so very isolated from other populations in Asia. Population size is not well known.

Essays Habitat Selection, p. 423.

Arabian Warbler

Sylvia leucomelaena

ATLAS 230; PMH -; PER - HFP -; HPCW 203; NESTS -; BWP6:406

1–3m

BLDS: ♂♀
Monogamy

2–3 (–4)
2–3 broods
INCU: ♂♀
15–16

FLDG: ♂♀
14–15(10–17)

Fruit

Bark glean

Breeding habitat Semi-desert with *Acacia* trees, along water courses.

Displays ♂s (and ♀s) sing from exposed perches. There is mutual preening between mated pairs.

Nesting Territorial; both sexes defend. Nest near top of an *Acacia*; a cup of plant stems and leaves, lined with finer materials. Young remain with parents for up to 6 weeks after fledging. Egg size not known apparently.

Diet Insects, particularly caterpillars taken from the trunks and branches of Acacias; also fruits. Also takes insects on ground, probing sand with its beak, and in mid-air.

Winters Resident; defends territories year-round.

Conservation Locally common in limited range along Red Sea, just into area covered by this guide.

Essays Habitat Selection, p. 423.

Refs Paz 1987.

within two days. There are four levels of precociality, although only three are found in European birds. Level 1 of development (precocial 1) is the pattern found in the chicks of megapodes (Australian Malleefowl, Brush-Turkeys, etc.), which are totally independent of their parents. The megapode eggs are incubated in a huge pile of decaying vegetation. Upon hatching the young dig their way out, already well feathered and able to fly. No European birds show this extreme precociality. Precocial 2 development is found in ducklings and the chicks of most waders, which follow their parents but find their own food. The young of gallinaceous birds, however, trail after their parents and are shown food; they are classified as precocial 3. Precocial 4 development is represented by the young of birds such as rails and grebes, which follow their parents and are not just shown food but are actually fed by them.

Semi-precocial: Hatch covered with down, with eyes open, and capable of leaving the nest soon after hatching (they can walk and often swim), but stay at the nest and are fed by parents. Basically precocial but nidicolous, this developmental pattern is found in the young of gulls and terns.

Semi-altricial: Covered with down, incapable of departing from the nest, and fed by the parents. In species classified as semi-altricial 1, such as hawks and herons, chicks hatch with their eyes open. Owls, in the category semi-altricial 2, hatch with eyes closed. If all young were divided into only two categories, altricial and precocial, these all would be considered altricial.

Altricial: Hatch with little or no down, with eyes closed, incapable of departing from the nest, and fed by the parents. All passerines are altricial.

Note that in the species treatments in this book we use the term 'fledging' (FLDG) for the number of days it takes for the young of an altricial or semi-altricial bird to acquire its full set of feathers, after which it leaves the nest. Thus for altricial and semi-altricial birds, the time needed to get fully feathered and time spent in the nest are essentially the same. In precocial and semi-precocial birds, FLDG: indicates not the number of days that pass before the young leave the nest, but generally from the time of hatching until they can fly.

Characteristics of nestlings (modified from O'Connor, 1984)

Type of development	Down present?	Eyes open?	Mobile?	Feed selves?	Parents absent?	Examples
Precocial 1	Yes	Yes	Yes	Yes	Yes	Megapodes
Precocial 2	Yes	Yes	Yes	Yes*	No	Ducks, most waders
Precocial 3	Yes	Yes	Yes	Yes†	No	Grouse, partridge
Precocial 4	Yes	Yes	Yes	Yes/No	No	Grebes, rails
Semi-precocial	Yes	Yes	Yes/No	No	No	Gulls, terns
Semi-altricial 1	Yes	Yes	No	No	No	Herons, hawks
Semi-altricial 2	Yes	No	No	No	No	Owls
Altricial	No	No	No	No	No	Passerines

* Precocial 2 follow parents but find own food.
† Precocial 3 are shown food.

Orphean Warbler

Sylvia hortensis

ATLAS 229; PMH 196; PER 174; HFP 232; HPCW 203; NESTS 253; BWP6:412

| Shrub 1–2m | BLDS: ♂♀? Monogamy? | 3–5 (6) 1 brood INCU: ♂♀ 12–13 | FLDG: ♂♀ 12–13 | Fruit | Ground glean |

Breeding habitat   Dry, open forest, olive groves, gardens.

Displays   ♂ sings from cover or tops of bushes; rarely in flight.

Nesting   Territorial. Nest is in branches of small trees or bushes; a cup of small twigs, grass, etc., lined with finer material, bound with silk from spiders' webs. Eggs whitish, with a few distinct light brown and grey blotches, 20mm. Hatch over 1–3 days; young fed for 1 week after fledging.

Diet   Insects, fruit; taken from trees, large bushes, from canopy. Sometimes pounces on insects on ground.

Winters   European populations to Africa S of Sahara, in dry areas with scattered trees and shrubs.

Conservation   Locally common, widely across Mediterranean to SW Asia.

Essays   Habitat Selection, p. 423; Timing of Migration, p. 405.

Refs   Dementiev et al. 1968.

Barred Warbler

Sylvia nisoria

ATLAS 228; PMH 196; PER 174; HFP 230; HPCW 203; NESTS 252; BWP6:424

| 0.5–3m | BLDS: ♂♀ Polygyny | 4–5 (2–6) 1 (2?) broods INCU: ♂♀ 12–13 | FLDG: ♂♀ 11–12 | 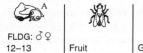Fruit | Ground glean |

Breeding habitat   Low vegetation in woodland edges, clearings, hedges.

Displays   ♂ sings from tops of bushes, or while flying between perches, rising at angle and then gliding downward.

Nesting   Territorial, but often in neighbourhood groups. Nest is often in bush or brambles, on forked branch; a tall cup of grass, lined with finer material. Eggs, whitish with fine light grey markings, 21mm. ♂ builds up to 3 'cock nests' – temporary nests which ♀ inspects, selecting the one in which to lay her eggs. Most ♂s try to acquire second ♀ after first mate starts laying,

giving early arriving ♂s an advantage. Second ♀ has to rear brood alone.

Diet   Insects, mostly from low bushes, but also in canopy; rarely from ground; fruits in early autumn.

Winters   E Africa, Arabia in thick dry scrub, along dry river beds.

Conservation   Some local declines, has spread in Scandinavia, Finland. Locally common in E Europe and C Asia. See p. 529.

Essays   Habitat Selection, p. 423; Timing of Migration, p. 405.

Refs   Dementiev et al. 1968.

Timing of Migration

IT is not surprising that the timing of major events in the annual cycle of migratory birds has evolved together with the requirements of migration. The onset and speed of feather moult, the deposition of fat stores to serve as fuel for flight, the growth and shrinkage of gonads in concert with breeding and non-breeding periods, and the actual departure on migration are all events that occur at 'the right time' of year as a result of natural selection. But what controls the precise timing of these events for the individual bird?

Biologists have known for some time that seasonal changes in photoperiod (the amount of daylight relative to darkness in a 24-hour period) and temperature both act as synchronizing cues for a variety of physiological activities in many vertebrate animals. Extensive studies with European species of long-distance migrants have revealed the existence of an endogenous rhythm that runs like an internal clock to set the timing of events in the bird's annual cycle. Hence this is referred to as a 'circannual rhythm', meaning an internal clock with a period of about one year. Experiments with hand-raised birds exposed only to constant environmental conditions in the laboratory demonstrate that the clock has an actual period of about ten months, so that in the absence of normal seasonal change in photoperiod, a captive bird's full annual cycle shifts forward and is completed more quickly. In nature, environmental cues provided by the external environment synchronize the genetically programmed internal rhythm with natural seasonal events.

Much of what we know about the relationship between circannual rhythms and the timing of migration comes from the research programme developed by ornithologists Eberhard Gwinner and Peter Berthold at Germany's Max-Planck-Institut für Verhaltensphysiologie. The first evidence for circannual rhythms in birds came from experiments with Willow and Garden Warblers that demonstrated a circannual periodicity regardless of photoperiod exposure in the laboratory. Individual Garden Warblers and Blackcaps were maintained continuously in the lab under constant photoperiod for nearly 10 years and continued to show a circannual moult rhythm with a period of approximately 10 months.

The tendency of most European passerines to migrate at night is expressed in captive birds by nocturnal fluttering ('migratory restlessness' or 'Zugunruhe') performed at the appropriate time of year and with the bird facing in the appropriate compass direction for migration. This behaviour revealed differences between species and among populations of migrants that correspond to differences in the onset of migration in free-living birds. For example, warblers that leave their breeding grounds in early autumn exhibit Zugunruhe earlier than later-migrating species. Young Willow and Garden Warblers from northern Sweden and southern Finland normally begin their first migration at an earlier age than conspecifics in Germany; these differences are seen

Lesser Whitethroat

Sylvia curruca

ATLAS 233; PMH 196; PER 174; HFP 230; HPCW 204; NESTS 251; BWP6:439

Decid tree 1–2m	BLDS: ♂♀ Monogamy	4–6 (2–7) 1(–2) broods INCU: ♂♀ 10–14
FLDG: ♂♀ 10–13	Fruit	Ground glean

Breeding habitat In low thick scrub, in woodland edges, openings, hedgerows. Overlaps extensively in habitat with Whitethroat but tends to prefer thicker ground cover.

Displays ♂ sings from thick cover, rarely in flight. ♂ chases ♀ around territory in courtship flights. May exclude Whitethroat from its territories

Nesting Territorial. Nest is low in a bush, brambles, or tree; a deep cup of fine twigs, grass, etc., lined with finer materials. Eggs white to cream, with a few grey to brown spots and blotches, 17mm.

Diet Insects, taken in bushes, trees, sometimes on ground; berries in early autumn.

Winters Africa S of Sahara, eastern populations to India; in *Acacia* scrub and other dry areas.

Conservation Local increases and decreases. Locally common across most of Europe and widely distributed in Asia.

Essays Bird Guilds, p. 77; Habitat Selection, p. 423; Timing of Migration, p. 405.

Refs Dementiev et al. 1968; Marchant et al. 1990.

Whitethroat

Sylvia communis

ATLAS 232; PMH 197; PER 174; HFP 230; HPCW 204; NESTS 250; BWP6:459

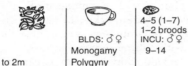 

to 2m	BLDS: ♂♀ Monogamy Polygyny	4–5 (1–7) 1–2 broods INCU: ♂♀ 9–14
FLDG: ♂♀ 10–12	Fruit	

Breeding habitat A variety of open areas with small bushes, brambles, hedgerows, orchards. Overlaps extensively with Lesser Whitethroat, but tends to prefer thicker bushes, thinner ground cover.

Displays ♂ sings from concealed or exposed perches. In song flight, rises into air, then dances upwards and downwards, eventually gliding down to new perch; with raised crown and tail spread. Threat includes bill-snapping.

Nesting Territorial. Nest is in low cover such as brambles; a deep cup of grasses, lined with finer material. ♂ starts building nest, ♀ may complete it or choose another. Eggs whitish with fine olive grey or brown spottings, 18mm. Some ♂s have second ♀ within their territory; if so, she must rear the brood alone. Young may remain with parents for up to 3 weeks.

Diet Insects; berries in early autumn

(and may be most important food in winter).

Winters Africa S of Sahara in savanna, thorn scrub.

Conservation Underwent a 75 per cent reduction in numbers after 1965, probably due to habitat losses in the Sahel where it winters. Eastern populations, however, winter in Asia, and were unaffected by the Sahelian drought and did not decline. Common across most of Europe and across Asia, into N Africa.

Essays Migration, p. 377; Birds and Agriculture, p. 365; Habitat Selection, p. 423; Ducking the Bird Laws, p. 523; Birds and Global Warming, p. 311; Declines in Forest Birds: Europe and America, p. 339; Orientation and Navigation, p. 503; Timing of Migration, p. 405; Population Dynamics, p. 515.

Refs Dementiev et al. 1968; Marchant et al. 1990.

also in caged birds from both populations of both species. Similarly, plumage development and moult proceed faster in birds from the northern populations of both species.

In addition to the timing of Zugunruhe, the duration of nocturnal activity also reveals striking correspondence to the distance of migration undertaken by a species. Among *Sylvia* warbler species, first-year Dartford, Sardinian, and Marmora's Warblers exhibit much shorter periods of migratory restlessness in autumn than do Blackcap, Whitethroat, Garden, Subalpine, and Barred Warblers. It appears that endogenous programmes of migratory restlessness can control the duration of migration in inexperienced migrants, enabling them to reach the approximate locale of their 'correct' wintering grounds.

Selective breeding experiments that cross individuals from populations with different migratory characteristics indicate a surprisingly high degree of genetic control over the quantity of migratory restlessness and migratory direction in *Sylvia* species. In autumn, Garden Warblers from southern Germany normally fly southwest to Spain and then south into Africa to reach their winter quarters. Under controlled laboratory conditions with handraised juveniles, birds correctly oriented southwest at the onset of migration and then shifted their heading to due south at the time when they would have reached southern Spain. Not all species show such complete genetic control over compass heading, however. Pied Flycatchers, which travel a similar route, apparently require exposure to the Earth's magnetic field in the breeding area to initiate orientation properly in their first autumn, and need properly timed exposure to the magnetic conditions they would meet en route to alter their compass heading to the south.

Even the question of whether or not an individual bird migrates or remains as a winter resident has been shown to have a strong genetically inherited basis in some species. In populations of partial migrants, in which only some individuals migrate, genetic inheritance for the tendency to migrate has been demonstrated with Blackcaps, Stonechats, Robins, and Blackbirds.

Taken together, experiments with a variety of *Sylvia* species under controlled experimental conditions indicate endogenous regulation of the timing of migration, migratory direction, and distance travelled to reach wintering areas. Work with other migratory species, however, indicates that there are complicated interactions between photoperiodic (and other environmental) cues with endogenous rhythms. These complexities remain to be sorted out before we have a more complete grasp of the mechanisms that govern the details of migration in other European species.

SEE: Migration, p. 377; Orientation and Navigation, p. 503; Wader Migration and Conservation, p. 167; Differential Migration, p. 323; Breeding Season, p. 293; Wintering Site Tenacity, p. 409; Breeding Site Tenacity, p. 219; Irruptions, p. 491; Wintering and Conservation, p. 409; Why Some Species Migrate at Night, p. 351; Hormones and Nest Building, p. 329. REFS: Beck and Wiltschko 1988; Berthold, 1988; Dhondt, 1983; Gwinner, 1986*a,b*.

Garden Warbler

Sylvia borin

ATLAS 229; PMH 197; PER 174; HFP 230; HPCW 250; NESTS 251; BWP6:479

Shrub to 2m	BLDS: ♂♀ Monogamy	4–5 (2–6) 1 (2) broods INCU: ♂♀ 10–12 (11–17)

FLDG: ♂♀ 9–12	Fruit	

Breeding habitat   Thick undergrowth in woodlands. Habitat overlaps extensively with Blackcap, although prefers a more open canopy with a dense and tall shrub layer. Despite common name, avoids gardens.

Displays   ♂ sings from low cover, in flight if courting a ♀. Often excludes Blackcap from its territory.

Nesting   Territorial. Nest is usually low in thick cover such as brambles; a cup of grasses, lined with finer materials. Eggs white to pale buff, with light brown spotting and blotching, 20mm. ♂ makes 'cock nests' — temporary nests which ♀ inspects, selecting the one in which to lay her eggs. A few ♂s are successively bigamous.

Diet   Insects; fruits in early autumn.

Forages mainly in shrub layer, sometimes in the canopy.

Winters   Africa S of Sahara in mixed grassland, forest.

Conservation   Common across most of Europe and into Asia. In UK and elsewhere, there was an up to 70 per cent decline in the population size in the mid-1970s, though populations have now recovered.

Essays   Interspecific Territoriality, p. 421; Brood Parasitism, p. 249; Declines in Forest Birds: Europe and America, p. 339; Habitat Selection, p. 423; Orientation and Navigation, p. 503; Timing of Migration, p. 405; Wintering Site Tenacity, p. 409.

Refs   Cody 1985*b*; Dementiev et al. 1968; Marchant et al. 1990.

Blackcap

Sylvia atricapilla

ATLAS 229; PMH 197; PER 174; HFP 232; HPCW 205; NESTS 252; BWP6:496

Shrub 0.5–2m	BLDS: ♂♀ Monogamy	4–6 (2–7) 1–2 broods INCU: ♂♀ 10–16

FLDG: ♂♀ 8–14	Fruit	

Breeding habitat   Similar to Garden Warbler (see above); more likely in undergrowth under conifers. Requires tall but not very dense undergrowth.

Displays   ♂ (♀ sometimes) sings from cover, below canopy. In courtship, ♂ may bow to ♀.

Nesting   Territorial. Nest is low in thick cover, often brambles; a cup of stems and grasses, lined with finer material. Eggs white to pale buff, with fine brown spotting and blotching, 20mm. Some ♂s are successively bigamous.

Diet   Insects taken from shrubs and canopy; fruits in autumn and winter.

Winters   Populations W of 12°E to the SW; others move SE. Winters mainly

in Africa, moves into drier habitats, savannahs with *Acacia*, forest edges; exploits locally abundant fruit and nectar, and may defend territories. Has recently changed winter range and substantial numbers now winter in SW Europe.

Conservation   Common and increasing across Europe into N Africa, Asia.

Essays   Migration, p. 377; Interspecific Territoriality, p. 421; Habitat Selection, p. 423; Orientation and Navigation, p. 503; Timing of Migration, p. 405; Wintering Site Tenacity, p. 409.

Refs   Cody 1985*b* Marchant et al. 1990.

Wintering Site Tenacity

JUST as many species show strong fidelity to breeding sites to which they return each year for nesting, many migrants show some degree of site fidelity to wintering areas as well. Ringing studies of wintering birds provide good evidence of strong site fidelity for Yellow Wagtails in Kenya and Nigeria, Reed Warblers in Uganda, and Great Reed Warblers in Zaïre. Fidelity to wintering sites is not limited to birds in Africa; similar studies of birds wintering along the Mediterranean have produced similar results for Firecrests and Dunnocks in Italy, Blackcaps and Chiffchaffs in Spain, and Robins in both Italy and Spain.

Some species show extreme site faithfulness to winter territories. It has become clear in recent years that many species have several African wintering grounds, among which they move regularly during their African stay. For example, Garden Warblers arrive in Uganda in November and occupy feeding territories for about six weeks while adding about five per cent additional body mass. They depart in December but return to the same individual territories in February, where they remain until March when they leave for the north. The implication is that individual Garden Warblers possess two or perhaps even three separate wintering sites within Africa. The strong seasonality of food resources such as insects and fruit may be the underlying cause of such 'step migration', but there is an alternative hypothesis for some species. Since vegetation has vanished from the Sahara only over the last 5000 years or so, birds may have been induced to take up temporary winter quarters immediately south of the desert in order to replenish their energy stores after the energetically demanding flight across the Sahara. Only then could they continue to their original winter areas further south.

SEE: Migration, p. 377; Orientation and Navigation, p. 503; Breeding Site Tenacity, p. 219; Wader Migration and Conservation, p. 167; Differential Migration, p. 323; Breeding Season, p. 293; Wintering and Conservation, p. 409; Spacing of Wintering Waders, p. 179. REFS: Bairlein, 1988; Curry-Lindahl, 1981; Gauthreaux, 1982; Lovei, 1989; Mead, 1983.

Wintering and Conservation

THE species treatments contain information on wintering ranges of European birds, primarily because of their importance to the birds' conservation. The connection between wintering range and conservation is emphasized here

Greenish Warbler

Phylloscopus trochiloides

ATLAS 237; PMH 198; PER 176; HFP 238; HPCW 206; NESTS 259; BWP6:523

  3–7 1 brood INCU: ♀ 12–13

to 1m

BLDS: ♀ Monogamy?

 FLDG: ♂♀ 12–14 (16)

 Ground glean

Breeding habitat Wide range of open woodlands, both deciduous and coniferous, up to scrub on mountains.

Displays ♂ (sometimes ♀) sings from canopy, sometimes shivering whole body; sometimes flutters from perch to perch while singing. Threat includes wing-flicking and bill-snapping.

Nesting Territorial. Nest is on ground among thick cover; a domed structure of grass, leaves, etc. lined with finer material. Eggs white, 15mm. Young remain with parents 1–2 weeks.

Diet Insects, gleaned from canopy foliage, down to ground. In winter, fly-catcher, or uses wing-flicks to disturb insects from foliage.

Winters Migrates E to India, SE Asia, in open woodland, gardens. May occur in mixed feeding flocks. Territorial and both sexes sing in winter.

Conservation Has extended range into Scandinavia, Finland, though populations fluctuate considerably from year to year. Common and widespread across NE Europe and much of Asia.

Notes A small population of the Green Warbler, *Phylloscopus nitidus*, breeds in an area in eastern Turkey covered by this guide.

Essays Nest Lining, p. 439; Mixed-species Flocking, p. 429; Why Some Species Migrate at Night, p. 351.

Refs Cody 1985*b*; Dementiev et al. 1968.

Arctic Warbler

Phylloscopus borealis

ATLAS 235; PMH 198; PER 176; HFP 238; HPCW 206; NESTS 259; BWP6:536

   6–7 (5–) 1 brood INCU: ♀ 11–13

Shrub to 1m

Crevice BLDS: ? Monogamy

FLDG: ♂♀ 13–14

Breeding habitat Wide range of boreal woodlands, birch with understory, mixed forests, and (sometimes stunted) coniferous forests, often near water.

Displays ♂ sings from near top of tree, or hidden perch; adopts an erect posture, ruffles throat and breast, droops wings, and shivers whole body. When moving between perches, quivers wings, producing rattling or buzzing sound.

Nesting Territorial, perhaps in neighbourhood groups. Nest is on ground or in natural crevice; a domed structure of grass, lined with finer material. Eggs white, with scattered light

red-brown spotting, 16mm. Occasionally simultaneous bigamy.

Diet Insects, from foliage of trees, bushes; sometimes on ground or in flight; will also hover-glean.

Winters Migrates E to tropical SW Asia, in forests (including rain forests), mangrove swamps.

Conservation Common in boreal forests from Scandinavia (where populations are small and local) across Asia to Alaska.

Essays Nest Lining, p. 439; Why Some Species Migrate at Night, p. 351.

Refs Dementiev et al. 1968.

because *the greatest threat to the preservation of many European birds either now occurs in their wintering range, or soon will.* At current growth rates, human populations in sub-Saharan Africa and western and southern Asia will double in the next 30 years or so, and remaining areas of undisturbed natural environment will be greatly reduced. Unlike the North American situation, however, continuing destruction of tropical forests is not likely to be a critical factor in the future of most species. Most of West Africa has long since been deforested, and relatively few migrants depend upon forests for wintering habitat (the Pied Flycatcher appears to be an important exception).

Many European passerines, however, spend the entire winter or stop while on migration in arid habitats that fringe the southern edge of the Sahara Desert — an area known as the Sahel. These important areas have suffered extensive degradation from livestock overgrazing during periodic droughts in the past several decades. The impact of droughts and desertification in the Sahel of West Africa has been seen in the diminishing numbers of breeding Whitethroats, Redstarts, and Sand Martins following extreme droughts in the late 1960s. In 1969, after a sudden failure of Sahel rains in the previous year, Whitethroat numbers in Britain dropped by about two-thirds. In Central Europe, 14 of the 15 species that have shown the most serious recent declines are long-distance migrants that winter in Africa.

In addition, numerous waders depend upon tropical estuarine and other wetland environments either for wintering or for resting habitat during migration. These areas are also likely to be destroyed as the numbers of people expand. And, finally, the use of pesticides dangerous to birds is not well regulated in most tropical nations. Some European birds doubtless never return after wintering, or suffer breeding failures when they do, because they were poisoned.

In short, much of the winter habitat required by some members of Europe's avifauna is likely to disappear or be contaminated in the next few decades. Outlining the extra-limital winter distribution of each species both gives a clue to its vulnerability and provides a reminder that conservation of many of our bird species requires steps to save tropical habitats. It is also of course true that many birds, both migratory and non-migratory, are threatened by environmental changes within Europe itself.

SEE: Declines in Forest Birds: Europe and America, p. 339; Pesticides and Birds, p. 115; Wader Migration and Conservation, p. 167; Migration, p. 377. REFS: Dobkin, 1994; Ehrlich and Ehrlich, 1981; Ehrlich *et al.*, 1992; Hagan and Johnston, 1992; Schreiber *et al.*, 1989; Terborgh, 1989.

Bonelli's Warbler

Phylloscopus bonelli

ATLAS 235; PMH 200; PER 176; HFP 236; HPCW 207; NESTS 259; BWP6:572

BLDS: ♀	5–6 (4–7)
Monogamy	1 (2) broods
	INCU: ♀
	12–13

| FLDG: ♂♀ | | |
| 12–13 | | Hover & glean |

Breeding habitat A variety of coniferous and deciduous woodlands, from open to closed canopies, on hillsides.

Displays Sings from top of tree, feathers ruffled and body shivering. Song flight is unusual.

Nesting Territorial, though locally in dense neighbourhood groups. Nest is on ground, often in a natural hollow; a domed structure of grass and other vegetation, with a side entrance, lined with finer materials. Eggs white, covered with brown spotting and blotching,

16mm. After fledging, brood may split and each group looked after by a single parent.

Diet Insects, taken from top or outermost twigs; sometimes hover-gleans, or fly-catches.

Winters Africa S of Sahara. In bushy savannah; holds winter territories.

Conservation Locally common S Europe to N Africa and Middle East. Has spread N to C Europe, including Belgium, Netherlands.

Essays Nest Lining, p. 439; Vocal Functions, p. 413.

Wood Warbler

Phylloscopus sibilatrix

ATLAS 236; PMH 201; PER 176; HFP 236; HPCW 207; NESTS 258; BWP6:585

BLDS: ♀	5–7 (2–10)
Monogamy	1 brood
Polygyny	INCU: ♀
	12–14

| FLDG: ♂♀ | | |
| 11–13 (–15) | | Hawks |

Breeding habitat Woodlands with more open understory and thicker canopy than that of Willow Warbler or Chiffchaff.

Displays ♂ sings from exposed perch below canopy. In song flight uses rapid, shallow, wing-beats as it flies along horizontal path between perches. Has sexual chases after ♀s arrive.

Nesting Territorial, but locally in neighbourhood groups. Nest is built on or into ground; a domed structure of grass, leaves, etc. lined with finer materials. Eggs white, heavily spotted brown, 16mm. Young fed by parents for up to 4 weeks after leaving nest. Some ♂s have two ♀s per territory (typically these birds have the larger territories). ♂s seek a second mate while the first

is laying. Other ♂s try to establish a second territory. ♀s in large territories may mate with other than the territory owner.

Diet Insects, taken from high in canopy or by hawking from there. Also hover-gleans.

Winters Africa S of Sahara; in savannah and humid, evergreen forest.

Conservation Has spread N, though there are local decreases. Common and widespread across N Europe, Asia.

Essays Habitat Selection, p. 423; Polygyny, p. 265; Nest Lining, p. 439; Hartley's Titmice and MacArthur's Warblers, p. 425; Vocal Functions, p. 413.

Refs Dementiev et al. 1968; Marchant et al. 1990.

Vocal Functions

THE advent of the breeding season in spring is heralded each dawn by a chorus of bird song that continues intermittently throughout the day. With practice, we can identify a species solely by its songs and calls, and we infer that birds similarly can distinguish between members of their own and other species by voice alone. This assumption has been verified experimentally for many passerine species by playing tapes of vocalizations in the field and carefully observing responses of individual listeners. By altering the tempo, frequency characteristics, length, or other features of tape-recorded songs, and then observing birds' responses to them, the actual components of songs used for species recognition can be identified. For example, Wren, Willow Warbler, Goldcrest, Woodlark, and Chaffinch encode identification mainly in the syntax (sequence of elements) of their songs. Robins, whose songs are very complex and composed of alternating high and low phrases, will respond vigorously even to artificially produced songs as long as they follow the basic syntactical rule of alternating high-low phrases. On the other hand, Skylarks pay little attention to syntax and instead encode species identification in the tempo and rhythm of their song. For many species, exemplified by Bonelli's Warbler, Chiffchaff, Firecrest, and Marsh Tit, the actual fine structure of elements within songs is important for species recognition.

Ornithologists differentiate, somewhat arbitrarily, between a call and a song by the length and complexity of the vocalization. Calls tend to serve specific functions and are generally innate rather than learned. For example, alarm calls serve to alert all within earshot that danger is present; they tend to be rather similar among groups of birds and often communicate their message across species. Contact calls are used among members of a flock or between mates to indicate the location of the caller. Many species in groups that lack song (such as gulls and parrots) have complex repertoires of calls that serve varied functions. Rooks in Norway possess 20 different calls, many of which function in the maintenance of pair bonds and include calls encoding individual identification.

Song is a well-developed feature primarily of oscine passerines (hence, they are referred to as 'songbirds'), and generally must be partly or entirely learned. Songs identify the species of the singer. In addition, the territorial or advertising song of males serves the dual function of territorial proclamation directed at other males and of mate attraction directed toward females. Thus the song warns the former to keep out of the defended territory and invites the latter to join the singer. There are other, more subtle functions and messages, as well. The motivation of the singer can be conveyed by the amount that he sings; in order to attract a mate, unpaired males devote more time to singing than do paired males. When excited, such as during and immediately following a territorial encounter with a rival male, the rapidity of

Chiffchaff
Phylloscopus collybita

ATLAS 236; PMH 201; PER 176; HFP 236; HPCW 208; NESTS 258; BWP6:612

		4–7 (3–9) 1 brood			
Vine tangle to 0.5m	BLDS: ♀ Monogamy	INCU: ♀ 13–15	FLDG: ♂♀ 12–15	Fruit	Ground glean

Breeding habitat Wide range of open deciduous and coniferous woodland, scrub, tall hedgerows.

Displays ♂ sings from cover. Threat includes wing-shivering and bill-snapping.

Nesting Territorial. Nest is on ground or just above it in brambles or thick bush; a domed structure of grass, leaves, etc. lined with feathers. Eggs white with a few brownish spots, 15mm. Usually 2 broods in S. ♂s only rarely bigamous. Young remain with adults up to 3 weeks.

Diet Insects, gleaned from foliage, often high in canopy (♂ feeds higher than ♀); fruit in late summer.

Winters Joins mixed species flocks in woods in autumn. Winters in S Europe, N Africa, SW Asia in scrub and woodlands. Some birds in flocks, others hold territories. The *tristis* subspecies often feeds on ground in winter.

Conservation Common and widespread across Europe, Asia, locally N Africa. Spreading in Eire, Scotland, Scandinavia.

Essays Habitat Selection, p. 423; Interspecific Territoritlity, p. 421; Mixed-species Flocking, p. 429; Nest Lining, p. 439; Species and Speciation, p. 325; Hartley's Titmice and MacArthur's Warblers, p. 425; Vocal Functions, p. 413; Wintering Site Tenacity, p. 409.

Refs Dementiev et al. 1968; Marchant et al. 1990.

Willow Warbler
Phylloscopus trochilus

ATLAS 236; PMH 202; PER 176; HFP 236; HPCW 208; NESTS 257; BWP6:639

		4–8 1 (2) broods			
	BLDS: ♀ Monogamy Polygyny	INCU: ♀ 12–14(10–17)	FLDG: ♂♀ 11–15 (8–19)		
Vine tangle				Fruit	Hawks

Breeding habitat A wide range of open woodlands and bushy habitats, from boreal forests to Mediterranean.

Displays ♂ sings from cover near top of tree; may shiver wings.

Nesting Territorial. Nest is on or built into ground, or in base of thick cover; a domed structure of grass and leaves, lined with feathers. Eggs white, with a few reddish spots or covered with fine light brown speckling, 15mm. Some ♂s are polygynous; these tend to be older birds and they arrive earlier.

Diet Insects gleaned from foliage in shrub layer; also fly-catches and sometimes hover-gleans. Takes fruit in late summer.

Winters May join mixed species flocks in autumn. Wide ranging in Africa S of Sahara in savannah to forests. Often in small groups.

Conservation Common and widespread across N Europe, Asia.

Essays Bird Guilds, p. 77; Birds and Agriculture, p. 365; Polygyny, p. 265; Interspecific Territoriality, p. 421; Nest Lining, p. 439; Population Dynamics, p. 515; Species and Speciation, p. 325; Hartley's Titmice and MacArthur's Warblers, p. 425; Timing of Migration, p. 405; Vocal Functions, p. 413; Breeding Site Tenacity, p. 219.

Refs Dementiev et al. 1968; Marchant et al. 1990.

singing often increases. Song length also may increase or decrease when the bird is agitated.

Males of approximately three-quarters of all songbirds sing two or more different songs and are said to possess 'song repertoires'. Each song having a particular configuration of syllables and phrases repeated in a stereotyped fashion is referred to as a 'song-type'. At the extreme end of the range in repertoire size is the male Brown Thrasher (*Toxostoma rufum*) of North America, estimated to sing in excess of 3000 song-types. The evolution of elaborate song repertoires is presumed to be the result of sexual selection arising from competition between males for females. In selecting a male with which to pair, females may use size and complexity of the song repertoire to assess a male's overall potential 'fitness' as a partner. In some species, such as Willow Warbler, these characteristics are known to increase with age, and may serve as an indirect gauge of breeding experience and health. Increased complexity and size of repertoire also have been shown to correlate with measures of territory quality in some species, thus providing further information to a female about to invest her immediate reproductive future on the basis of what she hears.

Field studies have shown that larger repertoire size in males is related positively to greater reproductive success in Great Reed Warbler, Willow Warbler, and Great Tit. Larger repertoires are also associated with an earlier date of pair formation in Willow Warbler and to higher probability of survival in male Great Tits. Ornithologist Clive Catchpole and others have demonstrated both a functional and an evolutionary dichotomy in the songs of leaf warblers (*Phylloscopus*) and reed warblers (*Acrocephalus*). Catchpole has proposed that the longer, more complicated songs of these species evolved through intersexual selection (by female choice of male mate) and are used for female attraction. The shorter, simpler songs of these warblers evolved through intrasexual selection (by competition among males) and function as aggressive, territorial signals directed at rival males. Both laboratory and field studies have been conducted with several species of these two genera and have provided firm support for these ideas. How general this dichotomy may be for other songbirds remains to be tested.

There is increasing experimental evidence that song is important in coordinating the reproductive cycle between mates in addition to its presumed role in maintaining the pair bond. Male song is known to stimulate ovarian development and egg-laying in Budgerigars and to accelerate nest-building activity in female Canaries. Laboratory experiments have shown that female Canaries exposed to large repertoires are more stimulated to build nests than are females exposed to impoverished repertoires. Similar experiments with female Great Tits and Great Reed Warblers demonstrate that larger song repertoires elicit more copulation-soliciting displays, indicating that females prefer to mate with males possessing larger repertoires of song- or syllable-types. For example, male Great Tits can have repertoires of one to six song-types, but females exposed to experimental tapes responded weakly to tapes of one or two song-types and responded strongly to repertoires of three to five songs.

Goldcrest

Regulus regulus

ATLAS 202; PMH 181; PER 178; HFP 238; HPCW 208; NESTS 260; BWP6:668

 2–15m | BLDS: ♂♀ Monogamy | 9–11 (6–13) 2 broods INCU: ♀ 16 (15–17) | A FLDG: ♂♀ 19 (17–22) | | Bark glean

Breeding habitat Widespread, but usually in coniferous or mixed woodland.

Displays ♂ high in canopy and often sings while foraging. Rival ♂s have long song duels. In display, ♂ bows head and shows brightly coloured crest; also has fast wing-flicks.

Nesting Territorial. Nest is usually suspended below the twigs at the end of a branch in a conifer; a tiny almost spherical cup of moss, lichens, and spiders' webs, lined with feathers. Eggs white, covered with very fine buff to brown spotting, 14mm. A second nest may be started, and a second clutch laid, while first brood still in nest.

Diet Small insects, picked from foliage in canopy, twigs, or tree trunks. Also hover-gleans .

Winters Mainly resident; N populations move S. Often in small territorial groups or moves in and out of mixed species flocks with tits and nuthatches.

Conservation Common and widespread across Europe and into Asia. Has declined in areas where acid rain has killed off conifers but has benefited from conifer plantations. Vulerable to cold winters.

Essays Bird Guilds, p. 77; Declines in Forest Birds: Europe and America, p. 339; Mixed-species Flocking, p. 429; Nest Lining, p. 439; Vocal Functions, p. 413.

Refs Dementiev et al. 1968; Marchant et al. 1990.

Firecrest

Regulus ignicapillus

ATLAS 240; PMH 203; PER 178; HFP 238; HPCW 209; NESTS 261; BWP6:685

 Conif tree | BLDS: ♀ Monogamy | 7–12 2 broods INCU: ♀ 14–16 | A FLDG: ♂♀ 22–24 | Hover & glean

Breeding habitat Deciduous woodland, but also in coniferous woodland, generally in areas where Goldcrest is absent. Prefers spruce trees in the UK, evergreen oaks in S.

Displays ♂ sings from concealed perch. In display, leans forward with feathers ruffled, and slowly raises wings one at a time.

Nesting Territorial. Nest is similar to that of the Goldcrest, suspended from terminal twigs and may take up to 3 weeks to build. Eggs whitish, often pinker than those of the Goldcrest's, with indistinct buffish markings, 14mm. Young stay with adults up to 4 weeks after fledging.

Diet Small insects, spiders, taken from trees, low shrubs, sometimes ground. Hover-gleans about 10% of time. A more active feeder than Goldcrest and takes larger prey.

Winters Resident or moves to lower elevations or to the SW. May join mixed species flocks with tits in the autumn.

Conservation Local across continental Europe outside Scandinavia, Turkey, and N Africa. Some spread NW and colonized UK in 1962.

Essays Decline of Forest Birds: Europe and America, p. 339; Vocal Functions, p. 413; Wintering Site Tenacity, p. 409.

Refs Dementiev et al. 1968

Individual males often can be identified by characteristic features of their songs, and birds of many species have been tested in the field for their ability to discriminate between the songs of neighbours (males that are already established on territories and pose no real threat) and strangers (males that are searching for a territory on which to establish themselves). The ability to distinguish between neighbours and strangers without being able to see them should afford considerable energy savings to a territory holder. The song of an established neighbour can be answered with a song or can be ignored; the song of a stranger, however, necessitates a vigorous physical as well as vocal rebuff. Territorial males identify each other using both song features and the location from which the song originates.

The ability to recognize neighbours by vocalizations alone has not been found in species that nest in dense colonies. This is true even for species (such as Gannet and Kittiwake) that can recognize their young or their mates by vocalizations. Presumably under conditions of unobstructed visual contact, natural selection has not favoured the development of vocal recognition of neighbours.

SEE: Vocal Development, p. 479; Vocal Copying, p. 383; Sonagrams: Seeing Bird Songs, p. 307; Visual Displays, p. 33; Sexual Selection, p. 149; Hormones and Nest Building, p. 329; Vocal Dialects, p. 477; Environmental Acoustics, p. 327. REFS: Aubin and Bremond, 1983; Baker, 1988; Becker, 1982; Catchpole and Leisler, 1989; Krebs and Kroodsma, 1980; Radesater and Jakobsson, 1988; Roskaft and Espmark, 1982; Temrin, 1986.

Songbird Foraging

WE tend to see passerines more often than other kinds of birds, and very frequently it is while they are looking for food. Songbird foraging is thus one of the most frequent and most interesting behaviours encountered by bird-watchers. Different birds go about it in different ways. A flycatcher can provide many minutes of entertainment as it sallies from a perch to snatch up passing insects. Warblers, which seem always on the move as they glean insects from foliage and bark, take on added interest when one realizes that different species tend to search in somewhat different places. Tits scramble through trees, often in flocks, frequently hanging upside down to search out an insect morsel (but in high winds and cold temperatures move lower in the trees and feed more on the ground). Crossbills also move in gangs, and resemble small parrots as they often hang upside down. Crossbills use their scissored bills to pry the seeds out of pine cones. Berry-eating Waxwings also flock but are more sedate. In the autumn, groups of Goldfinches make a lively sight as they swarm over the seed-heads of thistles. Wagtails may sneak up on flies on dung pats, pick prey from the ground or from the surface of shallow water in flooded meadows, or fly up and grab insects in mid-air.

Spotted Flycatcher

Muscicapa striata

ATLAS 243; PMH 203; PER 178; HFP 240; HPCW 209; NESTS 262; BWP7:10

to 2m	BLDS: ♂♀ Monogamy	4–6 (2–7) 1–2 broods INCU: ♀ 12–14(10–15)	FLDG: ♂♀ 12–16(10–17)		Swoops

Breeding habitat Open deciduous or mixed woodlands, woodland clearings, parks, gardens.

Displays ♂ sings inconspicuously from perch. Threat includes bill-snaps and wing-flicks. During nest-showing behaviour, ♀ begs food from ♂.

Nesting Territorial. Nest is placed against a tree trunk, supported by branch, or in hole in a tree, a crevice in a wall, or on ledge; a loose cup of grass, twigs, etc. lined with finer material including feathers. Eggs pale buff, blue-green, distinct reddish-brown blotches, 18mm. Young fed by parents for up to several weeks after leaving nest.

Diet Catches insects in mid-air, after flight from perch (see opposite page).

Often takes insects with stings, removing them by rubbing insect against perch. Especially in bad weather, will take prey from ground or tree trunks. See Collared Flycatcher.

Winters Africa S of Sahara in open forest.

Conservation Common across most of Europe, Asia, and parts of N Africa. Has declined in UK, Denmark, perhaps as a consequence of crossing the Sahelian region twice a year.

Essays Selection in Nature, p. 471; Bills, p. 391; Ducking the Bird Laws, p. 523; Birds and Global Warming, p. 311; Wintering and Conservation, p. 409.

Refs Dementiev et al. 1968; Marchant et al. 1990.

Red-breasted Flycatcher

Ficedula parva

ATLAS 243; PMH 204; PER 178; HFP 240; HPCW 210; NESTS 263; BWP7:26

2–10m	Cup BLDS: ♀,♂♀ Monogamy	5–6 (4–7) 1 brood INCU: ♀ 12–13 (–15)	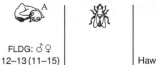 FLDG: ♂♀ 12–13(11–15)		Hawks

Breeding habitat Mainly mature mixed or deciduous forests (especially beech) with open understory.

Displays ♂ sings from perch, raising head and exposing throat. Also sings in horizontal flight from branch to branch, or descends from high to low branch while shivering wings. Threat includes wing- and tail-flicks. ♂ courtship-feeds ♀.

Nesting Territorial. Nest is either in a hole or against tree trunk, supported by branches; a cup of moss, lined with finer material. Eggs whitish to pale blue or

pale buff, with a covering of indistinct, fine brown markings, 16mm.

Diet Insects, especially caterpillars. Most common method (65 per cent of time) is to hover-glean from trees; also sallies for insects or pounces on them on the ground. See Collared Flycatcher.

Winters Migrates E to winter in India and adjacent regions in forest and more open habitats.

Conservation Locally common E Europe, across Asia. See p. 528.

Essays Bills, p. 391.

Refs Dementiev et al. 1968

A Spotted Flycatcher sallies from its perch in open woodland to hawk insects flying close to the ground.

Swallows and martins zoom along acting as speedy insect nets engulfing 'aerial plankton' (small flying insects).

Larks often dig in the ground with their bills or search under stones to obtain insect pupae and other edible items, but they may also extract seeds from seed-heads or even fly up from the surface to snatch insects in mid-air. Blackbirds run along the ground, pause, and pounce on insects or earthworms, and may sweep aside leaves with their bills as they search. Robins, in contrast, often perch on a low branch and fly down to capture prey on the ground. Shrikes may hover before dropping to take prey on the ground.

A given species of bird will often change its foraging behaviour from area to area, from season to season, and even from moment to moment, depending on the kinds of food items that are available. Watching and recording patterns of foraging can thus be a fascinating and useful activity. Ecologists have approached foraging theoretically, trying to create models that predict how an animal should behave when confronted by numerous food items that differ in how difficult each is to find, how long each takes to 'handle' (e.g. to kill an insect, husk a seed), how nutritious each is relative to the others, how long it takes an individual to travel from one concentration of food items (say, a seed-rich weed patch) to another, and so on. In fact, much of the work testing general foraging models has been done with birds. Some of the models have quite accurately predicted such things as when a bird will leave a certain patch of habitat where it has been feeding and seek another, and how a bird will select food items from a mix of big scarce and small common ones.

So whether you are a bird-lover who just enjoys watching them, or an ecologist interested in the details of how nature works, observing the foraging of songbirds has a great deal to offer.

SEE: Mixed-species Flocking, p. 429; Hartley's Titmice and MacArthur's Warblers, p. 425; Starlings, p. 463; Wader Feeding, p. 187; Raptor Hunting, p. 113. REFS: Davies, 1977; Elkins, 1983; Krebs *et al.*, 1977, 1983; Orians and Angell, 1985.

Collared Flycatcher

Ficedula albicollis

ATLAS 242; PMH 204; PER 178; HFP 240; HPCW 211; NESTS 263; BWP7:49

Conif tree 10–20m	BLDS: ♀ Monogamy Polygyny	5–7 (1–9) 1 brood INCU: ♀ 12–14	FLDG: ♂♀ 15–18	Foliage glean

Breeding habitat Openings in deciduous and coniferous forests.

Displays ♂ sings from near nest site with drooping wings; quivers and flicks tail. Nest hole is defended vigorously against other hole nesters.

Nesting Nest is in hole in tree (or nest box); a cup of vegetation lined with finer material. Eggs light blue, 17mm. Young remain with parents for about 1 week after fledging. Bigamy associated with ♂s that annex several nest holes. First mate gets most of the help from ♂ and second raises fewer, smaller young. ♂s are frequently cuckolded.

Diet Mainly caterpillars and other insects fed to young; sallies for insects, or gleans them from foliage or (in bad weather) ground. Flycatchers, in general, have feeding habits that vary with time of year, habitat, and especially the weather conditions.

Winters Africa S of Sahara; sometimes in forest. Winter habits not well known.

Conservation Locally common across C Europe (has spread N) and adjacent parts of W Asia. See p. 528.

Notes The Semi-collared Flycatcher has often been considered a SE subspecies of this species. BWP7, page 39, now considers it to be a separate species.

Essays Average Clutch Size, p. 31; Bills, p. 391; Sexual Selection, p. 149; Sleeping Sentries and Mate-guarding, p. 73.

Pied Flycatcher

Ficedula hypoleuca

ATLAS 241; PMH 204; PER 178; HFP 240; HPCW 211; NESTS 262; BWP7:64

Conif tree 2–6m	BLDS: ♀ Monogamy Polygyny	6–7 (5–8) 1 (2?) broods INCU: ♀ 13–15 (11–18)	FLDG: ♀, ♂♀ 14–17	Swoops

Breeding habitat Woodlands; mainly moist open oak in UK, also in conifers and gardens on continent.

Displays ♂ sings from high perch near nest hole, while drooping wings and flicking tail. Defends nest hole vigorously.

Nesting Nests in hole in tree or in nest box; a loose cup of vegetation lined with finer materials. Eggs light blue, 17mm. Some ♂s, typically the older ones, are bigamous, and try to set up a second territory after first mate starts to lay. Young ♂s may remain unpaired. Bigamous ♂ helps first mate, usually leaving the second to rear young alone. Cuckoldry is common (about 1/4 of all young are the product of extra-parental copulations) and it is especially likely when would-be bigamist leaves his mate unguarded.

Diet Takes insects from foliage, ground, or bark; especially caterpillars during nesting; also hawks for insects.

Winters Africa S of Sahara in a wide variety of forests, from savannah to almost rain forests.

Conservation Common across N Europe into Asia, locally into Spain, N Africa. Has increased, especially where aided by nest boxes.

Essays Acid and Eggshells, p. 287; Bills, p. 391; Declines in Forest Birds: Europe and America, p. 339; Habitat Selection, p. 423; Polygyny, p. 265; Population Dynamics, p. 515; Nest Evolution, p. 345; Sleeping Sentries and Mate-guarding, p. 73; Migration, p. 377; Orientation and Navigation, p. 503.

Refs Lundberg and Alatalo 1992 is a book about this species.

Interspecific Territoriality

MOST birds defend their territories only against members of the same species; some, however, defend against individuals of other species as well. Generally such interspecific territoriality occurs between species that are very similar — as might be expected if territoriality is a way of guarding resources or mates. Closely related species are most likely to have similar resource requirements, and are also most likely to attempt to copulate with the territory holder's mate. For instance, the Nightingale and Thrush Nightingale are interspecifically territorial in their narrow area of overlap. In that area they are very similar morphologically and ecologically, and Thrush Nightingale songs converge on those of Nightingales where the two species occur together. Chiffchaffs and Willow Warblers often defend their territories against each other, perhaps because this behaviour reduces interspecific interference in foraging. Interspecific territoriality between breeding Blackcaps and Garden Warblers appears to occur, at least partly, for similar reasons.

Similarly, on a Scottish island, Great Tits and Chaffinches defend their territories against one another, even though the birds belong to entirely different taxonomic families. On the mainland the two species do not exclude each other. Great Tits and Chaffinches have similar feeding habits and areas, and presumably the simpler island environment provides less opportunity for each to use different resources.

Ecologists generally expect to find interspecific territoriality when the habitat is relatively simple, restricting the variety of resources (usually kinds of food) available, and when the birds involved are specialists in their use of the same resources (so that it is not easy for one or both species to change its resource use in the face of competition from the other). When breeding, North American hummingbird species usually live in separate habitats, but during migration, more than one species often occur together, all use the same nectar resources, and interspecific territories are defended.

Some groups of birds defend interspecific territories communally. North American Acorn Woodpecker (*Melanerpes formicivorus*) groups attempt to exclude Acorn Woodpeckers belonging to other groups, Lewis' Woodpeckers (*M. lewis*), jays, and squirrels from the territories that they establish around their large caches of acorns. They also defend against Starlings, which may appropriate the woodpeckers' nest holes.

Finally, birds may even defend their territories against insects; some hummingbirds chase bees and butterflies away from nectar sources. It seems likely that sunbirds may behave similarly.

SEE: Territoriality, p. 397; Cooperative Breeding, p. 275; Hoarding Food, p. 453; Hybridization, p. 461; Species and Speciation, p. 325. REFS: Boyden, 1978; Cody, 1978; Fonstad, 1984; Garcia, 1983; Orians and Willson, 1964; Reed, 1982; Saether, 1983a, 1983b; Sorjonen, 1986, 1987.

Bearded Tit
Panurus biarmicus

ATLAS 262; PMH 205; PER 180; HFP 264; HPCW 211; NESTS 279; BWP7:88

to 0.5m	BLDS: ♂♀ Monogamy	4–8 (3–11) 2–4 broods INCU: ♂♀ 11–12 (10–13)

	FLDG: ♂♀ 12–13 (–16)	Ground glean

Breeding habitat Extensive reed-beds.

Displays ♂ sings all year, a three note song with head pumped up and down. Often in cohesive flocks, with frequent calling. Especially in late summer, the flocks rise high above reed-beds. This 'high flying' display is a precursor to irruptive movements.

Nesting Sometimes in loose colonies. Nest is in thick vegetation, low in reeds, for example where reeds have fallen over; a deep cup of dead vegetation, lined with softer material. Eggs off-white, with a few pale to brown streaks, 18mm. Clutch size decreases throughout year. Birds born early in a year may breed later the same year.

Diet Insects, taken low in the reeds or from water surface, seeds of marsh grasses in autumn and winter, often taken while hanging upside down on plant.

Winters Resident, but with irruptive movements; some N populations may wander S. Often in small flocks.

Conservation Common in restricted habitat, local across Europe and into Asia. Vulnerable to hard winters in N: In the UK, only 2–5 pairs survived the winter of 1946–7.

Notes Sometimes called the Bearded Reedling, this species is not in the tit family, but is allied to the babblers.

Essays Wetland Conservation, p. 145; Irruptions, p. 491.

Refs Dementiev et al. 1968.

Arabian Babbler
Turdoides squamiceps

ATLAS 263; PMH -; PER -; HFP 263; HPCW 212; NESTS 278; BWP7:114

1–7m	BLDS: ♂♀ * Cooperative	3–5 per ♀ 1–3 broods INCU: ♂♀ * 13–14

FLDG: ♂♀* 14	Probes

Breeding habitat Deserts with *Acacia* and other scrub, up into dry mountains.

Displays The birds move as a group, often remaining very close together and mutually preening. There is a peculiar dance ceremony, involving whole group before sunrise. One bird preens and attracts birds into a tight row, with individuals from the ends trying to push into the middle.

Nesting Territorial. Nest is in fork of *Acacia* bush, a large, loose cup of twigs and other vegetation, no obvious lining. Eggs bright blue, 22mm. This species is a cooperative breeder (see essay, p. 275). It forms territorial groups of between 2 and 22 birds. Most of the nest building and caring for the young is done by the dominant ♂ and ♀. More than one ♀ may lay in the nest, hence the sometimes large clutch sizes, up to 13. The ♂ may mate with other ♀s.

The remaining birds help to varying degrees. The dominant pair is generally the oldest. Breeders are usually 6–7 (3–14) years old. Group members are usually related, though ♀s disperse to other groups when 2–5 years old. Larger groups command larger territories.

Diet Omnivorous, taking insects, fruit, seeds, and small vertebrates (especially lizards) from ground, digging into soil, turning over leaf litter, or stripping bark to get to prey. Birds forage in groups.

Winters Resident.

Conservation Common around Arabian peninsula to extreme SE of the area covered by this guide.

Notes Also called Brown Babbler. See Fulvous Babbler.

Refs Paz 1987; Sibley and Monroe 1990.

*plus helpers.

Habitat Selection

ORNITHOLOGISTS are interested in answering two major questions about habitat selection — what determines the range of habitats in which a species occurs, and how does each individual determine when it's in an appropriate habitat? The first question is evolutionary: how has natural selection shaped habitat choices? The second is behavioural: what cues does a bird use in 'choosing' its home? We put choosing in quotes to emphasize the presumed absence of conscious choice. Indeed, some ecologists employ the term 'habitat use' rather than 'habitat selection' to avoid the connotation of birds making deliberate decisions among habitat alternatives.

Birds are nearly ideal subjects for studies of habitat selection, because they are highly mobile, often migrating thousands of kilometres (and in the process passing over an enormous range of environments), and yet ordinarily forage, breed, and winter in very specific habitats. Indeed, the lives of small migrant songbirds are replete with habitat choices — where to feed, where to seek a mate, where to build a nest, where to stop to replenish depleted stores of fat when migrating, and so on. Choices can be so finely tuned that often the two sexes of a species use habitats differently. In grassland of Sussex, England, male Blackbirds and Song Thrushes forage further afield during the breeding season than females. In North American woodlands female Red-eyed Vireos (*Vireo olivaceous*) seek their food closer to the height of their nest (3–9 metres), and males forage closer to the height of their song perches (6–18 metres).

Many studies have demonstrated the special habitat requirements of different species. Habitat selection by Pied Flycatchers depends heavily on the availability of suitable nest sites. Their distribution over the habitat is not what is known as 'ideal free' — where each individual is able to settle wherever its perception of the habitat dictates. Rather it is 'despotic', since the territorial behaviour of dominant males effectively bars some other males from suitable nest sites. When extra nest sites (nest boxes) are provided, extra males settle.

Avian habitat selection is a vast topic in part because both amateur and professional students of birds have accumulated an enormous body of information on which birds live where, and how they operate in their environments. But detailed observations can still add to our understanding of habitat selection — especially observations of bird behaviour made when habitats are being altered either by 'natural experiments' such as droughts and insect outbreaks or by human activities. And since similar species often select different habitats, knowledge of their choices can be a great aid to birdwatchers.

SEE: Bird Guilds, p. 77; Breeding Site Tenacity, p. 219; Seabird Nesting Sites, p. 233.
REFS: Alatalo *et al.*, 1985*a,b*; Alerstam and Högstedt, 1982; Cody, 1981, 1985*a, b*; Eriksson and Götmark, 1982; Greenwood and Harvey, 1978; Hanssen, 1984; Helle and Järvinen, 1986; Jedrzejewski and Jedrzejewska, 1988; Leck, 1987*b*; Williamson, 1971.

Fulvous Babbler

Turdoides fulvus

ATLAS 263; PMH -; PER -; HFP 262; HPCW 212; NESTS 278; BWP7:125

	BLDS: ?	4–5 (3–6) 1 brood? INCU: ?
1–2m	Cooperative	?

FLDG: ?		
?	Fruit	Ground glean

Breeding habitat Sandy desert plains with scattered scrub; oases.

Displays Not well known, the birds call throughout the year.

Nesting Holds group territories. Nests in a thick, thorny bush; a loose large cup of twigs, lined with softer material. Eggs bright blue, 25mm. Occurs in small groups of 4–6 (3–10) with helpers at the nest. See Arabian Babbler.

Diet Insects and fruit, taken from bushes, also ground.
Winters Resident.
Conservation Has been lost from Nile Valley; local in N Africa.
Notes On the basis of their DNA, babblers are now considered to be in the same family as warblers—see Sibley and Monroe 1990.
Essays Cooperative Breeding, p. 275; Eye Colour and Development, p. 85.

Long-tailed Tit

Aegithalos caudatus

ATLAS 264; PMH 205; PER 182; HFP 264; HPCW 213; NESTS 279; BWP7:133

	BLDS: ♂♀	8–12 (6–15) 1 brood INCU: ♀
Decid tree See below	Monogamy Cooperative	13–17

FLDG: ♂♀	
14–18	

Breeding habitat Open woodland, with thick understory; thick hedges.

Displays No territorial song. Display flight is jerky with tail alternatively fanned and closed, ascends to 6m, then dives down. May be made by 3–4 birds in quick succession.

Nesting Loosely defended territories. Pairs may roost with other pairs until nests are complete. Nest sites vary, but typically either low <3m in thick cover, such as gorse, brambles, hawthorn or high (6–10m) in tree against trunk. Nest is a domed structure densely packed with feathers, bound with spiders' webs, and covered with lichens. May take a month to build. Eggs white, with a few reddish spots, sometimes unmarked, 14mm. Often in small groups 8–10 (6–14) of parents and their young. In some nests the young help their parents and siblings; other helpers may be birds that have lost their nests (see essay on Cooperative Breeding, p. 275). Young

remain with parents for 1–2 weeks after fledging.
Diet Insects, especially lepidopteran eggs and larvae; spiders, taken from canopy and shrub layer. Does not hammer or dig for food like true tits.
Winters Resident in small flocks, which defend winter territories. Some continental populations partially migratory. Roost communally in sheltered places.
Conservation Common across most of Europe and across Asia. Vulnerable to cold winters.
Notes Despite its name, this species is not in the tit family, but is placed in a separate family, Aegithalidae, on the basis of its DNA.
Essays Communal Roosting, p. 81; Hartley's Titmice and MacArthur's Warblers, p. 425; Nest Sites and Materials, p. 443.
Refs Dementiev et al. 1968; Sibley and Monroe 1990.

Hartley's Titmice and MacArthur's Warblers

FAMED British ecologist David Lack pointed out a half century ago that closely related passerines that lived together almost always showed ecological differences. But at that time little was known about British titmice, which had wide areas of range overlap and were often found feeding together in the same habitats. They might, therefore, occupy the same 'niche' — in other words, they could play identical roles in the same bird community. The titmice would thus have been an exception to the ecological rule of competitive exclusion. That rule states that two species with essentially the same niche cannot coexist because one will always outcompete and displace the other.

Between 1947 and 1950 ornithologist P. H. T. Hartley of the Edward Grey Institute at Oxford carried out a classic study of the feeding behaviour of the Great, Blue, Marsh, Coal, and Long-tailed Tits in the region around the University. He found that 'the species of titmice are ecologically separated by their feeding habits; that each species has its characteristic height distribution, fixed or varying seasonally; that each species has its favoured foraging trees, and a tendency to seek its food in different parts of those trees; and that no two species are identical or even consistently similar in their food-seeking behaviour.'

For example, in February in one wood, Great Tits spent most of their time at the lowest levels, doing some 40 per cent of their feeding on the ground. Marsh Tits were better represented in the shrub layer than Blue Tits, which in turn foraged lower than Coal Tits. Blue Tits tended to be the dominant forager in oaks, Great Tits in sycamores, Coal Tits in conifers, and Marsh Tits in elders. Long-tailed Tits seemed to prefer ashes, sycamores, and conifers over oaks and elders. All species hunted in all of the kinds of trees — it was the frequency of their occurrence that differed. Thus the titmice did not appear to violate the rule of competitive exclusion.

Hartley's results coincided with those of Scandinavian investigators who had found that Blue Tits tended to forage high and Coal Tits preferred coniferous rather than deciduous trees. Of the closely similar Marsh and Willow Tits, the former inhabited rich deciduous woodlands and the latter coniferous forest.

Interestingly, experiments by ecologists Rauno Alatalo and Arne Lundberg in Sweden have shown that Willow Tits are more efficient foragers on both oak and spruce twigs than are Marsh Tits. The Willow Tits have a slightly more slender bill than the Marsh Tit, which may make them better able to take insects. The absence of the Marsh Tit from coniferous forest may be due to its relative inefficiency as a forager in winter when food is scarce and must be obtained quickly, or to a relative lack of nesting cavities (Willow Tits almost always excavate their own holes, Marsh Tits never do), or to interspecific competition, or all three. And Willow Tits may be kept from

Marsh Tit

Parus palustris

ATLAS 268; PMH 206; PER 180; HFP 268; HPCW 213; NESTS 285; BWP7:146

		7–12 (3–) 1 brood			
to 10m	BLDS: ♂♀ Monogamy	INCU: ♀ 13–15	FLDG: ♂♀ 17–21		Ground glean

Breeding habitat Moist deciduous woodland, typically oak and beech. Common name is misleading, though does occur near streams and marshes in CIS.

Displays ♂ sings from canopy or shrub layer, especially while visiting nest sites. Courtship-feeding common. Threat display like that of Great Tit.

Nesting Territorial. Nest is in a natural hole, often low down, such as in a rotten stump; a cup of moss lined with softer material. Not usually in found in nest boxes. Eggs white with a few reddish to brownish spots, 16mm. Parents feed young for about a week after fledging.

Diet Mostly insects and spiders in summer; seeds, berries at other times of year. Feeds in herb layer and on ground, often hanging upside down; will hover-glean. Holds seeds under feet and jabs with beak. Will store food.

Winters Resident and territorial in winter. Young without territories join flocks with other species of tits. Resident birds also join flocks when they move through territory.

Conservation Common across most of Europe. (Isolated subspecies in E Asia.)

Notes Does not occur in Ireland or a number of other islands – see essay on Island Biogeography, p. 303.

Essays How Long Can Birds Live?, p. 497; Finding Hidden Caches, p. 457; Hartley's Titmice and MacArthur's Warblers, p. 425; Nest Evolution, p. 345; Average Clutch Size, p 31.

Refs Dementiev et al. 1968; Marchant et al. 1990; Perrins 1979, is a book about this and other British tits.

Sombre Tit

Parus lugubris

ATLAS 267; PMH 206; PER 180; HFP 268; HPCW 214; NESTS 286; BWP7:161

		4–9 1(–2) broods			
Conif tree	BLDS: ♀ Monogamy	INCU: ♀ 12–14	FLDG: ♂♀ 21–24	Seeds	

Breeding habitat A wide range of usually montane woodlands, parkland, scrub, and along rivers.

Displays ♂ sings from top of bush or tree. Frequent courtship-feeding.

Nesting Territorial. Nests in a hole in a tree (sometimes among rocks); ♂ may help excavate hole; a cup of moss and dry vegetation lined with softer material. Eggs white with a few fine red to brown spots, 17mm.

Diet Small invertebrates, especially caterpillars; occasionally seeds; extent of seasonal diet shift is uncertain. Feeds in crowns of trees, and will hang from twigs, or work trunk like a Nuthatch. Also forages on ground. Hammers seeds like other tits.

Winters Resident.

Conservation Common in limited range in SE Europe, SW Asia.

Refs Dementiev et al. 1968.

deciduous forests by competition from Marsh Tits, for on the Åland Islands, which the Marsh Tits have not reached, the Willow Tits have expanded their habitat use to include deciduous woods.

In North America five species of insectivorous wood warblers were the subject of another classic study of community ecology (the science of interpreting species interactions). These species often share the same breeding grounds in mature coniferous forests, and were thought by some to occupy the same niche.

For his doctoral dissertation, the late Robert MacArthur, who became one of the world's leading ecologists, set out to determine whether the five species of warblers actually did occupy the same niche. By measuring distances down from the top and outward from the trunk of individual spruce, fir, and pine trees, he divided the trees into zones and recorded feeding positions of the different warblers within each. In all, 16 different positions were distinguished.

MacArthur found that each warbler species divided its time differently among various parts of the tree. One, for instance, stayed mostly toward the outside on the top, another fed mostly around the middle interior, while another moved from zone to zone more than either of the first two. Details of the warblers' foraging habits were also recorded, and they also differed. For example, one species of warbler hawks flying insects much more often than does another, and tends to move vertically rather than horizontally (matching its tendency to remain on the outside of the tree). In addition, MacArthur found evidence that food shortage limited the size of the warbler populations.

Overall, MacArthur concluded that 'the birds behave in such a way as to be exposed to different kinds of food'. They also have somewhat different nesting times, and thus the times of their peak food requirements are not the same. They are partitioning a limiting resource — their supply of insects, and, in the process, occupying different niches.

Hartley and MacArthur's work has been followed by many other studies of closely related birds, investigating how their niches differ. Typical of more modern studies is that of Erkki Korpimäki examining the ecological relationships of Great Grey, Ural, and Tawny Owls in Finland where they breed together. He found, for instance, that Ural and Tawny Owls exploit a similar array of foods and live in similar habitats, but that the Tawny differs strikingly from the Ural in being a specialist in hole-nesting and being somewhat more of a nocturnal hunter. The two may be similar enough for there to be some competition between the two species, perhaps accounting for the rather patchy distribution of the Tawny in the area of overlap. The Great Grey occupies a niche closer to the Ural than the Tawny. However its nomadic habits and generally more northerly range probably reduce competition with the other two species.

SEE: Wader Feeding, p. 187; Bird Guilds, p. 77; Songbird Foraging, p. 417. REFS: Alatalo *et al.*, 1985*a,b*; Alatalo and Lundberg, 1983; Hartley, 1953; Korpimäki, 1986*a*; MacArthur, 1958.

Willow Tit

Parus montanus

ATLAS 268; PMH 206; PER 180; HFP 268; HPCW -; NESTS 285; BWP7:168

 Conif tree to 3m	 BLDS: ♀♂ Monogamy	 6–9 (4–11) 1 brood INCU: ♀ 13–15	 FLDG: ♂♀ 17–20		

Breeding habitat A variety of woodlands; more often in conifers than is Marsh Tit and more often near water, in willows, alders, and damp birch forest.

Displays ♂ sings from song post, ruffling head and neck feathers. In courtship-feeding, ♀ solicits with begging calls.

Nesting Territorial. Nest is in a dead and rotting tree, with material soft enough for bird to excavate a hole; both sexes excavate. May also use natural holes; of wood fibres, with little softer material as lining. Eggs white with a few reddish-brown spots, 16mm.

Diet Insects in the summer, seeds and berries in winter. Will hang upside down, rarely hover-gleans. Less often on ground than Marsh Tit. May cache food. In winter, must find an insect on average once every few seconds to survive and may visit 1000 trees per day.

Winters Resident, though N populations move S. In the UK pairs keep territories, though will join mixed flocks when they move through. In Scandinavia, winter territories are defended by groups of 4–6 birds (adults plus their young). The young of these groups do not survive as well as adults, but they do survive better than young not in group.

Conservation Common; more northerly than Marsh Tit, and occurs across much of Europe and Asia. Has spread in N and C Europe.

Essays Dominance Hierarchies, p. 131; Flock Defence, p. 257; Bird Guilds, p. 77; Hartley's Titmice and MacArthur's Warblers, p. 425; Metabolism, p. 281; Mixed-species Flocking, p. 429; Population Dynamics, p. 515.

Notes See under Marsh tit, p. 426.

Refs Perrins 1979.

Siberian Tit

Parus cinctus

ATLAS 267; PMH 207; PER 180; HFP 268; HPCW -; NESTS 285; BWP7:187

 1–5m	 BLDS: ♀ Monogamy	 6–10 (4–11) 1 brood INCU: ♀ 15–18	 FLDG: ♂♀ 19–20		 Ground glean

Breeding habitat Boreal coniferous forests, riverside deciduous trees in such forests, birches.

Displays Song is inconspicuous and infrequent.

Nesting Territorial (though unpaired birds from winter territory may remain during the breeding season). Nest is in a hole in a rotten tree, which may be partly excavated, or in a nest box; a cup of moss, lined with softer material, including rodent hair, on a bed of decaying wood. Eggs white with a few reddish spots, 17mm.

Diet In summer, insects taken from foliage or by turning over leaf litter on ground, or probing bark. In winter, pine seeds, held under feet and hammered; caches seeds and insects. Typically taken from tips of conifer needles, but also trunks.

Winters Resident; northern populations may move S, but remain in coniferous forests. Social groups of 2–9 birds hold winter terriories.

Conservation Has declined in Finland and elsewhere as conifer plantations have replaced the preferred older forests with larger trees. Common across boreal forests from Scandinavia, across Russia and into Alaska.

Essays Declines in Forest Birds: Europe and America, p. 339; Metabolism, p. 281; Finding Hidden Caches, p. 457.

Refs Dementiev et al. 1968.

Mixed-species Flocking

IT is not uncommon to find birds of several species flocking together. Indeed, in the autumn and winter woodlands of northern and western Europe, most birds are likely to be in such flocks. Walking through the October woods of southern Finland in the autumn, for example, one is likely to come across Great, Blue, Coal, Willow, and Crested Tits moving along and feeding in company with Treecreepers and Goldcrests. One reason may be that such flocking increases the number of eyes and ears available to detect predators and may confuse predators as many individuals flee at once. Also a mixture of species can take advantage of different abilities. Near-sighted zebras with keen hearing associate on African plains with species such as wildebeest and giraffes with keen eyesight. Golden Plovers seem to join Lapwing flocks because they then have to spend less time scanning for predators. Willow Tits in winter mixed-species flocks in Norway are able to allocate more time to foraging, presumably because there are numerous lookouts.

Similarly, it has been shown experimentally in North America that tits are used as sentinels by Downy Woodpeckers (*Picoides pubescens*) foraging in mixed-species flocks. In Finland, Teal use the alarm cries of Black-headed Gulls as warnings of danger. In some cases, however, the increased skittishness observed in mixed-species flocks may simply reflect foraging interference between species, and only at the last minute when danger is imminent do the members of the flock benefit from the association.

Sentinels may benefit more from giving alarm calls than those that are alerted. First of all, the sentinel, being aware of the position of a predator, may have its own chances of escape enhanced by the sudden, confusing actions of the entire flock. In addition, some Amazonian flycatching birds give false alarm calls, distracting other birds from their pursuit of flushed insects. This apparently gives the birds that 'cry wolf' a better chance in multi-bird scrambles after insects.

Next to defence against predators, however, the most popular hypothesis to explain the formation of mixed-species flocks is an increase in feeding efficiency. Flocks, whether mixed species or single species, may function to overwhelm territorial defences, because moving groups are able to feed in areas from which single intruding individuals would be ejected by the 'owner' of the territory. Having more individuals searching for food also increases the likelihood that a rich feeding patch will be found. By moving together in a single- or mixed-species flock, birds with the same sorts of diets can avoid areas that have already been searched for food. Also, even in single-species flocks feeding efficiency may be enhanced by individuals capturing prey that was flushed by, but escaped from, other birds. Individuals in mixed flocks can also learn about new food sources from other species; tits have been observed to visit the site where a woodpecker was pecking at bark and to

Crested Tit
Parus cristatus

ATLAS 265; PMH 207; PER 180; HFP 268; HPCW 214; NESTS 285; BWP7:195

BLDS: ♀ Monogamy	6–7 (3–9) 1 brood INCU: ♀ 13–18	FLDG: ♂♀ 18–22	Ground glean

Breeding habitat Coniferous forests (mainly pine and spruce), less often mixed forests.

Displays ♂ sings from top of tree, with raised crest; song is not frequent and is inconspicuous. Courtship-feeding.

Nesting Territorial. Nest is in a hole excavated in stump of rotten tree; a cup of moss, lined with dense layer of softer material. Eggs white with a few reddish spots and blotches, 16mm. ♂ alone will feed fledged young, if ♀ starts second brood. Usually 2 broods in S. Young remain with parents for up to 3 weeks after fledging.

Diet Insects, spiders, taken from needles. In winter, conifer seeds extracted acrobatically, often hanging upside down from ends of twigs. Also feeds on ground. Caches seeds.

Winters Resident; has social groups of 2–4 individuals that maintain territories; some join mixed-species flocks.

Conservation Locally common across most of Europe, but not UK, apart from an isolated population in Scotland. This population was once more numerous, but now there are only about 1000 pairs. The cause appears to be the commercial forests that have replaced old-growth native pine forests. Commerical forests support lower densities of the tits. Has spread N in Finland. Colonized the Åland Islands in the Baltic in 1920s and is now common there: see essay on Island Biogeography, p. 303.

Essays Bird Guilds, p. 77; Mixed-species Flocking, p. 429.

Refs Dementiev et al. 1968; Perrins 1979.

Coal Tit
Parus ater

ATLAS 266; PMH 207; PER 182; HFP 266; HPCW 214; NESTS 283; BWP7:207

Bank to 1m	BLDS: ♀ Monogamy	8–9 (6–12) 1–2 broods INCU: ♀ 14–16	FLDG: ♂♀ 18–20	Hover & glean

Breeding habitat Mainly coniferous woodlands (especially spruce), but also mixed woodlands, more open habitats such as gardens.

Displays ♂ sings from high perch throughout year. In courtship-feeding, ♀ begs with shivering wings, crouching, and calling.

Nesting Territorial. Nest is generally near the ground in a hole in a tree, stump, or roots, sometimes in the ground or a bank; a cup of moss, lined with softer materials. Eggs white with a few reddish spots or blotches, 15mm. Young fed by parents for about 2 weeks after fledging. Brood sizes smaller around Mediterranean. Second brood averages 1 egg less.

Diet Insects in summer; often hangs below clusters of pine needles and

cones, probing for insects; seeds of conifers in winter. Will hover-glean and feed on ground; stores food.

Winters Resident; nothern populations may move S. Often joins mixed species flocks, sometimes large ones, but winter social behaviour not as well known as other tits. Some continental populations irrutpive when seed crops fail.

Conservation Common across most of Europe, across Asia, and locally in N Africa. Has benfited from afforestation.

Essays Acid and Eggshells, p. 287; Declines in Forest Birds: Europe and America, p. 339; Hartley's Titmice and MacArthur's Warblers, p. 425; Mixed-species Flocking, p. 429; Feeding Birds, p. 357.

Refs Dementiev et al. 1968; Marchant et al. 1990; Perrins 1979.

begin pecking in the same place. There is, however, some evidence from experiments with single-species flocks of Greenfinches that gains in searching efficiency may not be enough to compensate flocking birds for the depletion of food caused by their feeding companions. Birds in such flocks may, however, have a reduced chance of starvation, since the variation of food intake from bird to bird is reduced.

An interesting feature of mixed-species flocks is that the members often are convergent in appearance. This is the phenomenon called 'social mimicry'. Weaker species in the flocks may have evolved towards the appearance of the stronger, so as to reduce the amount of interspecific aggression they suffer. Or the species may have converged on each other in order to increase the economy of communication across species, or to make the flock appear more homogeneous to an approaching predator (making it more difficult for it to home in on one or a few distinctive individuals). The issue is still being debated.

Finally, by associating with birds of different species that have somewhat different food preferences and foraging techniques, each individual faces less competition than it would in a similar flock of conspecifics. In Sweden, Willow and Crested Tits that participate in winter mixed-species flocks form small (3–4 individuals) territorial groups of conspecifics. The groups move with mixed-species flocks within their territories, reaching territorial boundaries several times a day. The social groups presumably reduce competition for food within the territories by excluding conspecifics, which would have the most similar diets. Competition could be severe since these small birds may virtually deplete the food supplies in their area by the end of winter.

If the feeding efficiency hypothesis is correct, then the amount of flocking should be related to the availability of food; when food is superabundant, little can be gained by flocking. A test of this hypothesis was carried out in two woods in the US state of Ohio. One wood was left undisturbed; the other was provisioned in early November with an ample supply of sunflower seed and beef suet. Woodpeckers, tits, creepers, and nuthatches all participated much less frequently in mixed-species flocks in the provisioned wood than they did in the control wood. This result supports the hypothesis that increased feeding efficiency is a major cause of mixed-species flocking.

Similarly, flocks may occur because one species, in the course of its feeding, flushes prey that can be caught by the others. The foraging of the latter is called commensal feeding. In Australian rain forests, Yellow Robins follow Brush-Turkeys, pouncing on insects the turkeys stir up as they scratch through the dead leaves of the forest floor. Cattle Egrets 'flock' with cattle and kites with tractors for similar reasons.

There are other interesting aspects of mixed-species flocks. For instance, some species appear to take the lead in forming the flock — to serve as 'nuclear' or 'core' species. Such species often have conspicuous plumage or behaviour. Tits in Europe, Africa, and North America play this role, as do antbirds (which often follow army ants and snap up insects their raiding

Blue Tit
Parus caeruleus

ATLAS 266; PMH 208; PER 182; HFP 266; HPCW 214; NESTS 284; BWP7:225

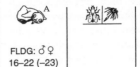

Cliff	Crevice	10–12 (–18)
1–3m	BLDS: ♀	1 brood
	Monogamy?	INCU: ♀
		13–16

FLDG: ♂ ♀
16–22 (–23)

Breeding habitat Wide range of mainly deciduous wooded areas including gardens, hedgerows.

Displays ♂ (sometimes ♀) sings from top of tree or other exposed perch. Also has 'moth flight' display (directed towards the nest hole) flying slowly with shallow, rapid wing-beats. Courtship-feeding is common.

Nesting Territorial. Nest is in a hole in a tree, stump, wall, or nest box; a cup of grass, moss, plant fibre, lined with feathers and other soft materials. Eggs white, with a few reddish spots or blotches, 16mm. 2 broods in some continental areas. Slightly larger clutches in N.

Diet Insects, spiders, taken from foliage; seeds in winter.

Winters Resident, joins winter feeding flocks; NE populations may move S. Some continental populations irruptive if seed crops fail.

Conservation Common across Europe into W Asia and N Africa. UK populations have benefited from the provision of nest boxes and from being fed in winter at bird tables.

Essays Acid and Eggshells, p. 287; Birds and Agriculture, p. 365; Mixed-species Flocking, p. 429; Hartley's Titmice and MacArthur's Warblers, p. 425; Metabolism, p. 281; Nest Evolution, p. 345; Feeding Birds, p. 357; Bird Badges, p. 433.

Refs Dementiev et al. 1968; Marchant et al. 1990; Perrins 1979 is a book about this and other British tits.

Azure Tit
Parus cyanus

ATLAS 266; PMH 208; PER -; HFP 266; HPCW 215; NESTS 284; BWP7:248

Conif tree	BLDS: ♀	9–11
2–5m	Monogamy?	1 brood
		INCU: ♀
		13–14

FLDG: ♂ ♀ ?
16?

Breeding habitat Wet deciduous woodlands, especially along river banks with willows; in thickets and undergrowth; also in marshes and reeds with bushes.

Displays Not well known; thought to be like those of the Blue Tit.

Nesting Nests in a hole in a tree; a cup of moss, grass, lined with finer material, often hair. Eggs white with a few purple-red spots, 16mm. Hatch over 2–3 days.

Diet Insects in summer, taken from small twigs, reed stems. Young fed caterpillars. Also takes seeds, fruit, in winter.

Winters Resident.

Conservation Uncommon in W of CIS, just into area covered by this guide. Locally very common further east, across C Asia.

Refs Dementiev et al. 1968.

columns disturb) in tropical America, babblers in tropical Asia, fairy wrens and thornbills (tit-like birds) in Australia, and gerygone warblers in New Guinea. Furthermore, it appears that, at least in waders, mechanisms for suppressing interspecific aggression have evolved that help to keep flocking individuals close together.

Mixed-species flocks in Europe are seen primarily in the non-breeding season. They tend to have a rapid turnover of species when they are just beginning to form in the late summer as migratory species depart or pass through from more northern locations. It is not in the temperate zones, however, that such flocking reaches its highest development. Mixed-species flocks are a dominant feature in tropical moist forests — so much so that their arrival can quickly transform an almost birdless patch of forest into an area alive with activity and calling. The composition of these tropical flocks and the complex relationships among their members are just beginning to be elucidated. Some European birds join these flocks on the wintering grounds in Africa and provide one reason for everyone interested in birds to make at least one trip to a tropical forest in winter.

SEE: Flock Defence, p. 257; Bird Guilds, p. 77; Commensal Feeding, p. 27; Geometry of the Selfish Colony, p. 15. REFS: Askenmo *et al.*, 1977; Barnard, 1982; Barnard *et al.*, 1982; Berner and Grubb, 1985; Diamond, 1981; Draulans and Van Vessem, 1982; Ehrlich and Ehrlich, 1973; Ekman, 1979; Ekman and Hake, 1988; Hake and Ekman, 1988; Hogstad, 1988*b*; Krebs, 1973; Krebs *et al.*, 1972; Morse, 1970; Moynihan, 1960, 1981; Munn, 1984, 1986; Pöysä, 1986; Stawarczyk, 1984; Stinson, 1988; Wagner, 1984.

Bird Badges

BULGING muscles and jewelled adornments are non-arbitrary symbols in human society, denoting strength and wealth, respectively. On the other hand, many arbitrary symbols — the bishop's mitre, the admiral's gold braid, the karate master's black belt, the judge's gown, the knight's title of 'Sir' — are also recognized. Such symbols are arbitrary because they signal status without having any inherent connection with the status signalled.

Non-arbitrary status symbols are readily found in non-human animals, a classic example being the size of horns in mountain sheep. In those creatures a small-horned male will avoid a large-horned stranger seen at a distance, even though the two have never determined their relative positions in a dominance hierarchy by actual combat.

Whether or not arbitrary symbols exist outside of human society is more problematic. British evolutionists Richard Dawkins and John Krebs adopted

Great Tit

Parus major

ATLAS 269; PMH 208; PER 182; HFP 266; HPCW 215; NESTS 283; BWP7:255

	Crevice	8–12(–18) 1–2 broods			
Cliff	BLDS: ♀ Monogamy	INCU: ♀ 12–14(10–22)	FLDG: ♂♀ 16–22		Ground glean

Breeding habitat A wide range of deciduous and mixed wooded areas, including hedgerows and gardens

Displays ♂ sings from high perch; in threat display, wings raised half open. Near nest hole, display flight with shallow wing-beats. Courtship-feeding is common.

Nesting Nest is in a hole, usually in tree or wall or nest box; a cup of moss, grass, lined with softer materials. Eggs white with a few reddish spots or blotches, 18mm. Hatch asynchronously. Young fed by parents for 1 week after fledging (first brood), or for 2–3 weeks (second brood). ♀ may start second brood in new nest while first nest still has young in it. Usually only one brood in the UK. Cuckoldry is common and mate guarding is important. Clutch sizes are unusually well studied. There is a typical clutch size for an individual. However, clutch sizes are generally smaller (1) later in the season, (2) in gardens and conifers (as compared to deciduous woods), and (3) in small nest cavitites.

Diet In summer, adults and young feed on insects (especially caterpillars) and spiders. In autumn and winter takes seeds and berries. Often forages on ground, especially in good beech mast years.

Winters Resident; N populations move S; irruptive in poor seed years. Joins mixed-species flocks.

Conservation Common across Europe, Asia, and into N Africa. Increase in the UK, spread N in Scandinavia. Helped by winter feeding at bird tables.

Essays Acid and Eggshells, p. 287; Altruism, p. 245; Average Clutch Size, p. 31; Birds and Agriculture, p. 365; Dawn Chorus, p. 369; Dominance Hierarchies, p. 131; Feeding Birds, p. 357; Hartley's Titmice and MacArthur's Warblers, p. 425; Interspecific Territoriality, p. 421; Mixed-species Flocking, p. 429; Pesticides and Birds, p. 115; Population Dynamics, p. 515; Nest Evolution, p. 345; Mobbing, p. 261; Visual Displays, p. 33; Vocal Development, p. 479.

Refs Dementiev et al. 1968; Marchant et al. 1990; Perrins 1979 is a book about this and other British tits.

Krüper's Nuthatch

Sitta krueperi

ATLAS 270; PMH 208; PER -; HFP 270; HPCW 215; NESTS 286; BWP7:283

		5–6 1 brood ?			
	BLDS: ♂♀ Monogamy?	INCU: ♀ 14–17	FLDG: ♂♀ 16–19		Ground glean

Breeding habitat Montane coniferous, mainly spruce forests.

Displays Not well known: ♂ sings vigorously, especially near nest hole.

Nesting Territorial. Nest is in a hole in a tree, including old woodpecker holes; a cup lined with finer and softer materials on a foundation of wood fragments; does not plaster entrance with mud (see Nuthatch). Eggs white, with dark red-brown spots and blotches, 17mm.

Diet Insects, taken from crowns of trees; seeds in winter, sometimes taken on ground. Wedges and hammers seeds like other nuthatches.

Winters Resident or some dispersal.

Conservation Not well known in restricted range in Turkey. Considered rare in the Caucasus; there is a small population on Lesbos (Greece).

Essays Tool-using, p. 459.

Refs Dementiev et al. 1968.

the term 'badge' for arbitrary animal symbols, and avian biologists, especially Sievert Rohwer, have carried out investigations to see if badges play a role in dominance relationships in bird flocks.

North American Harris' Sparrows (*Zonotrichia querula*) assemble in flocks of mixed ages in the winter. Individuals within the flocks show a great deal of variation in their plumage characteristics, especially in the amount of darkness on their heads and 'bibs'. In a series of experiments Rohwer darkened relatively light first-year birds with dye to make them look like adults. He found that dyed first-year birds are initially avoided by undyed 'control' first-year birds. Then the dyed birds began actively to dominate the controls. Rohwer thus concluded that the dominance status of a Harris' Sparrow can be communicated by a badge — a dark head and bib. The alternative explanation (that the dye in some way actually enhanced the combat ability of dyed birds) is too unlikely to merit serious consideration.

Differences in darkness do not, however, always correlate with status, as behaviourist Doris Watt has shown. In experiments Watt found that within age classes, at least in small groups, darker Harris' Sparrows are not always dominant over lighter individuals. She believes the darkness to be basically a badge of age, which signals to first-year birds the potential dominance of adults. Apparently among both young and adults, variation in breast spot patterns (as opposed to overall breast darkness) aids individuals in recognizing one another, but does not indicate status.

Perhaps the most ingenious experiment on avian badges involved the Great Tit. Torbjörn Järvi and Morten Bakken of Norway's University of Trondheim used radio-controlled motorized stuffed birds at a feeder to test the efficacy of the breast stripe as a badge. When a Great Tit approached the feeder, the stuffed bird could be rotated to face the incoming individual and to perform a 'head-up' aggressive display. When, and only when, the stuffed bird had a breast stripe wider than that of the incoming bird was the latter frightened away. Later work by Järvi and his associates showed that the status of male Great Tits could be enhanced when their breast stripe was enlarged and testosterone injections were given to increase aggressive behaviour.

Evidently badges can signal status in avian societies — but this presents evolutionists with a considerable mystery. Since they are arbitrary symbols, why isn't cheating widespread? Why don't first-year Harris' Sparrows grow dark plumage just like adults? Why don't weakling Great Tits develop broad breast stripes and monopolize the food at feeders? Badge systems seem to have built into them the seeds of their own evolutionary destruction, since frequent cheating should soon make all the signals ambiguous. One reason may be that naturally dominant birds may challenge the fakes, and chase them off. Indeed, that is what happens in Great Tits if only the badge is increased in size with no accompanying change in behaviour produced by testosterone.

Another reason that cheating does not become widespread has been suggested. Perhaps dominance in monogamous birds (as opposed to polygynous ones, where dominant males may get many more matings) does not

Corsican Nuthatch

Sitta whiteheadi

ATLAS 270; PMH 209; PER 184; HFP 270; HPCW -; NESTS 287; BWP7:287

		5–6 1 brood ? INCU: ♀	
	BLDS: ♂♀		FLDG: ♂♀
3–30m	Monogamy	?	22–24

Hover & glean

Breeding habitat Coniferous forests (especially of Coriscan pine) at elevations of 1000–1500 m, where trees are tall and old. Prefers areas with many dead and rotting trees.

Displays Not well known. In threat display has wing-flicking, and will ruffle all body feathers to look like a feathery ball.

Nesting Territorial. Nest is in a tree hole (often of Great Spotted Woodpecker). Does not plaster mud around entrance to nest hole (see Nuthatch). Hole is filled with wood fragments, moss, and lined with softer materials. Eggs white with a few reddish-brown spots and blotches, 17mm. Young remain with adults for several weeks after fledging.

Diet Insects in summer, pine seeds rest of year. Uses same feeding methods as those of the Nuthatch; also hovers to pick up insects and will hang from cones; caches seeds.

Winters Resident, has winter territories. Snow may force birds to lower elevations.

Conservation Total population about 2000 pairs in a very limited area on the island of Corsica.

Notes No nuthatches use the deciduous forests of Corsica, for the Nuthatch does not breed on the island.

Essays Declines in Forest Birds: Europe and America, p. 339; Finding Hidden Caches, p. 457.

Algerian Nuthatch

Sitta ledanti

ATLAS 270; PMH -; PER -; HFP 270; HPCW 216; NESTS 287; BWP7:292

Dead tree		?			
		3–4 1 brood? INCU: ♀			
	BLDS: ?		FLDG: ♂♀		
4–15m	Monogamy?	?	22–25?		Foliage glean

Breeding habitat Oak and cedar forests in two limited areas of Algeria above 2000m.

Displays ♂ sings from perch near nest, especially when young are in nest.

Nesting Territorial. Nest is an enlarged cavity in dying or dead tree, lined with wood fragments and conifer needles; no mud is plastered around entrance to nest hole (see Nuthatch). Eggs not described.

Diet Insects in cedars, firs; taken from trunks and branches with heavy growth of moss and lichens. Seeds in winter; will cache seeds.

Winters Resident, even though the habitats get a lot of snow (which can remain until May).

Conservation Known from only 4 localities in Algeria, one found in 1975, the second in 1989. The areas are within 40km of each other. The first area, Mount Babor, has a very unusual flora including fir, and a relict population of aspen. This important area is threatened by logging. It holds about 80 pairs. The second area, in the Taza National Park, is an area of oak woodland. It holds about 180 pairs.

Notes Called Kabyle Nuthatch in some field guides.

Essays Birds and the Law, p. 521.

in itself confer a selective advantage. Subordinate birds may not get access to the best resources, but they also may not have to expend much energy defending what they've got. Being subordinate may be just as good an evolutionary strategy as being dominant — both kinds of individual may be equally successful reproductively. If that is the case, there would be no advantage to cheating, and one would not expect such behaviour to evolve.

SEE: Visual Displays, p. 33; Sexual Selection, p. 149; Dominance Hierarchies, p. 131.
REFS: Järvi and Bakken, 1984; Järvi et al., 1987; Rohwer, 1985; Rohwer and Ewald, 1981; Roper, 1986; Watt, 1986; Whitfield, 1987.

Indeterminate Egg Layers

SOME birds, such as swallows, doves, lapwings, large raptors, and many small songbirds, lay a precise number of eggs in each clutch. Removing one or more eggs, adding additional ones, or the hatching of those first laid, will not lead the female to deviate from the predetermined number. Other birds, however, respond to the loss of eggs by laying more. The domestic hen is the best-known example; take away each egg she lays, and she can lay at a rate of very nearly an egg a day for a year (a talent which, of course, has been enhanced through selective breeding). A Mallard normally lays 7 to 10 eggs. When, however, one egg was removed daily from her nest, one female is said to have laid 80–100. Similarly a House Sparrow, when eggs were removed, laid a dozen eggs over 12 consecutive days.

Such 'indeterminate' layers, nonetheless, stop laying when they are sitting on the 'proper' number and are left undisturbed; whether the birds can visually 'count' the proper number is not certain, although there is good evidence that hens can. They will stop laying at a normal clutch size when the eggs they have produced are kept in sight but covered with a screen so that they can see them but not touch them. About half the individuals 'incubated' beside the screen basket covering the eggs. Whatever the mechanism, clearly there is some sort of feedback from the number of eggs being incubated to the hormonal system that controls production of eggs by the ovary (only the left ovary functions in the vast majority of birds). A clue to the mechanism has been provided by studies of Black-headed Gulls. Courtship in these birds stimulates the ovary to start producing eggs, and the female begins incubation with the first egg. The process of incubation starts to shut down the ovary. One or two eggs may already be far enough along to complete their development and be laid, but not three. Therefore the female gull will lay a total of two or three eggs, but not four. If she is supplied with a wooden egg

Nuthatch

Sitta europaea

Conif tree 2–20m	BLDS: ♀ Monogamy	6–8 (5–12) 1 brood INCU: ♀ 13–18	FLDG: ♂♀ 23–24 (–26)		Foliage glean

Breeding habitat Deciduous and mixed woodland, especially with large trees; also gardens. In N in conifer forests.

Displays ♂ sings in upright posture, at right angles to branch. Is often aggressive towards Great Spotted Woodpeckers (which may take their young).

Nesting Territorial. Nest is in a tree hole or old woodpecker hole; the ♀ plasters the entrance to the hole with mud to reduce its size. The mud sets hard to leave just enough space for the adults to squeeze through. See opposite page. The hole is replastered when young have feathers and no longer need brooding. Nest lining is bark flakes and leaves. Eggs white with a few reddish spots, 20mm. Hatch synchronously.

Diet Insects; seeds in winter. Climbs trees head up or head down, poking into crevices, or chiselling into soft wood. Also foliage-gleans, especially when caterpillars are abundant, feeding like a tit, inspecting small terminal twigs. Seeds grasped with foot, or pushed into crack and hammered with bill.

Winters Resident, and pairs hold territory throughout year. In N populations may move S, sometimes irruptively.

Conservation Common across Europe, Asia, and into N Africa. Increasing and spreading N and W; in the UK may benefit from bird tables.

Notes Does not occur in Ireland or many other islands: see essay on Island Biogeography, p. 303. Following irruptions, the N Asian subspecies may remain to breed in Sweden, Finland.

Essays Acid and Eggshells, p. 287; Population Dynamics, p. 515; Selection in Nature, p. 471; Feeding Birds, p. 357; Island Biogeography, p. 303; Irruptions, p. 491.

Refs Dementiev et al. 1968; Marchant et al. 1990.

Rock Nuthatch

Sitta neumayer

2–5m	Sphere BLDS: ♂♀ Monogamy	8–10 (6–13) 1 (2?) broods INCU: ♀ 15–18	FLDG: ♂♀ 23–30		Rock glean Foliage glean

Breeding habitat Rocks and cliffs (rather than trees), in dry mountains.

Displays ♂ sings from prominent rock. Pairs sing duets, first the ♂ and then ♀.

Nesting Usually territorial. Nest is in a crevice in rocks; the front of the nest is plastered over with mud, crushed insects and moistened with saliva, and a narrow tube is built out from this as an entrance. Inside is a cup lined with moss, hair, feathers, and other soft materials. Eggs white with a few reddish-brown to buff blotches, 21mm.

Diet In summer, insects, spiders, gleaned from ground and rocks; in winter takes seeds, also snails, and will cache food by burying it in ground. Pairs may forage together, one making frequent trips to a prominent perch to act as lookout.

Winters Resident and defends territories year-round; may move to lower elevations, and feed on trees.

Conservation Locally common in SE Europe and SW Asia.

Notes The Eastern Rock Nuhatch, *Sitta tethronota*, may just enter the area of eastern Turkey covered by this guide.

Essays Nest Sites and Materials, p. 443; Finding Hidden Caches, p. 457.

Refs Paz 1987.

to incubate before the development of the first egg in her ovary has proceeded far enough, she will lay no eggs at all.

SEE: Average Clutch Size, p. 31; Variation in Clutch Sizes, p. 55; Hormones and
Nest Building, p. 329. REFS: Moss and Watson, 1982; Steen and Parker, 1981.

A nuthatch plasters mud around the entrance to an old woodpecker nesthole reducing its size enough to use.

Nest Lining

THE bewildering array of materials that birds use to line their nests can in fact
be divided into five more or less discrete classes that include *finer materials,
feathers, concealing ornaments, remnants,* and *artefacts*. To condense some species
treatments in this *Handbook* these terms may be used to summarize materials
lining the nests; here we describe them in greater detail.

First, the lining may consist of loose, smaller bits of the same materials that
have been incorporated into the latticework of the nest. These *finer materials*
help cushion, insulate, shed water, deter pests, and conceal the eggs from
predators. Typically, finer materials include bits of vegetation (including
leaves, needles, twigs, sticks, reeds, mosses, lichen, grass, seaweed, etc.),
although birds may also add fur, shreds of dry cow dung, and other animal
products. According to one survey, some 71 per cent of European passerines

Wallcreeper

Tichodroma muraria

ATLAS 272; PMH 210; PER 182; HFP 272; HPCW 217; NESTS 289; BWP7:329

	A		Rock glean
BLDS: ♀	4–5 (3–) 1 brood INCU: ♀	FLDG: ♂♀	
Monogamy	19–20	28–30	Hawks

Breeding habitat Rocks and cliff faces of mountains to high elevations. Often in wet sites, above rivers.

Displays ♂ sings while perched or climbing or in flight when both birds are engaged in nest hunting. ♂ also flies in circles above nest hole, and if ♀ follows, he enters hole and sings inside it. Both sexes sing, the ♀ in winter. In threat display, wings are drooped, tail raised, and wings spread to show red.

Nesting Defends large territories. Nest is in deep rock crevice, hole, or cave; a cup of moss and grass, lined with softer materials, has two entrances. Eggs white with a very few black speckles, 21mm.

Diet Insects and spiders, usually gleaned from rocks, sometimes caught in air; moves across cliff, hopping and fluttering with wings half spread.

Winters Resident or moves to lower elevations. Also moves into towns, frequenting church, castle walls, etc. ♂s and ♀s hold winter territories.

Conservation Local in restricted and fragmented habitat across S Europe and Asia.

Essays Feet, p. 289.

Refs Dementiev et al. 1968; Paz 1987

Treecreeper

Certhia familiaris

ATLAS 273; PMH 210; PER 184; HFP 272; HPCW 217; NESTS 290; BWP7:346

Trees (see below)		A		
	BLDS:♂♀,♀	5–6 (3–9) 2 broods INCU: ♀	FLDG: ♂♀	
0.5–4m	Monogamy?	13–15	14–16	Seeds

Breeding habitat On the continent, in coniferous forest; in the UK, in deciduous and mixed forests, also hedgerows with large trees and only rarely in conifer plantations. Where its range overlaps with that of the Short-toed Treecreeper, this species tends to be at higher elevations and even more restricted to conifers.

Displays Sings, often while climbing tree.

Nesting Territorial. Nest is behind split in bark on tree trunk or similar concealed places such as behind ivy. A cup of small twigs, moss, etc. lined with finer materials, including spiders' webs. Eggs white with reddish-brown spots, 16mm. Thought to have only one brood in N.

Diet Insects and spiders taken by spirally creeping up trunks of trees and poking into crevices. Some seeds in winter.

Winters Mainly resident, though N populations partial migrants. Roosts communally in holes and other sheltered places.

Conservation Common across Europe and Asia. Increasing in UK, Norway, but vulnerable to cold winters.

Essays Bird Guilds, p. 77; Mixed-species Flocking, p. 429.

Refs Dementiev et al. 1968; Marchant et al. 1990.

regularly add hair to their nests. A diverse group of species including birds of prey and Starlings may also routinely add fresh greens — sanitizing sprigs containing hydrocyanic acid and other natural pesticides that may inhibit infestation by insect parasites or pathogens.

Feathers (including down) are typically plucked from the 'brood patch' (a ventral area stripped bare to ease heat flow between the adult and the eggs) of the nesting birds. Waterfowl are among the birds that, having plucked their brood patches, use the feathers to line the nest. A number of birds incorporate feathers from other species. Moulted feathers of Ptarmigan are routinely used by redpolls, Snow and Lapland Buntings.

On hatching, most nestlings are unable to stay warm without the help of their parents and young songbirds remain thus for at least a week. Among European passerines, feathers are most likely to be incorporated into nests of small birds that breed early in the year, and more feathers will be found in the nests of the more northerly distributed populations within a species. Feathering the nest may, in fact, determine the northern distribution of some passerines including Goldcrests and warblers that do not occupy the northernmost portion of what appears to be suitable breeding habitat. In one study Juha Tiainen, Ilpo Hanski, and Jaakko Mehtälä compared the nests of three Finnish *Phylloscopus* warblers to evaluate the role of insulation in determining their northernmost distributions. Of the three species studied (all of which build roofed nests that have a side entrance) the Willow Warbler and Chiffchaff line their nests with feathers whose tips often partially close the nest opening, while the Wood Warbler nest lacks feathers, its opening is wider, and the species is restricted to more southerly breeding. Interestingly, the Arctic Warbler which breeds from Fennoscandia east to Siberia, only rarely feathers its nest. Instead, the outer construction contains a thick layer of moss.

A third type of lining, often found in the minimal scrapes made by ground nesters, consists of *concealing ornaments* — collections of nearby objects that provide camouflage for otherwise exposed eggs. These ornaments, including stones, rock shards, shells, bits of wood, moss, lichen, withered leaves, or even nearby grasses plucked by the incubating adult, may also help to keep the eggs in place, provide insulation, or prevent the eggs from becoming embedded in mud or sand after accidental flooding of the nest.

Remnants include materials that have *not* been deliberately placed in the nests by the birds. Wood chips found in the excavations of cavity-nesting species, the remains from the winter nests of squirrels and mice occasionally found in tunnels and chambers of burrow-nesting species, bits of vegetation deposited by wind, and pieces of surrounding plants accidentally broken and matted into ground nests, are a few of the many items coincidentally cradling eggs. In simple scrapes some remnants may function as concealing ornaments, as well.

Artefacts include a large variety of objects, many of which are eye-catching and sometimes so poorly suited for use in a nest that their choice by adults is perplexing. In one study of Wrynecks, for example, the stomachs of 4 out of 14 nestlings contained potentially lethal, shiny stones or pieces of glass.

Short-toed Treecreeper
Certhia brachydactyla

ATLAS 273; PMH 211; PER 184; HFP 272; HPCW 218; NESTS 291; BWP7:365

|
1–9m |
BLDS: ♂♀
Monogamy? | 6–7 (4–)
1–2 broods
INCU: ♀
13–14 | 
FLDG: ♂♀
16–18 | | |

Breeding habitat Deciduous or mixed forests and other areas with large trees; Treecreeper tends to be at higher elevations, Short-toed Treecreeper at lower ones, though this species reaches high evelations in Turkey where its congener is absent.

Displays Not well known.

Nesting Nest similar to that of the Treecreeper. ♂ builds 2–3 foundations and ♀ then completes one. Eggs white with reddish-brown spots and blotches, 16mm. ♀ starts second nest when she is still feeding the first brood, then the ♂ feeds the first brood and the ♀ finishes second nest.

Diet Insects; seeds in winter. Like Treecreeper, creeps up trees, probing into crevices in bark, but moves more slowly, with more spirals around tree.

Winters Resident. Roosts communally—see Treecreeper.

Conservation Common in SE, S, and Central Europe, into N Africa, SW Asia. Has spread N in Denmark.

Notes Does not occur in the UK, despite its occurrence in adjacent areas on the continent – see essay on Island Biogeography, p. 303.

Penduline Tit
Remiz pendulinus

ATLAS 264; PMH 211; PER 182; HFP 264; HPCW 218; NESTS 280; BWP7:377

|
Reeds
1–8m |
BLDS: ♂♀
See below |
6–8 (5–10)
1 (2?) broods
INCU: ♂ or ♀
13–14 (–21) | 
FLDG:♂ or ♀
18–29 |
Seeds | |

Breeding habitat Thick vegetation, generally willows, poplars, and tamarisk along marsh edges and river banks; also reed-beds.

Displays Very little known.

Nesting Nest is suspended from the outermost twigs of willows or birches, often overhanging water, or slung between 2–3 stems in reed-beds. The nest is a pendant, domed structure. It is started with a loop, then followed with a bag to hold the nest and a downward-pointing tube with access to the nest at the top. Is decorated on the outside with seeds, bark, flowers. See illustration, p. 347. The ♂ makes up to 7 incomplete nests before attracting a ♀ to one of them. Eggs white, 16mm. The mating system is very unusual and involves both sequential polygyny and polygamy. All parental duties are carried out by one mate only. Of completed nests, about half are incubated only by the ♀, less than a quarter by the ♂, and the rest abandoned when the birds seek new mates. (Abandoned clutches are generally smaller than incubated ones, and it is usually the ♀ that abandons the nest first.) ♂s are more likely to incubate late in the breeding season. The success of the ♀'s incubation is about 4 times that of the ♂'s.

Diet Insects, spiders picked from the vegetation. Young fed larval insects, especially caterpillars and spider cocoons. Also takes seeds in winter.

Winters Mainly resident, in Europe; more migratory in E and N.

Conservation Common across E and S Europe and Asia; spreading N and W.

Notes First considered to be related to the tits, this species was then placed in a different family. DNA studies now show that it should indeed be in the tit family.

Essays Polygyny, p. 265; Polyandry, p. 195; Nest Evolution, p. 345.

Refs Dementiev et al. 1968; Sibley and Monroe 1990.

If by default or by design, the nest has no lining and eggs simply rest directly on the supporting lattice of twigs and so forth, it is described as *unlined*. Seasonal conditions may determine which materials are necessary or even available to line nests. In dry years, for example, the Song Thrush may forgo adding a smooth lining of woodpulp or dung, and may even forgo incorporating mud into the nest, leaving the structure soft and lined only with twigs and grasses.

Descriptions of nests published by early ornithologists allow us to identify changes in the availability of nest-building materials. For instance, in North America at the turn of the century, the Chipping Sparrow (*Spizella passerina*) was known as the 'hairbird' from the practice of lining its nest with horse hair. As automobiles replaced horses both the trait and the name disappeared. Similarly, plastic insulation and cellophane today substitute for snake skin in nests of some flycatchers and tits or may replace other once common materials. Perennial nests such as those of the White Stork (one still in use in 1930 dated from 1549) may serve as valuable archives for those studying the changing relationship of humanity and birds.

SEE: Nest Evolution, p. 345; Eggs and Their Evolution, p. 317; Incubation: Controlling Egg Temperatures, p. 273; Brood Patches, p. 3; Disease and Parasitism, p. 315; Hormones and Nest Building, p. 329; Precocial and Altricial Young, p. 401. REFS: Collias and Collias, 1984; Greig-Smith, 1986; Møller, 1984; Skutch, 1976; Terhivuo, 1977, 1983; Tiainen, *et al.*, 1983.

Nest Sites and Materials

NESTS not only provide protection from predators and brood parasites, they also allow birds to assert some control over the microclimate experienced by eggs and nestlings. By reducing the harshest effects of the environment, birds have been able to lengthen their breeding season and expand their breeding habitat. Various features of nests enhance breeding success. By floating their nests, for example, wetland-breeding Great Crested Grebes are less threatened by rising water than are Pochards or Moorhens which anchor theirs to vegetation. Similarly, by facing the entrance of their nest holes to increase warming from sunlight and reduce cooling from wind, some woodpeckers nesting in cool regions stay warmer. By orienting the nest entrance towards cooling afternoon breezes, some woodpeckers nesting in warm regions (or who double brood) minimize the potential for over-heating. The nests of Rooks are relatively exposed and more vulnerable to wind than are those of other corvids, so Rooks in windy areas usually select dense evergreens as nest sites.

In some wetland and ground-nesting birds, nest support may be expanded to form nest sides and is even sometimes extended to create a

Nile Valley Sunbird

Anthreptes metallicus

ATLAS 275; PMH -; PER -; HFP 264; HPCW 218; NESTS 282; BWP7:401

1.5–3m	BLDS: ♂♀ Monogamy	2–4 2 broods INCU: ♀

FLDG: ? ?	Insects	Hover & glean

Breeding habitat Dry desert scrub, wadis, gardens.

Displays ♂ sings from perch, accompanied by vigorous wing-flicks, and spreading and raising tail.

Nesting Territorial. Nest is in a bush, hung from fork or suspended from thin twig; a pendent structure made of grass and other plant material, with a high side entrance; bound with spiders' webs and decorated with leaves; thickly lined with fine plant material and feathers. Eggs white; with a few small pink spots, 17mm.

Diet Nectar, also insects. Takes nectar directly from small flowers, but pierces base of large flowers, robbing them without pollinating them. Wipes bill clean when finished. Takes insects by foliage-gleaning or hover-gleaning.

Winters Migrates short distances, movements probably determined by nectar availability. Typically in small feeding groups.

Conservation Common from Nile Valley southward. Has spread N.

Notes Also called Pygmy Sunbird.

Essays Territoriality, p. 397.

Palestine Sunbird

Nectarinia osea

ATLAS 275; PMH -; PER -; HFP 264; HPCW 219; NESTS 282; BWP7:407

1.5–2m	BLDS: ♀ Monogamy	1–3 2–3 broods INCU: ♀ 12–14

FLDG: ♂♀ 14–21	Insects	Hawks

Breeding habitat Desert scrub, juniper-covered hillsides, gardens, wadis.

Displays ♂ sings from high perches. Flies at intruding rivals, and chases are common. Intruding ♂s may try to kill young in nest and usurp the territory.

Nesting Territorial. Nest is like that of the Nile Valley Sunbird; a loose purse, with a side entrance and an awning, suspended from terminal twigs, bound together with hair and spiders' webs, and lined with soft material. Uses same nest for each brood and sometimes in successive years. Eggs with indistinct grey or purplish markings, 15mm. Receptive ♀ may attract 4–6 ♂s seeking

to cuckold resident ♂, which must then defend his mate.

Diet Nectar; may hover in front of flower like a hummingbird, but generally perches. Will also take sugar water from feeders. Takes insects from foliage or while in flight.

Winters Resident, nomadic, or short-distance migrant; in small flocks.

Conservation Increasing range into SE corner of area covered by this guide. May have benefited from honeysuckle and other nectar-producing garden plants.

Notes Also called Orange-tufted Sunbird.

Essays Territoriality, p. 397.

Refs Paz 1987.

relatively fragile, camouflaging canopy. In contrast, arboreal passerine nests are generally tiny and cryptic and few are domed (presumably since the absence of doming reduces overall size and visibility). Those that *are* domed and quite visible, such as the hanging nests of Long-tailed and Penduline Tits, are often attached to the far end of slender branches where they are relatively safe from nest robbers.

Because the form of the nest must be adapted to fit a vast diversity of supporting structures, it is not surprising that the variety of materials used in construction includes virtually anything that can be carried — from stones and mud to animal and plant products and human-made artefacts. Some binding materials are very specialized. Adhesive materials used to fasten adherent and hanging nests include mud gathered by swallows; saliva produced by swifts (Cave Swiftlet nests are the main ingredient in Chinese 'bird's nest' soup); and leaf mould, water-shedding lichens, and spider webs collected by passerines in at least 20 families. One of the most durable binding materials is cellulose, the major constituent of plant fibres. It is waterproof and, ounce for ounce, stronger than steel.

Some species, such as the Long-tailed Tit, may place their nests within protective brambles and thorny shrubs or near predator-deterring red ants (*Formica rufa*); many birds of prey apparently seek out ants which may clean parasites from the nest. Some birds of prey, such as Imperial Eagles, may accept House Sparrows or other small passerines as close neighbours or allow them to build their tiny nests in their ample platforms. These small birds sound the alarm when intruders approach, but are not threatened by their predatory 'hosts', which ordinarily do not hunt near their own nests.

Many bird species increasingly find themselves associating with people. Magpies, which lose eggs and young to Carrion Crows, may choose to nest nearer to people than the crows are willing to venture. As human and bird populations have been brought into closer contact, nest placement by some species has been changing. In 1774 Gilbert White recorded that very few Swallows entered further than the outlying streets of London, while the House Martin inhabited even the crowded sections of the city. Today's European cities are home to increasing numbers of nesting Swallows, Mallards, and feral Pigeons, and decreasing numbers of Rooks, Jackdaws, and House Martins (in contrast to White's eighteenth-century London). Ground-nesting Killdeers (*Charadrius vociferus*, a North American wader and vagrant in Europe) and Herring Gulls are both opportunistic, and adapt particularly well to urban sites, especially rooftops. Roof-reared Killdeer young have been known to survive falls of 15 m. These precocial young, however, have been unable to cope with parapets — traps from which they cannot escape before starving. At the other extreme, as old city buildings are replaced by streamlined skyscrapers and sleek office complexes, birds that nested on the ledges and nooks of the old edifices must now breed elsewhere. Roof-reared White Storks, for example, face a very uncertain future. Traditionally considered good omens, the storks have been encouraged for hundreds of years to nest near people. Wagon wheels dressed with straw are still used (as they were in the Middle Ages) to lure these birds who often return to nest within 100 metres

Golden Oriole

Oriolus oriolus

ATLAS 303; PMH 211; PER 184; HFP 302; HPCW 220; NESTS 314; BWP7:415

		 3–4 (2–6) 1 brood			
	BLDS: ♂♀	INCU: ♂♀	FLDG: ♂♀		
6–7m(1–20m)	Monogamy?	16–17(15–18)	16–17(13–20)	Fruit	Hawks

Breeding habitat Open deciduous woods, parks.

Displays Sexual chases through trees, with ♂ almost touching ♀'s tail.

Nesting Nest is suspended, hammock-like, between two twigs on outermost branches; a cup woven from grass, strips of bark, etc., and lined with finer materials. Eggs white to cream with distinct small black spots, 30mm.

Diet In summer, insects (especially large caterpillars gleaned from tops of trees); also insects taken while in flight; rest of year, berries and fruit.

Winters Africa S of Sahara and India, in dry open woodland to montane forest.

Conservation Has spread N. Has bred in UK since 1967, but only a few pairs appear each year. Common in adjacent areas of the continent (perhaps 5000 pairs each in Belgium and Holland). See essay on Island Biogeography, p. 303. Common across most of Europe into Asia.

Notes Under the recent DNA-based classification orioles are now placed in the crow family.

Essays The Colour of Birds, p. 137; Declines in Forest Birds: Europe and America, p. 339; Ducking the Bird Laws, p. 523.

Refs Ali and Ripley 1987; Sibley and Monroe 1990.

Black-crowned Tchagra

Tchagra senegala

ATLAS 215; PMH -; PER -; HFP 216; HPCW 221; NESTS 233; BWP7:434

		2–3 1 brood		
Decid tree	BLDS: ♂♀	INCU: ♂♀	FLDG: ♂♀	
0.5–5m	Monogamy	12–13	16	

Breeding habitat Desert scrub and dry woodlands, also around cultivated areas and gardens.

Displays ♂ sings from exposed perch or in flight. On perch, adopts upright posture, with head back and bill open wide. In flight, silently ascends steeply to 15m (sometimes much higher), then makes loud sounds with wings, and begins singing in a jerky downward glide. Pairs will duet.

Nesting Territorial. Nest in low thick cover, on a horizontal branch or in fork; a shallow cup of grass, thorny twigs, lined

with finer material. Eggs white, with a few dark red or purple blotches, 24mm.

Diet Invertebrates, especially beetles and grasshoppers, but also amphibians, reptiles, and fruit. Animal prey seized on ground or in low cover. Runs quickly, creeps under cover, and flicks debris, rather like a thrush.

Winters Resident.

Conservation Occurs In N Africa, S of Sahara, and locally in Arabia.

Notes Also called Bush Shrike. Under the recent DNA-based classification this genus is now placed in the crow family.

Refs Sibley and Monroe 1990.

of a previous site on a rooftop, telephone pole, or chimney. Sadly, however, the birds are in decline all along their migration route. Denmark's population declined by 50 per cent in only a decade, with only 15 birds returning in 1989. The future abundance and distribution of many bird species will be determined in no small part by their ability to nest in ever-changing human-altered landscapes.

SEE: Nest Evolution, p. 345; Nest Lining, p. 439; Nest Sanitation, p. 75; Hormones and Nest Building, p. 329; Disease and Parasitism, p. 315; Incubation: Controlling Egg Temperatures, p. 273; Precocial and Altricial Young, p. 401. REFS: Collias and Collias, 1984; Elkins, 1983, Fisk, 1978; Greenwood, 1985; Greig-Smith, 1986; Inouye, 1976; Inouye *et al.*, 1981; Louther, 1977; O'Connor, 1984; Parker, 1981; Powley, 1990; Skutch, 1976; Tiainen *et al.*, 1983; Wesolowski, 1983, White, 1789.

Life in the Egg

LIFE is a continuum, but in people, birds, and most other sexually reproducing organisms it is a continuum of alternating stages defined by the chromosomal complement of cells. Chromosomes are tiny structures of the cell that contain most of the DNA, the giant molecules (in the form of a double helix) that contain the coded genetic information. In the 'haploid' stage, the cells contain a single set of chromosomes — each represented only once. In the 'diploid' stage, which alternates with the haploid, each chromosome is represented twice in the cells. Eggs and sperm are the haploid stage; embryos and adults are the diploid stages.

In birds, the fusion of egg and sperm cells occurs while the egg cell is still high in the female's oviduct, before the shell is put on and development is initiated. (In chickens and turkeys, development has been observed to occur without fertilization, leading to an individual carrying copies of only the mother's chromosomes. This parthenogenetic type of development is presumed to be abortive in wild populations.) The 'genes', the genetic information in the chromosomes, control the development of the alternating stages. In the cell that results from the fusion of sperm and egg (the 'zygote'), genes oversee the transformation of that single cell into an adult bird containing many millions of cells. The process consists of a sequence of cell divisions; the zygote gives rise to two daughter cells, each of which divides to produce two granddaughters of the zygote. Division after division follows, through 8, 16, 32, 64 cells, and so on. At each division, the chromosomes are copied, and a complete set is deposited in each daughter cell.

Each cell, then, gets the same genetic information. A skin cell that helps form a feather, a muscle cell, and a brain cell, are all quite different from the original zygote and from each other, but they all have the same instructions. How they get to be so different is the central mystery of the science

Red-backed Shrike

Lanius collurio

ATLAS 213; PMH 212; PER 186; HFP 218; HPCW 222; NESTS 234; BWP7:456

1–3m	BLDS: ♂ Monogamy	5–6 (3–8) 1 brood INCU: ♀, ♂♥ 13–16

FLDG: ♂♀ 12–17	Sm verts	Hawks

Breeding habitat Open areas with bushes and trees; heaths.

Displays Sings from high perches around territory. Excludes rivals (and other birds up to the size of thrushes) vigorously, diving at intruder, calling, and snapping bill. Attracts ♀ with erratic display flight, exposing wing patches. ♂ courtship-feeds ♀.

Nesting Territorial. Nest is in a thick, usually thorny, bush; a cup of small twigs, grass, etc. lined with finer material. Eggs are variable and can be buffish, cream, or greenish with darker spots and blotches usually at larger end, 23mm. An unpaired ♂ may sometimes help rear brood of another pair (see essay on Cooperative Breeding, p. 275).

Diet Large insects (chiefly beetles), small birds, and a variety of other small vertebrates, taken on ground after dropping or gliding down from low, exposed perch. Also takes insects while in flight, acting like a flycatcher. Shrikes are predatory and act rather like small birds of prey. Some (♂s usually) cache extra food in a 'larder' by impaling the prey on the thorns of a bush or sometimes on barbed wire. See p. 451.

Winters Migrates to Africa, mainly S of Sahara, wintering in similar habitats to summer ones.

Conservation Has declined dramatically in the UK to the point of extinction, from more than 300 pairs in 1952. Has declined elsewhere in W, but expanded in Norway. Common across Europe and into Asia.

Essays Ducking the Bird Laws, p. 523; Hoarding Food, p. 453; Piracy, p. 213; Songbird Foraging, p. 417; Feeding Birds, p. 357.

Refs Dementiev et al. 1968; von Haartman 1969.

Lesser Grey Shrike

Lanius minor

ATLAS 214; PMH 213; PER 186; HFP 218; HPCW 223; NESTS 233; BWP7:482

Shrub 2–10m	BLDS: ♂♀ Monogamy?	5–6 (3–9) 1 brood INCU: ♂♥ 15–16 (12–)

FLDG: ♂♀ 16–18(13–19)	Sm verts	Hawks

Breeding habitat Open country, grasslands, with trees and bushes.

Displays Sings from exposed perch. Courtship includes display flight. On landing ♂ fans tail.

Nesting Territorial. Nest is high in a tree, on branch or against trunk, or in a bush; a cup of twigs etc. often with green plant stems; often unlined, but also lined with finer material including feathers. Eggs greenish to bluish, with brown or olive spots and blotches, 25mm.

Diet Almost entirely insects, mainly ground beetles. Swoops down from exposed perch to take insects on ground below. Sometimes takes flying insects, and will hover. Impales prey: see Red-backed Shrike and p. 451.

Winters In Africa, S of Sahara in savannah. Holds winter territories.

Conservation Has decreased in N and W. Locally common in S Europe and across Asia.

Essays Hoarding Food, p. 453; Piracy, p. 213; Songbird Foraging, p. 417; Feeding Birds, p. 357.

of embryology (or, as it is more commonly called today, 'developmental biology').

The cell nucleus, the tiny structure containing the chromosomes, has been removed experimentally from a frog zygote and replaced by the nucleus of a cell from an adult frog's intestine. That modified zygote, containing the nucleus with the genetic instructions from a gut cell, proceeded to develop into a complete adult frog. Why, then, isn't every gut cell in a frog producing adults? It is because the environment of the gut is very different from that of a zygote, and in the intestinal environment genes different from those that function in a zygote are active.

Thus a general solution to the mystery of development is known. It is believed that it is the environment of a cell — the chemical substances to which a cell is exposed and the other cells with which it is in contact — that turns genes on and off. Genes appropriate to cellular functioning in that environment give 'instructions' to the cell; inappropriate genes remain quiescent. In that way, the environment determines how the cells, and thus the tissues and organs of which the cells are the basic structural and functional units, develop in the proper manner. It sees to it that bills do not get placed on wingtips, and feathers do not grow inside kidneys.

Some of the details of bird embryology are well known, thanks to extensive research on the domestic chicken. Indeed, generations of biology students have studied the embryology of the chick. The zygote begins development on the surface of the yolk, which is the main energy source for the chick embryo. The 'white' (albumen) of the egg provides a sterile, protective, cushioned surrounding for the yolk and the developing embryo. A series of membranes carries out functions for the developing embyro; one (the amnion) cushions it so that no matter how an egg is turned, the embryo always remains 'up'.

Division of the zygote produces a flat disc of cells, which exist in different microenvironments. For instance, cells at the edge of the disc have less contact with other cells and more contact with the environment outside of the embryo than do those at the centre. These differences lead in a complex process to the formation of three layers of cells, creating further environmental differences among cells in different positions, and providing them with different destinies. For example, the skin and nervous system will be derived from the upper layer, the gut and lungs from the lower, and muscles and bones from the middle. Gradually, within two to three days after fertilization, the beginnings of a head, tail, nervous system, and limbs can be seen under a microscope. At this stage a chick embryo looks much like a pig or human embryo. Gradually the chick embryo takes on its avian character. Within eight to ten days the forelimbs can be seen developing into wings, and the start of feather development can be detected.

How far that development will go before hatching will depend on whether the bird is altricial or precocial — the former are hatched at an earlier developmental stage than the latter. In precocial birds, for example, the chicks 'mine' the shell for calcium and magnesium. The mining is concentrated at special protrusions into the egg membrane that were produced when the shell was formed. These protrusions are heavily eroded and often broken by the end of

Great Grey Shrike

Lanius excubitor

ATLAS 214; PMH 213; PER 186; HFP 218; HPCW 223; NESTS 233; BWP7:500

2–5m

BLDS: ♀,♂●
Monogamy?

5–7 (8–9)
1 brood
INCU: ♂●
15

FLDG: ♂♀
19–20

Sm verts

Breeding habitat Various subspecies are found in a remarkable range of open habitats; from areas with scattered trees and bushes, forest clearings, and wooded bogs in the N, through desert shrubs in the tropics.

Displays Defends large territory vigorously, often attacking small birds of prey if they intrude.

Nesting Territorial. Nest is in bushes (commonly thorn bushes in dry areas) or low trees; a cup of twigs and stems, lined with finer materials such as grass and feathers. Eggs whitish to pale greenish, heavily spotted and blotched reddish-brown, 26mm. Young remain with parents for 2 weeks or more after fledging. In Finland, clutch size increases when small rodents are unusually abundant.

Diet Large insects, birds, and other small vertebrates; feeding methods like that of Red-backed Shrike. Voles are major winter food in N.

Winters Southern populations resident; northern populations move S and may defend winter territories.

Conservation Local expansions and declines. Locally common across Europe from the Arctic, south across Africa, Asia, Africa, and N America.

Notes Does not breed in the UK, or many Mediterranean islands despite its occurrence in adjacent areas on the continent and despite its ability to utilize a wide range of habitats – see essay on Island Biogeography, p. 303.

Essays John Gould, p. 451.

Refs Paz 1987.

Woodchat Shrike

Lanius senator

ATLAS 213; PMH 214; PER 186; HFP 218; HPCW 224; NESTS 234; BWP7:523

 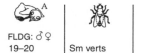

1–10m

BLDS: ♂♀
Monogamy?

5–6 (7)
1 (2) broods
INCU: ♀
14–15(–16)

FLDG: ♂♀
15–18

Sm verts

Hawks

Breeding habitat Dry open country with bushes and trees; maquis scrub.

Displays In courtship, there is a mutual head-bobbing display. Courtship feeding is frequent.

Nesting Nest is in outer branches of a tree; rarely in bushes; a large cup of fine twigs and similar material, lined with softer material such as feathers, hair. Eggs pale green to cream, blotched red-brown and grey, often concentrated near larger end, 23mm. Young remain with adults for about 3 weeks after fledging.

Diet Mainly insects, especially beetles; uses higher lookout than does Red-backed Shrike. From perch drops or glides down onto prey. Also makes sallying flights to catch insects in air. Will

take small mammals, particularly when temperature is low and insect activity reduced.

Winters Africa, S of Sahara, in open bush country, *Acacia* savannahs. Holds winter territories.

Conservation Dramatic contraction in range in N and W, no longer breeding regularly in Belgium, Holland, Luxembourg. Now breeds sporadically on Malta, where formerly common (see essay on Island Biogeography, p. 303). Locally common around Mediterranean and to SW Asia.

Essays Hoarding Food, p. 453; Piracy, p. 213; Songbird Foraging, p. 417; Feeding Birds, p. 357; Finding Hidden Caches, p. 457.

Refs Paz 1987.

development. By contrast the shells of altricial birds survive development essentially intact.

SEE: Eggs and Their Evolution, p. 317; Hatching, p. 487; Precocial and Altricial Young, p. 401; Incubation: Controlling Egg Temperatures, p. 273.

John Gould

JOHN Gould (1804–81), son of a gardener appointed to the Royal Gardens, was trained to be a gardener as well, but in 1825 at the age of 21 set up business as a taxidermist. Within two years the newly established Zoological Society of London (an offshoot of the Linnaean Society) appointed him

Male Great Grey Shrike adding a shrew to its cached prey. (Drawing by Darryl Wheye, after John Gould 1868.)

Masked Shrike

Lanius nubicus

ATLAS 213; PMH 214; PER 186; HFP 218; HPCW 221; NESTS 234; BWP7:542

| Shrub 1–10m | BLDS: ♂♀ Monogamy? | 4–7 (−8) 2 broods INCU: ♀ ? 15? | FLDG: ♂♀ 18–20 | Sm verts | Hawks |

Breeding habitat Open forest and shrubs; gardens, olive groves.

Displays Very little known. ♂ sings from exposed perch. Defends territory with loud calling and, ultimately, with fighting.

Nesting Territorial. Nest may be high in tree or low in thorny bush; a cup of coarse plant material, lined with feathers, hair. Eggs cream to buff, with dark brown and grey blotches, often in band near larger end, 21mm.

Diet Insects, especially grasshoppers, beetles, also lizards and small birds.

Drops down from exposed perch or takes prey in mid-air. Impales vertebrate and invertebrate prey – see Red-backed Shrike and p. 451.

Winters NE Africa and Arabia, in S edge of Sahara, in dry woodlands.

Conservation Locally common in limited range from Greece to Iran to Middle East. Has declined in Israel, perhaps because of pesticide use.

Essays Hoarding Food, p. 453; Piracy, p. 213; Songbird Foraging, p. 417; Feeding Birds, p. 357.

Refs Paz 1987.

Jay

Garrulus glandarius

ATLAS 307; PMH 214; PER 188; HFP 304; HPCW 225; NESTS 315; BWP8

| Conif tree 2–6m (−20m) | BLDS: ♂♀ Monogamy | 5–8 (3–10) 1 brood INCU: ♀, ♂♥ 16–17 (−19) | FLDG: ♂♀ 19–23 | | Ground glean |

Breeding habitat Deciduous or coniferous woodland; parks, gardens. In N, mainly spruce forests.

Displays Song weak and rarely heard. In threat display or towards ♀, rump, belly, and flank feathers are ruffled (making rump and wing pattern conspicuous); the crest may be raised, and bird may call. ♂ will hop around ♀ calling, offering her food. ♀ solicits by raising tail and rump feathers, spreading and quivering wings. Has 'ceremonial' gatherings, like those of the Magpie.

Nesting Territorial. Nest is in a tree, often relatively low in a fork of the branches; a cup of twigs, some earth, lined with fine materials. Eggs pale greenish to olive or buff with very fine brown speckles, 32mm. Clutch sizes may be smaller in SE. Young may remain in their parents' territory until winter.

Diet Omnivorous, but takes mostly acorns, and insects in the summer

(insects are also main item fed to young). Preys upon young of many bird species. Feeds in trees and bushes, less often on ground. Caches acorns in ground, sometimes in trees, and birds will dig through snow to recover them.

Winters Resident; N populations irruptive when acorn and other seed supplies fail. In small groups.

Conservation Common across most of Europe, Asia, and into N Africa. Increasing slightly in UK, expanding range in Ireland, following earlier persecution by gamekeepers.

Essays Anting, p. 469; Hoarding Food, p. 453; Interspecific Territoriality, p. 421; Walking vs. Hopping, p. 375; Finding Hidden Caches, p. 457; Irruptions, p. 491.

Refs Dementiev et al. 1968; Goodwin 1976; Paz 1987; Marchant et al. 1990; von Haartman 1969.

curator and preserver of its Museum and within another 16 years, the Royal Society would elect him a Fellow. In the interim, however, Gould turned his attention to developing a lithography studio and sketching birds.

Lithography, a method of printing that sends an acid-etched slab of stone through the press, had been invented in 1798. With its refinement, less technical skill was needed to create reproductions than that required for tool-engraved metal or wood. Gould left the elaboration of his sketched designs up to his wife, Elizabeth, and later hired Edward Lear to assist her. After Elizabeth's untimely death at the age of 37, Gould began a 40-year collaboration with lithographer Henry Constantine Richter who completed more than 1000 plates.

Like John James Audubon, John Gould blended scientific accuracy with artistic flair, but where the formally trained Audubon was seen as the more spectacular of the two, Gould's appeal was centred on his precision and quiet compositions.

Gould was phenomenally productive. The first among his major works was the *Birds of Europe* (1832–37), which had great general appeal. Gould gave up work on Charles Darwin's *Zoology of the voyage of H.M.S. Beagle* and resigned his position at the Zoological Society to travel to Australia to begin his *Birds of Australia* (1837–38). Pioneering work there led to the formation of the Gould League of Bird Lovers. The League was organized to protect Australian birds, many of which he named and had been the first to depict. His *Birds of Asia* (1850–83) was another massive undertaking, holding 530 lithographs. The five-volume *Birds of Great Britain* (1862–73) enlarged upon his *Birds of Europe*, and incorporated more biology into the compositions. It was Gould's last fully complete work and his most praised. By the end of his life, Gould had amassed more than 30 tonnes of book materials and completed 41 folio-sized volumes containing 2999 hand-coloured lithographs. A devoted collector of bird skins, his Australian material was sold to the Academy of Natural Sciences in Philadelphia and the remainder sent to the British Museum.

REF.: de Battisti, 1981.

Hoarding Food

BIRDS living in environments that produce food in abundance during one season of the year, and relatively little (or none) during others, may cope with the uneven supply in several different ways. One strategy is to leave the area during the periods of shortage, as many European birds do in migrating from barren, cold, polar or temperate regions to the relatively food-rich, warm

Siberian Jay

Perisoreus infaustus

ATLAS 308; PMH 215; PER 188; HFP 304; HPCW -; NESTS 315; BWP8

 2–10m

 BLDS: ♂♀ Monogamy

4 (3–5) 1 brood INCU: ♀ 16–20

 FLDG: ♂♀ 21–25

 Insects

 Ground glean

Breeding habitat Boreal coniferous and birch forests.

Displays ♂ hops towards ♀, has bowing display in front of her.

Nesting Nest in conifer near trunk; a large cup of twigs, lined with feathers and other softer materials. Egg whitish to very pale blue, with olive to grey spots and blotches, 30mm. Young may remain with parents through winter.

Diet Feeds on seeds and insects, foraging both from trees and on the ground.

Winters Resident; some may be nomadic.

Conservation Has declined in parts of Scandinavia because of forestry practices. Common across boreal forests of Europe and Asia.

Essays Hoarding Food, p. 453; Interspecific Territoriality, p. 421; Walking vs. Hopping, p. 375.

Refs Dementiev et al. 1968; Goodwin 1976; von Haartman 1969.

Azure-winged Magpie

Cyanopica cyana

ATLAS 308; PMH 215; PER 188; HFP 306; HPCW -; NESTS 316; BWP8

 3–5m

 BLDS: ♂♀ Monogamy?

 6–8 (5–9) 1 (2?) broods INCU: ♀ 15

 FLDG: ♂♀ ? Seeds Ground glean

Breeding habitat Cork oaks, olive groves, other dry areas with trees and bushes; often near water.

Displays Very little known.

Nesting Nests in small loose colonies; in fork of small tree, a large cup of twigs with mud, lined with hair, fur, and other soft materials. Egg cream, with distinct red-brown spots, 28mm. Often in small groups in the breeding season. Outside of Europe is a cooperative breeder (see essay), but whether there are helpers at the nest in Europe is not known.

Diet Mainly insects; will cache seeds, taken from bushes or ground.

Winters Resident; in small groups or flocks.

Conservation Locally common in its peculiar disjointed range: it occurs in Spain and Portugal, is absent from the rest of Euope, most of Asia, but occurs in parts of China and Japan. The theory that the European population was deliberately introduced is ususlly discounted.

Essays Cooperative Breeding, p. 275.

Refs Goodwin 1976.

tropics for the winter. The hazards of migration are endured in return for continuity of food supply and avoidance of severe weather. Another strategy is to stay through the time of shortages and scrounge hard for the food that is available, as do Ptarmigan and even tits, although throughout the northern winter the latter remain daily poised on the razor's edge of starvation.

A third strategy is to harvest more food than is needed during periods of seasonal abundance and to store it. This strategy, too, has its dangers; the store may be robbed or may spoil. Long-term storage — what might be called hoarding — is practised by various woodpeckers, owls, jays, Nutcrackers, and nuthatches. Only the two smallest owls in northern Europe (Pygmy and Tengmalm's) hoard — probably because their small body size makes them less able to fast through periods of inclement weather when hunting is difficult.

Techniques of storing differ from species to species. Groups of North American Acorn Woodpeckers (*Melanerpes formicivorus*) place surplus acorns in one or two storage sites near the centre of the group territory — dead trunks and limbs are studded with acorns jammed into shallow holes chiselled by the birds. Up to 50 000 acorns may be stored in the remains of a single dead tree, which is known as a granary. The woodpeckers aggressively defend their acorns, which are so tightly hammered into the holes that it is difficult for potential robbers to retrieve them without being detected or, in many cases, to remove them from the holes at all. Other woodpeckers that cache food do not chisel holes; they use natural cracks and cavities to store acorns and various other nuts.

Some birds, especially tits, some raptors, owls, shrikes, and (occasionally) woodpeckers, store animal prey, but this seldom extends beyond short-term storage of a few days, because such prey soon decay. Exceptions may be the victims of northern owls and tits, for autumn-stored mammals and insects may be preserved by cold and consumed over a longer period. This is indicated by the recent discovery that Tengmalm's Owls, and American Northern Saw-whet (*Aegolius acadicus*) and Great Horned Owls (*Bubo virginianus*) thaw frozen prey by incubating them as they would eggs! All the thoroughly studied, long-term-storing birds use conifer seeds, acorns, and other nuts that are energy-rich and yet have a hard, impervious coat that retards spoilage. Some acorns apparently can be stored for up to a year or more.

Careful observations are needed of hoarding behaviour, about which little is known. For instance, more information on the elapsed time before hoards are recovered would be desirable. Marking of the stores and repeated observations should help to solve the question of their 'shelf life' and their importance to the birds.

SEE: Finding Hidden Caches, p. 457; Coevolution, p. 239; Bills, p. 391. REFS: George and Sulski, 1984; Hutchins and Lanner, 1982; Källander and Smith, 1990; Korpimäki, 1987a; Roberts, 1979.

Magpie

Pica pica

ATLAS 308; PMH 215; PER 188; HFP 306; HPCW 225; NESTS 316; BWP8

Cliff
2–10m

BLDS: ♂♀
Monogamy

5–8 (2–10)
1 brood
INCU: ♀
17–18

FLDG: ♂♀
22–28

Foliage glean

Breeding habitat Woodland edges and open country with scattered trees.

Displays In threat display, raises plumage to display more white, and spreads wings slightly. Towards partner, will open wings and flutter them angled above back. 'Ceremonial' gatherings of several birds involve both territorial and non-territorial birds. Birds jump about on branches or ground, displaying and chasing each other, then fly back to perches.

Nesting Territorial. Nests in top of tree, sometimes in buildings; a large cup of twigs, mud, with a finer lining, with a loose mass of twigs forming the roof. Eggs variable; pale greenish to bluish, extensively spotted or blotched dark brown and grey, 34mm.

Diet In summer mainly insects, but a wide range of prey taken opportunistically, including the nestlings of smaller species; feeds mainly on ground, but also from bushes. In winter mainly plant material. Will scavenge. Caches surplus food.

Winters Mainly resident; in pairs or small groups.

Conservation Increasing in the UK (following declines where persecuted in last century) and may be having an impact on the breeding success of the smaller species whose nests it plunders. Common across Europe, Asia, into N Africa, N America.

Essays Birds and Agriculture, p. 365; Carrying Eggs, p. 99; Feeding Birds, p. 357; Nest Sites and Materials, p. 443; Piracy, p. 213; Hoarding Food, p. 453; Finding Hidden Caches, p. 457.

Refs Dementiev et al. 1968; Goodwin 1976; Marchant et al. 1990; Birkhead 1991 is a book about this species.

Nutcracker

Nucifraga caryocatactes

ATLAS 306; PMH 216; PER 188; HFP 304; HPCW 226; NESTS 315; BWP8

3–9m

BLDS: ♂♀
Monogamy

5–4 (2–5)
1 brood
INCU: ♂♀
17–19

?
FLDG: ♂♀
21–28

Insects

Ground glean

Breeding habitat Coniferous, sometimes mixed forests, at high elevations in C Europe, in boreal forest elsewhere.

Displays Not well known.

Nesting Territorial. Nest is in a tree, close to trunk and well hidden; a large untidy cup of twigs, moss, some earth, lined with grasses and softer materials. Eggs very pale greenish or bluish, with very fine dark brown spots, 34mm. Young remain with parents for 8–12 weeks. Clutches are larger in good seed years.

Diet Seeds of conifers (Siberian populations), Arolla pine (in the Alps), and hazel nuts; also insects and a variety of prey taken opportunistically.

Young fed seeds. Seeds are cached for the winter in the ground, birds digging through snow to retrieve them.

Winters Resident; some come down lower and into deciduous woods. Siberian populations often irruptive to rest of Europe, when seed crop fails (e.g in 1968). These Siberian populations remained and bred in Finland into the mid-1970s. In small flocks.

Conservation Locally common in mountains of C Europe, and boreal forests from Scandinavia across Asia.

Essays Finding Hidden Caches, p. 457; Hoarding Food, p. 453; Irruptions, p. 491.

Refs Dementiev et al. 1968; Goodwin 1976; von Haartman 1969.

Finding Hidden Caches

How does a long-term hoarder like a Nutcracker recover stored seeds when it needs them to feed its young? Ornithologists at first thought that the food was stored only in certain kinds of areas, and that the birds rediscovered it by later foraging in the same areas. A North American Clark's Nutcracker (*Nucifraga columbiana*, a close relative of Europe's Nutcracker), may store more than 30 000 pinyon pine seeds during a single season, placing them in caches of 4 to 5 seeds each. Recent aviary experiments with Clark's Nutcrackers and Gray Jays have shown clearly that individuals are able to recall where they have cached seeds. The birds remember where the seeds are in relation to certain landmarks, such as rocks. If the landmarks are moved, the areas the birds search are displaced an equivalent amount.

The results of these experiments confirmed observations by behaviourist Diana Tomback, who examined the distribution of beak marks in earth and snow where Clark's Nutcrackers had searched for caches. The marks were not random; unsuccessful probes were clustered in the vicinity of successful ones as indicated by the presence of pinyon-seed coats, which the birds had removed before eating the seeds. Later in the year rodents begin to find the caches, but prior to that the birds found caches on about two out of three attempts, far more frequently than one would expect if they were searching at random. Although Nutcracker cache recovery has not been as thoroughly studied as that of its American cousin, the European species reportedly can find caches under as much as 45 cm of snow. This capacity to remember the sites of stored food seems to be an evolutionary enhancement of a spatial memory that is widespread in birds. For example, Marsh Tits often store food in diverse places when it is abundant. They show excellent short-term (hours-days) memory for the storage locations, as elegant experiments by John Krebs and his colleagues have shown. Not unexpectedly, Hooded Crows appear to have no trouble in recovering cached food — indeed a female that watched a male caching eggs stolen from a nest returned two days later and ate one of the eggs.

SEE: Hoarding Food, p. 453; Bird-brained, p. 385. REFS: Elkins, 1988; Fjeld and Sonerud, 1988; Källander and Smith, 1990; Sherry *et al.*, 1981; Shettleworth, 1983; Stevens and Krebs, 1986; Tomback, 1980; Vander Wall, 1990.

Alpine Chough

Pyrrhocorax graculus

ATLAS 313; PMH 216; PER 188; HFP 306; HPCW 226; NESTS 317; BWP8

	BLDS: ♂♀ See below	4 (3–6) 1 brood INCU: ♀ 17–21

FLDG: ♂♀
 23–31 | Fruit | Probes

Breeding habitat Mountains, from tree line to snow line.

Displays Not well known.

Nesting Nest is in a crevice in the rock face or in a cave; fills crevice with a cup of small sticks, lined with finer material. Eggs buff to creamy, with olive-green to grey spots and blotches, 39mm. Breeding system not well known and may have helpers at nest – see essay on Cooperative Breeding, p. 275.

Diet Insects; picked or probed from ground; also takes fruit from bushes. Caches surplus food in rock crevices.

Winters Resident; descends in winter, but not to lowlands; in small flocks.

Conservation Locally common in fragmented habitats from N Africa, Spain, E into Asia.

Essays Finding Hidden Caches, p. 457; Hoarding Food, p. 453.

Refs Goodwin 1976.

Chough

Pyrrhocorax pyrrhocorax

ATLAS 313; PMH 216; PER 188; HFP 306; HPCW 226; NESTS 316; BWP8

	BLDS: ♂♀ Monogamy	3–5 (2–7) 1 brood INCU: ♀ 17–23

FLDG: ♂♀
 36–41 | Seeds | Probes

Breeding habitat Rocky areas in mountains, sea cliffs; often near grazed land.

Displays Has acrobatic aerial displays, rapidly changing direction, diving, turning on back. On ground, bowing, threat, and solicitation displays, similar to those of other corvids. Birds mutually preen.

Nesting Nests in a deep crevice in a cliff, rocks, or in a small cave; sometimes in buildings; a large cup of twigs, thickly lined with hair, wool, and other softer materials. Eggs buffish, with brown and grey blotches, 41mm. Young remain with adults for 3–4 weeks after fledging. Flocks contain non-breeders throughout year. Does not nest until 3 years old.

Diet Insects, especially ants in summer, taken on ground or by probing; will also take other invertebrates, seeds. Will cache surplus food.

Winters Resident. In small groups or flocks.

Conservation Decreasing in C and W, with local extinctions (e.g. SW UK). In the UK, some recovery after local decline. Locally common, but has a fragmented distribution from Ireland to N Africa and E into Asia. See p. 528.

Essays Hoarding Food, p. 453.

Refs Dementiev et al. 1968; Goodwin 1976; Marchant et al. 1990; Sharrock 1976.

Tool-using

At one time it was assumed that humans were unique among creatures in their ability to use tools. Now it is clear that tool-using is widespread in the animal kingdom. For instance, chimpanzees use twigs to fish termites out of termite mounds, and small wasps use pebbles to tamp down earth over their nests. Birds are no exception — tool use has been demonstrated in several species.

Perhaps the best-known avian tool user is the Woodpecker Finch (*Cactospiza pallida*), one of 'Darwin's finches', on the Galápagos Islands. It uses a cactus spine or wooden splinter to dig grubs or other insects out of holes. Although in general the Woodpecker Finch forages much like a true woodpecker, the two birds are unrelated. The woodpecker pries up bark with its bill, uncovering insects underneath and in holes and immediately devours those it can reach. But the finch has not evolved the long tongue that permits real woodpeckers to extract wood-boring insects from their deep holes. When such insects are found, the finch flies to a cactus, breaks off a spine, and returns to spear its prey. If a cactus spine is not available, the Woodpecker Finch may break a twig off a bush or tree, and if necessary even trim it of twiglets. In these cases the bird not only uses a tool, it 'manufactures' it.

Closer to home, a Blackbird was once observed using a twig about 8 cm long to sweep 4–5 cm of snow from an area of some 900 cm^2 in order to feed on bare ground. The closely related American Robin (*Turdus migratorius*) has been seen to use a twig to sweep leaves aside, so this behaviour should be anticipated in other *Turdus* thrushes.

Egyptian Vultures use stones as tools to assault the eggs of ostriches, often throwing rock after rock until an egg is breached and its contents can be consumed. The behaviour is not learned from other birds, and may be derived from the throwing of small eggs against rock anvils to break them (the vultures prefer to throw rounded, egg-like stones rather than jagged ones). White-winged Choughs (*Corcorax melanorhamphos*), Australian birds, are reported to employ pieces of mussel shell as hammers in their attempts to open other mussels.

One of the most astonishing examples of the employment of tools by a bird is the use of bait by fishing Green-backed Herons (*Butorides striatus*) in southern Japan. The herons obtain bait as diverse as live insects, berries, twigs, and discarded crackers, and cast them on the waters. They then crouch and wait for the curious or hungry fish that comes to inspect the lure. The birds have even been observed carefully trimming oversized twigs to the proper dimensions — so that like the Woodpecker Finch, the herons actually engage in tool-manufacturing. Young herons are less successful bait-fishers than their elders, in part because they tend to use twigs that are too large. Adults also probably differ in skill. While the herons can fish successfully

Jackdaw

Corvus monedula

ATLAS 312; PMH 217; PER 188; HFP 310; HPCW 226; NESTS 318; BWP8

Cliff	Crevice BLDS: ♂♀ Monogamy?	4–6 (3–9) 1 brood INCU: ♀ 17–18(16–20)	A FLDG: ♂♀ 30–35		Foliage glean

Breeding habitat A wide range of habitats; farmland, parks, cliffs.

Displays Has aerial displays with twists, dives, and swerving. In threat display, feathers on head and nape are ruffled, head is held up, bill downward, and bird struts. Mated pairs mutually preen. ♀ solicits by crouching and quivering tail.

Nesting Nests in colonies, wherever availability of suitable nest sites permit; in a hole in tree, building, cliff, rabbit burrow; a sometimes large pile of twigs; lined with softer materials. Eggs pale bluish-green, variably but distinctly spotted or blotched dark brown to black,

36mm.

Diet A wide variety of prey, generally taken on ground, by picking or probing, but also from vegetation.

Winters Mainly resident; N and E populations move S. Usually in flocks.

Conservation Recent increases in UK and on continent, perhaps benefiting from changes on farmlands. Common across Europe, W Asia, and into N Africa.

Essays Commensal Feeding, p. 27; Nest Sites and Materials, p. 443; Birds and Agriculture, p. 365.

Refs Dementiev et al. 1968; Goodwin 1976.

Rook

Corvus frugilegus

ATLAS 311; PMH 217; PER 190; HFP 310; HPCW 227; NESTS 317; BWP8

15–20m	BLDS: ♂♀,♂♀ Monogamy	3–5 (2–9) 1 brood INCU: ♀ 16–18	A FLDG: ♂♀ 29–33	Seeds	Ground glean

Breeding habitat Agricultural land and other open areas with scattered trees; open woodland.

Displays Display flights near colony start well before breeding season begins. In autumn, has mass acrobatic aerial displays, with tumbling, rolling, and diving. On ground, in bowing display, bird partly droops and opens wings, raises and spreads tail, bows forward, and calls. This display given in greeting as well as threat. ♀ solicits by crouching and quivering wings and tail.

Nesting Nests colonially in tops of tall trees (colonies may number up to 7000 pairs); defends area around nest. Nest is a large cup of twigs, lined with grass, leaves, often re-used in successive years. Eggs pale bluish-green, often heavily and variously marked with brown, 40mm; hatch asynchronously and in larger clutches, later young often die. Young may remain in colonies for a few days after fledging, and remain with

adults into late summer. Occasionally bigamous, when ♂ does not help second ♀ to build her nest, and provides little help with rearing young. Old ♂s try to mate with mates of young ♂s, who tend not to guard their mates so carefully.

Diet A wide variety of prey taken opportunistically. Earthworms are found by probing ground, insects are picked from ground; also takes spilled grain from fields. Will cache food, especially acorns.

Winters Resident in S, migrates S from N and E to most of Europe; in large flocks in agricultural fields.

Conservation A widespread decline in mid-20th century. Common across middle latitudes of Europe into Asia.

Essays Commensal Feeding, p. 27; Nest Sites and Materials, p. 443; Swallowing Stones, p. 135; Hoarding Food, p. 453; Finding Hidden Caches, p. 457.

without bait, their use of bait seems to enlarge the catch. It would be interesting to find similar behaviour in European herons.

Finally, it is not unusual to find birds using ants as tools for cleaning or disinfecting their plumage.

SEE: Anting, p. 469; Bird-brained, p. 385; Songbird Foraging, p. 417; How Woodpecker Tongues Work, p. 289. REFS: Higuchi, 1986; Thouless *et al.*, 1989.

Hybridization

WHEN two populations of distinct but closely related birds come into contact, members of those populations may mate with each other and successfully reproduce. That process of 'hybridization' creates problems for taxonomists, but is one sign of the continuous nature of the process of speciation — the evolutionary formation of new kinds of organisms. If hybrids are formed between two populations that are barely differentiated, they may remain undetected, since their features may fall within the range of variability of one or both of the populations. One would expect, if those populations were to remain in contact, that they would blend together and lose their distinctness. At the other extreme, two populations may each have diverged so far from their common ancestor that their individuals no longer recognize each other as potential mates. In that case, biologists are agreed that the two populations should be considered separate species. They will not fuse back into a single species.

It is between those two extremes of complete blending and total distinctness that hybridization can provide glimpses of the complex process of differentiation — of evolution in action. Speciation normally occurs in geographic isolation, but the distributions of birds are complicated and ever-changing. Populations previously isolated often come into contact, and when they do, the amount, duration, and results of hybridization will vary from instance to instance. For example, the Great Tit presents no evolutionary complexities within the range covered by this book. In Asia, however, the range of the Great Tit is complex, and a number subspecies have small zones of overlap in which intersubspecific hybridization takes place. However, in eastern Siberia one of these subspecies overlaps with the European form *without interbreeding*.

In most of Europe, the Hooded and Carrion Crows remain distinct, but in the middle of Scotland they hybridize extensively — forming a zone in which

Carrion / Hooded Crow

Corvus corone

ATLAS 312; PMH 217; PER 190; HFP 310; HPCW 227; NESTS 318; BWP8

Cliff

BLDS: ♂♀
Monogamy

4–6 (2–7)
1 brood
INCU: ♀
17–21

FLDG: ♂♀
28–36 (26–)

Foliage glean

Breeding habitat A wide range of habitats, generally where large trees are present, but also along shores. Spreading into more open habitats.

Displays Has a bowing display, followed by a upward head jerk, sometimes involving both birds. In threat display, head feathers are ruffled, bill is pointed downwards, and birds strut. ♀ solicits by crouching and quivering wings and tail. Birds mutually preen.

Nesting Territorial. Nest is in top of large tree, sometimes cliff, building, or bush, and occasionally on ground on offshore islands where trees are not available; a large cup of twigs, lined with finer material. Eggs pale bluish-green, heavily and variously spotted with dark browns and grey, 43mm. Young remain with parents, sometimes until the following breeding season.

Diet A wide variety of food taken on ground, sometimes from trees and bushes. Despite name, carrion is a minor portion of food in most areas.

Winters The Carrion Crow is largely resident. The Hooded Crow is resident in the S, while the N populations move S and W in flocks.

Conservation Common and widespread across Europe and Asia.

Notes There are two distinct subspecies: Carrion (all black) and Hooded (with grey body). The former has a restricted range in SW Europe, the latter is more widespread. The hybrid zone between them is narrow (<100km) suggesting that few hybrids survive. Another all-black subspecies occurs in E Asia.

Essays Bird-brained, p. 385; Birds and Agriculture, p. 365; Carrying Eggs, p. 99; Empty Shells, p. 199; Feathers, p. 363; Finding Hidden Caches, p. 457; Hybridization, p. 461; Piracy, p. 213; Species and Speciation, p. 325; Nest Sites and Materials, p. 443.

Refs Dementiev et al. 1968; Goodwin 1976; Marchant et al. 1990.

Brown-necked Raven

Corvus ruficollis

ATLAS 311; PMH -; PER -; HFP 308; HPCW 228; NESTS 319; BWP8

Decid tree

BLDS: ?
Monogamy

4–5 (1–7)
1 (2?) broods
INCU: ♀
20–22

FLDG: ?
37–38

Breeding habitat Desert scrub, from elevations below sea-level (such as the Dead Sea) to rocky mountains at high elevations.

Displays Not well known, but apparently similar to those of the Raven. During hot days will find shade or soar to high elevations.

Nesting Territorial. Nest is on a cliff or a tree if available; also on telephone poles, etc., a large cup of twigs, lined with softer material. Eggs are like those of Carrion/Hooded Crow, but with brown scribblings, 46mm. ♂ feeds ♀ on nest.

Diet Omnivorous; takes carrion; the bird's presence often attracts vultures to the site.

Winters Resident; adults hold territories year-round, young in large flocks, often near settlements, rubbish tips, etc.

Conservation Locally common and widespread across N Africa, SW Asia.

Refs Goodwin 1976.

birds with varying combinations of the characters of the all-black Carrion and grey-bodied Hooded can be found. Because they are known to inter-breed, Carrion and Hooded Crows are considered to be one species *Corvus corone*.

Something on the order of 10 per cent of North American birds that are considered specifically distinct hybridize with other species, and we suspect the percentage for Europe is similar. A complex example spanning a wide geographical area involves gulls of the Herring Gull group, where varying degrees of hybridization between species occur (and lead to endless debates on which should be considered 'good species'). The Herring Gull itself, for example, is involved in a 'ring of races' with the Lesser Black-backed Gull. The two overlap widely with little hybridization in Europe. But they are connected by a circle of hybridizing populations that extends across Siberia, North America, and the North Atlantic.

The situation is made more complex by the propensity of the Herring Gull also to hybridize with the Glaucous Gull (in Iceland 50 per cent of the popula-tion is hybrid), the Glaucous-winged Gull (in Alaska), and the Slaty-backed Gull (in Siberia). In turn, the Glaucous and Glaucous-winged Gulls hybridize around the Bering Sea. Furthermore, the Iceland Gull hybridizes with Thayer's Gull on Canada's Baffin Island. All of these gulls, together with North American California and Western Gulls, and the Mexican Yellow-footed Gull, compose one of the most interesting groups of birds showing many degrees of genetic differentiation. So when you are in the field trying to sort out which of these gulls you have in your binoculars, take heart. The gulls themselves also have problems telling who is who.

SEE: Species and Speciation, p. 325; Natural Selection, p. 297. REFS: Confer and Knapp, 1979; Gill, 1980; Perrins, 1987; Pierotti, 1987.

Starlings

NOT all Starlings are pests (although they apparently have associated closely with people since the advent of agriculture), nor have flocks always been the nuisance they are today. The bird was described in detail by Aristotle and Pliny and taught to mimic human speech by the Romans. One bought by Mozart and three years later publicly buried, was immortalized by a poem the musician wrote for the occasion. But the meagre mention of them by Euro-pean chroniclers before 1830 is thought to indicate that their numbers were rather limited. After 1830 things apparently changed. Milder European winters appear to have eliminated the need of Starlings to migrate (or shortened their migration route) while the increased conversion of forest into farms created more favourable open habitats and provided cereal grains for food. These concurrent changes presumably favoured double-brooding, breeding at an

Raven

Corvus corax

ATLAS 310; PMH 195; PER 190; HFP 308; HPCW 228; NESTS 319; BWP8

trees

BLDS: ♂♀
Monogamy

4–6 (3–7)
1 brood
INCU: ♀
20–21

FLDG: ♂♀
35–40

Breeding habitat Uplands, sea cliffs, forests (although not when disturbed).

Displays Has acrobatic aerial displays turning over and nose-diving, by ♂ alone or chasing ♀. In threat, ruffles head feathers, and struts. Has bowing display (like that of the Carrion/Hooded Crow), with tail spread and wings held away from body. ♀ solicits in a similar way to the Carrion/Hooded Crow.

Nesting Territorial. Nest is on a rock ledge or large tree; a large pile of twigs, earth, moss, lined with wool and other softer materials. Eggs pale bluish-green, heavily and variously spotted with dark brown and grey; sometimes only lightly marked, 50mm. Eggs laid early in year in N, often later in S. In the UK, nests in 1st week of March, allowing the young to be fed carrion at a time when many young lambs succumb to inclement weather. Young remain with adults for 20 weeks or more.

Diet Omnivorous, wide range of live and dead animals; takes food on ground and will cache surplus food.

Winters Resident; sometimes in small flocks.

Conservation Population has increased where former persecution has stopped, but remains absent from many lowland areas. Common across Europe, Asia, N America, and into N Africa.

Essays Feathers, p. 363; Feet, p. 289; Walking vs. Hopping, p. 375; Hoarding Food, p. 453.

Refs Dementiev et al. 1968; Goodwin 1976; Marchant et al. 1990; von Haartman 1969.

Fan-tailed Raven

Corvus rhipidurus

ATLAS 311; PMH -; PER -; HFP 308; HPCW 228; NESTS 311; BWP8:

BLDS: ?
Monogamy?

2–4?
1 brood?
INCU: ?
?

FLDG: ?
?

Breeding habitat Cliffs in desert regions to high elevations.

Displays Spends much time in aerobatic display, dropping stones or twigs and plunging to catch them while still airborne.

Nesting Nest is on a cliff; a large cup of twigs, lined with finer material. Egg pale bluish-green, with dark brown and grey spotting and blotching, 49mm. Sometimes several pairs nest close together.

Diet Omnivorous.

Winters Resident; sometimes in small groups.

Conservation Occurs across Middle East, Arabia, into NE Africa.

Refs Goodwin 1976.

earlier age, and formation of ever larger colonies (which probably have higher breeding success than small ones) and led to rapidly increased populations. By the turn of the century, not only was the species successful in Britain and on the Continent, but it also was transported across the Atlantic where it advanced 3700 kilometres to the Pacific within an astonishingly short 60 years.

Few people seem to like Starlings even though they are not always troublesome. The species becomes more interesting, however, when one knows more of its biology. According to DNA studies by Charles Sibley and Jon Ahlquist, starlings are most closely related to the family that contains American mockingbirds, diverging from a common ancestor some 23 to 28 million years ago. Within the 106-member starling family (Sturnidae), the Starling is unusual in that its jaw muscles work 'backward'. Instead of using most of their power to clamp the bill shut, these muscles spring the bill open. The closed bill is inserted between blades of grass in thick turf or other cover, and sprung open to expose hidden prey. In addition, as the bill opens, the eyeballs rotate forward to permit binocular vision. William Beecher, who first reported the behaviour, suggests that this manoeuvre is the key to their high rate of winter survival. Starlings forage in a wide array of habitats, and by using complex cues they are able to concentrate their efforts within the most profitable areas. In winter, Starlings may become partially nomadic, although they are able to find dormant insects under light snow. This highly adaptable, highly opportunistic species shows a marked preference for foraging for insects in short grass but will even rely on fungus to get by in the absence of more nutritious food.

Recent high-speed X-ray movies of Starlings during flight have uncovered another 'spring-like' adaptation in this species. Researchers report that the wishbone bends (expanding by almost 50 per cent) and recoils as the bird's wings move up-and-down. The function of this 'spring' is not yet clear, but the Starling breathes about three times a second during flight and the elastic wishbone may help to circulate air through adjacent air sacs.

Starling housekeeping is also highly adaptable, allowing the birds to utilize an especially wide variety of natural and human-built nest sites. Unlike most cavity nesters, Starlings add fresh green vegetation rich in natural fumigants that ward off insect parasites and pathogens. To maintain the nest's insulating properties they initially remove nestling fecal sacs, but as nestlings become feathered, nest insulation becomes superfluous, fecal sacs are no longer removed, and fresh greenery is no longer added. By the time the young fledge, the nest is a pest-ridden compost that precludes breeding success in less hardy cavity nesters. (Starlings can withstand the infestation of tens of thousands of mites per nest hole without increased mortality.) With nest construction that includes early incorporation of fumigants and minimal, but precisely timed sanitation, the Starling has reduced the energy costs of housekeeping while decreasing the value of its nest site for reuse by competing species.

Starlings are prolific. Breeding males may attempt to father a second and even third brood yearly and mate fidelity depends, in part, on the success of

Starling

Sturnus vulgaris

ATLAS 304; PMH 218; PER 190; HFP 302; HPCW 231; NESTS 313; BWP8

	BLDS: ♂♀	5–7 (4–9) 1–2 broods INCU: ♂♀	FLDG: ♂♀		
Cliff	Monogamy	12–15	20–22	Fruit	Foliage glean

Breeding habitat Widely distributed, common near habitation; agricultural land, towns, gardens, also cliffs.

Displays Singing birds are excellent mimics; when singing, droops and flutters wings, or waves them in exaggerated fashion. At roosts, birds may perform mass movements in air, diving quickly into roost site.

Nesting See essay, p. 463. Nest is in a hole in a tree, building, cliff; a cavity filled with grass, stems, and a finer lining that may sometimes include feathers. Eggs pale blue, 30mm.

Diet Insects and other invertebrates, picked or probed from ground; also berries from trees in autumn. Young fed insects.

Winters Resident in the SW, migrates to these areas from NE; in large flocks in agricultural fields; often roosts in very large concentrations.

Conservation Has moved into Spain and Iceland in 20th century, but some sharp declines in Scandinavia in last 20 years. Introduced to many areas of the world. Abundant and widespread across Europe, W Asia.

Notes Breeds only sporadically in Ireland – see essay on Island Biogeography, p. 303.

Essays Starlings, p. 463; Adaptations for Flight, p. 511; Anting, p. 469; Bird-brained, p. 385; Bird Droppings, p. 485; Birds and Agriculture, p. 365; Communal Roosting, p. 81; Dominance Hierarchies, p. 131; Eyes Like a Hawk, p. 89; Flock Defence, p. 257; Population Dynamics, p. 515; Temperature Regulation and Behaviour, p. 163; Who Incubates?, p. 285; Hormones and Nest Building, p. 329; Carrying Eggs, p. 99; Feeding Birds, p. 357; Nest Sanitation, p. 75; Sleeping Sentries and Mate-guarding, p. 73; Swallowing Stones, p. 135; Vocal Copying, p. 383.

Refs Dementiev et al. 1968; Marchant et al. 1990; Feare 1984 is a book about this species.

Spotless Starling

Sturnus unicolor

ATLAS 305; PMH 219; PER 190; HFP 302; HPCW 231; NESTS 313; BWP8

	BLDS: ?	4 ? brood INCU: ♀	FLDG: ♂♀		
Cliff	Monogamy	12–13	21–23		Foliage glean

Breeding habitat Similar to those of the Starling.

Displays Similar to those of the Starling.

Nesting Similar in its nesting habits to the Starling. Eggs pale blue, 31mm.

Diet Similar to that of the Starling.

Winters Resident.

Conservation Common in its restricted range around W end of Mediterranean; range barely overlaps that of Starling.

the previous brood. Starlings are colonial breeders and there may be a tendency toward cooperative breeding (which has been found in some tropical members of its family). There are reports of bachelor males feeding the young and, along with the breeding male, guarding the nest tree after the fledglings and the paired female depart to forage. A family unit usually forages within 200–500 yards of its nest. During nest-building and egg-laying, family members make an average of 30 visits a day to the nest; during incubation this decreases to 18, but when young are being fed, visits jump to 260.

Visits to the nest, however, are not restricted to bachelors and the breeding pair. Starlings are intraspecific brood parasites and visiting females dump their eggs in the active nests of others. A female is more likely to dump her eggs if she contests the nest site used by another pair, if she has had an unsuccessful clutch, if she is unpaired and copulates with a male(s) that already has a mate and nest site, or if she is a habitual brood parasite who characteristically distributes at least some of her eggs in one or more nests other than her own. The success of dumped eggs varies. Starlings, like many species including Swallows, will recognize and remove a foreign egg if it is added before their own clutch is started. To protect their own young from starvation as a result of extra mouths to feed, Starlings subject to brood parasitism tend to lay fewer than the optimal six eggs. That way, if they are conned into rearing extra young, their own offspring stand a better chance of surviving. Male Starlings also defend against cuckoldry (which would also divert their parental care into young they had not sired) and even avoid participating in incubation (which would leave their mates unattended) until egg-laying is completed.

Exotic 'weeds' that have left behind the natural controls that limit their numbers at home may, quite quickly, become a problem. In some of the Shetland Islands in Scotland, for example, the weedy Starling is viewed as one of the worst pests of newly sown grain fields. The Starlings dig up recently sprouted plants by probing down the side of the shoot into the soil to snap up what remains of the seed. Damage is most severe near winter roosts and pre-roosting assembly areas. A vast array of methods to control Starlings has been tried, from shooting cannons, electronic alarms, honking horns, to repellents and nets. Nonetheless, some value the birds for ridding pastures of insect infestations (although benefits have been demonstrated only under very special conditions). Their reputation for controlling pests apparently has prevailed in New Zealand and nest boxes for the birds can be found atop many pastureland fence posts. Similarly, it has been estimated that some 22.5 million Starling nestboxes are in place in the former Soviet Union. The use of Starlings to suppress European or North American insect outbreaks, however, is unlikely. Instead, programmes to control Starlings probably will become more common.

SEE: Birds and Agriculture, p. 367; Communal Roosting, p. 81; Bird Droppings, p. 485; Vocal Copying, p. 383; Cooperative Breeding, p. 275; Brood Parasitism, p. 249; Anting, p. 469; Bird-brained, p. 385; Interspecific Territoriality, p. 421. REFS: Anon, 1990b; Beecher, 1955; Clark and Mason, 1985; Eron, 1988; Evans, 1988; Feare, 1984; Goodwin, 1978; Harwood, 1988; Pool, 1988; Power, *et al.*, 1981; Suthers, 1978; Yom-Tov *et al.*, 1974.

Rose-coloured Starling
Sturnus roseus

ATLAS 305; PMH 219; PER 190; HFP 302; HPCW 231; NESTS 313; BWP8

Ground	BLDS: ?: Monogamy	4–6 (3–9) 1 brood INCU: ♀,♂♀? 11–15	FLDG: ♂♀ 14–19	Fruit	Foliage glean

Breeding habitat Open grasslands and agricultural land, to semi-deserts (with access to water) that provide suitable nesting sites.

Displays In courtship, ♂ moves around ♀ quivering his wings and raising throat feathers; ♀ solicits by crouching.

Nesting Nests in colonies, sometimes involving thousands of birds; in cliffs, buildings, rocks, or in holes in ground; a cavity filled with grass and other plant material, lined with finer materials. Eggs pale blue, 29mm.

Diet Insects, especially grasshoppers and relatives. Takes fruit in the autumn.

Winters Migrates E to India, wintering in flocks in dry areas.

Conservation Common from Ukraine, Turkey eastwards into Asia. An irruptive species that sometimes settles to nest in large numbers well to the W of its normal range.

Essays Irruptions, p. 491.

Refs Dementiev et al. 1968.

Tristram's Grackle
Onchognathus tristramii

ATLAS 305; PMH -; PER -; HFP 302; HPCW 230; NESTS 313; BWP8

	BLDS: ? Monogamy?	3–5 2 broods INCU: ♀ 16	FLDG: ♂♀ 28–30	Seeds

Breeding habitat Rocky gullies, in semi-desert; also near farms.

Displays Pairs mutually preen.

Nesting Nest is in crevice among rocks or in a cave; fills cavity with a pile of plant debris. Eggs pale blue, sometimes with a few small brown spots, 27mm. Pairs remain together throughout year.

Diet Fruits, seeds, and insects, taken from foliage; sometimes takes ticks from hides of large mammals. Also scavenges around settlements.

Winters Resident in extreme SE corner of area, S along Red Sea. In flocks.

Conservation Increasing in Israel, with spread of settlements in desert areas.

Essays Commensal Feeding, p. 27; Black and White Plumage, p. 7.

Refs Paz 1987.

Anting

MANY songbird species, including starlings, babblers, and weavers, have been observed picking up single ants or small groups and rubbing them on their feathers. Less commonly, other songbirds — such as the Jay — 'ant' by spreading their wings and lying on an anthill, and squirming or otherwise stimulating the ants to swarm up among their feathers. The Blackbird and some other thrushes use both techniques, but not simultaneously.

The purpose of anting is not well understood, but the most reasonable assumption seems to be that it is a way of acquiring the defensive secretions of ants, primarily for their insecticidal, miticidal, fungicidal, or bactericidal properties and, perhaps secondarily, as a supplement to the bird's own preen oil. The former explanation is reinforced by a growing body of evidence on the biocidal properties of ant secretions and by observations of a Jungle Myna (*Acridotheres fuscus*) and Robins 'anting' with millipedes, which have potent defensive secretions (evolved to fend off the millipede's enemies). Furthermore, North American Common Grackles (*Quiscalus quiscula*) and Starlings have been observed to 'ant' with mothballs, spheres of naphthalene, a compound widely used as an insect repellent. Likewise, the observed correlation of anting activity with high humidity might be explained by the documented fungicidal properties of ant secretions. Because the seasonal timing of anting and moulting (spring and summer) often correspond, some have suggested that anting may soothe the skin during feather replacement. It seems more likely that the seasonal relationship simply reflects the greater activity of ants during those periods.

There are basically two styles of anting: direct, in which ants are picked up and applied to feathers (e.g., starlings, weavers); and indirect, in which the bird squats in a characteristic posture on an ant nest and allows the insects to swarm into its feathers (some crows, Jay).

SEE: Preening, p. 349; Disease and Parasitism, p. 315; Bathing and Dusting, p. 355; Head Scratching, p. 371; Tool-using, p. 459. REFS: Beattie, 1985; Clark *et al.*, 1990; Ehrlich *et al.*, 1986; Potter, 1970; Simmons, 1966, 1986.

House Sparrow
Passer domesticus

ATLAS 300; PMH 220; PER 192; HFP 298; HPCW 233; NESTS 310; BWP8

	Sphere	3–6 (2–8)	A		
		1–3 broods			
	BLDS: ♂♀	INCU: ♂♀	FLDG: ♂♀		
Shrub	Monogamy	11–14 (10–17)	14–16(12–18)		Foliage glean

Breeding habitat Mainly urban, suburban, and agricultural areas, nearly always near settlements in Europe, although migratory races in Asia occur in wider range of habitats.

Displays ♂ calls on ground or on perch and courts with tail raised and spread, wings opened slightly and quivered, and head up, exposing black bib. Several ♂s may display thus, in a group. ♀ solicits by crouching.

Nesting Nests in small colonies; may be in thick bush or ivy, but usually in a hole in a building; an untidy dome of grass lined with feathers. Eggs whitish, with dark brown and grey speckling, 22mm. Clutch size varies with latitute (larger in the N); number of clutches declines with latitude (smaller in the N; from 3–4 broods in S). Behavioural observations suggested that this species is usually monogamous. Detailed genetic studies of the young demonstrate that there is a good deal of promiscuous mating.

Diet Adults and young eat insects in the summer. At other times of year, seeds, particularly spilled grain; also takes seeds from grass heads; household waste.

Winters Resident; some Asiatic populations are migratory. In flocks.

Conservation Abundant and widespread across Europe and Asia and introduced widely elsewhere.

Essays Bathing and Dusting, p. 355; Indeterminate Egg Layers, p. 437; Polygyny, p. 265; Population Dynamics, p. 515; Selection in Nature, p. 471; Sexual Selection, p. 149; Wing Shapes and Flight, p. 269; Hormones and Nest Building, p. 329; Commensal Feeding, p. 27; Feeding Birds, p. 357; Nest Sites and Materials, p. 443.

Refs Dementiev et al. 1968; Marchant et al. 1990; Summers-Smith 1968 is a book that provides many details about this and other sparrow species.

Spanish Sparrow
Passer hispaniolensis

ATLAS 300; PMH 220; PER 192; HFP 298; HPCW 233; NESTS 309; BWP8

		4–7 (2–8)			
		2 or 3 broods			
	BLDS:♂♀,●♀	INCU: ♂♀	FLDG: ♂♀		
	Monogamy	11–14	11–15		Foliage glean

Breeding habitat Generally associated with cultivation, but includes more rural areas (such as open woodlands) than those used by House Sparrow. WIll occupy settlements where that species is absent.

Displays ♂ calls (often from beginnings of nest site) and uses displays similar to those of the House Sparrow.

Nesting In colonies in trees, often in the basement of nests of birds of prey, herons, etc. Colonies can number in the thousands. Where House Sparrow absent, will use sites typical of that species. Nests are sometimes so close together that they fuse; an untidy dome of grass lined with finer plant material. Eggs whitish, with grey to brown speckling, 23 mm.

Diet Insects important in summer and for young. At other times of year, seeds taken from ground or from grass heads, and species can be a serious pest.

Winters Resident or moves S; in fields; in flocks.

Conservation Despite name, species is widely distributed around Mediterranean and into W and C Asia.

Essays Nest Evolution, p. 345.

Refs Dementiev et al. 1968; Summers-Smith 1968.

Selection in Nature

NATURAL selection, the differential reproduction of different genetic types in a population, is the motive force in evolution. Natural selection occurs when individuals of one genotype have more offspring represented among breeders in the next generation than do individuals of another genotype. In our essays we often attempt to show how selection has shaped the physical and behavioural characteristics of birds. The effects of selection are well known from both genetic theory and laboratory experiments. It has less frequently been investigated in natural populations, but several classic studies have involved birds.

In the winter of 1898, following an unusually severe ice and snow storm, biologist H. C. Bumpus brought 136 stunned House Sparrows into his laboratory at Brown University in the United States. Seventy-two of the sparrows recovered, and 64 died. Bumpus measured both groups, and modern analyses of his measurements indicate that large males were more likely to survive than small ones, and that intermediate-sized females were more likely to survive than either large or small ones. Thus it appeared that the storm acted as a selective agent on the sparrow population.

Since Bumpus's work, population geneticists have shown how efficacious natural selection can be. Very small differentials in survival or reproduction are sufficient to account for the whole sweep of evolution — the transformation of extremely simple ancestral organisms living in the seas shortly after life originated, into House Sparrows, people, and oak trees. The reason that such small changes could lead to such big differences is that around three billion years were available for the transformation. This means that selection often occurs at undetectably slow rates. For example, if birds with a wing length of 150 mm have a 1 per cent better chance of surviving and reproducing than members of the same population with 155 mm wings, then selection pressure could, over hundreds of years, lead to shorter wing length in a population. But that differential in reproduction is small enough and that period long enough to make it virtually impossible for observers to record the measurements and reproductive success of a sufficient number of individuals to demonstrate selection at work.

This problem accounts for the relative paucity of examples in which selection has actually been documented (rather than inferred) in nature. The Bumpus case is one of the very few in which selection operating on birds has been shown. Recently though, H. Lisle Gibbs and Peter Grant have shown the action of Darwin's mechanism in a most appropriate place — in the famous Darwin's finches (*Geospiza*) of the Galápagos Islands. They showed that climatic change altered the availability of different kinds of seeds. In response, selection altered bill and body dimensions of seed-eating finches first in one direction and then in the other. In periods with very heavy rainfall small birds were more likely to survive, while drought years favoured large birds with large bills.

Dead Sea Sparrow

Passer moabiticus

ATLAS 301; PMH 255; PER -; HFP 208; HPCW 233; NESTS 310; BWP8

Dead tree	BLDS: ♂♀	4–5 (3–7) 2–3 broods INCU: ♀	 FLDG: ♂♀		
2–10m	Monogamy	11–13	14–15	Insects	

Breeding habitat In bushes and trees along water-courses in desert areas, sometimes in orchards.

Displays ♂ sings from potential nest sites, or nest of previous year. ♂ hops with head and tail raised and wings partly spread.

Nesting Nests in loose colonies, in trees (often dead ones); a large well-insulated sphere of dead twigs, with a tunnel to the inside. ♂ makes several nests before one is selected. Eggs white to buff, with heavy grey to brown spotting, 19mm. To cool the nest ♀ may bring water soaked in her feathers or bill; she may be away from the nest for up to half the daylight hours. When on nest, will shade eggs.

Diet Grass seeds, some insects taken from the ground; young fed mainly insects.

Winters Resident or moves away from breeding areas. In flocks.

Conservation Has a restricted and fragmented distribution in SW Asia, but has increased in numbers and range, from beyond the area of the Dead Sea N and S. Also spreading across S Turkey to Cyprus.

Refs Paz 1987; Summers-Smith 1968.

Desert Sparrow

Passer simplex

ATLAS 467; PMH -; PER -; HFP 298; HPCW 234; NESTS 310; BWP8

Cliff	Sphere BLDS: ♂♀	2–5(–8) 2 broods? INCU: ♂♀	FLDG: ♂♀		Ground glean
1–4m	Monogamy?	12–13	12–14	Insects	

Breeding habitat Areas of tamarisks, palms, and bushes within deserts, generally near water.

Displays Little known; ♂ hops after ♀ with open, quivering wings.

Nesting Often not colonial (see other members of genus). Nests in holes in trees or among rocks, buildings, also among branches of trees, or in base of nests of birds of prey; a large untidy dome of grass and twigs, with a tubular entrance. Eggs white with brownish or grey blotches, 19mm.

Diet Seeds; also insects, buds, and flowers. Often found in the foliage of palms etc., though commonly feeds on the ground, and will feed around towns.

Winters Resident; in small flocks, not the large flocks typical of other members of this genus.

Conservation Uncommon, occurring in scattered locations in N Africa (and isolated places in SW Asia).

Refs Summers-Smith 1968.

Several important examples of selection in nature, however, do involve birds as selective agents. In the industrial Midlands of nineteenth-century England, pollution had blackened tree trunks and killed the lichens that grew on them. Simultaneously, populations of the peppered moths in those areas changed from mostly variegated, black-and-white (peppered) individuals to mostly all-black (melanic) individuals. It has been shown that this phenomenon of 'industrial melanism' in British moths was largely the result of selective predation by birds. In the 1950s motion pictures were made by Niko Tinbergen of both kinds of moths sitting on both pollution-blackened tree trunks near factories and lichen-covered tree trunks in unpolluted countryside. The films showed clearly that Spotted Flycatchers, Nuthatches, Yellowhammers, Robins, and Song Thrushes found and ate mostly peppered moths on blackened trunks and discovered and devoured melanic moths on the lichen-covered trunks.

Also in England, biologists measured selection under natural conditions in the field by taking advantage of Song Thrushes' propensity to crack the shells of many-patterned *Cepaea* land snails against favourite rocks (thrush anvils) within their territories. By comparing samples of snail shells from around the anvils with samples of live snails, they were able to show that the thrushes were selective in their choice of prey. They found that the birds differentially ate individuals with banded shells in an area where the background was rather uniform; snails with unbanded shells were apparently better camouflaged and thus somewhat protected from detection by the birds. When the snail population lived in rough herbage, the reverse was true, and the birds found and ate more unbanded individuals.

Another demonstration that birds act as selective predators was provided in a study by ecologists Deane Bowers, Irene Brown, and Darryl Wheye. They found the remains of over 300 chalcedon checkerspot butterflies on Stanford University's Jasper Ridge Biological Preserve in central California. Most of the wings were found with characteristic triangular beak marks where they were pulled from the body before it was eaten. California Thrashers (*Toxostoma redivivum*) were apparently the main culprit. Bowers and her colleagues compared the characteristics of the variable black-red-cream checkerspot butterflies eaten by birds with those of the butterfly population at large, and found that the birds preferentially attacked individuals with less red on their wings. The reason is not certain, but red is a 'warning colour' in many distasteful insects and the birds may simply avoid the redder individuals. Such field observations suggest that the butterfly-eating birds have at least some role in determining the evolution of wing colour in their prey.

There is every reason to believe that foraging birds are important evolutionary agents, helping to shape the characteristics not only of insects and other animals they prey upon, but also of such things as seed size, fruit colour, and flower shape in certain plants.

SEE: Natural Selection, p. 297; Coevolution, p. 239; Sexual Selection, p. 149. REFS: Bowers et al., 1985; Cain and Sheppard, 1954; Ehrlich, 1986a; Ehrlich and Roughgarden, 1987; Futuyma, 1987; Gibbs and Grant, 1987; Grant and Grant, 1989; Johnston et al., 1972; Kettlewell, 1973; Parkin, 1987.

Tree Sparrow

Passer montanus

ATLAS 300; PMH 220; PER 192; HFP 298; HPCW 234; NESTS 309; BWP8

Cliff	Crevice BLDS: ♂♀ Monogamy	4–6 (2–9) 2–3 broods INCU: ♂♀ 11–14	FLDG: ♂♀ 12–17		Foliage glean

Breeding habitat In agricultural land (where it overlaps with House Sparrow); in hedgerows, woodland edges; tends to avoid suburbs. In wooded areas where cliffs provide suitable nest sites. Locally becomes the urban sparrow if House Sparrow is absent (or in parts of Asia where that species occurs mainly in agricultural areas).

Displays ♂ often sings from potential nest site. Threat posture has wings and tail raised, head forward, and bill opened. Courtship is like that of House Sparrow and may also involve groups of displaying ♂s.

Nesting Loosely colonial. Nest is in a hole in tree, cliff, or building, sometimes in open in trees; a sphere of grass, lined with feathers. Eggs buff, with heavy dark brown to grey spotting, 19mm. Young fed by parents for about 2 weeks after fledging. Colonies may appear, build up in numbers, then disappear.

Diet In breeding season, young and adults feed on insects and other invertebrates. At other times, seeds, taken from ground or plants.

Winters Resident; N populations move S, some E populations may move to W in flocks.

Conservation A major decline in the UK perhaps due to use of pesticides. Common and widespread across most of Europe, Asia, and N Africa.

Notes Unlike most other sparrows, the plumage of the sexes is essentially identical.

Essays Feeding Birds, p. 357; Swallowing Stones, p. 135.

Refs Dementiev et al. 1968; Summers-Smith 1968; Marchant et al. 1990.

Pale Rock Sparrow

Petronia brachydactyla

ATLAS 302; PMH -; PER -; HFP 300; HPCW 235; NESTS 312; BWP8

Shrub	Cup BLDS: ? Monogamy?	4–5 ? ? brood INCU: ? 14	FLDG: ? ?		Greens

Breeding habitat Arid, rocky hillsides, with scattered trees and bushes, usually near water sources.

Displays Sings from perch, sometimes in flight.

Nesting Sometimes in loose colonies; nest is in a hole in rocks, buildings, or in low bush; a small well-constructed cup. (Compare this with untidy structures of other sparrows.) Eggs white with a few dark brown spots, 19mm.

Diet Seeds, green plant parts; also some insects.

Winters NE Africa, Arabia, generally in agricultural fields.

Conservation Local in SW of the area of this guide into Iran, Afghanistan.

Essays Birds and Agriculture, p. 365.

Refs Dementiev et al. 1968.

Bird Voices

THE organ that birds use to produce vocalizations (songs and calls) is very different in location and structure from our own. The mammalian larynx is located at the top of the windpipe (trachea) and contains hard membranes (vocal cords) whose vibration as air passes is controlled by a complex of muscles and cartilage. The vocal organ of birds, in contrast, is a unique bony structure called a syrinx, which lies at the lower end of the trachea, is surrounded by the clavicular air sac, and can be deep in the breast cavity. Thus situated, the syrinx becomes a resonating chamber (the air sac may resonate also) in conjunction with highly elastic vibrating membranes. Specialized sets of syringeal muscles control the movement of the syrinx, including the tension on the membranes (which can be adjusted like the skin of a drum). Birds can vary both the intensity (loudness) and frequency (pitch) of sounds by altering the air pressure passing from the lungs to the syrinx and by varying the tension exerted by the syringeal muscles on the membranes. The attributes of song that characterize individual species of songbirds result mostly from differences in the learning process rather than from differences in the structure of the vocal apparatus.

Neurobiologist Fernando Nottebohm has shown that the two sides of the syrinx can be controlled independently, which explains the 'two-voice' phenomenon seen in sonagrams of some species: simultaneous double tones that are non-harmonically related and therefore must be derived from two independent acoustic sources. Our understanding of how the syrinx works is based on studies of only a very few species (including the domestic chicken and Mallard, which hardly typify birds in general), and many of our ideas about how the passerine syrinx functions are based on 'informed guesswork'. Recent studies by ornithologist Abbot Gaunt have clarified some of these issues and point to the overriding influence of respiratory airflow control as the key to the tremendous variation heard in passerine song.

Nottebohm and his colleagues have identified the specific regions in the brain that control song production in passerines and have demonstrated differences between the sexes in the size of these regions. The substantially smaller size of these areas in female Canaries (*Serinus canaria*) and Zebra Finches (*Poephila guttata*) is probably related to their normal lack of song. The idea that singing ability is dependent on the amount of brain space allocated to it is further supported by Nottebohm's demonstration that superior singers among male Canaries, Zebra Finches, and Marsh Wrens (*Cistothorus palustris*) have larger song control regions in their brains. In fact, Pacific Coast Marsh Wrens, which have song repertoires that are three times larger than Atlantic Coast birds, have 30–40 per cent larger song control areas in their brains.

Among species overall, there now appears to be a correlation between complexity of learned vocalizations and complexity of the forebrain, with oscine

Rock Sparrow

Petronia petronia

ATLAS 302; PMH 221; PER 182; HFP 300; HPCW 237; NESTS 311; BWP8

		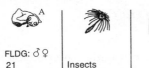		
Decid tree	Cavity BLDS: ? Monogamy	5–7 (4–8) 1 (2) broods INCU: ♂♀ 12–16	FLDG: ♂♀ 21	Insects

Breeding habitat Dry mountain areas, rocky gorges, rocky areas among agricultural fields.

Displays Very little known; has inconspicuous song.

Nesting Often in colonies; nest is in a hole in a wall, rock face, or tree, or in a burrow; a dome of grass and other plant material, lined with feathers. Eggs whitish, often heavily spotted and blotched with dark browns and greys, 22mm.

Diet Seeds, seedlings; young are fed insects.

Winters Mainly resident; in flocks.

Conservation Locally common around Mediterranean into C Asia.

Essays Bird Guilds, p. 77.

Refs Dementiev et al. 1968; Paz 1987.

Snow Finch

Montifringilla nivalis

ATLAS 303; PMH 221; PER 192; HFP 300; HPCW 237; NESTS 311; BWP8

	Burrow BLDS: ? Monogamy	4–5 (6–7) 1 (2) broods INCU: ♂♀ 13–14	FLDG: ♂♀ 21?	Insects

Breeding habitat High mountainous areas without trees or bushes; alpine tundra, rocky mountain tops, down to subalpine meadows.

Displays Very little known.

Nesting Nests in a hole or crevice among rocks, or in burrow; a cup of grass, moss, lined with feathers. Eggs white, 23mm.

Diet Seeds and some insects in the summer; forages on or near ground.

Winters Resident, though moves to lower elevations and may wander considerably in years of heavy snow.

Conservation Locally common in fragmented range from Spain to Himalayas.

Notes Occurs on 'islands' of alpine areas surrounded by a 'sea' of unsuitable lowland habitats. Consequently, population changes and distribution have much in common with species on real islands – see essay on Island Biogeography, p. 303.

Refs Dementiev et al. 1968.

songbirds and parrots possessing the most complex forebrain machinery. It is clear that voice production itself requires the close neural integration and control of both syringeal movement and respiration.

SEE: Vocal Development, p. 479; Sonagrams: Seeing Bird Songs, p. 307; Adaptations for Flight, p. 511; What Do Birds Hear?, p. 255; Vocal Copying, p. 383. REFS: Brackenbury, 1982; Gaunt, 1988; Gaunt and Gaunt, 1985; Konishi, 1985; Nottebohm, 1989; Nowicki and Capranica, 1986; Seller, 1988.

Vocal Dialects

JUST as our own speech patterns vary regionally, the songs of many avian species also show geographic variation. Although these regional differences are quite evident to the human ear, we still recognize the singer as a member of the species in question.

The songs of populations can differ markedly on a rather small geographic scale. Chaffinches in adjacent Scottish glens sound different. Such local variants are called dialects and are found commonly in songbirds with populations restricted to particular habitats and separated from other populations by unsuitable terrain. The separation can be on the order of a few kilometres, but in some species it can be much less. Among White-crowned Sparrow (*Zonotrichia leucophrys*) populations of coastal California, distinct dialects may be separated by as little as a few metres in what appears to be essentially continuous habitat!

Vocal dialects apparently are learned. Young birds hear the songs sung around their natal territories by their fathers and neighbouring males, and acquire the peculiarities of these renditions. Factors that determine the geographic pattern of dialects include the accuracy with which the pitch and temporal characteristics of individual song components are learned, the distance young males disperse from where they hatch to where they breed, and the timing of dispersal relative to the sensitive period for learning.

The 'why' of dialects, their functional significance, has proven more elusive than the question of how they arise. Many ornithologists have assumed that dialects serve as indicators of genetic adaptation to local conditions. The dialects thus enable females to choose males from their own birth area, who presumably are carrying genes closely adapted to the specific environment in which breeding occurs. In other words, dialects function to promote 'positive assortative mating' — the breeding together of similar individuals. Experimental work with several species (e.g. Corn Bunting) has shown that males or females (or both) are more responsive to their own song dialects than to more distant song dialects. Studies of White-crowned Sparrows along the coast of northern California have shown genetic differences between birds of different dialects.

Chaffinch

Fringilla coelebs

ATLAS 286; PMH 223; PER 194; HFP 284; HPCW 241; NESTS 299; BWP8

| Shrub 2–4m (15m) | BLDS: ♀ Monogamy | 4–5 (2–8) 1–2 broods INCU: ♀ 11–13 | FLDG: ♂♀ 12–15 | | Foliage glean |

Breeding habitat Widespread in almost any area with trees or bushes.

Displays Sings from tree or in flight. In courtship chases, ♂ flies close behind ♀. ♂ courts ♀ with drooped and fluttering wings, may perch erect with elevated crest, turn side to side exposing wing patches.

Nesting Nest is in a fork of a tree or bush; a neatly woven cup of grass, fibres, often decorated with lichens, and lined with hair, feathers, and softer materials. Eggs pale blue with dark brown spots which are sometimes large and blurred, 20mm. Young fed by both parents for several days after fledging.

Diet Insects in summer, seeds and berries rest of year; taken on ground or from foliage.

Winters Resident across much of Europe, migrates S and SW from NE; in flocks near forest edge and in agricultural fields.

Conservation One of the most common European birds, one of the most widely distributed, and probably the most common British bird. See Wren and Blackbird.

Notes Absent from some Scottish islands and only recently nested Iceland: see essay on Island Biogeography, p. 303.

Essays Interspecific Territoriality, p. 421; Bird-brained, p. 385; Dominance Hierarchies, p. 131; Bird Guilds, p. 77; Commensal Feeding, p. 27; Feeding Birds, p. 357; Sleeping Sentries and Mate-guarding, p. 73; Birds and Agriculture, p. 365; Adaptations for Flight, p. 511; Diet And Nutrition, p. 493; Vocal Development, p. 479; Breeding Site Tenacity, p. 219.

Refs Dementiev et al. 1968; Marchant et al. 1990.

Brambling

Fringilla montifringilla

ATLAS 285; PMH 223; PER 194; HFP 284; HPCW 241; NESTS 299; BWP8

| Conif tree 2–10m | BLDS: ♀ Monogamy | 6–7 (4–9) 1 (2 ?) broods INCU: ♀ 11–12 | FLDG: ♂♀ 11–13 | | Foliage glean |

Breeding habitat Mainly northern birch woods, edges of coniferous woodland.

Displays Similar to those of Chaffinch.

Nesting Nest is in a tree (often birch or conifer); like that of Chaffinch in forked branches; a neat cup of grass, etc., surfaced with lichens and strips of bark, and lined with softer materials. Eggs, like those of the Chaffinch; light greenish or bluish, with dark red-brown spots and blotches, 19mm.

Diet Insects in summer, seeds in winter; taken on the ground or from foliage.

Winters Over most of Europe; feeds in a wider range of habitats than in summer, especially beech woods, edges of fields; in flocks. Often depends on beech mast and concentrates where it is abundant.

Conservation Common and widespread across N Europe, Asia to Pacific; isolated populations in Scotland, Alps.

Essays Declines in Forest Birds: Europe and America, p. 339; Bird Guilds, p. 77.

Refs Dementiev et al. 1968; von Haartman 1969.

But nature is rarely that straightforward. Additional work has shown that females of some species are more responsive to songs of males with dialects other than their own, so that the assumption that a female breeds within the dialect region in which she was hatched is not always warranted. Further complicating the picture is the fact that males of many species disperse and settle to breed outside their natal dialect area where they learn and adopt the songs of their territorial neighbours, thus actually changing their own dialects! Such a system is now known for Redwings and Thrush Nightingales.

Perhaps most confounding is a series of experiments in which paired female White-crowned Sparrows were captured on their territories and injected with the male hormone testosterone (to induce singing). Surprisingly, they sang the song of nearby dialects, rather than their own local dialect. Presumably this indicates that they had chosen to mate with males from 'foreign' dialects and had dispersed out of their native dialect region. In addition, re-analysis of the genetic data from the White-crowned Sparrow studies has demonstrated that the results may be attributable to other factors. The data could be interpreted as indicating that environments are as heterogeneous within a dialect region as they are between dialect areas. If so, one might expect to find as much genetic differentiation between groups living in dramatically different habitats within a dialect region as between different dialects.

Thus, the adaptive significance of dialects remains to be demonstrated. It may be that no selective force has acted to promote dialects. Instead, dialects may be 'epiphenomena' that have arisen simply as a consequence of vocal learning, and may have no evolutionary significance.

See: Vocal Development, p. 479; Vocal Functions, p. 413; Vocal Copying, p. 383; Hybridization, p. 461; What Do Birds Hear? p. 255; Sonagrams: Seeing Bird Songs, p. 307. Refs: Espmark et al., 1989; Kroodsma et al., 1985; McGregor, 1983; Mundinger, 1982; Slater, 1986; Sorjonen, 1988.

Vocal Development

With practice, most birdwatchers learn to identify many species by their characteristic calls and songs. What are the underlying mechanisms that lead to 'standardized' repertoires for each species? Are these characteristic sounds learned or are they genetically determined and fixed without learning (innate)? Where learning is involved, when does it take place? And how does each species 'know' which sounds are appropriate and should be learned? The answers to these questions are as varied as birds themselves and have

Red-fronted Serin

Serinus pusillis

ATLAS 288; PMH 256; PER -; HFP 292; HPCW 241; NESTS 305; BWP8

Shrub

BLDS: ?
Monogamy?

3–5
2 broods
INCU: ♀
14

^A
FLDG: ♂♀
15–17

Foliage glean

Breeding habitat Scrub on rocky hillsides, often near water, to high elevations.

Displays Several ♂s may sing near each other from exposed perches; spread wings and tail, move about and circle around other rivals.

Nesting Nests in a crevice, hole among rocks, or low in bush; a cup of grass etc., with a lining of finer material. Eggs whitish to light blue with a few scattered pinkish to brown spots and scribbles, 17mm. Young remain with adults (mainly ♂) for about a week after leaving nest.

Diet Insects in summer; at other times, seeds of alpine plants, pine, cypress, alders, birch; taken from ground or foliage.

Winters Mainly resident, though moves to lower elevations, valleys, some move S; in flocks.

Conservation Common from Turkey to Himalayas.

Refs Dementiev et al. 1968.

Serin

Serinus serinus

ATLAS 287; PMH 223; PER 194; HFP 292; HPCW 242; NESTS 306; BWP8

2–5m

BLDS: ♀
Monogamy?

4 (3–5)
2 broods
INCU: ♂♀
13

^A
FLDG: ♂♀
13–17

Insects

Ground glean

Breeding habitat A variety of open woodland, parks, gardens to above tree line.

Displays ♂ sings from top of tree or in song flight like that of the Greenfinch.

Nesting Sometimes in loose colonies. Nest is in thick foliage, in forked branches of a tree, or at end of branches; a cup of grass, etc., lined with finer materials, such as hair. Eggs pale blue, with fine dark brown spotting, 17mm. Young fed by adults for about a week after leaving nest.

Diet Seeds of weeds, and trees such as alder and birch; also insects.

Winters Around Mediterranean; in small flocks.

Conservation Common. Has spread N from around Mediterranean to much of continent; benefits from its ability to use gardens. Occurs over much of continental Europe to N Africa and Turkey.

Notes Breeds in the UK only sporadically (1–5 pairs), despite its occurrence in adjacent areas on the continent and despite its ability to utilize a wide range of habitats – see essay on Island Biogeography, p. 303.

Essays Bird Voices, p. 475; Vocal Development, p. 479.

Refs Paz 1987; Marchant et al. 1990.

long served as a focus of research by ornithologists, ethologists, and neuro-biologists.

Most of this research has been concerned with song development in species of songbirds, but relatively few species have been examined in detail. Most songbirds must learn at least part of their song repertoire. What little we know of vocal development in non-passerines indicates that calls of those species (Mallard, American Coot, Ring-billed and Franklin's Gulls, domestic chicken, and Ringed Turtle Dove) are innate rather than learned, and that precocial young tend to have larger, better-developed repertoires of calls than do altricial young. Two exceptions among non-passerines are hummingbirds and parrots, for which there is evidence of vocal learning. Studies of many groups have yet to be done.

The learning of songs is a gradual process that takes place over a period of weeks or months. Typically, a vague, jumbled 'subsong' appears first which then gradually is transformed into a more structured, but still quite variable, 'plastic song'. The end point of this process is the production of a stable repertoire of 'crystallized' songs. Much more material may be developed than is actually needed for the eventual crystallized repertoire, leading to a process of attrition as the mature song takes shape. Chaffinches, for example, gener-ate several times more song material during development than they eventually express in the adult repertoire.

The most thorough studies of song development, pioneered by ethologists W. H. Thorpe and Peter Marler, involve detailed experimental procedures using birds that have been isolated in soundproof chambers as hatchlings or nestlings. The development of songs and calls can then be followed in these birds, which have been deprived of any chance to hear the normal song of their species. In most species that have been examined, the resulting songs bear only a slight resemblance to normal songs, and are not recognized by others of the same species. Isolated birds allowed to hear the singing attempts of other isolates form better, but still imperfect, songs, whereas isolates allowed to hear normal song during their 'sensitive phase' (the limited period during which song-learning can take place) develop normal songs.

Studies of song-learning have led to the 'auditory template hypothesis' — the idea that each species is born with a neurological model of what its song should sound like and develops that song by matching sounds that it hears with the template in its brain. This process enables a young bird to filter out inappropriate sounds and to produce sounds matching the template, which are then stored for future use when breeding the following spring. Recent neurological studies of young male Zebra Finches (an Australian species that is much used in laboratory studies of vocal development), have found an increase in brain cell production during the sensitive phase when song acquisition and development occur.

The template model is exemplified by studies of young White-crowned Sparrows (*Zonotrichia leucophrys*), which manifest a sensitive period for song acquisition roughly from day 10 until day 50 after hatching. Around day 150 they begin to practise what they have learned, and by day 200 they have

Tristram's Serin

Serinus syriacus

ATLAS 288; PMH -; PER -; HFP 292; HPCW 242; NESTS 305; BWP8

Shrub

BLDS: ?
Monogamy?

4
2 (3) broods
INCU: ?
?

FLDG: ?
?

?

Breeding habitat   Cedars and junipers on mountain slopes.

Displays   Sings from perch.

Nesting   Nests in trees and bushes. Eggs whitish to very pale blue with a few red-brown spots towards the larger end, 17mm. Moves to higher elevations for second brood.

Diet   Very little known about diet or feeding methods; often seen perching in trees, but known to feed on the ground.

Winters   Disperses away from nesting areas into more open habitats, in large noisy flocks.

Conservation   Common in extremely limited range in Middle East.

Notes   Sometimes called the Syrian Serin.

Refs   Paz 1987.

Citril Finch

Serinus citrinella

ATLAS 288; PMH 224; PER 194; HFP 292; HPCW 242; NESTS 306; BWP8

3–7m

BLDS: ♀
Monogamy?

4–5 (3–)
1 (2?) broods
INCU: ♀
13–14

FLDG: ♂♀
17–18

Insects

Ground glean

Breeding habitat   Open coniferous forest (mainly spruce) on mountain sides, in SW Europe.

Displays   Sings from top of trees or in Siskin-like song flight, circling over territory.

Nesting   Nest is in a tree; a small cup of grasses, lined with softer materials. Eggs greyish-white, with a few fine dark brown and purple spots, 16mm.

Diet   Seeds of firs, spruce, some insects; feeds in foliage, or on ground.

Winters   Mainly resident, but moves to lower elevations in winter; in small flocks.

Conservation   Has limited range in SW Europe.

Notes   The distribution of this species is quite curious – it is a species of southern montane coniferous forests. Unlike other species in these habitats, it does not occur in coniferous forests in the N of Europe. See notes for Three-toed Woodpecker, p. 294.

Essays   Nest Lining, p. 439; Nest Evolution, p. 345.

developed a stable 'crystallized' song that matches parts of the song heard during their sensitive phase. Song-learning is selective, so that if offered a choice, birds will learn their own species' song. If offered only songs of other species or if reared in isolation, learning does not occur and only a simplified approximation to the normal song develops. The importance of auditory feedback was shown by birds that were experimentally deafened after exposure to normal song during the sensitive phase but prior to day 150. Such birds failed to develop anything melodic. In contrast, birds deafened after their own song had crystallized will continue to sing normally. In essence, vocal learning appears to consist of two phases: (1) exposure to and memorization of species-specific sounds by matching them to the template during a sensitive period, and (2) production of those sounds.

In some species, the social bonds to the song tutor (often the male parent) have been shown to be important in determining which vocalizations are copied by young birds. Typical of such species might be the Nightingale which requires visual as well as vocal interaction with song tutors to learn songs fully. In contrast to White-crowned Sparrows, male Zebra Finches do not learn from birds with whom they cannot interact socially. In fact, young Zebra Finches learn preferentially from males that act aggressively toward them! Thus the social context and interactions with potential tutors during a young male's sensitive phase may be critical elements in determining the composition of a male's eventual song repertoire.

We know that the duration and timing of the sensitive phase varies among species, from those with song acquisition limited to their first few months following hatching to species (such as Canaries and Greenfinches) that continue to incorporate new songs and song elements into their repertoires beyond their first breeding season. Long-term studies of Great Tits in England have demonstrated that territorial males learn songs beyond their second year by copying new songs from newly-settled territorial neighbours. As additional long-term field studies are conducted on individually identifiable birds, many more species may be shown to possess the ability to alter their repertoires over time and replace song components each breeding season.

SEE: Vocal Dialects, p. 477; Vocal Functions, p. 413; Vocal Copying, p. 383; What Do Birds Hear?, p. 255; Bird Voices, p. 475; Parent–Chick Recognition in Colonial Nesters, p. 227. REFS: Kroodsma, 1982; Marler, 1984; McGregor and Krebs, 1989; Nordeen and Nordeen, 1990; Slater *et al.*, 1988.

Greenfinch
Carduelis chloris

ATLAS 290; PMH 224; PER 194; HFP 286; HPCW 244; NESTS 301; BWP8

Shrub 1–3m	BLDS: ♀ Monogamy?	4–6 (3–7) 2 (3) broods INCU: ♀ 12–14	FLDG: ♂♀ 13–17		Foliage glean

Breeding habitat A variety of open country with some bushes and trees, forest edges, hedgerows, gardens.

Displays ♂ sings from high perch and then, singing, flies up in erratic, bat-like flight, flapping wings slowly, and glides down to another perch.

Nesting Sometimes in loose colonies of up to 6 pairs. Nest is in forked branches or against tree trunk, sometimes in thick bush; a large cup of grass, etc. lined with softer materials. Eggs bluish-white, with a few dark brown to black spots, 21mm. ♂ may look after young while ♀ starts another clutch.

Diet Insects in summer (and fed to young); seeds, fruit at other times. In the

UK exploits agricultural crops (cereals, oil-seed rape, root, and vegetable crops) and has larger clutch sizes in these areas.

Winters Resident; N populations move S. In more open areas, including agricultural fields, often in small flocks.

Conservation Some local increases and decreases. Common across most of Europe into W Asia and N Africa.

Essays Birds and Agriculture, p. 365; Mixed-species Flocking, p. 429; Feeding Birds, p. 357; Vocal Copying, p. 383; Vocal Development, p. 479.

Refs Dementiev et al. 1968; Marchant et al. 1990; Sharrock 1976.

Goldfinch
Carduelis carduelis

ATLAS 289; PMH 225; PER 194; HFP 286; HPCW 244; NESTS 300; BWP8

Shrub 4–10m	BLDS:♀,♂♥ Monogamy?	4–6 (3–7) 2–3 broods INCU: ♀ 12–14	FLDG: ♂♀ 12–15	

Breeding habitat A range of open country with bushes and trees, forest clearings, gardens.

Displays ♂ sings from tree or in flight; courts ♀ swaying his body from side to side, expanding wings exposing gold coloured feathers.

Nesting Nest is on outermost twigs of tree branch; or in thick bush; a tidy cup of grass, etc., lined with softer materials. Eggs bluish-white, with a few fine dark brown spots and streaks, sometimes unmarked, 18mm. Young depend on adults for about 1 week after leaving nest.

Diet In summer, young and adults feed mainly on insects. At other times, seeds, particularly teasels and thistles, also birch, alder, usually taken from plants, rather than ground.

Winters Resident in S and W, moves to these areas from NE. Perhaps 80 per cent of UK population moves to France, Iberia. In more open areas than in summer.

Conservation In the UK declined in 19th century because of bird catchers – it was a popular cage bird. Recovered in this century, but with major declines in 1980s, probably due to use of herbicides to control weeds, the seeds of which form an important part of its diet. Common across Europe into N Africa and W Asia.

Essays Birds and Agriculture, p. 365; Songbird Foraging, p. 417; Hormones and Nest Building, p. 329.

Refs Dementiev et al. 1968; Marchant et al. 1990; Sharrock 1976.

Bird Droppings

'DROPPINGS' is a term ornithologists use to describe the excrement of birds because, unlike mammalian faeces, it includes both kidney products and alimentary wastes. Bird droppings, of course, vary: those of granivores are very hard and finely ground, those of frugivores are minimally cemented, and those of insectivores change consistency with the relative proportions of soft- and hard-bodied insects taken. Droppings also vary in their effect on the local community. Small amounts may go more or less unnoticed but in the Arctic, for example, the droppings of Snowy Owls, hawks, Gyrfalcons and other birds that perch on rocks provide a nutrient layer necessary for the growth of some lichens. Large accumulations, however, may be destructive, causing outbreaks of disease and killing plants. Accumulations in the now extinct Passenger Pigeon (*Ectopistes migratorius*) nesting colonies were thick enough to destroy the forest understory. Extensive local accumulations, as in the case of guano deposits, provide humanity with a resource that can be mined for use as fertilizer.

Some species are known to swallow the faecal sacs of their young thus gaining additional nutritional return for their foraging efforts. Like rabbits, certain birds reputedly recycle their own excrement. Some species are suspected of recycling the excrement of other birds, but reports such as those of Coots feeding on goose and gull droppings are generally anecdotal — the observations have not been made systematically. On the other hand, reports of seabirds using their excrement to 'dive bomb' a pirating foe or a predator at the nesting colony are true. Lesser Black-backed Gulls are particularly vicious in this respect. There are also claims that droppings are used to cement in place nests situated on windswept sites.

It was once thought that concentrations of waterfowl droppings were detrimental to farming, and flocks were discouraged from congregating in pastureland. The droppings, however, do little if any harm to forage or to grazing livestock, and their mineral load may be of value to plants and herbivores alike. The excrement of domestic birds, in fact, has several markets. Experiments using both poultry litter and conventional fertilizer in land reclamation around old coal mines have shown comparable germination rates for grass seeds. In another application, the replacement of up to 25 per cent (by volume) of sheep and cattle feed with chicken droppings has been shown to be a nutritionally sound practice.

Bird droppings are implicated in one human disease, histoplasmosis, a non-contagious respiratory ailment. Histoplasmosis is caused by the airborne spores of a fungus, *Histoplasma capsulatum*, that thrives in acid-rich soils fertilized by the droppings of chickens, Starlings, and other birds that closely associate with people. The elimination of massive flocks has been part of histoplasmosis control programmes.

Siskin

Carduelis spinus

ATLAS 290; PMH 225; PER 196; HFP 286; HPCW 245; NESTS 301; BWP8

10+m	BLDS: ♀ Monogamy?	3–6 (2–) 2 broods INCU: ♀ 11–14	FLDG: ♂♀ 13–15	Insects	

Breeding habitat Coniferous woodland, especially spruce, and birch forests.

Displays ♂ sings from top of tree or in song flight, as bird flutters into air, with exaggerated wing-beats, raising wings to almost touch above back; circles high above forest. In courtship ♂ may chase ♀ into air through trees, landing near her with wings drooped and quivering and breast feathers ruffled.

Nesting Nest is often high in a conifer at end of a branch; a small cup of grass, moss, and twigs, with a covering of lichens, lined with soft materials. Eggs whitish to pale blue, with a few lilac to red-brown spots, blotches around larger end, 16mm. ♂ feeds incubating ♀.

Diet Seeds of spruce, pine, grasses; other trees in winter, young also fed on insects. Feeds mainly from foliage, rather than the ground.

Winters Over much of Europe, moving SW in response to hard weather; in riverside alders, birches, in flocks often with Redpolls. Gardens may be locally an important habitat in winter. Large fluctuations in numbers, and is irruptive when seed crops fail.

Conservation Expanding in UK (towards S), as Sitka Spruce is planted over large areas. Common across much of Europe into Asia.

Essays Declines in Forest Birds: Europe and America, p. 339; Irruptions, p. 491.

Refs von Haartman 1969.

Linnet

Acanthis cannabina

ATLAS 291; PMH 225; PER 196; HFP 290; HPCW 245; NESTS 304; BWP8

1–3m	BLDS: ♀ Monogamy?	4–6 (7) 2–3 broods INCU: ♂♀ 10–14	FLDG: ♂♀ 11–17		

Breeding habitat Open country with scattered bushes, hedges, gorse, gardens.

Displays ♂ sings from high perch or circles territory, gliding down to new perch.

Nesting Sometimes in loose colonies of 4–6 pairs. Nest is in a thick bush, especially gorse; a large cup of grass and other vegetation, lined with softer materials. Eggs pale blue, with a few pink to red-brown spots and blotches, 18mm.

Diet Insects in the summer and fed to young. At other times, seeds,

particularly of weedy species. Feeds mainly on the ground.

Winters Resident; NE populations move SW; UK birds move to France and Iberia; in flocks on agricultural land .

Conservation A steep decline in the UK, Netherlands, Denmark, Finland, and probably elsewhere. In the UK, nest success and both summer and winter survival is lower now than in the past, probably because of herbicide and insecticide use. Common and widespread in Europe to Asia, N Africa.

Essays Birds and Agriculture, p. 365.

Refs Dementiev et al. 1968; Marchant et al. 1990.

Effective control programmes may also be critical for the timber industry. Entire plots in plantations may be damaged or killed by salts leaching from accumulated droppings of Starlings, Blackbirds, and other communally roosting birds. Foresters are presently trying to develop simple management practices that move the birds frequently enough from plot to plot to convert the problem into an asset.

Accumulated nitrogen- and phosphate-rich droppings at the sites of some large, perennial seabird colonies, particularly those along the South American Humboldt Current have long been mined. 'Guano' is the Spanish form of the Peruvian (Quechua Indian) word for the droppings of fish-eating seabirds, and 'guano birds' include cormorants, pelicans and boobies of that region. Along with our harvest of ocean fish and shell-fish, fish-eating seabirds play a crucial role in returning phosphorus to the land to complete its cycle. Nitrogen can exist as a gaseous compound and returns from sea to land via the atmosphere, but phosphorus cannot and has no easy return route after it is washed from the land.

SEE: Starlings, p. 463; Disease and Parasitism, p. 315; Parental Care, p. 171; Seabird Nesting Sites, p. 233; Communal Roosting, p. 81. REFS: Anderson and Braun, 1985; Boot, 1987; Bristow, 1989; Crockett and Hansley, 1977; Hardy, 1978; Lawes and Kenwood, 1970; Marriott, 1973.

Hatching

THE hard shell of a bird's egg is composed of a protein matrix in which a heavy deposit of calcium carbonate (largely) and other minerals is laid down. It is marvellously adapted to bear the weight of the incubating parent, conserve moisture, permit the exchange of gases, and resist the attacks of some predators. But it presents the developed chick with the problem of how to get out.

The chick solves the problem with two devices. It grows an 'egg tooth' at the end of the upper mandible, and it develops powerful 'hatching muscles' on the back of its head and neck. As hatching nears, the chick swallows much of the remaining liquid in the egg, and pulls the remaining membrane-wrapped yolk into its abdomen. It then works its head into the airspace in the egg (formed by evaporation of liquids from the egg and their absorption by the chick), where it can breathe air and peep. Finally, by contracting the hatching muscles the chick forces the egg tooth against the shell, making the first hole in the haven that has become its prison. With the use of its head and legs the breakout is completed. Soon after hatching, the egg tooth drops or wears off, and the hatching muscles atrophy. In some species, such as the Black Guillemot, the egg tooth may last several weeks.

From the first starring of the eggshell to emergence of the chick requires a few hours to several days, depending on the species. Albatrosses are the

Twite
Acanthis flavirostris

ATLAS 291; PMH 226; PER 196; HFP 290; HPCW 245; NESTS 304; BWP8

| Shrub | BLDS: ♀ Monogamy | 5–6 (4–7) 1–2 broods INCU: ♀ 12–13 | FLDG: ♂♀ ? | Insects | Foliage glean |

Breeding habitat Moorland, rough open country, alpine meadows (to high elevations in Asia).

Displays ♂ sings from rocks, bushes or in flight; in courtship exposes its pink rump.

Nesting Sometimes in loose colonies; nest is on ground, in a small bush, or in heather; a cup of grass, etc. lined with softer materials. Eggs like those of the Linnet, though more likely to have scrawls, 17mm. ♂ feeds ♀ while she is incubating.

Diet Seeds, also insects in summer, gathered from ground or low foliage.

Winters Moves to lower areas, often coastal fields, in NW. In flocks.

Conservation In the UK is probably decreasing as upland areas are planted in forests. Locally common in NW.

Notes The NW population is isolated from montane populations from Turkey to Himalayas. This species shows a distribution pattern that suggests it was more widespread when the climate was much colder. It has now retreated to geographically separated upland and northern areas. See notes about the Three-toed Woodpecker, p. 294.

Essays Birds and Global Warming, p. 311.

Refs Marchant et al. 1990.

Redpoll
Acanthis flammea

ATLAS 291; PMH 226; PER 196; HFP 290; HPCW 246; NESTS 303; BWP8

| Shrub 0.5–4m | BLDS: ♀ Monogamy? | 4–5 (3–7) 1–2 broods INCU: ♀ 10–14 | FLDG: ♂♀ 11–14 |  |

Breeding habitat Open northern or montane woodlands of birch, alder, mixed conifers.

Displays ♂ sings from perch or while looping or circling over territory, with jerky wing-beats, glides; courts ♀ with tail spread and wings raised above back.

Nesting Sometimes in loose colonies. Nest is in a small tree, bush, or on ground; a small cup of grass etc. lined with softer materials. Eggs like those of the Linnet; pale blue, with a few lilac to brown spots, blotches, or scrawls, 17mm.

Diet In summer, insects (also fed to young). At other times, seeds, especially birch, spruce, as well as those of shrubs, often extracting them acrobatically from ends of twigs.

Winters Resident in S; N populations move S over most of Europe; often in

alders along rivers, birches; in flocks. N populations may be irruptive.

Conservation Some breeding populations fluctuate greatly from year to year depending on the size of the birch seed crop. In the UK increased dramatically until 1976, then decreased by 50 per cent. Common across N Europe, Asia, N America, with fragmented populations in mountainous areas further S. Has spread so much on continent that alpine and other populations may no longer be isolated (see notes about Twite above).

Essays Nest Lining, p. 439; Irruptions, p. 491; Winter Feeding by Redpolls and Crossbills, p. 489.

Refs Dementiev et al. 1968; Marchant et al. 1990; von Haartman 1969.

record holders. Their chicks may take as many as six days to hatch. In most species hatching tends to occur in the morning, possibly because it allows time for feeding before nightfall. It appears that the alternation of day and night is perceived within the egg, thus permitting the chick to hatch at the best possible time.

SEE: Eggs and Their Evolution, p. 317; Incubation Time, p. 121; Incubation: Controlling Egg Temperatures, p. 273; Life in the Egg, p. 447.

Winter Feeding by Redpolls and Crossbills

ONE of the most important adaptations enabling redpolls and crossbills to cope with the energy demands imposed by severe arctic and subarctic winters is a structure that is somewhat analogous to the substantial crop of gallinaceous birds. The structure is a partially bilobed pocket situated about midway down the neck, technically an 'oesophageal diverticulum'. The pocket is used to store seeds, especially toward nightfall and during particularly severe weather. The 'extra' food helps carry the bird through low night-time temperatures and permits energy to be saved during bad weather by reducing foraging time and allowing the bird to 'feed' while resting in a sheltered spot.

Redpolls in winter feed primarily on birch seeds, and the presence of an oesophageal diverticulum permits feeding behaviour consisting of three distinct phases. In phase I, the birds acrobatically knock seeds from the birch catkins to the ground below. In phase II they gather the seeds from the often snow-covered ground and store them in their diverticula. The birds can then fly to a sheltered spot (phase III) where they are better protected from predators and where they can regurgitate, shell, and consume the seeds, which are exceptionally high in calories, at their leisure. In phase III, redpolls and crossbills seek the wind-protected shelter of dense conifers, remain stationary, and adopt a 'fluffed-ball' posture that further reduces heat loss.

Redpolls apparently are able to survive colder temperatures, down to −67 °C than any other songbirds that have been studied in detail. Large birds, of course, have a great advantage in saving heat because they have a relatively small surface area for their volume. Birds as large as Willow Grouse and as small as Snow Buntings may burrow into loose snow to sleep. Sixty centimetres down in the snow the temperature can be −4 °C when the air above the snow is colder than −45 °C. But neither a large bird nor a small one can survive long in an arctic or subarctic winter without an ample supply of food.

SEE: Feeding Birds, p. 357; Irruptions, p. 491; Temperature Regulation and Behaviour, p. 163; Metabolism, p. 281; Swallowing Stones, p. 135. REF.: Brooks, 1978.

Arctic Redpoll

Acanthis hornemanni

ATLAS 292; PMH 227; PER 196; HFP 290; HPCW -; NESTS 304; BWP8

Ground 1–2m	BLDS: ♀ Monogamy	5 (4–6) 1 (2?) broods INCU: ♀ 11–12	FLDG: ♂♀ 10–14	Ground glean

Breeding habitat Open tundra with small shrubs or trees.

Displays Like those of Redpoll.

Nesting Nest is in bush or on ground; a small cup of vegetation, with finer lining. Eggs similar to those of Redpoll, 18mm.

Diet Seeds, especially birch and alder; taken from terminal twigs, low bushes, or ground.

Winters Resident or moves S.

Conservation Locally common across arctic of Europe, Asia, N America.

Essays Nest Lining, p. 439; Winter Feeding by Redpolls and Crossbills, p. 489.

Refs Dementiev et al. 1968.

Two-barred Crossbill

Loxia leucoptera

ATLAS 293; PMH 227; PER 198; HFP 296; HPCW -; NESTS 308; BWP8

	BLDS: ? Monogamy	3–4 (5) 1 (2) broods INCU: ? ?	FLDG: ? ?		Ground glean

Breeding habitat Coniferous forests, especially larch.

Displays Continuous flight song as ♂ slowly beats wings while circling over ♀

Nesting Nest is high in tree among its branches; a small cup of twigs, etc., with a lining of grass and other softer materials. Eggs pale bluish-white, with a few dark purple spots and blotches, 24mm.

Diet Mainly larch and spruce seeds, extracted from the cones in the tree, and commonly from fallen cones.

Winters Resident or irruptive if food supply fails, to SW of range.

Conservation In Finland (W end or range) varies in numbers from one of the 10 most common species in coniferous forest, to being absent. Locally common from NE Europe across Asia into N America.

Essays Irruptions, p. 491; Winter Feeding by Redpolls and Crossbills, p. 489.

Notes Also called White-winged Crossbill.

Irruptions

SOUTHWARD autumn invasions (irruptions) by normally northern seed-eating birds are dramatic but apparently irregular events. Irruptive European species include Pine Grosbeak, Redpoll, Arctic Redpoll, Nutcracker, Jay, Great Spotted Woodpecker, Brambling, and Great, Coal, and Willow Tits. Aside from the redpolls, these species are widespread across Europe so that a change in their usual wintering numbers is not always dramatically noticeable. The species perhaps best associated with irruptive movements by their conspicuousness in regions well away from their normal wintering areas, are the Crossbill, Two-barred Crossbill, and Waxwing. The Rose-coloured Starling is another distinctive species that undergoes such movements when it appears in portions of Europe well west of its normal wintering range. These irruptive movements raise three major questions: What causes them? Are they really irregular events? Are they synchronized among populations within a species and between species?

Ornithologists generally concur that irruptions are triggered by food shortages, such as failure of coniferous cone crops over a large geographic area. Analyses of systematic North American winter counts (Audubon Christmas Counts) indicate that synchronous failure of seed crops in some high-latitude tree species leads to southward irruptions of species normally dependent on those seeds. Such failures often extend across the boreal zones of Europe and Asia as well, and are reflected by irruptions of high latitude birds into Europe in the same years as irruptions occur in North America.

Years of good seed crops, which presumably result in higher population densities of seed-eating birds, are often followed by years with poor crops. Thus, in a year of crop failure that follows one of abundant seeds, bird populations may be larger than normal. This increases pressure on scarce food resources and serves as additional impetus to migrate. It appears, then, that a poor seed crop is the primary cause of irruptions and that large population sizes may sometimes be a contributing factor. However, because many other factors (such as insect abundance during the breeding season) can affect population density in any given year, not all species will be affected synchronously by a seed crop failure.

Diurnal and nocturnal raptors that feed on small mammals with cyclic population fluctuations constitute another group of irruptive species whose food supply fluctuates from year to year in boreal regions. Among European species, Rough-legged Buzzard, Goshawk, and both Snowy and Short-eared Owls are known to irrupt periodically. Two main cycles are recognized in boreal small mammals: a four-year cycle among tundra and grassland rodents, and a ten-year cycle that characterizes snowshoe hares. Why populations of these species explode and crash with these approximate periodicities is not clear, but when they crash the predictable result is a southward irruption of

Crossbill

Loxia curvirostra

ATLAS 293; PMH 227; PER 198; HFP 296; HPCW 246; NESTS 307; BWP8

2–20m	BLDS: ♀ Monogamy	3–4 (2–5) 1 brood INCU: ♀ 13–16	FLDG: ♂♀ 16–25	Insects

Breeding habitat Coniferous forest, especially spruce, though will nest in pines in UK following irruptions.

Displays ♂ sings from exposed perch, sometimes in flight.

Nesting Will breed throughout year if food supplies permit, but generally in late winter (eggs in February - April) when spruce seeds are most available. Nests may be close together but ♂ defends nesting tree. Nest is in top of tree, usually sheltered by overhanging branch; a small cup of twigs, grasses lined with finer material. Eggs very pale blue, with purplish spots and scrawls, 22mm. Young depend on adults for 3–4 weeks after leaving nest; their bills do not become fully crossed for some time and they are unable to extract seeds efficiently.

Diet Conifer seeds extracted from cones. Insects fed to young.

Winters Resident, but irruptive across Europe when food supply fails.

Conservation Has wide though irregular distribution in the UK (including Scotland) and may have been absent until 1950s, except after irruptions. Has probably benefited from the great increase in spruce plantations. Crossbills occur across Europe, Asia, and N America.

Notes Recent studies in N America show that what was once considered one species of Crossbill is now several very similar species which differ in their calls and feeding habits and which do not interbreed where they overlap. In the area of this guide, one thin-billed form of Crossbill occurs in Cyprus, and another on islands in the W Mediterranean and adjacent N Africa.

Essays Winter Feeding by Redpolls and Crossbills, p. 489.

Refs Dementiev et al. 1968; Marchant et al. 1990; von Haartman 1969.

Scottish Crossbill

Loxia scotica

ATLAS 293; PMH 228; PER 198; HFP 296; HPCW -; NESTS -; BWP8

10–20m	BLDS: ♀ Monogamy?	3–4 (2–5) 1 brood? INCU: ♀ 13–15	FLDG: ♀ 17–20	Insects

Breeding habitat Mature coniferous forest, especiallly pine. (In contrast, the Crossbill is mainly in spruce.)

Displays In its song flight, glides with tail spread and rapidly beating wings from tree to tree.

Nesting Nest is in the top of pine tree; a small cup of twigs, lined with softer materials. Eggs like those of Crossbill, 22mm.

Diet Pine seeds, and seeds of other conifers, rowans, buds; young fed insects. Feeds in foliage, not usually on the ground.

Winters Resident.

Conservation Occurs only in a limited area of Scotland. The total population may number only 100–400 pairs. The increase of Crossbill with the extensive planting of alien spruce trees may pose a considerable threat to the survival of this, the UK's only endemic species. See p. 528.

Essays Winter Feeding by Redpolls and Crossbills, p. 489.

Refs Marchant et al. 1990; Nethersole-Thompson 1975 is a book about this species.

many of their avian predators. As in northern seed-eating birds, problems of food scarcity caused by the crash are often exacerbated by dense raptor populations that resulted from preceding years of relatively high prey abundance. Invasions by Rough-legged Buzzards and Snowy Owls often occur in the same year, with about a four-year periodicity, because both of these species feed largely on rodents. In contrast, invasions by Goshawks, which feed to a great extent on hares and rabbits, occur roughly in ten-year cycles.

SEE: Population Dynamics, p. 515; Bird Guilds, p. 77; Timing of Migration, p. 405; Raptor Hunting, p. 113; How Owls Hunt in the Dark, p. 251. REFS: Bock and Lepthien, 1976; Newton, 1979.

Diet and Nutrition

BIRDS eat many things that seem none too appealing to us: beetles, flies, spiders, earthworms, rotting fish, offal, weed seeds, and so on. Not only that, most birds have diets that are quite monotonous: some passerines may go for weeks on a diet composed largely of grasshoppers; Goosanders eat mostly fishes; Brent Geese rely heavily on eelgrass; Peregrines rarely dine on anything but birds; crossbills eat predominantly conifer seeds; and American Snail Kites (*Rostrhamus sociabilis*) rarely if ever taste anything but snails. In spite of this, the nutritional requirements of birds are not very different from ours: they need proteins, fats, carbohydrates, vitamins, and minerals.

Carbohydrates and fats are used primarily as energy sources, but proteins — more specifically the nitrogen-containing amino acids that are the building blocks of proteins — are needed to construct tissues, enzymes, and so on. Reproduction, growth, and moulting all require more nitrogen than routine maintenance of the body, and proteins are the source of that nitrogen. Birds, such as Chaffinches, that are omnivorous (eating both plant and animal food) increase the proportion of protein-rich animal food they eat during the breeding season. Many that are herbivorous (primarily eating plant foods), such as finches and buntings, may subsist for much of the year on a relatively low-protein vegetable diet, but in the breeding season take as many insects as possible, and often provide their young with a diet comprised entirely of insects. There may be parallel seasonal changes in the length of the gut which tends to be longer in winter when the diet includes more vegetable matter.

Similarly, warblers, which are considered insectivorous, will feed themselves and their young virtually exclusively on insects in the breeding season. Like many thrushes and other more omnivorous species, they may include berries and flower nectar as a substantial portion of their autumn–winter intake — their degree of frugivory being determined in no small part by their

Parrot Crossbill
Loxia pytyopsittacus

ATLAS 293; PMH 228; PER 198; HFP 296; HPCW ; NESTS 308; BWP8

	BLDS: ♀	2–4 (5)
	Monogamy?	1 (2?) broods
3–15m		INCU: ♀
		14–16?

FLDG: ♂♀
25

Fruit

Breeding habitat Mature coniferous forest, especially pine.

Displays Sings from perch but will also soar into air, fluttering wings and then returning to perch.

Nesting Loosely colonial. Nest is in top of pine; a large cup of twigs, lined with softer material. Eggs like those of the Crossbill, but slightly larger, 23mm.

Diet Pine seeds extracted from cones on trees; young fed regurgitated pine seeds; in winter also berries and buds.

Winters Resident or irruptive S and W when food supply fails.

Conservation Locally common from Scandinavia into Russia, but does not extend far to the E across northern forests, as do other coniferous forest specialists.

Notes In UK, bred in scattered locations following 1982 irruption. Pine crops probably fluctuate less than spruce and so species wanders less than Crossbill.

Essays Irruptions, p. 491; Winter Feeding by Redpolls and Crossbills, p. 489.

Refs Dementiev et al. 1968; Marchant et al. 1990; von Haartman 1969.

Crimson-winged Finch
Rhodopechys sanguinea

ATLAS 294; PMH -; PER -; HFP 288; HPCW 246; NESTS 303; BWP8

	BLDS: ?	4–5
	Monogamy	1 (2) broods
Shrub		INCU: ♀
		12

FLDG: ?
?

Breeding habitat Dry, open mountain sides and high tops.

Displays Very little known.

Nesting Nests on ground in cover of rock or bush or in low bush; a loose cup of grass, stems, twigs, lined with finer material. Eggs pale blue with a few dark brown spots, 22mm.

Diet Seeds, taken on ground; but diet is not well known.

Winters Resident; moves to lower elevations including fields; in small flocks.

Conservation Locally common, but has fragmented range from N Africa into Asia.

Refs Paz 1987.

body size (larger warblers are able to consume more kinds of fruits). And nectarivores, such as sunbirds and hummingbirds, must also catch insects to provide protein to balance their energy-rich but nitrogen-poor intake of nectar, especially when breeding. It is, of course, no miracle that protein-rich food sources just happen to be more abundant during the breeding season. Rather it is the reverse — evolution has timed the breeding season so that it occurs when the needed nitrogen can be obtained. In contrast, species such as Ptarmigan, that overwinter in the north, may lay down remarkable bodies of fat to see them through the high arctic winter when continuous darkness so impedes finding food.

Avian mineral requirements seem much like ours. Calcium, which is needed in large quantities for egg production, is a critical mineral nutrient for reproductively active female birds. During the laying period female Blue Tits and House Sparrows often collect snail shells before going to roost, thereby taking in the calcium required for the shell of the next egg. There is evidence that availability of easily metabolized calcium is an important factor in food choice by breeding gulls, whose individual food choices influence the survival of their offspring. It is also thought that shortage of calcium may restrict the reproductive output of vultures, which consume only the soft, calcium-poor parts of carcasses. This may be the reason that some American and Old World vultures, including the Egyptian Vulture, supplement their diets with small vertebrate prey that can be swallowed whole. Calcium, is of course, also critical for reproductively active female human beings, who must produce large amounts of calcium-rich milk. Avian needs for vitamins are also similar to the human requirements. Unlike us, however, many birds manufacture Vitamin C in their kidneys or liver, or in both. At least some birds clearly can choose their food according to its nutritional value. Willow Grouse, for instance, when in poor condition, select food that is high in nitrogen and phosphorus.

But, as with human beings, what birds eat is determined by more than their brute nutritional requirements. Various kinds of learning play important roles. For instance, once a bird has discovered a certain kind of palatable prey, it may form a 'search image' for that prey and specialize for a time in eating it. Experiments also indicate that a bird's feeding preferences can be influenced by its diet as a nestling. The best-documented learning pattern in birds is the speed with which North American Blue Jays (*Cyanocitta cristata*) learn to avoid foods that make them sick. Many monarch butterflies contain heart poisons, cardiac glycosides, which they obtain as caterpillars from the milkweed plants they feed on. A jay that has never seen such a monarch before will eat it and then suffer a bout of vomiting brought on by the glycosides. Subsequently the bird will not touch a monarch butterfly or even a viceroy butterfly, which closely mimics the monarch. Here again bird behaviour is much like human behaviour. A person who becomes violently ill soon after eating a particular food may be unable to stomach that food again, even if he or she knows that the sickness was caused, not by food, but by a virus. Nausea is a powerful teacher for both mammals and birds.

Desert Finch

Rhodopechys obsoleta

ATLAS 294; PMH -; PER -; HFP 288; HPCW 247; NESTS 302; BWP8

		4–6 (3–7) 1–2 broods	A		
Shrub 1–5m	BLDS: ♀ Monogamy?	INCU: ♀ 13–14	FLDG: ? 14	Insects	Foliage glean

Breeding habitat Arid areas with scattered trees, shrubs; gardens.

Displays ♀ has injury-feigning display on nest.

Nesting Loosely colonial. Nest is in a tree or bush; a cup of grass, stems, twigs, lined with softer materials. Eggs pale blue to bright green, with a few tiny black spots, 19mm.

Diet Feeds on seeds on ground, but also insects, buds, leaves on bushes. Young are fed seeds.

Winters Resident; in flocks.

Conservation Locally common across dry parts of S Asia. Erratic nester in Israel.

Essays Distraction Displays, p. 175.

Refs Dementiev et al. 1968; Paz 1987.

Trumpeter Finch

Rhodopechys githaginea

ATLAS 294; PMH 228; PER -; HFP 288; HPCW 248; NESTS 303; BWP8

		4–6 1 brood			
	BLDS: ? Monogamy	INCU: ♀ 13–14	A FLDG: ♂♀ 14	Insects	Foliage glean

Breeding habitat Rocky deserts, dry hillsides, usually with access to water.

Displays ♂ calls and throws head into vertical position with bill open. ♂ chases ♀, spreading wings out.

Nesting Nest is sheltered by a rock or bush; a cup of grass, stems, twigs, lined with softer materials, sometimes with small stones. Adults fly to water daily. Eggs pale blue, with a few purple-black

spots, 18mm. Young remain with adults 1–2 weeks after leaving nest.

Diet Seeds and insects taken on ground; sometimes leaves and buds from foliage.

Winters Resident; in flocks.

Conservation Common across N Africa (just into Europe) and across SW Asia. See p. 528.

Notes Also called Trumpeter Bullfinch.

Refs Dementiev et al. 1968; Paz 1987.

Changing availability of different kinds of food can also be a crucial factor in what is eaten. Many birds will opportunistically switch to a new food source that suddenly becomes abundant. In North America, when seventeen-year cicada broods emerge, many birds switch from whatever they have been eating to gorge on cicadas. Hobbies are reported to catch and eat more swifts in cool cloudy weather than in warm sunny weather. Apparently the lack of insects in the gloom weakens the swifts, making them easier prey for the Hobbies.

SEE: Breeding Season, p. 293; Feeding Young Petrels, p. 11; Hoarding Food, p. 453; Drinking, p. 313; Swallowing Stones, p. 135. REFS: Jordano, 1987; Mortensen, *et al.*, 1983; Pierotti and Annett, 1990; Savory, 1983.

How Long Can Birds Live?

PRECISE information on the longevity of birds is not easy to come by. It is usually impossible to follow large groups of individuals from hatching to death, so in addition to collecting data directly by ringing and recapturing individuals, many indirect methods of estimating age are used. Generally, it appears that the heaviest mortality occurs among inexperienced young birds, especially in the period after fledging. For adults, the probability of death each year remains roughly constant. In other words, few birds die of 'old age' — they just run the same gamut of risks year in and year out until they are killed. The annual risk of being killed varies from about 70 per cent in the smallest temperate-zone songbirds (adult life expectancy about 10 months) to 3 per cent in Royal Albatrosses (life expectancy slightly over 30 years). If a bird lasts long enough, however, the probability of it dying in a given year may once again rise. Common Terns reach old age after about 19 years, and their annual risk of dying then goes up.

Life expectancy in birds is closely correlated with size — the larger the species, the longer it is likely to live. But the relationship is far from exact, as there appears to be considerable variability from species to species and population to population. For instance, in one study Marsh Tits ringed as young survived an average of 2.5 years, about twice the average life expectancy of temperate-zone songbirds. Some groups of birds tend to have long lives for their sizes, especially the Procellariiformes (tubenoses — albatrosses, shearwaters, and petrels) and Charadriiformes (waders, gulls and terns, and auks). Some members of other groups, for instance tits, wrens, and game birds, are shorter-lived than their sizes would predict. In general there seems to be relatively little difference in the longevity of the two sexes of the same species, at least among common passerines studied in England.

Scarlet Rosefinch
Carpodacus erythrinus

ATLAS 296; PMH 229; PER 196; HFP 294; HPCW 248; NESTS 307; BWP8

Shrub to 3m	BLDS: ♀ Monogamy	4–6 (5–7) 1 brood? INCU: ♀ 11–15	FLDG: ♂♀ 9–12	Fruit	Ground glean

Breeding habitat Wet areas with thick bushes; on edge of forests; in mountains in the S to high elevations, in spruce.

Displays ♂ sings from exposed perch, raising crest, throat feathers, moves from one perch to the next. In courtship ♂ displays in front of ♀ with throat feathers ruffled, head and tail raised, shivering wings.

Nesting Territorial, but territories sometimes grouped into loose colonies. Nest is low in conifer or bush; a loose cup of stems, grass, lined with softer materials. Eggs pale blue, with a few black spots, 20mm. Hatch over 2–3 days. Pairs usually breed together in successive years.

Diet Seeds (especially of cereals), buds, berries, sometimes insects; taken from foliage or ground.

Winters Migrates SE to India, in open areas with bushes and trees; sometimes in large flocks.

Conservation Increased range in Finland starting in the 1940s (from about 10 000 pairs in 1940s to 360 000 pairs in the 1970s) into Sweden in the mid-1950s, Norway by 1970, and Denmark by 1972. Probably aided by habitat changes opening up forests. Common from E Europe across Asia.

Notes Also called Common Rosefinch, Scarlet Grosbeak.

Refs von Haartman 1969; Stjernberg 1979 is a monograph about this species.

Sinai Rosefinch
Carpodacus synoicus

ATLAS 296; PMH -; PER -; HFP 294; HPCW 248; NESTS 307; BWP8

	BLDS: ? Monogamy?	4–5 1 brood? INCU: ♂♀? 14?	FLDG: ♂♀ 14?	Greens	Foliage glean

Breeding habitat Rocky hillsides in deserts.

Displays Very little known.

Nesting Nest is in a crevice in cliff; a cup of twigs and grasses, lined with hair and fibres. Eggs pale blue, with delicate black or brown spots, 19mm. First nests at one year, before males have assumed complete adult plumage.

Diet Takes seeds on ground; less often buds, leaves, flowers, and fruit from plants. Young are fed seeds first softened in parents' crops.

Winters Resident, or moves short distances; in small flocks, which roost communally.

Conservation Has fragmented distribution; local in Sinai, other populations in C Asia.

Refs Paz 1987; Meinertzhagen 1954.

Birds can be very long-lived in captivity. One Sulphur-crested Cockatoo (*Cacatua galerita*), a common Australian parrot made famous in America by the television show 'Baretta'), lived most of his 80-plus years in a zoo. Captive Canada Geese have lived for 33 years, House Sparrows 23 years, and American Northern Cardinals (*Cardinalis cardinalis*) 22 years. In nature, the lifespans of these species are much shorter. As luck would have it, however, the record for a Starling in the wild, 20 years, is 3 years *longer* than for any Starling captives.

The table on the next page lists longevity records of wild birds. Small differences among these figures should not be taken too seriously. For one thing, they represent the upper end of a range — and the range of any measurement is a statistic that almost always increases with the number of measurements. If, for instance, you record the heights of a random sample of 10 English women, and then of another sample of a million English women, both the tallest and the shortest women are virtually certain to be in the larger sample. So the maximum lifespans of bird species that are frequently ringed are more likely to be greater than those of species rarely ringed, everything else being equal. At any rate, remember that with the exception of errors that may later be corrected, *the numbers on the list can only increase*. Remember also that these figures are maximum recorded ages. While at one point the maximum record for the North American Purple Finch (*Carpodacus purpureus*) was 10 years (it has since been extended to almost 12), of 1746 recoveries from 21 715 ringed individuals, only 1 lived 10 years, 6 lived 8 years, and 18 lived 7 years. All the remainder lived less than 7 years. In short, the maximum lifespan is far longer than the median lifespan (the length of life of the individual that lives longer than one-half the population and less long than the other half), which in songbirds is usually only a year or two.

Work on seabirds by the late American ornithologist Ralph Schreiber indicates that dramatic increases in longevity records of seabirds can be expected as more data are gathered. For example, there are now thousands of ringed Laysan Albatrosses that are in their thirties. It is likely that these and some others eventually will be shown to have lifespans of 50–70 years, longer than those of the rings used to mark them originally!

There is an interesting debate about why songbirds might be longer-lived in the tropics than in temperate zones. One possible explanation is that climate (especially severe winters) or the hazards of migration makes dying young more likely for birds that breed in colder climes. Another is that selection has 'designed' temperate zone birds to lay big clutches of eggs and die young — putting their energy into reproduction rather than into the costly process of fighting senescence.

Pine Grosbeak

Pinicola enucleator

ATLAS 297; PMH 229; PER 198; HFP 296; HPCW -; NESTS 308; BWP8

| 1–4m | BLDS: ♀ Monogamy | 4 (3–5) 1 brood INCU: ♀ 13–14? | FLDG: ♂♀ 13–20 | Fruit | Ground glean |

Breeding habitat Coniferous or mixed coniferous and birch forest.

Displays Sings from perch in tree.

Nesting Nest is relatively low in a tree, close to trunk; a loose cup of twigs, lined with finer material. Eggs pale blue, with black and lilac spotting and blotching, 26mm. ♂ feeds ♀ on nest.

Diet Seeds, berries (especially those of rowan trees), and insects; also buds of spruce. Feeds in foliage and on ground.

Winters Resident or moves S of breeding areas, irrupting if food supplies fail; in small flocks.

Conservation Locally common across N Europe, N Asia, and N America.

Essays Irruptions, p. 491.

Refs Dementiev et al. 1968; von Haartman 1969.

Bullfinch

Pyrrhula pyrrhula

ATLAS 286; PMH 230; PER 198; HFP 286; HPCW 249; NESTS 301; BWP8

| Shrub 1–2m | BLDS: ♀ Monogamy | 4–5 (6–7) 2 (3) broods INCU: ♂♀ 12–14 | FLDG: ♂♀ 12–18 | Fruit | Ground glean |

Breeding habitat Woodland (often coniferous on continent) with thick undergrowth, hedges, gardens.

Displays ♂ sings weak song from tops of trees or bushes, drooping wings, exposing breast feathers, spreading tail, turning in it different directions; bows towards ♀, moves around her, and birds touch bills.

Nesting Nest is in conifer or thick bush or brambles; a loose mass of twigs, with a tidy cup of finer material lining it. Eggs pale blue, with a few black spots on larger end, 20mm. Only one brood in N and E.

Diet Seeds of hardwoods (often rowan, ash) and conifers, berries; also herbs; insects fed to young. In spring takes buds, including those of commericaly important trees.

Winters Resident; N populations move S.

Conservation Has declined since mid 1970s in the UK, following earlier spread when birds moved into more open areas. On the continent, local declines and increases. Common and widespread across Europe, Asia.

Refs Dementiev et al. 1968; Marchant et al. 1990; Sharrock 1976.

Maximum recorded lifespan

Species	Years
Manx Shearwater	35.7
Arctic Tern	34.0
Guillemot	32.1
Black-headed Gull	32.1
Osprey	31.2
Mallard	29.0
Honey Buzzard	28.9
Long-eared Owl	27.7
Black-throated Diver	27.0
White Stork	26.2
Arctic Skua	25.8
Mute Swan	21.7
Common Swift	21.1
Shag	20.6
Blackbird	20.3
Starling	20.0
Rook	19.9
Grey Plover	18.9
Coot	18.3
Bullfinch	17.5
Kestrel	16.2
Swallow	16.0
Great Tit	15.0
Golden Oriole	14.9
House Sparrow	13.3
Robin	12.9
Cuckoo	12.9
Reed Warbler	11.0
Skylark	10.1
Pied Wagtail	9.9
Capercaillie	9.3
Dunnock	9.0
Long-tailed Tit	8.1
Common Quail	7.6
Goldcrest	7.0
Treecreeper	6.8

SEE: Population Dynamics, p. 515. REFS: Berndt and Winkel, 1987; Curio, 1989; Lindstedt and Calder, 1976; Rydzewksi, 1978a,b; Sutherland, 1989.

Hawfinch

Coccothraustes coccothraustes

ATLAS 298; PMH 230; PER 198; HFP 287; HPCW 250; NESTS 302; BWP8

	BLDS: ♀	4–5 (2–7) 1 (2) broods INCU:♀,♂♀ ?	FLDG: ♂♀		
3–10m	Monogamy	9–14	10–14	Fruit	Ground glean

Breeding habitat Deciduous or mixed woodland, parks, large orchards; locally in pine forests.

Displays Song is soft and quiet. In courtship, ♂ hops towards ♀ spreading wings and tail, prods her; also a bowing display and birds touch bills.

Nesting Nests in neighbourhood groups of 3–6 pairs. Nest is well concealed on small horizontal branch of tree; a cup of small twigs, with a finer lining. Eggs off-white, to light blue, with a few brown-black spots, blotches, and scribbles, 24mm.

Diet Seeds and fruit, readily cracking the nuts of cherries; locally, birds can damage orchard crops. Hornbean, beech, yew, and sycamore are important food sources. Seeds taken from trees or on ground. Young may be fed insects, buds are important in spring.

Winters Resident; N and E populations move S, depending on food supply, into a wider range of habitats. In flocks.

Conservation Numbers poorly known because of inconspicuous habits. Local across Europe, Asia, N Africa.

Essays Declines in Forest Birds: Europe and America, p. 339

Refs Dementiev et al. 1968; Marchant et al. 1990; Mountford 1957 is a book about this species.

Lapland Bunting

Calcarius lapponicus

ATLAS 276; PMH 232; PER 200; HFP 280; HPCW 250; NESTS 298; BWP9

	BLDS: ♀	5–6 (2–7) 1 brood INCU: ♀	FLDG: ♂♀	
Bank	Monogamy	10–14	8–10	

Breeding habitat Arctic and mountain tundra, generally wet areas.

Displays Sings in flight as bird slowly descends to the ground.

Nesting Nest is on ground, often in shelter of tussock, or in bank; a cup of moss, roots, grass, lined with finer materials. Eggs pale greyish to green to buff, heavily spotted brown with black scrawls, 21mm. Young leave the nest at 8–10 days, about 4 days before they can fly. ♂s arrive early on breeding grounds, when it can still be very cold. Clutch sizes decrease the later nesting starts.

Diet In summer, almost exclusively ground-feeding arthropods, especially flies and caterpillars. Seeds in winter.

Winters Migrates S to winter on coastal saltings, fields, or in grasslands of C Asia. In flocks, with other species, including Snow Buntings.

Conservation Locally common from Scandinavian mountains across arctic of Europe, Asia, N America.

Essays Nest Lining, p. 439.

Refs von Haartman 1969.

Orientation and Navigation

THE question of how birds find their way between breeding and wintering grounds has puzzled people for as long as humanity has been aware of the phenomenon of migration. Today we know many more parts of the puzzle's solution than we did even 25 years ago. Some would argue that there are really two puzzles: (1) how birds navigate over thousands of miles to find their way between breeding and wintering sites, and (2) how birds find their way back to precise nesting or roosting sites (homing behaviour). To do either, birds must be able to orient (that is, determine compass direction) and to navigate (judge their position while travelling).

The short explanation of these complex phenomena is that birds find their way by using a variety of cues in a hierarchical fashion. Different species may use these cues in different orders of priority, and some cues may always be used in preference to others. Birds acquire directional information from five primary sources: (1) topographic features, including wind direction which can be influenced by major features of the landscape, such as mountains, (2) stars, (3) sun, (4) Earth's magnetic field, and (5) odours.

Some of the most convincing experiments demonstrating the orientational abilities of birds were conducted by behavioural ecologist Stephen Emlen. To perform his experiments, Emlen made good use of the 'migratory restlessness' (*Zugunruhe*) displayed by caged migrant birds — nocturnal fluttering and hopping that tend to be oriented in the appropriate direction for migration. European workers previously had demonstrated the existence of this behaviour in laboratory studies carried out with several species of hand-raised *Sylvia* warblers. In a series of carefully controlled experiments in a planetarium, Emlen found that Indigo Buntings (*Passerina cyanea*) oriented in the proper migratory direction by using the stellar cues projected on to the planetarium ceiling. When Emlen shifted the position of the planetarium's stars, the birds shifted their orientation as well. The buntings were shown to learn a 'sky map' from their exposure to rotating stars while growing up. The young birds learn to recognize the area of least apparent movement around the pole; if maturing buntings were exposed to a false sky rotating around the star Betelgeuse (in the constellation Orion), they acted as if Betelgeuse were the North Star. Ornithologist Wolfgang Wiltschko and his colleagues have confirmed and extended Emlen's work by demonstrating that young Garden Warblers must observe the appropriate celestial rotation prior to their first migration in order to establish a correct star compass. A star compass has also been confirmed in Robins, Whitethroats, Blackcaps, and Pied Flycatchers.

But how do birds find their way on overcast nights? Apparently, they are able to set course by the setting sun, unless this too is obscured by cloud cover. Lacking either stars or sun for information, birds will orient by wind direction, although not always correctly. Studies using radar and portable

Snow Bunting
Plectrophenax nivalis

ATLAS 276; PMH 233; PER 200; HFP 280; HPCW 250; NESTS 298; BWP9

	Crevice	4–6 (7–8)			
	BLDS: ♀	1–2 broods	FLDG: ♂♀		
		INCU: ♀	10–14	Insects	
Cliff	Polyandry	10–15			

Breeding habitat Bare rocky screes, on mountains in the S to open tundra in the N.

Displays ♂ sings in a song flight, rather like that of the Skylark, or on ground. In courtship exposes striking black and white plumage.

Nesting ♂s defend territories in small colonies. Nest is on ground among rocks or in rock crevice; a large saucer of moss and grass, lined with finer materials, including ptarmigan feathers. ♀ may start more than one nest at the same time. Eggs pale bluish or greenish, variably spotted and blotched red to brown, sometimes only at larger end,

22mm. Clutch size varies with latitude. Young move in and out of nest from about 8 days. About half of the ♀s try to establish a second brood.

Diet Seeds and, in summer, also insects taken from the ground.

Winters Often along seashores, or grasslands across middle latitutes of Europe into Asia; in flocks.

Conservation Common across northern mountains and arctic of Europe, Asia, and N America.

Essays Nest Lining, p. 439.

Refs von Haartman 1969; Sharrock 1976; Nethersole-Thompson 1966 is a book about this species.

Yellowhammer
Emberiza citrinella

ATLAS 280; PMH 233; PER 200; HFP 276; HPCW 250; NESTS 294; BWP9

		3–5 (2–6)			
		2–3 broods			
Bank	BLDS:♂♀,♀	INCU:♀,♂●	FLDG:♂♀		
to 1m	Monogamy	11–14	12–13	Seeds	

Breeding habitat Open ground with shrubs, woodland edges, hedgerows. Where range overlaps with Cirl Bunting, this species tends to be more upland.

Displays ♂ sings from exposed perch.

Nesting Territorial. Nest is on ground, under bush, or in a bank; a cup of grass, lined with finer materials. Eggs are variable, often bluish to purplish-white, with fine black spots, 22mm. Young may leave nest before they can fly.

Diet Insects in summer. Also seeds,

berries (especially outside of breeding season).

Winters Resident; N populations move S; more likely on farmland; in flocks.

Conservation Declined during 1950s, 1960s, perhaps due to pesticides applied to seeds; numbers now stable. Common across most of Europe into Asia.

Essays Birds and Agriculture, p. 365; Selection in Nature, p. 471.

Refs Marchant et al. 1990; Sharrock 1976.

ceilometers (electronic devices for measuring the altitude of overcasts) to track nocturnal migrants found that birds frequently flew in the wrong direction by using wind as a cue when stars were unavailable. Interestingly, while most ornithologists believe that birds employ topographic features such as mountains, rivers, and tall buildings to navigate in the vicinity of the home site, there is little evidence to support this view.

We now know that homing pigeons and several songbird species are capable of detecting the Earth's magnetic field and can use it to orient and possibly to navigate. We still do not understand just how they manage to sense such weak electromagnetic fields, but birds are far more sensitive to them than are human beings. Robins, Whitethroats, and Blackcaps have demonstrated magnetic orientation in laboratory experiments, but the most impressive abilities were found in experiments with hand-raised Pied Flycatchers. The flycatchers initiate orientation in the proper migratory direction if exposed to the geomagnetic field of their natal area — even in the absence of any experience with stellar or solar cues!

The degree to which olfactory cues are used for navigation and orientation is still very controversial. Even among the researchers there is disagreement concerning the interpretation of experimental results. Homing pigeons in Italy and parts of Germany have been shown to use smell for at least short-distance orientation in returning to their loft, but attempts to repeat these studies in North America and in other parts of Europe have not been successful. These contradictory results might be explained if olfactory orientation is a genetically determined ability that is not present in all populations. If so, international cross-fostering experiments now underway should resolve the controversy. These results offer a picture of how birds determine compass direction. What remains less certain is how birds navigate, or judge their position while travelling. To some extent they may build up a mental map of the areas they visit in the course of their migrations. But birds can also return 'home' when released in unfamiliar locations. Such experiments provide evidence of true navigational ability. Particularly remarkable were G.V.T. Matthews' experiments involving the release of Manx Shearwaters from inland British locations. Despite never having visited these places — they are seabirds — the majority of Manx Shearwaters returned to their Skokholm breeding colony within four days of release under clear skies.

One clear message emerges from studies of avian orientation and navigation: birds do not rely on a single source of information to guide them on their travels. Instead, they possess the ability, shaped over evolutionary time, to use redundant cues from a variety of sources. Such a system enables birds to find their way under most conditions that they routinely encounter.

SEE: Migration, p. 377; The Avian Sense of Smell, p. 13; Timing of Migration, p. 405; Why Some Species Migrate at Night, p. 351; Wader Migration and Conservation, p. 167. REFS: Able and Bingman, 1987; Beck and Wiltschko, 1988; Emlen, 1975; Helbig, 1990; James, 1986; Mead, 1983; Moore, 1987; Papi, 1986; Schmidt-Koenig, 1987; Walcott and Lednor, 1983; Matthews, 1968; Waldvogel, 1989; Wiltschko et al., 1987.

Cirl Bunting

Emberiza cirlus

ATLAS 279; PMH 234; PER 200; HFP 276; HPCW 251; NESTS 294; BWP9

  3–4
2–3 broods
BLDS: ♀ INCU: ♀
Decid tree Monogamy 11–13

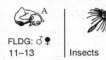
FLDG: ♂♀
11–13 Insects Ground glean

Breeding habitat Open country with bushes, small trees, hedgerows, vineyards.

Displays ♂ sings from top of bush.

Nesting Nest is low in a bush; a cup of moss, grass, etc., lined with finer materials. Eggs off-white to greenish, with distinct black spots and scrawls, 21mm.

Diet Seeds, insects, and berries; taken from foliage and ground; young fed insects.

Winters Resident, though moves into more open grasslands and farmlands.

Conservation Range contraction in N and W. Locally common in S and W Europe, N Africa, and W Turkey.

Essays Species and Speciation, p. 325.

Refs Sharrock 1976; Marchant et al. 1990.

Rock Bunting

Emberiza cia

ATLAS 284; PMH 234; PER 200; HFP 274; HPCW 251; NESTS 293; BWP9

  4–6
1–2 broods
BLDS: ? INCU: ♀
Shrub Monogamy 12–13

FLDG: ?
10–13 Insects

Breeding habitat Open rocky hillsides with bushes and small trees, into desert areas that have access to water.

Displays Very little known.

Nesting Nest is usually on the ground, among rocks, sometimes in a low bush; a cup of moss, grass, lined with softer materials. Eggs greyish to bluish-white, with long, fine black scribblings, 21mm.

Diet Seeds, insects, taken from ground or low foliage.

Winters Resident or moves to lower elevations; in small flocks.

Conservation Locally common from Mediterranean across Asia.

Hatching Asynchrony and Brood Reduction

WHETHER eggs in a single clutch will hatch simultaneously or sequentially over an extended period of time is determined by the onset of incubation. In many birds, including most precocial species, incubation does not begin until the last egg has been laid, resulting in all of the eggs hatching within a few hours of each other. In contrast, many species begin incubation before laying the last egg of the clutch. This results in asynchronous hatchings separated by anything from a few hours to several days, depending on how soon incubation commences following the start of egg-laying.

In altricial and semi-altricial species, asynchronous hatching gives the first chicks to leave the egg a head start at begging for food and successfully attracting parental attention. The influential British ornithologist David Lack viewed the evolution of asynchronous hatching as a parental strategy for raising the largest number of offspring that food resources will allow if the abundance of food for the chicks cannot be predicted when the eggs are laid. The matching of offspring number with food availability is thus achieved by means of brood reduction: with asynchronous hatching, the smallest chick or chicks do not garner 'their fair share' and will not survive in years of food scarcity.

Lack's hypothesis has been supported in the case of the Blackbird by a series of experiments by Robert Magrath when he was at Cambridge. By experimentally manipulating hatching synchrony in broods and by supplementing food in some territories, he was able to show that asynchronous broods were more productive than synchronous broods when food was scarce. Under conditions of food shortage, brood reduction occurred early, which resulted in more robust fledglings having greater probabilities of survival. When food was abundant, asynchronous and synchronous broods did not differ in offspring survival.

Elimination of the smallest chicks usually occurs by starvation as the result of competition with their larger siblings for parental feeding, from overt parental neglect, or through psychological and physical intimidation by their larger siblings. Brood reduction by means of starvation routinely occurs in almost all gulls and raptors, and is commonly seen in birds as diverse as cormorants, herons, egrets, terns, some woodpeckers, corvids, and wheatears. Bee-eaters exhibit an extreme degree of asynchrony, with hatching spread over as many as nine days within a single clutch. Size disparity among chicks is further exacerbated in gulls by the laying of different-sized eggs, with egg weight commonly decreasing from first to last egg laid. In three-egg clutches of the Shag, however, the second egg is the largest and the first egg is the smallest. Surprisingly, egg-size differences in Shag clutches are overridden by the greater asynchrony of hatching times between second and third eggs relative to the much shorter interval between first

House Bunting

Emberiza striolata

ATLAS 284; PMH -; PER -; HFP 274; HPCW 251; NESTS 293; BWP9

  3 (2–4)
1 (2?) broods
INCU: ?
?   FLDG: ?
?

BLDS: ?
Monogamy?

Insects

Breeding habitat   Human settlements in arid areas; rocky wadis, especially near cliffs.

Displays   ♂ sings from prominent rock.

Nesting   Nests in holes in the walls of buildings; a cup of grass lined with feathers. Eggs whitish or pale blue, with fine brownish spots, 20mm.

Diet   Mainly seeds, insects, also discarded domestic food.

Winters   Resident; in small groups, often near livestock.

Conservation   Locally common across N Africa, SW Asia.

Essays   Commensal Feeding, p. 27.

Refs   Paz 1987.

Cinereous Bunting

Emberiza cineracea

ATLAS 282; PMH 235; PER 200; HFP 278; HPCW 252; NESTS 296; BWP9

 ? 3
? brood
INCU: ?
?   FLDG: ?
?

BLDS:
?

Insects

Breeding habitat   Dry rocky mountain slopes.

Displays   Very little known.

Nesting   Nest is not well known. Eggs whitish or pale blue, with thin black scribbles, 20mm.

Diet   Seeds and insects, taken on ground.

Winters   Resident or migrates to NE Africa and Arabia.

Conservation   Has restricted and probably fragmented distribution from Turkey to Afghanistan. See p. 528.

Notes   Also called Ashy-headed Bunting.

and second eggs. The end result is higher mortality rates for last-hatched chicks.

Broods of some species typically exhibit 'siblicide', wherein the larger chick kills its smaller sibling. Eagles and boobies can be characterized as either 'obligately (i.e. virtually always) siblicidal', or 'facultatively siblicidal', in which the occurrence of siblicide may vary with food abundance or other ecological conditions. Among eagles, Imperial, Golden, Booted, and Bonelli's all display facultative siblicide, whereas Verreaux's, Tawny, Lesser Spotted, and Spotted Eagles demonstrate obligate siblicide. For example, of more than 200 records of two-egg clutches followed in Verreaux's Eagle (in southern Africa), only one record exists of both chicks surviving to fledging. Eagle species manifesting obligate siblicide tend to have longer hatching intervals between eggs, with a resulting greater size difference between siblings than eagle species that are facultatively siblicidal. Although rare among birds as a group, obligate siblicide has been documented in eight different families including pelicans, owls, and cranes. For species that exhibit obligate siblicide, which occurs even when food supplies are abundant, the second egg serves as insurance against loss of the first egg from infertility, predation, or damage, rather than as a means of rearing two chicks.

In the nearly 45 years since Lack's seminal publication, information about many additional species has accumulated, and hatching asynchrony is now thought to be more common than simultaneous hatching among altricial birds. Ornithologists today believe that for many species asynchronous hatching is not a strategy for achieving brood reduction and that other hypotheses might better explain its evolution. Sociobiologists Anne Clark and David Wilson argue that high nest predation rates can encourage the evolution of asynchronous hatching as a means of minimizing the total amount of time that eggs and nestlings spend in the nest and thus reduce the chances of predation causing a total nesting failure. Asynchronous hatching also can be interpreted for some insectivorous species as an adaptation to 'speed up' hatching so that at least some of the nestlings can capitalize on rapidly (but unpredictably) peaking food resources (such as outbreaks of forest caterpillars).

This 'new view' of the adaptive significance of hatching asynchrony helps to explain the increasing egg weight often seen from first to last egg laid among many asynchronously hatching passerines (just the opposite of what is seen in gulls). These weight differences represent differing proportions of nutrients and energy invested in different eggs within clutches, with the greatest investment going into the last egg of the clutch. This pattern is clearly inconsistent with the notion of facilitating brood reduction, and appears to be a means of compensating for the delay in hatching and development by initially providing the last chick with more resources.

SEE: Incubation Time, p. 121; Precocial and Altricial Young, p. 401; Eggs and Their Evolution, p. 317; Variation in Clutch Sizes, p. 55; Average Clutch Size, p. 31.
REFS: Anderson, 1990; Clark and Wilson, 1981; Edwards and Collopy, 1983; Hussell, 1985; Lack, 1968; Lessells and Avery, 1989; Magrath, 1989; Meyburg, 1987; Mock, 1984;

Ortolan Bunting

Emberiza hortulana

ATLAS 281; PMH 235; PER 202; HFP 278; HPCW 253; NESTS 295; BWP9

BLDS: ♀
Monogamy?

4–6
2 broods
INCU: ♀
11–14

FLDG: ♂♀
10–15

Insects

Breeding habitat Open areas with scrub, trees, woodland edges; often near water.

Displays ♂ sings from bush or tree.

Nesting Nest is on the ground in thick cover; a cup of grass, lined with finer materials. Eggs variable; pale blue to grey to purple, spotted, blotched, and scribbled darker, 20mm.

Diet Seeds and insects.

Winters Africa, S of Sahara in grasslands and savannahs, cultivated fields; in flocks.

Conservation Locally common from Europe across SW and C Asia. See p. 528.

Refs von Haartman 1969.

Cretzschmar's Bunting

Emberiza caesia

ATLAS 281; PMH 235; PER 202; HFP 278; HPCW 254; NESTS 296; BWP9

BLDS: ?
Monogamy?

4–6
2 broods
INCU: ♀
19

FLDG: ?
12

Insects

Breeding habitat Arid, open areas and rocky hillsides with scattered shrubs.

Displays ♂ sings from bush or tree.

Nesting Nest is on the ground, often at base of bush; a cup of plant stems, lined with softer materials. Eggs pale blue to purple, spotted and streaked black or purplish-black, 19mm. Young leave nest before they are able to fly.

Diet Small seeds, some insects, green plant parts; feeds on ground.

Winters In NE Africa, Arabia; in large flocks.

Conservation Locally common in restricted range in SE corner of the area covered by this guide. See p. 528.

Refs Paz 1987; Meinertzhagen 1954.

Mock *et al.*, 1990; Moreno, 1987*a,b*; O'Connor, 1978; Slagsvold, 1985; Slagsvold and Lifjeld, 1989; Stinson, 1979; Stokland and Amundsen, 1988; Wiklund, 1985.

Adaptations for Flight

THE evolution of flight has endowed birds with many physical features in addition to wings and feathers. One of the requirements of heavier-than-air flying machines, birds included, is a structure that combines strength and light weight. One way this is accomplished in birds is by the fusion of some bones, the elimination of others, and the 'pneumatization' (hollowing) of the remaining ones. Some of the vertebrae and some bones of the pelvic girdle of birds are fused into a single structure, as are some finger and leg bones — all of which are separate in most land vertebrates. And many tail, finger, and leg bones are missing altogether. Not only are some bones of birds hollow, unlike ours, but many of the hollows are also connected to the respiratory system.

The pneumatization of bird bones led to the belief that birds had skeletons that weighed proportionately less than those of mammals. Careful studies by H. D. Prange and his colleagues have shown this not to be the case. More demands are placed on a bird's skeleton than on that of a terrestrial mammal. The bird must be able to support itself either entirely by its forelimbs or entirely by its hindlimbs. It also requires a deep, solid breast-bone (sternum) to which the wing muscles can be anchored. Thus, while some bones are much lighter than their mammalian counterparts, others, especially the leg bones, are heavier.

Overall the skeleton constitutes about five per cent of a bird's weight. Evolution has created in the avian skeleton a model of parsimony, lightening where possible, adding weight and strength where required. To keep the cylindrical walls of a bird's major wing bones from buckling, for instance, the bones have internal strut-like reinforcements. The results can be quite spectacular: the skeleton of a frigatebird with a seven-foot wingspan weighs less than the feathers covering it!

Not all birds have the same degree of skeletal pneumatization. To decrease their buoyancy and make diving easier, some diving birds, such as divers and auklets, have relatively solid bones. These birds are generally less skilful fliers than birds with lighter skeletons.

Birds have found other ways to lighten the load in addition to hollowing out their bones. For instance, they keep their reproductive organs (testes, ovaries and oviducts) tiny for most of the year, greatly enlarging them only during the breeding season.

The respiratory system of birds is also adapted to the demands of flight; it is proportionately larger and much more efficient than ours — as might be

Rustic Bunting

Emberiza rustica

ATLAS 277; PMH 236; PER 202; HFP 280; HPCW 254; NESTS 297; BWP9

	BLDS: ?	4–6 1 (2 ?) broods INCU: ♀
Ground	Monogamy?	12–13

FLDG: ?
14 | Insects

Breeding habitat Marshy areas with undergrowth, scrubby woodland, often near water.

Displays Very little known.

Nesting Nest is near the ground in a shrub, or on ground; cup of moss, grass, etc., lined with finer materials. Eggs whitish-blue or whitish-green, with fine grey to olive spotting, 20mm.

Diet Seeds, some insects; taken on ground.

Winters Migrates SE to winter in India, SE Asia, in agricultural areas, gardens.

Conservation Locally common from Sweden E across Asia.

Refs von Haartman 1969.

Little Bunting

Emberiza pusilla

ATLAS 277; PMH 236; PER 202; HFP 280; HPCW 254; NESTS 287; BWP9

	BLDS: ?	4–5 (–7) 1 (2) broods INCU: ♂♀
	Monogamy?	11–12

FLDG: ♂♀
10–11 | Insects

Breeding habitat Bogs, or near water, in boreal forests

Displays Very little known.

Nesting Nest is on the ground in a small hollow, under shrub; a cup of moss, grass, etc., lined with finer materials. Eggs pale green to pink, with blackish spots, blotches, and scrawls, indistinct purplish markings, 19mm.

Young leave nest at about a week of age, but cannot fly for about another 4 days.
Diet Seeds; also insects in summer.
Winters Migrates SE to winter in SC Asia, India in fields, reed-beds, sometimes in large flocks.
Conservation From N Scandinavia, where generally rare, across Asia; locally common E of the Urals.
Refs von Haartman 1969.

expected, since flight is a more demanding activity than walking or running. An average bird devotes about one-fifth of its body volume to its respiratory system, an average mammal only about one-twentieth. Mammalian respiratory systems consist of lungs that are blind sacs and of tubes that connect them to the nose and mouth. Air moves in a two-way flow, in and out of the lungs. During each breath, only some of the air contained in the lungs is exchanged, since the lungs do not collapse completely with each exhalation, and some 'dead air' then remains in them.

In contrast, the lungs of birds are less flexible, and relatively small, but they are interconnected with a system of large, thin-walled air sacs in the front (anterior) and back (posterior) portions of the body. These, in turn, are connected with the air spaces in the bones to create an ingenious system that passes the air in a one-way, two-stage flow through the bird's lungs. A breath of inhaled air passes first into the posterior air sacs and then, on exhalation, into the lungs. When a second breath is inhaled into the posterior sacs, the air from the first breath moves from shrinking lungs into the anterior air sacs. When the second exhalation occurs, the air from the first breath moves from the anterior air sacs and out of the bird, while the second breath moves into the lungs. The air thus moves in one direction through the lungs. All birds have this one-way flow system; most have a second two-way flow system which may make up as much as 20 per cent of the lung volume.

In both systems, the air is funnelled down fine tubules that interdigitate with capillaries carrying oxygen-poor venous blood. At the beginning of the tubules the oxygen-rich air is in close contact with that oxygen-hungry blood; farther down the tubules the oxygen content of air and blood are in equilibrium. Birds' lungs are anatomically very complex (their structure and function are only barely outlined here), but they create a 'crosscurrent circulation' of air and blood that improves the exchange of oxygen and carbon dioxide. Together with the thin membranes intervening between blood and air, these features enable birds to extract some twenty per cent more oxygen from each breath than mammals.

Contrary to what was once believed, the rhythm of a bird's respiratory 'two-cycle pump' is not coupled to the beats of its wings. Flight movements and respiratory movements are largely independent, although recent research on Starlings (employing X-ray cinematography) has suggested that spring-like motion of the 'wishbone' in flight may help to move air between lungs and air sacs with which the bone is closely connected.

The heart does the pumping required to get oxygenated blood to the tissues and to carry deoxygenated blood (loaded with carbon dioxide) away from them. Because of the efficiency of the bird's breathing apparatus, the ratio of breaths to heartbeats can be quite low. A mammal takes about one breath for every four and one-half heartbeats (independent of the size of the mammal), a bird about one breath for every six to ten heartbeats (depending on the size of the bird).

A bird's heart is large, powerful, and of the same basic design as that of a mammal. It is a four-chambered structure of two pumps operating side by side. One two-chambered pump receives oxygen-rich blood from the lungs

Yellow-breasted Bunting

Emberiza aureola

ATLAS 277; PMH 236; PER 202; HFP 276; HPCW 254; NESTS 294; BWP9

0.5–1m	BLDS: ♂♀ Monogamy?	4–5 (6) 1 brood INCU: ♂♀ 13	FLDG: ♂♀ 13–15	Seeds

Breeding habitat Open areas with shrubs, often near water.

Displays ♂ sings from top of bush.

Nesting Nests in neighbourhood groups. Nest is low in a bush or on ground; a cup of grass, lined with softer materials. Eggs pale greenish to grey, with dark brown spots and blotches, 21mm. Young remain with parents for about 2 weeks after fledging.

Diet In summer, mainly insects; also seeds at other times of year.

Winters Migrates SE to winter in India, SE Asia in agricultural and other open areas; sometimes in large flocks.

Conservation Occurs from Finland (where population is a few hundred pairs), E across Asia where locally common.

Essays Species and Speciation, p. 325.

Refs von Haartman 1969.

Reed Bunting

Emberiza schoeniclus

ATLAS 278; PMH 237; PER 202; HFP 280; HPCW 254; NESTS 297; BWP9

Reeds 0–1m	BLDS: ♀ Monogamy?	4–5 (6–7) 2–3 broods INCU: ♂♀ 12–14	FLDG: ♂♀ 10–13	Insects

Breeding habitat Marshes, water meadows, reed-beds, but moving more recently into drier areas, particularly when densities are high.

Displays ♂ sings from top of low vegetation.

Nesting Nests on or just above ground in thick cover; a cup of grass, reeds, lined with softer material. Eggs olive to buff, with black spots, scrawls, and blotches, 20mm.

Diet Seeds, plus insects in summer.

Winters Resident in W and N. E populations move S and W, as far S as N Africa. Moves onto cultivated fields.

Conservation In the UK, a steep decline since mid-1970s, probably as a result of increased use of herbicides to control weeds. Common across Europe, most of N and C Asia, to Japan.

Essays Birds and Agriculture, p. 365.

Refs Marchant et al. 1990; Sharrock 1976.

and pumps it out to the waiting tissues. The other pump receives oxygen-poor blood from the tissues and pumps it into the lungs. This segregation of the two kinds of blood (which does not occur completely in reptiles, amphibians, and fishes) makes a bird's circulatory system, like its respiratory system, well equipped to handle the rigours of flight.

The flight muscles of most birds are red in colour ('dark meat') because of the presence of many fibres containing red oxygen-carrying compounds, myoglobin, and cytochrome. They are also richly supplied with blood and are designed for sustained exertion. Lighter-coloured flight muscles ('white meat'), with many fewer such fibres, are found in pheasants, grouse, quail, and other gallinaceous birds. These are also well supplied with blood and are apparently capable of carrying a heavy work load for a short time, but fatigue more rapidly. If a quail is flushed a few times in a row, it will become too exhausted to fly.

Finally, of course, it does little good to be able to sustain flight or fly rapidly if you are always crashing into things. Although birds have found many ways to streamline, lighten, or totally eliminate parts (like urinary bladders), they have not stinted on nervous systems. The brains of birds are proportionally much larger than those of lizards and comparable, in fact, with those of rodents. The brain is connected to sharp eyes, and has ample processing centres for coordinating the information received from them. A bird's nerves can rapidly transmit commands of the brain to the muscles operating the wings. It is the combination of visual acuity, quick decision-making, and high-speed nerve transmission along short nerves that permits a Chaffinch to weave rapidly among the branches of a thicket, escaping the clutches of a pursuing Sparrowhawk.

SEE: Temperature Regulation and Behaviour, p. 163; Metabolism, p. 281; Feathered Dinosaurs?, p. 299; Eyes Like a Hawk, p. 89. REFS: Calder, 1984; Dunker, 1974; Jenkins et al., 1988; Prange et al., 1979; Rayner, 1988; Scheid, 1982.

Population Dynamics

THE 'dynamics' of bird populations, the ways in which their numbers grow and shrink as time goes by, are controlled by the same general factors that control the size of human populations. An avian or human population has two kinds of input — birth (natality) and immigration. And each population has the same two outputs — death (mortality) and emigration. If the inputs are greater than the outputs, the population will grow. If the outputs are higher than the inputs, it will shrink. If the two are in balance, the population size will not change, or as ecologists would say, the population 'density' is constant. Population density is, technically, the number of individuals per

Black-headed Bunting

Emberiza melanocephala

ATLAS 282; PMH 238; PER 202; HFP 276; HPCW 255; NESTS 295; BWP9

Shrub to 3m	BLDS: ? Monogamy?	4–5 (6–7) 1 brood INCU: ♀ 14	FLDG: ♀? ?	Insects

Breeding habitat Open areas with scattered trees and bushes, gardens.

Displays ♂ sings from exposed perch or in flight, with legs dangling rather like the display of the Corn Bunting.

Nesting Nest is in dense herbage, vines, or low, thick bush, or on ground; a cup of grass, leaves, lined with softer materials. Eggs pale greyish-blue, with distinct, fine red-brown spots, 22mm.

Diet Seeds; also insects in summer.

Winters Migrates SE to India, in agricultural areas; often in very large flocks.

Conservation Locally common from Italy E to SW Asia.

Corn Bunting

Emberiza calandra

ATLAS 279; PMH 238; PER 202; HFP 274; HPCW 255; NESTS 292; BWP9

  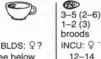 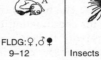

Shrub to 2m	BLDS: ♀? See below	3–5 (2–6) 1–2 (3) broods INCU: ♀ ˙ 12–14	FLDG:♀,♂♥ 9–12	Insects

Breeding habitat Open grassland, farmland (especially barley) with scattered bushes or hedges.

Displays ♂ sings from top of bush, flying between perches with legs dangling, or parachuting downwards. Near ♀ on ground ♂ makes short upward flight, hovering above her.

Nesting Nest is on the ground, often at base of bush, or in thick bush such as gorse; a cup of grass, lined with softer materials. Eggs pale grey to purplish, spotted, streaked, and scribbled grey to purplish-brown, 24mm. Probably has promiscuous mating system with many ♂s polygamous (up to 7♀s). ♀s too, may have several mates.

Diet Seeds, grassheads, buds; also insects.

Winters Mainly resident; may form flocks with other seed-eaters.

Conservation Is closely tied to barley fields (which also have more polygamous ♂s). As wheat has replaced barley, populations have declined greatly in the UK and also elsewhere in NW. Is now rare and local in Ireland. Locally common from UK across Europe (not N) to N Africa, SW Asia.

Notes ♂s are about 20 per cent heavier than ♀s – which is unusual for this genus.

Essays Polygyny, p. 265; Polyandry, p. 195; Birds and Agriculture, p. 365; Vocal Dialects, p. 477; Vocal Functions, p. 413.

unit area. But since a population normally occupies a limited area of suitable habitat, its size increases, decreases, or remains stable along with its density.

In an average lifetime, the average breeding female in each bird population lays many more eggs than are required to replace her and her mate. Mortality, however, intervenes. Eggs are destroyed by nest robbbers; chicks starve, freeze, are killed by disease or parasites, or are carried off by predators; juveniles are devoured by hawks, crash into obstacles on migration, or die of cold or starvation in their first winter. In general, birds that have high adult mortality produce more and larger clutches, and mature early.

The availability of food is critical to the dynamics of almost all bird populations, from owls to passerines. For example, in Norway some 85 per cent of all Goldcrests perish during the winter, with the heaviest mortality being associated with the combination of high snowfall and low temperature. The former tends to make spiders, the most common prey, more difficult to find, while the latter increases food requirements. Winter temperatures have also been shown to be the major cause of mortality in Great Tit populations in the Harz Mountains of Germany.

As a result of such mortality, the sizes of bird populations are often more or less constant over time in spite of their large reproductive potential. Over the long run each female in one generation of a bird population is replaced in the next generation by, on the average, just one female. If she were replaced by two females, and just one generation per year were produced, and if each bird weighed a pound, then in less than a century the bird population would outweigh Earth. Such is the power of exponential increase. If each female were replaced by much less than one female each generation, then the population would soon be extinct. In the following example, the constraints of mortality have been relaxed, and one can see a bird population begin expansion in the direction of Earth weight.

In 1937, two male and six female Common Pheasants were introduced on to a 180-hectare island off the coast of the western United States. The island had not previously had a pheasant population, but with super-abundant food and few predators, the population exploded. Even though many birds died each winter, the original flock of eight became a horde of nearly two thousand within six breeding seasons. During that period, however, the rate of growth of the population was gradually slowed. This decrease in growth rate was probably due, at least in part, to diminishing space for male territories and possibly to decreased food supply, leading to higher juvenile mortality.

Limited space for territories may often put a cap on the size of bird populations. In their well-known study of Florida Scrub Jays (*Aphelocoma coerulescens*), American ornithologists Glen Woolfenden and John Fitzpatrick found that the density of breeding pairs remained quite constant. The habitat is saturated with breeding pairs; surplus mature birds must wait until space opens for them, often in the interim helping at the nests of their parents.

Florida Scrub Jay territories tend to be relatively constant in size, but those of other birds may vary. When territorial males are abundant, territories may be small. If, in contrast, few males seek territories, territories may expand.

And if a severe winter or some other factor significantly reduces the number of potentially breeding males, parts of the habitat that previously were used for territories will remain unoccupied in the spring. The size of populations of Short-eared Owls in conifer plantations in Scotland rise, and fall, with populations of the voles they eat — and the owls hold smaller territories when both their numbers and those of their prey are high.

In a classic study of Song Sparrows (*Melospiza melodia*) by pioneer American ornithologist Margaret Morse Nice, the number of males fluctuated over six years between 17 (much habitat unoccupied, territories large) and 44 (most habitat occupied, territories small). The two-and-a-half-fold range of population sizes of the sparrow may seem far from constancy, but compared with fluctuations of, say, the sort found in insect populations, the Song Sparrow population was quite stable. For example, in 30 years of study, a single population of checkerspot butterflies (*Euphydryas editha*) in California has gone through more than 20-fold changes in size, and enormously greater changes are commonly observed in organisms ranging from phytoplankton (minute water plants) to lemmings. Indeed, some bird populations are even more constant in size than those of the Song Sparrow. At Noss in the Shetlands, the number of pairs of Arctic Skuas varied from 25 to 60, and between 1948 and 1964 the number of Pied Flycatcher females in the Forest of Dean only varied between about 50 and 100.

Migration and nomadism can greatly influence the size of a bird population in a given area. Crossbills, for example, may move in large numbers into a habitat providing a rich, seasonal supply of conifer seeds. The crossbills breed and then move on. Immigration creates a large local population, and emigration removes it. Crossbills are an extreme case, and their sort of nomadic behaviour is normally not considered in studies of the dynamics of individual populations (since crossbills are not moving into and out of a population, but into and out of a location). The major influence of immigration on the size of bird populations is through the short-range movement of non-territorial males into unoccupied space that is suitable for territories.

Note also that migration between wintering and breeding grounds is not ordinarily important in the dynamics of populations except as it affects the mortality of migrants. Birds of a given breeding population usually return to nest in the same area each year (a phenomenon known as 'site tenacity' or 'philopatry', meaning 'site faithfulness'). The entire population moves south and then returns north. Some migrants, such as Swallows, tend to have their population sizes limited by the amount of breeding habitat; others, including Redstarts and Pied Flycatchers, seem to be largely unaffected by population density on the breeding grounds, but are instead limited by factors on the wintering grounds. Furthermore, trans-Saharan migrants such as the Whitethroat, Sedge Warbler, Redstart, and Sand Martin have had their population sizes greatly reduced because of drought in their Sahelian winter homes. Resident (non-migrating) passerines like the Nuthatch and Great and Willow Tits seem also to have their population sizes controlled largely in winter, by competition for food and, in some instances, for roosting sites.

The nature of the mechanisms that determine the size of animal populations, especially to the degree that they are 'regulated' in a manner that depends upon their density — to grow when they are sparse and shrink when dense — has long been a matter of debate. Some of the most important work bearing on such questions has been done by Dutch scientists on Great Tits and British scientists on Red Grouse, and shows that the effect of density on population dynamics can be very complex. Red Grouse, an economically important bird in Britain (where hunters bag about 400 000 per year) have been subject to a long-term decline associated with the degradation of their habitat. Moorlands and bogs have been overgrazed, drained, and converted to tree plantations. But on top of this general drop in population size is a pattern of cyclic change that appears related to grouse density. Possible causes include build-up of parasites as the population becomes more dense, changes in territoriality and aggressiveness related to density, and (least likely from the data in hand), increases in predator abundance.

As we indicated, *Homo sapiens* is subject to the same basic population dynamic factors as birds. The human population has increased about 40-fold in the eighty generations since the time of Christ, as mortality rates have dropped without compensating declines in natality, and the entire planet has become overpopulated. One result of human overpopulation and continuing rapid growth has been a decline in many bird populations, as *Homo sapiens* has hunted them, appropriated their food, and destroyed their habitats. In contrast, other bird populations have benefited from human activities. In England Great Crested Grebes have increased in response to the creation of new aquatic habitats such as flooded gravel pits, and Goldcrests, Coal Tits, and Siskins have multiplied with the creation of conifer plantations. Other populations that have undergone increases include those of some gulls, Starlings, and House Sparrows, which have thrived by exploitation of resources supplied by people and by occupation of human-modified habitats. As the human population shoots past six billion we can expect to see further increases in the populations of these 'garbage birds'.

SEE: Territoriality, p. 397; Irruptions, p. 491; Breeding Site Tenacity, p. 219; Cooperative Breeding, p. 275. REFS: Bennett and Harvey, 1988; Bergerud and Gratson, 1988; Berndt and Winkel, 1987; Campbell, 1968; Dobkin, 1994; Dobson, 1990; Ehrlich and Ehrlich, 1990; Einarsen, 1945; Harvey et al., 1988; Hogstad, 1984; Klomp, 1980; Korpimäki, 1987b; Krebs, 1970; Krebs and May, 1990; Marchant et al., 1990; Møller 1989a; Nice, 1964; Pimm, 1982; Saether, 1988, 1990; Tinbergen et al., 1985; Village, 1987; Woolfenden and Fitzpatrick, 1984; Zang, 1988.

Appendix
Legal Protection for Birds

Wildlife and the Law

SINCE the 1940s, eight major international treaties that include birds (but are not restricted to them) have been written. *The Western Hemisphere Convention* (1940), *The African Convention* (1968), and *The Berne Convention* (1979) all pay particular attention to habitat preservation by requiring parties to establish protected areas and to protect wildlife (both within and outside of those areas). *The Convention on the Conservation of Antarctic Marine Living Resources (CCAMLR)*, signed in 1980 by members of the Antarctic Treaty, limits fishing in Antarctic waters. It obliges parties to adopt an ecosystem approach to conservation and to prevent the overharvesting of krill, the principal food of numerous species including whales, penguins, and such European migrants as Arctic Terns.

The additional four conventions, when taken together, affect the conservation of an enormous number of the planet's plants and animals. These four are neither restricted to limited species nor confined to geographic areas, but emphasize protecting what is *irreplaceable*, and acknowledge that wildlife is a global heritage. The *Convention on Wetlands of International Importance Especially As Waterfowl Habitat* (Ramsar — named after the Iranian town where the treaty was signed in 1971) addresses the problem of wetland preservation. The *World Heritage Convention* was signed in 1972 and protects some 100 areas of outstanding natural (rather than cultural) value. The *Convention on International Trade in Endangered Species of Wild Fauna and Flora* (CITES) was signed in 1973 and manages international trade in endangered species by clamping down on poachers (to shrink the supply) and by making imports illegal in consumer countries (to lessen the demand). While the convention is an excellent example of international cooperation, especially between rich and poor nations, with so many countries and organisms involved, it runs the risk of becoming unenforceable. Not only is the problem of re-export increasing, especially of products in different forms, so too is the difficulty of distinguishing endangered species from others that look similar. The latest treaty, the *Bonn Convention*, was signed in 1979 and protects migratory species throughout their ranges. Collectively these conventions close the gaps in preceding treaties and presumably facilitate international cooperation.

The breakthrough in protective legislation in the 1970s coincided with public concern that the importance of birds extends beyond utilitarian values.

Birds were seen previously as sources of food, opportunities for sport and trade, and aids to agriculture (especially to control insect pests). Now they are recognized for their aesthetic, recreational, and scientific value, as well as for their importance as integral parts of the natural environment. Regional wildlife treaties cover Africa, Europe, and the Antarctic, and an Asian wildlife treaty is pending, but enactment of a worldwide treaty for protection of habitats of endangered species or endangered ecosystems has yet to be drafted.

SEE: Birds and the Law, p. 521; Ducking the Bird Laws, p. 523; Listing Birds in Danger, p. 526; European Community Birds Directive, p. 528; Conservation of Raptors, p. 103; Birds on Borders, p. 95; Wintering and Conservation, p. 409. REFS: Lyster, 1985; Mrosovsky, 1988.

Birds and the Law

EUROPEAN wildlife was once the property of royalty. In the Middle Ages, the right to hunt tended to be a lordly privilege with the 'chase' sometimes viewed as a sport to keep noblemen battle-ready. As such, vast stretches of forest were protected from poaching and over-hunting, setting the stage for some of the first European nature reserves.

But things changed. While John James Audubon was dining on Dunlin in America 150 years ago, wild birds, except for those found on private land, were the property of no one; if shot or trapped, they became the property of the shooter or trapper. Then, as European population centres grew, hunting regulations tightened — and they continue to tighten. In some cases, it has been a matter of cutting quotas. Hebridean hunting of young Gannets, for example, has gone on for at least 600 years, but the yearly cull has recently been dropped from 3000 to 2000 birds. In other cases, total bans have been imposed. The yearly five-tonne production of Corsican Blackbird paté is now, presumably, history. Today, all wild European birds are protected in principle, and most, in practice, require it.

While about 900 of the world's 9000 or so bird species are threatened with global extinction during our lifetime, few occur exclusively in the area covered by this book. The recently discovered Algerian Nuthatch, confined to a small area in Algeria, is amongst them. However, some species whose ranges include the area covered may soon disappear from the Western Palearctic. Thus, the main thrust of regional protective legislation is to maintain or enhance the range and numbers of naturally occurring birds, especially species for which there is international responsibility, and species that are particularly valuable as indicators of environmental quality.

Concern over species exploitation had been expressed off and on for centuries, but the first international law to protect European birds focused on species of value to farmers. In 1868 the General Assembly of German agriculturalists and foresters urged the Austro-Hungarian government to enter into an agreement to protect insectivorous birds. Interestingly, the Assembly also recommended the destruction of birds seen as humanity's competitors, including granivorous birds, fish-eating birds, and birds of prey. A resolution (the *1902 Convention*) calling for the protection of some 150 species useful to agriculture eventually was signed by 12 European countries. Its effectiveness was limited, however, for cooperation among countries located along migration flyways was not assured (Italy, the Netherlands, Norway, the UK and Russia had not signed), and the document contained an escape clause that emasculated the agreement.

European law reached a turning point a half-century later, with the signing of the *1950 Convention*. Safeguards were extended (theoretically) to all European birds during spring migration and breeding, and species threatened with extinction were off-limits throughout the entire year. Protection was also extended to habitats, and safeguards were required against hazards such as oil and other forms of water pollution, lighthouses, electric cables, and insecticides. Yet, even this Convention proved too vague; in failing to list the species thought to be threatened, it eventually became a 'sleeping treaty', devoid of practical impact.

The signing by Belgium, The Netherlands, and Luxembourg of the *Benelux Convention* in 1970 standardized hunting regulations and regulated the exploitation of selected birds in those countries. It allowed unlimited exploitation of three species, provided 16 others with limited protection from capture, and granted complete protection to the remaining non-game species. But as in the *1902 Convention*, it addressed only the exploitation of species, overlooking both habitat protection and the elimination of hazards.

Then, in 1979, the *Birds Directive* was adopted. It applied to *all naturally occurring wild birds in the European Economic Community* (except for Greenland, then a member but considered too anomalous). The Directive listed species considered threatened (see p. 528) and assigned legal responsibility to each Member State to conserve avian habitats and to maintain naturally occurring bird populations at ecologically appropriate levels. Member States agreed on signing to regulate trade in birds (and their parts and products), limit hunting to species that can withstand it, eliminate some methods of capture and killing (such as shooting from aeroplanes), promote scientific research, pay special attention to species introductions, and report all progress in these areas every three years. For the first time, economic considerations were made secondary to ecological, scientific, and cultural ones — at least on paper.

In May 1992 the EEC *Habitats Directive* was adopted. It extends to other groups of plants and animals, and to habitats, the protection afforded to birds by the earlier Birds Directive. By seeking to ensure the 'favorable conservation status' of habitats, the 1992 Directive recognizes the paramount importance of maintaining suitable habitat for Europe's beleaguered fauna and flora.

Each country can best persuade others to take international responsibility for nature conservation when its own record can withstand criticism. As public alarm builds in Britain and Europe over deliberate damage to habitat and overhunting, we hope that more stringent regulations with higher penalties for non-compliance will be adopted.

SEE: Wildlife and the Law, p. 520; Ducking the Bird Laws, p. 523; Listing Birds in Danger, p. 526; European Community Birds Directive, p. 528; Conservation of Raptors, p. 103; Wintering and Conservation, p. 409; Pesticides and Birds, p. 115. REF.: Lyster, 1985.

Ducking the Bird Laws

NINETEEN wildlife treaties that apply directly or indirectly to migrating birds have been signed since the turn of the century and, in theory, have eliminated many threats to the birds of Britain and the Continent. Those treaties are not without loop-holes, however, and threats continue from illegal bird trade, egg thefts, spring hunts, and illegal trapping and shooting, as well as from the destruction of bird habitats.

A single bird of prey illegally taken from its nest may fetch £25 000 in Britain and £80 000 in the Middle East. Previously when adult birds of prey were transported as contraband they were subject to high mortality from shock, suffocation, and sedatives, but traffickers now avoid most hazards by shipping incubated eggs, which are more likely to survive and are much more difficult for authorities to intercept. Insisting on irrefutable certification for new purchases does not always protect today's falconers; the forging of wildlife documents has become extremely sophisticated.

Trade in illegal cagebirds is also lucrative and difficult to control. (It is also an avenue through which diseases are spread.) Rather than shipping eggs, however, importation is commonly accomplished by 'laundering' export birds. That is, birds captured in countries where the European Community has banned trade may be shipped through neighbouring countries where trade is allowed. For example, Grey Parrots illegally trapped in Gabon and bound for Europe may be exported through Senegal, the source of nearly half of all wildbirds imported by Britain. Some 70 million pairs of exotic birds have been captured legally in Senegal and shipped during the past 15 to 20 years. Laundered birds are easily concealed in a trade of that magnitude. Paraguay, although one of the 95 signatory nations to the CITES treaty (the international agreement limiting trade in endangered species), is a well-known source of illegally-trapped exotic birds bearing forged documentation and destined for European, Asian, and North American markets.

Although the majority of Europe's 100 000 aviculturalists abhor illegal harvesting, the practice remains a multi-million pound business. While this situation prevails, cagebird fanciers and pet store owners must be monitored with diligence. That alone, however, is probably not the final answer. Even in legal harvesting, many birds are injured and killed (or their nesting disrupted) in the process of capture, and many die in transit. Legislation to forbid the trade of all wild-caught birds must eventually be put in place, and the sooner the better. To encourage compliance with such legislation, incentives to develop a more extensive captive breeding industry will be necessary, and captive-bred birds must be identifiable. One means of registering fledglings reared by aviculturalists and dealers involves fitting them with snug, seamless leg rings (called close rings) that distinguish them from (illegal) wild-reared birds.

While cagebird fanciers may unknowingly foster illegal trade in exotics, egg collectors — those seeking the shell, rather than the contents — are quite aware that they are breaking any number of regulations. In some cases strict, explicit laws with fines of up to £2000 per egg have been put in place. Nonetheless, egg-robbing, particularly in Britain, continues as hobbyists remain deeply entrenched, and spectacular seizures of collections containing up to 10 000 eggs still take place. There are reputedly 500 active egg collectors and 1000 reports of alleged egg thefts yearly. Because egg-collecting is a hobby where rarity is prized, individual nests of such highly threatened species as White-tailed Eagles, Red Kites, Ospreys, Golden Eagles, and Merlins may require (and are sometimes provided with) round-the-clock surveillance.

Perhaps the most emotionally-charged legal question surrounds the problem of spring shoots. The EC outlawed spring shoots in 1979 (Birds Directive, 79/409/EEC), but France, Greece, Italy, Spain, and Portugal (or portions of those countries) are either exempt (except during actual nesting) or their national laws are not enforced. For example, the taking of Turtle Doves was legal in France and Italy when they became signatories of the Birds Directive (Greece and Portugal at the time were not members). Not only is the hunt still legal today, it also appears to provide a front for the illegal shooting of protected species.

As Turtle Doves make their way from central Africa to northern Europe, other accompanying north-bound species such as Golden Orioles, Red-footed Falcons, Bee-eaters, and Cuckoos suffer tremendous losses from marksmen. Apparently losses have not been the result of just a few early (and busy) hunters. It is said, for example, that 40 000 of Greece's 300 000 hunters go after Turtle Doves. With that many participants, the issue of spring shoots is bound to remain contentious, and centuries-old hunting clubs, reluctant to forgo traditional hunts, will continue to run up against adverse popular opinion. In Italy (important as a land bridge for birds migrating between Europe and Africa), hunting has generated a substantial anti-hunting crusade; some 85 per cent of Italians would like to see reforms — shorter hunting seasons, a ban on spring shooting and net-trapping, fewer huntable species, and a general moratorium until scientists complete species inventories. As it stands, the size of many avian populations are unknown and bag limits are arbitrary and rarely enforced. Protests also occur in France where an estimated 40 per cent of its bird species are threatened and 90 per cent of the people polled are even against the shooting of Turtle Doves. Nonetheless, the hunt continues.

A decade ago, informal estimates indicated that 150–170 million birds might be falling to European hunters each year. More recent estimates indicate that some 15 per cent of Mediterranean migratory birds are hunted or trapped and perhaps 35 per cent of common songbirds in central Europe may vanish within a single generation. While hunting licences are required and help to assure the knowledge of hunters (in most countries skill in species identification must be exhibited before a licence will be issued), hunting is poorly regulated, if at all. The highest concentration of hunters in the world is in Malta where 30 000 of its 300 000 inhabitants kill some 4 million wild birds yearly. Italy follows, with hunters reportedly killing 50 million protected birds yearly. Hunters there are so dense that each stalks an area only about the size of two football fields. Egypt, the site of 25 per cent of the wetland in the Mediterranean, also traces declines to overhunting. While responsibility lies in part with local people who net large quantities of passerines and Quail for food, trapping falcons is alarmingly common, and foreign hunters on holiday, especially those from Malta, Italy, and France, are seriously depleting formerly common residents such as legally-protected Black-winged Kite, Little Green Bee-eaters, and Kestrel.

Non-compliance with laws protecting strategic habitats also continues. If appeals to national laws fail to halt threats, conservation organizations can appeal to the European Directive. This approach succeeded in the case of Duich Moss when malt distillers sought permission to extract peat from a bog on the Hebridean island of Islay. Duich Moss, the winter home of the second largest European aggregation of the Greenland White-fronted Goose was not only granted protection, but proceedings were brought against the British government. Despite the national and international safeguards in place, however, concern remains over continued losses (Whitethroat, Redstart, Spotted Flycatcher, Sedge Warbler, Red-backed Shrike, and Marsh Warbler are just a well-known few among the many in decline) and the chronic pressure to develop what is left of critical habitat.

One further safeguard involves creating computerized species inventories, especially for areas in contention. Inventories not only reduce the chance for developers to plead ignorance after the fact, they also substantiate the assertions of conservationists opposed to habitat alteration. Additional programmes include outlining the threats facing individual bird species. A study conducted in Britain by the Royal Society for the Protection of Birds (RSPB) identified 119 species that currently (1990) qualify as internationally significant, rare, vulnerable, declining, or thought to be in trouble. The RSPB aims to maintain or enhance the range and numbers of all naturally occurring birds, especially those for which Britain has an international accountability and those which are important as indicators of environmental quality.

Despite numerous innovative efforts, perhaps one-third of Europe's bird populations are declining. Difficulties in protection may stem from the limitations of the Birds Directive itself. Compliance of the signatories is required, but enforcement is up to each Member State; the treaty is a *directive*, not a *regulation*. As such, conditions fostering obsolete attitudes toward wildbird trade, egg-collecting, and spring shooting will continue, and chronic economic pressures can't help but encourage laxness in habitat protection at the national level. It should also be remembered that the combined territories of the Member States only partially cover the migratory ranges of most bird species, leaving them open to exploitation elsewhere. Guaranteeing protection of the birds of Britain and Europe just while they are in residence depends more on relentless public interest and pressure. The RSPB, with more members than any British political party is now Europe's largest voluntary conservation organization. Doubtless its efforts will continue to make the deciding difference when specific laws appear too difficult or too expensive to enforce.

SEE: European Community Birds Directive, p. 528; Listing Birds in Danger, p. 526; Birds and the Law, p. 521; Wildlife and the Law, p. 520; Conservation of Raptors, p. 103; Wintering and Conservation, p. 407. REFS: Anon, 1990a; Brooke, 1989; Cramp, 1977; Graham, 1988; Hudson, 1990; Lyster, 1985; Starr, 1989; Telander, 1990.

Listing Birds in Danger

AFTER a full discussion on the conservation of wild birds, the European Economic Community adopted Council Directive of 2 April 1979. The Directive relates to the conservation of *all* naturally occurring wild birds within its jurisdiction, but it lists separately (Annex I) those species requiring special protection. Annex I birds are considered 'in danger of extinction, vulnerable to specific changes in their habitat, considered rare because of the small size of their populations or because of their restricted distribution, or, finally, requiring special attention because of the specificity of their habitat'. As a result of subsequent surveys, Annex I has been repeatedly amended (1981, 1985, 1991) and 101 species and subspecies have now been added to the 74 originally listed.

On p. 528 we list the 175 birds (including 156 species and 19 subspecies) requiring special protection (Annex I) as of 1991. We also cite 72 species that may be hunted (Annex II-1, -2), 17 that may be marketed with permits (Annex III-1, -2), and 9 targeted to encourage additional research both on their biological status and on the effects of marketing on that status (Annex III-3).

Will listing in Annex I provide adequate protection for European wild birds now considered at risk? In North America, where a federal 'listing' system was established in 1973, serious concern arose among conservationists that specifying endangerment would not, in itself, suffice. Annex I may be seen as somewhat analogous to the US Threatened and Endangered Species List. Both have drawbacks. In Annex I no differentiation is made between highly endangered species and comparatively less threatened ones, and in North America, specification of endangerment is reserved for species at severe risk, so that by the time a species is officially listed it may be on the verge of extinction.

In North America, the National Audubon Society publishes an unofficial 'Blue List' to provide early warning of range reductions and impending losses in bird populations. The list is updated periodically to make it easier to identify both serious ongoing regional losses and increases in formerly imperilled populations. So far, two summarizing decade lists have also been published. The decade lists include the birds nominated for current listing as well as all species previously listed. These lists, although unofficial, aid in confirmation of the changing status of species and identification of those requiring further study.

The effectiveness of such an early warning system depends on the accuracy of the recommendations for nomination or deletion supplied by regional Blue List compilers and the responsiveness of government agencies charged with species conservation. Submission of data to compilers is a way for field observers to influence policies of local and national agencies concerned with bird species protection. More information on the North American approach is available from: American Birds Blue List, c/o *American Birds*, National Audubon Society, 700 Broadway, New York, NY 10003, USA.

In a programme similar to Blue Listing, the Royal Society for the Protection of Birds (RSPB) and the former Nature Conservancy Council have given priority to 116 species listed in the *Red Data Book for Birds in Britain*. In addition, preparations have been made for a series of 'Action Plans' entailing the steps the Society will take to secure the future of each species and its habitats in the UK and other parts of the species' range. Thus, rather than focusing attention on the breeding species that are candidates for imperilled status worldwide (such as the Corncrake, Red Kite and White-tailed Eagle), emphasis will be placed on species at risk within Britain even though they may be secure outside of the UK. More information on this approach is available from The Royal Society for the Protection of Birds, The Lodge, Sandy, Bedfordshire, SG19 2DL.

An alternative to lists for birds in trouble has been suggested by Christoph Imboden, Director General of the International Council for Bird Preservation (ICBP), who proposed compilation of 'Green Lists' containing those species definitely known to be secure. By shifting the burden of proof to those who maintain that 'all is well', a more realistic indication of the extinction crisis may be provided. Red Data books are most valuable where species are well studied and there are large numbers of amateur birdwatchers. Green lists would be most helpful in providing a true picture of endangerment in the tropics where birdwatchers and field guides are less common and information on rarity is often scanty.

SEE: European Community Birds Directive, p. 528; Birds and the Law, p. 521; Ducking the Bird Laws, p. 523; Wildlife and the Law, p. 520; Wintering and Conservation, p. 409. REFS: Arbib, 1971; Bibby, *et al.*, 1989; Diamond, 1988; Ehrlich *et al.*, 1992; OJEC 1979, 1985, 1991; Tate, 1981, 1986.

European Community Birds Directive

Annex I: Species or subspecies afforded special protection
*Not treated in this book

Avocet
Bittern: Eurasian; Little
Bluethroat
Bullfinch: Azores*
Bunting: Cinereous; Cretzschmar's;
    Ortolan
Bustard: Great; Little; Houbara
Buttonquail: Common (Andalusian
    Hemipode)
Buzzard: Honey; Long-legged
Capercaillie
Chaffinch: (Hierro subspecies);*
    Canary Island*
Coot: Crested
Cormorant: Great (Continental
    subspecies); Pygmy
Corncrake
Chough
Courser: Cream-coloured
Crake: Baillon's; Little; Spotted
Crane: Common
Crossbill: Scottish
Curlew: Slender-billed*; Stone
Diver: Black-throated; Great
    Northern; Red-throated
Dotterel
Duck: Ferruginous; White-headed
Eagle: Bonelli's; Booted; Golden;
    Imperial; Lesser Spotted; Short-
    toed; Spanish Imperial; Spotted
Egret: Great White; Little
Falcon: Eleonora's; Lanner;
    Peregrine
Finch: Trumpeter
Flamingo: Greater
Flycatcher: Collared; Red-breasted;
    Semi-collared*

Freira* (Soft-plumaged Petrel,
    Madeira subspecies. Also known
    as Madeira Petrel)
Gallinule: Purple
Gon-gon* (Soft-plumaged Petrel,
    Cape Verde subspecies. Also
    known as Cape Verde
    Petrel)
Goose: Barnacle; Lesser White-
    fronted; Red-breasted; White-
    fronted; (Greenland subspecies)
Goshawk (Corsican-Sardinian
    subspecies)
Grebe: Slavonian
Grouse: Black (Continental species);
    Hazel
Guillemot (Iberian subspecies)
Gull: Audouin's; Mediterranean;
    Slender-billed
Harrier: Hen; Marsh; Montagu's;
    Pallid
Heron: Purple; Squacco
Ibis: Glossy
Kestrel: Lesser
Kingfisher: Common
Kite: Black; Black-winged;
    Red
Lammergeier (Bearded Vulture)
Lark: Calandra; Dupont's; Short-
    toed; Thekla
Merlin
Night Heron
Nightjar
Nuthatch: Corsican; Kruper's
Osprey
Owl: Eagle; Pygmy; Short-eared;
    Snowy; Tengmalm's

Partridge: (Iberian and Italian subspecies); Barbary; Rock (Alpine and Sicilian subspecies)
Pelican: Dalmatian; White
Petrel: Bulwer's*; Frigate (White-faced Storm-Petrel); Storm
Phalarope: Red-necked
Pigeon: Bolle's Laurel*; Laurel*; Long-toed*
Pipit: Tawny
Plover: Golden; Spur-winged
Pratincole: Collared
Ptarmigan (Pyrenean and Alpine sub-species)
Roller: European
Ruff
Sandgrouse: Pin-tailed; Black-bellied
Sandpiper: Wood
Sea Eagle: White-tailed
Shag (Mediterranean subspecies)
Shearwater: Cory's; Manx (Balearic subspecies); Little*
Shelduck: Ruddy
Shrike: Lesser Grey; Red-backed
Snipe: Great

Sparrowhawk (Canarian-Madeirian subspecies); Levant
Spoonbill: Eurasian
Stilt: Black-winged
Stonechat: Canary Islands
Stork: Black; White
Storm-Petrel: Leach's; Madeiran*
Swan: Bewick's; Whooper
Swift: White-rumped
Teal: Marbled
Tern: Arctic; Black; Caspian; Common; Gull-billed; Little; Roseate; Sandwich; Whiskered
Vulture: Black; Egyptian; Griffon (see Lammergeier)
Warbler: Aquatic; Barred; Dartford; Marmora's; Moustached; Olive-tree; Rüppell's
Wheatear: Black
Woodlark
Woodpecker: Black; Great Spotted (Gran Canaria and Tenerife subspecies); Grey-headed; Middle Spotted; Syrian; Three-toed; White-backed
Woodpigeon (Azores subspecies)
Wren (Fair Isle subspecies)

Annex II: 72 Birds which may be hunted
(1 = hunting permitted throughout area; 2 = hunting limited to some member states)

Blackbird (2)
Capercaillie (2)
Coot: Common (1)
Curlew (2)
Dove: Collared (2); Rock/Feral Pigeon (1); Stock (2); Turtle (2)
Duck: Long-tailed (2); Tufted (1)
Eider: Common (2)
Fieldfare (2)
Gadwall (1)
Garganey (1)
Godwit: Bar-tailed (2); Black-tailed (2)
Goldeneye (2)

Goosander (2)
Goose: Bean (1); Brent (2); Canada (1); Greylag (1); Pink-footed (2); White-fronted (2)
Greenshank (2)
Grouse: Black (2); Hazel (2); Red/Willow (1)
Gull: Black-headed (2); Common (2); Great Black-backed (2); Herring (2); Lesser Black-backed (2)
Knot* (2)
Lapwing (2)
Mallard (1)

Merganser: Red-breasted (2)
Moorhen (2)
Oystercatcher (2)
Partridge: (1); Barbary (2);
   Red-legged (1); Rock (1)
Pheasant: Common (1)
Pigeon: Wood (1)
Pintail (1)
Plover: Golden (2); Grey (2)
Pochard: (1); Red-crested (2)
Ptarmigan (1)
Quail: Common (2)
Rail: Water (2)
Redshank: (2); Spotted (2)

Redwing (2)
Ruff (2)
Scaup (2)
Scoter: Common (2);
   Velvet (2)
Shoveler (1)
Skylark (2)
Snipe: Common (1); Jack (1)
Swan: Mute (2)
Teal (1)
Thrush: Mistle (2); Song (2)
Whimbrel (2)
Wigeon (1)
Woodcock (1)

Annex III (1,2): 17 Species which may be marketed with permits
(1 = marketing permitted throughout area; 2 = marketing limited to some
member states)

Capercaillie (2)
Coot: Common (2)
Duck: Tufted (2)
Eider: Common (2)
Goose: Greylag (2)
Grouse: Red/Willow (1)
Mallard (1)
Partridge: (1); Barbary (1);
   Red-legged (1)

Pheasant: Common (1)
Pigeon: Wood (1)
Pintail (2)
Pochard (2)
Ptarmigan (2)
Teal (2)
Pigeon (2)

Annex III: 9 Species targeted for further research

Goose: White-fronted
Grouse: Black
Plover: Golden
Scaup

Scoter: Common
Shoveler
Snipe: Common; Jack
Woodcock

REFS: Lyster, 1985; *OJEC* 1979, 1985, 1991.
SEE: Listing Birds in Danger, p. 526.

Able, K. P. and Bingman, V. P. (1987). The development of orientation and navigation behavior in birds. *Quarterly Review of Biology*, **62**, 1–29.

Alatalo, R. V. (1982). Multidimensional foraging niche organization of foliage-gleaning birds in northern Finland. *Ornis Scandinavica*, **13**, 56–71.

Alatalo, R. V. and Lundberg, A. (1983). Laboratory experiments on habitat separation and foraging efficiency in Marsh and Willow Tits. *Ornis Scandinavica*, **14**, 115–22.

Alatalo, R. V. and Lundberg, A. (1984). Polyterritorial polygyny in the Pied Flycatcher *Ficedula hypoleuca* — evidence for the deception hypothesis. *Ann. Zool. Fenn.*, **21**, 217–28.

Alatalo, R. V., Carlson, A., Lundberg, A., and Ulfstrand, S. (1981). The conflict between male polygyny and female monogamy: the case of the Pied Flycatcher (*Ficedula hypoleuca*). *American Naturalist*, **117**, 738–53.

Alatalo, R. V., Lundberg, A., and Stählbrandt, K. (1982). Why do Pied Flycatcher females mate with already-mated males? *Animal Behaviour*, **30**, 586–93.

Alatalo, R. V., Gustafsson, L., and Lundberg, A. (1984). High frequency of cuckoldry in Pied and Collared Flycatchers. *Oikos*, **42**, 41–7.

Alatalo, R. V., Lundberg, A., and Ulfstrand, S. (1985a). In *Habitat selection in birds*, (ed. M. L. Cody), pp. 59–83. Academic Press, New York.

Alatalo, R. V., Gustafsson, L., Lundberg, A., and Ulfstrand, S. (1985b). Habitat shift of the Willow Tit *Parus montanus* in the absence of the Marsh Tit *Parus palustris*. *Ornis Scandinavica*, **16**, 121–8.

Alatalo, R. V., Gottlander, K., and Lundberg, A. (1987). Extra-pair copulations and mate guarding in the polyterritorial Pied Flycatcher, *Ficedula hypoleuca*. *Behaviour*, **101**, 139–55.

Alerstam, T. (1981). The course and timing of bird migration. In *Animal migration*. (ed. D. J. Aidley), pp. 9–54. Cambridge University Press, London.

Alerstam, T. and Hogstedt, G. (1981). Evolution of hole-nesting in birds. *Ornis Scandinavica*, **12**, 188–93.

Alerstam, T. and Hogstedt, G. (1982). Bird migration and reproduction in relation to habitats for survival and breeding. *Ornis Scandinavica*, **13**, 25–37.

Alerstam, T. and Hogstedt, G. (1985). Sheltered nesting in birds: a reply to Greenwood and an evaluation of the Canadian avifauna. *Ornis Scandinavica*, **16**, 158–62.

Ali, S. and Ripley, S. D. (1987). *Compact handbook of the birds of India and Pakistan*. Oxford University Press.

Alison, R. M. (1975). Breeding biology and behavior of the Oldsquaw (*Clangula hyemalis* L.). *Ornithological Monographs*, **No. 18**.

Alonso, J. C., Alonso, J. A., and Veiga, J. P. (1987). Flocking in wintering Common Cranes *Grus grus*: influence of population size, food abundance and habitat patchiness. *Ornis Scandinavica*, **18**, 53–60.

Amat, J. A. (1985). Nest parasitism of Pochard *Aythya ferina* by Red-crested Pochard *Netta rufina*. *Ibis*, **127**, 255–62.

Amat, J. A. and Aguilera, E. (1990). Tactics of Black-headed Gulls robbing egrets and waders. *Animal Behaviour*, **39**, 70–7.

Amat, J. A. and Soriguer, R. (1984). Kleptoparasitism of Coots by Gadwalls. *Ornis Scandinavica*, **15**, 188–94.

Anderson, D. J. (1990). Evolution of obligate siblicide in boobies. I. A test of the insurance-egg hypothesis. *American Naturalist*, **135**, 334–50.

Anderson, G. L. and Braun, E. J. (1985). Postrenal modifications of urine in birds. *American Journal of Physiology*, 248, **17**, R93–8.

Anderson, D. J., Stoyan, N. C., and Ricklefs, R. E. (1987). Why are there no viviparous birds? A comment. *American Naturalist*, **130**, 941–7.

Andersson, M. (1982). Female choice selects for extreme tail length in a widowbird. *Nature*, **299**, 818–20.

Andersson, M. and Eriksson, M. O. G. (1982). Nest parasitism in Goldeneyes *Bucephala clangula*: some evolutionary aspects. *American Naturalist*, **120**, 1–16.

Andrew, R. J. (1961). The displays given by passerines in courtship and reproductive fighting: a review. *Ibis*, **103A**, 315–48, 549–79.

Anon. (1990*a*). A traveler's guide to European border parks. *Natural History*, June, pp. 64–70.

Anon. (1990*b*). Sneaky starlings. *Discover*, June, p. 10.

Arbib, R. (1971). Announcing—The Blue List: an 'early warning system' for birds. *American Birds*, **25**, 948–9.

Arcese, P. and Smith, J. N. M. (1985). Phenotypic correlates and ecological consequences of dominance in Song Sparrows. *Journal of Animal Ecology*, **54**, 817–30.

Armstrong, E. A. (1949). Diversionary display: the nature and origin of distraction display. *Ibis*, **91**, 88–97, 179–88.

Arvidsson, B. and Klaesson, P. (1986). Territory size in a Willow Warbler *Phylloscopus trochilus* population in mountain birch forest in Swedish Lapland. *Ornis Scandinavica*, **17**, 24–30.

Ashmole, N. P. (1963). The regulation of numbers of tropical oceanic birds. *Ibis*, **103B**, 458–73.

Askenmo, C., Brömssen, A., von Ekman, J., and Jansson, C. (1977). Impact of some wintering birds on spider abundance in spruce. *Oikos*, **28**, 90–4.

Askins, R. A., Lynch, J. A., and Greenberg, R. (1990). Population declines in migratory birds in eastern North America. In *Current ornithology*, (ed. D. M. Power), pp. 1–57.

Aubin, T. and Bremond, J.-C. (1983). The process of species-specific song recognition in the Skylark *Alauda arvensis*. An experimental study by means of synthesis. *Z. Tierpsychol.*, **61**, 141–52.

Audubon, J. J. (1840–1844). *Birds of America*, Vols. 1–9. (Published by the author).

Avery, M. and Sherwood, G. (1982). The lekking behaviour of Great Snipe. *Ornis Scandinavica*, **13**, 72–8.

Baerends, G. P. (1975). An evaluation of the conflict hypothesis as an explanatory principle for the evolution of displays. In *Function and evolution in behavior*, (eds. G. Baerends, C. Beer, and A. Manning), pp. 187–227. Clarendon Press, Oxford.

Bailey, R. E. (1952). The incubation patch of passerine birds. *Condor*, **54**, 121–36.

Baines, D. (1988). The effects of improvement of upland, marginal grasslands on the distribution and density of breeding wading birds (Charadriiformes) in northern England. *Biological Conservation*, **45**, 221–36.

Bairlein, F. (1988). How do migratory songbirds cross the Sahara? *Trends in Ecology and Evolution*, **3**, 191–4.

Baker, M. C. (1988). Sexual selection and size of repertoire in songbirds. *Acta Congr. Ornithol. Internat.* **XIX**, 1358–65.

Baker, R. R. and Parker, G. A. (1979). The evolution of bird coloration. *Philos. Trans. Royal Soc. London*, **B287**, 63–130.

Balfour, E. and Cadbury, C. J. (1979). Polygyny, spacing and sex ratio among Hen Harriers *Circus cyaneus* in Orkney, Scotland. *Ornis Scandinavica*, **10**, 133–41.

Bang, B. G. and Wenzel, B. M. (1985). The nasal cavity and olfactory system. In *Form and function in birds*, (eds. A. S. King and J. McLelland), pp. 195–225, Vol. 3. Academic Press, New York.

Baptista, L. F. and Catchpole, C. K. (1989). Vocal mimicry and interspecific aggression in songbirds: experiments using White-crowned Sparrow imitation of Song Sparrow song. *Behaviour*, **109**, 247–57.

Barash, D. P. (1975). Evolutionary aspects of parental behavior: distraction behavior of the Alpine Accentor. *Wilson Bulletin*, **85**, 367–73.

Barnard, C. J. (1982). Social mimicry and interspecific exploitation. *American Naturalist*, **120**, 411–15.

Barnard, C. J. (1984*a*). When cheats may prosper. In *Producers and scroungers*, (ed. C. J. Barnard), pp. 6–33. Croom and Helm, London.

Barnard, C. J. (1984*b*). The evolution of food-scrounging strategies within and between species. In *Producers and scroungers*, (ed. C. J. Barnard), pp. 95–126. Croom and Helm, London.

Barnard, C. J., Thompson, D. B. A., and Stephens, H. (1982). Time budgets, feeding efficiency and flock dynamics in mixed species flocks of lapwings, golden plovers and gulls. *Behaviour*, **80**, 44–69.

Barrentin, C. D. (1980). Ingestion of grit by nesting Barn Swallows. *Journal of Field Ornithology*, **51**, 368–71.

Beattie, A. J. (1985). *The evolutionary ecology of ant-plant mutualisms*. Cambridge University Press, Cambridge.

Beaver, D. L. (1980). Recovery of an American Robin population after early DDT use. *Journal of Field Ornithology*, **51**, 220–8.

Bech, C. and Reinertsen, R. E. (1989). *Physiology of cold adaptation in birds*. Plenum Press, London.

Beck, W. and Wiltschko, W. (1988). Magnetic factors control the migratory direction of Pied Flycatchers (*Ficedula hypoleuca* Pallas). Acta Congr. Internat. Ornithol. **XIX**, Vol. 2, pp. 1955–62. University of Ottawa Press.

Becker, P. H. (1982). The coding of species-specific characteristics in bird sounds. In *Acoustic communications in birds*, (eds. D. E. Kroodsma and E. H. Miller), Vol. 1. Academic Press, New York.

Beecher, M. D., Beecher, I. M., and Hahn, S. (1981). Parent–offspring recognition in Bank Swallows (*Riparia riparia*): II. Development and acoustic basis. *Animal Behaviour*, **29**, 95–101.

Beecher, W. J. (1955). *Attracting birds to your backyard*. All-Pets Books, Inc., Fond du Lac, Wisconsin.

Beehler, B. and Foster, M. S. (1988). Hotshots, hotspots, and female preference in the organization of lek mating systems. *American Naturalist*, **131**, 203–19.

Beer, C. G. (1979). Vocal communication between Laughing Gull parents and chicks. *Behaviour*, **70**, 118–46.

Beintema, A. J. (1988). Conservation of grassland bird communities in the Netherlands. In *Ecology and conservation of grassland birds*, (P. D. Goriup), pp. 105–11. ICBP Technical Publication No. 7.

Bengtson, S. A. (1984). Breeding ecology and extinction of the Great Auk (*Pinguinus impennis*): anecdotal evidence and conjectures. *Auk*, **101**, 1–12.

Benkman, C. W. (1988). On the advantages of crossed mandibles: an experimental approach. *Ibis*, **130**, 288–93.

Bennett, P. and Harvey, P. (1988). How fecundity balances mortality in birds. *Nature*, **333**, 216.

Bent, A. C. (1926). *Life histories of North American marsh birds*. United States National Museum, Washington, DC. Reprinted by Dover, New York, [1962–1968].

Bergerud, A. T. and Gratson, M. W. (eds.). (1988). *Adaptive strategies and population ecology of northern grouse*. University of Minnesota Press, Minneapolis.

Berman, C. (1978). Why animals form groups. *New Scientist*, 26 January, pp. 212–14.

Berndt, R. and Winkel, W. (1987). Bestandsentwicklung und Brutzeit-Daten der Sumpfmeise (*Parus palustris*) Befunde aus dem südöstlichen Niedersachsen. *Die Vogelwelt*, **108**, 121.

Berner, T. O. and Grubb, Jr. T. C. (1985). An experimental analysis of mixed-species flocking in birds in deciduous woodland. *Ecology*, **66**, 1229–36.

Berthold, P. (1988). The control of migration in European warblers. Acta Congr. Internat. Ornithol. **XIX**, Vol. 1, pp. 215–49. University of Ottawa Press.

Bezzel, E. (1961). Über Mischgelege bei Enten. *Die Vogelwelt*, **82**, 97–101.

Bezzel, E. and Engler, U. (1985). Dynamik binnenländischer Rastbestände des Höckerschwans (*Cygnus olor*) und das Bläffhuhns (*Fulica atra*). *Die Vogelwelt*, **106**, 161–84.

Bezzel, E. and Hashmi, D. (1989). Nimmt der Zwergtaucher (*Tachybaptus ruficollis*) Indextrends von Rastbeständen aus Sübayern. *Die Vogelwelt*, **110**, 42–51.

Bibby, C. J. (1982). Polygyny and breeding ecology of the Cetti's Warbler *Cettia cetti*. *Ibis*, **124**, 288–301.

Bibby, C., Housden, S., Porter, R., and Thomas, G. (1989). *A conservation strategy for birds*. Royal Society for the Protection of Birds. pp. 1–74.

Birkhead, M. and Perrins, C. M. (1986). *The Mute Swan*. Croom Helm, London.

Birkhead, T. R. (1977). The effect of habitat and density on breeding succession in the common guillemot (*Uria aalgae*). *Journal of Animal Ecology*, **46**, 751–64.

Birkhead, T. R. (1979). Mate guarding in the Magpie (*Pica pica*). *Animal Behaviour*, **27**, 866–74.

Birkhead, T. R. (1982). Timing and duration of mate-guarding in Magpies (*Pica pica*). *Animal Behaviour*, **30**, 277–83.

Birkhead, T. R. (1987). Sperm competition in birds. *Trends in Ecology and Evolution*, **2**, 268–71.

Birkhead, T. R. (1988). Behavioral aspects of sperm competition in birds. *Adv. Study Behavior*, **18**, 35–72.

Birkhead, T. R. (1989). Studies of west Palearctic birds: 189 Magpie. *British Birds*, **82**, 583–600.

Birkhead, T. R. (1991). *The magpies: the ecology and behaviour of Black-billed and Yellow-billed Magpies*. Poyser, Academic Press, London.

Blackburn, D. G. and Evans, H. E. (1986). Why are there no viviparous birds? *American Naturalist*, **128**, 165–90.

Blem, C. R. (1990). Avian energy storage. In *Current ornithology*, (ed. D. M. Power), pp. 59–113. Plenum, New York.

Blockstein, D. E. and Tordoff, H. B. (1985). Gone forever: a contemporary look at the extinction of the Passenger Pigeon. *American Birds*, **39**, 845–51.

Boag, D. A. (1982). *The Kingfisher*. Blandford Press, Poole.

Boag, D. A. and Alexander, M. (1986). *The Atlantic Puffin*. Blandford Press, Poole.

Bock, C. E. and Lepthien, L. W. (1976). Synchronous eruptions of boreal seed-eating birds. *American Naturalist*, **110**, 559–71.

Boersma, P. D. (1986). Ingestion of petroleum by seabirds can serve as a monitor of water quality. *Science*, **231**, 373–6.

Böhning-Gaese, K. (1992). Ursachen für Bestandseinbusen europäischer Singvögel: eine Analyse der Fangdaten des Mettnau-Reit-Illmitz-Programms. *Journal für Ornithologie*, **133**, 413–25.

Bollinger, R. C. and Bowes, E. (1973). Another chapter in the 'ornithological mystery story'. *American Birds*, **27**, 741–2.

Bonney, R. E. (1986). Dicofol stays on the market. *Audubon*, January, 124–5.

Boot, A. S. (1987). Coot feeding on Black-headed Gull droppings. *British Birds*, **80**, 573.

Borowiec, M. and Lontkowski, J. (1988). Polygyny in the Sedge Warbler *Acrocephalus schoenobaenus*. *Die Vogelwelt*, **109**, 222–6.

Botkin, D., Woodby, D., and Nisbet, R. (1991). Kirtland's Warbler habitats: a possible early indicator of climatic warming. *Biological Conservation*, (in press).

Bowers, M. D., Brown, I. L., and Wheye, D. (1985). Bird predation as a selective agent in a butterfly population. *Evolution*, **39**, 93–103.

Boyden, T. C. (1978). Territorial defense against hummingbirds and insects by tropical hummingbirds. *Condor*, **80**, 216–21.

Brackenbury, J. H. (1982). The structural basis of voice production and its relationship to sound characteristics. In *Acoustic communication in birds*, Vol. 1 (eds. D. E. Kroodsma and E. H. Miller), pp. 53–73. Academic Press, New York.

Bradbury, J. W. and Gibson, R. (1983). Leks and mate choice. In *Mate choice* (ed. P. Bateson), pp. 109–38. Cambridge University Press.

Brent, R., Pedersen, P. F., Bech, C., and Johansen, K. (1985). Thermal balance in the European Coot *Fulica atra* exposed to temperatures from −28 °C to 40 °C. *Ornis Scandinavica*, **16**, 145–50.

Brichetti, P. and Di Capi, C. (1987). Conservation of the Corsican Nuthatch *Sitta whiteheadi* Sharpe, and proposals for habitat management. *Biological Conservation*, **39**, 13–21.

Bristow, P. (1989). Ring-billed Gulls apparently feeding on gulls' droppings. *British Birds*, **82**, 76.

Brittingham, M. C. and Temple, S. A. (1983). Have cowbirds caused forest songbirds to decline? *BioScience*, **33**, 31–5.

Brockmann, H. J. and Barnard, C. J. (1979). Kleptoparasitism in birds. *Animal Behaviour*, **27**, 487–514.

Brooke, M. de L. (1989). A birthday for birds. *New Scientist*, February 4, pp. 54–7.

Brooke, M. de L. (1990). *The Manx Shearwater*. Poyser, Academic Press, London.

Brooke, de L. M. and Davies, N. B. (1988). Egg mimicry by cuckoos *Cuculus canorus* in relation to discrimination by hosts. *Nature*, **335**, 630–2.

Brooks, W. S. (1978). Triphasic feeding behavior and the esophageal diverticulum in redpolls. *Auk*, **95**, 182–3.

Brower, J. V. Z. (1958). Experimental studies of mimicry in some North American butterflies. I. *Danaus plexippus* and *Limenitis archippus archippus*. *Evolution*, **12**, 32–47.

Brown, C. R. (1986). Cliff Swallow colonies as information centers. *Science*, **234**, 83–5.

Brown, C. R. and Brown, M. B. (1986). Ectoparasitism as a cost of coloniality in Cliff Swallows (*Hirundo pyrrhonota*). *Ecology*, **67**, 1206–18.

Brown, C. R. and Brown, M. B. (1988). A new form of reproductive parasitism in Cliff Swallows. *Nature*, **331**, 66–8.

Brown, J. L. (1987). *Helping and communal breeding in birds*. Princeton University Press, Princeton, NJ.

Brown, L. and Amadon, D. (1968). *Eagles, hawks, and falcons of the world*, Vols 1 and 2. McGraw-Hill, London.

Buchheister, C. W. and Graham, Jr., F. (1973). From the swamp back: a concise and candid history of the Audubon movement. *Audubon*, January, pp. 4–43.

Bull, E. L. and Henjum, M. G. (1987). The neighborly great gray owl. *Natural History*, September, pp. 32–40.

Bunn, D. S., Warburton, A. B., and Wilson, R. D. S. (1982). *The Barn Owl*. Poyser, Calton, Staffordshire.

Burger, J. and Olla, B. L. (eds.). (1984). *Shorebirds: Migration and foraging behavior, behavior of marine animals*, Vol. 6. Plenum, New York.

Burke, T. and Bruford, M. W. (1987). DNA fingerprinting in birds. *Nature*, **327**, 149–52.

Burton, R. (1985). *Bird behavior*. Granada, London.

Burtt, E. H. and Hailman, J. P. (1978). Head-scratching among North American wood-warblers (Parulidae). *Ibis*, **120**, 153–70.

Busche, G. (1989). Drastische Bestandseinbussen der Feldlerche *Alauda aevensis* au Grunlandflächen in Schleswig-Holstein. *Die Vogelwelt*, **110**, 51–9.

Butcher, G. S. and Rohwer, S. (1990). The evolution of conspicuous and distinctive coloration for communication in birds. *Current Ornithology*, **7**, 51–108.

Butcher, G. S., Niering, W. A., Barry, W. J., and Goodwin, R. H. (1981). Equilibrium biogeography and the size of nature reserves: an avian case study. *Oecologia*, **49**, 29–37.

BWP, *Birds of the Western Palearctic*. *See references under* Cramp and co-authors.

Cade, T. J. (1982). *The falcons of the world*. Cornell University Press, Ithaca, NY.

Cain, A. J. and Sheppard, P. M. (1954). Natural selection in *Cepaea*. *Genetics*, **39**, 89–116.

Calder, W. A. (1974). Consequences of body size for avian energetics. In *Avian energetics*, (ed. R. A. Paynter, Jr.), pp. 86–151. Nuttall Ornithology Club, Publication 15. Cambridge, MA.

Calder, W. A. (1984). *Size, function, and life history*. Harvard University Press, Cambridge.

Calder, W. A. and King, J. R. (1974). Thermal and caloric relations in birds. In *Avian biology*, (eds. D. S. Farner, J. R. King, and K. C. Parkes), Vol. 4, pp. 259–413. Academic Press, New York.

Campbell, B. (1968). The Dean nestbox study, 1942–1964. *Forestry*, **41**, 27–46.

Caple, G., Balda, R. P., and Willis, W. R. (1983). The physics of leaping animals and the evolution of preflight. *American Naturalist*, **121**, 455–76.

Carey, C. (1983). Structure and function of avian eggs. *Current Ornithology*, **1**, 69–103.

Carlson, A. and Moreno, J. (1983). Sexual size dimorphism and its effect on load size and loading efficiency in Wheatears *Oenanthe oenanthe*. *Ornis Scandinavica*, **14**, 198–201.

Carson, R. (1962). *Silent spring*. Houghton Mifflin, Boston, MA.

Catchpole, C. K. (1987). Bird song, sexual selection, and female choice. *Trends in Ecology and Evolution*, **2**, 94–7.

Catchpole, C. K. and Leisler, B. (1989). Variation in the song of the Aquatic Warbler *Acrocephalus paludicola* in response to playback of different song structures. *Ethology*, **82**, 125–38.

Chapuis, C. (1971). Un exemple de l'influence du milieu sur les emissions vocales des oiseaux: l'evolution des chants en foret equatoriale. *Terre et Vie*, **25**, 183–202.

Charig, A. (1979). *A new look at the dinosaurs*. Mayflower Books, New York.

Churcher, P. B. and Lawton, J. H. (1989). Beware of well-fed felines. *Natural History*, July, pp. 40–6.

Clark, A. B. and Wilson, D. S. (1981). Avian breeding adaptations: hatching asynchrony, brood reduction, and nest failure. *Quarterly Review of Biology*, **56**, 253–277.

Clark, C. C., Clark, L., and Clark, L. (1990). 'Anting' behavior by comon grackles and European starlings. *Wilson Bulletin*, **102**, 167–9.

Clark, G. A., Jr. (1969). Spread-wing postures in Pelecaniformes, Ciconiiformes, and Falconiformes. *Auk,* **86,** 136–9.

Clark, L. and Mason, J. R. (1985). Use of nest material as insecticidal and antipathogenic agents by the European Starling. *Oecologia,* **67,** 169–76.

Clark, R. G. and Ohmart, R. D. (1985). Spread-wing posture of Turkey Vultures: single or multiple function? *Condor,* **87,** 350–5.

Cody, M. L. (1978). Habitat selection and interspecific territoriality among sylviid warblers of England and Sweden. *Ecological Monographs,* **48,** 351–96.

Cody, M. L. (1981). Habitat selection in birds: the roles of habitat structure, competitors, and productivity. *BioScience,* **31,** 107–13.

Cody, M. (ed.) (1985*a*). *Habitat selection in birds.* Academic Press, New York.

Cody, M. L. (1985*b*). Habitat selection in the sylviine warblers of western Europe and North Africa. In *Habitat selection in birds,* (ed. M. L. Cody), pp. 85–129. Academic Press, New York.

Collias, N. E. and Collias, E. C. (1984). *Nest building and bird behavior.* Princeton University Press, Princeton.

Condor, P. (1989). *The Wheatear.* Croom and Helm, London.

Confer, J. L. and Knapp, K. (1979). The changing proportion of Blue-winged and Golden-winged Warblers in Tompkins County and their habitat selection. *Kingbird,* **29,** 8–14.

Costello, D. F. (1971). *The world of the gull.* J. B. Lippincott, Philadelphia.

Cracraft, J. (1986). The origin and early diversification of birds. *Paleobiology,* **12,** 383–99.

Cracraft, J. (1988). Early evolution of birds. *Nature,* **331,** 389–90.

Cramp, S. (1977). *Bird conservation in Europe: a report prepared for the Environment and Consumer Protection Service,* Her Majesty's Stationery Office, London.

Cramp, S. and Simmons, K. E. L. (eds.) (1977). *Handbook of the birds of Europe, the Middle East, and North Africa: The birds of the Western Palearctic. Volume I.* Oxford University Press.

Cramp, S. and Simmons, K. E. L. (eds.) (1979). *Handbook of the birds of Europe, the Middle East, and North Africa: The birds of the Western Palearctic, Volume II.* Oxford University Press.

Cramp, S. and Simmons, K. E. L. (eds.) (1982). *Handbook of the birds of Europe, the Middle East, and North Africa: The birds of the Western Palearctic, Volume III.* Oxford University Press.

Cramp, S. (ed.) (1985). *Handbook of the birds of Europe, the Middle East, and North Africa: The birds of the Western Palearctic, Volume IV.* Oxford University Press.

Cramp, S. (ed.) (1988). *Handbook of the birds of Europe, the Middle East, and North Africa: The birds of the Western Palearctic, Volume V.* Oxford University Press.

Cramp, S. (ed.) (1992). *Handbook of the birds of Europe, the Middle East, and North Africa: The birds of the Western Palearctic, Volume VI.* Oxford University Press.

Cramp, S. and Perrins, C. M. (eds.) (1993). *Handbook of the birds of Europe, the Middle East, and North Africa: The birds of the Western Palearctic, Volume VII.* Oxford University Press.

Cramp, S. and Perrins C. M. (eds.). (1994) *Handbook of the birds of Europe, the Middle East, and North Africa: The birds of the Western Palearctic, Volume VIII.* Oxford University Press.

Cramp, S. and Perrins, C. M. (eds.) (1994) *Handbook of the birds of Europe, the Middle East, and North Africa: The birds of the Western Palearctic*, Volume IX. Oxford University Press.

Crocker, J. (1985). Respect your feathered friends. *New Scientist,* 10 October, pp. 47–50.

Crockett, A. B., Jr. and Hansley, P. L. (1977). Coition, nesting, and post-fledging behavior in Wiliamson's Sapsucker in Colorado. *Living Bird,* **16,** 7–19.

Curio, E. (1989). Is avian mortality preprogrammed? *Trends in Ecology and Evolution,* **4,** 81–2.

Curio, E., Ernst, U., and Veith, W. (1978). The adaptive significance of avian mobbing. II. *Z. Tierpsychol.,* **21,** 223–34.

Curio, E. and Regelmann, K. (1985). The behavioural dynamics of Great Tits (*Parus major*) approaching a predator. *Z. Tierpsychol.,* **69,** 3–18.

Curry-Lindahl, K. (1981). *Bird migration in Africa,* Vols. 1 and 2. Academic Press, London.

Dagy, A. I. (1977). The walk of the Silver Gull (*Larus novaehollandiae*) and of other birds. *Journal of Zoology* (London), **182,** 529–40.

Dane, B. and Van Der Kloot, W. (1964). An analysis of the display of the Goldeneye Duck (*Bucephala clangula*). *Behaviour,* **22,** 282–328.

Davies, N. B. (1977). Prey selection and social behaviour in wagtails (*Aves: Motacillidae*). *Journal of Animal Ecology,* **46,** 37–57.

Davies, N. B. (1983). Polyandry, cloaca-pecking and sperm competition in dunnocks. *Nature,* **302,** 334–6.

Davies, N. B. (1988). Dumping eggs on conspecifics. *Nature,* **331,** 19.

Davies, N. B. (1990). Dunnocks: cooperation and conflict among males and females in a variable mating system. In *Cooperative breeding in birds,* (eds. P. B. Stacey and W. D. Koenig), Cambridge University Press, pp. 457–85.

Davies, N. B. (1992). *Dunnock behaviour and social evolution.* Oxford University Press.

Davies, N. B. and Brooke, M. de L. (1989*a*). An experimental study of co-evolution between the Cuckoo, *Cuculus canoris,* and its hosts. I. Host egg discrimination. *Journal of Animal Ecology,* **58,** 207–224.

Davies, N. B. and Brooke, M. de L. (1989*b*). An experimental study of co-evolution between the Cuckoo, *Cuculus canoris*, and its hosts. II. Host egg markings, chick discrimination and general discussion. *Journal of Animal Ecology*, **58**, 225–36.

Davies, N. B. and Lundberg, A. (1985). The influence of food on time budgets and timing of breeding of the dunnock *Prunella modularis*. *Ibis*, **127**, 100–10.

Davies, N. B., Bourke, A. F. G., and Brooke, M. de L. (1989). Cuckoos and parasitic ants: interspecific brood parasitism as an evolutionary arms race. *Trends in Ecology and Evolution*, **4**, 274–8.

de Battisti, M. (ed.) (1981). *John Gould's birds of Great Britain*. Bloomsbury, London.

De Graaf, R. and Payne, B. (1975). Economic values of non-game birds and some urban wildlife research needs. *Trans. North American Wildlife and Natural Resources Conf.*, **40**, 281–7.

De Laet, J. F. (1985). Dominance and anti-predator behaviour of Great Tits *Parus major*: a field study.

Dementiev, G. P. and Gladkov, N. A. (eds.) (1968). *Birds of the Soviet Union*. (6 volumes). Israel Program for Scientific Translations. U.S. Department of Commerce, Springfield, Virginia.

Desmond, A. J. (1975). *The hot-blooded dinosaurs*. Warner Books, New York.

Dhondt, A. A. (1983). Variations in the number of overwintering Stonechats possibly caused by natural selection. *Ringing and Migration*, **4**, 155–8.

Dhondt, A. A. (1987). Reproduction and survival of polygynous and mono-gamous Blue Tit *Parus caeruleus*. *Ibis*, **129**, 327–34.

Diamond, J. M. (1981). Mixed-species foraging groups. *Nature*, **292**, 408–9.

Diamond, J. M. (1982). How eggs breathe while avoiding desiccation and drowning. *Nature*, **295**, 10–11.

Diamond, J. M. (1984). Evolution of stable exploiter-victim systems. *Nature*, **310**, 632.

Diamond, J. M. (1986). Animal art: variation in bower decorating style among male bowerbirds *Amblyornis inornatus*. *Proceedings of the National Academy Science USA*, **83**, 3042–6.

Diamond, J. M. (1987*a*). Learned specializations of birds. *Nature*, **330**, 16–17.

Diamond, J. M. (1987*b*). Will grebes provide the answer? *Nature*, **325**, 16–17.

Diamond, J. M. (1988). Red books or green lists? *Nature*, **332**, 304–5.

Diamond, J. M., Fraga, M., Wiakibu, J., Maru, T., and Feni, S. (1977). Fruit consumption and seed dispersal by New Guinea birds. *Wildlife in Papua New Guinea Publication*, **77**, 9.

Diehl, O. (1988). Lebensraum Obstwiese — Gefährdung und Massnahmen zur Erhaltung. *Die Vogelwelt*, **109**, 141–4.

Dobkin, D. S. (1979). Functional and evolutionary relationships of vocal copying phenomena in birds. *Z. Tierpsychol.*, **50**, 348–63.

Dobkin, D. S. (1984). Flowering patterns of long-lived *Heliconia* inflorescences: implications for visiting and resident nectarivores. *Oecologia, 64*, 245–54.

Dobkin, D. S. (1994). *Conservation and management of Neotropical migrant landbirds in the Northern Rockies and Great Plains.* University of Idaho Press, Moscow.

Dobkin, D. S. and Wilcox, B. A. (1986). Analysis of natural forest fragments: riparian birds in the Toiyabe Mountains, Nevada. In *Wildlife 2000: modeling habitat relationships of terrestrial vertebrates,* (eds. J. Verner, M. L. Morrison, and C. J. Ralph), pp. 293–9. Univ. Wisconsin Press, Madison.

Dobkin, D. S., Holmes, J. A., and Wilcox, B. A. (1986). Traditional nest-site use by White-throated Swifts. *Condor, 88*, 252–3.

Dobson, A. P. (1990). Survival rates and their relationship to life-history traits in some common British birds. In *Current ornithology,* (ed. D. M. Power), pp. 115–46. Plenum, New York.

Dooling, R. J. (1982). Auditory perception in birds. In *Acoustic Communication in Birds,* (eds. D. E. Kroodsma and E. H. Miller), Vol. 1, pp. 95–130. Academic Press, New York.

Doughty, R. W. (1975). *Feather fashions and bird preservation.* University of California Press, Berkeley.

Draulans, D. and van Vessem, J. (1982). Flock size and feeding behaviour of migrating Whinchats *Saxicola rubetra. Ibis, 124*, 347–51.

Drent, P. J. and Woldendorp, J. W. (1989). Acid rain and eggshells. *Nature, 339*, 431.

Dresser, H. E. (1871–1881). *A history of the birds of Europe.* Taylor and Francis, London.

Dunker, H.-R. (1974). Structure of the avian respiratory tract. *Respiratory Physiology, 22*, 1–19.

Dunn, E. H. (1990). Feeding Birds in Europe. *Feederwatch News, 3*, 9.

East, M. L. and Perrins, C. M. (1986). The effect of nestboxes on breeding populations of birds in broadleaved temperate woodlands. *Ibis, 130*, 393–401.

Edwards, T. C., Jr. and Collopy, M. W. (1983). Obligate and facultative brood reduction in eagles: an examination of factors that influence fratricide. *Auk, 100*, 630–5.

Ehrlich, P. R. (1970). Coevolution and the biology of communities. In *Biochemical coevolution,* (ed. K. L. Chambers), pp. 1–11. Oregon State Univ. Press, Corvallis.

Ehrlich, P. R. (1986*a*). *The machinery of nature.* Simon and Schuster, New York.

Ehrlich, P. R. (1986*b*). Which animal will invade? In *Ecology of biological invasions of North America and Hawaii,* (eds. H. A. Mooney and J. A. Drake), pp. 79–95. Springer-Verlag, New York.

Ehrlich, P. R. and Ehrlich, A. H. (1973). Coevolution: heterotypic schooling in Caribbean reef fishes. *American Naturalist*, **107**, 157–60.

Ehrlich, P. R. and Ehrlich, A. H. (1981). *Extinction: the causes and consequences of the disappearance of species*. Random House, New York.

Ehrlich, P. R. and Ehrlich, A. H. (1990). *The population explosion*. Simon and Schuster, New York.

Ehrlich, P. R. and Ehrlich, A. H. (1991). *Healing the planet*. Addison Wesley, New York.

Ehrlich, P. R. and Roughgarden, J. (1987). *The science of ecology*. Macmillan, New York.

Ehrlich, P. R., Ehrlich, A. H., and Holdren, J. P. (1975). *Ecoscience: population, resources, environment*. Freeman, San Francisco.

Ehrlich, P. R., Dobkin, D. S., and Wheye, D. (1986). The adaptive significance of anting. *Auk*, **103**, 835.

Ehrlich, P. R., Dobkin, D. S., and Wheye, D. (1988). *The birder's handbook: a field guide to the natural history of North American birds*. Simon and Schuster, New York.

Ehrlich, P. R., Dobkin, D. S., and Wheye, D. (1992). *Birds in jeopardy*. Stanford University Press, Palo Alto.

Einarsen, A. S. (1945). Some factors affecting Ring-necked Pheasant population density. *Murrelet*, **26**, 3–9, 39–44.

Ekman, J. (1979). Coherence, composition and territories of winter social groups of the Willow Tit *Parus montanus* and the Crested Tit *P. cristatus*. *Ornis Scandinavica*, **10**, 56–68.

Ekman, J. and Hake, M. (1988). Avian flocking reduces starvation risk: an experimental demonstration. *Behavioral Ecology Sociobiology*, **22**, 91–4.

Elgar, M. and Harvey, P. (1987). Colonial information centers. *Trends in Ecology and Evolution*, **2**, 34.

Elkins, N. (1983). *Weather and bird behavior*. Poyser, Calton, Staffordshire.

Elkins, N. (1988). *Weather and bird behavior*. (2nd edn.). Poyser, Calton.

Ellis, H. I. (1980). Metabolism and solar radiation in dark and white herons in hot climates. *Physiological Zoology*, **53**, 358–72.

Elowson, A. M. (1984). Spread-wing postures and the water repellency of feathers: a test of Rijke's hypothesis. *Auk*, **101**, 371–83.

Emlen, S. T. (1975). The stellar-orientation system of a migratory bird. *Scientific American*, **233**, 102–11.

Emlen, S. T. and Oring, L. W. (1977). Ecology, sexual selection, and the evolution of mating systems. *Science*, **197**, 215–23.

Emlen, S. T. and Wrege, P. H. (1988). The role of kinship in helping decisions among white-fronted bee-eaters. *Behavioral Ecology and Sociobiology*, **23**, 305–15.

Emlen, S. T., Demong, N. J., and Emlen, D. J. (1989). Experimental induction of infanticide in female Wattled Jacanas. *The Auk*, **106**, 1–7.

Ens, B. J., Esselink, P., and Zwarts, L. (1990). Kleptoparasitism as a problem of prey choice: a study on mudflat-feeding curlews, *Numenius arquata*. *Animal Behaviour*, **39**, 219–30.

Erckmann, W. J. (1983). The evolution of polyandry in shorebirds: an evaluation of hypotheses. In *Social behavior of female vertebrates*, (ed. S. K. Wasser), pp. 113–68. Academic Press, New York.

Eriksson, M. O. G. and Göttmark, F. (1982). Habitat selection: Do passerines nest in association with Lapwings *Vanellus vanellus* as defence against predators? *Ornis Scandinavica*, **13**, 189–92.

Eron, C. (1988). Starlings Star in X-Ray Movies. *Science News*, **134**, 181.

Espmark, Y. O., Lampe, H. M., and Bjerke, T. K. (1989). Song conformity and continuity in song dialects of Redwings *Turdus iliacus* and some ecological correlates. *Ornis Scandinavica*, **20**, 1–12.

Evans, M. E. (1975). Breeding behaviour of captive Bewick's Swans. *Wildfowl*, **26**, 117–30.

Evans, P. G. H. (1982). Associations between seabirds and cetaceans: a review. *Mammal Review*, **12**, 187–206.

Evans, P. G. H. (1988). Intraspecific nest parasitism in the European Starling *Sturnus vulgaris*. *Animal Behaviour*, **36**, 1282–94.

Evans, P. R., Goss-Custard, J. D., and Hale, W. G. (eds.). (1984). *Coastal waders and wildfowl in winter*. Cambridge University Press.

Ezaki, Y. (1990). Female choice and the causes and adaptations of polygyny in great reed warblers. *Journal of Animal Ecology*, **59**, 103–20.

Falls, J. B. (1982). Individual recognition by sounds in birds. In *Acoustic communication in birds*, (eds. D. E. Kroodsma and E. H. Miller), Vol. 2, pp. 237–78. Academic Press, New York.

Fay, R. R. and Feng, A. S. (1987). Mechanisms for directional hearing among nonmammalian vertebrates. In *Directional hearing*, (eds. W. A. Yost and G. Gourevitch). Springer-Verlag, New York, pp. 179–213.

Feare, C. (1984). *The Starling*. Oxford University Press, Oxford.

Feare, C. J., Spencer, P. L., and Constantine, D. A. T. (1982). Time of egg-laying of starlings *Sturnus vulgaris*. *Ibis*, **124**, 174–8.

Fisk, E. J. (1978). The growing use of roofs by nesting birds. *Bird Banding*, **49**, 134–41.

Fjeld, P. E. and Sonerud, G. A. (1988). Food caching, cache recovery, and the use of an egg shell dump in Hooded Crows *Corvus corone cornix*. *Ornis Scandinavica*, **19**, 268–74.

Folz, H.-G. (1989). Das Artenspektrum der Brutvögel auf einer landwirtschaftlich intensiv genutzten Fläche Rheinhessens. *Die Vogelwelt*, **110**, 12–23.

Fonstad, T. (1984). Reduced territorial overlap between the willow warbler *Phylloscopus trochilus* and the brambling *Fringilla montifringilla* in heath birch forest: competition or different habitat preferences? *Oikos*, **42**, 314–22.

Forshaw, J. M. (1978). *Parrots of the world*. Neptune Publications, New Jersey.

Fry, H. (1984). *The Bee-eaters*. Poyser, Calton, Staffordshire.

Furness, R. W. (1987). *The Skuas*. Poyser, Calton, Staffordshire.

Futuyma, D. J. (1987). *Evolutionary biology*, 2nd edn. Sinauer Associates, Sunderland, MA.

Futuyma, D. J. and Slatkin, M. (1983). *Coevolution*. Sinauer Associates, Sunderland, MA.

Garcia, E. F. J. (1983). An experimental test of competition for space between Blackcaps *Sylvia atricapilla* and Garden Warblers *Sylvia borin* in the breeding season. *Journal Animal Ecology*, **52**, 795–805.

Gargett, V. (1993). *The Black Eagle: Verreaux's Eagle in southern Africa*. Academic Press, New York.

Gärtner, K. (1982). Zur Ablehnung von Eiern und Jungen des Kuckucks (*Cuculus canorus*) durch die Wirtsvögel—Beobachtungen und experimentelle Untersuchungen am Sumpfrohrsänger. *Die Vogewelt*, **103**, 201–24.

Gates, J. E. and Geysel, L. W. (1978). Avian nest dispersion and fledging success in field-forest ecotones. *Ecology*, **59**, 871–83.

Gaunt, A. S. (1988). Interaction of syringeal structure and airflow in avian phonation. *Acta Congr. Internat. Ornithol.*, **19**, 915–24.

Gaunt, A. S. and Gaunt, S. L. L. (1985). Syringeal structure and avian phonation. *Current Ornithology*, **2**, 213–45.

Gauthreaux, S. A., Jr. (1982). The ecology and evolution of avian migration systems. *Avian Biology*, Vol. 6. Academic Press, New York, pp. 93–168.

George, W. G. and Sulski, R. (1984). Thawing of frozen prey by a Great Horned Owl. *Canadian Journal of Zoology*, **62**, 314–15.

Gibbs, H. L. and Grant, P. R. (1987). Oscillating selection on Darwin's finches. *Nature*, **327**, 511–13.

Gibbons, D. W. (1987). Juvenile helping in the Moorhen *Gallinula chloropus*. *Animal Behaviour*, **35**, 170–81.

Gill, F. B. (1980). Historical aspects of hybridization between Blue-winged and Golden-winged Warblers. *Auk*, **97**, 1–18.

Gill, F. B. and Wolf, L. L. (1975). Economics of feeding territoriality in the Golden-winged sunbird. *Ecology*, **56**, 333–45.

Gillis, A. M. (1990). What are birds hearing? *BioScience*, **40**, 810–16.

Giroux, J. (1981). Interspecific nest parasitism by Redheads on islands in southeastern Alberta. *Canadian Journal of Zoology*, **59**, 2053–7.

Gish, S. L. and Morton, E. S. (1981). Structural adaptations to local habitat acoustics in Carolina Wren songs. *Z. Tierpsychol.*, **56**, 74–84.

Gjershaug, J. O., Järvi, T., and Røskaft, E. (1989). Marriage entrapment by 'solitary' mothers: a study on male deception by female Pied Flycatchers. *American Naturalist*, **133**, 273–76.

Goldsmith, T. H. (1980). Hummingbirds see near ultraviolet light. *Science*, **207**, 786–8.

Gonzalez, L., Hiraldo, F., Delibes, M., and Calderon, J. (1989). Reduction in the range of the Spanish Imperial Eagle (*Aquila adalberti* Brehm, 1861) since AD 1850. *Journal of Biogeography*, **16**, 305–15.

Goodburn, S. F. (1984). Mate guarding in the Mallard *Anas platyrhynchos*. *Ornis Scandinavica*, **15**, 261–5.

Gooders, J. (1983). *Birds that came back*. Tanager Books, Dover, New Hampshire.

Goodwin, D. (1976). *Crows of the world*. British Museum (Natural History), London.

Goodwin, D. (1978). *Birds of man's world*. British Museum (Natural History), London.

Goodwin, D. (1983). *Pigeons and doves of the world*. (3rd edn.). British Museum (Natural History), London.

Gori, D. F. (1988). Colony-facilitated foraging in Yellow-headed Blackbirds: experimental evidence for information transfer. *Ornis Scandinavica*, **19**, 224–30.

Gorman, M. L. and Milne, H. (1972). Creche behavior in the Common Eider *Somateria m. mollissima*. *Ornis Scandinavica*, **3**, 21–6.

Goslow, C. E., Jr. (1971). The attack and strike of some North American raptors. *Auk*, **88**, 815–27.

Götmark, F. (1990). A test of the information-centre hypothesis in a colony of sandwich terns *Sterna sandvicensis*. *Animal Behaviour*, **39**, 487–95.

Gould, L. L. and Heppner, F. (1974). The vee formation of Canadian Geese. *Auk*, **91**, 494–506.

Gould, S. J. (1985). The Flamingo's smile. *Natural History*, March, pp. 6–19.

Gowaty, P. A. and Mock, D. W. (eds.) (1985). Avian monogamy. *Ornithological Monographs*, No. 37.

Graham, F., Jr. (1988). A bird in the hand is worth . . . plenty! *Audubon*, March, pp. 97–9.

Grant, B. R. and Grant, P. R. (1989). *Evolutionary dynamics of a natural population: the Large Cactus Finch of the Galapagos*. University of Chicago Press, Chicago.

Grant, P. J. (1986). *Gulls: a guide to identification*. Buteo Books, Vermillion, SD.

Greene, E. (1987). Individuals in an osprey colony discriminate between high and low quality information. *Nature*, **329**, 239–41.

Greenwood, J. J. D. (1985). Comments on hole-nesting in birds. *Ornis Scandinavica*, **16**, 153–8.

Greenwood, P. J. and Harvey, P. H. (1978). Foraging and territory utilization of Blackbirds (*Turdus merula*) and Song Thrushes (*Turdus philomelos*). *Animal Behaviour*, **26**, 1222–36.

Greig-Smith, P. (1986). Avian ideal homes. *New Scientist*, 2 January, pp. 29–31.

Grimmett, R. (1987). *A review of the problems affecting Palearctic migratory birds in Africa*. ICBP Study Rept. 22, Cambridge.

Grubb, T. C., Jr. (1974). Olfactory navigation to the nesting burrow in Leach's Petrel (*Oceanodroma leucorhoa*). *Animal Behaviour*, **22**, 192–202.

Gustafsson, L. and Sutherland, W. J. (1988). The costs of reproduction in the Collared Flycatcher, *Ficedula albicollis*. *Nature*, **335**, 813–15.

Gwinner, E. (1986a). *Circannual rhythms*. Springer-Verlag, Berlin.

Gwinner, E. (1986b). Circannual rhythms in the control of avian migrations. *Adv. Study. Behav.*, **16**, 191–228.

Haartman, L. von (1969). The nesting habits of Finnish Birds I: Passeriformes. *Commentiones Biologicae Societas Scientiarum Fennica*, **32**, 1–187.

Haartman, L. von (1978). Changes in the bird fauna in Finland and their causes. *Fennia*, **150**, 25–32.

Haartman, L. von (1981). Coevolution of the Cuckoo *Cuculus canorus* and a regular Cuckoo host. *Ornis Fennica*, **58**, 1–10.

Haftorn, S. (1988). Incubating female passerines do not let the egg temperature fall below the 'physiological zero temperature' during their absences from the nest. *Ornis Scandinavica*, **19**, 97–110.

Haftorn, S. and Reinertsen, R. E. (1982). Regulation of body temperature and heat transfer to eggs during incubation. *Ornis Scandinavica*, **13**, 1–10.

Hagan, J. M., III and Johnston, D. W. (eds.) (1992). *Ecology and conservation of Neotropical migrant landbirds*. Smithsonian Institution Press, Washington.

Haila, Y. (1988). Calculating and miscalculating density: the role of habitat geometry. *Ornis Scandinavica*, **19**, 88–92.

Hailman, J. P. (1973). Double-scratching and terrestrial locomotion in Emberizines: some complications. *Wilson Bulletin*, **85**, 348–50.

Hake, M. and Ekman, J. (1988). Finding and sharing depletable patches: when group foraging decreases intake rates. *Ornis Scandinavica*, **19**, 275–9.

Halliday, T. (1978). *Vanishing birds: their natural history and conservation*. Holt, Rinehart and Winston, New York.

Hamilton, W. D. (1971). Geometry for the selfish herd. *Journal of Theoretical Biology*, **31**, 295–311.

Hamilton, W. D. and Zuk, M. (1982). Heritable true fitness and bright birds: a role for parasites? *Science*, **218**, 384–7.

Hanssen, O. J. (1984). Habitat selection of shorebirds in an archipelago in SE Norway. *Ornis Scandinavica*, **15**. 253–60.

Hardy, J. W. (1978). Damage to loblolly pine by winter roosting blackbirds and starlings. *Proceedings of the Annual Conference of the Southeast Association Fish and Wildlife Agencies*, **30**, 466–70.

Harris, M. P. (1984). *The Puffin*. Poyser, Calton, Staffordshire.

Harrison, C. (1982). *An atlas of the birds of the Western Palaearctic*. Collins, London.

Harrison, C. (1985). *A field guide to the nests, eggs, nestlings of British and European birds*. Collins, London.

Hartley, P. H. T. (1953). An ecological study of the feeding habits of the English titmice. *Journal of Animal Ecology*, **22**, 261–88.

Harvey, P. H. and Partridge, L. (1988). Of cuckoo clocks and cowbirds. *Nature*, **335**, 586–7.

Harvey, P., Stenning, M., and Campbell, B. (1988). Factors influencing reproductive success in the pied flycatcher. In *Reproductive success*, (ed. T. H. Clutton-Brock), pp. 189–200. University of Chicago Press, Chicago.

Harwood, M. (1988). In praise of starlings? *Audubon*, March, p. 75.

Hébert, P. N. (1988). Adoption behaviour by gulls: a new hypothesis. *Ibis*, **130**, 216–20.

Hecht, J. (1990). Fossil birds force an evolutionary rethink. *New Scientist*, 3 November, p. 26.

Hedge, S. (1973). Composition of pigeon milk and its effect on growth in chicks. *Indian Journal of Experimental Biology*, **11**, 238–9.

Heinrich, B. (1986). Why is a robin's egg blue? *Audubon*, July, pp. 65–71.

Heinzel, H., Fitter, R. S. R., and Parslow, J. (1979). *The Birds of Britain and Europe with North Africa and the Middle East*. Collins, London.

Helbig, A. J. (1990). Are orientation mechanisms among migratory birds species-specific? *Trends Ecology Evolution*, **5**, 365–7.

Helle, P. (1985). Effects of forest fragmentation on bird densities in northern boreal forests. *Ornis Fennica*, **62**, 35–41.

Helle, P. and Järvinen, O. (1986). Population trends of North Finnish land birds in relation to their habitat selection and changes in forest structure. *Oikos*, **46**, 107–15.

Heller, H. C. (1989). Sleep, hypometabolism, and torpor in birds. In *Physiology of cold adaptation in birds*, (eds. C. Bech and R. E. Reinertsen), pp. 231–45. Plenum Press, London.

Hennemann, W. W., III. (1982). Energetics and spread-winged behavior of Anhingas in Florida. *Condor*, **84**, 91–6.

Hennemann, W. W., III. (1983). Environmental influences on the energetics and behavior of Anhingas and Double-crested Cormorants. *Physiological Zoology*, **56**, 201–16.

Hennemann, W. W., III. (1985). Energetics, behavior and the zoogeography of Anhingas and Double-crested Cormorants. *Ornis Scandinavica*, **16**, 19–23.

Heppleston, P. B. (1971). Feeding techniques of the Oystercatcher. *Bird Study*, **18**, 15–20.

Heredia, R. and Luke, A. (1990). Ménage à trois for Spain's vultures. *New Scientist*, 128 (No. 1747), 45–7.

Higuchi, H. (1986). Bait-fishing by the Green-backed Heron, *Ardeola striata* in Japan. *Ibis*, **128**, 285–90.

Hinde, R. A. (1954*a*). Factors governing the changes in strength of a partially inborn response, as shown by the mobbing behavior of the Chaffinch (*Fringilla coelebs*), I. The nature of the response and examination of its course. *Proceedings of the Royal Society London, Series B*, **142**, 306–30.

Hinde, R. A. (1954*b*). Factors governing the changes in strength of a partially inborn response, as shown by the mobbing behavior of the Chaffinch (*Fringilla coelebs*), II. The waning of the response. *Proceedings of the Royal Society London B Biological Science*, **142**, 331–58.

Hinde, R. A. (1955). A comparative study of the courtship of certain finches (*Fringillidae*). *Ibis*, **97**, 706–44; **98**, 1–222.

Hogstad, O. (1984). Variation in numbers, territoriality and flock size of a Goldcrest *Regulus regulus* population in winter. *Ibis*, **126**, 296–306.

Hogstad, O. (1988*a*). Advantages of social foraging of Willow Tits *Parus montanus*. *Ibis*, **130**, 275–83.

Hogstad, O. (1988*b*). Rank-related resource access in winter flocks of Willow Tit *Parus montanus*. *Ornis Scandinavica*, **19**, 169–74.

Hohman, W. L. (1985). Feeding ecology of Ring-necked Ducks in northwestern Minnesota. *Journal of Wildlife Management*, **49**, 546–57.

Hohn, E. O. (1977). The 'snowshoe effect' of the feathering on ptarmigan feet. *Condor*, **79**, 380–2.

Holley, A. J. F. (1984). Adoption, parent–chick recognition and maladaption in the Herring Gull *Larus argentatus*. *Z. Tierpsychol.*, **64**, 9–14.

Hollom, P. A. D., Porter, R. F., Christensen, S. and Willis, I. (1988). *Birds of the Middle East and North Africa*. T. and A. D. Poyser, Calton, Staffordshire.

Hölzinger, J. von and Kroymann, B. (1984). Auswirkungen des Waldsterbens in Südwestdeutschland auf die Vogelwelt. *Ökol. Vögel*, **6**, 203–12.

Hoogland, J. L. and Sherman, P. W. (1976). Advantages and disadvantages of Bank Swallow (*Riparia riparia*) coloniality. *Ecological Monographs*, **46**, 33–58.

Howe, M. A. (1987). Wetlands and waterbird conservation. *American Birds*, **41**, 204–9.

Hudson, P. J. (1986). *The Red Grouse: the biology and management of a wild gamebird*. Game Conservancy Trust, Fordingbridge, Hampshire.

Hudson, R. L. (1990). Tough bird laws mean little when it's time for dinner. *Wall Street Journal*, January 18, p. 1.

Hudson, P. J. and Rands, M. R. W. (eds.) (1988). *Ecology and management of gamebirds*. Blackwell Scientific Publications, Oxford.

Hughes, A. L. (1987). The chivalrous pigeon: pigeons help their mates to obtain resources. *Trends in Ecology and Evolution*, **2**, 113.

Hulscher, J. B. (1985). Growth and abrasion of the Oystercatcher bill in relation to dietary switches. *Netherlands Journal of Zoology*, **35**, 124–54.

Hume, R. (1993). *The Common Tern.* Hamyln.

Hunt, G. L., Jr., Eppley, Z. A., and Schneider, D. C. (1986). Reproductive performance of seabirds: the importance of population and colony size. *Auk,* **103,** 306–17.

Hurxthal, L. M. (1986). Our gang, Ostrich style. *Natural History,* December, pp. 34–41.

Hussell, D. J. T. (1985). On the adaptive basis for hatching asynchrony: brood reduction, nest failure and asynchronous hatching in Snow Buntings. *Ornis Scandinavica,* **16,** 205–12.

Hussell, D. J. T. (1988). Supply and demand in tree swallow broods: a model of parent-offspring food-provisioning interactions in birds. *American Naturalist,* **131,** 175–202.

Hutchins, H. E. and Lanner, R. M. (1982). The central role of Clark's Nutcracker in the dispersal and establishment of whitebark pine. *Oecologia,* **55,** 192–201.

Illner, H. (1988). Langfristiger Rückgang von Schleiereule *Tyto alba,* Waldohreule *Asio otus,* Steinkauz *Athene noctua* und Waldkauz *Strix aluco* in der Agrarlandschaft Mittelwestfalens 1974–1986. *Die Vogelwelt,* **109,** 145–51.

Inouye, D. W. (1976). Nonrandom orientation of entrance holes to woodpecker nests in aspen trees. *Condor,* **78,** 101–2.

Inouye, R. S., Huntley, N. J., and Inouye, D. W. (1981). Non-random orientation of Gila Woodpecker nest entrances in Saguaro cacti. *Condor,* **83,** 88–9.

James, P. C. (1986). How do Manx Shearwaters *Puffinus puffinus* find their burrows? *Ethology,* **71,** 287–94.

Järvi, T. and Bakken, M. (1984). The function of variation in the breast stripe of the Great Tit (*Parus major*). *Animal Behaviour,* **32,** 590–6.

Järvi, T., Walsø, Ø., and Bakken, M. (1987). Status signalling by *Parus major*: an experiment in deception. *Ethology,* **76,** 334–42.

Jedrzejewski, W. and Jedrzejewska, B. (1988). Nest site selection by the Buzzard *Buteo buteo* L. in the extensive forests of eastern Poland. *Biological Conservation,* **43,** 145–58.

Jenkin, P. M. (1957). The filter feeding and food of flamingoes (Phoenicopteri). *Phil. Trans. Royal Society London, Series B,* **240,** 401–93.

Jenkins, F., Dial, K., and Goslow, G. (1988). A cineradiographic analysis of bird flight: the wishbone in starlings is a spring. *Science,* **242,** 1495–8.

Jenkinson, M. A. and Mengel, R. M. (1970). Ingestion of stones by goatsuckers (Caprimulgidae). *Condor,* **72,** 236–7.

Johnsgard, P. A. (1965). *Handbook of waterfowl behaviour.* Cornell University Press, Ithaca, New York.

Johnsgard, P. A. (1983). *Cranes of the world.* Indiana University Press, Bloomington, Indiana.

Johnsgard, P. A. and Kear, J. (1968). A review of parental carrying of young by waterfowl. *Living Bird*, **7**, 89–102.

Johnston, R. F., Miles, D. M., and Rohwer, S. A. (1972). Hermon Bumpus and natural selection in the House Sparrow *Passer domesticus*. *Evolution*, **26**, 20–31.

Jones, P. J. (1978). A possible function of the 'wing-drying' posture in the Reed Cormorant *Phalacrocorax africanus*. *Ibis*, **120**, 540–2.

Jönsson, P. E. (1987). Sexual size dimorphism and disassortive mating in the Dunlin *Calidris alpina schinzii* in southern Sweden. *Ornis Scandinavica*, **18**, 257–64.

Jordano, P. (1987). Frugivory, external morphology and digestive system in mediterranean sylviid warblers *Sylvia* spp. *Ibis*, **129**, 175–89.

Kacelnik, A. and Krebs, J. (1982). The dawn chorus in the great tit (*Parus major*): proximate and ultimate causes. *Behaviour*, **83**, 287–309.

Källander, H. and Smith, H. G. (1990). Food storing in birds: an evolutionary perspective. In *Current ornithology*, (ed. D. M. Power), pp. 147–207, Vol. 7. Plenum, New York.

Kenyon, K. W. (1942). Hunting strategy of Pigeon Hawks. *Auk*, **59**, 443–4.

Kerlinger, P. (1989). *Flight strategies of migrating hawks*. University of Chicago Press.

Kerlinger, P. and Moore, F. R. (1989). Atmospheric structure and avian migration. *Current Ornithology*, **6**, 109–42.

Ketterson, E. D. and Nolan, V., Jr. (1983). The evolution of differential bird migration. *Current Ornithology*, **1**, 357–402.

Kettlewell, H. B. D. (1973). *The evolution of melanism*. Clarendon Press, Oxford.

Kharitonov, S. P. and Siegel-Causey, D. (1988). Colony formation in seabirds. In *Current ornithology*, (ed. R. Johnston), pp. 223–72, Vol. 5. Plenum, New York.

Kilham, L. (1980). Association of Great Egret and White Ibis. *Journal of Field Ornithology*, **51**, 73–4.

King, B. (1988). Water Pipit feeding in close association with man. *British Birds*, **81**, 183.

Klomp, H. (1980). Fluctuations and stability in Great Tit populations. *Ardea*, **68**, 205–24.

Knudsen, E. I. (1980). Sound localization in birds. In *Comparative studies of hearing in vertebrates*, (eds. A. N. Popper and R. R. Fay), pp. 289–322. Springer-Verlag, New York.

Koenig, W. D. (1984). Geographic variation in clutch size in the Northern Flicker (*Colaptes auratus*): support for Ashmole's hypothesis. *Auk*, **101**, 698–706.

Konishi, M. (1983). Night owls are good listeners. *Natural History*, September, pp. 56–9.

Konishi, M. (1985). Birdsong: from behavior to neuron. *Annual Review Neurosci.*, **8**, 125–70.

Korpimäki, E. (1986*a*). Niche relationships and life-history tactics of three sympatric *Strix* owl species in Finland. *Ornis Scandinavica*, **17**, 126–32.

Korpimäki, E. (1986*b*). Reversed size dimorphism in birds of prey, especially in Tengmalm's Owl *Aegolius funereus*: a test of the 'starvation hypothesis.' *Ornis Scandinavica*, **17**, 326–32.

Korpimäki, E. (1987*a*). Prey caching of breeding Tengmalm's Owls *Aegolius funereus* as a buffer against temporary food shortage. *Ibis*, **129**, 499–510.

Korpimäki, E. (1987*b*). Timing of breeding of Tengmalm's Owl *Aegolius funereus* in relation to vole dynamics in western Finland. *Ibis*, **129**, 58–68.

Krasinski, Z. (1990). The border where the bison roam. *Natural History*, **6**, 62–3.

Krebs, J. R. (1970). Territory and breeding density in the Great Tit, *Parus major*. *Ecology*, **52**, 2–22.

Krebs, J. R. (1973). Social learning and the significance of mixed-species flocks of Chickadees (*Parus* spp.). *Canadian Journal of Zoology*, **51**, 1275–88.

Krebs, J. R. and Davies, N. B. (eds.) (1984). *Behavioural ecology: an evolutionary approach*, 2nd edition. Sinauer Associates, Sunderland, MA.

Krebs, J. R. and Harvey, P. H. (1988). Lekking in Florence. *Nature*, **333**, 12.

Krebs, J. R. and Kroodsma, D. E. (1980). Repertoires and geographical variation in bird song. *Advances in the Study of Behaviour*, **11**, 143–77.

Krebs, J. R. and May, R. (1990). The moorland owners' grouse. *Nature*, **343**, 310–11.

Krebs, J. R., MacRoberts, M., and Cullen, M. (1972). Flocking and feeding in the Great Tit *Parus major* — an experimental study. *Ibis*, **114**, 507–30.

Krebs, J. R., Erickson, J. T., Webber, M. I., and Charnov, E. L. (1977). Optimal prey selection in the Great Tit (*Parus major*). *Animal Behaviour*, **25**, 30–8.

Krebs, J. R., Stephens, D. W., and Sutherland, W. J. (1983). Perspectives in optimal foraging. In *Perspectives in ornithology*, (eds. G. A. Clark and A. H. Brush). Cambridge University Press, New York.

Kress, S. W. (1985). *Audubon Society guide to attracting birds*. Charles Scribner's Sons, New York.

Kroodsma, D. E. (1982). Learning and the ontogeny of sound signals in birds. In *Acoustic communication in birds*, (eds. D. E. Kroodsma and E. H. Miller), Vol. 2, pp. 1–23. Academic Press, New York.

Kroodsma, D. E., Baker, M. C., Baptista, L. F., and Petrinovich, L. (1985). Vocal 'dialects' in Nuttall's White-crowned Sparrow. *Current Ornithology*, **2**, 103–33.

Kruuk, H. (1976). The biological function of gulls' attraction towards predators. *Animal Behaviour*, **24**, 146–53.

Kushlan, J. A. (1978). Commensalism in the Little Blue Heron. *Auk*, **95**, 677–81.

Lack, D. (1947). The significance of clutch-size. I, II. *Ibis*, **89**, 302–52.

Lack, D. (1956). *Swifts in a tower*. Methuen, London.

Lack, D. (1958). The significance of colour in turdine eggs. *Ibis*, **100**, 145–66.

Lack, D. (1965). *Life of the Robin*. H. F. and G. Witherby, London.

Lack, D. (1968). *Ecological adaptations for breeding in birds*. Methuen, London.

Lang, E. M. (1963). Flamingos raise their young on a liquid containing blood. *Experientia*, **19**, 532–3.

Lanier, G. A. (1982). A test for conspecific egg discrimination in three species of colonial passerine birds. *Auk*, **99**, 519–25.

Larochelle, J., Delson, J., and Schmidt-Nielsen, K. (1982). Temperature regulation in the Black Vulture. *Canadian Journal of Zoology*, **60**, 491–4.

Lawes, G. and Kenwood, M. (1970). Poultry droppings feed cows and reclaim tips. *New Scientist*, 12 March, p. 508.

Lawn, M. R. (1982). Pairing systems and site tenacity of the Willow Warbler *Phylloscopus trochilus* in southern England. *Ornis Scandinavica*, **13**, 193–9.

Leck, C. F. (1978). Temperature and snowfall effects on feeding station activity. *Bird Banding*, **49**, 283–4.

Leck, C. F. (1987a). Update on House Finch range. *Records of NJ Birds*, **13**, 18–19.

Leck, C. F. (1987b). Habitat selection in migrant birds: seductive fruits. *Trends in Ecology and Evolution*, **2**, 33.

Lefebvre, L. and Henderson, D. (1986). Resource defense and priority access to food by the mate in pigeons. *Canadian Journal of Zoology*, **64**, 1889–92.

Lendrem, D. A. (1983). Safer life for the peeking duck. *New Scientist*, 24 February, pp. 514–15.

Lenington, S. (1983). Commentary. In *Perspectives in ornithology*, (eds. A. Brush and G. Clark), pp. 85–91. Cambridge University Press, Cambridge.

Lessells, C. M. and Avery, M. I. (1989). Hatching asynchrony in European Bee-eaters *Merops apiaster*. *Journal of Animal Ecology*, **58**, 815–35.

Lessells, C. M. and Krebs, J. R. (1989). Age and breeding performance of European Bee-eaters. *Auk*, **106**, 375–82.

Lewin, R. (1985). Why are male hawks so small? *Science*, **228**, 1299–300.

Lewin, R. (1986). Egg laying is for the birds. *Science*, **234**, 285.

Lewin, R. (1988). Hotshots, hotspots, and female preference. *Science*, **240**, 1277–8.

Lifjeld, J. T. (1984). Prey selection in relation to body size and bill length of five species of waders feeding in the same habitat. *Ornis Scandinavica*, **15**, 217–26.

Lindstedt, S. L. and Calder, W. A. (1976). Body size and longevity in birds. *Condor*, **78**, 91–145.

Lissaman, P. B. S. and Schollenberger, C. A. (1970). Formation flight of birds. *Science*, **168**, 1003–5.

Löhrl, H. (1986). Verhalten zum Schutz der Beine bei grosser Kälte. *Die Vogelwelt*, **107**, 238–40.

Long, J. L. (1981). *Introduced birds of the world*. David and Charles, London.

Louther, J. K. (1977). Nesting biology of the Sora at Vermillion, Alberta. *Canadian Field-Naturalist*, **91**, 63–7.

Lovei, G. L. (1989). Passerine migration between the Palaearctic and Africa. *Current Ornithology*, **6**, 143–174.

Loye, J. E. and Zuk, M. (1991). *Bird–parasite interactions*. Oxford University Press.

Lowe, V. P. W. (1972). Distraction display by a Woodcock with chicks. *Ibis*, **114**, 106–7.

Lucas, P. H. C. (1990). A glasnost-era park is born. *Natural History*, June, p. 61.

Lundberg, A. (1986). Adaptive advantages of reversed sexual size dimorphism in European owls. *Ornis Scandinavica*, **17**, 133–40.

Lundberg, A. and Alatalo, R. V. (1992). *The Pied Flycatcher*. Poysner, Calton, Staffordshire.

Lustick, S., Battersby, B., and Kelty, M. (1978). Behavioral thermoregulation: orientation toward the sun in Herring Gulls. *Science*, **200**, 81–3.

Lynch, J. F. and Whigham, D. F. (1984). Effects of forest fragmentation on breeding bird communities in Maryland, USA. *Biological Conservation*, **28**, 287–324.

Lyster, S. (1985). *International wildlife law: an analysis of international treaties concerned with the conservation of wildlife*. Grotius, Cambridge.

MacArthur, R. H. (1958). Population ecology of some warblers of northeastern coniferous forests. *Ecology*, **39**, 599–619.

MacArthur, R. H. and Wilson, E. O. (1967). *The theory of island biogeography*. Princeton University Press, Princeton.

Mace, R. (1987). The dawn chorus in the Great Tit *Parus major* is directly related to female fertility. *Nature*, **330**, 745–7.

McGregor, P. K. (1983). The response of Corn Buntings to playback of dialects. *Z. Tierpsychol.*, **62**, 256–60.

McGregor, P. K. and Krebs, J. R. (1989). Song learning in adult Great Tits (*Parus major*): effects of neighbours. *Ethology*, **82**, 139–59.

McKinney, F. (1975). The evolution of duck displays. In *Function and evolution in behaviour*, (eds. G. Baerends, C. Beer, and A. Manning), pp. 331–57. Clarendon Press, Oxford.

McNamara, J., Mace, R., and Houston, A. (1987). Optimal daily routines of singing and foraging in a bird singing to attract a mate. *Behavioral Ecology and Sociobiology*, **20**, 399–405.

McNicholl, M. K. (1975). Larid site tenacity and group adherence in relation to habitat. *Auk*, **92**, 98–104.

Magrath, R. D. (1989). Hatching asynchrony and reproductive success in the blackbird. *Nature*, **339**, 536–8.

Mahoney, S. A. (1984). Plumage wettability of aquatic birds. *Auk*, **101**, 181–5.

Marchant, J. H., Hudson, R., Carter, S. P., and Whittington, P. (1990). *Population trends in British breeding birds*. British Trust for Ornithology, Tring.

Marler, P. (1984). Song learning: innate species differences in the learning process. In *The Biology of learning*, (eds. P. Marler and H. S. Terrace), pp. 289–309. Springer-Verlag, Berlin (Dahlem Konferenzen).

Marriott, R. W. (1973). The manurial effect of Cape Barren Goose droppings. *Wildfowl*, **24**, 131–3.

Marshall, A. J. and Serventy, D. L. (1959). The experimental demonstration of an internal rhythm of reproduction in a transequatorial migrant, the Short-tailed Shearwater, *Puffinus tenuirostris*. *Nature*, **184**, 1704–5.

Martin, G. R. (1986). Sensory capacities and the nocturnal habit of owls (Strigiformes). *Ibis*, **128**, 266–77.

Martin, L. D. (1983). The origin and early radiation of birds. In *Perspectives in ornithology*, (eds. A. H. Brush and G. A. Clark, Jr.), pp. 291–338. Cambridge Univ. Press, Cambridge, *See also* commentaries by D. W. Steadman (pp. 338–45) and P. V. Rich (pp. 345–53), following this article.

Martin, T. E. (1988). Processes organizing open-nesting bird assemblages: competition or nest predation? *Evolutionary Ecology*, **2**, 37–50.

Mattes, H., Eberle, C., and Schreiber, K.-F. (1980). Über den Einfluss von Insektizidspritzungen im Ostbau auf die Vitalität und Reproduktion von Kohlmeisen (*Parus major*). *Die Vogelwelt*, **100**, 81–98, 132–40.

Matthews, G. V. T. (1968). *Bird navigation*, 2nd edn. Cambridge University Press.

Matthysen, E. (1990). Nonbreeding social organization in *Parus*. In *Current ornithology*, (ed. D. M. Power), Vol. 7, pp. 209–49. Plenum, New York.

May, R. M. (1979). Flight formations in geese and other birds. *Nature*, **282**, 778–80.

Mayr, E. (1969). *Principles of systematic zoology*. McGraw-Hill, New York.

Mead, C. (1983). *Bird migration*. Facts on File, New York.

Meanly, B. (1985). *The marsh hen—a natural history of the Clapper Rail of the Atlantic Coast salt marsh*. Tidewater Publishers. Centreville, MD.

Meinerzhagen, R. (1954). *Birds of Arabia*. Oliver and Boyd, Edinburgh.

Meyburg, B.-U. (1987). Clutch size, nestling aggression and breeding success of the Spanish Imperial Eagle. *British Birds*, **80**, 308–20.

Midtgard, U. (1989). Circulatory adaptations to cold in birds. In *Physiology of cold adaptation in birds*, (eds. C. Bech and R. E. Reinertsen), pp. 211–22. Plenum Press, London.

Mikkola, H. (1983). *The owls of Europe*. Poyser, Calton, Staffordshire.

Mikkonen, A. V. (1983). Breeding site tenacity of the Chaffinch *Fringilla coelebs* and the Brambling *F. montifringilla* in northern Finland. *Ornis Scandinavica*, **14**, 36–47.

Miller, E. H. (1984). Communication in breeding shorebirds. In *Shorebirds: breeding behavior and populations*, (eds. J. Burger and B. L. Olla), pp. 169–241. Plenum, New York.

Mock, D. W. (1984). Infanticide, siblicide, and avian nestling mortality. In *Infanticide — comparative and evolutionary perspectives*, (eds. G. Hausfater and S. B. Hrdy), pp. 3–30. Aldine, New York.

Mock, D. W., Drummond, H., and Stinson, C. H. (1990). Avian siblicide. *American Scientist*, **78**, 438–49.

Moknes, A. and Røskaft, E. (1987). Cuckoo host interactions in Norwegian mountain areas. *Ornis Scandinavica*, **18**, 168–72.

Moknes, A. and Røskaft, E. (1988). Responses of Fieldfares *Turdus pilaris* and Bramblings *Fringilla montifringilla* to experimental parasitism by the Cuckoo *Cuculus canorus*. *Ibis*, **130**, 535–9.

Møller, A. P. (1983a) Changes in Danish farmland habitats and their populations of breeding birds. *Holarctic Ecology*, **6**, 95–100.

Møller, A. P. (1983b). Song activity and territory quality in the Corn Bunting *Milaria calandra*; with comments on mate selection. *Ornis Scandinavica*, **14**, 81–9.

Møller, A. P. (1984). On the use of feathers in birds' nests: predictions and tests. *Ornis Scandinavica*, **15**, 38–42.

Møller, A. P. (1986). Mating systems among European passerines: a review. *Ibis*, **128**, 234–50.

Møller, A. P. (1988a). False alarm calls as a means of resource usurpation in the Great Tit *Parus major*. *Ethology*, **79**, 25–30.

Møller, A. P. (1988b). Female choice selects for male sexual tail ornaments in the monogamous swallow. *Nature*, **332**, 640–2.

Møller, A. P. (1989a). Population dynamics of a declining swallow *Hirundo rustica* population. *Journal Animal Ecology*, **58**, 1051–63.

Møller, A. P. (1989b). Viability costs of male tail ornaments in a swallow. *Nature*, **339**, 132–5.

Møller, A. P. (1990). Male tail length and female mate choice in the monogamous swallow *Hirundo rustica*. *Animal Behaviour*, **39**, 458–65.

Moore, F. R. (1987). Sunset and the orientation behaviour of migrating birds. *Biological Reviews*, **62**, 65–86.

Moreno, J. (1987a). Parental care in the Wheatear *Oenanthe oenanthe*: effects of nestling age and brood size. *Ornis Scandinavica*, **18**, 291–301.

Moreno, J. (1987b). Nestling growth and brood reduction in the Wheatear *Oenanthe oenanthe*. *Ornis Scandinavica*, **18**, 302–9.

Morley, A. (1943). Sexual behavior in birds from October to January. *Ibis*, **85**, 132–58.

Morse, D. H. (1970). Ecological aspects of some mixed-species foraging flocks of birds. *Ecology*, **40**, 119–68.

Mortensen, A., Unander, S., Kolstad, M., and Blix, A. S. (1983). *Ornis Scandinavica*, **14**, 144–8.

Morton, E. S. (1971). Nest predation affecting the breeding season of the Clay-colored Robin, a tropical songbird. *Science*, **171**, 920–1.

Morton, E. S. (1975). Ecological sources of selection in avian sounds. *American Naturalist*, **109**, 17–34.

Moss, R. and Watson, A. (1982). Determination of clutch size in Red Grouse without implying the Egg-'munerostat'. A reply to Steen and Parker. *Ornis Scandinavica*, **13**, 249–50.

Moss, W. W. and Camin, J. H. (1970). Nest parasitism, productivity, and clutch size in Purple Martins. *Science*, **168**, 1000–3.

Mountford, G. (1957). *The Hawfinch*. Collins, London.

Moynihan, M. (1960). Some adaptations which help to promote gregariousness. *Proceedings of XII International Ornithological Congress*, **1958**, 523–41.

Moynihan, M. (1981). The coincidence of mimicries and other misleading coincidences. *American Naturalist*, **117**, 372–8.

Mrosovsky, N. (1988). The CITES conservation circus. *Nature*, **331**, 563.

Mudge, G. P. (1983). The incidence and significance of ingested lead pellet poisoning in British wildfowl. *Biological Conservation*, **27**, 333–72.

Mueller, H. C. and Meyer, K. (1985). The evolution of reversed sexual dimorphism in size: a comparative analysis of the Falconiformes of the western Palearctic. *Current Ornithology*, **2**, 65–101.

Mundinger, P. C. (1982). Microgeographic and macrogeographic variation in acquired vocalizations of birds. In *Acoustic communication in birds*, (eds. D. E. Kroodsma and E. H. Miller), Vol. 2, pp. 147–208. Academic Press, New York.

Munn, C. A. (1984). Birds of different feather also flock together. *Natural History*, November, pp. 34–42.

Munn, C. A. (1986). Birds that 'cry wolf.' *Nature*, **319**, 143–5.

Munroe, J. and Bédard, J. (1977a). Creche formation in the Common Eider. *Auk*, **94**, 759–71.

Munroe, J. and Bédard, J. (1977b). Gull predation and creching behaviour in the Common Eider. *Journal Animal Ecology*, **46**, 799–810.

Murphy, E. C. and Haukioja, E. (1986). Clutch size in nidicolous birds. *Current Ornithology*, **4**, 141–80.

Murphy, M. T. (1986). Temporal components of reproductive variability in Eastern Kingbirds (*Tyrannus tyrannus*). *Ecology*, **67**, 1483–92.

Murton, R. K. (1965). *The Woodpigeon*. Collins, London.

Myers, J. P. (1981). A test of three hypotheses for latitudinal segregation of the sexes in wintering birds. *Canadian Journal of Zoology*, **59**, 1527–34.

Myers, J. P. (1984). Spacing behavior of nonbreeding shorebirds. In *Shorebirds: migration and foraging behavior, behavior of marine animals*, (eds. J. Burger and B. L. Olla), Vol. 6, pp. 271–321. Plenum Press, New York.

Myers, J. P. (1985). Making sense of sexual nonsense. *Audubon*, July.

Myers, J. P., Connors, P. G., and Pitelka, F. A. (1979). Territoriality in nonbreeding shorebirds. *Studies in Avian Biology No. 2, Cooper Ornithological Society*, pp. 231–246.

Myers, J. P., Morrison, R. I. G., Antas, P. Z., Harrington, B. A., Lovejoy, T. E., Sallaberry, M., Senner, S. E., and Tarak, A. (1987). Conservation strategy for migratory species. *American Scientist*, **75**, 19–26.

Necker, R. (1985). Observations on the function of a slowly adapting mechanoreceptor associated with filoplumes in the feathered skin of pigeons. *Journal of Comparative Physiology A*, **156**, 391–4.

Nelson, B. (1978). *The Gannet*. Poyser, Calton, Staffordshire.

Nethersole-Thompson, D. (1966). *The Snow Bunting*. Oliver and Boyd, Edinburgh.

Nethersole-Thompson, D. (1973). *The Dotterel*. Collins, London.

Nethersole-Thompson, D. (1975). *Pine Crossbills: a Scottish contribution*. Poyser, Calton, Staffordshire.

Nethersole-Thompson, D. and Nethersole-Thompson, M. (1979). *Greenshanks*. Poyser, Calton, Staffordshire.

Nettleship, D. N. and Birkhead, T. R. (eds.) (1985). *The Atlantic alcidae: the evolution, distribution and biology of the auks inhabiting the Atlantic Ocean and adjacent water areas*. Academic Press, London.

Newell, R. G. (1989). *Locustella* locomotion in Eilat, Israel. *British Birds*, **82**, 331.

Newton, I. (1979). *Population ecology of raptors*. T. and A. D. Poyser, Beckhamsted, Hertfordshire.

Newton, I. (1985). *The Sparrowhawk*. T. and A. D. Poyser, Calton, Staffordshire.

Newton, I., Bogan, J., Meek, E., and Little, B. (1982). Organochlorine compounds and shell-thinning in British merlins *Falco columbarius*. *Ibis*, **124**, 328–55.

Nice, M. (1964). *Studies in the life history of the Song Sparrow*, Vols. 1 and 2. Dover, New York (originally published 1937, 1943).

Nilsson, S. G. (1984). The evolution of nest-site selection among hole-nesting birds: the importance of nest predation and competition. *Ornis Scandinavica*, **15**, 167–75.

Nisbet, I. C. T. (1977). Courtship-feeding and clutch size in Common Tern *Sterna hirundo*. In *Evolutionary ecology*, (eds. B. Stonehouse and C. M. Perrins). Macmillan, London.

Noer, H. and Secher, H. (1983). Survival of Danish Kestrels *Falco tinnunculus* in relation to protection of birds of prey. *Ornis Scandinavica*, **14**, 104–14.

Norberg, U. M. (1986). Evolutionary convergence in foraging niche and flight morphology in insectivorous aerial-hawking birds and bats. *Ornis Scandinavica*, **17**, 253–60.

Norton-Griffiths, M. (1967). Some ecological aspects of the feeding behaviour of the Oystercatcher (*Haematopus ostralegus*) on the edible mussel (*Mytilus edulis*). *Ibis*, **109**, 412–24.

Nottebohm, F. (1989). From bird song to neurogenesis. *Scientific American*, **260**, 74–9.

Nowicki, S. and Capranica, R. R. (1986). Bilateral syringeal interaction in vocal production of an oscine bird sound. *Science*, **231**, 1297–9.

Nur, N. (1987). Alternative reproductive tactics in birds: individual variation in clutch size. *Perspectives in Ethology*, **7**, 49–77.

Nygård, T. (1983). Pesticide residues and the shell thinning in eggs of Peregrines in Norway. *Ornis Scandinavica*, **14**, 161–6.

Obst, B. S. and Hunt, Jr., G. L. (1990). Marine birds feed at gray whale mud plumes in the Bering Sea. *Auk*, **107**, 678–88.

O'Connor, R. J. (1978). Brood reduction in birds: selection for fratricide, infanticide, and suicide? *Animal Behaviour*, **26**, 79–96.

O'Connor, R. J. (1984). *The growth and development of birds*. Wiley, New York.

O'Connor, R. and Shrubb, M. (1986). *Farming and birds*. Cambridge University Press, Cambridge.

O'Donald, P. (1983). *The Arctic Skua: a study of the ecology and evolution of a seabird*. Cambridge University Press, Cambridge.

Official Journal of the European Communities Legislation. (1979). **103**, 22, 25 April.

Official Journal of the European Communities Legislation. (1985). **233**, 33, 25 July.

Official Journal of the European Communities Legislation. (1991). **115**, 41, 6 March.

Olson, S. L. and Feduccia, A. (1980). Relationships and Evolution of Flamingos (Aves: Phoenicopteridae). *Smithsonian Contributions in Zoology*, No. 316.

Orell, M. (1989). Population fluctuations and survival of Great Tits *Parus major* dependent on food supplied by man in winter. *Ibis*, **131**, 112–27.

Orians, G. H. (1967). On the evolution of mating systems in birds and mammals. *American Naturalist*, **103**, 589–603.

Orians, G. and Angell, T. (1985). *Blackbirds of the Americas*. University of Washington Press, Seattle, London.

Orians, G. H. and Willson, M. F. (1964). Interspecific territories of birds. *Ecology*, **45**, 736–45.

Oring, L. W. (1982). Avian mating systems. In *Avian biology*, (eds. D. S. Farner, J. R. King, and K. C. Parkes), Vol. 6, pp. 1–92. Academic Press, New York.

Oring, L. W. (1986). Avian polyandry. *Current Ornithology*, **3**, 309–51.

Ormerod, S. J. (1985). The diet of breeding Dippers *Cinclus cinclus* and their nestlings in the catchment of the River Wye, mid-Wales: a preliminary study by faecal analysis. *Ibis*, **127**, 316–31.

Ormerod, S. J., Boilstone, M. A., and Tyler, S. J. (1985). Factors influencing the abundance of breeding Dippers *Cinclus cinclus* in the catchment of the River Wye, mid-Wales. *Ibis*, **127**, 332–40.

Ostrom, J. H. (1979). Bird flight: how did it begin? *American Scientist*, **67**, 46–55.

Pain, S. (1990*a*). Modern farming puts small birds to flight. *New Scientist*, 25 August, p. 21.

Pain, S. (1990*b*), Developers drive Britain's birds away from estuaries. *New Scientist*, September 8, p. 28.

Palfery, J. (1989). Migrating steppe eagles taking prey disturbed by farm machinery. *British Birds*, **82**, 330.

Papi, F. (1986). Pigeon navigation: Solved problems and open questions. *Monit. Zool. Ital. (N.S.)*, **20**, 471–517.

Parker, J. W. (1981). Nest associates of the Mississippi Kite. *Journal of Field Ornithology*, **52**, 144–5.

Parkin, D. T. (1987). Evolutionary genetics of house sparrows. In *Avian genetics*, (eds. F. Cooke and P. A. Buckley), pp. 381–406. Academic Press, London.

Patterson, I. J., Jalil, S. A., and East, M. L. (1989). Damage to winter cereals by greylag and pink-footed geese in north-east Scotland. *Journal of Applied Ecology*, **26**, 879–95.

Payne, R. B. (1977). The ecology of brood parasitism in birds. *Annual Review of Ecology and Systematics*, **8**, 1–28.

Payne, R. B. (1984). Sexual selection, lek and arena behavior, and sexual size dimorphism in birds. *Ornithological Monographs*, No. 33.

Paynter, R. A., Jr. (ed.). (1974). *Avian energetics*. Nuttall Ornith. Club. Publ. No. 15, Cambridge, MA.

Paz, U. (1987). *The birds of Israel*. Stephen Greene, Lexington, Massachusetts.

Pedersen, H. C. and Steen, J. B. (1979). Behavioural thermoregulation in Willow Ptarmigan chicks *Lagopus lagopus*. *Ornis Scandinavica*, **10**, 17–21.

Pedersen, H. C., Steen, J. B. and Andersen, R. (1983). Social organization and territorial behaviour in a Willow Ptarmigan population. *Ornis Scandinavica*, **14**, 263–72.

Pennycuick, C. J. (1975). Mechanics of flight. In *Avian biology*, (eds. D. S. Farner and J. R. King), Vol. 5, pp. 1–76. Academic Press, New York.

Pennycuick, C. J. (1982). The flight of petrels and albatrosses (Procellariiformes), observed in South Georgia and its vicinity. *Phil. Trans. R. Soc. Lond, B*, **300**, 75–106.

Pennycuick, C. J. (1989). *Bird flight performance*. Oxford University Press, Oxford.

Perrins, C. (1987). *New generation guide to birds of Britain and Europe*. Collins, London.

Perrins, C. M. (1979). *British tits*. Collins, London.

Perrins, C. M. and Geer, T. A. (1980). The effects of Sparrowhawks on Tit populations. *Ardea*, **68**, 133–42.

Perrins, C. M. and Middleton, A. L. A. (1985). *The encyclopedia of birds*. Facts on File, New York.

Peterson, R., Mountford, G. and Hollom, P. A. D. (1993). *Birds of Britain and Europe*. (5th edn.). Collins, London.

Petretti, F. (1988). An inventory of steppe habitats in southern Italy. In *Ecology and conservation of grassland birds*, (ed. P. D. Goriup), pp. 125–43. ICBP Technical Publication No. 7.

Petrie, M. (1986). Reproductive strategies of male and female Moorhens (*Gallinula chloropus*). In *Ecological aspects of social evolution*, (eds. D. I. Rubenstein and R. W. Wrangham), pp. 43–63. Princeton University Press, Princeton.

Pettifor, R. A., Perrins, C. M., and McCleery, R. H. (1988). Individual optimization of clutch size in Great Tits. *Nature*, **336**, 160–2.

Phillips, J. G., Butler, P. J., and Sharp, P. J. (1985). *Physiological strategies in avian biology*. Blackie, London.

Picozzi, N. (1984*a*). Breeding biology of polygynous Hen Harriers *Circus c. cyaneus* in Orkney. *Ornis Scandinavica*, **15**, 1–10.

Picozzi, N. (1984*b*). Sex ratio, survival and territorial behaviour of polygynous Hen Harriers *Circus c. cyaneus* in Orkney. *Ibis*, **126**, 356–65.

Pienkowski, M. W. (1983). The effects of environmental conditions on feeding rates and prey-selection of shore plovers. *Ornis Scandinavica*, **14**, 227–38.

Pienkowski, M. W. and Evans, P. R. (1984). Migratory behavior of shorebirds in the western Palearctic. In *Behavior of marine animals, current perspectives in research*, Vol. 6, (eds. J. Burger and B. L. Olla), pp. 73–123. Plenum Press, New York.

Pierotti, R. (1987). Isolating mechanisms in seabirds. *Evolution*, **41**, 559–70.

Pierotti, R. and Annett, C. A. (1990). Diet and reproductive output in seabirds. *BioScience*, **40**, 568–74.

Pimm, S. L. (1982). *Food webs*. Chapman and Hall, London.

Pitelka, F. A., Holmes, R. T., and MacLean, S. F. (1974). Ecology and evolution of social organization in arctic sandpipers. *American Zoologist*, **14**, 185–204.

Pomiankowski, A. (1989*a*). Mating success in male pheasants. *Nature*, **337**, 696, 23 February.

Pomiankowski, A. (1989*b*). Choosing parasite-free mates. *Nature*, **338**, 9 March.

Pool, R. (1988). Wishbones on Display. *Science,* **241,** 1430–31.

Poole, A. F. (1989). *Ospreys: a natural and unnatural history.* Cambridge University Press, Cambridge.

Potter, E. F. (1970). Anting in wild birds, its frequency and probable purpose. *Auk,* **87,** 692–713.

Potts, G. R. (1986). *The partridge: pesticides, predation, and conservation.* Collins, London.

Power, H. W., Litovich, E., and Lombardo, M. P. (1981). Male starlings delay incubation to avoid being cuckolded. *Auk,* **98,** 386–8.

Powley, F. (1990). Fables 'baby-carrying' White Storks near extinction, ornithologists say. *New York Times,* March 28.

Pöysä, H. (1983*a*). Morphology-mediated niche organization in a guild of dabbling ducks. *Ornis Scandinavica,* **14,** 317–26.

Pöysä, H. (1983*b*). Resource utilization pattern and guild structure in a waterfowl community. *Oikos,* **40,** 295–307.

Pöysä, H. (1986). Foraging niche shifts in multispecies dabbling duck (*Anas* spp.) feeding groups: harmful and beneficial interactions between species. *Ornis Scandinavica,* **17,** 333–46.

Pöysä, H. (1988). Do foraging Teals exploit gulls as early warners? *Ornis Scandinavica,* **19,** 70–2.

Prange, H. D., Anderson, J. F., and Rahn, H. (1979). Scaling of skeletal mass to body mass in birds and mammals. *American Naturalist,* **113,** 103–22.

Price, F. E. and Bock, C. E. (1983). *Population ecology of the Dipper (Cinclus mexicanus) in the Front Range of Colorado.* Studies in Avian Biology No. 7, Cooper Ornithol. Society, Los Angeles.

Prinzinger, R. and Siedle, K. (1988). Ontogeny of metabolism, thermoregulation and torpor in the House Martin *Delichon u. urbica* (L.) and its ecological signficance. *Oecologia,* **76,** 307–12.

Quinlan, S. E. (1983). Avian and river otter predation in a storm-petrel colony. *Journal of Wildlife Management,* **47,** 1036–43.

Quinn, T. W., Quinn, J. S., Cooke, F., and White, B. N. (1987). DNA marker analysis detects multiple maternity and paternity in single broods of the lesser snow goose. *Nature,* **326,** 392–4.

Radesater, T. and Jakobsson, S. (1988). Intra- and intersexual functions of song in the Willow Warbler (*Phylloscopus trochilus*). *Acta Congr. Ornithol. Internat.,* **XIX,** 1382–90.

Raspet, A. (1950). Performance measurements of a soaring bird. *Aeronautical Engineering Review,* **9,** 1–4.

Ratcliffe, D. (1993). *The Peregrine Falcon,* 2nd edn. Poyser, Berkhamsted, Hertfordshire.

Rayner, J. M. V. (1988). Form and function in avian flight. *Current Ornithology,* **5,** 1–66.

Read, A. F. (1987). Comparative evidence supports the Hamilton and Zuk hypothesis on parasites and sexual selection. *Nature,* **328,** 68–70.

Read, A. F. and Weary, D. M. (1990). Sexual selection and the evolution of bird song: a test of the Hamilton–Zuk hypothesis. *Behavioral Ecology Sociobiology,* **26,** 47–56.

Redpath, S. (1988). Vigilance levels in preening Dunlin *Calidris alpina. Ibis,* **130,** 555–7.

Reed, T. M. (1982). Interspecific territoriality in the Chaffinch and Great Tit on islands and the mainland of Scotland: playback and removal experiments. *Animal Behaviour,* **30,** 171–81.

Reichholf, J. H. (1988). Auswirkung des Angelns auf die Brutbestände von Wasservögeln im Fuechtgebiet von internationaler Bedeutung 'Unter Inn.' *Die Vogelwelt,* **109,** 206–21.

Reinertsen, R. E. and Haftorn, S. (1986). Different metabolic strategies of northern birds for nocturnal survival. *Journal of Comparative Physiology, B,* **156,** 655–63.

Reynard, G. B. and Harty, S. T. (1968). Ornithological 'mystery' song given by male Virginia Rail. *Casinia,* **50,** 3–8, (1966–7 issue; issued Nov. 1968).

Reynolds, J. D. (1987). Mating system and nesting biology of the Red-necked Phalarope, *Phalaropus lobatus*: what constrains polyandry? *Ibis,* **129,** 225–42.

Rhijn, J. G., van (1983). On the maintenance and origin of alternative strategies in the Ruff *Philomachus pugnax. Ibis,* **125,** 482–98.

Rhijn, J. G. van (1991). *The Ruff.* Poyser, Academic Press, London.

Rich, A. C., Dobkin, D. S., and Niles, L. J. (1994). Defining forest fragmentation by corridor width: the influence of narrow forest-dividing corridors on forest-nesting Neotropical migrant landbirds in southern New Jersey. *Conservation Biology,* in press.

Ricklefs, R. E. (1980). Geographical variation in clutch size among passerine birds: Ashmole's hypothesis. *Auk,* **97,** 38–49.

Ricklefs, R. E. (1989). Nest predation and the species diversity of birds. *Trends in Ecology and Evolution,* **4,** 184–6.

Ricklefs, R. E., Day, C. H., Huntington, C. E., and Williams, J. B. (1985). Variability in feeding rate and meal size of Leach's Storm-Petrel at Kent Island, New Brunswick. *Journal of Animal Ecology,* **54,** 883–98.

Ripley, S. D. (1977). *Rails of the world.* Godine, Boston, Massachusetts.

Robbins, C. S., Dawson, D. K., and Dowell, B. A. (1989). Habitat area requirements of breeding forest birds of the Middle Atlantic States. *Wildlife Monographs,* **103,** 1–34.

Robbins, J. (1985). Anatomy of a sting. *Natural History,* July, pp. 4–10.

Roberts, R. C. (1979). The evolution of avian food-storing behavior. *American Naturalist,* **114,** 418–38.

Rohwer, F. C. and Anderson, M. G. (1988). Female-biased philopatry, monogamy, and timing of pair formation in migratory waterfowl. *Current Ornithology*, **5**, 187–221.

Rohwer, S. A. (1985). Dyed birds achieve higher social status than controls in Harris' Sparrows. *Animal Behaviour*, **33**, 1325–31.

Rohwer, S. A. and Ewald, P. W. (1981). The cost of dominance and advantage of subordination in a badge signalling system. *Evolution*, **35**, 441–54.

Rohwer, S. and Spaw, C. D. (1988). Evolutionary lag versus bill-size constraints: a comparative study of the acceptance of cowbird eggs by old hosts. *Evolutionary Ecology*, **2**, 27–36.

Root, R. B. (1967). The niche exploitation pattern of the Blue-gray Gnatcatcher. *Ecological Monographs*, **37**, 317–50.

Roper, T. (1986). Badges of status in avian societies. *New Scientist*, 6 February, pp. 38–40.

Roskaft, E. and Espmark, Y. (1982). Vocal communication by the Rook *Corvus frugilegus* during the breeding season. *Ornis Scandinavica*, **13**, 38–46.

Rudolph, S. G. (1982). Foraging strategies of American Kestrels during breeding. *Ecology*, **63**, 1268–76.

Rundel, W. D. (1982). A case for esophageal analysis in shorebird food studies. *Journal of Field Ornithology*, **53**, 249–57.

Rüppell, G. (1977). *Bird-flight*. Van Nostrand and Reinhold, New York.

Rusterholz, K. A. and Howe, R. W. (1979). Species-area relations of birds on small islands in a Minnesota lake. *Evolution*, **33**, 468–77.

Ryan, M. R. (1981). Evasive behavior of American Coots to kleptoparasitism by waterfowl. *Wilson Bulletin*, **93**, 274–5.

Rydzewski, W. (1978a). The longevity of ringed birds. *The Ring*, **96–7**, 218–62.

Rydzewski, W. (1978b). The longevity of ringed birds. *The Ring*, **98–9**, 8.

Saether, B.-E. (1983a). Habitat selection, foraging niches and horizontal spacing of Willow Warbler *Phylloscopus trochilus* and Chiffchaff *P. collybita* in an area of sympatry. *Ibis*, **125**, 24–32.

Saether, B.-E. (1983b). Mechanism of interspecific spacing out in a territorial system of the Chiffchaff *Phylloscopus collybita* and the Willow Warbler *P. trochilus*. *Ornis Scandinavica*, **14**, 154–60.

Saether, B.-E. (1988). Pattern of covariation between life-history traits of European birds. *Nature*, **331**, 616–17.

Saether, B.-E. (1990). Age-specific variation in reproductive performance of birds. In *Current ornithology*, (ed. D. M. Power), pp. 251–83. Plenum, New York.

Safriel, U. N. (1985). 'Diet dimorphism' within an Oystercatcher *Haematopus ostralegus* population — adaptive significance and effects on recent distribution dynamics. *Ibis*, **127**, 287–305.

Safriel, U. N. and Lavee, D. (1988). Weight changes of cross-desert migrants at an oasis — do energetic considerations alone determine the length of stopover? *Oecologia*, **76**, 611–19.

Sanderson, G. C. and Bellrose, F. C. (1986). *A review of the problem of lead poisoning in waterfowl*. Illinois Natural History Survey, Special Publication No. 4.

Sanz, J. L., Bonaparte, J. F., and Lacasa, A. (1988). Unusual early Cretaceous birds from Spain. *Nature*, **331**, 433–5.

Sasvári, L. (1985). Different observational learning capacity in juvenile and adult individuals of congeneric bird species. *Z. Tierpsychol.*, **69**, 293–304.

Sasvári, L., Török, J., and Tóth, L. (1987). Density dependent effects between three competitive bird species. *Oecologia*, **72**, 127–30.

Savory, C. J. (1983). Selection of heather age and chemical composition by Red Grouse in relation of physiological state, season and time of day. *Ornis Scandinavica*, **14**, 135–43.

Schantz, T. von, Göransson, G., Andersson, G., Fröberg, I., Grahn, M., Helgée, A., and Wittzell, H. (1989). Female choice selects for a viability-based male trait in pheasants. *Nature*, **337**, 166–9.

Schardien, B. J. and Jackson, J. A. (1979). Belly-soaking as a thermoregulatory mechanism in nesting Killdeers. *Auk*, **96**, 604–6.

Scheid, P. (1982). Respiration and control of breathing. In *Avian biology*, (eds. D. S. Farner and J. R. King), Vol. 6, pp. 406–54. Academic Press, New York.

Schmidt, K.-H. and Einloft-Achenbach, H. (1984). Können isolierte Meisenpopulationen in Städten ihren Bestand erhalten? *Die Vogelwelt*, **105**, 97–105.

Schmidt-Koenig, K. (1987). Bird navigation: has olfactory orientation solved the problem? *Quarterly Review Biology*, **62**, 31–47.

Schmutz, J. K., Robertson, R. J., and Cook, F. (1982). Female sociality in the Common Eider duck during brood rearing. *Canadian Journal of Zoology*, **60**, 3326–31.

Schneider, M. (1987). Wassersportler stören Wasservögel auch im Winter. *Die Vogelwelt*, **108**, 201–9.

Schneider, S. H. (1989). *Global warming*. Sierra Club Books, San Francisco.

Schnell, G. D. and Hellack, J. J. (1978). Flight speeds of Brown Pelicans, Chimney Swifts, and other birds. *Bird-Banding*, **49**, 109–12.

Schnell, G. D. and Hellack, J. J. (1979). Bird flight speeds in nature: optimized or a compromise? *American Naturalist*, **113**, 53–66.

Schoener, T. W. and Spiller, D. A. (1987). High population persistence in a system with high turnover. *Nature*, **303**, 474–7.

Schreiber, R. K. and Newman, J. R. (1988). Acid precipitation effects on forest habitats: implications for wildlife. *Conservation Biology*, **2**, 249–59.

Schreiber, R. L., Diamond, A. W., Peterson, R. T., and Cronkite, W. (1989). *Save the birds*. Houghton Mifflin, Boston.

Scott, D. K. (1988). Breeding success in Bewick's Swans. In *Reproductive success* (ed. T. H. Clutton-Brock), pp. 220–36. University of Chicago Press.

Scott, P. and the Wildfowl Trust. (1972). *The swans*. Houghton Mifflin, Boston.

Seger, J. (1987). El Nino and Darwin's finches. *Nature*, **327**, 461.

Seller, T. J. (1988). Central control of sound production in birds. *Acta Congr. Internat. Ornithol.*, **19**, 925–34.

Shawyer, C. (1987). *The Barn Owl in the British Isles — its past, present, and future*. The Hawk Trust, Freepost, Beckenham, Kent.

Sharrock, J. T. R. (1976). *The atlas of breeding birds in Britain and Ireland*. Poyser, Calton, Staffordshire.

Shedd, D. H. (1985). A propensity to mob. *Living Bird*, **4**, 8–11.

Sherry, D. F., Krebs, J. R., and Cowie, R. J. (1981). Memory for the location of stored food in Marsh Tits. *Animal Behaviour*, **29**, 1260–6.

Shettleworth, S. J. (1983). Memory in food-hoarding birds. *Scientific American*, **248**, 102–10.

Sibley, C. G. and Ahlquist, J. E. (1985). The phylogeny and classification of the Australo-Papuan passerine birds. *Emu*, **85**, 1–14.

Sibley, C. G. and Monroe, B. L. (1990). *Distribution and taxonomy of birds of the world*. Yale University Press, New Haven.

Siegel-Causey, D. and Kharitonov, S. P. (1990). The evolution of coloniality. In *Current ornithology*, (ed. D. M. Power), Vol. 7, pp. 285–330. Plenum, New York.

Siegfried, W. R. and Underhill, L. G. (1975). Flocking as an antipredator strategy in doves. *Animal Behaviour*, **23**, 504–8.

Simmons, K. E. L. (1966). Anting and the problem of self-stimulation. *Journal of Zoology, London*, **149**, 145–62.

Simmons, K. E. L. (1986). *The sunning behaviour of birds*. Bristol Ornithological Club, Bristol.

Simmons, K. E. L. (1987). Wing-oiling by birds. *British Birds*, **80**, 573–4.

Simmons, R., Barnard, and Smith, P. C. (1987). Reproductive behaviour of *Circus cyaneus* in North America and Europe: a comparison. *Ornis Scandinavica*, **18**, 33–41.

Skutch, A. F. (1976). *Parent birds and their young*. University of Texas Press, Austin.

Skutch, A. F. (1987). *Helpers at birds' nests: a worldwide survey of cooperative breeding and related behavior*. University Iowa Press, Iowa City.

Slagsvold, T. (1982a). Clutch size variation in passerine birds: the nest predation hypothesis. *Oecologia*, **54**, 159–69.

Slagsvold, T. (1982b). Sex, size, and natural selection in the Hooded Crow *Corvus corone cornix*. *Ornis Scandinavica*, **13**, 165–75.

Slagsvold, T. (1985). Asynchronous hatching in passerine birds: influence of hatching failure and brood reduction. *Ornis Scandinavica*, **16**, 81–7.

Slagsvold, T. (1986). Nest site settlement by the Pied Flycatcher: does the female choose her mate for the quality of his house or himself? *Ornis Scandinavica*, **17**, 210–20.

Slagsvold, T. and Lifjeld, J. T. (1988). Why are some birds polyterritorial? *Ibis*, **130**, 65–8.

Slagsvold, T. and Lifjeld, J. T. (1989). Constraints on hatching asynchrony and egg size in Pied Flycatchers. *Journal Animal Ecology*, **58**, 837–49.

Slater, P. J. B. (1986). The cultural transmission of bird song. *Trends in Ecology and Evolution*, **1**, 94–7.

Slater, P. J. B., Eales, L. A., and Clayton, N. S. (1988). Song learning in Zebra Finches (*Taeniopygia guttata*): progress and prospects. *Advances in the Study of Behaviour*, **18**, 1–33.

Slessers, M. (1970). Bathing behavior of land birds. *Auk*, **87**, 91–9.

Smith, M. (1986). From a strike to a kill. *New Scientist*, 29 May, pp. 44–7.

Smith, P. H. (1989). Great White Egrets feeding in wake and robbing Black-headed Gulls. *British Birds*, **82**, 27.

Smith, S. A. and Paselk, R. A. (1986). Olfactory sensitivity of the Turkey Vulture (*Cathartes aura*) to three carrion-associated odorants. *Auk*, **103**, 586–92.

Snow, B. K. and Snow, D. W. (1984). Long-term defence of fruit by Mistle Thrushes *Turdus viscivorus*. *Ibis*, **126**, 39–49.

Snow, B. and Snow, D. (1988). *Birds and berries: a study of an ecological interaction*. Poyser, Calton, Staffordshire.

Snyder, A. W. and Miller, W. H. (1978). Telephoto lens system of falconiform eyes. *Nature*, **275**, 127–9.

Solheim, R. (1983). Bigyny and biandry in the Tengmalm's Owl, *Aegolius funereus*. *Ornis Scandinavica*, **14**, 51–7.

Sonerud, G. A. and Fjeld, P. E. (1987). Long-term memory in egg predators: an experiment with a Hooded Crow. *Ornis Scandinavica*, **18**, 323–5.

Sorjonen, J. (1983). Transmission of the two most characteristic phrases of the song of the Thrush Nightingale *Luscinia luscinia* in different environmental conditions. *Ornis Scandinavica*, **14**, 278–88.

Sorjonen, J. (1986). Mixed singing and interspecific territoriality — consequences of secondary contact of two ecologically and morphologically similar nightingale species in Europe. *Ornis Scandinavica*, **17**, 53–67.

Sorjonen, J. (1987). Interspecific territoriality in *Luscinia*: an example of interspecific competition for space. *Ornis Scandinavica*, **18**, 65.

Sorjonen, J. (1988). Song dialects and vocal traditions of the Thrush Nightingale (*Luscinia luscinia*) in different parts of the species distribution. *Congr. Internat. Ornithol.*, **19**, 1613–20.

Spitzer, P. R., Risebrough, R. W., Walker, W., Hernandez, R., Poole, A., Puleston, D., and Nisbet, I. C. T. (1978). Productivity of Ospreys in Connecticut–Long Island increases as DDE residues decline. *Science*, **202**, 333–5.

Squibb, R. C. and Hunt, Jr., G. L. (1983). A comparison of nesting-edges used by seabirds on St. George Island. *Ecology*, **64**, 727–34.

Stacey, P. B. and Koenig, W. D. (eds.) (1990). *Cooperative breeding in birds.* Cambridge University Press.

Stamps, J., Clark, A., Arrowood, P., and Kus, B. (1985). Parent–offspring conflict in budgerigars. *Behaviour*, **94**, 1–40.

Starr, D. (1989). Civilizing the Hunt. *International Wildlife*, Nov.–Dec., pp. 17–19.

Stawarczyk, T. (1984). Aggression and its suppression in mixed-species wader flocks. *Ornis Scandinavica*, **15**, 23–37.

Steen, J. B. and Parker, H. (1981). The egg-'numerostat'. A new concept in the regulation of clutch-size. *Ornis Scandinavica*, **12**, 109–10.

Stenmark, G., Slagsvold, T., and Lifjeld, J. (1988). Polygyny in the pied flycatcher, *Ficedula hypoleuca*: a test of the deception hypothesis. *Animal Behaviour*, **36**, 1646–57.

Stevens, T. A. and Krebs, J. R. (1986). Retrieval of stored seeds by Marsh Tits *Parus palustris* in the field. *Ibis*, **128**, 513–25.

Still, E., Monaghan, P., and Bignal, E. (1987). Social structuring at a communal roost of Choughs *Pyrrhocorax pyrrhocorax*. *Ibis*, **129**, 398–403.

Stinson, C. H. (1979). On the selective advantage of fratricide in raptors. *Evolution*, **33**, 1219–25.

Stinson, C. H. (1988). Does mixed-species flocking increase vigilance or skittishness? *Ibis*, **130**, 303–4.

Stjernberg, T. (1979). Breeding biology and population dynamics of the Scarlet Rosefinch, *Carpodacus erythrinus*. *Acta Zoologica Fennica*, **157**, 1–88.

Stokland, J. N. and Amundsen, T. (1988). Initial size hierarchy in broods of the Shag: relative significance of egg size and hatching asynchrony. *Auk*, **105**, 308–15.

Strebeigh, F. (1988). Letters from Selborne. *Audubon*, November, pp. 105–13.

Summers-Smith, J. D. (1968). *The sparrows*. T. and A. D. Poyser, Calton, Staffordshire.

Sutherland, W. J. (1987). Why do animals specialize? *Nature*, **325**, 483–4.

Sutherland, W. J. (1989). Asynchronous hatching in birds. *Nature*, **339**, 510.

Suthers, H. B. (1978). Analysis of a resident flock of starlings. *Bird Banding*, **49**, 35–46.

Swennen, C., De Bruijn, L., Duiven, D., Leopold, M., and Marteijn, E. (1983). Differences in bill form of the oystercatcher *Haematopus ostralegus*; a dynamic adaptation to specific foraging techniques. *Netherlands Journal of Sea Research*, **17**, 57–83.

Tasker, C. R. and Mills, J. A. (1981). A functional analysis of courtship feeding in the Red-billed Gull, *Larus novaehollandiae scopulinus*. *Behaviour*, **77**, 221–41.

Tate, J., Jr. (1981). The Blue List for 1981: the first decade. *American Birds*, **35**, 3–10.

Tate, J., Jr. (1986). The Blue List for 1986. *American Birds*, **40**, 227–36.

Telander, R. (1990). Warriors in the Parrot Game. *International Wildlife*, Sept.–Oct., pp. 4–11.

Temeles, E. J. (1985). Sexual size dimorphism of bird-eating hawks: the effect of prey vulnerability. *American Naturalist*, **125**, 485–99.

Temple, S. A. (ed.). (1978). *Endangered birds: management techniques for preserving threatened species*. University of Wisconsin Press, Madison.

Temrin, H. (1986). Singing behaviour in relation to polyterritorial polygyny in the Wood Warbler (*Phylloscopus sibilatrix*). *Animal Behaviour*, **34**, 146–52.

Temrin, H. and Arak, A. (1989). Polyterritoriality and deception in passerine birds. *Trends in Ecology and Evolution*, **4**, 106–9.

Temrin, H. and Jakobsson, S. (1988). Female reproductive success and nest predation in polyterritorial wood warblers (*Phylloscopus sibilatrix*). *Behavioral Ecology and Sociobiology*, **23**, 225–31.

Temrin, H., Mallner, Y., and Windén, M. (1984). Observations on polyterritoriality and singing behaviour in the Wood Warbler *Phylloscopus sibilatrix*. *Ornis Scandinavica*, **15**, 67–72.

Terborgh, J. W. (1980). The conservation status of neotropical migrants: present and future. In *Migrant birds in the neotropics: ecology, behavior, distribution, and conservation*, (eds. A. Keast and E. S. Morton), pp. 21–30. Smithsonian Institution Press, Washington, DC.

Terborgh, J. (1989). *Where have all the birds gone?* Princeton University Press, Princeton, N.J.

Terhivuo, J. (1977). Occurrence of strange objects in nests of the Wryneck, *Jynx torquilla*. *Ornis Fennica*, **54**, 66–72.

Terhivuo, J. (1983). Why does the Wryneck *Jynx torquilla* bring strange items to the nest? *Ornis Fennica*, **60**, 51–7.

Terrace, H. S. (1987). Chunking by a pigeon in a serial learning task. *Nature*, **325**, 149–51.

Thompson, D. B. A., Thompson, P. S., and Nethersole-Thompson, D. (1988). Fidelity and philopatry in breeding Redshanks (*Tringa totanus*) and Greenshanks (*T. nebularia*). *Acta XIX Congr. Internat. Ornithol.*, Vol. 1, pp. 563–74. University of Ottawa Press.

Thompson, J. N. (1982). *Interaction and coevolution*. Wiley, New York.

Thouless, C. R., Fanshawe, J. H., and Bertram, B. C. R. (1989). Egyptian Vultures *Neophron percnopterus* and Ostrich *Struthio camelus* eggs: the origins of stone-throwing behaviour. *Ibis*, **131**, 9–15.

Threlfall, W. (1985). Stacked on a cliff. *International Wildlife*, **15**, 40–3.

Tiainen, J., Hanski, I. K., and Mehtälä, J. (1983). Insulation of nests and the northern limits of three *Phylloscopus* warblers in Finland. *Ornis Scandinavica*, **14**, 149–53.

Tinbergen, J. M., Van Balen, J. H., and Van Eck, H. M. (1985). Density dependent survival in an isolated Great Tit population: Kluyver's data reanalysed. *Ardea*, **73**, 38–48.

Tinbergen, N. (1953). *The Herring Gull's world*. Collins, London.

Tinbergen, N. and Falkus, H. (1970). *Signals for survival*. Clarendon Press, Oxford.

Tinbergen, N. and Norton-Griffiths, M. (1964). Oystercatchers and mussels. *British Birds*, **57**, 64–70.

Tinbergen, N., Impekoven, M., and Franck, D. (1967). An experiment in spacing-out as a defense against predation. *Behaviour*, **28**, 307–21.

Tomback, D. F. (1980). How nutcrackers find their seed stores. *Condor*, **82**, 10–19.

Townshend, D. J. (1985). Decisions for a lifetime: establishment of spatial defence and movement patterns by juvenile Grey Plovers *Pluvialis squatarola*. *Journal of Animal Ecology*, **54**, 267–74.

Trauger, D. L. (1974). Eye color of female Lesser Scaup in relation to age. *Auk*, **91**, 243–54.

Trivers, R. L. (1974). Parent–offspring conflict. *American Zoologist*, **14**, 249–64.

Trost, C. H. and Webb, C. L. (1986). Egg moving by two species of Corvid. *Animal Behaviour*, **34** 294–5.

Truslow, F. K. (1967). Egg-carrying by the Pileated Woodpecker. *Living Bird*, **6**, 227–35.

Tubbs, C. R. (1974). *The Buzzard*. David and Charles, London.

Tye, A. (1984). Attacks by shrikes *Lanius* spp. on wheatears *Oenanthe* spp.: competition, kleptoparasitism or predation? *Ibis*, **126**, 95–101.

Ueda, K. (1986). A polygamous social system of the Fan-tailed Warbler *Cisticola juncidis*. *Ethology*, **73**, 43–55.

U.S. Fish and Wildlife Service and U.S. Bureau of the Census. (1980). *National survey of fishing, hunting, and wildlife-associated recreation*. Washington, DC.

Váisánen, R. A., Járvinen, O., and Rauhala, P. (1986). How are extensive, human-caused habitat alterations expressed on the scale of local bird populations in boreal forests? *Ornis Scandinavica*, **17**, 282–92.

Vander Wall, S. B. (1990). *Food hoarding in animals*. University Chicago Press, Chicago.

Veiga, J. P. (1990). Infanticide by male and female House Sparrows. *Animal Behaviour*, **39**, 496–502.

Verner, J. and Willson, M. F. (1966). The influence of habitats on mating systems of North American passerine birds. *Ecology*, **47**, 143–7.

Vessem, J. van and Draulans, D. (1986). The adaptive significance of colonial breeding in the Grey Heron *Ardea cinerea*: inter- and intra-colony variability in breeding success. *Ornis Scandinavica*, **17**, 356–62.

Village, A. (1987). Numbers, territory-size and turnover of Short-eared Owls *Asio flammeus* in relation to vole abundance. *Ornis Scandinavica*, **18**, 198–204.

Village, A. (1990). *The Kestrel*. T. and A. D. Poyser, Academic Press, London.

Vitousek, P. M., Ehrlich, P. R., Ehrlich, A. H., and Matson, P. A. (1986). Human appropriation of the products of photosynthesis. *BioScience*, **36**, 368–73.

Wagner, J. L. (1981). Seasonal change in guild structure: oak woodland insectivorous birds. *Ecology*, **62**, 973–81.

Wagner, J. L. (1984). Post-breeding avifauna and mixed insectivorous flocks in a Colorado spruce-fir forest. *Western Birds*, **15**, 81–4.

Walcott, C. and Lednor, A. J. (1983). Bird navigation. In *Perspectives in ornithology*, (eds. A. H. Brush and G. A. Clark, Jr.), pp. 513–42, Cambridge University Press, Cambridge.

Waldvogel, J. A. (1989). Olfactory orientation by birds. *Current Ornithology*, **6**, 269–321.

Waldvogel, J. A. (1990). The bird's eye view. *American Scientist*, **78**, 342–53.

Walsberg, G. E. (1982). Coat color, solar heat gain, and conspicuousness in the *Phainopepla*. *Auk*, **99**, 495–502.

Walsberg, G. E. (1983). Avian ecological energetics. In *Avian biology*, (eds. D. S. Farner and J. R. King), Vol. 7, pp. 161–220. Academic Press, New York.

Walsberg, G. E., Campbell, G. S., and King, J. R. (1978). Animal coat color and radiative heat gain: a re-evaluation. *Journal of Comparative Physiology*, **126**, 211–22.

Walter, H. (1979). *Eleonora's Falcon: adaptation to prey and habitat in a social raptor*. University of Chicago Press, Chicago.

Wander, W. (1985). Sharing the shore. *Living Bird*, **4**, 12–19.

Ward, P. and Zahavi, A. (1973). The importance of certain assemblages of birds as 'information-centres' for food-finding. *Ibis*, **115**, 517–34.

Warren, R. B. (1989). Red Kite and Black Kite following mowing machine. *British Birds*, **82**, 116.

Watt, D. J. (1986). Relationship of plumage variability, size, and sex to social dominance in Harris' Sparrows. *Animal Behaviour*, **34**, 16–27.

Watt, D. J. and Mock, D. W. (1987). A selfish herd of martins. *Auk*, **104**, 342–3.

Weatherhead, P. J. (1979a). Do savannah sparrows commit the Concorde fallacy. *Behavioral Ecology and Sociobiology*, **5**, 373–81.

Weatherhead, P. J. (1979b). Behavioral implications of the defense of a Shoveler brood by Common Eiders. *Condor*, **81**, 427.

Weatherhead, P. J. (1985). The birds' communal connection. *Natural History*, February, pp. 34–40.

Wellnhofer, P. (1988). A new specimen of *Archaeopteryx*. *Science*, **240**, 1790–2.

Wenzel, B. M. (1973). Chemoreception. In *Avian biology*, (eds. D. S. Farner and J. R. King), Vol. 3, pp. 389–416. Academic Press, New York.

Wesolowski, T. (1983). Conjectures, venturous suggestions or 'Evolution of hole-nesting in birds'? *Ornis Scandinavica*, **14**, 63–5.

West, M. J. and King, A. P. (1988). Female visual displays affect the development of male song in the cowbird. *Nature*, **334**, 244–6.

Westneat, D. F., Sherman, P. W., and Morton, M. L. (1990). The ecology and evolution of extra-pair copulations in birds. In *Current ornithology*, (ed. D. M. Power), Vol. 7, pp. 331–69. Plenum, New York.

Wetton, J. H., Carter, R. E., Parkin, D. T., and Walters, D. (1987). Demographic study of a wild house sparrow population by DNA fingerprinting. *Nature*, **327**, 147–9.

Wheelwright, N. T. (1988). Fruit-eating birds and bird-dispersed plants in the tropics and temperate zone. *Trends in Ecology and Evolution*, **3**, 270–4.

White, F. N. and Kinney, J. L. (1974). Avian incubation. *Science*, **186**, 107–15.

White, G. (1789). *The natural history and antiquities of Selborne in the county of Southampton*. B. White and Son, Horace's Head, Fleet Street, London.

Whitfield, D. P. (1985). Raptor predation on wintering waders in southeast Scotland. *Ibis*, **127**, 544–58.

Whitfield, D. P. (1987). Plumage variability, status signalling and individual recognition in avian flocks. *Trends in Ecology and Evolution*, **2**, 13–18.

Whitlock, R. (1981). *Birds at risk: a comprehensive world-survey of threatened species*. Moonraker Press, Bradford-on-Avon, Wiltshire.

Wickler, W. (1968). *Mimicry in plants and anmals*. McGraw-Hill, New York.

Wiemeyer, S. N., Spann, J. W., Bunck, C. M., and Krynitsky, A. J. (1989). Effects of kelthane on reproduction of captive eastern screech-owls. *Environmental Toxicology and Chemistry*, **8**, 903–13.

Wiklund, C. G. (1985). Fieldfare *Turdus pilaris* breeding strategy: the importance of asynchronous hatching and resources needed for egg formation. *Ornis Scandinavica*, **16**, 213–21.

Wilcove, D. S. (1985). Nest predation in forest tracts and the decline of migratory songbirds. *Ecology*, **66**, 1211–14.

Wilcove, D. S. and Terborgh, J. W. (1984). Patterns of population decline in birds. *American Birds*, **38**, 10–13.

Wiley, R. H. (1978). The lek mating system of the Sage Grouse. *Scientific American*, **238**, 114–25.

Wiley, R. H. and Richards, D. G. (1982). Adaptations for acoustic communication in birds: sound transmission and signal detection. In *Acoustic communication in birds*, (eds. D. E. Kroodsma and E. H. Miller), Vol. 1, pp. 131–81. Academic Press, New York.

Williams, G. G. (1953). Wilson Phalaropes as commensals. *Condor*, **55**, 158.

Williams, M. (1974). Creching behaviour of the Shelduck *Tadorna tadorna*. L. *Ornis Scandinavica*, **5**, 131–43.

Williamson, M. (1981). *Island populations*. Oxford University Press, Oxford.

Wiliamson, M. (1989). The MacArthur and Wilson theory today: true but trivial. *Journal of Biogeography*, **16**, 3–4.

Williamson, P. (1971). Feeding ecology of the Red-eyed Vireo (*Vireo olivaceus*) and associated foliage-gleaning birds. *Ecological Monographs*, **41**, 129–52.

Willis, E. O. and Oniki, Y. (1978). Birds and army ants. *Annual Review of Ecology and Systematics*, **9**, 243–63.

Willson, M. F. (1986). Avian frugivory and seed dispersal in eastern North America. *Current Ornithology*, **3**, 223–79.

Wilson, E. O. (1975). *Sociobiology: the new synthesis*. Harvard University Press, Cambridge, MA.

Wiltschko, W., Daum, P., Fergenbauer-Kimmel, A., and Wiltschko, R. (1987). The development of the star compass in Garden Warblers, *Sylvia borin*. *Ethology*, **74**, 285–92.

Wimberger, P. H. (1984). The use of green plant material in bird nests to avoid ectoparasites. *Auk*, **101**, 615–18.

Winkler, D. W. and Walters, J. R. (1983). The determination of clutch size in precocial birds. *Current Ornithology*, **1**, 33–68.

Wittenberger, J. F. and Hunt, Jr. G. L. (1985). The adaptive significance of colonality in birds. In *Avian biology*, (eds. D. S. Farmer, J. R. King, and K. C. Parkes), Vol. 8, pp. 1–78. Academic Press, New York.

Woolfenden, G. E. and Fitzpatrick, J. W. (1984). *The Florida Scrub Jay*. Monogr. Pop. Biol. No. 20. Princeton University Press, Princeton, NJ.

Wunder, B. A. (1979). Evaporative water loss from birds: effects of artifical radiation. *Comparative Biochemistry and Physiology*, **63A**, 493–4.

Wyllie, I. (1981). *The Cuckoo*. Batsford, London.

Yom-Tov, Y. (1975). Synchronization of breeding and intraspecific interference in the Carrion Crow. *Auk*, **92**, 778–85.

Yom-Tov, Y. (1979). The disadvantage of low positions in colonial roosts: an experiment to test the effect of droppings on plumage quality. *Ibis*, **121**, 331–2.

Yom-Tov, Y. (1980). Intraspecific nest parasitism in birds. *Biological Reviews*, **55**, 93–108.

Yom-Tov, Y., Dunnet, G., and Anderson, A. (1974). Intraspecific nest parasitism in the Starling, *Sturnus vulgaris*. *Ibis*, **116**, 87–90.

Yong, W. and Moore, F. R. (1990). 'Foot-quivering' as a foraging maneuver among migrating *Catharus* thrushes. *Wilson Bulletin*, **102**, 542–4.

Zahavi, A. (1990). Arabian Babblers: the quest for social status in a cooperative breeder. In *Cooperative breeding in birds*, (eds. P. B. Stacey and W. D. Koenig), pp. 105–30. Cambridge University Press.

Zang, H. (1988). Regulation von Kohlmeisen (*Parus major*) — Beständen im Harz. *Die Vogelwelt*, **109**, 107–14.

Zink, R. M. and Remsen, Jr., J. V. (1986). Evolutionary processes and patterns of geographic variation in birds. *Current Ornithology*, **4**, 1–69.

Index of English and scientific bird names

Page numbers in **boldface** refer to species treatment paragraphs; pages in roman type refer to essays and appendix.

Index of bird names in German, French, Dutch, Spanish, and Swedish

German bird names

French bird names

Lagopède des Alpes 122
des saules 122
Linotte à bec jaune 488
mélodieuse 486
Locustelle fluviatile 376
luscinioïde 376
tachetée 374
Loriot 446
Lusciniole à moustaches 378

Macareux moine 234
Macreuse brune 70
noire 68
Marouette de Baillon 142
ponctuée 140
poussin 140
Martin roselin 468
Martinet alpin 272
cafre 274
des maisons 274
noir 270
pâle 272
Martin-pêcheur d'Europe 276
de Smyrn 276
Mergule nain 232
Merle bleu 364
noir 366
à plastron 364
de roche 362
Mésange azurée 432
bleue 432
boréale 428
charbonnière 434
huppée 430
lapone 428
à longue queue 424
lugubre 426
à moustaches 422
noire 430
nonnette 426
rémiz 442
Mésangeai imitateur 454
Milan noir 80
royal 80
Moineau blanc 472
domestique 470
espagnol 470
friquet 474
de la mer Morte 472
soulcie 476
soulcie pâle 474
Mouette mélanocéphale 204
pygmée 204
rieuse 206
de Sabine 206
tridactyle 214

Nette rousse 60
Niverolle 476

Oedicnème criard 156
du Sénégal 158

Oie à bec court 40
cendrée 44
d'Egypte 48
des moissons 40
naine 42
rieuse 42
Outarde barbue 152
canepetière 150
houbara 150

Pélican blanc 20
frisé 20
Percnoptère d'Egypte 84
Perdrix bartavelle 128
choukar 126
gambra 130
grise 134
de Hey 130
rouge 128
Perruche à collier 246
Pétrel culblanc 14
fulmar 10
tempête 14
Phalarope à bec étroit 196
à bec large 198
Phragmite aquatique 378
des joncs 380
Pic cendré 284
à dos blanc 292
épeiche 288
épeichette 292
de Levaillant 286
mar 290
noir 288
syriaque 290
tridactyle 294
-vert 286
Pie bavarde 456
-bleue 454
Pie-grièche écorcheur 448
grise 450
masquée 452
à poitrine rose 448
à tête rousse 450
Pigeon biset 240
colombin 240
ramier 242
Pingouin Grand 230
Petit 230
Pinson des arbres 478
du Nord 478
Pintade sauvage 136
Pipit des arbres 320
à gorge rousse 322
à long bec 320
maritime 324
des prés 322
rousseline 318
spioncelle 324
Plongeon arctique 2
à bec blanc 4
catmarin 2

Dutch bird names

Spanish bird names

Swedish bird names

Subject Index

Page numbers in **boldface** refer to entire essays devoted to a subject. For mention of birds, see Index of English and scientific bird names, pp. 575–90. This index is in word-by-word alphabetical order.

anatomy (*continued*)
　　skin; skull; tail; thumbs; tissues; vessels,
　　　blood; wings; wishbone
　　alimentary canal 87
　　arteries 163
　　bladder, urinary 515
　　capillaries 513
　　cartilage 475
　　diverticula 489
　　eustachian tube 371
　　gastrointestinal tract 137, 241, 243, 317
　　heart 513
　　intestines 135
　　kidneys 225, 313, 485, 495
　　liver 225, 495
　　lungs 65, 313, 449, 475, 513, 515
　　oesophageal diverticulum 489
　　oesophagus 137, 243
　　rectum 239
　　reproductive organs, *see* organs, reproductive
　　stomach 11, 135
　　throat 313
　　trachea 475
　　vocal cords 475
ancestral organisms 471, *see also* evolutionary
　　ancestors of birds; fossils
Andersson, Malte 151
anecdotal information, *see* information on bird
　　biology
anemometers 65
animals, domestic 359
Annex I–III and amendments, *see* Directive,
　　Birds
Anser (Skanes Ornitologiska Förening) xxxix
Antarctic 222, 233, 243, 521
anting **469**
ants
　　and bactericidal secretions 461, 469
　　in commensal associations 29, 431
　　nests of 469
　　as predator defence in bird nests 445
anvils, *see* tool use by birds
Aosta 95
appearance, convergence in 431
aquatic birds 59, 89, 137, 375
　　and botulism 59
Aquila (Institutus Ornithologicus Hungaricus)
　　xxxviii
arctic, *see* areas, arctic
Ardea (Netherlandse Ornithologische Unie)
　　xxxviii
Ardeola (Sociedad Española de Ornithología)
　　xxxix
areas 271, 491, 520
　　arctic 57, 293, 295, 311, 335, 349, 379, 453, 485
　　arid 7, 311, 313, 355
　　boreal 491
　　loafing 109
　　moulting 171
　　natal 109
　　northern 193
　　polar 453
　　resting 379
　　staging 41, 95, 145, 171

subarctic 283, 293
temperate 57, 241, 283, 293, 295, 311, 339,
　　373, 433, 453, 497, 499
tropic, *see* tropics
tundra, *see* tundra
wintering 171, 411; *see also* wintering
Areas of Outstanding Natural Value 520
arena 123
　　transient 123
Aristotle 463
Ashmole, N. P. 55, 57
Asia 241, 379, 433, 491, 521, 523
　　southeastern 16, 381
aspergillosis 315
Aspergillus fumigatus 361
associations, feeding, *see* feeding, commensal
Atlantic Ocean 465
　　coast of 379, 475
Atlas of the birds of the Western Palearctic xviii, xix
atmosphere
　　and greenhouse gases 311
　　night time 353
　　structure of and evolution of migration 353
attendants in commensal associations, *see*
　　feeding, commensal
attenuation 183
auditory space, neural map of 253
Audubon, John James 143, 151, 195, 231, 453,
　　521
Australasia 273
Australia 25, 113, 257, 279, 297, 321, 387, 403,
　　431, 433, 453, 459, 499
Austro-Hungaria, government of 522
automata 391
autumn, mobbing in 261
auxiliaries 275, 277
Avebury, Lord 27
Aves 3, 351
Aves (Société d'Etudes Ornithologiques) xxxvii
avian seed dispersers, *see* seeds
avian sense of smell, *see* sense of smell
avian snowshoes, *see* snowshoes, avian
aviculturalists, *see* captives
avifauna 305, 325, 343, 367, 411
Avocetta (Centro Italiano Studi Ornitologici)
　　xxxviii

backcross 325
bacteria 75, 315, 349
　　anaerobic 59
　　and botulism 59
　　and nests, *see* nest sanitation
Baden-Württemberg 343
badges **433–7**
　　as arbitrary symbols 435
　　bibs and stripes as 435
Baffin Island 463
bait 459, 461
　　-fishers 459
Bakken, Morten 435
Balda, Russel 159
bananas 389, 393
Banks, Joseph 273

bans, *see* conservation efforts
barbials 363
barbs, zipping of 363
barbules 363
  rotation of and iridescence 139
Bardsey 307
Baretta 499
bathing 143, 312, **355–7**, 391; *see also* dusting
  frequency of 357
  and moulting 373
  passive 355
bathing, sun 17, 165; *see also* postures;
  temperature regulation
bats 271, 321
  and ultrasonic frequencies 255
Bavaria 147, 299
Bay of Fundy 11, 13
beak 101, 163, 187, 313, 391
  horny plates of 37
  and use in preening, *see* bills, functions of
beak marks
  on butterfly wings 473
  near cache sites 457
Bears, Polar 231
beaters in commensal associations 29
Beaulieu River 145
bedbugs 317
Bedfordshire 527
Beecher, William 465
Beehler, Bruce 125
beetles
  and commensal feeding 29
  as grinding agents 135
behaviour 17, 37, 75, 107, 141, 143, 146, 151,
    195, 197, 199, 211, 241, 251, 267, 349, 399,
    405, 423, 461, 465, 503; *see also listings under*
    displays
  geographic variation and xxx
  and local environmental conditions xxix
behaviour, breeding
  brooding 331
  egg-tossing 279
  guarding 47
  helping 277
  hormone-driven 331
  infanticide 197
  nest building 329
  nest lining xxix
  parental 331
  post-season breeding 331
  sexual 209, 331
  shell-disposal 199, 201
behaviour, foraging 233, 417; *see also listings*
    under foraging
  caching, *see listings under* caches
  changes in 419
  courtship feeding, *see* feeding during
    breeding
  eliciting feeding by young 173
  and exposure to food 427
  and interference 421
  and kleptoparasitism, *see* piracy
  and leg length, *see* foraging; walking
  milk-robbing 387

three-phase 489
throwing eggs at anvils 459; *see also* tool use
  by birds
and winter guilds 77
behaviour, group 43; *see also* altruism;
    dominance; flocking; flocks; flocks,
    coherence of; groups; mobbing
behaviour and intelligence; *see also* intelligence;
    tool use by birds
  behaviour spread by learning 387
  evolved versus learned behaviour 387, 391
  similarity between bird and human 495
behaviour, migratory, *see* migrants; migration
behaviour and temperature regulation, *see*
    temperature regulation
  effects of weather on 41
  and heat loss, *see* heat
  sunbathing and wing-drying, *see* bathing;
    postures
behaviour, territorial 299, 399; *see also*
    territoriality
behaviourists 35, 73, 435, 457
Belgium 307, 359, 522
belly-wetting 236; *see also* temperature
  regulation
Bering Sea 463
Bernoulli, Daniel 217
Berthold, Peter 405
Betelgeuse 503
Bewick's of Slimbridge, the **39–43**
biandry 197
bibliography xxxi
bigamy 267, 269
bills 115, 155, 157, 187, 199, 205, 237, 241, 249,
    289, 313, 349, **397**, 417, 419, 465, 471
bills, adaptations of 157, 393, 397
  crossing 397
  length and prey size 187
  sensory receptors 157
  serrations 129, 391, 393
  tips 157, 391
  touch receptors 391
bills, colour and appearance
  changes in 393
  and exfoliation of horny sheath 391
  and identification 41
  parasites or diseases and 155
  and red spot 205, 211
  and size 393
  and unique markings 38
  and wear 391
bills and feeding habits 157, 393, 397; *see also*
  guilds
bills, functions of 391; *see also listings under*
    displays; egg-turning; hatching; nest-
    building; patches, brood; preening;
    scratching; sound
  climbing 393
  and prey-carrying 397
bills, shape of 299, 397
  broad 39
  downcurved 397
  hooked 129
  pickaxe-shaped 393

clavicle 301
derived from 449
elimination and fusion of 511
fish 137
hyoid 289
internal strut-like reinforcements 511
and pellets 257
pneumatization of 511
solid versus hollow 511
sternum 129, 301, 511
borders, international and conservation 95
Austrian–German 97
Belgium–Luxembourg 95
Franco–German 95
Franco–Italian 95
German–Luxembourg 95
German–Netherlands–Danish 95
Hungarian–Austrian 97
Macedonia–Greece 97
Polish–Belorussian 97
Polish–Czechoslovakian 97
Swiss–Italian 95
Turkey–Greece 97
boreal species and global warming 311
Borneo 57
Bosporus, the, *see* wintering
botulism 59
bower style, cultural transmission of 387
Bowers, Deane 473
Bradbury, Jack 125
brain 11, 39, **385–91**, 481, 515
midbrain 253
olfactory centre of 13
regions of and song production 475
and sensitive period for cell production 481
breast 355, 475
positions during displays 209
stripe as badge, *see* badges
breeding 97, 219, 233, 281, 303, 307, 329, 423,
427, 441, 471, 477, 481, 522; *see also* system,
mating
and abundance of migrating prey 331
age of onset 463
in autumn 331
and brood parasitism, *see* parasites, brood
and clutch size, *see* clutch size
colonial, *see* coloniality; colonies
communal, *see* cooperative
cooperative, *see* system, mating
disadvantages of premature 133
early 153
failure, *see* nest failure
first-time 201
first-year 179
late, and clutch size 57
limited opportunities for 279
and nest-robbing, *see* nest robbers
proximate triggers versus ultimate causes of
295
season, *see* season, breeding
selective 437
solitary 55, 109
success 237, 247, 387, 465
survival to 299

and syllable repertoires 385
synchronous 337
timing of 295
Breeding Bird Survey 339
breeding habitat xx, 41, 149, 153, 169, 205, 207,
221, 231, 243, 261, 269, 295, 335, 405, 427,
441, 503, 518
amount of 518
arctic 193
distribution and polygyny 267
and females and resources, *see* resources
island 169
and site tenacity, *see* site tenacity
see also areas; habitat
Brest 97
bristles 365, 393
British Birds xxxvii, xxxviii
British Columbia 121, 133
British Ministry of Agriculture 117
British Museum 453
British Ornithologists' Union (Zoological
Museum) xxxv
British Trust for Ornithology xxxv, 361, 367
brooding 5, 167, 173, 331
brood parasitism, *see* parasites, brood
broods ix, 331, 467, 507
and crèches 45
defence of 197
double 59, 175, 463
first versus subsequent 277
intermixing of 227, 229
large versus small 57
loss of 173, 267, 295
number of xviii, xix, xxiv, xxx, 295, 465
reduction of 199, **507–11**; *see also* hatching;
siblicide
run away chicks 199
brothers 247
Brower, Jane Van Zandt 387
Brown, Charles 317
Brown, Irene 473
Brown, Mary 317
Brown University 471
bubules 513
bugs, swallow 317
Bumpus, H. C. 471
buoyancy 143, 511
and oil contamination 225
burrows, *see* nest types
butterflies 137, 295, 399
checkerspot 473, 518
monarch versus viceroy 387, 389, 495
palatable versus distasteful 387, 389
poisonous chemicals stored in 239
wing patterns of 387, 473
buzzes 307

caches 239, 391, 451, **453–5**
of acorns, nuts or seeds 239, 455
of animal prey 455
of eggs 457
of frozen prey and 'incubating' 455
caches, finding hidden 457

ducks
  blue-winged 49
  dabbling 49
  displays of, *see* displays, general forms
  diving 61
  diving versus dabbling in crèches 45
  and down 275
  migratory 43
  parasitized, *see* parasites, brood
  puddle 49
  river 49
Duich Moss 525
dusting **355–7**; *see also* anting; bathing
  antiparasite function of 355
  and moulting 373
  in wallows 357
dynamics, population, *see* population dynamics

ears 255
  asymmetrical openings of 253
  scratching of, *see* scratching
Earth 107
earthworms 13, 117, 157
East Indies 273
East, Marion 345
Eastern Hemisphere and clutch size 57
echidna 319
echolocation 255
ecologists 161, 303, 337, 341, 387, 419, 421, 423,
  425, 427, 473, 515
  behavioural 15, 155, 177, 335, 503
  evolutionary 133
ecology 133, 143, 146, 233
  community 427
  distinctiveness of 324
  factors of and shared incubation 287
  and foot structure 289
  foraging and bills 397
  and loop migrations 383
  and similar but unrelated birds 233
economic versus cultural, ecological, or
  scientific considerations 522
economists 297
ecosystems
  natural and global warming 311
  services of 43
  wetland 43; *see also* conservation and human
    pressure; wetlands
ectoparasites 371; *see also* egg-laying; nest
  sanitation; parasites, insect
ectotherms 283, 285
Edinburgh, Duke of 145
Edward VII 25
Edward Grey Institute xxxvii, 425
EEC, *see* European Economic Community
egg ix, 3, 5, 83, 87, 109, 111, 121, 151, 171, 175,
  195, 197, 199, 201, 229, 231, 233, 237, 243,
  247, 249, 251, 265, 277, 279, 285, 293, 295,
  297, 299, 317, 323, 331, 337, 345, 349, 403,
  439, 441, 443, 445, 509; *see also* care,
  parental; colour; eggshells; embryos;
  hatching; incubation
egg-burying 345

egg caching, *see* caches
egg carrying, *see* carrying
egg collectors, *see* conservation and human
  pressure
egg colour xxx, **161**
  and camouflage 201
  and discoloration from guano 161
  and eggshell removal 201
  and patterns 161
  and pigments 161
  see also colour
egg development **447–51**; *see also* development;
  developmental stage at hatching; embryos
  and airspace 487
  and albumen 449
  arrested prior to laying 439
  and breathing 487
  and chilling 191, 275
  completed prior to laying 437
  as haploid stage 447
  and heat loss 275
  and oil contamination 225
  and protection from sun 275
  and storage of nitrogenous wastes 315
  and temperature 273, 275
  and uric acid 315
  and water loss during 5, 487
  and weather 275
  and the white 449
  and the yolk 319, 321, 449
egg evolution, *see* evolution of
  and ammonia excretion from fish and
    amphibian eggs 315
egg hatching intervals 507, 509
egg identification xxx
egg incubation 5, 101, 275, 455
  of last laid egg 507
  and number of eggs laid 55, 223
egg-laying 135, 467
  and courtship feeding 223
  and dawn chorus 371
  and ectoparasites 75
  and hatching 507
  indeterminate 69, **437–9**
  and mate-guarding 73
  and supplemented diets 295
  timing of 293
egg marked versus unmarked xviii, xix, xxiv
egg and nest type xxii
egg number per clutch; *see also* clutch size
  counted by female 437
  predetermined 437
egg parasitism, *see* parasites, brood
egg production
  and calcium 495
  and disadvantages of retention within
    female 321
  and female size 101
egg recognition 69, 71, 161
  wooden 437
egg, risks to
  and defence 399
  from ectoparasites 371
  from embedding 441

European Economic Community (*continued*)
  Member States of 522, 526, 529–30
Europe, Central 411
Europe, Eastern 97
Europe, Southern 97
Europe, Western 25, 95
Evans, Howard 321
evaporation 313; *see also* temperature
    regulation
  and spread-wing postures 19
evolution 89, 133, 175, 215, 241, 297, 325, 461,
    471
evolution of
  altruism 245, 247
  annual migratory cycle 405
  Archaeopteryx 157
  asynchronous hatching 507, 509
  behavioural characteristics 153
  bird colours 139
  birds as shaped by flight 301
  black plumage 9
  bright plumage 149
  brood parasitism 69
  cheating in dominance hierarchies 437
  chick recognition by adults 199
  clutch size 31, 57
  coloniality 107
  colour and colour vision 93
  colour patterns in butterflies 239
  competition for nest holes 347
  cooperative breeding systems 279
  crèching 45
  day length as a signal 295
  deep voices in men 149
  defensive secretions of millipedes 469
  dialect systems 383
  displays 37, 49, 53
  distasteful butterflies 239
  distraction displays 177
  efficient circulatory systems 301
  egg discrimination 249
  egg mimicry 241
  eggs **317–23**
  eggshell removal from nests 201
  eggshells 317
  elaborate song repertoires 415
  eye structure 91
  feathers 159
  flight 153, 159, 511
  flocking behaviour 257
  flower shape 473
  frugivores and fruit 241
  fruit colour 473
  functioning temperature 283
  habitat choice 423
  hair 159
  insects 473
  intelligence 301
  large breeding aggregations 111
  lek mating system 125, 193
  long complex songs 415
  loop migrations 383
  migratory flight altitude and time 353
  mimicry in butterflies and other insects 387

nests **345–9**
new organisms 461
offspring recognition 229
passerines 351
patterns of communication 205
Peacock tails 149
physical characteristics 153
piercing calls 181
piracy 213, 215
plant characteristics 241
polyandry 193
powered flight 159
prey 473
promiscuous mating system 127
redundant navigation and orientation cues
    505
Ruff necks 149
seed size 473
sequential polyandry 197
short simple songs 415
sickle-shaped bills 241
site tenacity 221
social mimicry 239
songs and calls 327
spatial memory 457
specialized tongues 459
spur length in Common Pheasants 153
suppressed interspecific aggression 433
synchronous moult 375
tail length in Widowbirds 153
temperature regulation 301
the timing of breeding seasons 293, 295, 495
uric acid 315
viviparity 321
weaker towards appearance of stronger 431
white plumage 9
wing colour in butterflies 473
evolutionary agents 473
evolutionary ancestors of birds 461, 465; *see also*
    bones; fossils; *Hesperornis* and other
    missing links
  Archaeopteryx 157, 159
  bipedal insectivores as 159
  feathered dinosaurs as **299–303**
  and egg colour 161
  and modern birds 159
  and the origin of modern birds 129
  the 'other birds' as 129
  reptiles as 161, 301
  toothed birds as 129
  winged 129
evolutionary costs of brood parasitism 71
evolutionary history 249
  of loop migrations 383
evolutionary interests
  of parents versus young 175
evolutionary significance of
  dialects 479
  eye colour change 87
  monogamy 337
evolutionists 35, 159, 433, 435
excrement, recycling of 485
excretion 313
  and evaporative cooling 163

exoskeletons in pellets 257
experiments, field
    altering tail length in Widowbirds 151
    Clark's Nutcrackers and Grey Jays recovering
        caches 457
    cross-fostering 505
    dialects of Corn Buntings and White-
        crowned Sparrows 477
    dusting to discourage bird lice 355
    eliciting distraction displays at nests 177
    establishment of peck order in flocks 131
    flocking and extra food supplied to woods
        431
    flying models of predators over gull colonies
        203
    fumigated versus non-fumigated nests 317
    Greenfinch flocks and foraging efficiency 431
    gulls removing eggshells from their nests
        201
    homing behaviour of Leach's Storm-Petrel
        14
    infanticide by Northern Jacana females 197
    land reclamation and poultry litter 485
    Laughing Dove flight reaction time 259
    measuring nest predation in fragmented
        habitat 341
    memory of nest-robbing Hooded Crows 389
    natural 423
    placing cuckoo eggs in host nests 251
    playback of local song types 329
    predation and nest failure among hole
        nesting birds 345
    predation and spacing of gull nests 191
    removing males and effect on brood-rearing
        335
    sentinals in mixed-species flocks 429
    tape recorded songs and species 413
    tits feeding in Scandinavia 425
    White-crowned Sparrow singing after
        testosterone injections 479
    winter foraging of tits 425
experiments, laboratory 471
    Blue Jays avoiding monarch butterflies 495
    motorized model and breast badge in Harris'
        Sparrows 435
    breast stripe width as badge in Great Tits 435
    breeding 407
    caged migrants and Zugunruhe 503
    Canary females and nest-building 415
    chick weights after crop milk supplement
        243
    circannual periodicity in warblers 405
    constant light and biological clocks of Short-
        tailed Shearwaters 297
    deafening and effects on song learning 483
    demonstrating owls hunting by sound 253
    dominance status and badges in Harris's
        Sparrows 435
    female preference and song 385
    instinct versus learning in nest-building 331
    learning to avoid distasteful prey 387
    learning from other birds who to mob 261
    learning of progressions by Hooded Crow
        389

manipulating hatching synchrony 507
parasite infection and plumage coloration
    155
Pied Flycatchers orienting using natal area
    geomagnetic field 505
pigeons combining learned skills 389
replacing frog zygote cell nucleus with that of
    adult 449
Robins, White-throats, Black Caps and
    magnetic orientation 505
seasonal changes in photoperiod 405
short-term memory of Marsh Tits 457
song and call development in isolated
    soundproof chamber 481
songs coordinating reproductive cycle 415
species showing they hear vocalizations of
    other species 257
supplemental diets and early breeding 295
Sylvia juveniles correctly switch orientation
    407
Sylvia and regulation of migraton, timing,
    and direction 407
exploitation 231, 233, 526
    regulation of 522
extinction, see conservation status
extramarital 49
Exxon Valdez 227
eyes 4, 13, 84, 89, 253, 403
    adaptions of 2, 91
    colour of and development **85–7**, 93
    and eyeball 465
    and focal length 91
    and lens 91
    like a hawk **89–93**, 515
    open versus closed at hatching 401
    and overlapping visual fields 89
    positions held during displays 207
    and pupil 91
    and salt glands 237
    as signals of maturity 87
    size of in birds versus people 91
    and sleep 73
    and third eyelid 333
    see also vision
Eyrie 113

facial ruff, see feathers, types of; head; hunting
    by birds
faecal sacs 75, 465, 485
faeces
    mammalian 485
    and sealing nesthole entrance 285
Faeroe Islands 95
Fair Isle 153
falconry 103, 523
    policing by RSPB 27; see also conservation
        efforts; raptors
Falsterbo Peninsula 93; see also wintering
family 3, 59, 85, 123, 250, 251, 267, 315, 336,
    351, 362, 421, 422, 424, 442, 446, 465, 467, 509
Far North 295
farming 339, 365, 367, 369; see also conservation
    and human pressure

of songbirds 417–19
time available for 429
time and crèches 45
of waders 187–9
forebrain
complexity in parrots and songbirds 477
and vocalizations 475
forelimbs 299, 511
clawed 301
feathered 159
mammal 391
and origin of flight 159; *see also* bones;
evolutionary ancestors of birds; fossils
Forest of Dean 518
foresters, informed by RSPB 27
forests, birds of 97, 329, 339, 343, 347, 367, 485;
see also conservation and declines;
conservation and human pressure
canopy 381
coniferous 343
continuous 341
interiors 343
and lekking 125
lowland moist 241
old growth 339
patches of deciduous 305
thorn 57
tropical 105, 241, 341, 365, 381, 387, 411, 431,
433
forests, declines of 105
and conversion 343, 463
and damage from acid precipitation 287, 289
and death 343
and destruction 339, 341, 343, 411
and edge species xxxi, 339, 341
and extermination of populations 367
and global warming 311
and isolation of remnants 341
and protection 521
and wintering habitat 411
see also listings under conservation;
fragmentation
Formica rufa as predator defence 445
forms, intergrading 325
related 325
fossils 129
claws 301
morphological features of 301
opposable first digits 301
record of, *see* records
tail feathers and fused tail vertebrae 301
foster breeding programs and insurance eggs
33
Foster, Mercedes 125
foxes xxxi, 191, 203
fragmentation 339, 341
and abundance of nest-robbers 307
and habitat requirements 307
and invaders 307
and territories 307
see also conservation and range contraction;
forests, declines of; habitat
France 25, 41, 137, 169, 381, 524–5
Frankfurt 95

frugivores 135, 241, 485, 493
fruit
colour and odour of and seed dispersal 241
fermenting 332
flesh of 241
pits and commensal feeding 29
pits as grinding agent 135
seasonal dependence on 241
Fuglevaern xxxvii
fumigants, natural added to nests 465
fungi 315, 349, 465, 485
and nests, *see* nest sanitation
fungicidal properties of ant secretions 469
furcula 301

Gabon 523
Galápagos Islands 239, 459, 471
gallinaceous birds 69, 135, 215, 243, 269, 403,
489, 515
and brood parasitism 69
game birds 5, 87, 113, 120, 293, 357,
497
Game Conservancy xxxvi
game, wild 103
gamekeepers 103
policing by RSPB 27; *see also* conservation
efforts
gangplanks 231
gape 241, 393
and eliciting feeding 173
positions held during displays 207
Garden Bird Feeding Survey 361
Garefowl 231
gases, greenhouse 311; *see also* climate; global
warming
Gaunt, Abbot 475
Geirfuglasker 231
genera 253, 287, 373
General Assembly of German Agriculturalists
and Foresters 522
generations 241
genes 45, 197, 201, 245, 247, 265, 281, 297, 447,
471
activation of 449
adapted to specific environments 477
and breeds shaped by stockmen 297
and brood parasitism 71
and chromosomes 447, 449
and degree of migratory restlessness 407
as determinants of egg patterns 249
and genetic analysis 337, 479
and genetic basis for partial migration 407
and inherited characteristics 149
and polymorphic populations 153
and reflection of quality 155
and relatedness 247
geneticists, population 471
genetics 297
evolutionary 297
genotypes 297, 299, 471
gens 251
gentes 251
genus 3, 349, 392, 446, 516

hovering, *see* flight, types of
how birds fly, *see* flight mechanics and
    remaining airborne
how fast and high birds fly, *see* flight mechanics
    and remaining airborne
how long birds can live, *see* age
how owls hunt in the dark, *see* hunting by birds
how woodpecker tongues work, *see* tongues
humans 233, 313, 485; *see also* bird-human
    interactions; conservation and human
    pressure; *Homo sapiens*; hunting by people;
    people
  activities of, as natural experiments 423
  tool use by 459
humidity
  and anting 469
  noctural 353
Hunstanton 221
hunting by birds 393
  diurnal 115
  and efficiency of female raptors 115
  and mobbing raptors 263
  owls and other nocturnal predators 13, **251–
    5**, 427; *see also* predators, nocturnal
  and risks during 101
  specializing on one group of prey 203
  and success 11, 101, 113, 223
  techniques of 113, 115; *see also* foraging
    techniques
  using sight alone 187
  and wing shape 271
hunting by people xxxi, 97, 105, 519, 521, 525
  for feathers, *see* plume trade
  and illegal shooting 105, 107, 523–4
  and lead poisoning 137
  legal 141, 526, 529
  and overhunting 521, 525
  and regulations 522, 524, 525
  and spring shoots 523–24, 526
  see also conservation and human pressure;
    laws
Huxley, Julian 35
hybridization 51, 205, **461–3**
  in gulls 205
  inability for 325, 327
  intersubspecific 461
hybrids 53
  detection of 461
hydro-developers, informed by RSPB 27
hypothermia
  nocturnal 167
  regulated 167
hypotheses 57, 279, 321, 323
  arrival-times, body-size, dominance and
    differential migration 323
  asynchronous hatching and lower nest
    predation 509
  auditory template 481
  decorative males and pathogens and
    parasites 155
  eggshell lining and attraction of predators
    199
  elaborate displays and pathogens and
    parasites 155

explanations for nocturnal migration 351
flocking and increased feeding efficiency
    429, 431
Hamilton–Zuk 155
information-centre versus mutual predator
    defence as incentive for flocking 83, 107,
    109, 111, 429
limited discrimination ability and
    intraspecific adoption 199
move-along 261
number of offspring matches food
    availability 507
rise of nest predation with rise in forest
    fragmentation 341
size dimorphism in raptor pairs 101
size dimorphism and speed of prey 99
temporary nature of African wintering sites
    409

Iberian Peninsula 383
Ibis (British Ornithologists' Union) xxxv,
    xxxviii
ice 163
  pack 233
Ice Age, Little 231
Iceland 95, 231, 233, 463
Idaho 99
iguanas, marine 239
illnesses, *see* disease
image, search 345, 495
Imboden, Christoph 527
imitation, vocal 383
immigration 303, 305, 515, 518
increase
  exponential 517
  rate of 305
incubation 3, 5, 121, 151, 171, 191, 193, 195,
    197, 243, 249, 277, 285, 287, 295, 321, 331,
    335, 337, 349, 403, 437, 439, 467
  attentiveness during 275
  and controlling egg temperatures **273–5**
  and courtship feeding 223
  and DDT 119; *see also* conservation and
    human pressure
  and egg colour 161
  and genetic control of constancy 121
  geographic variation in xxv, xxxiii
  heat from non-bird sources 171
  and insulation 275
  length of ix, xviii, xxiv, xxv, **121**
  and maximum clutch size 55
  and oil contamination 225
  onset of 507
  shared 285; *see also* ecology; foraging;
    climate; predation
  shutting down ovary 437
  and who sits xviii, ix, xix, xxiv, 121, **285–7**
indeterminate egg layers, *see* egg-laying
India 25, 27, 381
Indians, Quechua 487
individuals 179
  and clutch size 55
  marked 43; *see also* ringing birds

industries with marked effect on birds
  fashion 25
  pesticide 119
  timber 487
infanticide 197
infections, fungal 315; *see also* disease
infidelity 337; *see also* mate-guarding;
  monogamy
influenza, avian 315; *see also* disease
information on bird biology
  and anecdotal or unconfirmed reports xx,
    xxxiii, 9, 485
  and birds targeted for further research 530
  and censusing or monitoring populations
    147, 522
  collected by amateurs 423
  and contributing observations to birding
    community xxxv, 491
  and data and submission of ix, xxxv, 361
  and field notebook and record-keeping xxxiii
  and field research 17
  and incomplete and informed guesswork
    xxxiii, 475
  and influence of field observations on
    policies 527
  observations and recording ix, xxxiii, xxxv;
    see also observations
  and ornithological or technical literature
    xxxii, xxxv
  and ornithological research 59
  and permits xxxiv
  and promoting scientific research 522
  and quantitative analysis 237
  and recording and analysing behaviour
    xxxiv, 53, 455
  and recording copulation 89
  and recording patterns of foraging 419
  and research 193, 227
  research on biological status 526
  research on effects of marketing 526
  and tropical rarities 527
  and wetland refuges as resource for studying
    birds 41
  see also birdwatching; conservation efforts;
    displays, recording observations of
information, directional 503
information exchange among birds
  in flocks 111
  see also calls; communication; *listings under*
    displays; signals; songs, functions of
information, genetic; *see* genes
Inn River 97
insecticidal properties of ant secretions 469; *see
  also* anting; ants
insecticides 119, 367
insectivores 135, 485, 493
  bipedal 159
insects 75, 465
  abundance of and breeding season 293, 295,
    509
  as bait 459
  distasteful 473; *see also* butterflies
  outbreaks as natural experiments 423
  and protein 495

instincts 201; *see also* intelligence; learning
  feeding 173
  killer 101
  nest building 331
insulation 19, 165; *see also* incubation
  body 5; *see also* feathers; feet; legs
  nest 5, 441; *see also* nest lining
  and oil contamination 225
  thermal 123
intelligence 385; *see also* instincts; learning; tool
  use by birds
  ability to generalize 203
  and abstract ideas 389
  and capacity for thinking 391
  discriminating between figures 389
  problem-solving 389, 391
  reasoning 387
  replacing instinct 391
interactions;
  agonistic 207, 215
  bird–human, *see* bird–human interactions
  coevolutionary 251; *see also* coevolution
  display–response 51
  hormone–environment 333; *see also*
    breeding; nest-building
  male–male 125
  social and foraging 107
  territorial 267; *see also* territoriality
  see also displays
interbreeding 205, 461, 463, 492
  capability of 325
  prevention of 325
interest, public 526
International Council for Bird Preservation
  (ICBP), *see* BirdLife International
International Waterfowl and Wetlands
  Reserves Bureau 43
interspecific interactions, *see* flocking; parasites,
  brood; territoriality
intraspecific brood parasitism, *see* parasites,
  brood 67
intraspecific encounters 377
introductions 517, 531
  species 522; *see also listings under*
    conservation
intruders 175, 183, 209, 445
  warning away of 399
inventories, species 524, 525
invertebrates and bird nests 75
investment 321
  male 127
Iowa 361
Iran 520
Ireland 25, 41, 303, 320, 326, 346, 384, 426, 438,
  466
Ireland, Northern 41, 65
Irish Bird Report (Irish Ornithologists' Club)
  xxxviii
Irish Wildbird Conservancy xxxvii
irruptions 238, **491–3**
  causes of 491
  irregularity of 491
  southward autumn 491
  synchronization of 491

irruptions (*continued*)
  see also conservation and fluctuations in
    population size
island biogeography, theory of 288, **303–7**, 320,
    326, 346, 354, 370, 384, 386, 390, 394, 426,
    430, 438, 442, 446, 450, 466, 476, 478, 480;
    see also theory
  and forecasting 305
islands
  barrier 169
  breeding on 231
  fragments of alpine habitat as 476
  invasion and colonization of volcanic 303
  offshore 231, 233
  and offshore colonies 345
  roosting on 83
Islay 525
Isle of Sheppey 147
isolates 481
isolation, geographic 325, 488
Israel 277
Italy 369, 381, 383, 409, 505, 522, 524

Jakobsson, S. 267
Japan 41, 265, 459
jargon, scientific 213, 401
Järvi, Torbjörn 435
Java 57, 305
jaw 135, 301, 391, 465
  musculature of Hawfinch 397
  reversal of 39
Job, Herbert 23
Journal für Ornithologie (Deutsche Ornithologen-
    Gesellschaft) xxxviii
journals, avian xxxvii; *see also* information on
    bird biology
Jurasic Period 299
Jutland 367
juveniles 133, 245, 256, 277, 293, 323, 387, 397
  mortality of 517
  and piracy 215

keepers, *see* gamekeepers
Kelthane 105
Kent 145
Kent Island 13
Kenya 151, 409
Kerlinger, Paul 353
kidneys, *see* anatomy
killing
  eliminating methods of 522
  surplus 203
kilohertz 309
kin protection by mobbing 261
kiss, cloacal 87
kleptoparasitism, *see* piracy
Knudsen, Eric 253
Koenig, Walter 57
Konishi, Mark 253
Korpimäki, Erkki 427
Krakatoa and extermination of flora and fauna
    305
Krebs, John 433, 457

krill, prevention of overharvesting 520
laboratory, *see* experiments, laboratory
Labrador 231
Lack, David 55, 425, 507
Lack, Peter 367
Lake Ferto 97
lakes
  acidification of 287
  salt 97
lampreys, guts of 39
Lancashire 43
land birds 67, 167, 237, 271, 313, 357
  birds adapted to open lands 367
landfalls 95
landing 219
landscape, directional information from 503
Landscape Protection Area, *see* Protection Area
Landscape Protection Zone, *see* Protection Zone
language, acquisition of 389
Lapland, Swedish 399
Larus (Institute of Ornithology, University of
    Zagreb) xxxvii
Latin America 241, 343
latitudes
  and clutch size 57
  and daylight 379
  high and irruptions 491
  and migration 377
laws ix, xxxiv, 105, 107, 521, 522, 525
  bird **521–3**
  ducking the bird **523–6**
  enforcement of 524, 526
  and plume trade 27; *see also* plume trade
  unenforceable 520
  wildlife and 147, **520–1**; *see also* wildlife
  see also conservation efforts; Directive;
    legislation
lead
  and ban on anglers' weights 137
  versus non-toxic pellets 137
  see also conservation and human pressure
Lear, Edward 453
learning 201, 285, 475
  ability 387
  to associate patterns 387
  and combining learned skills 389
  concepts 391
  dialects 477
  by experience 387
  and feeding preference 495
  to follow trains 387
  from other birds 389
  local dialect 479
  phases and vocalizations 483
  about predators by mobbing 261
  progressions 389
  purposive behaviour, *see* behaviour and
    intelligence
  songs in isolation 483
  songs of other species 483
  vocal 255
legislation 105, 520
  banning trade of wild-caught birds 524; *see
    also* captives

and soaring 353
spring and fall 93
tracking with ceilometers 505
trans-Saharan 343, 518
tropical 341
migration 65, 169, 175, 179, 193, 241, 273, 335,
    339, **377–83**, 411, 423, 433, 453, 463, 491,
    503
  autumn 353
  and avoidance of severe weather 455
  behavioural preparation for 379
  and continuity of food supply 455
  direction of 407
  and duration of nocturnal activity 407
  hazards of and effects on longevity 499
  and homing 503
  and interspecific territoriality 421
  long-distance 381
  mechanisms governing 407
  and migratory divide 381
  and moult 71
  and nomadism 518
  and older versus younger birds 323
  partial 381
  patterns of 359
  physiological preparation for 379
  seasonal 377, 379
  spring 353, 522
  timing of **405–7**
  wader **167–71**
migration flight
  and clouds 503
  daytime 353
  and density of air 353
  and directional information from buildings
    505
  and distance travelled 407
  diurnal 351, 379
  duration of 407
  hazards of 455, 517
  and magnetic conditions of route 407
  nocturnal **351–3**, 379, 405
  and optimal time of day for 353
  and overcast nights 503
  and proper orientation during 407
  and stellar cues 503
  and thermals 32
migration route 41, 147, 171, 381, 447,
    463
  and land bridge 524
  loop 383
  mental map of 505
  overwater 93, 379
  autumn versus spring 383
  step 409
  teaching of 43
  trans-Saharan 379
milk
  ability to produce 243
  bird **243**
  human and calcium 495
  mammal 243
milk bottles, pilfering 387, 389
milkweed 495

Miller, Edward H. 183
millinery and plume trade 25; *see also* plume
    trade
millipedes, defensive secretions of 469
mimicry 239, 385, 495
  and deception 383
  of human speech 463
  social 239, 431
  vocal 383, 385
mimics 249, 387
minerals 135, 493; *see also specific
    minerals*
  in droppings 485
  requirement of 495
Mississippi River 105, 339
mites 75, 317
  infestation of 465
miticidal properties of ant secretions 469
mixed-species, flocking, *see* flocking
mobbing 17, 47, 111, 215, **261–3**
  and altruism 245
  and audio tape 261
  see also behaviour, group; flocking
models 17, 125, 159, 239, 259, 383
  climatic 311
  computer 311
  of foraging 419
  of predators 203
  mathematical/physical 159
  neurological of song 481
  showing why animals form aggregaions 15
molluscs 155, 157, 393
  bivalve 173
Mongolia 301
monogamy xviii, xix, xxiii, 73, 151, 153, 173,
    191, 193, 209, 265, 267, 277, 279, 285, **335–9**,
    399, 435
  and dominance hierarchies 133
  facultative 337
  social patterns of 339
Moore, Frank 353
Morecambe Bay 169
Morley, A. 331
Morocco 169
morphology and thermoregulation 163
Morris, Francis O. Rev. 25
mortality 237, 251, 515
  of inexperienced young birds 497
mortality rates, human 519
  declines in 519
Morton, Eugene 327, 329
Moscow University 389
mosquitoes 57, 293, 315
mothballs, anting with 469
moths 137
  peppered versus melanic 473
moult 53, 407; *see also* feathers, care of;
    migration; plumage, seasonal changes in
  flightless period during 53
  gradual 375
  synchronous 375
moulting 287, 297, **373–5**
  and adaptiveness of pattern 373
  and anting 469

moulting (*continued*)
  and migration 405
  and nitrogen 493
Mount Babor 436
Mount-Temple, Lady 25
mountains, directional information from 503, 505
mouths, bristles around 365
movements; *see also* displays; postures; posturing
  ritualized 205
  stereotyped 355, 357
mowing, times of 369
muscles 285
  adductor 155, 157
  anchoring wings 511
  atrophy of hatching 487
  derived from 449
  and feather rotation 365
  flight 301, 515
  hatching 487
  jaw 465
  light-coloured and fatigue 515
  red-coloured 515
  reptile 301
  syringeal 475
mussels 173, 187
mutation 297
myglobin 515

names xviii, 325
  common xix
  scientific (latinized) xvii, xviii, xix, 3, 231
Naphthalene as insect repellent 469
natality 515; *see also* areas; territory types
  rates of human 519
National Audubon Society 527
  Christmas Count 491
national parks, *see* parks
nations, signatory to CITES 523; *see also* conservation efforts; *listings under* Convention
Natural history of Selborne 271, 273, 357
natural selection, *see* selection, natural
  naturalists 273, 393
nature 231, 241, 249, 297, 305, 307, 325, 387
Nature Conservancy Council 527
Nature Conservation Area, *see* Conservation Area
Nature Protection Area, *see* Protection Area
Nature Reserves, *see* Reserves
nausea, as a teacher 495
navigation; *see also* migration flight; orientation
  between breeding and wintering sites 503
  and judging position while travelling 503
  and reliance on multiple cues 505
  and sense of smell 15
necks 143, 489; *see also* prey
  evolution of Ruff, *see* evolution of
  and hatching 487
  position held during display 207, 209, 211
  white plumage of 136

nectar 241
  energy-rich 495
  and interspecific territoriality 421
  nitrogen-poor 495
nectarivores 135, 495
neighbours 199, 201, 209, 213, 279, 371, 417, 445
  adopting songs of territorial 479
  recognition of by vocalizations 417
  songs of 477
  territorial 483
nerve 285, 515
  endings 157
  olfactory 13
  and highspeed transmission 515
nest xx, xxiv, 23, 115, 121, 123, 171, 175, 183, 199, 203, 229, 249, 251, 261, 267, 275, 337, 341, 439, 443; *see also listings under* displays
  active 151, 467
  and adaptive advantage of fragility 75
  as an archive 443
  and DDT 119
  density 17, 191, 193, 345
  and enhancing breeding success 443
  evolution of **345–9**
  insect parasites in an empty 317; *see also* parasites, insect
  legal protection of eggs and young and xxx
  number of visits to 467
  perennial 443
  remaining in 401
  repairs to 277
  size and clutch size 59
  see also nesting; *specific nest listings*
nest building xviii, ix, xix, xxiii, 71, 207, 211, 293, 331, 467
  breeding habitat and xxx
  and diversity of supporting structures 349, 445
  environmental triggers for 329
  and hormones, *see* hormones and nest building
  origins of 345
nest defence 209, 269, 335, 397, 399, 443, 445
  and brood parasitism 71, 443; *see aslo* parasites; brood
  and camouflage 275, 445
  and conspicuousness 175, 201, 345
  and guarding 51, 193, 467, 524
  and immediate threat 203, 445
  and predation 17, 172, 191, 201, 267, 339, 367, 509; *see also* nest robbers
nest failure 173, 221, 277, 347, 411
  and abandonment 75, 199, 221, 249
  flooding and embedding eggs 441
  frequency of 71
nest hole xxii, 267, 285, 335, 345, 347, 393, 421, 425, 427, 441, 465
  entrance of 75
  infestation of 465
  and interspecific territoriality 421
  and roosting 83
  secondary use of 75, 349

nitrogen 495
  water-soluble compounds and fish or
    amphibian eggs 315
nocturnal birds 91
nomadism, see conservation and fluctuations in
    population sizes; population dynamics
nomenclature, see classification
non-passerines, see passerines, non-
nonvocal sounds 263
Norfolk 221
North Atlantic 225, 231, 233, 463
North Star 503
Northern Hemisphere 53, 216, 222, 231, 287
northern penguin, see penguin, northern
northern seed-eating birds and irruptions 491,
    493
Norway 131, 133, 233, 267, 435, 517, 522
Nos Oiseaux (Société Romande pour l'Etude et la
    Protection des Oiseaux) xxxix
Noss 518
nostrils 11, 237, 365, 391
  external 391
  gannet 391
  and nasal passages 13
  woodpecker 391
notes, of interest xx, xxxi
notochord 3
Nottebohm, Fernando 475
nourish, to (as Latin root) 401
nourishment, see food availability; nutrition
numbers, maintaining or enlarging 525; see also
    listings under conservation; population
    dynamics
nutrients 315, 495
  in droppings 485
nutrition 115, 239, 315, 357, 397, 465
  and crop milk 243
  and fecal sacs 75
  see also diet; food availability

Oaxaca 57
observations 17, 83, 121, 135, 153, 169, 205,
    211, 241, 259, 273, 305, 337, 389, 413, 419,
    423, 455, 459, 469, 473, 485
  of beak marks in the ground 457
  field 527
  of noctural migration 353
  see also information on bird biology
observatories, bird 307
oceans, southern 233
  air flow over 81
O'Connor, Raymond 367
O'Donald, Peter 153
odours 317
  detection at high altitude 15
  directional information from 503
  dissipation of 89
  and locating nests by 11
  perception of dispersed 13
offal 21, 357; see also feeding, commensal
offspring 149, 153, 157, 159, 173, 175, 183, 227,
    245, 247, 265, 267, 269, 277, 299, 335, 467,
    471

care of and egg retention 323
  communication with 263
  diets of 173
  extended care of 171
  genetic differences among 149
  parentage of 335
  syllable repertoires and 385
  unrelated 197
  see also fledglings; hatchlings; parent;
    parental care; parasites, brood
Ohio 431
oil contamination of birds 225–7
  from facilities 225
  and oceanic pollution 225
  and rescuing oiled birds 225; see also
    conservation efforts; conservation and
    human pressure
  from spills 225
  from spills used as a weapon 227
oil production by birds 19
  preen 355, 371, 469; see also feathers, care of;
    glands; preening
  in the stomach of Storm Petrels 227
L'Oiseau (Ligue Française pour la Protection des
    Oiseaux) xxxvii
Old World 251, 285
olfactory, brain centre of 11
omnivores 397, 493
opportunism 191, 193, 357, 445, 465, 497
orchards 369
order, peck 131
orders 138, 282, 315, 351
organizations
  conservation 27, 145, 525
  humane 25
  natural history 25
  see also conservation efforts
organs 475
  and bird milk 243
  development of 449
  and parasites 317
  sensory 89
  see also anatomy
organs, reproductive 329, 511
  and alimentary canal 87
  breeding versus non-breeding 405
  and cloaca 87, 337
  and effects of light regimes on 297
  female 87
  oviduct 87, 447, 511
  oviduct and egg colour 161
  and ovulation 329
  regression of 295, 331
  see also hormones
orientation 379
  and compass direction 503
  and directional information from stars 503,
    505
  magnetic 505
  and navigation 503–5
  and reliance on multiple cues 505
  short-distance 505
  see also migrants; migration flight; navigation
Origin of species 297

and pattern 181; *see also* coloration of
  plumage
and sexes with identical 474
plumage and development 85, 205, 407
  as badge of age 435
plumage, maintenance 355, 371
  cleaning and disinfecting 461
  and oil contamination 225
  and parasites or diseases 155, 317
plumage, properties of 165
  insulating and roosting 85
  protection from saturation 333
plumage, seasonal changes in
  eclipse 53, 75
  winter or breeding 53, 75, 27, 139, 153, 205,
    375
plume trade 6, **23–7**, 28; *see also* legislation;
  laws
  and Age of Extermination 27
  French Revolution and 23
  Greeks and 23
  and Importation of Plumage (Prohibition)
    Bill 27
  and Plumage League 25
  and Selbourne League/Selbourne Society 25
pneumonia 225
poaching 520; 521
poison
  heart 389, 495
  human sources of 107, 117, 137, 225, 411; *see
    also* conservation and human pressure
  and learning to avoid 387
  and storage of nitrogenous wastes 315
pollination 241
pollution 103, 115, 343; *see also* conservation
    and human pressure
  and industrial melanism 473
polyandry xxiii, 75, 173, 193, **195–7**, 279, 287,
    337
  cooperative simultaneous 195
  and dominance hierarchies 131
  sequential versus simultaneous 195
  serial 191
  and sexual selection 149
polygamy 153, 193, 516
polygynandry 279
polygyny xxiii, 125, 151, 173, 191, 193, 197,
    265–9, 279, 285, 337, 385, 399, 435
  and resource availability 269
  and territoriality 269
polymorphism 153
polyterritoriality 267, 399
  and deception 269
population 109, 153, 157, 171, 241, 249, 279,
    305, 327, 337, 343, 359, 365, 381, 383, 405,
    407, 410, 441, 461, 471, 497
  and ecological differences 324
  founder 288, 306
  hybridizing 463
  local 518
  and non-overlapping ranges 325
  wild 447
population, breeding 147, 289, 345, 518
  and clutch size 55

density of 191
population declines, *see* conservation and
  declines
population density 191, 491
  and clutch size 55
  constant 515
  cyclic change in 519
  and parasites and predators 519
  and territoriality 519
population dynamics 303, **515–19**
  and changes in size 147, 251, 476, 518
  and changes in wintering numbers 491
  and cyclic fluctuations 491
  and emigration and immigration 515
  and impact of parasites and pathogens 317
  and migration and nomadism 465, 518
  and mortality and natality 515
  and regional and short-term changes 147
population, human 311, 411, 515, 519; *see also*
    bird–human interactions; humans; people
  in sub-Saharan Africa 411
  in western and southern Asia 411
population increases, *see* conservation and
  increases
population size 303, 517, 519, 518, 525
  large 491
  maintaining 522
  and mortality from raptors 115
  stability of 359, 517
Population trends in British breeding birds xxxii
populations and imperilment, *see* conservation
    status
Portugal 169, 524
postures
  bathing and showering 357
  convection and 19
  fluffed-ball 489
  spread-wing **17–19**
  stance and camouflage 22
  sunbathing 165, 357
  temperature regulation and 19; *see also*
    temperature regulation
  threat 185; *see also* displays, defence
posturing 205
potential, reproductive 265
poultry 359
power lines, high-voltage 105
pox, avian 315
Prange, H. D. 511
precipitation, acid, *see* acid precipitation
precocial and altricial young, *see* developmental
    stage at hatching
precociality, gradient and levels of 401, 403
precocious, as Latin root 401
predation 167, 181, 193, 261, 295, 341, 347
  and coloniality 107, 139, 345, 221
  pressure 109, 287
predators xxxi, 17, 47, 89, 91, 109, 159, 173,
    191, 259, 261, 269, 285, 315, 385, 485, 517
  avian 493
  and brood parasitism 69
  and clutch size 59
  conspicuousness to 75
  and crèches 45

ratio
  breaths-to-heartbeats in birds and mammals
    513
  surface-to-volume 5
receptors 91
  sensory 365
reclamation and use of droppings 485
recognition
  individual 435
  pair 263
  parent–chick 227
  of unique objects 389
recombination 297
recorders, portable tape 307
  video cassette 53
recordings 143, 309
records 257
  fossil 299
  of longevity and maximum age 499
recrudescence, autumnal 331
recycling and commensal feeding, see feeding,
    commensal
Red data book for birds in Britain 527
red data books
  and amateur birdwatchers 527
  value of 527
  and well-studied species 527
Reed, Chester 161
reeds, exploitation of 147
references, in bibliography xx, xxxi
reflection, angle of 139
reflectors, parabolic 309
refuse 357
regions, see areas
regulation, endogenous 407
regulations; see also conservation efforts;
    Convention; Directive; laws; legislation;
    treaties
  controlling deliberate habitat damage 523
  controlling hunting 27, 521, 523
  trade 27
regurgitation 11, 137, 173, 205, 211, 215, 223,
    243, 489
  and oil pollution 227
  of pellets 257
  of stomach oil 173
relatedness, genetic, see genes
relationships, ecological 427
relatives 247, 277, 279, 293
  and altruism 245
repertoires, see songs, repertoires of
reports, see information on bird biology
reproduction 205, 265, 297, 493, 499
  differential 297, 471
  lifetime 33
  rates of 121
  and survivorship per brood 33
reproductive
  contribution 197, 267
  efforts, variation in 191
  fitness, see fitness, reproductive
  output, see output, reproductive
  success 75, 221, 223, 245, 267, 279, 299, 437,
    471

reptiles 157, 159, 283, 313, 319, 515
  and birds as feathered descendants of
    299
  and eggs 171, 317, 345
  metabolism of 301
requirements, nutritional 493, 495
research, see information on bird biology
reserves 147, 369; see also conservation efforts;
    parks
  Belovezhskaya Pushcha State Hunting 97
  Evros Delta 97
  Gala Golu Proposed 97
  nature 145, 521
  network of wetland 147
  purchasing of by RSPB 27
  Vadehavet Wildlife 95
  Waddenzee State Nature 95
residents 518, 525
  winter 407
resource partitioning 187
  of a limited food suppy 427
  of prey 101
resource-guarding and interspecific
    territoriality 421
resources 107, 133, 149, 197, 303, 437
  abundance of 55, 181, 189, 197, 269, 366
  and attempts to monopolize 397
  and breeding females 149
  density of 51, 179, 181
  distribution of food 189, 269
  food 51, 109, 171, 189, 409, 491; see also
    resource partitioning
  and guilds 77
  and interspecific territoriality 421
  supplied by people 359, 519
  unpredictability of 279
respiration, cellular 313
respiratory tract; see also anatomy; *listings under*
    flight; migration
  and breathing apparatus 513
  and crosscurrent circulation 513
  and dead air 513
  and evaporative cooling 163
  and two-cycle respiratory pump 513
restlessness, migratory 405, 407, 503
retina 91, 139
Revue Française d'Ornithologie, La (Société
    Ornithologique de France) xxxvii
rhythms
  altering of during darkness by nocturnal
    migrants 379
  circannual 405
  endogenous 405, 407
  genetically programmed internal 405
Ribble Estuary 169
Richter, Henry Constantine 453
rickettsiae 315
Ricklefs, Robert 57
Ring, The (Polish Zoological Society) xxxviii
ringing birds 169, 221, 222, 497
  frequency of and lifespan determination
    499
  and recapturing 41, 497
  and seamless leg (close) ring 524

risk
  annual of being killed 497
  and degree of endangerment 527
  maternal and egg retention 321
rivers
  productivity of and Dippers 333
  and provision of directional information 505
Rivista Italiana di Ornithologia (Societa Italiana di
  Scienze Naturali) xxxviii
rodents 105, 493, 515
  grassland 491
  population density of 369
  tundra 491
rods 91
Rohwer, Sievert 435
Romans 23, 39, 463
roosting 379, 495
  and benefits of joining aggregations 83, 85
  cold weather and 270, 272
  communal 81–5, 487
  and competition for sites 518
  and dawn chorus 371
  mixed-species 83
  and nocturnal aggregations 17
  and pellets 257
  and positions taken 83
  pre-assembly 467
  solitary 83
  sites 83, 93, 163, 221
  winter 467
Ross-shire, West 103
rotation, celestial 503
Rothwell, Philip 145
Royal Gardens 451
Royal Society 453
Royal Society for Nature Conservation 145
Royal Society for the Protection of Birds (RSPB)
  xxxvi, 25, 27, 525, 527
  as largest voluntary conservation
    organization 526
Ruhr University 261
Rumania 147
running 513
  and energy use 283
Russia 43, 329, 522
  Arctic 43, 233

Sahara 169, 343, 379, 411; *see also* desert;
  migration; wintering
  migratory flight over 409
  sub- 343
Sahel, the 311, 312; *see also* desert; migration;
  wintering
  desertification of 343, 411
  and drought and rain 411
  overgrazing of 411
sailplanes 79
salinity 239
salt 313
  content in seawater 237
  excretion of 239
  glands, *see* glands
  leached from droppings 487

sanctuary, bird 97, 145
sand, as grinding agent 135
sandpipers, social systems, and territoriality
  189–93
saturation, predator 111
scales 123
  elongated 301
  reptilian 159
Scandinavia 267, 287, 339, 425
Schjelderup-Ebbe, Thorleif 131
Schnell, Gary 65
schools of fish 17
Schreiber, Ralph 499
scientists 117, 131, 519, 524; *see also individual*
  names
  atmospheric 311
  biological 159
  physical 159
Scotland 41, 45, 105, 107, 115, 153, 221, 369,
  421, 461, 477, 478, 518
Scott, Sir Peter 39
Scottish Birds (Scottish Ornithologists' Club)
  xxxviii
Scottish Ornithologists' Club xxxvi
scratching
  ears 371
  and foot structure 293
  in ground birds versus arboreal 373
  head 373; *see also* head
  methods of and ecology 373
  patterns of 371, 373
sea crossings
  concentrations at 93
  and migrants and weather 93
  raptors and, *see* raptors
sea lanes and offal 357; *see also* feeding,
  commensal; offal
Seabird (Seabird Group) xxxviii
seabirds 29, 55, 57, 61, 63, 65, 75, 81,
  83, 107, 117, 161, 202, 212, 215, 219, 227,
  233, 287, 317, 335, 357, 399, 485, 487, 499,
  505
  and depredation by river otters 17
  fish-eating 487
  and nesting sites, *see* nest sites
seaducks 67
search image, *see* image, search
season, breeding 53, 55, 73, 87, 99, 145, 147,
  149, 173, 181, 221, 223, 277, 293–97, 335,
  339, 349, 375, 377, 397, 413, 423, 483, 491,
  493, 495, 511, 517
  and changes in bills 393
  and flying north to breed 379
season, growing 191
season, mating 263
season, non-breeding 171, 335
Second World War, *see* World War II
seeds
  avian dispersal of 241
  conifer 518
  as grinding agent 135
  impervious to digestive tracts 241
  and internal storage of 489
  obtaining water from 313

stimulating nest-building or egg-laying 415
stimulating ovarian development 415
in territorial display 303, 371, 413
songs, repertoire of 383, 385, 415, 475, 481
  adult or crystallized 481
  and complexity and territorial quality 415
  and determining composition 483
  and genetic determination 479
  and intimidating rivals 385
  large versus small 385
  learned versus innate 479
  and mate attraction 385
  and replacing components 483
  size of 307, 415
  standardized 479
  and stimulating females 385
  and syllable 385
songs, variation in
  geographic 307
  passerines 475
  populations 383
Sorjonen, Jorma 329
sound 263, 307, 309, 329; see also calls; signals;
    listings under songs; vocalizations; voices
  acquiring alien 383
  during displays 183
  non-vocal 183
  species-specific 483
  and temporal complexity 255
  time differential and 253
  variety of 183
sound, frequency of 475
  and transmission through different habitats
    327, 329
sound, perception of 255
  discrimination of loudness and frequency
    255, 475
  and locating prey 13, 253
sound, transmission of 327, 369, 385
  and absorption 327
  and acoustic complexity 255
  and attenuation 327
  and coastal habitat 183
  and degradation 327
  and environmental influences on 327
  and intensity 475
  and intensity differential 253
  and low-frequency 181
  and pitch 475
  and scattering 327
soup, Chinese bird's nest 445
South America 137, 241, 301, 465
South American Humboldt Current 487
South Asia 121
South Atlantic 81
Southern Hemisphere 39, 297
Soviet Union, former 41, 369, 467
Spain 129, 169, 213, 233, 301, 407, 409, 524
speciation 461
  and geographic isolation 461
  rate of 351
  and species, see species
species 3, 107, 237, 314, 315, 323, 324, 327, 349,
    383, 393, 397, 405, 407, 409, 419, 420, 422,

423, 424, 427, 441, 461, 463, 492, 497, 520,
    526-7
  abundance and conservation 171; see also
    listings under conservation
  and clutch size 55
  conspicuousness of nuclear 431
  distinct or 'good' 463
  ecological or morphological similarity and
    territoriality 421
  and interpretation of interactions 427
  recognition of 155, 385, 413
  and speciation 325-7
spectrograph, sound 307
spectrum, electromagnetic 139
speculum 49
Spencer, Herbert 299
sperm 127, 247, 265, 297
  competition 73
  ejection of 337
  as haploid stage 447
  shelf-life or storage of 73, 87
Spitsbergen 233
spread-wing postures, see postures
spring 369
  arrival of migrants 377
spurs, length of 153
stability, social 131
staging or staging grounds, see areas
Stanford University 473
Starlings 463-7
  adaptability of 465
  and insect infestations 467
  and programmes to control 467
starvation 455
  and brood parasitism 71
  pesticide-induced 119
  safeguards against 11
stations, feeding 357-61, 435
  and aspergillosis 361
  and beef suet 361
  and diseases 359
  and fruit or seed abundance 361
  and surveys 361
  and weather 361
status, conservation, see conservation status
status, nutritional
  determinants of 223
status, social and relative dominance 131
stealing
  risks of 215
  versus foraging 213
Stenmark, G. 267
steppes, conversion of, see conservation and
    human pressure
Sterna (Stavanger Museum) xxxviii
stoneflies 333
stones
  as grinding agent 135
  swallowing 135-7
storms, risk of
  and breeding season 295
Straits of Gibraltar 32
strangers 417
Strasbourg 95